Evaluation Guide for
Merrill Applications of Mathematics

P9-BIM-245

Merrill Applications of Mathematics provides a comprehensive course in general mathematics. This text provides every opportunity for student success.

To further strengthen the presentation of the text material, many special features have been included.

Please turn to the following pages to examine selected examples of these features of *Merrill Applications of Mathematics*.

pp. 221–223	**Annotations in the Teacher Annotated Edition,** printed in red, present an objective for each lesson, teaching suggestions, assignment guides, and answers to problems.
p. 32	**Student Annotations,** printed in blue, explain steps in solving problems and help students identify important concepts.
p. 259	**Key Skills** features are provided to allow students to review specific skills before they apply the skills in the lesson.
pp. 420–461	**Basic Skills Appendix** pages provide exercises for those students needing more practice or review.
pp. 198, 412	**Problem Solving** is developed sequentially throughout the text using four steps.
p. 245	**Math Break** features provide general topics to expand the students' knowledge of mathematics.
p. 173	**Mental Math** features help students estimate and compute without pencil and paper.
p. 67	**Calculator** features show ways a calculator can be used and reinforce mathematical concepts.
p. 343	**Computer** features provide topics to help students understand the uses and limitations of computers.
pp. 12–13, 278	**Review and Test** materials in each chapter include a Practice Page, a two-page Chapter Review, a Chapter Test, and a Cumulative Review.
pp. 478–498	**Selected Answers** allow students to check their answers as they work.

Merrill Teacher Annotated Edition
Applications of Mathematics

Authors

Jack Price
Superintendent of Schools
Palos Verdes, California

Michael Charles
San Diego College
San Diego, California

Olene Brame
Arts Magnet High School
Dallas, Texas

Miriam Clifford
Bay View High School
Milwaukee, Wisconsin

Consultants

Les Winters
Mathematics Supervisor
Los Angeles Unified School District
Los Angeles, California

Bill Leschensky
Glenbard South High School
Glen Ellyn, Illinois

MERRILL
PUBLISHING COMPANY
A Bell & Howell Information Company

London • Toronto • Sydney

Contents

Permission is specifically granted by the publisher to reproduce the tests in this Teacher Guide entirely or in part.

ISBN 0-675-05718-3

Published by
Merrill Publishing Company
A Bell & Howell Information Company
Columbus, Ohio 43216

Copyright © 1988 by Merrill Publishing Company. All rights reserved. No part of this book may be reproduced in any form, electronic or mechanical, including photocopy, recording or any information storage or retrieval system, without permission in writing from the publisher.

Printed in the United States of America

Teacher Guide Preface for
Merrill Applications of Mathematics

Merrill Applications of Mathematics is a high school mathematics textbook written by classroom teachers for today's student. It presents the fundamental concepts and skills required in a technological society. The relevant and student-motivating approach as well as the comprehensive presentation of essential skills appeal to and meet the needs of all students.

Relevant Real-Life Applications   Research has shown that students learn best that for which they see a need. This premise is the basis for this general mathematics program. Mathematical proficiency and understanding will follow as the student is given practice in relevant problem-solving situations.

Easy-to-Read Presentation   Throughout the text, the reading level has been carefully controlled. It resents an open format to facilitate reading and comprehension. In addition, many color photographs, illustrations, charts, and graphs are used. These features help students visualize the ideas presented and help them read with improved understanding.

Organization   *Merrill Applications of Mathematics* is organized into eighteen chapters. For easy management, each chapter is composed of primarily two-page lessons. The daily routine can be varied by using the Reviews and the Special Features. This design allows the flexibility to structure a program to meet the needs of students.

Problem Solving   Learning to solve problems is the principal reason for studying mathematics. *Merrill Applications of Mathematics* presents a sequential and comprehensive development of problem solving. The format guides the student through problem-solving processes that reveal the underlying relationships in problems. In this manner, students can examine many aspects of problem solving.

Plenty of Practice   The text contains an ample selection of exercises, problem solving, and applications. An extra practice section is included in each chapter.

Review   A one-page cumulative review in each chapter provides students with constant review and reinforcement of the basic skills presented up to that point. This research-proven review method is most effective in increasing student retention of mathematical skills. Each chapter also includes a two-page Chapter Review that reinforces vocabulary and concepts, and provides exercises and problem solving. At the back of the text, there is a 42-page Basic Skills Appendix section that provides students with a review of skills. The appropriate pages are assigned in each lesson.

Testing   Each chapter ends with a Chapter Test to help students check their own progress.

America's most dynamic

**MERRILL APPLICATIONS OF MATHEMATICS
. . . it's the ideal choice to keep your students
motivated to learn mathematics.**
No other program does a better job of integrating
applications and basic skills. And no other high
school general mathematics course covers such a
wide range of real-world applications.

It's mathematics with a purpose from beginning to
end—so your students will be motivated right from
the start.

And because MERRILL APPLICATIONS OF MATH-
EMATICS is based on concrete situations rather
than abstract concepts, your students will understand concepts more readily.

Each lesson focuses on everyday applications and
basic computational skills—with interesting situations, step-by-step examples, a comfortable pace,
and plenty of opportunities for practice and review.
This dynamic combination builds success for every
student—and gives your students a reason for
mastering each skill.

T4

general mathematics program

Compared to other general mathematics courses, MERRILL APPLICATIONS OF MATHEMATICS has more of these features:

- real-life situations
- problem solving
- estimation and mental math
- review and maintenance
- teaching examples
- integrated use of calculators

MERRILL APPLICATIONS OF MATHEMATICS is ideal for students of varying math backgrounds, including

- first-year general mathematics students
- second-year general mathematics students
- students taking business or technical mathematics
- students taking a course between pre-algebra and algebra

A teaching package that makes your job easier

The **Teacher Annotated Edition** supports your daily teaching completely—and gives you extra help to meet the needs of students with varying math backgrounds and interests. Included are teaching suggestions and assignment guides for three different ability levels—plus complete cross-referencing to the Basic Skills Appendix in the Student Edition and extra worksheets in the Teacher Resource Book.

The **Teacher Resource Book** offers something for everyone. Worksheets and tests supplement every chapter—more than 300 pages in all—organized with tabbed dividers in a convenient three-ring binder.

Components

- Student Edition
- Teacher Annotated Edition
- Teacher Resource Book with Binder
- Software Package

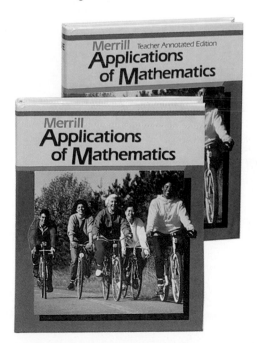

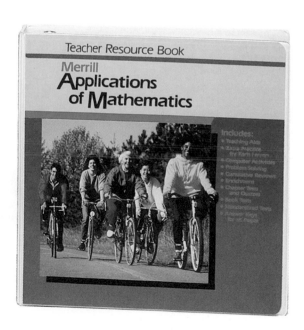

Students begin each lesson seeing mathematics in use.

This typical lesson shows an easy-to-follow progression from introduction to independent practice.

(1) Motivating real-life situation . . . to get students' attention

(2) Step-by-step examples . . . to explain exactly how to get the answers . . . including estimation skills

(3) Key Skills section . . . to review computational skills students will use in the exercises

(4) Plenty of practice exercises . . . to ensure mastery

(5) Word problems . . . to apply the skills in problem-solving situations

Tips for using a calculator are included in the examples and features where applicable.
A "Career" lesson in every chapter features an on-the-job application of mathematics.
A "Problem Solving" lesson in each chapter teaches the four-step method for solving problems.

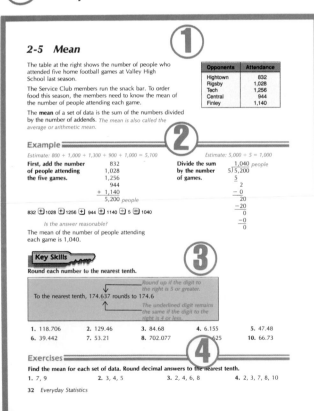

2-5   Mean

The table at the right shows the number of people who attended five home football games at Valley High School last season.

The Service Club members run the snack bar. To order food this season, the members need to know the mean of the number of people attending each game.

The **mean** of a set of data is the sum of the numbers divided by the number of addends. *The mean is also called the average or arithmetic mean.*

Opponents	Attendance
Hightown	832
Rigsby	1,028
Tech	1,256
Central	944
Finley	1,140

Example

Estimate: 800 + 1,000 + 1,300 + 900 + 1,000 = 5,100

First, add the number of people attending the five games.	
	832
	1,028
	1,256
	944
	+ 1,140
	5,200 *people*

Estimate: 5,000 ÷ 5 = 1,000

Divide the sum by the number of games.

```
        1,040 people
5)5,200
    5
    2
  - 0
    20
  - 20
     0
   - 0
     0
```

832 ⊞ 1028 ⊞ 1256 ⊞ 944 ⊞ 1140 ⊟ 5 ⊟ 1040

Is the answer reasonable?

The mean of the number of people attending each game is 1,040.

Key Skills

Round each number to the nearest tenth.

> *Round up if the digit to the right is 5 or greater.*
> To the nearest tenth, 174.637 rounds to 174.6
> *The underlined digit remains the same if the digit to the right is 4 or less.*

1. 118.706	2. 129.46	3. 84.68	4. 6.155	5. 47.48
6. 39.442	7. 53.21	8. 702.077	9. .625	10. 66.73

Exercises

Find the mean for each set of data. Round decimal answers to the nearest tenth.

1. 7, 9	2. 3, 4, 5	3. 2, 4, 6, 8	4. 2, 3, 7, 8, 10

32 Everyday Statistics

---

5. 5, 10, 15, 20, 25, 30, 35	6. 10, 40, 60, 80, 30, 50
7. 129, 215, 327, 242, 183	8. $1.10, $1.25, $1.34, $1.18, $3.13
9. 0.98, 0.8, 0.75, 0.85	10. 68, 62, 78, 79, 83, 91, 70, 67
11. $4\frac{1}{2}$, $2\frac{1}{4}$, $3\frac{3}{4}$, 5, $3\frac{1}{2}$, 4	12. 4.8, 4.8, 6.4, 7.2, 3.2, 2.4, 4.5

Find the mean for each of the following.

13. Miguel's bowling scores are 84, 111, and 150.

14. Sue buys 5 baseball tickets at $3.50 each, 4 tickets at $4.50, and 2 tickets at $5.50.

Solve. Round answers to the nearest tenth.

15. During this football season, Alonzo made the following punts (in yards): 32, 45, 50, 33, 36, 39, 27, 45, 10, 19, 20, 55, 32, 56, 43, 46, and 53. What is the average length of a punt?

16. Last month Wilda paid $57.63 for gasoline, $6.10 for oil, $238.27 for a car payment, and $32.16 for car insurance. She drove 1,326 miles. What did it cost per mile for Wilda to drive her car?

17. Refer to the rainfall chart on page 31. What was the total rainfall in Jacksonville for the year? Find the mean of the monthly rainfall.

Math Break

The **mean variation** is the average amount each measurement differs from the mean.

Find the mean variation of the temperatures (Celsius) 28°, 23°, 27°, 25°, 22°, and 24° as follows.

1. Find the mean of the temperatures (to the nearest tenth).
2. Find the difference between each number and the mean.
3. Add the differences.
4. Then the mean variation is the sum in exercise 3 divided by the number of addends.
5. What kind of changes would greatly affect the mean variation?
6. What kind would not?

Chapter 2 **33**

T6

Special features focus on motivating topics.

In every chapter, optional special features offer students a change of pace and a chance to expand their knowledge and skills beyond the regular lessons.

"**Computer**" features familiarize students with different uses of computers.

"**Calculator**" features offer additional instruction in calculator skills.

"**Math Break**" features look at chapter topics from a slightly different angle.

Mental math . . . no other program does it better!

"**Mental Math**" features offer instruction and practice in a variety of mental math skills. But MERRILL APPLICATIONS OF MATHEMATICS doesn't stop there with mental math. Estimation skills are treated as an important part of every computation—and are clearly demonstrated in the daily lesson examples.

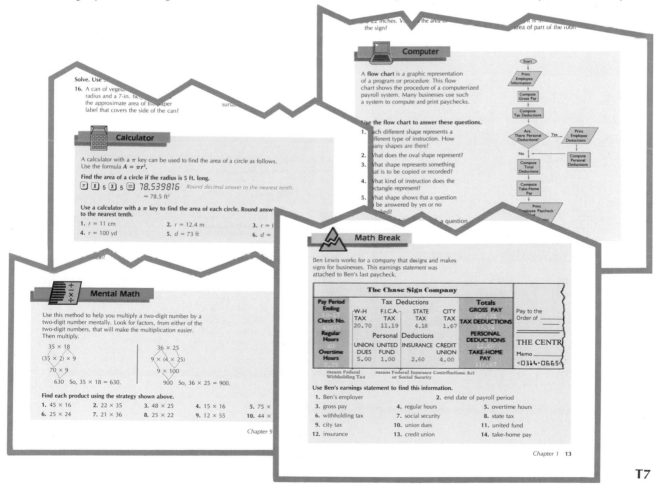

Continuous review puts skills at your students' command.

Plentiful review throughout the program helps your students maintain every skill they learn.

Regular review in every chapter includes
- Extra Practice pages . . . two pages of skills practice
- Chapter Review . . . two pages of vocabulary, skills practice, and problem-solving review
- Cumulative Review . . . one-page review of topics covered earlier in the book

Key Skills are reviewed in the lessons whenever necessary.

A Basic Skills Appendix offers 42 extra pages of computational practice for students having difficulty. These exercise sets are referenced wherever appropriate in the Student Edition and Teacher Annotated Edition.

PRACTICE

Estimate.

1. $379 + 120$	2. $42.06 - 21.98$	3. 384×32	4. $\$39.16 \times 19$	5. 68
6. $751 + 486$	7. $3.98 - 1.45$	8. 297×54	9. $\$6.98 \times 30$	10. 23

Add, subtract, multiply, or divide.

11. $7.56 + 6.2$	12. 14.21×0.03	13. $1,561 - 562$	14. $126 \div 7$	15. $\times$
16. 0.002×36	17. $22\overline{)319}$	18. $463 + 537$	19. $17\overline{)952}$	20. $-$
21. $86.9 + 27.1$	22. 37.8×0.46	23. $3.1\overline{)465}$	24. $86.9 - 71.8$	25. $+$

26. $\frac{1}{3} + \frac{5}{6}$ 27. $\frac{5}{7} + \frac{2}{5}$ 28. $\frac{3}{4} - \frac{3}{5}$ 29. $\frac{2}{3} \div \frac{4}{15}$

30. $\frac{2}{5} - \frac{1}{4}$ 31. $1\frac{1}{2} \times 6$ 32. $6 \div 2\frac{1}{2}$ 33. $\frac{3}{5} + \frac{5}{3}$

34. $1\frac{1}{3} + \frac{3}{4}$ 35. $4\frac{3}{4} - 2\frac{1}{4}$ 36. $\frac{3}{4} \div 1\frac{1}{3}$ 37. $1\frac{1}{3} \times 1$

38. $3\frac{1}{2} + 2\frac{1}{4}$ 39. $6\frac{7}{8} + 3\frac{3}{8}$ 40. $6\frac{3}{4} - 3\frac{3}{8}$ 41. $10\frac{1}{3} \div$

42. $\frac{7}{8} - \frac{3}{4}$ 43. $\frac{9}{10} + \frac{3}{5}$ 44. $1\frac{2}{3} \times \frac{1}{10}$ 45. $3\frac{5}{6} \times 1$

46. 10×29 47. 4.2×10 48. $3.6 \div 10$ 49. $49 \div 1$

50. 100×0.012 51. $46 \times 1,000$ 52. 0.085×10 53. $100 \times$

54. 100×0.12 55. $36 \div 10$ 56. 3.9×100 57. $360 \div$

58. 465×100 59. 0.88×10 60. $1,000 \times 0.008$ 61. $3.45 \div$

62. $490 \div 100$ 63. 10×0.23 64. $4.9 \div 100$ 65. $0.42 \times$

Complete.

66. $69 \text{ min} = \blacksquare \text{ h} \blacksquare \text{ min}$ 67. $86 \text{ s} = \blacksquare \text{ min} \blacksquare \text{ s}$ 68. $2 \text{ h } 45 \text{ min} = \blacksquare$

69. $500 \text{ h} = \blacksquare \text{ days} \blacksquare \text{ h}$ 70. $2 \text{ qt } 1 \text{ c} = \blacksquare \text{ c}$ 71. $1 \text{ h} = \blacksquare \text{ s}$

72. $14 \text{ g} = \blacksquare \text{ mg}$ 73. $2.75 \text{ L} = \blacksquare \text{ mL}$ 74. $5 \text{ pt} = \blacksquare \text{ qt}$

216 *Geometry*

CHAPTER 7 REVIEW

Vocabulary/Concepts

Choose a word or numeral from the list at the right to complete each sentence.

1. The ___?___ is a nonstandard unit of length.
2. The ___?___ is the basic unit of length in the metric system.
3. There are 1,000 meters in one ___?___ .
4. One hundred ___?___ (s) equals one meter.
5. The most commonly used ___?___ units of length are the inch, foot, yard, and mile.
6. There are ___?___ feet in one mile.
7. Thirty-six inches equals one ___?___ .
8. The measurement 2.7380 meters has ___?___ significant digits.

4
5
1,760
5,280
centimeter
customary
foot
kilometer
meter
metric
millimeter
span
yard

Exercises

Name the larger unit. Pages 137–138

9. pace or span 10. cubit or span 11. thumb or pace

Name the larger unit. Pages 139–141

12. centimeter or meter 13. kilometer or meter
14. millimeter or centimeter 15. meter or millimeter

Measure the length of each line segment. Give the measurement in centimeters and then in millimeters. Pages 139–141

16. _____ 17. _____
18. _____ 19. _____

Tell whether you would multiply or divide to complete the following. Pages 142–143

20. $2 \text{ m} = \blacksquare \text{ mm}$ 21. $450 \text{ cm} = \blacksquare \text{ m}$ 22. $5 \text{ km} = \blacksquare \text{ m}$
23. $2.4 \text{ cm} = \blacksquare \text{ mm}$ 24. $1,300 \text{ mm} = \blacksquare \text{ m}$ 25. $85 \text{ mm} = \blacksquare \text{ cm}$
26. $1,250 \text{ m} = \blacksquare \text{ km}$ 27. $5 \text{ m} = \blacksquare \text{ cm}$ 28. $300 \text{ mm} = \blacksquare \text{ m}$

Complete. Pages 142–143

29. $7 \text{ m} = \blacksquare \text{ cm}$ 30. $4,200 \text{ mm} = \blacksquare \text{ m}$ 31. $200 \text{ m} = \blacksquare \text{ km}$
32. $56 \text{ cm} = \blacksquare \text{ m}$ 33. $51 \text{ cm} = \blacksquare \text{ mm}$ 34. $163.2 \text{ cm} = \blacksquare \text{ m}$
35. $1,700 \text{ m} = \blacksquare \text{ km}$ 36. $1.4 \text{ m} = \blacksquare \text{ cm}$ 37. $3.3 \text{ cm} = \blacksquare \text{ mm}$

156 *Length*

Tests make evaluation quick and convenient.

Numerous tests throughout the program give you more options for make-up tests and for testing students of different ability levels . . . or they can be used for further review and reinforcement.

Chapter Tests are included in the Student Edition, in the Teacher Annotated Edition, and in the Teacher Resource Book.

The **Teacher Resource Book** also contains Quizzes, Standardized-Format Tests, and Book Tests.

CHAPTER 16 TEST

Find the number named by each of the following.

1. 1^6 2. 2^3 3. 3^2 4. 2^4 5. 4^3

Find the value of each expression.

6. $3 + 4 \times 2 - 6$ 7. $28 \div 2^2$ 8. $(4 + 4^2) \div 5$ 9. $6 + [4 \times (8 \div 2)]$

Find the value of each expression if $x = 4$, $y = 6$, **and** $z = {}^-3$.

10. $4x + 7$ 11. $x - 2y$ 12. xy 13. $x^2 + z^2$

14. $(x + y)^2$ 15. $\frac{2y}{3}$ 16. $\left(\frac{y}{z}\right)^2$ 17. z^3

Use the formula $rt = d$ **to solve for the missing value.**

18. $r = 40$ mph, $t = 5$ hours 19. $r = 125$ mph, $t = 2.5$ hours

20. $d = 344$ miles, $t = 4$ hours 21. $d = 5.25$ miles, $r = 3.5$ mph

Use the gas mileage formula, $s = \frac{m}{g}$, **to solve for the missing value.**

22. $m = 135$, $g = 9$ 23. $m = 340$, $s = 42.5$ 24. $s = 32$, $g = 7.3$

Use the formulas for circumference, C solve for the indicated variable. Use 3.1

25. $d = 9$ ft, $C \approx$ ■ ft 26.

Find each square root.

28. $\sqrt{36}$ 29. $\sqrt{81}$

Use the table on page 419 or a calculat to the nearest thousandth.

33. $\sqrt{7}$ 34. $\sqrt{12}$

Use the Pythagorean Theorem to find th

38. $a = 6$, $b = 8$ 39. $a = 12$,

Solve.

42. Use the formula $I = prt$ to find the i owed for a loan of \$800 for 1 year annual rate of 13%.

44. Mary traveled 135 miles at an avera rate of 45 mph. Use the formula $rt = d$ to find how many hours Mary traveled.

374 *Using Formulas*

Independent Test for Chapter 17

Use $n \times 100 = p$ **to change each fraction to a percent.**

1. $\frac{4}{5}$ 2. $\frac{1}{2}$ 3. $\frac{2}{5}$ 4. $\frac{3}{5}$ 5. $\frac{8}{10}$

Write a mathematical expression for each verbal expression.

6. 7 times a number 7. 3 less than a number

8. 2 more than a number 9. a number divided by 5

Use the values in each table to find the function rule.

10.

x	y
14	7
27	20
31	24
42	35

rule: y = ■■■

11.

x	y
$\frac{1}{2}$	$\frac{1}{4}$
1	1
2	4
4	16

rule: y = ■

12.

x	y

Find the next three terms in each arithmetic sequ

13. 10, 20, 30, 40, ■■, ■■, ■■

15. ${}^-15$, ${}^-10$, ${}^-5$, 0, ■■, ■■, ■■

Find the next three terms in each geometric sequ

17. 9, 27, 81, 243, ■■, ■■, ■■

19. 3, ${}^-6$, 12, ${}^-24$, ■■, ■■, ■■

Determine the pattern in each sequence to find th

21. 2, 4, 7, 11, 16, ■■, ■■, ■■

Express each number in scientific notation.

23. 789 24. 6,140

Express each number in standard notation.

27. 4.5×10^3 28. 8.31×10^6

Solve.

31. The perimeter (p) of a triangle with sides 15 ft and 19 ft depends on the length of the third side (s). Write a rule for this function.

T78

Name _____ **Chapter 6, Quiz A**
(Lessons 6-1 through 6-4)

A nickel and a dime are tossed. Find the odds for each toss.

1. both are tails 2. dime is tails 3. nickel is heads, dime is tails 1.

2.

Write each chance as a probability in simplest form.

3.

4. The Broncos have a 40% chance of winning the series. 4.

5. Brenda has an 80% chance of making her next free throw. 5.

Find the odds for each event given its probability or chance. 6.

6. Marta has a 60% chance of being elected class president. 7.

7. The probability of winning the school raffle is 1%. 8.

Suppose all the answers are guesses. Find the expected score for each test. 9.

8. 36 questions, 4 choices each 10.

9. 48 questions, 3 choices each

10. 50 true-false questions; 50 multiple choice questions, 5 choices each

Copyright ©1988 by Merrill Publishing Co. Applications of Mathematics

Name _____ **Chapter 6, Quiz B**
(Lessons 6-5 through 6-7)

Use the poll results at the right to complete the following.

Who do you support for Fire Commissioner?

The teaching package helps you

Teacher Notes

Chapter 1   Charts and Tables

Chapter Overview

In this chapter, students will learn how to read and use data from charts and tables. Those included are bus schedules, federal income tax tables, mileage charts, postal and telephone rates, pay schedules, and sales tax tables. The emphasis is not on computation, but rather on the accurate reading of schedules and charts that can reduce the amount of computation.

Lesson Notes

1-1   Page 3   As part of the preparation for the lesson, remind the students that columns are vertical and rows are horizontal on charts and tables. Bring in several types of maps with mileage charts. Additional information may be found on these charts such as the average travel time by automobile and distances in kilometers.

Chalkboard Exercises   Find the distance between the two cities.

1. row: Louisville, column: Toledo   (301)

2. row: Denver, column: New York   (1,771)

Find the total mileage for a trip that includes the following cities.

1. Atlanta to Chicago to Omaha to Denver to Atlanta
(1,968)

1. 11:16 A.M.   (10:54 A.M.)

2. 3:46 P.M.   (3:24 P.M.)

Activity   Locate a map of the nearest city with a transit system. Obtain several different route maps. Plan a trip by tracing the transit route on the city map. Plan this trip in an unfamiliar area of the city.   (See students' work.)

1-3   Page 6   Although postal rates may change, the basic method for computing postage for first-class letters is given. When rates change, you may want the students to figure postage costs at the new rate.

The Zip + 4 is a voluntary code that uses 9 digits to speed mail delivery. The original 5-digit code remains the same. The 4 new digits indicate the following local

In addition to helping you with planning and daily instruction, the **Teacher Annotated Edition** contains more support materials to help you reach students of every ability level.

(1) Teacher Notes include chalkboard exercises you can use to explain concepts to your students.

(2) A year-long assignment guide shows you all of your teaching options for every lesson, including Teacher Resource Book pages.

(3) Clearly stated learning objectives help you customize the program to your class.

(4) Assignment Guides identify exercises for basic, average, and enriched ability levels.

Chapter 14

Day	Lesson and Page Number	Practice/Review	Testing	Special Features	Teacher Resource Book
121	p. 304 14-1, p. 305 14-2, pp. 306–307	Basic Skills Appendix, p. 453			pp. 309–310
122	14-3, pp. 308–309				p. 311
	14-4, pp. 310–312	Key Skills, p. 311 Basic Skills Appendix, pp. 450, 452, 454–457		Calculator, p. 312	p. 312
24	14-5, pp. 313–315			Computer, p. 315	pp. 308A, 313
125	14-6, pp. 318–319	Practice, pp. 316–317 Basic Skills Appendix, p. 459		Math Break, p. 319	p. 314
126	14-7, pp. 320–321			Mental Math, p. 321	p. 315
127	14-8, pp. 322–323			Calculator, p. 323	p. 316
128	14-9, pp. 324–325			Math Break, p. 325	pp. 308B, 317–318
129		Chapter 14 Review, pp. 326–327	Chapter 14 Test, p. 328		pp. 305–307
130		Cumulative Review, p. 329	Independent Test, p. T75		pp. 319–320

Chapter 15

Day	Lesson and Page Number	Practice/Review	Testing	Special Features	Teacher Resource Book
131	p. 330 15-1, p. 331 15-2, pp. 332–333	Basic Skills Appendix, pp. 421–422, 425, 428, 453			pp. 329–330
132	15-3, pp. 334–335	Key Skills, p. 334 Basic Skills Appendix, pp. 435–436, 455–456		Math Break, p. 335	p. 331
133	15-4, pp. 336–337	Basic Skills Appendix, pp. 450, 454, 457		Calculator, p. 337	pp. 328A, 332
134	15-5, pp. 338–339	Key Skills, p. 338 Basic Skills Appendix, pp. 443–444, 460		Mental Math, p. 339	p. 333
135	15-6, pp. 342–343	Practice, pp. 340–341 Basic Skills Appendix, pp. 438–439		Computer, p. 343	p. 334
136	15-7, pp. 344–345	Basic Skills Appendix, pp. 435, 436, 456			p. 335

T23

7-6   Using Customary Measures of Length

Objective: To add, subtract, multiply, and divide customary units of length.

Rose is making a skirt and a blouse. She needs 2 feet 8 inches of ribbon for the skirt and 3 feet 7 inches of ribbon for the blouse. How much ribbon does she need?

When you add, subtract, multiply, or divide measurements, you may need to rename some of the units.

Examples

A. Add.

$$\begin{array}{r} 2 \text{ ft } 8 \text{ in.} \\ + \ 3 \text{ ft } 7 \text{ in.} \\ \hline 5 \text{ ft } 15 \text{ in.} \end{array}$$

Add the inches, then the feet.

Rename the sum.   *15 in. = 1 ft 3 in.*

5 ft 15 in. = 6 ft 3 in.

B. Subtract.

$$\begin{array}{r} 9 \text{ ft } 4 \text{ in.} \to Rename. \to \ \overset{8}{\cancel{9}} \overset{16}{\cancel{4}} \text{ ft } \ \text{in.} \\ - \ 3 \text{ ft } 7 \text{ in.} \qquad\qquad - \ 3 \text{ ft } 7 \text{ in.} \\ \hline \qquad\qquad\qquad 5 \text{ ft } 9 \text{ in.} \end{array}$$

C. Multiply.

$$\begin{array}{r} 3 \text{ yd } 1 \text{ ft} \\ \times \qquad 4 \\ \hline 12 \text{ yd } 4 \text{ ft} \end{array}$$

Multiply the units separately.

Rename the product.   *4 ft = 1 yd 1 ft*

12 yd 4 ft = 13 yd 1 ft

D. Divide.

2)7 yd 1 ft   2)6 yd 4 ft
= 3 yd 2 ft

Rename.

Basic: 2–22 even; Average: 1–22; Enriched: 1–15 odd, 17–22

Exercises

Add, subtract, multiply, or divide.

1.
$$\begin{array}{r} 2 \text{ ft } 9 \text{ in.} \\ + \ 11 \text{ ft } 2 \text{ in.} \\ \hline 13 \text{ ft } 11 \text{ in.} \end{array}$$

2.
$$\begin{array}{r} 6 \text{ ft } 8 \text{ in.} \\ + \ 3 \text{ ft } 6 \text{ in.} \\ \hline 10 \text{ ft } 2 \text{ in.} \end{array}$$

3.
$$\begin{array}{r} 3 \text{ yd } 24 \text{ in.} \\ + \ 4 \text{ yd } 22 \text{ in.} \\ \hline 8 \text{ yd } 10 \text{ in.} \end{array}$$

4.
$$\begin{array}{r} 4 \text{ mi } 900 \text{ yd} \\ + \ 7 \text{ mi } 900 \text{ yd} \\ \hline 12 \text{ mi } 40 \text{ yd} \end{array}$$

5.
$$\begin{array}{r} 8 \text{ ft } 11 \text{ in.} \\ - \ 3 \text{ ft } 6 \text{ in.} \\ \hline 5 \text{ ft } 5 \text{ in.} \end{array}$$

6.
$$\begin{array}{r} 13 \text{ ft} \\ - \ 6 \text{ ft } 8 \text{ in.} \\ \hline 6 \text{ ft } 4 \text{ in.} \end{array}$$

7.
$$\begin{array}{r} 7 \text{ yd } 1 \text{ ft} \\ - \ 5 \text{ yd } 2 \text{ ft} \\ \hline 1 \text{ yd } 2 \text{ ft} \end{array}$$

8.
$$\begin{array}{r} 6 \text{ mi } 1,200 \text{ ft} \\ - \ 3 \text{ mi } 4,700 \text{ ft} \\ \hline 2 \text{ mi } 1,780 \text{ ft} \end{array}$$

9.
$$\begin{array}{r} 4 \text{ ft } 4 \text{ in.} \\ \times \qquad 2 \\ \hline 8 \text{ ft } 8 \text{ in.} \end{array}$$

10.
$$\begin{array}{r} 6 \text{ ft } 8 \text{ in.} \\ \times \qquad 3 \\ \hline 20 \text{ ft} \end{array}$$

11.
$$\begin{array}{r} 13 \text{ yd } 2 \text{ ft} \\ \times \qquad 3 \\ \hline 41 \text{ yd} \end{array}$$

12.
$$\begin{array}{r} 2 \text{ mi } 500 \text{ yd} \\ \times \qquad 5 \\ \hline 11 \text{ mi } 740 \text{ yd} \end{array}$$

150   *Length*

---

succeed with every student.

The **Teacher Resource Book** includes a wealth of blackline masters to help you meet every need . . . making MERRILL APPLICATIONS OF MATHEMATICS one of the most comprehensive general mathematics programs available!
- Teaching Aids
- Extra Practice
- Problem Solving
- Use a Computer
- Enrichment
- Cumulative Review
- Quizzes
- Standardized-Format Tests
- Book Tests

This convenient teaching aid is completely organized by chapter . . . and it comes with a binder and tabbed dividers for easy storage.

Name _____ Problem Solving

Missing Facts

Always study a verbal problem carefully to determine what facts are given and what facts are needed. Sometimes facts that you need are missing from the problem.

Each bookshelf will hold about 30 books.
How many shelves will Kim need for her books?

You need to know how many books Kim has. The problem does not have all the facts you need to solve it.

EXERCISES Tell what facts are needed in order to solve each of the following.

1. Jeff added up the scores on his five tests to find his average score. What is his average score?

   What are Jeff's test scores?

2. After the salesperson added the tax, Sue's shoe bill was $32.84. How much change will she get?

   How much money did she give the salesperson?

3. Leon and his friends decided to go to a double feature. Each movie is about 1 hour 50 minutes long. At what time will they get out of the movies?

   What time does the movie start?

4. After the restaurant began to advertise on the radio, they had about 30 more customers per day. About how many customers per week do they now serve?

   How many customers did they have before they advertised?

5. One-half of the money from the Drake High School car-wash was to

6. Vickie won the election by 85 votes over Naomi. How many votes did

---

Name _____ Extra Practice
(Lesson 3-6)

Percent of a Number

The table below shows how four families budget their expenses.

Family	Take-Home Pay	Housing	Food	Clothing	Enter-tainment	Trans-portation	Savings
Adams	$2,500	25%	31%	18%	9%	12%	5%
Brown	$1,875	27%	38%	12%	11%	5%	7%
Correa	$2,125	31%	37%	15%	6%	9%	2%
Davis	$1,650	16%	43%	20%	8%	10%	3%

Use the table above to find the amount that the families spend on the following types of expenses.

1. Adams; housing
2. Brown; food
3. Correa; clothing
4. Davis; entertainment
5. Adams; transportation
6. Brown; savings
7. Correa; housing
8. Davis; clothing
9. Adams; entertainment
10. Brown; transportation
11. Correa; food
12. Davis; savings

Solve.

13. What number is 50% of 30?
14. 20% of 64 is what number?
15. 40% of 22 is what number?
16. What number is 15% of 19.05?
17. 20% of 30 is what number?
18. What number is 12% of 162?

Copyright ©1988 by Merrill Publishing Co. Application of Mathematics

---

Name _____ Enrichment

Magic Squares

A magic square is an arrangment of numbers where the sum of each row, column, and diagonal all equal the same total.

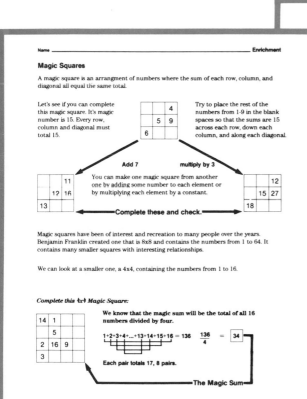

Let's see if you can complete this magic square. It's magic number is 15. Every row, column and diagonal must total 15.

Try to place the rest of the numbers from 1-9 in the blank spaces so that the sums are 15 across each row, down each column, and along each diagonal.

Add 7 You can make one magic square from another one by adding some number to each element or by multiplying each element by a constant. **multiply by 3**

Complete these and check.

Magic squares have been of interest and recreation to many people over the years. Benjamin Franklin created one that is 8x8 and contains the numbers from 1 to 64. It contains many smaller squares with interesting relationships.

We can look at a smaller one, a 4x4, containing the numbers from 1 to 16.

Complete this 4x4 Magic Square:

We know that the magic sum will be the total of all 16 numbers divided by four.

$1+2+3+4+...+13+14+15+16 = 136$ $\dfrac{136}{4} = 34$

Each pair totals 17, 8 pairs.

The Magic Sum

Copyright ©1988 by Merrill Publishing Co. Applications of Mathematics

Learning Objectives

Objectives for Chapter 1
Charts and Tables

1-1: To learn how to read a mileage chart.

1-2: To interpret transit system schedules.

1-3: To learn how to read postal rate charts.

1-4: To find the lowest long distance rates.

1-5: To read pay schedules and withholding tax tables.

1-6: To use a tax table to find tax owed.

1-7: To read sales tax schedules.

1-8: To make a table in order to solve a problem.

Objectives for Chapter 2
Everyday Statistics

2-1: To gather and record data from a survey.

2-2: To know what a sample is and to use data in a frequency table.

2-3: To become familiar with calculator functions.

2-4: To determine the range and mode of a set of data.

2-5: To determine the mean of a set of data.

2-6: To determine the median of a set of data.

2-7: To determine whether the mean, median, or mode yields the desired result.

2-8: To choose the best average for a given situation.

Objectives for Chapter 3
Ratio, Proportion, and Percent

3-1: To use a ratio to compare two numbers and to write ratios as fractions.

3-2: To find unit rates.

3-3: To use cross products to solve proportions.

3-4: To learn how ratios are used in scale drawings.

3-5: To change a fraction, mixed numeral, or decimal to a percent. To change a percent to a fraction, mixed numeral, or decimal.

3-6: To find the percent of a number.

3-7: To find the percent one number is of another.

3-8: To find a number when a percent of it is known.

3-9: To solve verbal problems involving ratios, proportions, and percents.

Objectives for Chapter 4
Graphs

4-1: To interpret pictographs. To draw pictographs from data.

4-2: To interpret bar graphs. To draw bar graphs from data.

4-3: To interpret line graphs and to draw line graphs from data.

4-4: To interpret circle graphs.

4-5: To interpret histograms.

4-6: To determine what makes a graph misleading.

4-7: To use graphs to predict and estimate the solution to word problems.

Objectives for Chapter 5
Probability

5-1: To determine all the possible outcomes.

5-2: To use a tree diagram to determine all possible outcomes of a given situation.

5-3: To use more than one method to solve word problems.

5-4: To find the probability of an outcome and to express a probability as a fraction.

5-5: To find the probability of independent events.

5-6: To find the probability of dependent events.

5-7: To find the probability of an event using addition.

5-8: To find the probability of an event using estimation.

Objectives for Chapter 6
Using Probability and Statistics

6-1: To find the odds, given the probability.

6-2: To change chance to probability and vice versa.

6-3: To change odds to probability and vice versa.

6-4: To compare probabilities and expected values.

6-5: To use statistics to make predictions.

6-6: To find the expected winnings.

6-7: To solve problems using Venn diagrams.

Objectives for Chapter 7
Length

7-1: To recognize and use nonstandard units of measure.

7-2: To identify and use metric units of length.

7-3: To change from one metric unit of length to another.

7-4: To identify and use customary units of length.

7-5: To change from one customary unit of length to another.

7-6: To add, subtract, multiply, and divide customary units of length.

7-7: To determine the number of significant digits in a given measurement. To determine the more precise of two measurements.

7-8: To compare units of length in the metric and customary systems.

Objectives for Chapter 8
Other Common Measurements

8-1: To familiarize students with the different metric units for weight.

8-2: To identify the appropriate metric unit for measuring capacity in a given situation.

8-3: To change from one metric unit to another.

8-4: To change from one customary unit of weight or capacity to another.

8-5: To identify the appropriate Celsius temperature for a given situation. To change Fahrenheit to Celsius, and Celsius to Fahrenheit.

8-6: To familiarize students with time measurement and to change units of time.

8-7: To solve multi-step word problems involving measurements.

Objectives for Chapter 9
Reading Measures

9-1: To read an odometer and to use odometer readings to find the distance traveled.

9-2: To learn how to find routes, distances, and driving times on travel maps.

9-3: To tell time on a 24-hour clock.

9-4: To read a stopwatch and a graduated cylinder.

9-5: To read electric, gas, and water meters.

9-6: To measure and draw angles using a protractor.

9-7: To solve word problems that give too much information.

Objectives for Chapter 10
Geometry

10-1: To name and represent basic terms of geometry.

10-2: To classify angles as acute, right, or obtuse.

10-3: To recognize and use complementary and supplementary angles.

10-4: To recognize parallel and perpendicular lines and vertical angles.

10-5: To identify the parts of triangles and circles.

10-6: To classify triangles by sides and by angles.

10-7: To find squares and square roots. To find the hypotenuse of a right triangle.

10-8: To use number patterns and geometrical patterns to solve word problems.

10-9: To identify the parts of a conditional statement, and to write the converse of a statement.

10-10: To use and distinguish between deductive and inductive reasoning.

Objectives for Chapter 11
Constructions

11-1: To identify congruent figures.

11-2: To construct a line segment congruent to a given line segment. To construct a circle with a given radius.

11-3: To construct an angle congruent to a given angle.

11-4: To construct the bisector of a given line segment and a given angle.

11-5: To construct a line perpendicular to a given line.

11-6: To construct a line parallel to a given line through a point not on the line.

11-7: To construct a triangle congruent to a given triangle using the SSS, SAS, or ASA rule.

Objectives for Chapter 12
Polygons and Circles

12-1: To determine if a given figure is a polygon.

12-2: To classify quadrilaterals.

12-3: To use proportions to find missing lengths in similar figures.

12-4: To find the perimeter of a polygon.

12-5: To find the circumference of a circle.

12-6: To find the area of rectangles and parallelograms.

12-7: To find the area of a triangle.

12-8: To find the area of a trapezoid.

12-9: To find the area of a circle.

12-10: To use diagrams and formulas to find composite areas.

Objectives for Chapter 13
Surface Area and Volume

13-1: To find the surface area of rectangular prisms.

13-2: To find the surface area of pyramids.

13-3: To find the surface area of a cylinder.

13-4: To find the surface area of a cone.

13-5: To find the volume of prisms.

13-6: To find the volume of cylinders.

13-7: To find the volume of pyramids and cones.

13-8: To find the surface area and volume of spheres.

13-9: To compare volumes by subtraction and division.

Objectives for Chapter 14
Rational Numbers

14-1: To recognize integers and their opposites.

14-2: To recognize rational numbers, their opposites, and their absolute value.

14-3: To investigate patterns on number lines.

14-4: To add rational numbers using rules for addition.

14-5: To subtract rational numbers.

14-6: To multiply rational numbers.

14-7: To divide rational numbers.

14-8: To learn the order of operations.

14-9: To solve problems involving rational numbers.

Objectives for Chapter 15
Solving Open Sentences

15-1: To discover how placeholders are used in mathematics.

15-2: To solve open sentences using a replacement set and the guess-and-check method.

15-3: To solve equations by using subtraction.

15-4: To solve equations by using addition.

15-5: To solve equations by using division.

15-6: To solve equations by using multiplication.

15-7: To solve equations that involve two operations.

15-8: To solve inequalities.

15-9: To solve verbal problems using equations and inequalities.

Objectives for Chapter 16
Using Formulas

16-1: To write powers as a product of the same factor and vice versa, and to evaluate powers.

16-2: To use the order of operations to evaluate expressions.

16-3: To solve problems using formulas.

16-4: To practice using formulas.

16-5: To compute squares and square roots, and to use a square root table.

16-6: To use the Pythagorean Theorem to find unknown lengths.

16-7: To use formulas to solve problems.

Objectives for Chapter 17
Patterns and Functions

17-1: To write expressions and to organize information in a table.

17-2: To complete a function table given a function rule.

17-3: To find a rule for a function given a table.

17-4: To find the terms in an arithmetic sequence.

17-5: To find the terms in other kinds of sequences.

17-6: To change numbers in standard notation to scientific notation, and vice versa.

17-7: To use geometrical patterns and numerical patterns to solve word problems.

Objectives for Chapter 18
The Coordinate Plane

18-1: To locate and name points by using ordered pairs.

18-2: To learn more about the coordinate system.

18-3: Select values for x and find the corresponding values for y from a linear equation in x and y.

18-4: To graph linear equations.

18-5: To obtain information by reading a graph.

18-6: To identify or graph a reflection, rotation, translation, or dilation of a figure in a coordinate plane.

18-7: To solve problems using graphs.

Assignment Guide

The Assignment Guide is provided as an aid in planning the year's work. This guide gives examples of pacing and assignments. You should use the assignment guide in relation to the interests and ability levels of your students.

Use this assignment guide to help you in supplementing the daily assignments with exercises from the Reviews, Practice pages, Tests, Special Features, and the *Teacher Resource Book*.

Chapter 1

Day	Lesson and Page Number	Practice/ Review	Testing	Special Features	Teacher Resource Book
1	p. 2 1-1, p. 3 1-2, pp. 4–5			Math Break, p. 5	pp. 49–50
2	1-3, pp. 6–7			Math Break, p. 7	p. 51
3	1-4, pp. 8–9			Mental Math, p. 9	pp. 48A, 52
4	1-5, pp. 10–11			Math Break, p. 11	p. 53
5	1-6, pp. 14–15	Practice, pp. 12–13 Basic Skills Appendix, p. 420		Math Break, p. 15	p. 54
6	1-7, pp. 16–17			Computer, p. 17	p. 55
7	1-8, pp. 18–19				pp. 48B, 56–58
8		Chapter 1 Review, pp. 20–21	Chapter 1 Test, p. 22		pp. 45–47
9		Cumulative Review, p. 23	Independent Test, p. T62		pp. 59–60

Chapter 2

Day	Lesson and Page Number	Practice/ Review	Testing	Special Features	Teacher Resource Book
10	p. 24 2-1, p. 25 2-2, pp. 26–27			Mental Math, p. 27	pp. 69–70
11	2-3, pp. 28–29			Computer, p. 29	p. 71
12	2-4, pp. 30–31	Basic Skills Appendix, pp. 422, 433			pp. 68A, 72
13	2-5, pp. 32–33	Key Skills, p. 32 Basic Skills Appendix, pp. 421, 424, 428, 432, 434		Math Break, p. 33	p. 73
14	2-6, pp. 36–37	Practice, pp. 34–35 Basic Skills Appendix, pp. 435, 441		Calculator, p. 35 Mental Math, p. 37	p. 74

Day	Lesson and Page Number	Practice/ Review	Testing	Special Features	Teacher Resource Book
15	2-7, pp. 38–39	Basic Skills Appendix, pp. 426, 428			p. 75
16	2-8, pp. 40–41				pp. 68B, 76–78
17		Chapter 2 Review, pp. 42–43	Chapter 2 Test, p. 44		pp. 65–67
18		Cumulative Review, p. 45	Independent Test, p. 63		pp. 79–80

Chapter 3

Day	Lesson and Page Number	Practice/ Review	Testing	Special Features	Teacher Resource Book
19	p. 46 3-1, p. 47 3-2, pp. 48–49	Bas. Sk. App., pp. 445–446, 448–449 Key Skills, p. 48 Basic Skills Appendix, pp. 441, 443			pp. 89–90
20	3-3, pp. 50–51	Basic Skills Appendix, pp. 438–439			p. 91
21	3-4, pp. 52–53	Key Skills, p. 52 Basic Skills Appendix, pp. 458–459		Math Break, p. 53	pp. 88A, 92
22	3-5, pp. 56–58	Practice, pp. 54–55 Key Skills, p. 58 Basic Skills Appendix, pp. 451, 461		Math Break, p. 55	p. 93
23	3-6, pp. 59–60	Basic Skills Appendix, pp. 427, 431		Mental Math, p. 60	p. 94
24	3-7, pp. 61–62				p. 95
25	3-8, pp. 63–64	Basic Skills Appendix, p. 460		Computer, p. 64	p. 96
26	3-9, pp. 65–67			Calculator, p. 67	pp. 88B, 97–99
27		Chapter 3 Review, pp. 68–69	Chapter 3 Test, p. 70		pp. 85–87
28		Cumulative Review, p. 71	Independent Test, p. 164		pp. 100–101

Chapter 4

Day	Lesson and Page Number	Practice/ Review	Testing	Special Features	Teacher Resource Book
29	p. 72 4-1, p. 73 4-2, pp. 74–76			Math Break, p. 76	pp. 111–112
30	4-3, pp. 77–79			Mental Math, p. 79	p. 113
31	4-4, pp. 80–81	Key Skills, p. 80 Basic Skills Appendix, pp. 432, 438, 461		Calculator, p. 81	pp. 110A, 114

Day	Lesson and Page Number	Practice/ Review	Testing	Special Features	Teacher Resource Book
32	4-5, pp. 84–85	Practice, pp. 82–83		Math Break, p. 83 Computer, p. 85	p. 115
33	4-6, pp. 86–87				p. 116
34	4-7, pp. 88–89				pp. 110B, 117–118
35		Chapter 4 Review, pp. 90–91	Chapter 4 Test, p. 92		pp. 107–109
36		Cumulative Review, p. 93	Independent Test, p. T65		pp. 119–120

Chapter 5

Day	Lesson and Page Number	Practice/ Review	Testing	Special Features	Teacher Resource Book
37	p. 94 5-1, p. 95 5-2, pp. 96–97			Math Break, p. 97	pp. 129–130
38	5-3, pp. 98–99	Basic Skills Appendix, p. 425			pp. 131, 137–138
39	5-4, pp. 100–101	Basic Skills Appendix, pp. 421, 449			pp. 128A, 132
40	5-5, pp. 104–105	Practice, pp. 102–103 Key Skills, p. 104 Bas. Sk. App., pp. 447, 449, 458		Math Break, p. 103	p. 133
41	5-6, pp. 106–107	Basic Skills Appendix, pp. 449, 458		Calculator, p. 107	p. 134
42	5-7, pp. 108–109	Key Skills, p. 108 Basic Skills Appendix, pp. 450, 454, 458		Computer, p. 109	p. 135
43	5-8, pp. 110–111	Basic Skills Appendix, p. 449		Mental Math, p. 111	pp. 128B, 136
44		Chapter 5 Review, pp. 112–113	Chapter 5 Test, p. 114		pp. 125–127
45		Cumulative Review, p. 115	Independent Test, p. T66		pp. 139–140

Chapter 6

Day	Lesson and Page Number	Practice/ Review	Testing	Special Features	Teacher Resource Book
46	p. 116 6-1, p. 117 6-2, pp. 118–119	Key Skills, p. 118 Basic Skills Appendix, pp. 428, 449, 460		Math Break, p. 119	pp. 149–150
47	6-3, pp. 120–121	Basic Skills Appendix, p. 449		Computer, p. 121	p. 151
48	6-4, pp. 122–123	Basic Skills Appendix, p. 458		Math Break, p. 123	pp. 148A, 152

Day	Lesson and Page Number	Practice/ Review	Testing	Special Features	Teacher Resource Book
49	6-5, pp. 126–127	Practice, pp. 124–125 Key Skills, p. 127 Bas. Sk. App., pp. 421, 430–431, 458		Mental Math, p. 125	p. 153
50	6-6, pp. 128–129	Basic Skills Appendix, pp. 421, 442, 449		Calculator, p. 129	p. 154
51	6-7, pp. 130–131	Basic Skills Appendix, pp. 421–422			pp. 148B, 155–156
52		Chapter 6 Review, pp. 132–133	Chapter 6 Test, p. 134		pp. 145–147
53		Cumulative Review, p. 135	Independent Test, p. T67		pp. 157–158

Chapter 7

Day	Lesson and Page Number	Practice/ Review	Testing	Special Features	Teacher Resource Book
54	p. 136 7-1, pp. 137–138			Computer, p. 138	p. 167
55	7-2, pp. 139–141			Math Break, p. 141	p. 168
56	7-3, pp. 142–143	Key Skills, p. 142 Basic Skills Appendix, p. 440			p. 169
57	7-4, pp. 144–145				pp. 166A, 170
58	7-5, pp. 148–149	Practice, pp. 146–147 Basic Skills Appendix, pp. 427, 430		Calculator, p. 149	p. 171
59	7-6, pp. 150–151			Mental Math, p. 151	p. 172
60	7-7, pp. 152–153				p. 173
61	7-8, pp. 154–155				pp. 166B, 174–176
62		Chapter 7 Review, pp. 156–157	Chapter 7 Test, p. 158		pp. 163–165
63		Cumulative Review, p. 159	Independent Test, p. T68		pp. 177–178

Chapter 8

Day	Lesson and Page Number	Practice/ Review	Testing	Special Features	Teacher Resource Book
64	p. 160 8-1, p. 161 8-2, pp. 162–163			Math Break, p. 163	pp. 187–188
65	8-3, pp. 164–165	Key Skills, p. 165 Basic Skills Appendix, pp. 426, 442			pp. 186A, 189

Day	Lesson and Page Number	Practice/ Review	Testing	Special Features	Teacher Resource Book
66	8-4, pp. 166–169	Key Skills, p. 167 Basic Skills Appendix, pp. 458–459		Computer, p. 169	p. 190
67	8-5, pp. 172–173	Practice, pp. 170–171 Basic Skills Appendix, p. 458		Mental Math, p. 173	p. 191
68	8-6, pp. 174–175			Calculator, p. 175	p. 192
69	8-7, pp. 176–177				pp. 186B, 193–194
70		Chapter 8 Review, pp. 178–179	Chapter 8 Test, p. 180		pp. 183–185
71		Cumulative Review, p. 181	Independent Test, p. T69		pp. 195–196

Chapter 9

Day	Lesson and Page Number	Practice/ Review	Testing	Special Features	Teacher Resource Book
72	p. 182 9-1, p. 183 9-2, pp. 184–185	Basic Skills Appendix, pp. 423, 436–437			pp. 205–206
73	9-3, pp. 186–187			Mental Math, p. 187	p. 207
74	9-4, pp. 188–189			Calculator, p. 189	pp. 204A, 208
75	9-5, pp. 192–195	Practice, pp. 190–191 Key Skills, p. 193 Basic Skills Appendix, p. 422		Computer, p. 195	p. 209
76	9-6, pp. 196–197				p. 210
77	9-7, pp. 198–199			Math Break, p. 199	pp. 204B, 211–212
78		Chapter 9 Review, pp. 200–201	Chapter 9 Test, p. 202		pp. 201–203
79		Cumulative Review, p. 203	Independent Test, p. T70		pp. 213–214

Chapter 10

Day	Lesson and Page Number	Practice/ Review	Testing	Special Features	Teacher Resource Book
80	p. 204 10-1, pp. 205–206 10-2, p. 207				pp. 223–224
81	10-3, pp. 208–209			Mental Math, p. 209	p. 225
82	10-4, pp. 210–211				p. 226
83	10-5, pp. 212–213			Math Break, p. 213	pp. 222A, 227

Day	Lesson and Page Number	Practice/Review	Testing	Special Features	Teacher Resource Book
84	10-6, pp. 214–215			Math Break, p. 215	p. 228
85	10-7, pp. 218–220	Practice, pp. 216–217 Basic Skills Appendix, p. 419			p. 229
86	10-8, pp. 221–223			Calculator, p. 223	pp. 230, 233
87	10-9, pp. 224–225			Computer, p. 225	p. 231
88	10-10, pp. 226–227				pp. 222B, 232
89		Chapter 10 Review, pp. 228–229	Chapter 10 Test, p. 230		pp. 219–221
90		Cumulative Review, p. 231	Independent Test, p. T71		pp. 234–235

Chapter 11

Day	Lesson and Page Number	Practice/Review	Testing	Special Features	Teacher Resource Book
91	p. 232 11-1, p. 233				p. 245
92	11-2, pp. 234–235			Calculator, p. 235	p. 246
93	11-3, pp. 236–237				p. 247
94	11-4, pp. 238–239			Mental Math, p. 239	pp. 244A, 248
95	11-5, pp. 242–243	Practice, pp. 240–241			p. 249
96	11-6, pp. 244–245			Math Break, p. 245	p. 250
97	11-7, pp. 246–249			Computer, p. 249	pp. 244B, 251–254
98		Chapter 11 Review, pp. 250–251	Chapter 11 Test, p. 252		pp. 241–243
99		Cumulative Review, p. 253	Independent Test, p. T72		pp. 255–256

Chapter 12

Day	Lesson and Page Number	Practice/Review	Testing	Special Features	Teacher Resource Book
100	p. 254 12-1, p. 255 12-2, pp. 256–257			Math Break, p. 257	pp. 265–266
101	12-3, pp. 258–259	Key Skills, p. 259			p. 267
102	12-4, pp. 260–261	Basic Skills Appendix, p. 435			p. 268

Day	Lesson and Page Number	Practice/Review	Testing	Special Features	Teacher Resource Book
103	12-5, pp. 262–263	Basic Skills Appendix, pp. 425, 438–439		Calculator, p. 263	pp. 264A, 269
104	12-6, pp. 266–267	Practice, pp. 264–265 Basic Skills Appendix, pp. 425, 438–439		Math Break, p. 267	p. 270
105	12-7, pp. 268–269	Basic Skills Appendix, pp. 425, 438–439		Computer, p. 269	p. 271
106	12-8, pp. 270–271	Basic Skills Appendix, pp. 425, 435, 438–439		Mental Math, p. 271	p. 272
107	12-9, pp. 272–273	Basic Skills Appendix, pp. 425, 438–439			p. 273
108	12-10, pp. 274–275	Basic Skills Appendix, pp. 421, 425, 435, 438–439			pp. 264B, 274–275
109		Chapter 12 Review, pp. 276–277	Chapter 12 Test, p. 278		pp. 261–263
110		Cumulative Review, p. 279	Independent Test, p. T73		pp. 276–277

Chapter 13

Day	Lesson and Page Number	Practice/Review	Testing	Special Features	Teacher Resource Book
111	p. 280 13-1, p. 281 13-2, pp. 282–283				pp. 287–288
112	13-3, pp. 284–285	Key Skills, p. 284 Basic Skills Appendix, pp. 438–439		Calculator, p. 285	p. 289
113	13-4, pp. 286–287				pp. 286A, 290
114	13-5, pp. 288–289				p. 291
115	13-6, pp. 292–293	Practice, pp. 290–291		Math Break, p. 293	p. 292
116	13-7, pp. 294–295			Mental Math, p. 295	p. 293
117	13-8, pp. 296–297			Computer, p. 297	p. 294
118	13-9, pp. 298–299				pp. 286B, 295–297
119		Chapter 13 Review, pp. 300–301	Chapter 13 Test, p. 302		pp. 283–285
120		Cumulative Review, p. 303	Independent Test, p. T74		pp. 298–299

Chapter 14

Day	Lesson and Page Number	Practice/ Review	Testing	Special Features	Teacher Resource Book
121	p. 304 14-1, p. 305 14-2, pp. 306–307	Basic Skills Appendix, p. 453			pp. 309–310
122	14-3, pp. 308–309				p. 311
123	14-4, pp. 310–312	Key Skills, p. 311 Basic Skills Appendix, pp. 450, 452, 454–457		Calculator, p. 312	p. 312
124	14-5, pp. 313–315			Computer, p. 315	pp. 308A, 313
125	14-6, pp. 318–319	Practice, pp. 316–317 Basic Skills Appendix, p. 459		Math Break, p. 319	p. 314
126	14-7, pp. 320–321			Mental Math, p. 321	p. 315
127	14-8, pp. 322–323			Calculator, p. 323	p. 316
128	14-9, pp. 324–325			Math Break, p. 325	pp. 308B, 317–318
129		Chapter 14 Review, pp. 326–327	Chapter 14 Test, p. 328		pp. 305–307
130		Cumulative Review, p. 329	Independent Test, p. T75		pp. 319–320

Chapter 15

Day	Lesson and Page Number	Practice/ Review	Testing	Special Features	Teacher Resource Book
131	p. 330 15-1, p. 331 15-2, pp. 332–333	Basic Skills Appendix, pp. 421–422, 425, 428, 453			pp. 329–330
132	15-3, pp. 334–335	Key Skills, p. 334 Basic Skills Appendix, pp. 435–436, 455–456		Math Break, p. 335	p. 331
133	15-4, pp. 336–337	Basic Skills Appendix, pp. 450, 454, 457		Calculator, p. 337	pp. 328A, 332
134	15-5, pp. 338–339	Key Skills, p. 338 Basic Skills Appendix, pp. 443–444, 460		Mental Math, p. 339	p. 333
135	15-6, pp. 342–343	Practice, pp. 340–341 Basic Skills Appendix, pp. 438–439		Computer, p. 343	p. 334
136	15-7, pp. 344–345	Basic Skills Appendix, pp. 435, 436, 456			p. 335

Day	Lesson and Page Number	Practice/ Review	Testing	Special Features	Teacher Resource Book
137	15-8, pp. 346–347	Key Skills, p. 347 Basic Skills Appendix, pp. 435, 457–458			p. 336
138	15-9, pp. 348–349	Basic Skills Appendix, pp. 421–422, 436		Math Break, p. 349	pp. 328B, 337–339
139		Chapter 15 Review, pp. 350–351	Chapter 15 Test, p. 352		pp. 325–327
140		Cumulative Review, p. 353	Independent Test, p. T76		pp. 340–341

Chapter 16

Day	Lesson and Page Number	Practice/ Review	Testing	Special Features	Teacher Resource Book
141	p. 354 16-1, p. 355 16-2, pp. 356–357	Key Skills, p. 357		Math Break, p. 357	pp. 351–352
142	16-3, pp. 358–360	Basic Skills Appendix, pp. 427, 438, 441, 458		Computer, p. 360	p. 353
143	16-4, pp. 361–362	Basic Skills Appendix, pp. 425, 428, 438, 443		Calculator, p. 362	pp. 350A, 354
144	16-5, pp. 365–366	Practice, pp. 363–364		Math Break, p. 366	p. 355
145	16-6, pp. 367–368				p. 356
146	16-7, pp. 369–371	Basic Skills Appendix, pp. 435, 439		Mental Math, p. 371	pp. 350B, 357–358
147		Chapter 16 Review, pp. 372–373	Chapter 16 Test, p. 374		pp. 347–349
148		Cumulative Review, p. 375	Independent Test, p. T77		pp. 359–360

Chapter 17

Day	Lesson and Page Number	Practice/ Review	Testing	Special Features	Teacher Resource Book
149	p. 376 17-1, p. 377 17-2, pp. 378–379	Basic Skills Appendix, pp. 431, 439		Mental Math, p. 379	pp. 369–370
150	17-3, pp. 380–381				pp. 368A, 371
151	17-4, pp. 382–383	Key Skills, p. 383 Basic Skills Appendix, pp. 435–436, 450			p. 372

Day	Lesson and Page Number	Practice/ Review	Testing	Special Features	Teacher Resource Book
152	17-5, pp. 386–387	Practice, pp. 384–385 Key Skills, p. 387 Basic Skills Appendix, p. 459		Math Break, p. 387	p. 373
153	17-6, pp. 388–389	Basic Skills Appendix, p. 426		Computer, p. 389	p. 374
154	17-7, pp. 390–391			Calculator, p. 391	pp. 368B, 375–376
155		Chapter 17 Review, pp. 392–393	Chapter 17 Test, p. 394		pp. 365–367
156		Cumulative Review, p. 395	Independent Test, p. T78		pp. 377–378

Chapter 18

Day	Lesson and Page Number	Practice/ Review	Testing	Special Features	Teacher Resource Book
157	p. 396 18-1, p. 397				p. 387
158	18-2, pp. 398–399				p. 388
159	18-3, pp. 400–401			Math Break, p. 401	p. 389
160	18-4, pp. 402–403			Mental Math, p. 403	pp. 386A, 390
161	18-5, pp. 406–407	Practice, pp. 404–405			p. 391
162	18-6, pp. 408–410			Calculator, p. 410 Computer, p. 411	
163	18-7, pp. 412–413				pp. 386B, 393–394
164		Chapter 18 Review, pp. 414–415	Chapter 18 Test, p. 416		pp. 383–385
165		Cumulative Review, p. 417	Independent Test, p. T79		pp. 395–396

Teacher Notes

Chapter 1   Charts and Tables

Chapter Overview

In this chapter, students will learn how to read and use data from charts and tables. Those included are bus schedules, federal income tax tables, mileage charts, postal and telephone rates, pay schedules, and sales tax tables. The emphasis is not on computation, but rather on the accurate reading of schedules and charts that can reduce the amount of computation.

Lesson Notes

1-1   Page 3   As part of the preparation for the lesson, remind the students that columns are vertical and rows are horizontal on charts and tables. Bring in several types of maps with mileage charts. Additional information may be found on these charts such as the average travel time by automobile and distances in kilometers.

Chalkboard Exercises   Find the distance between the two cities.

1. row: Louisville, column: Toledo   (301)

2. row: Denver, column: New York   (1,771)

Find the total mileage for a trip that includes the following cities.

1. Atlanta to Chicago to Omaha to Denver to Atlanta (3,068)

2. San Francisco to Denver to Dallas to New Orleans to St. Louis to San Francisco   (5,274)

1-2   Page 4   Students will find learning to read transit system schedules useful for travel in their city or when visiting another city. The route map and timetable help passengers orient themselves in the city and plan their traveling time.

Chalkboard Exercises   Suppose you want to arrive at Sunlawn and Miami at each of the following times. Use the timetable on page 4 to tell when you should board at Maple and Lenox.

1. 11:16 A.M.   (10:54 A.M.)

2. 3:46 P.M.   (3:24 P.M.)

Activity   Locate a map of the nearest city with a transit system. Obtain several different route maps. Plan a trip by tracing the transit route on the city map. Plan this trip in an unfamiliar area of the city.   (See students' work.)

1-3   Page 6   Although postal rates may change, the basic method for computing postage for first-class letters is given. When rates change, you may want the students to figure postage costs at the new rate.

The Zip + 4 is a voluntary code that uses 9 digits to speed mail delivery. The original 5-digit code remains the same. The 4 new digits indicate the following local areas.

$$\underbrace{8\ 4\ 2\ 7\ 5} \qquad \underbrace{3 \qquad 4} \qquad \underbrace{0 \qquad 5}$$

| original code | sector (10 to 20 blocks) | segment (one side of a street) |

Chalkboard Exercises   For each of the following weights, give the number of pounds used to find Priority Mail Rates on page 6.

1. $1\frac{1}{4}$ lb   (2)   **2.** 5 lb 6 oz   (6)

Have the students find the Zip + 4 Code for each student in the class and answer the following questions.

1. How many sectors and segments are represented in the class?
2. How many students are in the same sectors?

1-4 Page 8 Since telephone rates vary from city to city, use your local directory to find some typical charges for the full rate, 40% discount, and 60% discount dial-direct calls. Discuss the operator-assisted calls and the type of calls charged this highest rate.

Chalkboard Exercises Use the charts on page 8 to answer each of the following. What rate would you be charged, when calling dial-direct to Marietta at 9:30 P.M.

1. on a Sunday? (40% discount)
2. on a Saturday? (60% discount)

Answer yes or no to each of the following.
1. The full rate to Lancaster is lower than the one to Zanesville. (No)
2. Night rates are lower than evening rates. (Yes)

1-5 Page 12 This lesson shows how to read pay schedules and withholding tax tables. Point out to the students that schedules like the pay schedule shown save having to do certain computations over and over again.

Chalkboard Exercises Use the pay schedule on page 12 to answer each of the following. The hourly rate and number of hours worked are given.
1. $4.10 for 34 h   ($139.40)
2. $4.60 for 38 h   ($174.80)

Use the withholding tax table on page 12 to answer each of the following.
1. Number of allowances is 3, amount of earnings: $226.00. What is the amount of withheld tax? ($18.00)
2. The amount of withheld tax is $25, the amount of earnings is $286.50. What is the number of allowances claimed?   (4 allowances)

1-6 Page 14 You may wish to point out that if certain criteria are met, students may claim themselves as dependents and their parents may also claim them as dependents. This is explained in the tax booklet and other IRS material. Some students may be interested in researching this and reporting back to the class.

Chalkboard Exercise Use the information in the chart below and the tax table on page 14 to find the tax for a single person claiming one exemption. Then find the amount of the payment or refund.

Taxable Income	Tax Withheld	Tax Owed	Payment (P) or Refund (R)
$10,179	$1,000	**1.** ($1,082)	**2.** ($82 P)
$10,290	$2,010	**2.** ($1,098)	**4.** ($912 R)

1-7 Page 16 Students as consumers should become aware of the tax rates and the amount of tax added to the total cost.

Chalkboard Exercises Use the tax table on page 16 to find the sales tax on each of the following purchases.
1. $12.35   ($0.68)
2. $6.20   ($0.35)

Use the tax schedule on page 16 to complete each of the following.
1. The tax on $25 is ($1.38) .
2. The tax on $34 is ($1.87) .

1-8 Page 18 This lesson focuses on the process of using information from a table of data to solve problems. First, the student should understand what the problem is and what he is looking for. Then, by using some common sense search techniques, the answer can be located.

Activity Have the students study the table of data and list some interesting facts about Mickey Mantle's batting record that were not asked for on page 19. Then, have them write 3 questions that can be answered using the table.   (See students' work.)

Chapter 2   *Everyday Statistics*

Chapter Overview

In this chapter, the students will be introduced to the mode, mean, and median, which are measures of central tendency. Effects of additional data, misleading data, and frequency tables will be introduced.

Lesson Notes

2-1   Page 25   Students are introduced to tallying. Due to the reading and counting ease, tally marks are separated into groups of five.

Chalkboard Exercises   Use tally marks to represent each of the following.

1. 18   (卌 卌 卌 |||)   2. 6   (卌 |)

Activity   Surveys and elections lend themselves to tallying. Have a student find a survey on a newspaper and distribute it to the math class. Have them record the results with tally marks.

2-2   Page 26   The concept of sampling is introduced. Stress the point that a sample should be representative of many different areas. For example, a basketball team would not be a good group to sample for shoe sizes. They would have larger shoe sizes than the average person.

Chalkboard Exercises   Construct a frequency table using the following shoe sizes. List the shoe sizes from smallest to largest.

$6\frac{1}{2}$, 7, 5, $6\frac{1}{2}$, 6, $8\frac{1}{2}$, 7, $7\frac{1}{2}$, $6\frac{1}{2}$, $8\frac{1}{2}$, $7\frac{1}{2}$, 5, $6\frac{1}{2}$, 8, $6\frac{1}{2}$, 7, 6, 6, 7

Activity   Have a marketing researcher speak to the class. Ask the researcher to bring to class several surveys developed by the company.

2-3   Page 28   This lesson instructs students in using a calculator. Ask students to identify other commands on their calculators that are not identified in the text.

Point out to students the flowchart on page 28. Explain that it is a graphic representation of the different steps involved to perform an operation on a calculator. Point out that the oval $\bigcirc$ calls for the beginning and the end of the operation, and the rectangles $\square$ mean that the variables need to be entered to process the calculations.

Chalkboard Exercises   Use a calculator to evaluate the following.

1. $6 \times 2 - 4 \times 2$ (4)
2. $6 \times 3 \div 9 - 1$ (1)
3. $42 - 54 \div 6$ (33)

2-4   Page 30   The range and mode are introduced as the easiest measures of central tendency to understand. Numbers can be taken from a telephone book to illustrate the range and mode. The mode can have three cases. (1) There is no mode if no element is listed more than once. (2) There is one mode if one element is listed more than once. (3) There is more than one mode if several elements are listed the same number of times and more than once.

Chalkboard Exercises   Find the mode and range for each of the following.

1. 5, 8, 6, 5, 9, 12, 5, 6   (5; 7)

2. 3.1, 4.9, 2.7, 3.1, 4.5, 3.1, 4.9   (3.1; 2.2)

Activity   Since astrology is popular, take a survey of the astrological signs of the students in your class. Find the mode. Astrology makes a good bulletin board display.

2-5   Page 32   The mean is commonly known as the average. All three measures of central tendency are averages. Only the mean has kept the title "average."

Chalkboard Exercises   Find the mean for each of the following.

1. 2, 3, 7, 5, 6, 12, 15, 4, 9   (7)

2. 4, 9, 3, 13, 8, 6, 15, 16 $(9\frac{1}{4})$

Activity   Use a metric ruler to measure the height of each student. Round each height to the nearest centimeter. Find the mean, and range of the heights for the class and the mode and range.

2-6   Page 36   The median is the most difficult of the central tendencies to understand. To determine the median, the set of data must be put in order. Listing the data vertically might make it easier for the student to determine the median. If there is an odd number of data, the median will be the middle element. If there is an even number of data, the median is the mean of the two middle elements.

Chalkboard Exercises   Find the median for each of the following.

1. 4, 7, 8, 12, 15, 21, 27, 36, 42   (15)

2. 3, 7, 5, 6, 2, 9, 1, 13, 5, 6 $(5\frac{1}{2})$

Activity   Have the students write 3 sets of data: a set that has no median, a set whose median is not in the set, and a set whose median is in the set.

no median—[a, b, c, d]

not in the set—[1, 2, 3, 4]

in the set—[3, 4, 6, 8, 9]

2-7   Page 38   It is important to know which statistical measure is being used when the word "average" is employed. The mean, mode, and median are all types of statistical averages.

Chalkboard Exercises   Use the data listed below to answer the following questions.

2, 2, 6, 74

1. What is the mode, mean, and median?
   (2; 21; 4)

2. Which of the averages are more misleading and most descriptive? (The mode and the mean are misleading. The median best describes the data.)

Activity   Have the students develop a topic, take a survey, and show how the statistical averages could be misleading.

2-8   Page 40   The problem-solving section involves the mode, mean, and median. Given the situation, the student will have to recognize which average best describes the answer for that particular situation.

Chalkboard Exercises   Find the mode, mean, and median for each of the following.

1. 3, 7, 6, 13, 5, 3, 10, 11, 14   (3; 8; 7)

2. 2, 8, 5, 1, 2, 7, 2, 5 $(2; 4; 3\frac{1}{2})$

Find a set of data that contains different numbers and whose mode, mean, and median are the same number.   ([3, 4, 5, 4, 4])

Chapter 3   Ratio, Proportion, and Percent

Chapter Overview

In this chapter, students will explore ratio, ratio as a rate, proportions, percent, proportion and percent, similar figures, and scale drawings. Mathematical skills will involve writing ratios as fractions, writing ratios as rates, finding cross products for a proportion, changing ratios to percents, changing percents to fractions, and changing decimals to percents and percents to decimals.

Lesson Notes

3-1   Page 47   Point out the four ways that a ratio can be written. Have students discuss the way each can be used. Emphasize that ratios are comparisons and they are useful in everyday life. An interest rate is a ratio. For example, an interest rate of 14% means $14 on each $100.

Chalkboard Exercises   Write each ratio as a fraction in simplest form.

1. 5 to 10 $\left(\frac{1}{2}\right)$ **2.** 12 to 8 $\left(\frac{3}{2}\right)$ **3.** 8 to 12 $\left(\frac{2}{3}\right)$

3-2   Page 48   Emphasize the difference between rate and unit rate. Discuss the similarities of unit rate and unit pricing. Mention how rate and unit rate can be used in everyday life. For example, a store has a sale on batteries; buy 2, get 2 free (4 to 2) or 2 for the price of 1 (2 to 1).

Chalkboard Exercises   Solve.
Twelve ounces of ham cost $3.29. At that rate, how much do 16 ounces of ham cost?   ($4.39)

Activity   Have students use grocery ads to set up a shopping situation in which they must determine the better buy. Students should solve their own problems first, then, trade their list with other students. Have students check to see if they agree with each other.

3-3   Page 50   A proportion can be used to compare two sets of data. Cross products make com-

paring 2 sets of data, or finding missing numerators and denominators quick and easy.

Chalkboard Exercises   Replace each ▒ with the missing number.

1. $\frac{21}{12} = \frac{▒}{4}$ (7)   **2.** $\frac{3}{4} = \frac{9}{▒}$ (12)

Activity   Have students answer a coded joke or question by solving proportions. Make up a coded joke and give each student a copy. For example, why does a chicken cross the road? $\underline{\text{T}}$ $\underline{\text{O}}$ _ _ _ _ _ _ _ _ _ _ _ _ _ _ _ _ _ _ _.

Use the alphabet A through Z and a number to go with each letter. As the students solve the proportion, they find a letter in the puzzle. Put problems in order so that each answer corresponds to the order of the blanks.

3-4   Page 52   Display a scale drawing of your classroom and the furniture. Point out that the scale drawing and the actual room and furniture are similar figures. Given the scale on the scale drawing and the scale size, proportions can be used to find the actual size. Measure some furniture on the scale drawing and find the corresponding actual size. You may want to think of a scale drawing as an aerial photograph with only the outline of shapes showing.

Chalkboard Exercises   On a certain scale drawing, 1 inch represents 36 inches. Find the actual size for the following.

1. 10 in. (360 in.)   **2.** 6 in. (216 in.)

T30

3-5   Page 56   Using a ratio as a percent makes it easier to compare ratios in two or more situations. Discuss why percent can mean per one hundred or hundredths. It is important to be able to write a decimal as a percent. Most research or descriptive material will use percents rather than decimals to relate findings. Changing a percent to a decimal is used in everyday life. Sales and state taxes, interest, and commissions are figured on a percent, which must be changed to a decimal before computation.

Chalkboard Exercises   Write each percent as a fraction in simplest form.

1. 30% $\left(\frac{3}{10}\right)$ **2.** 25% $\left(\frac{1}{4}\right)$ **3.** 48% $\left(\frac{12}{25}\right)$

3-6   Page 59   Emphasize the terms *rate, base,* and *percentage.* Point out that the base and percentage are numbers, while the rate is a percent. Stress that the rate must always be written as a fraction or a decimal before computing an answer. The equation $\frac{\text{Percentage}}{\text{Base}}$ = Rate can also be written Rate × Base = Percentage.

Chalkboard Exercises   Solve.

1. 10% of 420   (42)   **2.** 15% of 40   (6)

3. 48% of 85   (40.8)   **4.** 61$\frac{1}{2}$% of 90   (55.35)

3-7   Page 61   The proportion $\frac{P}{B} = \frac{r}{100}$ is used to find the percent one number is of another. Be sure students understand that when finding the percent one number is of another, their final answers should be percents and therefore, a percent sign should be placed after the numbers.

Chalkboard Exercises   Solve.

1. 4$\frac{1}{2}$ is what percent of 9?   (50%)

2. What percent of 25 is 5?   (20%)

3. 29.7 is what percent of 90?   (33%)

3-8   Page 63   Discuss with students when it is best to change the percent to a decimal and when it is best to change the percent to a fraction. Point out that percents such as 33$\frac{1}{3}$% can only be written as repeating decimals, and therefore should be changed to fractions. However, this is not true of all fractional percents. For example, 37$\frac{1}{2}$% can be written as 37.5% and then as 0.375. Remind students that when no decimal point appears in a percent, the decimal point should be placed *after* the number.

Chalkboard Exercise   Name the percentage, base, or rate. Then solve.

Jose left $1.90 as a 15% tip for dinner at a restaurant. What was his bill for dinner?   (P = 1.90, r = 15, b = 12.6$\overline{6}$)

3-9   Page 65   Stress the "Decide" step. Students must determine the values for *P, B,* and *r.* Once values have been determined, solve the problem and give an answer. Have students reread the problems and determine whether the answer is reasonable. Students should also check their solutions.

Chalkboard Exercises   You may want to have students use a calculator to find the following percents and percentages to the nearest tenth.

1. 7 is what percent of 8?   (87.5%)

2. What number is 5% of 48?   (2.4)

Chapter 4   *Graphs*

Chapter Overview

In this chapter, graphing is introduced as a method of organizing data. Students learn how to interpret pictographs, bar graphs, line graphs, circle graphs, and histograms.

Lesson Notes

4-1   Page 73   A pictograph uses symbols to show quantities of objects. It attracts attention and enables a quick comparison. Each picture represents many actual items. To find the total number of items represented, multiply the number of pictures by the number of items represented by each picture. Fractional parts are represented by partial pictures.

Chalkboard Exercises   Suppose you want to construct a pictograph to show the number of telephones in several different cities. A picture of a telephone will represent 1,000,000 telephones. Answer the following questions.

1. If there are 6,500,000 telephones in a city, how many pictures of a telephone will be shown in the pictograph? $(6\frac{1}{2})$

2. If there are 250,000 telephones in a city, how many pictures of a telephone will be shown in the pictograph? $(\frac{1}{4})$

4-2   Page 74   Call attention to the parts of a graph. They are the title, labels, and scales. A well-constructed graph can be interpreted with little or no written description. The vertical scale should always begin with 0 (zero) and end with a number slightly greater than any numerical data to be displayed. Starting the scale at 0 allows for a better comparison of the data.

Chalkboard Exercises   The flying speeds of six birds are: swallow, 148 mph; crow, 125 mph; eider duck, 100 mph; falcon, 70 mph; bald eagle, 50 mph; and wild goose, 45 mph.

1. To make a bar graph for the data, what is the best

scale for the horizontal axis? (intervals of 20 mph)

2. Construct a bar graph for the data. (See students' work.)

4-3   Page 77   Line graphs are often used to show change over a period of time. Line graphs show change and trends better than any other type of graph. Line graphs must be accurately drawn.

Chalkboard Exercises   Refer to the graph below to answer the following questions.

Number of Daily Sales

1. What is the number of sales for each day? (M, 300; T, 280; W, 320; Th, 450; F, 540; S, 560)

2. Between which two days did the sales increase the most?   (Wed. and Thurs.)

4-4   Page 80   Circle graphs are used to compare parts to the whole. Budgets, percentages, component parts, and so on are often graphed using circle graphs. The entire circle represents 100% or the whole. The largest sector of the circle represents the greatest percentage. All percentages must total 100% as all sectors must total the complete circle. Review how to change percents to decimals.

Chalkboard Exercises Suppose a family's income is $30,000. Use the circle graph to find the amount spent on each of the following.

Family Spending

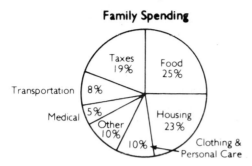

1. Food ($7,500) 2. Housing ($6,900)
3. Taxes ($5,700) 4. Medical ($1,500)

4-5 Page 84 Histograms are used to show the frequency of certain occurrences. The data is grouped in intervals. The bars' widths represent the class intervals, and the heights represent the number of observations per interval.

Chalkboard Exercises Answer the following.

1. How is a histogram different from a bar graph? (There are no spaces between the bars of a histogram.)

2. When intervals for histograms are being chosen, what happens when a group has no members? (The space will be left empty.)

4-6 Page 86 The importance of starting the vertical scale at 0 is shown in two pairs of graphs on page 87. The width of the bars on the graphs on page 86 tends to make the graphs misleading.

Activity Have students use their math test scores for six weeks to make a misleading line graph.

4-7 Page 88 Graphs are sometimes used to estimate future events. Continuing the path of a line graph usually results in a good estimate. This process is known as extrapolation.

Chalkboard Exercises The following chart shows the number of athletes on a school's track team from 1984 through 1987. Use the chart to answer the following questions.

Year	1984	1985	1986	1987
no. of athletes	33	39	43	48

1. What is the estimate for the number of members on the 1988 track team? (53)

2. What year should the team have 70 members? (1991 or 1992)

Chapter 5   Probability

Chapter Overview

The main objective of the chapter is to give the students a solid base in probability. Counting outcomes starts the students through single and multiple probabilities.

Lesson Notes

5-1   Page 95   After you discuss the Cotter's possible outcomes for their travel plans, go through an example that has 3 parts. Have the students write the possible outcomes given the letters A, B, and C. Ask them to find the number of ways the 3 letters can be arranged.   (6 ways)

Chalkboard Exercises   There are 2 white disks, 3 red disks, 6 blue disks, and 1 green disk. Choose one disk. How many ways are there for drawing each of the following?

1. a red disk   (3)

2. a white or a blue disk   (8)

Activity   Draw one card from a standard deck of 52 cards. How many ways are there for drawing each of the following?

1. a king   (4)   **3.** a red card   (26)

3. a diamond   (13)   **4.** an 8   (4)

5-2   Page 96   A coin toss is another good example in which to use a tree diagram. Toss a penny and a dime. On the chalkboard, develop a tree diagram similar to the one on page 96. Use H for heads and T for tails. Ask students the following questions. How many possible outcomes are there?   (4) Are the outcomes equally likely?   (yes)

Chalkboard Exercises   Suppose there are 2 spinners, each divided into halves. One half is A, the other B. Spin both spinners. Find the number of possible outcomes for each of the following.

1. AA   (1)   **2.** not BA   (3)

Use a tree diagram to list the possible outcomes of tossing a penny, nickel, and dime.

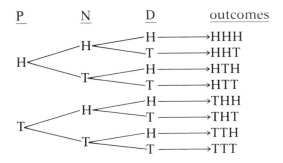

5-3   Page 98   Three alternate methods for finding the number of outcomes are discussed. They are lists, tree diagrams, and multiplication. Multiplication is the principle method of counting outcomes. Many kinds of choices could serve as additional examples.

Chalkboard Exercise   How many different autos can be ordered given the following information?

Auto: 3 colors, 2 body styles, 3 kinds of radios, 2 types of tires   (36)

5-4   Page 100   After completing three lessons on the number of outcomes, the students should be ready for probability. Use the letter F for favorable outcomes and N for unfavorable outcomes. What would represent total number of outcomes? $(F + N)$

$$\text{probability} = \frac{\text{number of favorable outcomes}}{\text{number of possible outcomes}}$$

$$P = \frac{F}{F + N}$$

Chalkboard Exercises   Find the probability of drawing each of the following from a deck of 52 playing cards.

1. a 7 $\left(\frac{4}{52} \text{ or } \frac{1}{13}\right)$

2. a club $\left(\frac{13}{52} \text{ or } \frac{1}{4}\right)$

3. a 5 or a queen $\left(\frac{8}{52} \text{ or } \frac{2}{13}\right)$

5-5   Page 104   The fundamental principle of counting, multiplication, pertains to probability as well as outcomes. Show the tree diagram for the example· on page 104. You can find the number of outcomes: 3 × 5 = 15. Find the favorable number of outcomes: 1 × 2 = 2.
Probability $= \frac{2}{15}$ or $\frac{\text{favorable}}{\text{total}}$.

Chalkboard Exercises   A bag contains 2 green, 3 red, and 4 gold marbles. Find the probability of drawing each of the following with and without replacement.

1. 2 green marbles $\left(\frac{4}{81}\right)\left(\frac{1}{36}\right)$

2. 2 red marbles $\left(\frac{1}{9}\right)\left(\frac{1}{12}\right)$

5-6   Page 106   Additional problems dealing with probability are discussed. The replacement of articles and its effect on the answer is discussed. Be sure to discuss the probabilities of 1 and 0. Go over several examples having a probability of 1 and a probability of 0.
Another example of multiplying probabilities is as follows. A bag contains 5 red marbles and 2 blue marbles. The probability of picking 2 blue marbles in a row changes a great deal if the first marble is replaced or not replaced. The probability of picking a blue marble first is $\frac{2}{7}$. By not replacing the blue marble and picking again, the probability of picking another blue marble is $\frac{1}{6}$ not $\frac{2}{7}$. The probability of picking 2 blue

marbles is $\frac{2}{42}$ or $\frac{1}{21}$. What is the probability of picking 2 blue marbles if the first marble is replaced? $\left(\frac{4}{49}\right)$

Activity   The first example on page 106 shows a probability of $\frac{1}{6}$ that the first key opens the blue room and the second key opens the green room. What happens to the probability if the number of keys is increased to 4?   (The probability is cut in half from $\frac{1}{6}$ to $\frac{1}{12}$.) Suppose there are 6 keys. $\left(\frac{1}{30}\right)$ Can you identify a pattern? If so, what is the probability if there are 20 keys? $\left(\frac{1}{380}\right)$

5-7   Page 108   For events that cannot occur at the same time A and B, $P(A \text{ or } B) = P(A) + P(B)$.

Chalkboard Exercise   Solve. Suppose you spin the spinner shown below. What is the probability of spinning an even number or 5? $\left(\frac{2}{3}\right)$

5-8   Page 110   Point out to students that in the example on page 110, the second statement can be assumed to be true only if this is a representative sample of SoundMaster AM radios produced by the company.

Chalkboard Exercise   Solve. (Answers may vary. Typical answer is given.)

There are 32 defective TV's out of 3,314 TV's produced. One TV is chosen at random to be tested. Estimate the probability of choosing a defective TV. $\left(\frac{1}{100}\right)$

Chapter 6   Using Probability and Statistics

Chapter Overview

The material in this chapter deals with probability and topics relating to probability. Other lessons deal with probability and percents, multiplying probabilities, and odds.

Lesson Notes

6-1   Page 117   If S represents the number of ways an event *can* occur (successes), and F represents the number of ways an event *cannot* occur (failures), then the odds for an event are $\frac{S}{F}$. Odds are commonly written as "6 to 2" or "6:2." These odds should be read "six to two."

Chalkboard Exercises   There are 3 cubes in a bag. Two cubes are red and one cube is white. Find the odds for each of the following.

1. picking a white cube   (1 to 2)

2. picking a red cube   (2 to 1)

Activity   Set up several different chance events and have students pick at random. Record the results. Do the experiment at least 20 times to get a good result.

6-2   Page 118   The lesson is a review of changing percents to fractions and changing probabilities in the form of fractions to percents. No new concept is taught. Review how to change a decimal to a percent and how to change a fraction to a decimal using division.

For the Math Break on page 119: Use the given scores and percentiles to better illustrate percentiles.

Score	Percentile
70	100th
68	90th
68	90th
62	70th
57	60th
50	50th
46	40th
46	40th
32	20th
25	10th

Chalkboard Exercises   Write each percent as a probability in fraction form.

1. 25% $\left(\frac{1}{4}\right)$ **2.** 40% $\left(\frac{2}{5}\right)$ **3.** 90% $\left(\frac{9}{10}\right)$

Arrange the following probabilities in order from least to greatest.

78%, $\frac{9}{12}$, 5 out of 7, $\frac{74}{100}$, 0.8, $\frac{121}{160}$ (5 out of 7, $\frac{74}{100}$, $\frac{9}{12}$, $\frac{121}{160}$, 78%, 0.8)

6-3   Page 120   This section shows the relationship between odds and probability. Review the expressions of $\frac{S}{F}$ and $\frac{S}{F+S}$.

Chalkboard Exercises   Find the probability for each of the following odds. Express the probability as a fraction in simplest form and as a percent.

1. 3 to 7 $\left(\frac{3}{10}\right)$ (30%)   **2.** 4 to 1 $\left(\frac{4}{5}\right)$ (80%)

Suppose the probability for an event is given as x. Write a formula for the odds for the same event. Test your formula with probabilities such as 0.4, $\frac{1}{4}$, and 20%. (In terms of x, the odds are "x to $(1 - x)$.")

6-4   Page 122   Stress the fact that events are never certain to happen exactly as predicted.

Chalkboard Exercises   A spinner is divided into fourths labeled red, green, blue, and gold. Out of 80 spins, how many times would you expect the spinner to stop:

1. on the blue?   (20)

2. not on the red?   (60)

Activity   Pass answer sheets out to the class. Each contains 10 answer lines each having the letters "a" through "e." Pick a letter in each and ask the students to guess which letter you picked in each line. Record their success and the predicted results.

6-5   Page 126   Statistics are used to estimate how many weeks supplies will last, how many votes a candidate will receive, and other real-world occurrences.

Chalkboard Exercises   Solve.

1. Of the first 100 votes cast, 42 votes were in favor of candidate A. How many votes would you predict candidate A to receive if 1,000 votes were cast? (420)

2. A regular octahedron has 8 congruent faces. The faces are numbered 1 through 8. Suppose you roll it 160 times. How many times would you expect each of the following?

1. a 7   (20)   **2.** a 5 or a 6   (40)

6-6   Page 128   The probability of winning a lottery is talked about in this section. If your state has a lottery, use information concerning the lottery for a class discussion.

Chalkboard Exercises   Find the expected winnings for the following raffle.   ($0.50)

1. 1,000 tickets sold at $2 each
        1—$300 prize

10—$10 prizes
20—$5 prizes

Solve.

2. Using 500 tickets at $1 each, what would the total prize money be for the game to be fair?   ($500)

6-7   Page 130   The problem-solving section uses Venn Diagrams to solve statistical problems. Point out in the example on page 130 that the rectangle represents the total number of television viewers. The circles represent the viewers in each satellite region, and the intersection of the circles represents the viewers in both satellite regions.

Chalkboard Exercises   Answer the following for the given Venn Diagram.

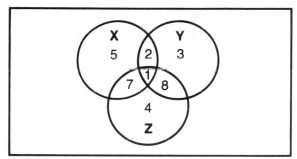

1. What is the total number in region X?   (15)
2. What is the total number in region Y?   (14)
3. What is the total number in the intersection of regions X and Z?   (8)

Chapter 7   Length

Chapter Overview

Nonstandard, metric, and customary units of length are discussed in this chapter. Estimation of length is emphasized to help students gain an intuitive idea of different units of length.

Lesson Notes

7-1   Page 137   Historically, many measurements were developed using parts of the human body. The obvious variability caused problems and confusion. This lesson is intended to point out the need for standard units of measurement.

Have the students measure a variety of objects using thumbs, spans, cubits, and paces. The variation of results should convince them of the need for standard units of measurement.

Activities   Ask students to measure the width of their math book using thumbs. Collect this data from all the students. Find the average number of thumbs by adding the individual findings and dividing by the number of students. Who had the greatest number of thumbs? The fewest? To what can you attribute this difference? (Different people have different sized thumbs.)

Cubit and span are very old measures. Have the students research to find other ancient units of measurement.

7-2   Page 139   The metric system is introduced as one measurement system used in the manufacturing of automobiles. The meter is the current world standard for measuring length. The United States is the last major country to adopt the metric system. Metric units of length are introduced and metric prefixes are shown in relation to place-value position. Emphasize that km,

m, cm, and so on are symbols, not abbreviations. No period follows the symbol.

Chalkboard Exercises   Choose the best estimate.

1. length of a ski	**a.** 2 m	**b.** 2 mm
2. thickness of a nickel	**a.** 2 km	**b.** 2 mm
3. width of a window	**a.** 1.5 km	**b.** 1.5 m
4. length of a race	**a.** 1 km	**b.** 1 cm

Answer the following questions.

5. Which is longer—310 millimeters or 310 centimeters?   (310 centimeters)

6. Which is shorter—68 meters or 68 kilometers?   (68 meters)

7-3   Page 142   In this lesson conversion of metric units is taught. Emphasis is on the most commonly used units of length: kilometer, meter, centimeter, and millimeter. Conversion within the system is demonstrated with the units most commonly used: kilometers to meters, meters to centimeters, centimeters to millimeters, and vice versa.

Chalkboard Exercises   Answer the following.

1. Cindy runs 350 meters every day. How many centimeters is this?   (35,000 centimeters)

2. The distance from home to school is 120 km. How many meters is this?   (120,000 meters)

T38

3. To complete 3,500 mm = ▨ m.
Do you multiply or divide? (÷)
Would you use 10, 100, or 1,000? (1,000)

7-4   Page 144   Customary units of length are treated here the same way metric units of length were treated in the previous lesson. Estimation is emphasized. Discuss why the United States continues to use the customary system of measurement.

Chalkboard Exercises   Choose the best estimate.

1. length of a paper clip   **a.** 1.1 in.   **b.** 1.1 ft
2. width of a desk   **a.** 2.6 yd   **b.** 2.6 ft
3. length of a river   **a.** 100 mi   **b.** 100 in.
4. thickness of a book   **a.** 2 in.   **b.** 2 yd

Answer the following.

5. Which is longer—0.8 inches or 0.8 feet?
(0.8 feet)
6. Which is shorter—41 yards or 41 miles?
(41 yards)

7-5   Page 148   In this lesson conversion of customary units is taught. Do not assume that students are totally familiar with customary conversion.

Chalkboard Exercise   Solve.

The common unit we use for auto speed is miles per hour. Braking speed is measured in feet per second. At 55 mph, a car travels about 80 feet per second. The estimated time for reaction in an emergency is about $\frac{3}{4}$ second. At 55 mph, how far does a car travel before the driver begins to brake? (60 ft) Discuss how 80 feet per second is derived from 55 miles per hour. (Change 55 miles to 240,400 feet and 1 hour to 3,600 sec. Then 55 mph becomes 80 ft/sec.)

7-6   Page 150   The purpose of this lesson is to help students add, subtract, multiply, and divide customary units of length.

Chalkboard Exercises   Add, subtract, multiply, or divide.

1.   3 ft 6 in.
    +2 ft 6 in.
    (5 ft 12 in.)

2.   4 yd 2 ft
    ×   5
    (20 yd 10 ft)

Rename each of the above.

3. (6 ft)   **4.** (23 yd 1 ft)

7-7   Page 152   Students will learn to determine the number of significant digits in a measurement and the more precise of two measurements. Be sure students understand examples D, E, F, and G on page 152.

Activity   Ask students to orally respond to the following.

1. Name a number with 3 significant digits.
2. Name a decimal with 5 significant digits.

7-8   Page 154   After becoming familiar with the metric units of length and the customary units of length, students will compare them.

Chalkboard Exercise   Solve.

The average driver drives about 10,000 miles per year. How many miles is this in seven years? How many kilometers is this? (70,000 miles, 112,000.0 kilometers)

Chapter 8   Other Common Measurements

Chapter Overview

The previous chapter dealt with measurements of length. Length is but one of the physical properties that an object may have. In this chapter, students will explore customary and metric units of weight, capacity, temperature, and time. The students need many experiences of measuring to develop an ability to estimate in different units.

Lesson Notes

8-1   Page 161   The term "mass" is well known in science laboratories but has not gained popularity as a quantity of matter to be measured. The term "weight" is used in the text. Mass is the measure of the amount of matter and is constant anywhere. Weight depends upon gravity and may vary from place to place on earth. At sea level a mass of 1 kilogram weighs 2.2 pounds. The familiar example used to distinguish mass and weight is an astronaut who has a mass of 75 kg. His mass is constant, but on a scale, he weighs nothing in space.

Chalkboard Exercises   Choose the best estimate for each of the following.

1. weight of a nickel	**a.** 5 mg	**b.** 5 g
2. weight of an apple	**a.** 8 oz	**b.** 8 lb
3. weight of a dog	**a.** 90 tons	**b.** 90 lb

Activity   A few granules of salt have a mass of 1 milligram. Have the students make a list of objects that would be measured using the milligram unit.

8-2   Page 162   The liter is almost equivalent to one quart. (1 liter ≈ 1.056 quarts) This fact will probably help students recognize reasonable measures of capacity. Use the Special Feature, on page 163, to discuss how measures in the metric system are related. One cubic decimeter holds one liter and weighs one kilogram. One cubic centimeter holds one milliliter and weighs one gram. A visual impression of 1 milliliter can be given by centimeter cubes, a common aid.

Chalkboard Exercises   Complete the following.
1. 16 cubic centimeters of water is 16 milliliters of water and weighs _____. (16 grams)
2. 128 cubic decimeters of water is _____ of water and weighs 128 kilograms.   (128 liters)

Activity   Have the students bring in food containers that are labeled with milliliters and liters. Ask them if they can bring in a one-kiloliter container.

8-3   Page 164   Students who have difficulty multiplying and dividing by 1,000 should review the Key Skills on page 165. Additional problems are found in the Basic Skills Appendix.

Chalkboard Exercises   Use the diagram on page 164 to complete each statement.
1. To change milligrams to grams, divide by _____. (1,000)
2. To change grams to milligrams, _____ by 1,000. (multiply)
3. To change milliliters to liters, _____ by 1,000. (divide)
4. To change liters to milliliters, multiply by _____. (1,000)

Solve.
5. A new nickel coin has a mass of about 5 g. How many milligrams is this?   (5,000 mg) How many kilograms does a roll of nickels weigh?   (0.2 kg)

8-4   Page 166   In this lesson, the emphasis is on customary units of weight and capacity. Food purchased at the grocery store is usually labeled with customary units of weight and capacity. You may want to ask students to write down some of the customary units used on food labels and bring the list to class. Then you may want to ask students to change from one unit to another.

Chalkboard Exercises   Solve.

1. A 46-fluid ounce can of juice sells for 97¢. Find the cost of one ounce to the nearest tenth of a cent. (2.1¢)

2. Milk is purchased in quarts at 79¢ each. How much will it cost for 9 one-cup servings?   ($2.37)

8-5   Page 172   A Celsius thermometer is essential to present this lesson. Use a Celsius thermometer to record indoor and outdoor temperatures over a period of time. This scale was proposed by Anders Celsius, a Swedish astronomer.

Chalkboard Exercises   Change each Fahrenheit reading to a Celsius reading.

1. 149°F (65°C)	**2.** 113°F (45°C)
3. 122°F (50°C)	**4.** 239°F (115°C)
5. 194°F (90°C)	**6.** 374°F (190°C)

Change each Celsius reading to a Fahrenheit reading.

7. 35°C (95°F)	**8.** 5°C (41°F)
9. 95°C (203°F)	**10.** 23°C (73.4°F)
11. 54°C (129.2°F)	**12.** 82°C (179.6°F)

8-6   Page 174   Note that the symbols for time are s, min, h, d, wk, and yr. Because they are symbols and not abbreviations, no period follows.

Chalkboard Exercises   Complete.

1. 1 h = ▧ s   (3,600)   **2.** 1 min ▧ s = 65 s   (5)

3. 700 s = ▧ min ▧ s   (11, 40)

4. 1 h ▧ min = 100 min   (40)

Activity   Use your calculator and the table on page 174 to answer these questions.

1. How old are you in weeks?

2. How old are you in days?

8-7   Page 176   Most of the problems on pages 176 and 177 require more than one computation. Read the first two problems aloud and have students discuss how to solve them. Is there more than one correct way?   (yes)

Chalkboard Exercises   Solve.

1. Ali has a 1,000-mL can of juice. He drinks 250 mL of juice a day. How many days does he need to drink the 1,000-mL can of juice?   (4 days)

2. Alice walks to school and back. The distance from her house to school is 1,800 m. How many kilometers does she walk each week?   (18 km)

Chapter 9   Reading Measures

Chapter Overview

The ability to read different measures is developed by showing the many measurements that are used today. Real world situations are given to emphasize the importance of knowing the measure unit systems. Some of those situations include reading odometers to find distances traveled, reading the gas meter to find out how much gas has been consumed, etc.

Lesson Notes

9-1   Page 183   Discuss the uses of learning to read the odometer. For example, you can figure out how much gasoline is used for a certain amount of miles traveled. If a car is running out of gas, you will be able to know how many more miles you can travel before filling up the tank.

Chalkboard Exercises   Write the reading for each odometer.

1. | 2 | 4 | 6 | 1 | 2 | 0 | (24, 612.0)
2. | 8 | 9 | 0 | 4 | 3 | 6 | (89, 045.6)
3. | 1 | 0 | 1 | 1 | 2 | 3 | (10,112.3)

Solve.

4. Sophia rented a car that had an odometer reading of 38,840.2 miles. When she returned the car, the odometer reading was 40,640.3 miles. How far did Sophia drive?   (1,800.1 miles)

9-2   Page 184   Discuss the interstate highway system shown on the map on page 184. Discuss the advantages and disadvantages of traveling on interstate routes versus the scenic state roads.
Travelers use the driving distance map to compute distance and driving time to cities not included in the mileage chart.

Chalkboard Exercises   Use the map on page 185 to find the total mileage for a trip that includes the following cities.

1. Kansas City to Tulsa to Houston   (726)
2. Salt Lake City to Minneapolis to Chicago   (1,591)
3. Atlanta to New York City to Columbus to Atlanta (2,071)

Activity   Plan a trip from New York City to Albuquerque. Suppose the average driving time per day is 8 hours. Choose the interstate routes. Then find the total miles and the number of days of travel.   (Answers may vary.)

9-3   Page 186   In this lesson, many examples are given to familiarize students with the 24-hour clock. Also, the conversion from a 12-hour time to a 24-hour time, and vice versa, is practiced to make sure students understand the concept.

Chalkboard Exercises   Solve.

1. Kathy White eats dinner at 1915 hours. Using A.M. or P.M., what time does Kathy eat dinner?   (7:15 P.M.)

Express each time as a 12-hour time, using A.M. or P.M.

2. 1814   (6:14 P.M.)   3. 0801   (8:01 A.M.)
4. 0002   (12:02 A.M.)   5. 2359   (11:59 P.M.)

9-4   Page 188   A stopwatch and a graduated cylinder are discussed. Stopwatches are usually

T42

marked in tenths of a second. Graduated cylinders are usually marked in tenths of a milliliter.

Activity   Have the students bring in several different measurement instruments. Display as many different types as possible. Have the students research the instruments that record the lightest and heaviest weights imaginable.

9-5   Page 192   The fourth utility, not mentioned in the section, is the telephone. Point out that to get a reading on the electric meter, you must determine which direction the arrow rotates on each dial. Be sure that students understand that to get a gas meter reading in cubic feet, they must multiply by 100.

Chalkboard Exercises   Match the utility with its unit of measure.

1. electricity   (c)   **a.** cubic feet

2. natural gas   (a)   **b.** gallons

3. water   (b)   **c.** kilowatt hour

Activities   As a project let students record the readings at different times on their home water meters.
You may want to arrange to have a meter reader from a utility company come to your classroom to talk about his or her job.

9-6   Page 196   A demonstration of measuring and drawing angles using an overhead projector is an effective way to begin this lesson. Show how small angles can be measured by using a straightedge to lengthen one ray. The most common error in measuring angles is reading the wrong scale.

Activity   Draw five triangles on a sheet of paper. Measure the three angles of each triangle and record the results. What can you conclude about the sum of the measures of a triangle?   (The sum of the measures of the angles of a triangle equals 180°.)

9-7   Page 198   Many problems contain more than enough information. Each problem in the problem-solving section has too much information. The student will have to analyze the problem and decide what information should be used to solve it.

Chalkboard Exercises   Solve.
A radio costs $39.95 and four speakers total $65.00. If each speaker costs the same price, what does one speaker cost?   ($16.25)

Activity   Have the students write three problems containing too much information. Exchange the problems with classmates and solve them.

Chapter 10   Geometry

Chapter Overview

Students will develop an intuitive understanding of points, lines, planes, rays, angles, and so on. Models of these concepts are related to the everyday experiences of students wherever possible.

Lesson Notes

10-1   Page 205   Students should understand that line segments, lines, and rays have different numbers of endpoints as follows.

line segment	2 endpoints
ray	1 endpoint
line	no endpoints

Exercises 9 through 13 would be valuable for class discussion.

Chalkboard Exercises   Match.

1. point Z (c)

2. line segment DE (a)

3. angle GHI (b)

4. ray PQ (d)

a. $\overline{DE}$

b. $\angle GHI$

c. Z

d. $\overrightarrow{PQ}$

10-2   Page 207   Students learn to classify right, acute, and obtuse angles.

Chalkboard Exercises   Use the symbols $<$, $>$, and $=$ to describe the measure of the following.

1. right angle   (measure $= 90°$)

2. acute angle   ($0° <$ measure $< 90°$)

3. obtuse angle   ($90° <$ measure $< 180°$)

10-3   Page 208   Students learn to recognize complementary and supplementary angles.

Chalkboard Exercises   Tell whether each pair of angles described below is complementary, supplementary, or neither.

1. $64°, 26°$ (C)

2. $147°, 23°$ (N)

3. $16°, 160°$ (N)

4. $90°, 90°$ (S)

What type(s) of angle has no complement?   (right and obtuse)

10-4   Page 210   Lines in a plane either intersect or are parallel. You may wish to introduce skew lines. Skew lines lie in different planes and neither intersect nor are parallel. An example of skew lines is the base of the chalkboard and a diagonal of the opposite wall. Point out that perpendicular lines are a special case of intersecting lines.

Chalkboard Exercises   State whether each of the following is true or false. Refer to the figure for exercises 26–30 on page 211.

1. $\overleftrightarrow{CR} \parallel \overleftrightarrow{QS}$ (true)

2. $\overleftrightarrow{MA} \parallel \overleftrightarrow{RS}$ (false)

3. $\angle JMR$ and $\angle ACR$ are vertical angles.   (false)

4. $\overleftrightarrow{QS} \perp \overleftrightarrow{JB}$ (false)

Activity   After completion of exercises 6 through 9, discuss why vertical angles have the same measure. (They are supplementary to the same angle.)

10-5   Page 212   Students learn that three points (not in a line) will determine a plane, a circle, or a triangle. Three points drawn on a chalkboard might represent a plane. A circle could be drawn including these points. Finally, a triangle could be drawn.

Activity   The "tri" in triangle means three. Name parts of a triangle that come in threes.   (3 sides, 3 angles, 3 vertices or corners)

10-6   Page 214   Triangles are classified by sides and by angles. Be sure that students understand that certain triangles, such as triangles with two right angles, do not exist.

Chalkboard Exercises   Determine whether each of the following exist. Write yes or no.

1. an acute scalene triangle   (yes)

2. an obtuse right triangle   (no)

3. a right isosceles triangle   (yes)

10-7   Page 218   You may want to explain that 5 is the positive square root of 25. It is also true that $^-5 \cdot {}^-5 = 25$, therefore another square root of 25 is the negative square root $^-5$.

In this book we will address only the positive square root, which is also called the principle square root.

Draw squares that are from 1 up to 10 units on a side. Make a chart of side length and area as shown.

side	1	2	3	. . .	10
area	1	4	9	. . .	100

The numbers in the bottom row are the squares of those on top. Also, the numbers in the top row are square roots of those in the bottom row.

Show the class that a ruler or straightedge placed across the square root table makes it easier to read the numbers.

The hypotenuse of a right triangle is always the longest side, opposite the right angle. Its length is represented in the Pythagorean Theorem by the letter c. The letters a and b represent the lengths of the legs.

You may want students to show how the Pythagorean Theorem works for the right triangle surrounding the fountain on the Example on page 218.

Chalkboard Exercises   Square each number. Then find the sum of the squares.

1. 3, 4   (9, 16; 25)

2. 5, 12   (25, 144; 169)

10-8   Page 221   This problem-solving lesson combines geometry and number theory.

You may wish to have students repeat the activity on page 221 using triangles with different shapes.

Activity   Answer the following.

1. How many triangles will be formed when the figure has 15 sides?   (13 triangles)

2. Nine triangles are formed when the vertices of a figure are connected by line segments from one vertex. How many sides does the figure have?   (11 sides)

10-9   Page 224   Point out that not all conditional statements are written in if-then form, such as those in exercises 6–8.

Chalkboard Exercises   Identify the condition and the conclusion in each sentence.

1. If it rains, then I will stay home.

2. x = 2, when x + 3 = 5.

10-10   Page 226   Students learn to use and differentiate between deductive and inductive reasoning.

Chalkboard Exercises   Use inductive reasoning to guess the next two numbers in each list of numbers.

1. 3, 6, 9, 12, (15), (18)

2. 8, 16, 24, (32), (40)

Chapter 11   Constructions

Chapter Overview

Students will learn six basic compass and straightedge constructions. The constructions are listed below.
1. congruent line segment
2. congruent angle
3. bisect a line segment
4. bisect an angle
5. perpendicular line
6. parallel line
7. triangles

Lesson Notes

11-1   Page 233   Students will learn to identify congruent figures. The concept of correspondence is important to understand the idea of congruence.

Chalkboard Exercises   For each of the following, name the corresponding part.

1. ∠A (∠E)   **2.** ∠D (∠B)
3. $\overline{BC}$ ($\overline{DF}$)   **4.** $\overline{EF}$ ($\overline{AC}$)
5. $\overline{DE}$ ($\overline{BA}$)   **6.** ∠C (∠F)

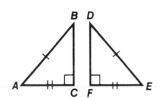

11-2   Page 234   If possible, each student should actually do each construction. Students may use compasses or make their own compass from a pencil and string.

Activities   Have each student draw a line segment on a sheet of paper. Then, construct a line segment congruent to the one drawn. (See students' work.)

Construct a segment three times as long as a given segment. (See students' work.)

11-3   Page 236   Students should become proficient at constructing congruent angles. This skill is needed in constructing parallel lines. Be sure students are able to construct all types of angles—acute, right, and obtuse.

Activities   Draw an acute angle and an obtuse angle. Construct an angle congruent to each angle drawn. (See students' work.)

Draw an acute angle and an obtuse angle. Construct an angle whose measure is the measure of the obtuse angle minus the measure of the acute angle. (See students' work.)

11-4   Page 238   In constructions A and B, students learn how to bisect line segments and angles. As the constructions are done, the student locates the midpoint of a line segment and an angle bisector.

Activities   Draw an acute angle and an obtuse angle. Bisect each angle drawn. (See students' work.)

Draw a triangle. Locate the midpoint of each side of the triangle. Draw a line segment from each vertex to the midpoint of the opposite side. Do research on these three line segments called medians. (The medians meet at a point called the centroid. The centroid is the center of gravity, or balance point, of the triangle.)

11-5   Page 242   The construction of a line perpendicular to a line at a given point depends heavily on the ideas used in bisecting a segment.

Activity   Have students draw an acute triangle. Construct the perpendicular bisector of each side of the triangle. (See students' work. The bisectors meet at a point inside the triangle.)

11-6   Page 244   The construction of a parallel line depends on congruence of corresponding angles. In the Example on page 244, the corresponding angles are $\angle BAP$ and $\angle RPQ$. Since these angles are congruent, lines PQ and AB are parallel.

Activities   Have each student draw a line and a point not on the line on a sheet of paper. Then, construct a line parallel to the line drawn through the point. (See students' work.)
Construct a trapezoid using the construction example on page 244. (See students' work.)

11-7   Page 246   Constructions B and C are more complicated than any of the previous constructions. It may be well to demonstrate these before students do them alone.
Students should understand that the triangles constructed in each of exercises 8 through 19 should be congruent. Point out that exercises 17 through 19 result in equilateral triangles.

Activities   Have each student draw a triangle on a sheet of paper. Then, construct a triangle congruent to the one drawn. (See students' work.)

Draw an acute triangle. From each vertex, construct a line segment perpendicular to the opposite side. Do research on these three line segments called altitudes. (The altitudes meet at a point called the orthocenter.)

Chapter 12   Polygons and Circles

Chapter Overview

In this chapter, the definition of a polygon is discussed. Students will learn to distinguish among different kinds of polygons. The perimeter, circumference, and area of various polygons and circles are presented. The problem-solving lesson brings together many of these concepts.

Lesson Notes

12-1   Page 255   Polygons are defined. Students can try to draw polygons with as few sides as possible, leading to a line, and with as many sides as possible, leading to a circle. Students can draw pentagons, triangles, and quadrilaterals of varied shapes. Point out that the singular of vertices is vertex.

Activity   Have students find out if there are other polygons with specific names, excluding those defined on page 256.

12-2   Page 256   The relationships among different quadrilaterals are emphasized, especially those among parallelograms, rhombuses, rectangles, and squares. You may want to use the following diagram to classify quadrilaterals. From least specific to most specific:

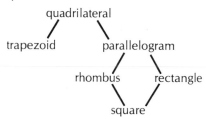

Activity   Using the same instructions given for problems 6 through 13, change the key word to rhombus, changing number 8 to square. Then change the key word to rectangle, changing number 6 to square.

12-3   Page 258   You may want to make a transparency to discuss similar triangles. Stress your explanation of corresponding sides, then vary the location

of the corresponding sides to see if students understand. Once they understand this, it will be easier for them to find missing lengths in similar figures. Another transparency would be valuable to explain missing lengths. Show how the proportion is used to find the missing length in similar figures. Have extra problems for students to solve.

Activity   Have students make their own transparencies with geometric figures, showing the measurement of each side of the figure as it appears. Then, project it onto the screen. This projection will be the corresponding figure. Have a student measure 1 or more sides of the projection. From this, they can compute the rest of the missing lengths.

12-4   Page 260   Perimeter is a linear measurement. It is the distance around a polygon.
Students can measure doors, windows, chalkboards, and desk tops to gain practice in finding perimeters. Students should develop a systematic method for finding perimeter. They can start at one vertex and list the lengths of the sides as they go around the figure back to the starting vertex. A formula for the perimeter of a rectangle may be presented, $P = 2\ell + 2w$, where P is perimeter, ℓ is length, and w is width. The formula can also be written as $P = 2(\ell + w)$.

Activity   Cut a length of string. Have students make as many different polygons with the same perimeter as possible, using pins and a corkboard.
This will demonstrate that different polygons can have the same perimeter. Polygons with the same perimeter are called isoperimetric.

12-5   Page 262   Circumference is a linear measurement. It is the distance around a circle. Discuss its similarity to perimeter by pointing out both are distances around plane, closed figures.

Chalkboard Exercises   Pi is not an arbitrary number. Have students measure the circumference and diameter of various circular objects to verify that $\frac{C}{d} = \pi$. The ratio $\frac{355}{113}$ was discovered centuries ago to be a close approximation for π. On a calculator, the quotient is very close to the actual value of π. Using a calculator and the formula $C = \frac{355}{133} \times d$, find the circumference of a circle with each diameter given below.

Round answers to two decimal places.

1. 2.81 m   (8.83)   **2.** 45.3 in.   (142.31)

12-6   Page 266   Graph paper may be helpful to distinguish between length and area. Counting out the number of squares in rectangles drawn on the graph paper helps students understand square units.

Activity   Use drinking straws strung together to form a parallelogram that is not a rectangle. Measure the lengths of the base and height. Find its area. Move the same straws to form a rectangle. Measure the length and width. Find its area. Students will see that the areas are not the same.

12-7   Page 268   To show that the formula for the area of a triangle, $A = \frac{1}{2} \times b \times h$, holds true, cut out parallelograms of varying sizes and shapes. Have students find the area of each parallelogram, cut it into two triangles, and find the area of each triangle. Be sure students correctly identify the base and height of each triangle before using the formula.

Chalkboard Exercises   Find the area of each triangle described below.

base	height
1. 4 m	3 m (6 m²)
2. 21 in.	22 in. (231 in²)
3. 11.2 cm	10 cm (56 cm²)
4. $14\frac{1}{2}$ yd	16 yd (116 yd²)

12-8   Page 270   In discussing the area of trapezoids, emphasize that the lengths of the bases must be added before doing multiplication. The height is always perpendicular to the bases; the bases are always parallel to each other.

Chalkboard Exercises   Find the area of each trapezoid described below.

base (a)	base (b)	height (h)
1. 3 cm	4 cm	2 cm (7 cm²)
2. 8 in.	10 in.	9 in. (81 in²)
3. 9.2 m	11.4 m	13 m (133.9 m²)
4. 2.3 yd	4.5 yd	6 yd (20.4 yd²)

12-9   Page 272   The formula for the area of a circle is developed from the formula for the area of a parallelogram. Separating the circle into parts does not make a perfect parallelogram, but if smaller and smaller pieces were used the dimensions of the parallelogram, $b \times h$, would become closer and closer to $\left(\frac{1}{2} \times C\right) \times r$.

Chalkboard Exercises   Use a calculator to find the area of each circle with the given radius. Use 3.1416 for π.

1. 47 cm   (6,939.7944 cm²)

2. 3.912 m   (48.078242 m²)

3. 913 mm   (2,618,740.4 mm²)

12-10   Page 274   In this lesson, various word problems are given, and for each one there is a diagram. This will enable students to recognize the type(s) of figure(s) in order to solve the problems.

Chalkboard Exercise   Solve.

The figure below is to be tiled. Find its area. (560.52 m²) Would you order that amount of tile?   (No) Why or why not? (Order extra tile to allow for breakage.)

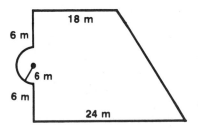

Chapter 13   *Surface Area and Volume*

Chapter Overview

The surface area of various solid figures is discussed. The cubic units of volume are introduced, followed by the volume of several solid figures. The problem-solving lesson shows how to compare the volumes of containers of different sizes.

Lesson Notes

13-1   Page 281   The concepts of surface area and rectangular prism are shown by examples. Using a shoe box or other model of a rectangular prism, slit the sides so that the box lies flat. Have students identify the 3 sets of congruent rectangles making up the rectangular prism. The surface area of the box is the sum of the areas of the 6 rectangular faces. Have students find the area of each face and add them together. Then ask them to find a "shortcut" for finding the surface area by using the 3 sets of congruent rectangles.

Activity   Have students estimate the surface area of several rectangular prisms, such as boxes. Then have them measure the sides of each prism and calculate its surface area. Compare the estimated and calculated surface areas.

13-2   Page 282   A pyramid is a solid figure with a polygonal base. The problems given in this lesson present pyramids with different polygonal bases. The illustrations on page 282 show examples of regular polygonal bases; there are also pyramids with bases that are not regular polygons. These pyramids will have triangular faces that are not congruent.

Chalkboard Exercise   Solve. Round decimal answers to the nearest tenth.

A tent is shaped like an hexagonal pyramid. Each wall is a triangle measuring 10 ft wide and 12 ft high. Find the surface area of the walls of the tent.   (360 ft²)

13-3   Page 284   An oatmeal or salt container can be cut apart to show the two circular bases and the rectangular lateral surface of a cylindrical shape.

Rolling one circular base along the width of the lateral surface will help students understand why the width of the lateral surface equals the circumference of the circular base.

Chalkboard Exercises   Find the surface area of each of the cylinders described below. Use 3.14 for π. Round decimal answers to the nearest tenth.

1. $r = 5$ cm; $h = 11$ cm   (502.4 cm²)

2. $r = 3.4$ in.; $h = 6$ in.   (200.7 in²)

3. $r = 7$ m; $h = 15$ m   (967.1 m²)

13-4   Page 286   As the illustration on page 286 shows, a cone can be considered to be a kind of pyramid. The problems in the text deal with a highly specialized cone, a right circular cone, shown in (a) below. The figure (b) below shows a cone in which a segment from the common vertex to the center of the base does not meet the base at a right angle. This is called an oblique cone.

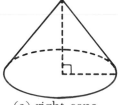   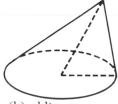

(a) right cone   (b) oblique cone

Chalkboard Exercises   Find the surface area of each cone with the given dimensions. Use 3.14 for π. Round decimal answers to the nearest tenth.

1. $r = 6$ ft; $s = 11$ ft   (320.3 ft²)

2. $r = 3.8$ yd; $s = 7.2$ yd   (131.3 yd²)

3. $r = 15.3$ mm; $s = 19$ mm   (1,647.8 mm²)

13-5   Page 288   The volume of a rectangular prism is discussed. Be sure students understand cubic units are different from square units and linear units. Boxes are good models of rectangular prisms. Stack cubic units into a box to find the volume of the box. Remove all but the bottom layer of cubic units. Lead students to see that the bottom layer is $\ell \times w$, which multiplied by the height of the box, h, results in the volume. But $\ell \times w$ is also the area of the bottom, or the area of the base of the box. The volume formula, then, can be written as $V = B \times h$ where B is the area of the base and h is the height of the rectangular prism.

Activity   Measure the length, width, and height of a box in centimeters. Calculate the volume of the box. Turn the box so that a different face serves as the base. Calculate the volume again. Can any face be used as the base?   (yes)

13-6   Page 292   In common speech, the word "cylinder" usually means a right, circular cylinder. In this lesson, *only* right, circular cylinders are used in problems. However, students should understand that a right, circular cylinder is a specialized form of cylinder. Cylinders may have bases that are not circular, and may have sides that do not meet the bases at right angles, as shown below.

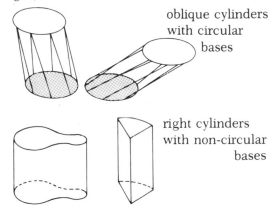

oblique cylinders with circular bases

right cylinders with non-circular bases

Chalkboard Exercises   Find the volume of each cylinder described below. Use 3.14 for π. Round decimal answers to the nearest hundredth.

1. $r = 14$ cm; $h = 22$ cm   (13,539.68 cm³)
2. $B = 58$ ft²; $h = 15$ ft   (870 ft³)
3. $B = 71$ yd²; $h = 22$ yd   (1,562 yd³)

13-7   Page 294   Pyramids and cones are similar in that they both have a base, and the sides extended evenly to a single point. In this lesson, only pyramids with rectangular and square bases, and cones with circular bases are used. As noted in lessons 13-2 and 13-4, students should become familiar with other kinds of pyramids and cones. A visual demonstration of the comparison of the volumes of the square prism and square pyramid, and of the cylinder and cone, is very helpful. If possible, have students do their own demonstrations.

Chalkboard Exercises   Find the volume of each of the following. Use 3.14 for π. Round decimal answers to the nearest tenth.

1. A cone. $r = 12$ m; $h = 16$ m   (2,411.5 m³)
2. A pyramid. $\ell = 10$ ft; $w = 9$ ft; $h = 7$ ft   (210 ft³)
3. A pyramid. $\ell = 13$ m; $w = 13$ m; $h = 8$ m   (450.7 m³)

13-8   Page 296   Students will study the formulas for the surface area and volume of a sphere. Ask students to name objects that are shaped like spheres. Some examples are basketballs, the planets, and oranges.

Chalkboard Exercises   Solve. Use 3.14 for π. Round decimal answers to the nearest tenth. A spherical water tank has a radius of 18.1 meters.

1. What is the surface area of the tank?   (4,114.8 m²)
2. What is the volume of the tank?   (24,825.8 m³)

13-9   Page 298   In determining the volume of cylinders and cones, the radius is more significant than the height because the radius is squared.

Chalkboard Exercise   Solve.
Which box appears to hold more and which box does hold more?   (Answers may vary. Box A)

A.
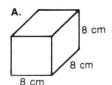
8 cm

8 cm
8 cm

B.
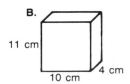
11 cm
10 cm
4 cm

Chapter 14   Rational Numbers

Chapter Overview

This chapter considers the ordering of rational numbers as well as adding, subtracting, multiplying, and dividing rational numbers. It is expected that students have some familiarity with the real number line, which is used throughout the chapter to illustrate various concepts. At the conclusion of this chapter, students should be able to demonstrate competence in using the four basic operations with rational numbers.

Lesson Notes

14-1   Page 305   Introduce the signs for positive and negative. Point out that 9 is greater than 3, but ⁻9 is less than ⁻3. You may wish to review the symbols > and <.

Point out to students that the + sign can be omitted when writing positive numbers because positive numbers are also whole numbers.

Chalkboard Exercises   Which statements are true and which are false?

1. 23 < 26   (T)   **2.** 15 > 9   (T)
3. ⁻7 > 4   (F)   **4.** 104 < 98   (F)

14-2   Page 306   The concept of absolute value will be used throughout the rest of the chapter when adding, subtracting, multiplying, and dividing integers. Make sure that students understand this concept.

Chalkboard Exercises   Use the number line to order these integers from least to greatest.

1. 0, ⁻4, ⁻14   (⁻14, ⁻4, 0)   **2.** 7, ⁻3, 10   (⁻3, 7, 10)
3. 8, ⁻9, ⁻12   (⁻12, ⁻9, 8)   **4.** 0, 13, 2   (0, 2, 13)

14-3   Page 308   The symbols used in graphing on the number line should be explained to students; i.e., a solid dot is used to indicate one number, a hollow dot does not include the number it is centered upon, a ray indicates all numbers greater or less than a certain number. Also, explain the meaning of points of ellipsis (. . .) as used in infinite sequences.

Activity   Students may gain insight by considering such questions as:

1. What is the greatest number?

2. What is the least positive number?
3. How many integers are there?

14-4   Page 310   This suggestion is offered as a means of helping students visualize addition of integers on the number line: construct a number line large enough that a playing card may represent one unit (integer). Movement in the positive direction is done by picking up cards consecutively; cards are put down over each unit when moving to the left. To compute an addition such as 3 + ⁻5, start on zero.

Move to the right three units by picking up the first three cards, then move to the left five units by putting down five cards. The last card represents the sum, ⁻2.

Chalkboard Exercises   Add.

1. 500 + 200   (700)
2. 740 + ⁻820   (⁻80)
3. ⁻1,500 + 2,400   (900)

14-5   Page 313   To find the difference or interval, between any two numbers, subtraction is used. Rather than appeal to the number line to find the difference between two numbers, which can be an impractical approach in many cases, students must learn the algebraic rules for the subtraction of positive and negative numbers.

Chalkboard Exercises   Find the difference between each pair.

1. 56¢, $1.00   (44¢)
2. 8 mph, 5 mph   (3 mph)
3. 1 min, 86 s   (26 s)

14-6   Page 318   If the number line can be used to illustrate addition, it can also be used for multiplication. Give students multiplication exercises to do on the number line. What difficulties are there in illustrating the multiplication of two negative numbers on the number line?

Point out that the product of zero and any integer is zero.

Chalkboard Exercises   Solve.

A 1,000 gallon pool is being filled at the rate of 100 gal per hour. At 2:00 P.M. the pool is half full. How many gallons of water are in the pool at 4:00 P.M.? (700 gal) at 5:00 P.M.? (800 gal) at 12:00 noon? (300 gal) at 11:00 A.M.? (200 gal)

14-7   Page 320   Students may benefit from seeing the relationship between division and multiplication, i.e., that they are inverse operations. This relationship can be illustrated by using specific examples.

Chalkboard Exercises   Divide.

1. $16 \div {}^-4$ $({}^-4)$
2. ${}^-18 \div {}^-6$ (3)
3. ${}^-1{,}095 \div 3$ $({}^-365)$

14-8   Page 322   Without a convention such as the order of operations, the same expression could mean different things to different people. To convey the importance of agreement on such a convention, have students speculate on what would happen if people no longer agreed on the order in which things are done, for example, in a baseball game.

Activity   Could another order of operations have been agreed upon? Suppose the order was to do all operations from left to right. Would the same expression mean the same thing to different people if they used this order of operations?   (yes)

14-9   Page 324   In this lesson, different word problems involving rational numbers are presented. Students will analyze the problems to decide what type of operation is needed in each case to solve the problems.

Chalkboard Exercises   Solve.

1. Sandy's scores in a game were, 110, ${}^-60$, ${}^-80$, and 90. What was her total score?   (60)
2. The altitude at sea level is 0. Point A has an altitude of 150 m, and point B has an altitude of ${}^-40$ m. How much greater is the altitude of point A than point B?   (190 m)

Chapter 15   *Solving Open Sentences*

Chapter Overview

This chapter introduces students to the meaning, uses, and solution of open sentences. This approach provides students with tangible examples of the uses of open sentences, and gives to the teacher a basis for classroom experiments that could involve students in writing and solving open sentences. Point out that the extensive use of letters as variables distinguishes algebra from arithmetic.

Lesson Notes

15-1   Page 331   Whereas English is the language we use in common, everyday affairs, mathematics is the language used in science to describe the world. Since both are languages, they have a number of things in common. For example, they both allow for the expression of statements that can be judged true, false, or open. Does mathematics have a grammar? (yes) a vocabulary? (yes) punctuation? (yes)

Chalkboard Exercises   Identify the pronoun in each sentence that acts as a placeholder. Replace each pronoun with a noun that makes the sentence true.

1. It is a star.   **2.** It is a planet.

3. He discovered the law of gravity.

15-2   Page 332   To solve an open sentence is to find a replacement for the variable that makes the sentence true. An open sentence is solved when we transform it into another sentence containing the variable, a constant, and the relation between them, i.e., $=, <, \geq$.

Chalkboard Exercises   Write an open sentence to correspond with each statement.

1. Two more would make a dozen. $(x + 2 = 12)$

2. Ten times as many would be 300. $(10x = 300)$

3. A year ago, she was 16 years old. $(x - 1 = 16)$

15-3   Page 334   We can use an equation to state that two beakers contain equal amounts of water. If we add or subtract the same amount of water from both beakers, the end result is that they still contain equal amounts of water. What does this tell us about adding or subtracting the same quantity from each side of an equation? (Each side will name the same number.)

Chalkboard Exercises   Let $a = 4$, $b = {}^-5$, and $c = 9$. Which statements are true and which are false?

1. $a + 4 = 8$ (T)   **2.** $9 - b = 4$ (F)

3. $5 - a = 1$ (T)   **4.** $a + b = {}^-1$ (T)

15-4   Page 336   The same number can be added to or subtracted from both sides of an equation. The result is an equivalent equation; i.e., an equation having the same solution set as the original equation. To solve an equation involving addition or subtraction, we can use this knowledge to find an equivalent equation in which the variable is isolated on one side of the equation.

Chalkboard Exercises   Solve each equation for z.

1. $z + 2 = 5$ $(z = 3)$

2. $4 + z = 10$ $(z = 6)$

3. $z - 5 = {}^-14$ $(z = {}^-9)$

15-5   Page 338   When dealing with variables, multiplication is commonly denoted by juxtaposition rather than by using the multiplication symbol. This correlates with our use of English in that we refer to two pounds rather than two times a pound. This connection with English usage may help students understand this notation.

Chalkboard Exercise   Solve.

An empty pool is to be filled with water from a hose. The volume of the pool is 500 gal and water is delivered from the hose at 50 gal per h. Write an equation, with time *(t)* being the variable, which describes this situation. Solve for time to find how long it takes to fill the pool. $(500 = 50 \times t)$ $(10h)$

15-6   Page 342   The two sides of an equation may be multiplied or divided by the same amount to obtain an equivalent equation. As an illustration, consider how one unit of measurement is converted to another unit of measurement.

Chalkboard Exercises   Solve for *x* in each equation.

1. 12 in. = *x* ft $(x = 1)$

2. 3 ft = *x* in. $(x = 36)$

3. 5 min = *x* s $(x = 300)$

15-7   Page 344   Consider the equation $3x + 5 = 23$. This equation may be solved in either of two ways:

$$3x + 5 = 23 \qquad 3x + 5 = 23$$
$$3x = 18 \qquad x + \tfrac{5}{3} = \tfrac{23}{3}$$
$$x = 6 \qquad x = \tfrac{23}{3} - \tfrac{5}{3}$$
$$x = \tfrac{18}{3}$$
$$x = 6$$

As can be seen, one method involves less work than the other. Is there any advantage to performing addition before division in solving an equation such as $2t - 4 = 8$?   (no)

Chalkboard Exercises   Solve each equation for *F*.

1. $\frac{F}{a} = m$ $(F = ma)$ **2.** $\frac{2}{k} = \frac{x^2}{F}$ $(F = \tfrac{1}{2}kx^2)$

3. $r = \sqrt{\frac{gm_1m_2}{F}}$ $\left(F = \frac{gm_1m_2}{r^2}\right)$

15-8   Page 346   The method for solving inequalities is essentially the same as that used in solving equations. The solution to an inequality is usually a set of values rather than just one value.

Chalkboard Exercises   Solve each inequality.

1. $r + 350 < 500$ $(r < 150)$

2. $p + {}^-24 > 12$ $(p > 36)$

3. $a + 3\tfrac{1}{3} \leq 5$ $(a \leq 1\tfrac{2}{3})$

15-9   Page 348   This lesson gives a series of word problems that help students solve equations and inequalities.

Chalkboard Exercises   Solve.

The equation $d = r \times t$ describes the relationship between the distance traveled by an object, the rate of speed of the object, and the amount of time spent traveling at that speed. The equation can be rewritten $t = \frac{d}{r}$. How?   (Divide both sides of the equation by *r*.) For a given distance, what happens to *t* as *r* increases? (*t* decreases)

Chapter 16   Using Formulas

Chapter Overview

This chapter ties together many of the ideas and concepts presented in earlier chapters. It is intended to help students appreciate how the different topics in mathematics combine in the solution of physical problems. In the previous chapter, students learned how to solve equations. In this chapter they learn how to write equations to solve several types of problems. The subject matter of this chapter is, essentially, algebraic equations.

Lesson Notes

16-1   Page 355   Studying the chart on page 355 should help students see the relationship of the intensity of one earthquake to another.

Be sure students understand the terms factor, base, and exponent.

Chalkboard Exercises   Write using exponents.

1. $6 \times 6 \times 6$ (6^3) **2.** 14×14 (14^2)

3. 9 cubed (9^3)

4. 5 squared (5^2)

5. 12 to the fifth power (12^5)

6. x to the fourth power (x^4)

16-2   Page 356   The order of operations is a convention that ensures that a mathematical expression has a unique value, i.e., two people evaluating the same expression will arrive at the same result. To illustrate the chaos that results when people do not agree on the meaning of some expression, stage a classroom dialogue in which the two parties do not agree on the meaning of some statement.

Chalkboard Exercises   Evaluate each expression. Let $x = {}^-1$, $y = 2$, and $z = 3$.

1. $(x + y)^2$ (1)   **2.** $\frac{1}{x^2 + y^2}$ $\left(\frac{1}{5}\right)$

3. $\frac{1}{(x + y)^2}$ (1)   **4.** x^3z (-3)

Another way of expressing $x + x + x$ is $3x$. Another way of expressing $x \cdot x \cdot x$ is x^3. Also, $2x + 3x = 5x$. How else may $x^2 \cdot x^3$ be written? (x^5)

16-3   Page 358   The formulas for the work needed to move an object and for the circumference of

a circle are used as examples in this lesson. Students learn through these examples how formulas may be used in the solution of problems. Point out to students that to solve a problem by using some formula, a certain amount of data is required. Only one unknown can be found by solving one equation.

Chalkboard Exercises   Find the missing value.

1. $x = \frac{1}{2}gt^2$; $x = 72$, $t = 4$ $(g = 9)$

2. $D = \frac{m}{v}$; $D = 3.6$, $v = 6.4$ $(m = 23.04)$

3. $a^2 = c^2 - b^2$; $b = 3$, $c = 5$ $(a = 4)$

16-4   Page 361   Physical properties are measured in reference to some standard unit. In the customary system, rate could be measured in miles per hour, time could be measured in hours, and distance could be measured in miles. In the metric system, rate could be measured in kilometers per hour, time could be measured in hours, and distance could be measured in kilometers.

Chalkboard Exercises   Solve.

A circular race track has a diameter of $\frac{1}{2}$ mile. How long does it take a car traveling at 120 mph to make a lap around the track?   (47 s)

16-5   Page 365   This lesson expands on some of the material presented in lesson 16-1. Given the increasing availability and use of calculators, students may benefit from being shown how to find the powers and roots of a number on a calculator.

Chalkboard Exercises   Find the square and the square root of each number.

1. 8   (64, 2.828)   **2.** 11   (121, 3.317)

3. $\frac{1}{2}$ $\left(\frac{1}{4}, 0.707\right)$ **4.** 16   (256, 4)

Solve.

5. If the side of a square were increased by 1 unit, its area would increase by 7 square units. What is the area of the square?   (9 square units)

1. $\ell = 3$, $w = 2$ $(\sqrt{13})$

2. $\ell = 5$, $w = 3$ $(\sqrt{34})$

3. $\ell = 4$, $w = 4$ $(4\sqrt{2})$

4. $\ell = \frac{1}{2}$, $w = \frac{1}{4}$ $\left(\frac{1}{4}\sqrt{5}\right)$

16-6   Page 367   To help students understand the meaning of the Pythagorean Theorem, use the figure below to prove the theorem.

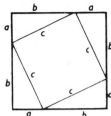

Write an equation that expresses the relationship between the areas of the larger square, the inner square, and the four triangles.

$$(a + b)^2 = c^2 + 2ab$$

Chalkboard Exercises   Find the diagonal for a rectangle having the given length and width.

16-7   Page 369   A formula and the required data are given for each problem presented in this lesson. Students should be able to replace the variables in the formula with the numerical values listed in the problem. Be sure to explain the difference between simple interest and compound interest.

Chalkboard Exercises   Solve.

1. A machine is capable of lifting a 900-lb weight to a height of 14 ft. How high can the machine lift a 100-lb weight?   (126 ft) How much weight can it lift to a height of 24 ft?   (525 lb)

2. A person is caught going 62 mph in a 55 mph zone. The fine is $5 for every mph in excess of the speed limit. How much is the person fined?   ($35)

Chapter 17   Patterns and Functions

Chapter Overview

In this chapter, the definition of a function will be discussed. Students will learn about patterns and function rules. This will enable them to organize data in tables. Also, given a table, students will be able to use the data to find patterns or function rules. Arithmetic and geometric sequences, and the concept of scientific notation are introduced.

Lesson Notes

17-1   Page 377   In Chapter 1, students learned how to read and use data from a table. In this lesson, given an expression, students will learn how to find a certain pattern to make a table.

Chalkboard Exercises   Make a table to organize the following fractions and their equivalent decimals.
$\frac{1}{4}$, $\frac{5}{8}$, $2\frac{1}{4}$, $3\frac{3}{8}$ (0.25, 0.625, 2.25, 3.375)

Change each fraction to a percent to complete the table. Use $n \times 100 = p$.

fraction	percent	
$\frac{1}{5}$		(20%)
$\frac{1}{4}$		(25%)
$\frac{1}{3}$		($33\frac{1}{3}$%)
$\frac{1}{2}$		(50%)

17-2   Page 378   Point out that functions can be represented in several ways. Some of these are tables, arrow diagrams, and function rules.

Chalkboard Exercises   Use $A = \pi r^2$ to complete the following table. Use 3.14 for π. Round your answers to the nearest tenth.

r	πr^2	A	
2	(3.14) (2^2)		(12.6)
3	(3.14) (3^2)		(28.3)
4	(3.14) (4^2)		(50.2)
5	(3.14) (5^2)		(78.5)

Draw an arrow diagram for the function $y = 3x + 1$. The replacement set is $\{-1, 0, \frac{1}{2}, 1\}$.

Replacement Set	Solution Set
$^-1$	$^-2$
0	1
$\frac{1}{2}$	2.5
1	4

17-3   Page 380   The information learned in lesson 17-2 will help students use tables to find function rules.

Chalkboard Exercises   Use the values in each table to find the function rule.

1.

x	y
$\frac{1}{2}$	$\frac{1}{4}$
$\frac{1}{4}$	$\frac{1}{16}$
13	169
29	841

rule: $y = $ ▒▒ (x^2)

2.

x	y
$\frac{1}{8}$	0
$\frac{1}{16}$	$-\frac{1}{2}$
8	63
$\frac{1}{10}$	$-\frac{1}{5}$

rule: $y = $ ▒▒ $(8x - 1)$

17-4   Page 382   You may want to explain to students what the term arithmetic means.

Chalkboard Exercises   Find the next two terms in each arithmetic sequence.

1. 62,   66,   70,   ▒,
    ▒   (74, 78)

2. 21, 26, $^-$31, 36, ▒,
    ▒   (41, 46)

3. 3.09, 3.11, 3.13, ▓, ▓ (3.15, 3.17) **4.** ⁻9, ⁻7, ⁻5, ⁻3, ▓, ▓ (⁻1, 1)

Find the tenth number in this sequence.

5. 0.6, 0.9, 1.2, 1.5, . . . (3.3)

17-5   Page 386   The concept of geometric sequences and other types of sequences are developed in this lesson.

You may want to mention that the Fibonacci Sequence found in the Math Break on page 387, is a special sequence named after Leonardo Fibonacci who published the sequence in 1202.

Chalkboard Exercises   Find the next three terms in each geometric sequence.

1. 86, 43, 21.5, ▓, ▓, ▓ (10.75, 5.375, 2.6875)

2. 110, 330, 990, ▓, ▓, ▓ (2,970; 8,910; 26,730)

Find the number each term is multiplied by in each geometric sequence.

3. $\frac{3}{4}$, $\frac{6}{20}$, $\frac{12}{100}$, $\frac{24}{500}$ $\left(\frac{2}{5}\right)$

4. $\frac{1}{5}$, $\frac{4}{15}$, $\frac{16}{45}$, $\frac{64}{135}$ $\left(\frac{4}{3}\right)$

17-6   Page 388   This lesson is an extension of lesson 16-1, exponents. Point out that the power of 10 indicates where to place the decimal point when writing the number in standard form.

Chalkboard Exercises   Determine how many places the decimal point should be moved to find a number that is at least 1 but less than 10.

1. 47 (1)   **2.** 1,300 (3) **3.** 65,000 (4)

4. 520,000 (5) **5.** 906.3 (2) **6.** 1,000,000,000 (9)

Express each number in scientific notation.

1. 915 (9.15×10^2) **2.** 810,000 (8.1×10^5)

3. 604,000 (6.04×10^5) **4.** 206,000,000 (2.06×10^8)

17-7   Page 390   This problem-solving lesson combines geometry and number theory. Triangular and square numbers are known as figurate numbers.

Chalkboard Exercises   Match.

1. third square number (b)   **a.** 1,600

2. first triangular number (c)   **b.** 9

3. eighth triangular number (d)   **c.** 1

4. fortieth square number (a)   **d.** 36

Solve.

5. For a rectangular number, the figure is one dot wider than it is high. Draw and name the first six rectangular numbers. (See students' figures. 2, 6, 12, 20, 30, 42)

Chapter 18 The Coordinate Plane

Chapter Overview

This chapter introduces students to the graphing of ordered pairs and linear equations in the coordinate plane. They will learn how to solve linear equations by algebraic and graphic methods. Students will explore transformations such as reflection, translation, rotation, and dilation. In the problem-solving lesson, they will use graphs to solve word problems.

Lesson Notes

18-1   Page 397   Point out to students the importance of the order of the numbers in an ordered pair. Show students that (5, 6) and (6, 5) do not name the same point.

Chalkboard Exercises   Name the letter for each ordered pair.

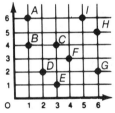

1. (3, 1) (E) **2.** (1, 6) (A)
3. (6, 5) (H) **4.** (6, 2) (G)
5. (2, 2) (D) **6.** (4, 3) (F)
7. (1, 4) (B) **8.** (3, 4) (C)

18-2   Page 398   In this lesson, students will learn to locate and name points in a coordinate plane. It is important that you emphasize the one-to-one correspondence between ordered pairs and points on a plane.

Activities   Draw a map of the classroom, showing each student's desk, the door, closets, and other features. List letters along one side of the map and numbers along an adjacent side. Then make an index for the map, listing each student's name and the ordered pair that represents the location of each student's desk.

Play "buried treasure." Separate the class by twos. Each student locates a trunk full of buried treasure of at least 6 squares in size, on a piece of graph paper. The opposing student calls out ordered pairs. The "captain" responds by saying "hit" or "miss." Each takes a turn questioning the other. Three "hits" mean the buried treasure is found.

18-3   Page 400   In this lesson, students will learn how to find the algebraic solutions for linear equations. Point out that equations of the form $ax + by = c$, where a, b, and c are real numbers, are linear equations. Students will use charts to organize the given information.

Chalkboard Exercises   Determine whether each of the following are linear equations. Write yes or no.

1. $3x + 2y = 6$ (yes)   **2.** $y = 3x - 1$ (yes)
3. $y = 8$ (yes)   **4.** $3x + 4y^2 = 1$ (no)
5. $9x + 4y = {}^-2$ (yes)   **6.** $\frac{1}{x} + \frac{3}{4}y = 7$ (no)

18-4   Page 402   Graphic solutions to linear equations are introduced in this lesson.
Point out to students that it is helpful to find at least three ordered pairs before graphing each equation. Explain that this will help ensure that the points chosen are correct.

Chalkboard Exercises   Graph the solutions to each equation.

1. $x - 4 = y$ **2.** $x + 2 = y$
3. $\frac{x}{3} = y$ **4.** $5x = y$
5. $6x - 2 = y$ **6.** ${}^-3x - 1 = y$
(See students' work.)

Each of the following are the coordinates of three vertices of a rectangle. Graph them. Then, find the fourth vertex.

7. (3, 1), (3, ${}^-$3), (${}^-$5, ${}^-$3)   (${}^-$5, 1)
8. (${}^-$1, 0), (1, 1), (0, 3)   (${}^-$2, 2)
9. (2, 0), (0, 2), (${}^-$4, ${}^-$2)   (${}^-$2, ${}^-$4)

18-5   Page 406   In this lesson, different types of problems and their corresponding graphs are given. Students will have to solve the problems by analyzing the graphs.

Chalkboard Exercise   Find the value of y when x is −1. (⁻4)

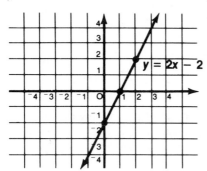

18-6   Page 408   Emphasize the definitions for reflection, rotation, translation, and dilation. Stress the differences among these transformations, and how to recognize each type.

Chalkboard Exercises   Solve.

1. Draw a trapezoid with vertices at A(0, 1), B(3, 1), C(3, 3), and D(1, 3). Then multiply the second coordinate of each vertex by ⁻1. Draw the new trapezoid. Which type of transformation is this? (reflection)

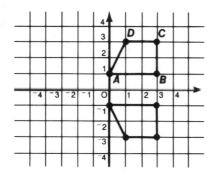

2. Draw a triangle with vertices at X(⁻3, 7), Y(⁻5, 6), and Z(⁻1, 5). Then add 6 to the first coordinate of each vertex. Draw the new triangle. Which type of transformation is this?   (translation)

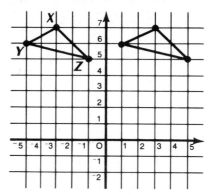

18-7   Page 412   This lesson presents an opportunity for students to apply concepts and skills learned throughout this chapter.

Chalkboard Exercises   In each problem, state which of the two points named lie on the graph of each equation.

1. x − y = 5   **a.** (14, 9)   **b.** (2, 3)
2. x = y + 1   **a.** (1, 1)   **b.** (0, ⁻1)
3. x + 2y = 1   **a.** (1, 0)   **b.** (⁻1, 1)

Independent Test for Chapter 1

Use the mileage chart on page 3 to find each distance.

1. Des Moines to Minneapolis

2. Philadelphia to Cincinnati

3. St. Louis to Tulsa

4. New Orleans to San Francisco

Use the timetable on page 4 to answer the following.

5. Suppose you board at Starr and Third at 10:52 A.M. When will you arrive at Sunlawn and Miami?

6. Suppose you board at Price and Lenox at 11:53 A.M. When will you arrive at Starr and Third?

Use the chart on page 6 to find the cost of sending each package fourth class with the given weight to the given zone.

7. 3.4 lb; 4

8. 2 lb; 6

9. 4.1 lb; 1

10. 5 lb; local

11. 2 lb 6 oz; 7

12. 4.9 lb; 5

Use the chart on page 8 to find whether each call will be charged full rate, 40% discount, or 60% discount.

13. 3:01 A.M.; Sun.

14. 10:00 P.M.; Fri.

15. 12:45 P.M.; Tues.

16. 2:45 A.M.; Wed.

17. 12:00 P.M.; Sat.

18. 6:30 P.M.; Mon.

Use the tax table on page 10 to find the withholding tax. The weekly wages and the number of allowances are given.

19. $149.80; 1

20. $261.90; 2

21. $197.30; 3

22. $238.41; 2

23. $136.64; 0

24. $272.0; 1

Use the federal tax table on page 14 to find the tax for single (s), married filing jointly (mj), married filing separately (ms), or head of household (hh).

25. $10,155; s

26. $10,711; mj

27. $10,449; hh

28. $10,620; ms

29. $10,020; s

30. $10,230; ms

Use the tax table on page 16 to find the sales tax on the following purchases.

31. $13.25

32. $5.89

33. $7.63

34. $17.40

Use Mickey Mantle's batting record on page 19 to answer the following.

35. In what years did he play more than 150 games?

36. What was his lowest number of home runs made in any one season? What year was that?

Independent Test for Chapter 2

Use tally marks to represent each number.

1. 7   **2.** 15   **3.** 32   **4.** 55

The number of people attending a science club per day is listed at the right.

5. Make a frequency table for the data. Use tally marks.

6. Find the range.   **7.** Find the mode.

8. Find the mean.   **9.** Find the median.

30	29	31	30
41	38	29	32
26	33	30	44
47	36		

Which average—mode, mean, or median—would best describe each of the following?

10. income made in a year

11. scores on a basketball game

12. favorite subject of high-school students

13. heights of a team's players

The number of jumping-jacks each student did on a fitness test are listed at the right.

14. Find the mode.   **15.** Find the mean.

16. Find the median.

17. Which average—mode, mean, or median—best describes the test results?

60	57	174
42	66	57
47	60	40

The heights (in centimeters) of the members of the orchestra are listed at the right.

18. Find the range.   **19.** Find the mode.

20. Find the mean.   **21.** Find the median.

148	167	154
172	167	148
163	154	154
181	174	

The ages of the members of a baseball team are listed at the right.

22. Find the median age.

23. Find the mean age.

24. Which average—median or mean—is most descriptive of the ages?

25. Suppose the youngest member was 21 and the oldest 52. How would the mean and median be affected?

30	24	25
26	30	27
30	31	29

Independent Test for Chapter 3

Write each ratio as a fraction in simplest form.

1. 6 out of 18   **2.** 49 to 63   **3.** 148:36

Use cross products to determine whether each pair of ratios forms a proportion. Write yes or no.

4. $\frac{9}{21}$ and $\frac{3}{7}$ **5.** $\frac{3}{8}$ and $\frac{5}{12}$ **6.** $\frac{16}{4}$ and $\frac{8}{2}$

Change each decimal, fraction, or mixed numeral to a percent.

7. $6\frac{1}{2}$ **8.** $\frac{3}{2}$ **9.** 0.42

Change each percent to a decimal.

10. 22%   **11.** 36.7%   **12.** $5\frac{1}{5}\%$

Change each percent to a fraction or mixed numeral.

13. 40%   **14.** 120%   **15.** $5\frac{3}{4}\%$

Solve.

16. What number is 18% of 85?

17. 6 is 15% of what number?

18. 32% of what number is 80?

19. What percent of 25 is 9?

20. 21 is what percent of 50?

21. 13% of 200 is what number?

22. The total cost of a dryer is $324. The sales tax is $24. If the original price is $500, what percent of the original price is the sale price?

23. The Gomez family traveled 72 miles on 3.6 gallons of gasoline. How far can they travel on 9.2 gallons?

24. There are 17 girls and 9 boys in Mrs. White's science class. What percent of the students are girls?

25. A $12\frac{1}{5}$-ounce can of orange juice sells for 98¢ and a 13-ounce can sells for $1.01. Which is the better buy?

Independent Test for Chapter 4

Use the pictograph at the right to answer each question.

1. How many strawberries were produced at Martin Farms?

2. How many were produced at Steven Farms?

3. How many more were produced at Martin Farms than Moore Farms?

Strawberries Produced	
Martin Farm	🍓🍓🍓🍓🍓🍓🍓🍓
Steven Farm	🍓🍓🍓🍓🍓🍓🍓🍓🍓
Moore Farm	🍓🍓🍓🍓🍓🍓🍓🍓

Each 🍓 stands for 10,000 strawberries

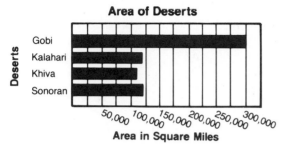

Area of Deserts

Use the bar graph at the left to answer each question.

4. Which desert has the greatest area?

5. Which desert has the least area?

6. Which two deserts have nearly the same area?

Use the circle graph at the right to answer each question.

7. What percent of the income is spent on food?

8. What percent of the income is spent on clothing?

9. What is the sum of the percents?

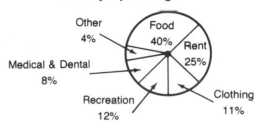

Family Spending

Other 4%
Food 40%
Rent 25%
Medical & Dental 8%
Recreation 12%
Clothing 11%

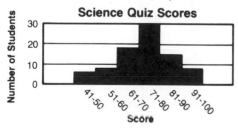

Science Quiz Scores

Use the histogram at the left to answer the following.

10. How many students scored in the interval 81–90?

11. In what interval did 30 students score?

12. During which months is the average temperature greater than 75°F?

13. Which of the bar graphs below is misleading? Explain.

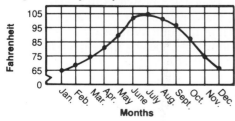

Average Monthly Temperatures in Phoenix

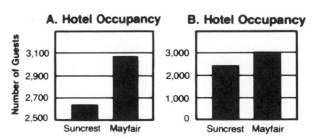

A. Hotel Occupancy   B. Hotel Occupancy

Independent Test for Chapter 5

Tell how many outcomes are possible for the following.

1. all different arrangements of the letters C, D, and E

2. spinning this spinner three times

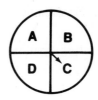

Suppose a penny, a nickel, and a quarter are tossed at the same time. Complete the following.

3. Draw the tree diagram.

4. How many outcomes are possible?

5. How many outcomes have heads on the penny?

Each spinner is spun once. Find each probability.

6. two L's

7. two M's

8. an M on spinner I and an L on spinner II

A box contains 6 green, 4 blue, and 2 yellow marbles. One is chosen, replaced, and a second marble is chosen. Find each probability.

9. both marbles are blue

10. a blue marble, then a yellow one

Suppose two cards are chosen at random from those shown at the right. Each card chosen is not replaced. Find each probability.

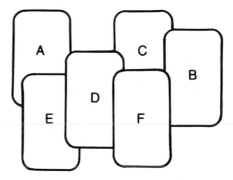

11. both consonants

12. a consonant, then a vowel

13. both vowels

14. a vowel, then a consonant

Solve.

15. There are 2 science books, 3 health books, and 4 social studies books on a shelf. One book is to be chosen at random. What is the probability of choosing a health book?

16. A box contains 5 brown, 3 red, and 4 white marbles. Three marbles are to be chosen at random. What is the probability of choosing three marbles of the same color?

Independent Test for Chapter 6

Two coins are tossed. Find the odds for the following.

1. no tails

2. no heads

3. at least one tail

Write each percent as a probability in simplest form.

4. 12.5%

5. 40%

6. 25%

Find the probability of an event given its odds. Express the probability as a fraction in simplest form and as a percent.

7. 2 to 4

8. 3 to 3

9. 5 to 4

10. 3 to 1

Find the odds for an event given its probability or chance.

11. $\frac{2}{3}$

12. 50%

13. 25%

14. $\frac{6}{7}$

Use the poll results at the right to complete the following.

15. How many people were polled?

16. What fraction is in favor of the increase?

17. Suppose another 1,200 people are polled. Predict how many would support the increase.

Bus Fare	Increase
For	41
Against	162

If 1,000 tickets are sold, find the expected winnings for the following.

18. 2 $100 prizes

19. 1 $500 prize

20. 8 $20 prizes

The numbers in the Venn Diagram at the right represent the population in each region. Find the population in each region if the population of B is 92.

21. Region A

22. Region B

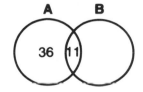

Answer the following.

23. A test has 50 questions each having 5 choices. Suppose all answers are guesses. Find the expected score.

24. A die is rolled 2,000 times. How many times would you expect an even number?

25. Out of 30 students polled, 10 students were science majors, 11 students were math majors, and 6 students were both science and math majors. How many students were neither science majors nor math majors?

Independent Test for Chapter 7

Name the larger unit.

1. cm or mm   **2.** ft or yd   **3.** yd or mi

4. in. or ft   **5.** m or mm   **6.** cm or km

Measure each line segment. Give the measurement in inches.

7. |—————|

8. |——————————|

9. |————————————|

10. |———————————————————|

Choose the best estimate.

11. height of a mountain   **a.** 700 km   **b.** 700 m   **c.** 700 cm

12. thickness of a book   **a.** 2 cm   **b.** 2 mm   **c.** 2 m

13. length of a wall   **a.** 3 mm   **b.** 3 m   **c.** 3 cm

Complete.

14. 24 in. = ▨ ft   **15.** 3.5 ft = ▨ in.   **16.** 10,560 yd = ▨ mi

17. 3 km = ▨ m   **18.** 971 cm = ▨ m   **19.** 600 m = ▨ km

20. 15.4 m = ▨ cm   **21.** 161 mm = ▨ m   **22.** 8.2 m = ▨ mm

Add, subtract, multiply, or divide.

23.
$$\begin{array}{r} 4 \text{ ft } 7 \text{ in.} \\ \times \quad 3 \\ \hline \end{array}$$

24. $5\overline{)16 \text{ ft } 23 \text{ in.}}$

25.
$$\begin{array}{r} 8 \text{ ft } 2 \text{ in.} \\ - \ 3 \text{ ft } 4 \text{ in.} \\ \hline \end{array}$$

26.
$$\begin{array}{r} 1 \text{ ft } 7 \text{ in.} \\ + \ 9 \text{ ft } 6 \text{ in.} \\ \hline \end{array}$$

Give the number of significant digits in each measurement.

27. 21.5 mm   **28.** 1,684 m   **29.** 0.03 cm   **30.** 439 km

Solve.

31. Luis ran one mile in 6 minutes 38.1 seconds. At the same rate, would her time for a 1,700-meter race be more or less?

32. On the highway a speed limit of 45 miles per hour is posted. About how many kilometers per hour is this?

Independent Test for Chapter 8

Complete.

1. 420 mL = ▦ L   **2.** 7,040 mg = ▦ g   **3.** 100 g = ▦ kg

4. 13.41 kg = ▦ g   **5.** 36 oz = ▦ lb   **6.** 24 qt = ▦ gal

7. 3,100 lb = ▦ tons   **8.** 9.01 L = ▦ mL   **9.** 87.2 kL = ▦ L

10. 2 gal = ▦ qt   **11.** 6 c = ▦ pt   **12.** 2.1 tons = ▦ lb

Replace each ● with >, <, or = to make a true sentence.

13. 9 c ● 5 pt   **14.** 300 mL ● 2.5 L   **15.** 35 qt ● 7 gal

16. 44 kg ● 4,000 g   **17.** 13 tons ● 26,000 lb   **18.** 80.0 mg ● 0.7 g

19. 10 lb ● 150 oz   **20.** 7 kL ● 7,000 L   **21.** 3 gal ● 11 qt

Add or subtract.

22.   3 wk 5 d
      + 2 wk 4 d

23.   8 h 15 min
      − 3 h 20 min

24.   2 d 13 h
      + 1 d 11 h

25.   4 wk 6 d 10 h
      − 3 wk 7 d 9 h

26.   23 h 45 min 57 s
      + 7 h 30 min 20 s

27.   3 d 18 h 45 min
      − 2 d 22 h 59 min

Change each Fahrenheit reading to a Celsius reading.

28. 95°F   **29.** 131°F   **30.** 203°F   **31.** 50°F

Change each Celsius reading to a Fahrenheit reading.

32. 40°C   **33.** 110°C   **34.** 66°C   **35.** 25°C

Choose the better temperature for the following.

36. iced tea ⁻5°C or 5°C   **37.** walking 25°C or 45°C

Solve.

38. The temperature in Dallas is 25°C. The temperature in Miami is 66°F. Which city has the colder temperature?

39. Tracey weighs 130 pounds. She lost 1.8 pounds in one week. How many ounces did she lose?

Independent Test for Chapter 9

Find the number of miles driven for each pair of odometer readings.

1. | 8 | 2 | 3 | 1 | 5 | 6 |

   | 8 | 2 | 5 | 7 | 9 | 8 |

2. | 1 | 3 | 6 | 8 | 7 | 0 |

   | 1 | 4 | 5 | 4 | 3 | 2 |

3. | 6 | 6 | 1 | 2 | 3 | 5 |

   | 6 | 7 | 4 | 3 | 8 | 9 |

Use the travel maps on pages 184–185 to answer the following.

4. Name the route that is most direct from St. Louis, Missouri, to Little Rock, Arkansas.

5. What is the distance and average driving time between Denver, Colorado, and Houston, Texas going by way of Kansas City and Tulsa?

Express each time as 12-hour time, using A.M. or P.M.

6. 1545   7. 0715   8. 2320   9. 0801   10. 0044

How many kilowatt hours are shown on each electric meter below?

11.   12.

How many cubic feet of natural gas are shown on each water meter below?

13.    14.   15.   16.

Use a protractor to measure each angle.

17.   18.   19.   20.

Use a protractor to draw angles having each measurement.

21. 31°   22. 57°   23. 92°   24. 160°   25. 175°   26. 14°

Solve.

27. The odometer reading yesterday was 47,380.5 miles. Suppose the car was driven 105.0 miles after that reading. What is today's odometer reading?

28. A gas meter reading is now 7,258 ccf. The previous reading was 7,123 ccf. How many hundred cubic feet of natural gas were used?

Independent Test for Chapter 10

Use symbols to name each figure.

1.

2.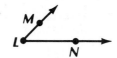

3.

4.

Use the figure at the right to complete the following.

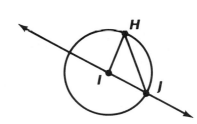

5. Name a line.

6. Name three line segments.

7. Name the center of the circle.

8. Name a segment that represents the radius of the circle.

Classify each angle as acute, right, or obtuse.

9.

10.

11.

For each angle whose degree measure is given below, find the degree measure of the complement and supplement.

12. 18°　　　　**13.** 23°　　　　**14.** 89°　　　　**15.** 60°　　　　**16.** 45°

Use the Pythagorean Theorem to find the length of the hypotenuse in each right triangle.

17.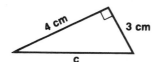

18.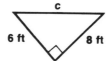

19.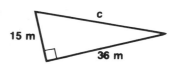

Write the converse of the following statement. Then determine whether each statement (original and converse) is true.

20. If the month of February has 29 days, then there is a leap year.

Determine whether the following is an example of deductive or inductive reasoning.

21. Sonia has spent $40.00 on groceries every two weeks for the past three months. Sonia's sister says, "Sonia always spends $40.00 on groceries every two weeks."

Solve.

22. Donald wants to save $10 for a gift. He begins by saving 40¢ the first week. Each week he saves twice as much as the week before. In how many weeks will he have saved at least $10?

Independent Test for Chapter 11

Trace each figure. Construct a figure congruent to the figure you traced.

1.

2.

Trace each figure. Then, bisect each line segment or angle you traced.

3.

4.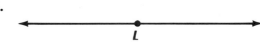

Trace each line and point. Construct a line perpendicular to the line you traced at the given point.

5.

6.

Trace each line segment. Construct the perpendicular bisector of the line segment you traced.

7.

8.

Trace each line and point. Construct a line parallel to the line you traced through the point not on the line.

9.

10.

Use the congruent triangles at the right to complete the following.

11. ∠KML ≅ ▨

12. $\overline{XZ}$ ≅ ▨

13. $\overline{ZY}$ ≅ ▨

14. ∠XYZ ≅ ▨

Trace the triangle at the right. Construct a triangle congruent to the triangle you traced using each rule.

15. SSS **16.** ASA **17.** SAS

Independent Test for Chapter 12

Find the missing length for each pair of similar figures.

1.

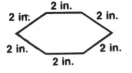

2.

 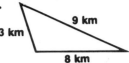

Find the perimeter of each polygon.

3.

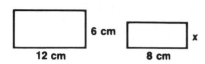

4.

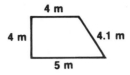

5.

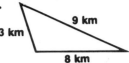

Find the circumference of each circle. Use 3.14 for π.

6.

15 cm

7.

6 m

8.

11 in.

Find the area of each rectangle or parallelogram described below.

9. base, 4 ft; height, 10 ft

10. base, 2.8 m; height, 9 m

11. length, 21 cm; width, 11.5 cm

12. length, 15 in.; width, 9 in.

Find the area of each triangle described below.

base	height
13. 26 m	9 m

base	height
14. 18 yd	7.5 yd

Find the area of each trapezoid.

15.

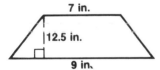

16.

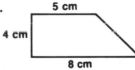

Find the area of each circle with the given radius. Use 3.14 for π.
Round decimal answers to the nearest tenth.

17. 4 km   **18.** 7.5 ft   **19.** 16 m   **20.** 13 in.

Solve.

21. The side of the house will be covered
with siding. What is the entire area
of the side of the house, including
the area under the roof?

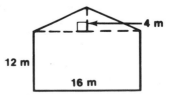

Independent Test for Chapter 13

**Find the surface area of each figure. Use 3.14 for π.
Round decimal answers to the nearest tenth.**

1.

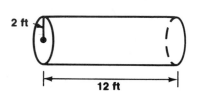

2.

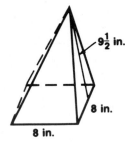

$9\frac{1}{2}$ in.

8 in.

8 in.

3.

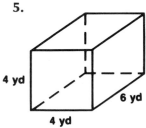

2 ft

12 ft

4.

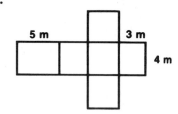

6 cm

24 cm

4 cm

**Find the volume of each figure. Use 3.14 for π.
Round decimal answers to the nearest tenth.**

5.

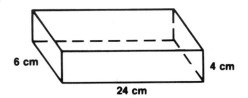

4 yd

6 yd

4 yd

6.

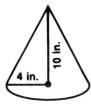

10 in.

4 in.

7.

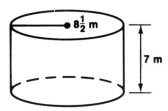

$8\frac{1}{2}$ m

7 m

Solve. Use 3.14 for π. Round decimal answers to the nearest tenth.

8. A storage silo is cylindrical. Its radius is $3\frac{1}{2}$ ft and its height is 15 ft. Find the volume of the silo.

9. The base of a steel bar measures 2.1 centimeters by 2 centimeters. Its height is 9 centimeters. Find the volume of the beam.

10. A cone-shaped funnel has a radius of 18 meters and a slant height of 26 meters. Find the surface area of the funnel.

11. A cylindrical water tank has a radius of 4 km and a height of 6 km. Find the surface area of the tank.

12. Box A measures 14 in. long, 11 in. wide, and 15 in. high. Box B measures 15 in. long, 12 in. wide, and 11 in. high. Which box has the greatest volume? How much greater?

Independent Test for Chapter 14

Replace each ● with <, >, or = to make a true sentence.

1. ⁻8 ● ⁻9   **2.** ⁻6 ● ⁻5   **3.** 1 ● ⁻4

Graph each set of numbers on a number line.

4. $\left\{\frac{1}{2}, \frac{1}{4}, \frac{1}{8}, \frac{1}{16}\right\}$ **5.** {all numbers greater than 5}   **6.** $\left\{\frac{1}{3}, \frac{2}{5}, \frac{3}{7}, \frac{4}{9}\right\}$

Add.

7. 13 + 4   **8.** ⁻5 + 7   **9.** 31 + ⁻6   **10.** $\frac{1}{4} + \frac{1}{8}$

11. ⁻24 + 18   **12.** 15.1 + ⁻2.1   **13.** $-\frac{8}{5} + \frac{2}{3}$ **14.** ⁻4 + 11

Subtract.

15. 12 − 6   **16.** 0 − ⁻2   **17.** ⁻45 − ⁻15   **18.** $\frac{3}{4} - \frac{1}{2}$

19. $\frac{7}{3} - \frac{⁻8}{6}$ **20.** 9 − 4   **21.** 13 − 8   **22.** ⁻23 − ⁻19

Multiply.

23. 3 × 7   **24.** ⁻5 × 4   **25.** 8 × ⁻9   **26.** 0 × 3

27. 4.5 × ⁻1.6   **28.** $-\frac{3}{5} \times \frac{2}{7}$ **29.** $\frac{1}{4} \times \frac{1}{8}$ **30.** 1 × ⁻2.9

Divide.

31. 81 ÷ 9   **32.** ⁻63 ÷ 14   **33.** ⁻12.4 ÷ ⁻6.2   **34.** ⁻243 ÷ ⁻27

35. $\frac{5}{4} \div \frac{6}{7}$ **36.** 6 ÷ 8   **37.** $\frac{1}{3} \div \frac{⁻12}{3}$ **38.** ⁻13 ÷ ⁻4

Compute.

39. 5 + 2 × 3   **40.** ⁻8 ÷ 2 − 4   **41.** 21 − 7 × 2 + 10

42. 44 × (6 + 2) − 13   **43.** (81 + 9) ÷ 3   **44.** 8 × 4 − 16

Solve.

45. Joan is 8 years older than Amelia. Amelia is 19. How old is Joan?

46. An airplane has an altitude of 8,700 feet, a helicopter has an altitude of 2,000 feet. The helicopter is how many feet lower than the airplane?

Independent Test for Chapter 15

Determine whether each sentence is true, false, or open.

1. She is a good scientist.

2. Oxygen is a gas.

3. $\frac{1}{2} < \frac{1}{4}$

4. $y - 3 = 7$

Translate each sentence into an equation. Then solve the equation and check your solution.

5. c divided by 3 is $^-9$.

6. Ten increased by $6d$ is 22.

7. The sum of y and $\frac{8}{7}$ is 8.

8. Six less than $\frac{x}{3}$ is $\frac{^-5}{3}$.

Solve each equation. Check your solution.

9. $4a + 6 = 26$

10. $x - 18 = 23$

11. $41 - 2b = 11$

12. $\frac{e}{5} - 4 = 2$

13. $72 = \frac{m}{21}$

14. $3g + 4\frac{1}{4} = 10\frac{1}{4}$

Solve each inequality and check your solutions. Then graph each solution set on a number line.

15. $2x < 12$

16. $5m + 3 > 8$

17. $7b - 4 > 17$

18. $\frac{n}{9} < 2$

19. $\frac{h}{4} > \frac{1}{2}$

20. $f - 6 < ^-10$

Solve. Write an equation or inequality.

21. Tina and her sister spent more than $185.00 on clothes. Tina spent $82.50. How much did her sister spend?

22. Enrique has three times as many stamps as David has. Enrique has 120 stamps. How many stamps does David have?

23. Kathy studied more than 7 hours for her biology and literature tests. She studied literature for 2.5 hours. How long did she study biology?

24. Four times a number is increased by 9. The result is 33. What is the number?

Independent Test for Chapter 16

Find the number named by each of the following.

1. 5^3 **2.** 8^2 **3.** 4^4 **4.** 1^8 **5.** 2^5

Find the value of each expression.

6. $8 \div 2 + 3^2 (5 - 4)$ **7.** $31 - [10 \div (3 - 1)]$ **8.** $16 \div 2^2$ **9.** $7(3^2 - 2)$

Find the value of each expression if $a = 2$, $b = {}^-1$, and $c = 4$.

10. $5a^2 - 3c$ **11.** ab **12.** $\frac{c}{a} - b$ **13.** $\left(\frac{c}{b}\right)^2 + 8$

14. $(a - c)^2$ **15.** $a^2 - c^2$ **16.** $\frac{b^2}{c} + 6$ **17.** $b^3 + 2a^2$

Use the formula $rt = d$ to solve for the missing value.

18. $r = 65$ mph, $t = 3$ hours   **19.** $r = 80$ mph, $t = 1.5$ hours

20. $d = 630$ miles, $t = 5$ hours   **21.** $d = 1{,}110$ miles, $t = 12$ hours

Use the gas mileage formula, $s = \frac{m}{g}$, to solve for the missing value.

22. $m = 189$, $g = 15$ **23.** $s = 29$, $g = 14$ **24.** $s = 41$, $g = 9$

Use the formulas for circumference, $C = \pi d$ and $C = 2\pi r$, to solve for the indicated variable. Use 3.14 for π.

25. $C = 37.68$ m, $d \approx$ ▓ m   **26.** $d = 6$ ft, $C \approx$ ▓ ft   **27.** $r = 7$ cm, $C \approx$ ▓ cm

Find each square root.

28. $\sqrt{400}$ **29.** ${}^-\sqrt{1600}$ **30.** $\sqrt{169}$ **31.** $\sqrt{49}$ **32.** ${}^-\sqrt{256}$

Use the table on page 419 or a calculator to approximate each square root.

33. $\sqrt{13}$ **34.** $\sqrt{23}$ **35.** ${}^-\sqrt{94}$ **36.** $\sqrt{83}$ **37.** $\sqrt{71}$

Use the Pythagorean Theorem to find the third side of each triangle.

38. $a = 3$, $c = 5$ **39.** $a = 8$, $b = 6$ **40.** $b = 15$, $c = 39$ **41.** $a = 13$, $b = 12$

Solve.

42. The radius of a circle is 9 ft. Use the formula $A = \pi r^2$ to find the area of the circle. Use $\frac{22}{7}$ for π.

43. Angie traveled 512.4 miles in 9 hours. Use the formula $rt = d$ to find her average rate.

Independent Test for Chapter 17

Use $n \times 100 = p$ to change each fraction to a percent.

1. $\frac{4}{5}$　　　　**2.** $\frac{1}{2}$　　　　**3.** $\frac{2}{5}$　　　　**4.** $\frac{3}{5}$　　　　**5.** $\frac{8}{10}$

Write a mathematical expression for each verbal expression.

6. 7 times a number

7. 3 less than a number

8. 2 more than a number

9. a number divided by 5

Use the values in each table to find the function rule.

10.

x	y
14	7
27	20
31	24
42	35

rule: $y =$ ▩

11.

x	y
$\frac{1}{2}$	$\frac{1}{4}$
1	1
2	4
4	16

rule: $y =$ ▩

12.

x	y
$\frac{1}{2}$	$\frac{1}{2}$
1	2
2	8
4	32

rule: $y =$ ▩

Find the next three terms in each arithmetic sequence.

13. 10, 20, 30, 40, ▩, ▩, ▩

14. 1.75, 1.85, 1.95, 2.05, ▩, ▩, ▩

15. ⁻15, ⁻10, ⁻5, 0, ▩, ▩, ▩

16. 2.3, 2.5, 2.7, 2.9, ▩, ▩, ▩

Find the next three terms in each geometric sequence.

17. 9, 27, 81, 243, ▩, ▩, ▩

18. 4, 16, 64, 256, ▩, ▩, ▩

19. 3, ⁻6, 12, ⁻24, ▩, ▩, ▩

20. 4, 2, 1, $\frac{1}{2}$, ▩, ▩, ▩

Determine the pattern in each sequence to find the next three terms.

21. 2, 4, 7, 11, 16, ▩, ▩, ▩

22. 16, 18, 22, 30, ▩, ▩, ▩

Express each number in scientific notation.

23. 789　　　　**24.** 6,140　　　　**25.** 5,670,000　　　　**26.** 25,000

Express each number in standard notation.

27. 4.5×10^3　　　**28.** 8.31×10^6　　　**29.** 1.1×10^2　　　**30.** 7.25×10^4

Solve.

31. The perimeter (p) of a triangle with sides 15 ft and 19 ft depends on the length of the third side (s). Write a rule for this function.

32. A ball dropped 60 cm bounces $\frac{1}{2}$ of the height from which it fell on each bounce. How far does the ball travel after the fourth bounce?

Independent Test for Chapter 18

Use the grid to find the letter for each ordered pair.

1. (3, 0)   **2.** (4, 6)   **3.** (3, 4)

Use the grid to find the ordered pair for each letter.

4. P   **5.** J   **6.** M

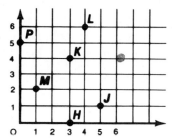

Draw coordinate axes on graph paper. Then graph each ordered pair. Label each point with the given letter.

7. R(1, 3)   **8.** S(4.5, 2.5)   **9.** T(0, 5)   **10.** X(4, 0)   **11.** Y(3, 1)

12. Copy and complete the chart at the right for the equation $y = 3x + 1$.

x	3x + 1	y
⁻3		
⁻1		
0		
2		

Choose 4 values for x and find the corresponding values for y in each equation. Write your answers in chart form.

13. $y = 2x$ **14.** $y = {}^-x + \frac{1}{2}$ **15.** $y = 3x - 2$

Graph each equation on graph paper. Write the equation on the graph.

16. $y = x + 1$ **17.** $x + y = 5$ **18.** $y = {}^-2x + 4$

19. Graph the equation $y = {}^-x + 2$ and $y = 2x - 2$ on the same coordinate system. Then describe what their relationship appears to be.

State whether each pair of figures shows a reflection, a translation, a rotation, or a dilation.

20.

21.
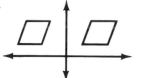

22.
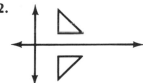

Complete.

23. Mr. Campos begins a 210-mile trip at 2:00 P.M. After 1 hour, he had traveled 60 miles. An hour and a half later, he had traveled 150 miles. At what time did he complete his trip? Use a graph to solve the problem. Assume a constant rate of travel.

24. Draw a rectangle that has vertices at A(⁻2, ⁻2), B(⁻5, ⁻2), C(⁻5, ⁻4), and D(⁻2, ⁻4). Draw the 180° rotation about the origin.

Answers to Independent Tests

Chapter 1, Page T62   **1.** 252 mi   **2.** 567 mi   **3.** 396 mi   **4.** 2,249 mi   **5.** 11:31 A.M.   **6.** 12:22 P.M.
7. $2.08   **8.** $2.13   **9.** $1.65   **10.** $1.52   **11.** $2.99   **12.** $2.86   **13.** 60% discount   **14.** 40% discount
15. full rate   **16.** 60% discount   **17.** 60% discount   **18.** 40% discount   **19.** $13   **20.** $29   **21.** $14
22. $23   **23.** $15   **24.** $34   **25.** $1,089   **26.** $897   **27.** $1,057   **28.** $1,324   **29.** $1,058   **30.** $1,248
31. $0.73   **32.** $0.33   **33.** $0.42   **34.** $0.96   **35.** 1960, 1961   **36.** 13; 1951

Chapter 2, Page T63   **1.** 卌 || **2.** 卌 卌 卌   **3.** 卌 卌 卌 卌 卌 卌 卌 || **4.** 卌 卌 卌 卌 卌 卌 卌 卌 卌 卌 卌

5.

#	Tally	Frequency
26	|	1
29	||	2
30	|||	3
31	|	1
32	|	1
33	|	1
36	|	1
38	|	1
41	|	1
44	|	1
47	|	1

6. 21   **7.** 30   **8.** 34   **9.** 31.5   **10.** mean or median
11. median   **12.** mode   **13.** mean   **14.** 57, 60   **15.** 67
16. 57   **17.** median   **18.** 33   **19.** 154   **20.** 162
21. 167   **22.** 29   **23.** 28   **24.** either one   **25.** median: no
change; mean becomes 30.6

Chapter 3, Page T64   **1.** $\frac{1}{3}$ **2.** $\frac{7}{9}$ **3.** $\frac{37}{9}$ **4.** yes   **5.** no   **6.** yes   **7.** 650%   **8.** 150%   **9.** 42%   **10.** 0.22
11. 0.367   **12.** 0.052   **13.** $\frac{2}{5}$ **14.** $1\frac{1}{5}$ **15.** $\frac{23}{400}$ **16.** 15.30   **17.** 40   **18.** 250   **19.** 36%   **20.** 42%   **21.** 26
22. 60%   **23.** 184 miles   **24.** 65.4%   **25.** 13-ounce at $1.01

Chapter 4, Page T65   **1.** 80,000 strawberries   **2.** 100,000 strawberries   **3.** 5,000 more   **4.** Gobi
5. Khiva   **6.** Kalahari and Sonoran   **7.** 40%   **8.** 11%   **9.** 100%   **10.** 15   **11.** 71-80   **12.** April, May, June,
July, August, September, October   **13.** Graph A; starting the vertical scale at 2,500 magnifies the difference.

Chapter 5, Page T66   **1.** 6 outcomes   **2.** 64 outcomes   **3.**
4. 8 outcomes   **5.** 4 outcomes   **6.** $\frac{1}{6}$ **7.** $\frac{2}{6}$ or $\frac{1}{3}$ **8.** $\frac{2}{6}$ or $\frac{1}{3}$
9. $\frac{1}{9}$ **10.** $\frac{1}{18}$ **11.** $\frac{6}{15}$ or $\frac{2}{5}$ **12.** $\frac{4}{15}$ **13.** $\frac{1}{15}$ **14.** $\frac{4}{15}$ **15.** $\frac{1}{3}$
16. $\frac{3}{44}$

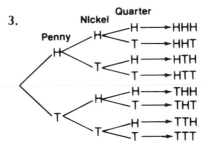

Chapter 6, Page T67   **1.** 1 to 3   **2.** 1 to 3   **3.** 3 to 1   **4.** $\frac{1}{8}$ **5.** $\frac{2}{5}$ **6.** $\frac{1}{4}$ **7.** $\frac{1}{3}$; 33%   **8.** $\frac{1}{2}$; 50%   **9.** $\frac{5}{9}$; 55%
10. $\frac{3}{4}$; 75%   **11.** 2 to 1   **12.** 1 to 1   **13.** 1 to 3   **14.** 6 to 1   **15.** 203 people   **16.** $\frac{41}{203}$ **17.** 242 people
18. 20¢   **19.** 50¢   **20.** 16¢   **21.** 47   **22.** 81   **23.** 10   **24.** 1,000 times   **25.** 15 students

Chapter 7, Page T68   **1.** cm   **2.** yd   **3.** mi   **4.** ft   **5.** m   **6.** km   **7.** 1 in.   **8.** $1\frac{3}{4}$ in.   **9.** 2 in.   **10.** 3 in.
11. b   **12.** a   **13.** b   **14.** 2   **15.** 42   **16.** 6 mi   **17.** 3,000   **18.** 9.71   **19.** 0.6   **20.** 1,540   **21.** 0.161
22. 8,200   **23.** 13 ft 9 in.   **24.** 3 ft 7 in.   **25.** 4 ft 10 in.   **26.** 11 ft 1 in.   **27.** 3   **28.** 4   **29.** 1   **30.** 3
31. more   **32.** about 72

Chapter 8, Page T69 **1.** 0.42 **2.** 7.04 **3.** 0.1 **4.** 13,410 **5.** 2.25 **6.** 6 **7.** 1.55 **8.** 9,010 **9.** 87,200 **10.** 8 **11.** 3 **12.** 4,200 **13.** < **14.** < **15.** > **16.** > **17.** = **18.** < **19.** > **20.** = **21.** > **22.** 6 wk 2 d **23.** 4 h 55 min **24.** 4 d **25.** 6 d 1 h **26.** 31 h 16 min 17 s **27.** 19 h 46 min **28.** 35°C **29.** 55°C **30.** 95°C **31.** 10°C **32.** 104°F **33.** 230°F **34.** 150.8°F **35.** 77°F **36.** 5°C **37.** 25°C **38.** Miami **39.** 28.8 ounces

Chapter 9, Page T70 **1.** 264.2 miles **2.** 856.2 miles **3.** 1,315.4 miles **4.** 55 S to 40 W **5.** 1,320 miles, 28:15 **6.** 3:45 P.M. **7.** 7:15 A.M. **8.** 11:20 P.M. **9.** 8:01 A.M. **10.** 12:44 A.M. **11.** 46,903 **12.** 90,162 **13.** 953,210 **14.** 368,321 **15.** 247,590 **16.** 856,123 **17.** 110° **18.** 74° **19.** 22° **20.** 163° **21–26.** See students' work. **27.** 47,485.0 miles **28.** 135 ccf

Chapter 10, Page T70 **1.** $\overleftrightarrow{AB}$ **2.** $\angle MLN$ (or $\angle NLM$) **3.** $\triangle IHJ$ **4.** $\overrightarrow{OP}$ **5.** $\overleftrightarrow{IJ}$ (or $\overleftrightarrow{JI}$) **6.** $\overline{IH}$ (or $\overline{HI}$), $\overline{IJ}$ (or $\overline{JI}$), $\overline{HJ}$ (or $\overline{JH}$) **7.** point I **8.** $\overline{HI}$ or $\overline{IH}$, $\overline{IJ}$ or $\overline{JI}$ **9.** obtuse **10.** acute **11.** right **12.** 72°, 162° **13.** 67°, 157° **14.** 1°, 91° **15.** 30°, 120° **16.** 45°, 135° **17.** 5 cm **18.** 10 ft **19.** 39 m **20.** If there is a leap year, then the month of February has 29 days; true, true **21.** Inductive **22.** 5 weeks

Chapter 11, Page T71 **1–10.** See students' work. **11.** $\angle YXZ$ **12.** $\overline{ML}$ **13.** $\overline{LK}$ **14.** $\angle MKL$ **15–17.** See students' work.

Chapter 12, Page T72 **1.** 4 **2.** 6 **3.** 12 in. **4.** 17.1 m **5.** 20 km **6.** 47.1 cm **7.** 37.7 m **8.** 69.1 in. **9.** 40 ft² **10.** 25.2 m² **11.** 241.5 cm² **12.** 135 in² **13.** 117 m² **14.** 67.5 yd² **15.** 100 in² **16.** 26 cm² **17.** 50.2 km² **18.** 176.6 ft² **19.** 803.8 m² **20.** 530.7 in² **21.** 224 m²

Chapter 13, Page T73 **1.** 94 m² **2.** 216 in² **3.** 175.8 ft² **4.** 528 cm² **5.** 96 yd³ **6.** 167.5 in³ **7.** 1,588.1 m³ **8.** 577.0 ft³ **9.** 37.8 cm³ **10.** 2,486.9 m³ **11.** 251.2 km³ **12.** A; 330 in³ more

Chapter 14, Page T74 **1.** > **2.** < **3.** > **4–6.** See students' work. **7.** 17 **8.** 2 **9.** 25 **10.** $\frac{3}{8}$ **11.** ⁻6 **12.** 13 **13.** $-\frac{14}{15}$ **14.** 7 **15.** 6 **16.** 2 **17.** ⁻30 **18.** $\frac{1}{4}$ **19.** $3\frac{2}{3}$ **20.** 5 **21.** 5 **22.** ⁻4 **23.** 21 **24.** ⁻20 **25.** ⁻72 **26.** 0 **27.** ⁻7.2 **28.** $-\frac{6}{35}$ **29.** $\frac{1}{32}$ **30.** ⁻2.9 **31.** 9 **32.** ⁻4.5 **33.** 2 **34.** 9 **35.** $1\frac{11}{24}$ **36.** 0.75 **37.** $-\frac{1}{12}$ **38.** 3.25 **39.** 11 **40.** ⁻8 **41.** 17 **42.** 339 **43.** 30 **44.** 16 **45.** 27 **46.** 6,700

Chapter 15, Page T75 **1.** open **2.** true **3.** false **4.** open **5.** $\frac{c}{3} = -9$; ⁻27 **6.** $10 + 6d = 22$; 2 **7.** $y + \frac{8}{7} = 8$; $\frac{48}{7}$ **8.** $\frac{x}{3} - 6 = -\frac{5}{3}$; 13 **9.** 5 **10.** 41 **11.** 15 **12.** 30 **13.** 1,512 **14.** 2

15. $x < 6$; **16.** $m > 1$;

17. $b > 3$; **18.** $n < 18$;

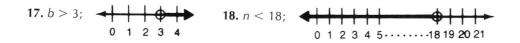

19. $h > 2$; **20.** $f < -4$; **21.** $x + 82.50 > 185$; $102.50 or more

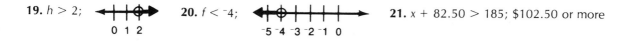

22. $3t = 120$; 40 stamps **23.** $2.5 + r > 7$; 4.5 hours or more **24.** $4n + 9 = 33$; 6

Chapter 16, Page T76 **1.** 125 **2.** 64 **3.** 256 **4.** 1 **5.** 32 **6.** 13 **7.** 26 **8.** 4 **9.** 49 **10.** 8 **11.** $^-2$
12. 3 **13.** 24 **14.** 4 **15.** $^-12$ **16.** $6\frac{1}{4}$ **17.** 9 **18.** 195 miles **19.** 120 miles **20.** 126 mph **21.** 92.5 mph
22. 12.6 **23.** 406 **24.** 369 **25.** 12 m **26.** 18.84 ft **27.** 43.96 cm **28.** 20 **29.** $^-40$ **30.** 13 **31.** 7
32. $^-16$ **33.** 3.606 **34.** 4.796 **35.** 9.695 **36.** 9.110 **37.** 8.426 **38.** $b = 4$ **39.** c = 10 **40.** a = 36
41. $\approx$17.7 **42.** $\approx$255 ft^2 **43.** $\approx$56.9 mph

Chapter 17, Page T77 **1.** 80% **2.** 50% **3.** 40% **4.** 60% **5.** 80% **6.** 7x **7.** x $-$ 3 **8.** x + 2 **9.** $\frac{x}{5}$
10. x $-$ 7 **11.** x^2 **12.** $2x^2$ **13.** 50, 60, 70 **14.** 2.15, 2.25, 2.35 **15.** 5, 10, 15 **16.** 3.1, 3.3, 3.5
17. 729; 2,187; 6,561 **18.** 1,024; 4,096; 16,384 **19.** 48, $^-96$, 192 **20.** $\frac{1}{4}, \frac{1}{8}, \frac{1}{16}$ **21.** 22, 29, 37 **22.** 46, 78,
142 **23.** 7.89 $\times$ 10^2 **24.** 6.14 $\times$ 10^3 **25.** 5.67 $\times$ 10^6 **26.** 2.5 $\times$ 10^4 **27.** 4,500
28. 8,310,000 **29.** 110 **30.** 72,500 **31.** $p = 34 + s$ **32.** 3.75 cm

Chapter 18, Page T78 **1.** H **2.** L **3.** K **4.** (0, 5) **5.** (5, 1) **6.** (1, 2)

7 -11.

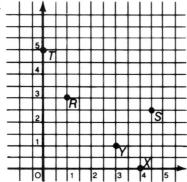

12.

x	3x + 1	y
$^-3$	3($^-3$) + 1	$^-8$
$^-1$	3($^-1$) + 1	$^-2$
0	3(0) + 1	1
2	3(2) + 1	7

13.

x	2x	y
$^-1$	2($^-1$)	$^-2$
0	2(0)	0
1	2(1)	2
2	2(2)	4

14.

x	$-x + \frac{1}{2}$	y
$^-3$	$-(^-3) + \frac{1}{2}$	$\frac{7}{2}$
$^-1$	$-(^-1) + \frac{1}{2}$	$\frac{3}{2}$
0	$-(0) + \frac{1}{2}$	$\frac{1}{2}$
3	$-(3) + \frac{1}{2}$	$\frac{-5}{2}$

15.

x	3x $-$ 2	y
$^-2$	3($^-2$) $-$ 2	$^-8$
0	3(0) $-$ 2	$^-2$
1	3(1) $-$ 2	1
2	3(2) $-$ 2	4

16.

17.

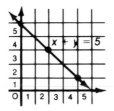

18.

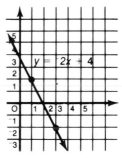

19.

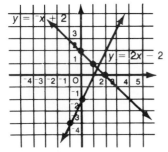

T82

20. rotation   **21.** translation   **22.** reflection

23.

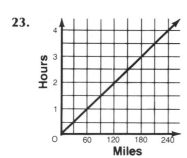

24.

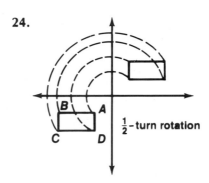

$\frac{1}{2}$-turn rotation

On the graph, 210 miles corresponds to $3\frac{1}{2}$ hours. Mr. Campos completed his trip at 5:30 P.M.

Teacher Answer Key

Chapter 1   Charts and Tables

Page 19   Exercises

1.

	Black	Brown	White	Navy
Size 9	|||| — 4	|| — 2	|||| — 4	﷼ — 5
Size 10	||| — 3	﷼ || — 7	|| — 2	||| — 3
Size 11	﷼ | — 6	0	0	|| — 2
Size 12	|| — 2	|||| — 4	| — 1	||| — 3

2.

	Week 1	Week 2	Week 3	Week 4
food	$43.20	$56.47	$37.26	$41.19
health and beauty aids	6.72		2.49	4.57
snacks	5.89	2.89	3.89	4.56
beverages	8.46	2.99	5.74	5.56
cookware	12.67		3.16	
pet food	4.99		4.99	

The most money is spent on food.   The least money is spent on pet food.

Chapter 2   Everyday Statistics

Page 27   Exercises

7. no; people are all from same party
9. yes; variety of people

8. no; may be there to see star actor
10. no; some apartments don't allow dogs

11.

Wages	Tally	Frequency
$11,300	|||	3
13,000	﷼	5
14,500	﷼ |	6
16,000	|||	3
19,400	||	2
28,600	|	1

13.

Score	Tally	Frequency
12	||	2
13	|	1
14	|||	3
15	|||	3
16	|	1
17	|	1
18	|||	3
20	||	2
22	||	2
24	|	1
25	|	1

Page 31 Exercises

14.

Number	Tally	Frequency
0	||	2
1	|	1
2	|||	3
3	||||	4
4	||||	4
5	|||	3
6	||	2
8	|	1

16.

Number	Tally	Frequency
2	|||	3
4	⊮||	7
8	⊮|||	8
9	||	2

Page 38 Exercises

2. People who can afford higher priced homes want to live in higher priced neighborhoods.

11. Group A. Group A had both a higher mean and a higher median because of more higher scores than group B.

Page 38 Exercises

2. People who can afford higher priced homes want to live in higher priced neighborhoods.

11. Group A. Group A had both a higher mean and a higher median because of more higher scores than group B.

Page 41 Exercises

17.

Passengers	Tally	Frequency
1	||||	4
2	⊮||	7
3	⊮ ⊮	10
4	⊮|||	8
5	⊮|	6
6	||	2
7	|	1
8	|	1
9	|	1

21. The best answer for the owners is the mean, because this tells what the income is for the ride.

Page 42 Exercises

16. no, too many people go to a dealer because of the make of car sold there
17. no, people attend concert because of who is performing
18. no, football is just one sport

19. yes, variety of food offered

Page 43 Exercises

37.

#	Tally	Frequency
5	|	1
6	|	1
7	|||	3
8	||||	4
9	||	2
10	|||	3
12	||	2

48. 162.8 cm, mean, or 160 cm, median
50. Brown hair, mode
52. Basketball, mode

49. 56.4 kg, mean, or 57 kg, median
51. Chicken, mode
53. Female 163 cm tall, mass of 56.4 kg, has brown hair, likes chicken and basketball.

Page 44 Exercises

5.

#	Tally	Frequency
22	||	2
26	|	1
28	||	2
30	|	1
31	|||	3
36	|	1
38	|	1
40	|	1
42	|	1
47	|	1

Page 45 Exercises

22.

Score	Tally	Frequency
37	|	1
59	|	1
68	||||	4
72	|	1
75	||||	4
77	|	1
80	|	1
81	|	1
83	|	1
86	|	1
87	|	1
92	|	1
93	||	2
94	|	1
100	||	2

Chapter 4   *Graphs*

Page 73 Exercises

6.

FM Radio Stations

Austin
Boston
Honolulu
Miami
Oklahoma City
San Antonio

Each ▨ stands for 4 stations

14.

Vehicles Passing by Each 15 Minutes		
Vehicle	Tally	Frequency
Car	JHT JHT JHT JHT JHT JHT JHT JHT JHT JHT JHT JHT JHT JHT JHT	75
Bus	JHT III	8
Van	JHT JHT JHT JHT JHT III	28
Pickup	JHT JHT II	12
Truck	JHT JHT JHT IIII	19

Page 76   Exercises

52.

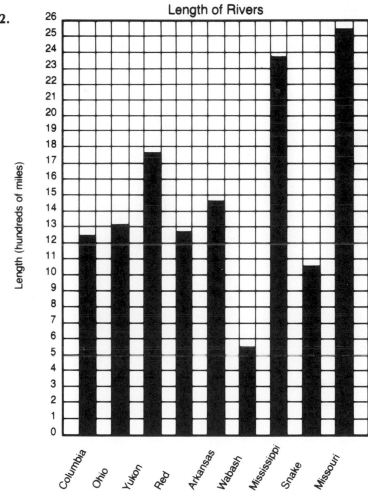

Length of Rivers

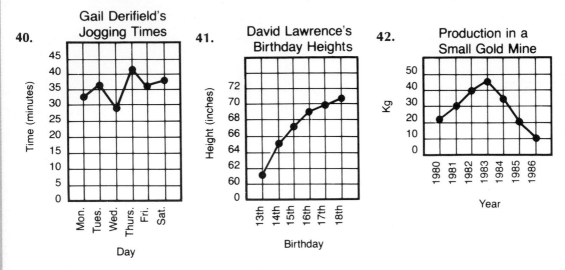

40. **Gail Derifield's Jogging Times**
(y-axis: Time (minutes), 0–45; x-axis: Day — Mon., Tues., Wed., Thurs., Fri., Sat.)

41. **David Lawrence's Birthday Heights**
(y-axis: Height (inches), 60–72; x-axis: Birthday — 13th, 14th, 15th, 16th, 17th, 18th)

42. **Production in a Small Gold Mine**
(y-axis: Kg, 0–50; x-axis: Year — 1980, 1981, 1982, 1983, 1984, 1985, 1986)

14.

Families with Children		
Number of Children	Tally	Frequency
1	ⅻ|||	8
2	ⅻ ⅻ ⅻ	15
3	ⅻ ⅻ ||	12
4	ⅻ		6
5					3
7				2
8 or more			1

30. Cars in a Parking Lot

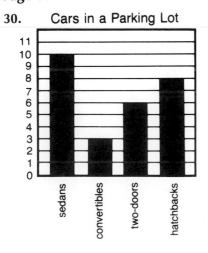

(bar graph; y-axis 0–11; bars: sedans = 10, convertibles = 3, two-doors = 6, hatchbacks = 8)

Chapter 5   Probability

1. travel to Denver by bus; return home by bus
2. travel to Denver by rail; return home by air
3. travel to Denver by bus; return home by rail
4. travel to Denver by air; return home by bus

Page 97   Exercises

25.

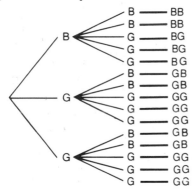

26.

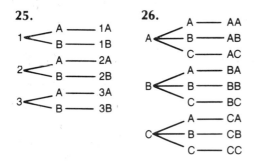

27.

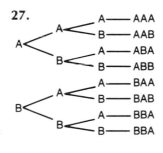

28.

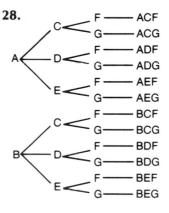

Page 104   Example

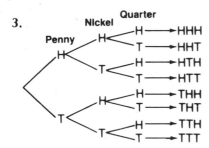

Page 114   Chapter 5 Test

3.

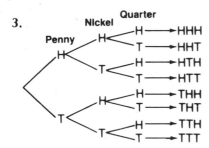

Chapter 6   Using Probability and Statistics

Page 131   Exercises

8.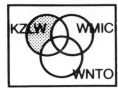

9.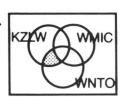

10.

11.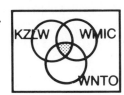

Page 131   Exercises

16.

Page 135   Cumulative Review

9.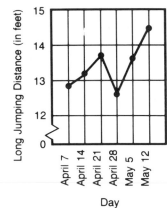

Chapter 10   Geometry

Page 215   Exercises

19.

20.

21.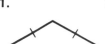

23.

24.

Page 225 Exercises

9. If an animal is a mammal, then it is a bear. original—true, converse—false

10. If a number is divisible by three, then it is six. original—true, converse—false

11. If a triangle is equilateral, then it has three congruent sides. original—true, converse—true

12. If a triangle has no congruent sides, then it is scalene. original—true, converse—true

13. If the sum of the degree measures of two angles is 90, then the angles are complementary. original—true, converse—true

14. If two lines are perpendicular, then they form right angles. original—true, converse—true

15. If a month has 31 days, then it is named May. original—true, converse—false

16. If I do not have to go to school, then today is Saturday. original—true, converse—false

Chapter 11   Constructions

Page 243 Exercises

14.

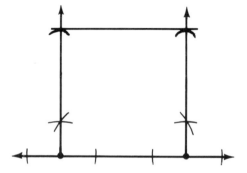

15.

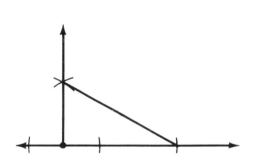

Page 245 Exercises

17.

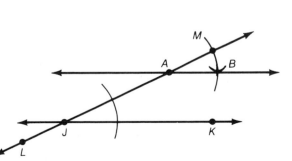

18.

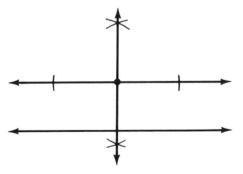

Chapter 12   Polygons and Circles

Page 257   Math Break   1.
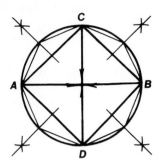

Chapter 13   Surface Area and Volume

Page 281   Exercises   6. 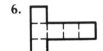   7.

Chapter 14   Rational Numbers

Page 307   Exercises

21. ⁻2, 0, 4, 5, 7   **22.** ⁻7, ⁻3, ⁻2, 1, 12
23. ⁻15, ⁻8, 3, 6, 7   **24.** $\frac{-4}{2}$, $\frac{-1}{2}$, 0, $\frac{2}{3}$, 3
25. ⁻3.5, ⁻3, 0, 3, 3.5   **26.** 0, |4|, 5, |⁻6|, 8

Page 309   Exercises

12. 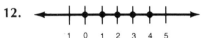   13.    14.

15.    16.    17.

18. 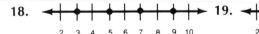   19.    20.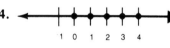

21.    22.

23. 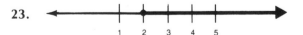   24.

25.    26.

37.    38.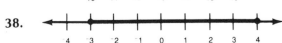

Page 311 Exercises

4.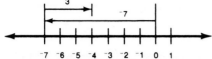

5.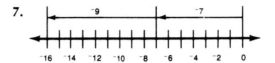

6.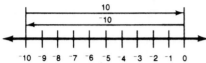

7.

8.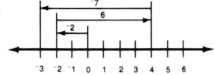

Page 325 Exercises

12. Fill 2-L container and empty into 5-L container. Repeat. Fill 2-L container and finish filling 5-L container. One liter remains in the 2-L container. Another solution is possible.

Page 329 Exercises

24.

25.

26.

27.

28.

29.

Chapter 15   Solving Open Sentences

Page 347 Key Skills

1.

2.

3.

4.

5.

6.

Page 347 Exercises

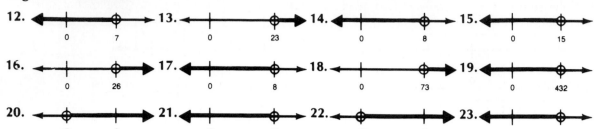

Page 351 Chapter 15 Review

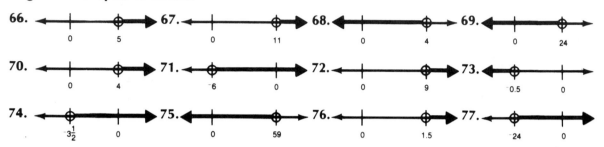

Page 352 Chapter 15 Test

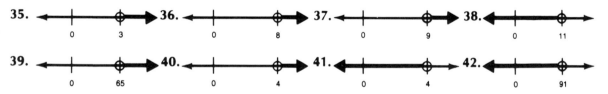

Chapter 17   Patterns and Functions

Page 377 Exercises

15.

fraction	decimal
$\frac{1}{2}$	0.5
$\frac{3}{4}$	0.75
$\frac{4}{5}$	0.8
$1\frac{1}{4}$	1.25
$3\frac{5}{8}$	3.625

1. If the sum of the measures of two angles is 180°, then they are supplementary. original—true, converse—true
2. If you can buy a car, then you have $10,000. original—true, converse—false
3. If two lines in a plane are parallel, then they are perpendicular to the same line. original—true, converse—false
4. If a polygon has 2 parallel sides, then it is a trapezoid. original—true, converse—false

Chapter 18   The Coordinate Plane

Page 397   Exercises

21–28

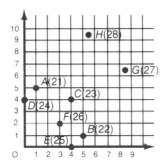

Page 399   Exercises

29–44

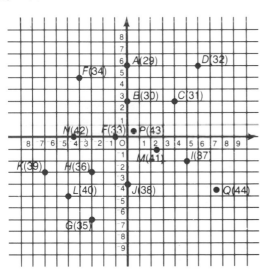

45–53

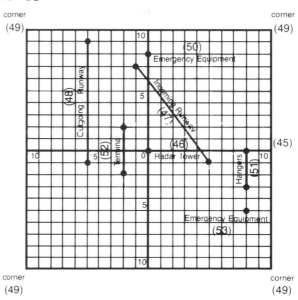

Page 401 Exercises

Answers may vary. Typical answers are given.

7. (x, y)
(⁻1, ⁻2)
(0, 0)
(1, 2)
(2, 4)

8. (x, y)
(⁻1, ⁻3)
(0, 0)
(1, 3)
(2, 6)

9. (x, y)
(⁻1, ⁻5)
(0, 0)
(1, 5)
(2, 10)

10. (x, y)
(⁻1, 4)
(0, 0)
(1, ⁻4)
(2, ⁻8)

11. (x, y)
(⁻1, 6)
(0, 0)
(1, ⁻6)
(2, ⁻12)

12. (x, y)
(⁻1, 1)
(0, 0)
(1, ⁻1)
(2, ⁻2)

13. (x, y)
(⁻1, ⁻2)
(0, 1)
(1, 4)
(2, 7)

14. (x, y)
(⁻1, ⁻6)
(0, ⁻4)
(1, ⁻2)
(2, 0)

15. (x, y)
(⁻1, 0)
(0, 5)
(1, 10)
(2, 15)

16. (x, y)
(⁻1, 0)
(0, ⁻1)
(1, ⁻2)
(2, ⁻3)

17. (x, y)
(⁻1, 7)
(0, 3)
(1, ⁻1)
(2, ⁻5)

18. (x, y)
(⁻1, 1)
(0, ⁻2)
(1, ⁻5)
(2, ⁻8)

19. (x, y)
(⁻1, $-\frac{1}{2}$)
(0, 0)
(1, $\frac{1}{2}$)
(2, 1)

20. (x, y)
(⁻1, $-\frac{2}{3}$)
(0, 0)
(1, $\frac{2}{3}$)
(2, $\frac{4}{3}$)

21. (x, y)
(⁻1, $-\frac{3}{4}$)
(0, 0)
(1, $\frac{3}{4}$)
(2, $\frac{3}{2}$)

22. (x, y)
(⁻1, $\frac{3}{4}$)
(0, 1)
(1, $1\frac{1}{4}$)
(2, $1\frac{1}{2}$)

23. (x, y)
(⁻1, $-2\frac{1}{3}$)
(0, ⁻2)
(1, $-1\frac{2}{3}$)
(2, $-1\frac{1}{3}$)

24. (x, y)
(⁻1, $-\frac{7}{3}$)
(0, ⁻1)
(1, $\frac{1}{3}$)
(2, $\frac{5}{3}$)

25. (x, y)
(⁻1, 5)
(0, 3)
(1, 1)
(2, ⁻1)

26. (x, y)
(⁻1, 9)
(0, 5)
(1, 1)
(2, ⁻3)

27. (x, y)
(⁻1, 8)
(0, 7)
(1, 6)
(2, 5)

28. (x, y)
(⁻1, $3\frac{2}{3}$)
(0, 3)
(1, $2\frac{1}{3}$)
(2, $1\frac{2}{3}$)

29. (x, y)
(⁻1, 11)
(0, 6)
(1, 1)
(2, ⁻4)

30. (x, y)
(⁻1, $-2\frac{3}{5}$)
(0, ⁻2)
(1, $-1\frac{2}{5}$)
(2, $-\frac{4}{5}$)

31. y = x ⁻3
(x, y)
(40, 37)
(30, 27)
(20, 17)
(4, 1)

32. y = 2 x + 3
(x, y)
(0, 0)
(1, 4.75)
(2, 9.50)
(3, 14.25)

33. y = 0.1 x + 100
(x, y)
(10, 101)
(100, 110)
(200, 120)
(500, 150)

34. y = 4.75 x
(x, y)
(2, 7)
(4, 11)
(6, 15)
(8, 19)

Page 402 Exercises

1.

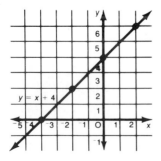

2.

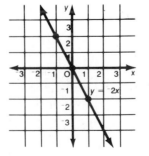

Page 403 Exercises

3.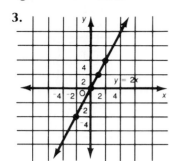

4.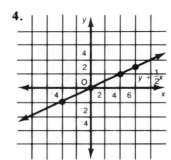

5.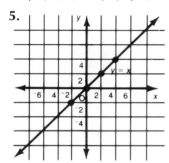

6.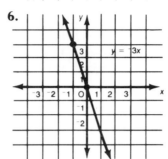

7.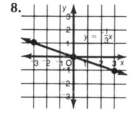

8.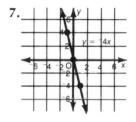

9.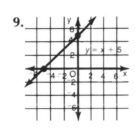

10.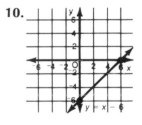

11.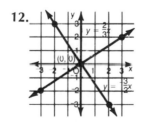

12.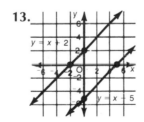

13.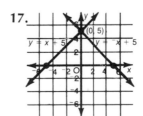

14.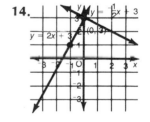

15.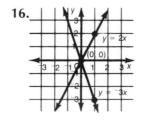

16.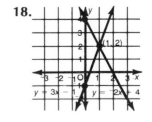

17.

18.

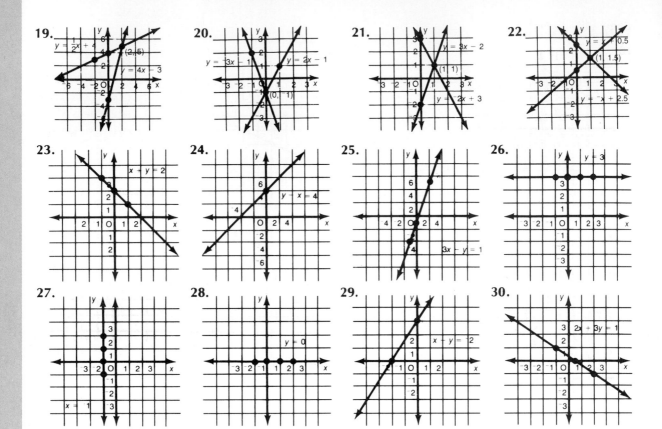

Page 405 Exercises

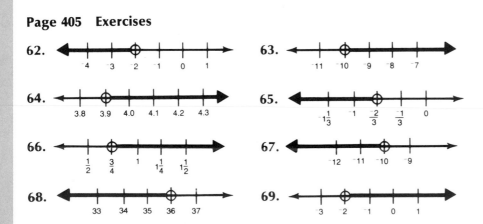

Page 410 Exercises

10.

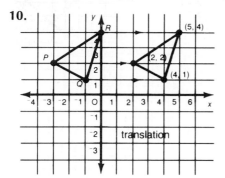

translation

11.

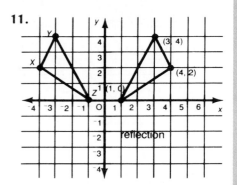

reflection

12.

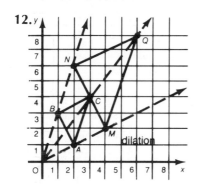

dilation

13.

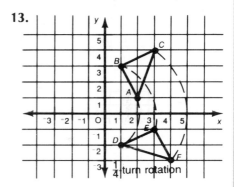

$\frac{1}{4}$ turn rotation

14.

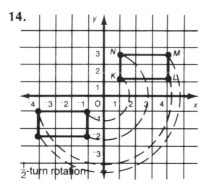

$\frac{1}{2}$-turn rotation

Page 413 Exercises

3.

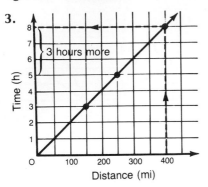

4.

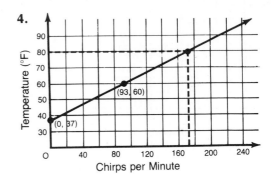

5.

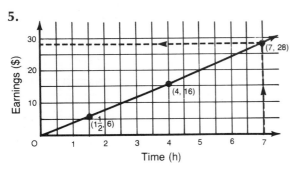

6.

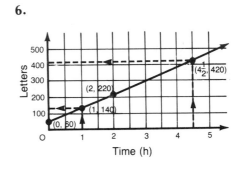

Page 414 Exercises

23. – 30.

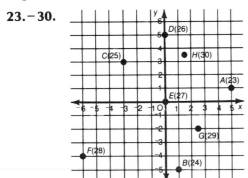

Page 415 Exercises

34.

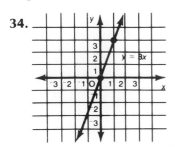

35.

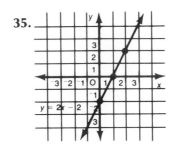

T100

36.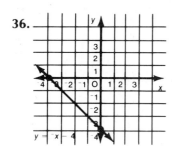

$y = x - 4$

37.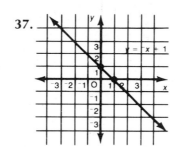

$y = -x + 1$

38.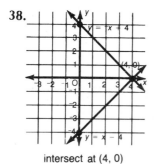

$y = x + 4$

$(4, 0)$

$y = x - 4$

intersect at (4, 0)

39.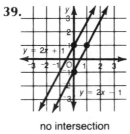

$y = 2x + 1$

$y = 2x - 1$

no intersection

40.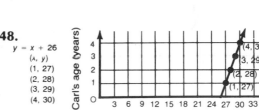

$y = x + 4$

$(-3, 1)$

$y = -x - 2$

intersect at (-3, 1)

47.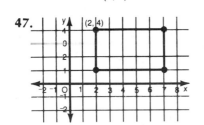

(2, 4)

48.

$y = x + 26$

(x, y)

$(1, 27)$

$(2, 28)$

$(3, 29)$

$(4, 30)$

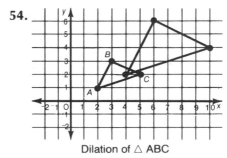

Carl's age (years)

(4, 30)

(3, 29)

(2, 28)

(1, 27)

Edna's age (years)

50.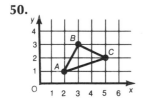

51.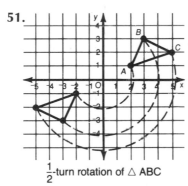

$\frac{1}{2}$-turn rotation of △ ABC

52.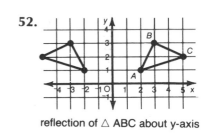

reflection of △ ABC about y-axis

53.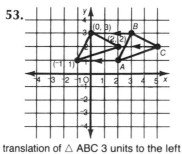

(0, 3)

(2, 2)

B

C

(-1, 1)

A

translation of △ ABC 3 units to the left

54.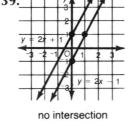

B

C

A

Dilation of △ ABC

7.-11.

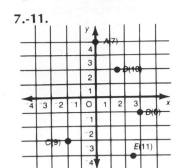

13. (x, y)
(⁻1, ⁻8)
(0, ⁻5)
(1, ⁻2)
(2, 1)

14. (x, y)
(⁻1, $2\frac{3}{4}$)
(0, 2)
(1, $1\frac{1}{4}$)
(2, $\frac{1}{2}$)

15. (x, y)
(⁻1, ⁻1.2)
(0, 0)
(1, 1.2)
(2, 2.4)

16.

17.

18.

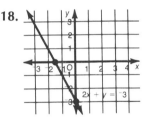

19.

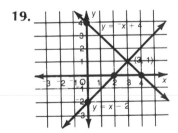

The graphs of their equations intersect at (3, 1).

24.

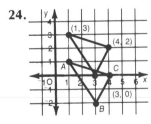

Translation of △ ABC 3 units upward

15. (x, y)
(⁻1, $1\frac{3}{8}$)
(0, 1)
(1, $\frac{5}{8}$)
(2, $\frac{1}{4}$)

16. (x, y)
(⁻2, ⁻12)
(⁻1, ⁻6)
(0, 0)
(3, 18)

17. (x, y)
(⁻2, 1)
(⁻1, $\frac{3}{2}$)
(0, 2)
(2, 3)

18.

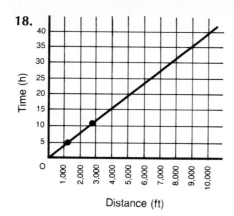

19.

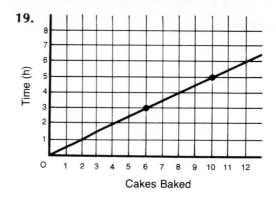

Notes

Merrill
Applications
of Mathematics

Authors

Jack Price is currently Superintendent of Schools in Palos Verdes, California, and a former Director of Curriculum Coordination for the San Diego City Schools. He has taught elementary and secondary mathematics in Detroit, Michigan. Dr. Price received his M.Ed. and Ed.D. from Wayne State University. His dissertation dealt with discovery and its effect on achievement and critical thinking of general mathematics students. He is a member of many state and national professional organizations including the Mathematical Sciences Education Board, National Research Council and the National Advisory Committee on Mathematics Education.

Michael Charles is Associate Dean of Learning Resources at San Diego College, San Diego, California. Mr. Charles taught in the Sweetwater Union High School District, California. He also taught learning skills and secondary mathematics for five years at San Diego City College, San Diego, California. He received his B.A. and M.A. from San Diego State University. He is a member of several state and national organizations.

Olene Brame teaches mathematics and is Department Chairman at Arts Magnet High School, Dallas, Texas. Dr. Brame received her B.A. from Texas Woman's University, her M.Ed. from the University of Texas, and her Ph.D. from North Texas State University. She has served on numerous special committees and curriculum projects.

Miriam Clifford teaches mathematics at Bay View High School in Milwaukee, Wisconsin. Mrs. Clifford received her B.S. from Texas Tech University and her M.Ed. from the University of Texas. She has served on several curriculum committees and has conducted numerous workshops.

Consultants

Les Winters
Mathematics Supervisor
Los Angeles Unified School District
Los Angeles, California

Bill Leschensky
Glenbard South High School
Glen Ellyn, Illinois

Reviewers

Catherine Cotton
Mathematics Teacher
Columbia High School
Columbia, Mississippi

Tom Donoughe
Mathematics Teacher
Mayfield High School
Mayfield Heights, Ohio

Richard Frankenberger
Mathematics Consultant
Hazelwood School District
Florissant, Missouri

Sandra L. Moore
Mathematics Teacher
Alvin High School
Alvin, Texas

Ralph Schubothe
Chairperson, Mathematics Department
Banks High School
Banks, Oregon

Wanda S. Davis
Chairperson, Mathematics Department
Gordon Central High School
Calhoun, Georgia

Sandra Dorsey
Chairperson, Mathematics Department
Ocean View High School
Huntington Beach, California

Ruth Mooney
Mathematics Supervisor
Hamilton Township School District
Trenton, New Jersey

Diane Pors
Mathematics Coordinator
Eastside Union High School District
San Jose, California

Glenda Young
Mathematics Teacher
Bryant High School
Bryant, Arkansas

Credits

Project Editor: Jeanne Huffman; *Editors:* Susan E. Bailey, James M. Bruce, Jr., Gladys Martinez Suber;
Book Design: David Germon: *Project Artist:* Jeffrey Clark; *Photo Editor:* David Dennison; *Production Editor:* Kimberly Munsie;
Illustrator: Glenn Wasserman

ISBN 0-675-05717-5

Published by
Merrill Publishing Company
A Bell & Howell Information Company
Columbus, Ohio 43216

Copyright © 1988 by Merrill Publishing Company. All rights reserved. No part of this book may be reproduced in any form, electronic or mechanical, including photocopy, recording or any information storage or retrieval system, without permission in writing from the publisher.

Printed in the United States of America

Preface

Merrill Applications of Mathematics is a high school mathematics textbook written by classroom teachers for today's student. It presents the fundamental concepts and skills required in a technological society. The relevant and student-motivating approach as well as the comprehensive presentation of essential skills appeal to and meet the needs of all students.

Relevant Real-Life Applications Research has shown that students learn best that for which they see a need. This premise is the basis for this general mathematics program. Mathematical proficiency and understanding will follow as the student is given practice in relevant problem-solving situations.

Easy-to-Read Presentation Throughout the text, the reading level has been carefully controlled. It presents an open format to facilitate reading and comprehension. In addition, many color photographs, illustrations, charts, and graphs are used. These features help students visualize the ideas presented and help them read with improved understanding.

Organization *Merrill Applications of Mathematics* is organized into eighteen chapters. For easy management, each chapter is composed of primarily two-page lessons. The daily routine can be varied by using the Reviews and the Special Features. This design allows the flexibility to structure a program to meet the needs of students.

Problem Solving Learning to solve problems is the principal reason for studying mathematics. *Merrill Applications of Mathematics* presents a sequential and comprehensive development of problem solving. The format guides the student through problem-solving processes that reveal the underlying relationships in problems. In this manner, students can examine many aspects of problem solving.

Plenty of Practice The text contains an ample selection of exercises, problem solving, and applications. An extra practice section is included in each chapter.

Review A one-page cumulative review in each chapter provides students with constant review and reinforcement of the basic skills presented up to that point. This research-proven review method is most effective in increasing student retention of mathematical skills. Each chapter also includes a two-page Chapter Review that reinforces vocabulary and concepts, and provides exercises and problem solving. At the back of the text, there is a 42-page Basic Skills Appendix section that provides students with a review of skills. The appropriate pages are assigned in each lesson.

Testing Each chapter ends with a Chapter Test to help students check their own progress.

CONTENTS

1

Charts and Tables

2

Everyday Statistics

3

Ratio, Proportion, and Percent

4

Graphs

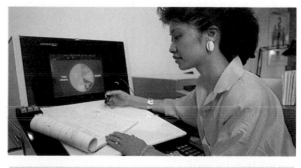

5

Probability

6

Using Probability and Statistics

7

Length

Special Features:

8

Other Common Measurements

Special Features:

9

Reading Measures

10

Geometry

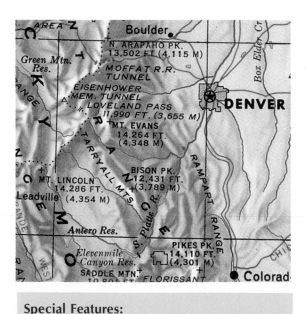

11

Constructions

12

Polygons and Circles

13

Surface Area and Volume

Special Features:

14

Rational Numbers

Special Features:

15

Solving Open Sentences

16

Using Formulas

17

Patterns and Functions

18

The Coordinate Plane

Basic Skills Appendix

Special Features

Career

Charts and Tables

1-1 Mileage Chart

Objective: To learn how to read a mileage chart.

A **mileage chart** shows the number of miles between two cities.

Find the distance from Cheyenne to New York City.

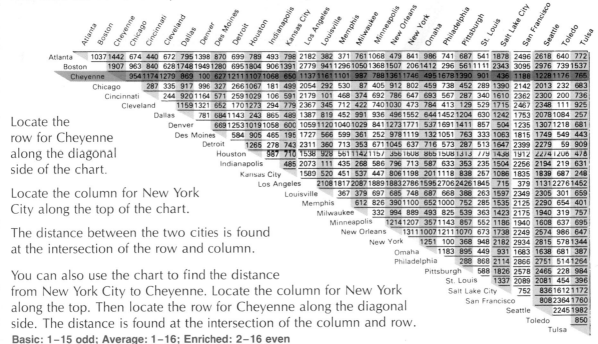

Locate the row for Cheyenne along the diagonal side of the chart.

Locate the column for New York City along the top of the chart.

The distance between the two cities is found at the intersection of the row and column.

You can also use the chart to find the distance from New York City to Cheyenne. Locate the column for New York along the top. Then locate the row for Cheyenne along the diagonal side. The distance is found at the intersection of the column and row.

Basic: 1–15 odd; Average: 1–16; Enriched: 2–16 even

Exercises

Use the chart to find each distance.

1. Cheyenne to New York City 1,746 mi

2. New York City to Cheyenne 1,746 mi

3. Atlanta to Dallas 795 mi

4. Boston to Cleveland 628 mi

5. Chicago to Denver 996 mi

6. Des Moines to Pittsburgh 763 mi

7. Detroit to Memphis 713 mi

8. Kansas City to Denver 600 mi

9. Louisville to Milwaukee 379 mi

10. New Orleans to New York 1,311 mi

11. Omaha to St. Louis 449 mi

12. Tulsa to Cheyenne 765 mi

13. Houston to Los Angeles 1,538 mi

14. Cincinnati to Minneapolis 692 mi

15. Philadelphia to Salt Lake City 2,114 mi

16. San Francisco to Toledo 2,364 mi

1-2 Bus Schedules

Objective: To interpret transit system schedules.

Maria Lopez is a bus driver in a metropolitan area. In addition to picking up and discharging passengers, she collects fares, answers questions about schedules, and follows a time schedule.

To qualify for the job, Maria had to have a high school education and a chauffeur's license. She also had to be at least 21 years old. She was given eight weeks of classroom and behind-the-wheel instruction by the local transit system.

Example

The timetable shows the departure (leave) and arrival (due) times for Maria's route.

The light type times indicate A.M.
The bold type times indicate P.M.

One departure from Starr and Third is at 9:37 A.M.
The bus arrives at Sunlawn and Miami at 10:16 A.M.
One departure from Sunlawn and Miami is at **1:12 P.M.**
The bus arrives at Starr and Third at **1:52 P.M.**

5 LENOX

MON THROUGH FRI — WEST						MON THROUGH FRI — EAST					
LEAVE	LEAVE	DUE	LEAVE	LEAVE	DUE	LEAVE	LEAVE	DUE	LEAVE	LEAVE	DUE
STARR AND THIRD	MAPLE AND LENOX	SUNLAWN AND MIAMI	STARR AND THIRD	MAPLE AND LENOX	SUNLAWN AND MIAMI	SUNLAWN AND MIAMI	PRICE AND LENOX	STARR AND THIRD	SUNLAWN AND MIAMI	PRICE AND LENOX	STARR AND THIRD
8:22	8:39	9:01	**12:07**	**12:24**	**12:46**	8:12	8:23	8:52	**12:12**	**12:23**	**12:52**
8:37	8:54	9:16	**12:22**	**12:39**	**1:01**	8:27	8:38	9:07	**12:27**	**12:38**	**1:07**
8:52	9:09	9:31	**12:37**	**12:54**	**1:16**	8:42	8:53	9:22	**12:42**	**12:53**	**1:22**
9:07	9:24	9:46	**12:52**	**1:09**	**1:31**	8:57	9:08	9:37	**12:57**	**1:08**	**1:37**
9:22	9:39	10:01	**1:07**	**1:24**	**1:46**	9:12	9:23	9:52	**1:12**	**1:23**	**1:52**
9:37	9:54	10:16	**1:22**	**1:39**	**2:01**	9:27	9:38	10:07	**1:27**	**1:38**	**2:07**
9:52	10:09	10:31	**1:37**	**1:54**	**2:16**	9:42	9:53	10:22	**1:42**	**1:53**	**2:22**
10:07	10:24	10:46	**1:52**	**2:09**	**2:31**	9:57	10:08	10:37	**1:57**	**2:08**	**2:37**
10:22	10:39	11:01	**2:07**	**2:24**	**2:46**	10:12	10:23	10:52	**2:12**	**2:23**	**2:52**
10:37	10:54	11:16	**2:22**	**2:39**	**3:01**	10:27	10:38	11:07	**2:27**	**2:38**	**3:07**
10:52	11:09	11:31	**2:37**	**2:54**	**3:16**	10:42	10:53	11:22	**2:42**	**2:53**	**3:22**
11:07	11:24	11:46	**2:52**	**3:09**	**3:31**	10:57	11:08	11:37	**2:57**	**3:08**	**3:37**
11:22	11:39	**12:01**	**3:07**	**3:24**	**3:46**	11:12	11:23	11:52	**3:05**	**3:16**	**3:45**
11:37	11:54	**12:16**	**3:22**	**3:39**	**4:01**	11:27	11:38	**12:07**	**3:12**	**3:23**	**3:52**
11:52	**12:09**	**12:31**	**3:37**	**3:54**	**4:16**	11:42	11:53	**12:22**	**3:20**	**3:30**	**4:00**
						11:57	**12:08**	**12:37**			

Exercises

Use the timetable to answer the following.

1. What three locations are used for this route to see if the bus is on time when heading west? **Starr and Third, Maple and Lenox, Sunlawn and Miami**

2. What three locations are used for this route to see if the bus is on time when heading east? **Sunlawn and Miami, Price and Lenox, Starr and Third**

3. What is the route number and route name? **5, Lenox**

4. How long is the riding time for the entire one-way ride east? **40 minutes**

5. What are the possible transfer points going west or east? **Maple and Lenox, Sunlawn and Miami, Price and Lenox, Starr and Third**

6. Suppose you board at Sunlawn Street and ride to Price Avenue. Are you heading east or west? **east**

7. Suppose you board at Starr and Third, west, at 10:52 A.M. When will you arrive at Sunlawn and Miami? **11:31 A.M.**

8. The Youngs want to arrive at Sunlawn and Miami around 10:30 A.M. When should they board at Starr and Third? **9:52 A.M.**

9. Mr. Lamar has a business appointment at Price and Lenox at 3:00 P.M. What is the latest time he can board at Sunlawn and Miami? **2:42 P.M.**

10. Angie Huffman has a dance class at Maple and Lenox at 12:00 noon. The class lasts 1 hour. How much time does she have to catch the next bus for Sunlawn and Miami? **9 minutes**

This feature presents general topics.

Math Break

Interstate highways with odd numbers run north and south. Interstate highways with even numbers run east and west. Highways that make a loop around a city have three digits.

Answer the following.

1. Which direction does route 25 run? **north and south**

2. Which direction does route 40 run? **east and west**

3. Where does route 270 go? **around a city**

1-3 Postal Rates

Objective: To learn how to read postal rate charts.

Tai Ling wants to mail a letter that weighs six ounces. He knows that items weighing 12 ounces or less are sent by *first-class letter rates*. The first-class letter rates are shown below. Tai Ling pays postage of $1.07 for a six-ounce letter.

A weight with a fraction is charged as if it were the next higher weight.

What is the cost of sending a $9\frac{1}{2}$-ounce letter? **$1.75**

FIRST CLASS

LETTER RATES:

1st ounce......................................22¢
Each additional ounce...........................17¢

For Pieces Not Exceeding (oz.)	The Rate Is	For Pieces Not Exceeding (oz.)	The Rate Is
1	$0.22	7	$1.24
2	0.39	8	1.41
3	0.56	9	1.58
4	0.73	10	1.75
5	0.90	11	1.92
6	1.07	12	2.09

Items weighing over 12 ounces can be sent by *priority mail* (first class) or *parcel post* (fourth class).

FIRST-CLASS ZONE RATED (PRIORITY) MAIL

Weight over 12 ounces and not exceeding-pound(s)	Rate					
	Local zones 1, 2, and 3	Zone 4	Zone 5	Zone 6	Zone 7	Zone 8
1	$ 2.40	$ 2.40	$ 2.40	$ 2.40	$ 2.40	$ 2.40
2	2.40	2.40	2.40	2.40	2.40	2.40
3	2.74	3.16	3.45	3.74	3.96	4.32
4	3.18	3.75	4.13	4.53	4.92	5.33
5	3.61	4.32	4.86	5.27	5.81	6.37
6	4.15	5.08	5.71	6.31	6.91	7.66
7	4.58	5.66	6.39	7.09	7.80	8.67
8	5.00	6.23	7.07	7.87	8.68	9.68
9	5.43	6.81	7.76	8.66	9.57	10.69
10	5.85	7.39	8.44	9.44	10.45	11.70

A package weighing $2\frac{3}{4}$ pounds is sent as first-class mail to Cheyenne, Wyoming. Cheyenne is in zone 6.

The postage is $3.74.

FOURTH CLASS (PARCEL POST)

Weight 1 Pound and not exceeding (pounds)	Local	Zones 1-2	Zone 3	Zone 4	Zone 5	Zone 6	Zone 7	Zone 8
2	1.35	1.41	1.51	1.66	1.89	2.13	2.25	2.30
3	1.41	1.49	1.65	1.87	2.21	2.58	2.99	3.87
4	1.47	1.57	1.78	2.08	2.54	3.03	3.57	4.74
5	1.52	1.65	1.92	2.29	2.86	3.47	4.16	5.62

Postage for the same package sent as fourth-class mail will cost $2.58.

Basic: 2–30 even; Average: 1–30; Enriched: 1–29 odd

Exercises

Find the cost of sending each letter first class with the given weight.

1. 2 oz 39¢
2. 3 oz 56¢
3. $4\frac{1}{2}$ oz 90¢
4. 1 oz 22¢
5. $7\frac{3}{4}$ oz $1.41

6. $1\frac{1}{2}$ oz 39¢
7. $6\frac{1}{4}$ oz $1.24
8. 10 oz $1.75
9. $8\frac{1}{2}$ oz $1.58
10. 12 oz $2.09

Find the cost of sending each package first class with the given weight to the given zone.

11. 3 lb; 7 **$3.96**

12. 2.5 lb; 5 **$3.45**

13. 4.5 lb; 2 **$3.61**

14. 4.0 lb; 6 **$4.53**

15. 3.4 lb; 3 **$3.18**

16. 7.6 lb; 2 **$5.00**

17. 8 lb 7 oz; 4 **$6.81**

18. 6 lb 11 oz; local **$4.58**

19. 5 lb 9 oz; 8 **$7.66**

20. 9.2 lb; 7 **$10.45**

Find the cost of sending each package fourth class with the given weight to the given zone.

21. 1.5 lb; 7 **$2.25**

22. 2.8 lb; 1 **$1.49**

23. 3.2 lb; 3 **$1.78**

24. 4 lb; 4 **$2.08**

25. 3.5 lb; 8 **$4.74**

26. 5 lb; local **$1.52**

27. 2 lb 3 oz; 2 **$1.49**

28. 4 lb 1 oz; 4 **$2.29**

Solve.

29. Ms. Andrews wants to mail a package weighing 3.6 pounds. What is the least expensive way to send it?
Fourth-Class Parcel Post

30. Dave Kutil's package weighs 8.6 pounds. How could he send it so that the package is delivered quickly?
First-Class Priority Mail

This feature presents general topics.

Math Break

A ZIP (Zone Improvement Plan) Code is a 5-digit code that identifies areas within the United States and its territories for distributing mail. The first digit of the code indicates a large group of states. The second and third digits indicate areas within the large group. The last two digits identify local delivery areas. In which state group area do you live?

8	4	2	7	5
state group area	large city or central delivery area		local delivery area	

See the Teacher Guide for an explanation of the zip + 4.

1-4 Telephone Rates

Objective: To find the lowest long distance rates.

Ben and Cindy Adams are planning a trip to Fish Creek, Wisconsin. They want to rent a cottage that is close to Lake Michigan and to the places they want to visit. Before calling long distance to make a reservation, the Adamses check the front section of the telephone book. There they can find out when the lowest direct-dial rate is in effect.

The chart shows a comparison of the direct-dial long-distance rates for various times and days of the week.

On what day can you call at any time and still get the lowest rate? **Saturday**

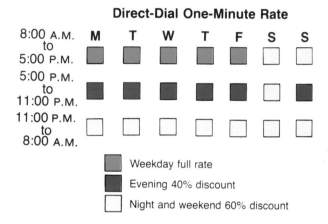

Direct-Dial One-Minute Rate

Weekday full rate

Evening 40% discount

Night and weekend 60% discount

The table below shows the rates for direct-dial and operator-assisted long distance telephone calls.

Which type of long distance call is the most expensive?
Operator assisted person-to-person

Sample rates from the city of Columbus to

| City | DIRECT DIAL | | | | | | OPERATOR ASSISTED | | | |
| | Full Rates | | Evening Rates | | Night Rates | | Station-to-Station | | Person-to-Person | |
	1st Min.	Add.	1st Min.	Add.	1st Min.	Add.	1st Min.	Add.	1st Min.	Add.
Coshocton	.57	.37	.34	.23	.22	.15	2.12	.37	3.57	.37
Gallipolis	.57	.37	.34	.23	.22	.15	2.12	.37	3.57	.37
Lancaster	.48	.28	.28	.17	.19	.12	2.03	.28	3.48	.28
Marietta	.57	.37	.34	.23	.22	.15	2.12	.37	3.57	.37
Steubenville	.58	.39	.34	.24	.23	.16	2.13	.39	3.58	.39
Wash. C.H.	.48	.28	.28	.17	.19	.12	2.03	.28	3.48	.28
Zanesville	.48	.28	.28	.17	.19	.12	2.03	.28	3.48	.28

Exercises

Use the chart to find the time period during which a person should call to get the lowest rate.

1. Wednesday **before 8:00 A.M.; after 11:00 P.M.**
2. Friday **before 8:00 A.M.; after 11:00 P.M.**
3. Sunday **before 5:00 P.M.; after 11:00 P.M.**
4. Monday **before 8:00 A.M.; after 11:00 P.M.**
5. Saturday **all day**
6. Thursday **before 8:00 A.M.; after 11:00 P.M.**

Find whether each call will be charged full rate, 40% discount, or 60% discount.

7. 8:15 A.M.; Mon. **full rate**
8. 5:30 P.M.; Tues. **40% discount**
9. 7:00 A.M.; Sun. **60% discount**
10. 4:55 P.M.; Sat. **60% discount**
11. 9:30 A.M.; Mon. **full rate**
12. 8:45 P.M.; Sun. **40% discount**
13. 1:10 A.M.; Thurs. **60% discount**
14. 11:30 P.M.; Thurs. **60% discount**

Use the table to answer the following.

15. What is the least expensive type of long distance call? **direct dial night rate**

16. What is the least expensive operator-assisted long distance call? **station to station**

17. Are there discount rates for operator-assisted long distance calls? **no**

18. What is the cost of a person-to-person one-minute call to Coshocton? **$3.57**

19. Is it cheaper to call Zanesville or Marietta? **Zanesville**

20. Which city is the most expensive to call? **Steubenville**

21. What is the cost of a direct-dial one-minute call to Gallipolis at 11:30 P.M.? **22¢**

22. Tell which type of long distance call would suit your needs. Why? **Answers may vary.**

This feature promotes students' mental abilities in computation and reasonableness.

Mental Math

To subtract mentally, add any number to the minuend that will make the problem easier. Then be sure to subtract that same number from the difference.

$$\underset{\text{Add 1 to 176.}}{176 - 47} \rightarrow 177 - 47 = 130 \rightarrow \underset{\text{Subtract 1 from 130.}}{130 - 1 = 129}$$

Find each difference using the strategy shown above.

1. 74 − 45 **29**
2. 187 − 58 **129**
3. 152 − 44 **108**
4. 374 − 165 **209**
5. 242 − 124 **118**
6. 4,372 − 2,472 **1,900**
7. 7,431 − 4,181 **3,250**
8. 563 − 483 **80**

1-5 Pay Schedules and Withholding Tax

Objective: To read pay schedules and withholding tax tables.

Suppose you earn $4.50 per hour (h) and work 36 hours one week.
How much would you earn in one week?

Use the pay schedule below to locate the column for the hourly
rate of $4.50. Then locate the row for 36 hours worked. The
amount earned is $162.00.

Pay Schedule							
Hours Worked	Hourly Rate (in dollars)						
	$4.00	$4.10	$4.20	$4.30	$4.40	$4.50	$4.60
34	136.00	139.40	142.80	146.20	149.60	153.00	156.40
35	140.00	143.50	147.00	150.50	154.00	157.50	161.00
36	144.00	147.60	151.20	154.80	158.40	162.00	165.60
37	148.00	151.70	155.40	159.10	162.80	166.50	170.20
38	152.00	155.80	159.60	163.40	167.20	171.00	174.80
39	156.00	159.90	163.80	167.70	171.60	175.50	179.40

Before a paycheck is issued, federal income tax is withheld from
the wages by the employer. The amount of federal **withholding tax**
depends on the amount earned and the number of allowances claimed.

Suppose you earn $209.00 each week. You are single and claim
one allowance. How much tax is withheld from your paycheck?

Use the withholding tax table to locate the row that contains
your wages. $209.00 is more than $200.00 but less than $210.00.
Locate the column for one allowance. The amount of tax withheld
is $22.00.

SINGLE Persons–WEEKLY Payroll Period

And the wages are–		And the number of withholding allowances claimed is–										
At least	But less than	0	1	2	3	4	5	6	7	8	9	10
		The amount of income tax to be withheld shall be–										
125	130	13	10	7	4	2	0	0	0	0	0	0
130	135	14	11	8	5	2	0	0	0	0	0	0
135	140	15	11	9	6	3	1	0	0	0	0	0
140	145	15	12	9	6	4	1	0	0	0	0	0
145	150	16	13	10	7	4	2	0	0	0	0	0
150	160	17	14	11	8	5	3	0	0	0	0	0
160	170	19	16	13	10	7	4	1	0	0	0	0
170	180	20	17	14	11	8	5	3	0	0	0	0
180	190	22	19	16	12	9	6	4	1	0	0	0
190	200	24	20	17	14	11	8	5	2	0	0	0
200	210	25	22	19	15	12	9	6	4	1	0	0
210	220	27	24	20	17	14	11	8	5	2	0	0
220	230	29	25	22	18	15	12	9	6	4	1	0
230	240	31	27	23	20	17	14	11	8	5	2	0
240	250	32	29	25	22	18	15	12	9	6	4	1
250	260	34	31	27	23	20	17	14	10	8	5	2
260	270	36	32	29	25	22	18	15	12	9	6	3
270	280	38	34	30	27	23	20	17	13	10	7	5
280	290	40	36	32	28	25	21	18	15	12	9	6
290	300	43	38	34	30	27	23	20	16	13	10	7

Basic: 2–46 even; Average: 1–46; Enriched: 1–45 odd

Exercises

**Use the pay schedule to find the amount earned.
The hourly rate and number of hours worked are given.**

1. $4.30; 35 h **$150.50**   **2.** $4.00; 38 h **$152.00**   **3.** $4.60; 34 h **$156.40**

4. $4.20; 39 h **$163.80**   **5.** $4.10; 36 h **$147.60**   **6.** $4.40; 37 h **$162.80**

7. $4.50; 34 h **$153.00**   **8.** $4.40; 34 h **$149.60**   **9.** $4.00; 35 h **$140.00**

10. $4.60; 36 h **$165.60**   **11.** $4.20; 35 h **$147.00**   **12.** $4.30; 38 h **$163.40**

13. $4.10; 38 h **$155.80**   **14.** $4.50; 37 h **$166.50**   **15.** $4.20; 36 h **$151.20**

16. $4.40; 39 h **$171.60**   **17.** $4.30; 34 h **$146.20**   **18.** $4.60; 37 h **$170.20**

**Use the tax table to find the withholding tax.
The weekly wage and the number of allowances are given.**

19. $234; 1 **$27**   **20.** $265; 3 **$25**   **21.** $217; 2 **$20**   **22.** $144; 1 **$12**

23. $186.85; 0 **$22**   **24.** $251; 2 **$27**   **25.** $245.50; 4 **$18**   **26.** $269.50; 7 **$12**

27. $147.15; 2 **$10**   **28.** $169; 8 **0**   **29.** $152.75; 5 **$3**   **30.** $250; 6 **$14**

31. $237; 7 **$8**   **32.** $220; 5 **$12**   **33.** $197.60; 4 **$11**   **34.** $180; 0 **$22**

35. $139.45; 3 **$6**   **36.** $142; 0 **$15**   **37.** $243.50; 2 **$25**   **38.** $247.25; 4 **$18**

39. $193; 5 **$8**   **40.** $211.19; 6 **$8**   **41.** $204.35; 0 **$25**   **42.** $240; 3 **$22**

Solve. Each person in exercises 45–48 is single.

43. How does the tax change as the number of allowances increases? **decreases**

44. Suppose two workers earn the same amount of money each week. Will their withholding tax always be the same? Why?
Yes or no. The tax depends on the number of allowances.

45. Sue Mentor earns $4.10 per hour. She works 38 hours a week. How much federal tax is withheld from her paycheck each week if she claims one allowance? **$14.00**

46. Josh Crum claims two allowances. His withholding tax is $34.00. In what range is his income? **$290–$299**

PRACTICE

Express each number in words.

1. 333 three hundred thirty-three

2. 1,006 one thousand six

3. 16,890 sixteen thousand eight hundred ninety

4. 300,000 three hundred thousand

5. 2,873,042 two million eight hundred seventy-three thousand forty-two

6. 80,651 eighty thousand six hundred fifty-one

7. 5,002 five thousand two

8. 154,903 one hundred fifty-four thousand nine hundred three

State the number named by each digit in 4,328.

9. 4 4,000

10. 3 300

11. 2 20

12. 8 8

Round each number to the underlined place-value position.

13. 346 300

14. 21,368 21,400

15. 2,964 2,960

16. 196 200

17. 227 230

18. 12,882 13,000

19. 2,806 2,810

20. 349 350

21. 46 50

22. 52,408 50,000

23. 6,628 7,000

24. 84,715 85,000

Estimate. Answers may vary. Typical answers are given.

25.	**26.**	**27.**	**28.**	**29.**
99	75	107	159	397
+ 10	+ 49	+ 39	+ 64	+ 284
110	130	150	220	700

30.	**31.**	**32.**	**33.**	**34.**
99	68	209	268	992
− 10	− 52	− 39	− 36	− 841
90	20	170	230	200

Add or subtract.

35.	**36.**	**37.**	**38.**	**39.**
293	671	921	2,958	9,510
+ 57	+ 399	+ 311	+ 711	+ 721
350	1,070	1,232	3,669	10,231

40.	**41.**	**42.**	**43.**	**44.**
13,498	47,987	240	759	935
+ 116	+ 2,153	721	289	168
13,614	50,140	+ 470	+ 681	+ 754
		1,431	1,729	1,857

45.	**46.**	**47.**	**48.**	**49.**
6,289	862,500	$3,608	72,954	1,750
20,453	45,761	1,495	486	8,624
+ 82,970	+ 27,049	+ 827	+ 6,785	+ 5,092
109,712	935,310	$5,930	80,225	15,466

50.	**51.**	**52.**	**53.**	**54.**
135	127	237	798	999
− 72	− 55	− 139	− 654	− 389
63	72	98	144	610

55.	**56.**	**57.**	**58.**	**59.**
646	1,189	1,143	1,476	1,514
− 218	− 909	− 801	− 823	− 611
428	280	342	653	903

Add or subtract.

60. 72 + 25 + 83 180

61. 58 − 23 35

62. 173 − 39 134

63. 254 + 32 + 50 336

64. 763 + 9 + 50 822

65. 847 − 265 582

66. 4,273 − 921 3,352

67. 8,652 − 3,409 5,243

68. 35 + 294 + 862 1,191

69. 9,642 + 84 + 108 9,834

70. 15,000 − 14,837 163

71. 47,054 + 9,283 56,337

Solve.

72. Bill Ortega orders a sandwich at $1.75, french fries at 50¢, and salad at 95¢. What is the cost of his lunch? **$3.20**

73. Lois Borge has 2 one-dollar bills, 3 quarters, 2 dimes, 1 nickel, and 4 pennies. What is the total amount? **$3.04**

This feature presents general topics.

Math Break

Ben Lewis works for a company that designs and makes signs for businesses. This earnings statement was attached to Ben's last paycheck.

The Chase Sign Company						
Pay Period Ending 10–17 **Check No.** 43075 **Regular Hours** 40 **Overtime Hours** 2.25	**Tax Deductions**				**Totals**	Pay to the Order of _____ THE CENTR Memo _____ 1:0314ᵐ0665ᵗ
	W-H TAX 20.70	F.I.C.A. TAX 11.19	STATE TAX 4.18	CITY TAX 1.67	GROSS PAY 167.01 TAX DEDUCTIONS 37.74	
	Personal Deductions				PERSONAL DEDUCTIONS 12.60	
	UNION DUES 5.00	UNITED FUND 1.00	INSURANCE 2.60	CREDIT UNION 4.00	TAKE-HOME PAY 116.67	

means Federal Withholding Tax   means Federal Insurance Contributions Act or Social Security

Use Ben's earnings statement to find this information.

1. Ben's employer Chase Sign Co.

2. end date of payroll period 10–17

3. gross pay $167.01

4. regular hours 40

5. overtime hours 2.25

6. withholding tax $20.70

7. social security $11.19

8. state tax $4.18

9. city tax $1.67

10. union dues $5.00

11. united fund $1.00

12. insurance $2.60

13. credit union $4.00

14. take-home pay $116.67

1-6 Federal Income Tax

Objective: To use a tax table to find tax owed.

All employees with taxes withheld receive **W-2 Forms** in January. This form shows the total earnings and the total amount withheld for the previous year. Income taxes are computed using this information.

1 Control number		OMB No. 1545-0008			
2 Employer's name, address, and ZIP code		3 Employer's identification number 63-7098020		4 Employer's State number	
Ayers Trucking Co. 1300 Creek Rd. Hometown, Wyoming		5 Stat employee □ Deceased □ Legal rep □ 942 emp □ Subtotal □ Void □			
		6 Allocated tips		7 Advance EIC payment	
8 Employee's social security number 615-04-1492	9 Federal income tax withheld $1,032	10 Wages, tips, other compensation $10,762		11 Social security tax withheld $769.48	
12 Employee's name, address, and ZIP code		13 Social security wages $10,762		14 Social security tips	
Ines H. Novelli 27 N. Town Hometown, Wyoming 82053		16			
		17 State income tax $269.05	18 State wages, tips, etc. $10,762	19 Name of State Wy	
		20 Local income tax $161.43	21 Local wages, tips, etc. $10,762	22 Name of locality Hometown	

Form **W-2 Wage and Tax Statement**   Copy B To be filed with employee's Federal tax return
This information is being furnished to the Internal Revenue Service   Department of the Treasury Internal Revenue Service

A partial federal income **tax table** is shown at the left. An employee can find the tax owed by locating the total earnings on the chart.

If line 37 (taxable income) is—		And you are—			
At least	But less than	Single	Married filing jointly *	Married filing separately	Head of a household
			Your tax is—		
10,000					
10,000	10,050	1,058	799	1,212	989
10,050	10,100	1,066	806	1,221	997
10,100	10,150	1,074	813	1,230	1,006
10,150	10,200	1,082	820	1,239	1,014
10,200	10,250	1,090	827	1,248	1,023
10,250	10,300	1,098	834	1,257	1,031
10,300	10,350	1,106	841	1,266	1,040
10,350	10,400	1,114	848	1,275	1,048
10,400	10,450	1,122	855	1,284	1,057
10,450	10,500	1,130	862	1,293	1,065
10,500	10,550	1,138	869	1,302	1,074
10,550	10,600	1,146	876	1,313	1,082
10,600	10,650	1,154	883	1,324	1,091
10,650	10,700	1,162	890	1,335	1,099
10,700	10,750	1,170	897	1,346	1,108
10,750	10,800	1,178	904	1,357	1,116

Example

$10,183 is more than $10,150 but less than $10,200.

The tax for an employee who is single is $1,082.

Sometimes more tax is withheld than the amount owed. Then a refund can be obtained. If not enough tax is withheld, then an additional payment is required.

Basic Skills Appendix, Page 420
Basic: 1–12, 13–30 odd; Average: 1–30; Enriched: 1–12, 14–30 even

Exercises

Use Ines Novelli's W-2 Form to answer the following.

1. How much was Ines's gross pay for the year? **$10,762**

2. How much social security (FICA) was withheld? **$769.48**

3. How much state income tax was withheld? **$269.05**

4. How much city income tax was withheld? **$161.43**

5. How much federal income tax was withheld? **$1,032**

6. Use the tax table to find the tax owed by Ines. Ines is single. **$1,178**

7. Does Ines receive a refund or make an additional payment? **make an additional payment**

8. What should she do if the W-2 Form is incorrect?

9. What company employs Ines?

10. In what state does she live? **Wyoming**

11. What is Ines's social security number? **615-04-1492**

12. What is her house number and street name? **27 N. Town**

8. Contact her employer.   9. Ayers Trucking Company

Use the federal income tax table to find the tax for single (s), married filing jointly (mj), married filing separately (ms), or head of household (hh).

13. $10,414; s
$1,122

14. $10,500; ms
$1,302

15. $10,015; hh
$989

16. $10,742; mj
$897

17. $10,386; ms
$1,275

18. $10,128; s
$1,074

19. $10,649; mj
$883

20. $10,799; hh
$1,116

21. $10,200; s
$1,090

22. $10,475; ms
$1,293

23. $10,701; hh
$1,108

24. $10,350; mj
$848

25. $10,194; s
$1,082

26. $10,089; s
$1,066

27. $10,572; mj
$876

28. $10,265; ms
$1,257

Solve. Use the federal income tax table.

29. Maggie Sims is single. She earns $10,228 a year. Her withholding tax is $1,045. Does she receive a refund or make an additional payment?
additional payment

30. Karen Downing files as single one year. The following year she files as married filing separately. If her income is the same both years, are her taxes more or less the second year?
more

This feature presents general topics.

 Math Break

Each time you begin working for a new employer, an Employee's Withholding Allowance Certificate (W-4) must be filled out. Allowances usually include you, your spouse, and your children. Whenever your number of allowances changes, you sign a new W-4.

Form **W-4** Department of the Treasury Internal Revenue Service	**Employee's Withholding Allowance Certificate** ► For Privacy Act and Paperwork Reduction Act Notice, see instructions.	OMB No. 1545-0010 19**87**

1 Type or print your full name
Ted Blaine Harris

2 Your social security number
937 - 65 - 3420

Home address (number and street or rural route)
9 Oval Drive

3 Marital Status
☐ Single ☑ Married
☐ Married, but withhold at higher Single rate
Note: *If married, but legally separated, or spouse is a nonresident alien, check the Single box.*

City or town, state, and ZIP code
Homedale, Arizona 85250

4 Total number of allowances you are claiming (from the Worksheet on page 3) *3*
5 Additional amount, if any, you want deducted from each pay (see Step 4 on page 2) . . . . . . $ *0*
6 I claim exemption from withholding because (see Step 2 above and check boxes below that apply):
  a ☐ Last year I did not owe any Federal income tax and had a right to a full refund of **ALL** income tax withheld, **AND**
  b ☐ This year I do not expect to owe any Federal income tax and expect to have a right to a full refund of **ALL** income tax withheld. If both a and b apply, enter the year effective and "EXEMPT" here ► 19 | Year 19
  c If you entered "EXEMPT" on line 6b, are you a full-time student? . . . . ☐ Yes ☐ No

Answer the following.

1. How many allowances is Ted claiming? **3**

2. What is Ted's marital status?
married

3. Does he want an additional amount deducted from each pay? **no**

1-7 Sales Tax Table

Objective: To read sales tax schedules.

Karl Johnson owns his own bookstore. For each sale, he computes the total amount of purchase. Then Karl charges sales tax on the total.

A **sales tax** is a way to raise money for states and cities. It is a percentage of the total amount purchased.

Instead of calculating the tax on each purchase, Karl uses the tax schedule.

BRACKETED TAX COLLECTION SCHEDULE
SALES & USE TAX FOR STATE, COUNTY AND/OR TRANSIT TAX – TOTAL ⟨5 1/2%⟩ TAX LEVY
SALES 15¢ AND UNDER – NO TAX

Each Sale		Tax	Each Sale		Tax
.16 to	.18	.01	8.19 to	8.36	.46
.19 to	.36	.02	8.37 to	8.54	.47
.37 to	.54	.03	8.55 to	8.72	.48
.55 to	.72	.04	8.73 to	8.90	.49
.73 to	.90	.05	8.91 to	9.09	.50
.91 to	1.09	.06	9.10 to	9.27	.51
1.10 to	1.27	.07	9.28 to	9.46	.52
1.28 to	1.46	.08	9.47 to	9.64	.53
1.47 to	1.64	.09	9.65 to	9.82	.54
1.65 to	1.82	.10	9.83 to	10.00	.55
1.83 to	2.00	.11	10.01 to	10.18	.56
2.01 to	2.18	.12	10.19 to	10.36	.57
2.19 to	2.36	.13	10.37 to	10.54	.58
2.37 to	2.54	.14	10.55 to	10.72	.59
2.55 to	2.72	.15	10.73 to	10.90	.60
2.73 to	2.90	.16	10.91 to	11.09	.61
2.91 to	3.09	.17	11.10 to	11.27	.62
3.10 to	3.27	.18	11.28 to	11.46	.63
3.28 to	3.46	.19	11.47 to	11.64	.64
3.47 to	3.64	.20	11.65 to	11.82	.65
3.65 to	3.82	.21	11.83 to	12.00	.66
3.83 to	4.00	.22	12.01 to	12.18	.67
4.01 to	4.18	.23	12.19 to	12.36	.68
4.19 to	4.36	.24	12.37 to	12.54	.69
4.37 to	4.54	.25	12.55 to	12.72	.70
4.55 to	4.72	.26	12.73 to	12.90	.71
4.73 to	4.90	.27	12.91 to	13.09	.72
4.91 to	5.09	.28	13.10 to	13.27	.73
5.10 to	5.27	.29	13.28 to	13.46	.74
5.28 to	5.46	.30	13.47 to	13.64	.75
5.47 to	5.64	.31	13.65 to	13.82	.76
5.65 to	5.82	.32	13.83 to	14.00	.77
5.83 to	6.00	.33	14.01 to	14.18	.78
6.01 to	6.18	.34	14.19 to	14.36	.79
6.19 to	6.36	.35	14.37 to	14.54	.80
6.37 to	6.54	.36	14.55 to	14.72	.81
6.55 to	6.72	.37	14.73 to	14.90	.82
6.73 to	6.90	.38	14.91 to	15.09	.83
6.91 to	7.09	.39	15.10 to	15.27	.84
7.10 to	7.27	.40	15.28 to	15.46	.85
7.28 to	7.46	.41	15.47 to	15.64	.86
7.47 to	7.64	.42	15.65 to	15.82	.87
7.65 to	7.82	.43	15.83 to	16.00	.88
7.83 to	8.00	.44	16.01 to	16.18	.89
8.01 to	8.18	.45	16.19 to	16.36	.90

Example

Find the sales tax for a purchase totaling $15.85.

$15.85 is more than $15.83 but less than $16.00.

The tax on $15.85 is $0.88.

Basic: 1–23 odd; Average: 1–25; Enriched: 2–20 even, 21–25

Exercises

Use the tax table to find the sales tax on the following purchases.

1. $0.25 $0.02
2. $0.51 $0.03
3. $0.14 0
4. $0.96 $0.06
5. $2.54 $0.14
6. $1.96 $0.11
7. $13.72 $0.76
8. $9.28 $0.52
9. $16.08 $0.89
10. $6.18 $0.34
11. $4.92 $0.28
12. $7.25 $0.40
13. $8.03 $0.45
14. $10.47 $0.58
15. $12.65 $0.70
16. $16.18 $0.89
17. $3.10 $0.18
18. $15.36 $0.85
19. $1.88 $0.11
20. $11.56 $0.64

Use the tax schedule to complete the following.

21. What is the rate of sales tax for the schedule? $5\frac{1}{2}$%

22. When is there no tax charged on a purchase? **15¢ or less**

23. Bonnie buys a book for $3.95. How much sales tax is charged? **$0.22**

24. Gary wants to buy a book that costs $7.95. He has $8.00. Does he have enough money to buy the book? **no**

25. How could you find the tax on $32.00 using the chart? **Find the amount of tax on $16 and double it.**

26. Find the tax on $20.00 using the chart. **$1.10**

16 *Charts and Tables*

This feature provides general topics about the uses of a computer.

Computer

All computer systems are made up of an internal memory, an input device, a processing unit, and an output device. Information must be put into the computer using *input devices*. Once the information is in the computer, it can be temporarily stored in *internal memory* and/or *processed*. The processed information is then made available to the person using the computer by an *output device*.

This is a Universal Product Code symbol known as a UPC symbol.

Stores and libraries use input devices that can read this type of symbol.

A grocery store's computer system might be described like this.

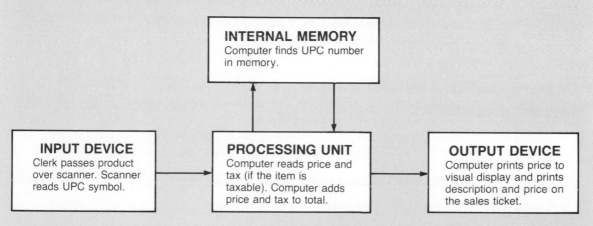

INTERNAL MEMORY
Computer finds UPC number in memory.

INPUT DEVICE
Clerk passes product over scanner. Scanner reads UPC symbol.

PROCESSING UNIT
Computer reads price and tax (if the item is taxable). Computer adds price and tax to total.

OUTPUT DEVICE
Computer prints price to visual display and prints description and price on the sales ticket.

The first two questions should be used for discussion.

Complete.

1. Name two other types of input devices. **joystick, disk drive, cassette player**

2. Name three stores or other places where you have seen input devices. **Answers may vary.**

Label each action as *input, processing,* or *output*.

3. A library clerk types in the card number of a patron. **input**

4. A computer shows a list of overdue books on the monitor screen. **output**

5. A computer calculates the total fine on overdue books. **processing**

6. A computer prints a list of books on the topic "women in science." **output**

7. A computer figures the amount of tax on a purchase. **processing**

8. A clerk types in the amount of money the customer has handed him. **input**

1-8 Problem Solving: Make a Table

Objective: To make a table in order to solve a problem.

Zac Early hires high school students to work in his ice cream shop for the summer. The shop is open from 10 A.M. to 10 P.M. Monday through Saturday. Each week Zac makes a work schedule for Susan, Bill, Alan, Katie, Ann, and Ken. Zac wants each student to work the same number of hours and have the same number of days off. Two students work at a time and there are two shifts a day. Make a possible schedule showing the days and hours each student will work.

 Read

You know the days and hours the shop is open. You know how many students work for Zac. You need to find the hours and days each student works.

Decide

The shop is open 12 hours a day. There are two shifts a day. Divide 12 by 2 to find the number of hours each student works. Since there are 6 students, 4 will each work 6-hour shifts and 2 will have the day off. Making a table is a convenient way to find the hours and days each student works.

Days and hours worked for each student may vary from week to week.

Solve

Employee	Days					
	Mon.	Tues.	Wed.	Thur.	Fri.	Sat.
Susan	10–4	4–10	–	10–4	4–10	–
Bill	10–4	4–10	–	10–4	4–10	–
Alan	4–10	–	10–4	4–10	–	10–4
Katie	4–10	–	10–4	4–10	–	10–4
Ann	–	10–4	4–10	–	10–4	4–10
Ken	–	10–4	4–10	–	10–4	4–10

The table shows the hours worked and days off for each student. 10–4 is 10 A.M. to 4 P.M. 4–10 is 4 P.M. to 10 P.M.

 Examine

Refer to the chart to answer each question. Does each student have the same number of days off? Does **Yes** each student work the same number of hours each week? **Yes** The schedule is correct.

Exercises

Solve. Make a table.

1. Sam Baker sells men's socks. Each week he needs to know how many pairs of each color and size he has sold. The letter and number on the sales receipt stand for the color and size. The color code is B-black, BB-brown, W-white, and N-navy. How many pairs of each size and color of socks were sold in one week?

B9	BB9	W10	N11	B11	BB10
BB10	N10	B9	BB10	B9	N9
N11	W9	BB12	BB12	W9	B9
W12	B10	N9	B11	N10	N9
B11	B12	W10	N9	BB9	B11
N9	BB10	BB10	N12	N12	W9
BB12	N12	BB10	B10	B12	B10
BB10	B11	N10	W9	BB12	B11

2. Mr. and Mrs. Gomez want to see what they spend their money on at the grocery store. They have saved their grocery receipts for one month. Week 1: food $43.20, health and beauty aids $6.72, snacks $5.89, beverages $8.46, cookware $12.67, pet food $4.99; Week 2: food $56.47, snacks $2.89, beverages $2.99; Week 3: food $37.26, health and beauty aids $2.49, snacks $3.89, beverages $5.74, cookware $3.16, pet food $4.99; Week 4: food $41.19, health and beauty aids $4.57, snacks $4.56, beverages $5.56. On what item do they spend the most money? the least money?

Use Mickey Mantle's batting record to answer the following. The code is G-game, R-runs, H-hits, HR-home runs, RBI-runs batted in, and AVG-batting average. The * means he led the league in this category.

3. How many years did Mickey Mantle play baseball for the New York Yankees? **18 years**

4. What was his greatest number of hits made in any one season? **188 hits**

5. What year did he have his lowest average? What was that average? **1968; .237**

6. What year did he have his most runs scored? How many runs were scored? **1956 and 1961; 132 runs**

7. In what year did he have the most runs batted in of his career? How many RBI's was this? **1956; 130 RBI's**

8. Name the years he led the league in home runs. **1955, 1956, 1958, 1960**

9. In what year did he hit the most home runs? How many did he hit? **1961; 54 home runs**

10. What was his total number of hits? **2,415 hits**

11. How many years did he have an average of 0.300 or over? **10 years**

Mickey Mantle's Batting Record

	G	R	H	HR	RBI	Avg
1951	96	61	91	13	65	.267
1952	142	94	171	23	87	.311
1953	127	105	136	21	92	.295
1954	146	129*	163	27	102	.300
1955	147	121	158	37*	99	.306
1956	150	132*	188	52*	130*	.353*
1957	144	121*	173	34	94	.365
1958	150	127*	158	42*	97	.304
1959	144	104	154	31	75	.285
1960	153	119*	145	40*	94	.275
1961	153	132*	163	54	128	.317
1962	123	96	121	30	89	.321
1963	65	40	54	15	35	.314
1964	143	92	141	35	111	.303
1965	122	44	92	19	46	.255
1966	108	40	96	23	56	.288
1967	144	63	108	22	55	.245
1968	144	57	103	18	54	.237
Total	2401	1677	2415	536	1509	.298

CHAPTER 1 REVIEW

Vocabulary/Concepts

Use a word from the list at the right to complete each sentence.

1. Taxes withheld from a paycheck by an employer are called _____?_____ .**withholding tax**

2. The _____?_____ shows the total earnings and the total amount withheld for the previous year.**W-2 Form**

3. A _____?_____ is a way to raise money for states and cities.**sales tax**

4. A _____?_____ shows the number of miles between two cities.**mileage chart**

5. An employee can find the tax owed for one year by locating the total earnings on a _____?_____ .**tax table**

> bus schedule
> mileage chart
> pay schedule
> sales tax
> tax table
> withholding tax
> W-2 Form

Exercises

Use the mileage chart on page 3 to find each distance.   Page 3

6. Houston to Milwaukee **1,142 mi**

7. Des Moines to Salt Lake City **1,063 mi**

8. Cleveland to Memphis **712 mi**

9. Boston to Dallas **1,748 mi**

10. Toledo to Los Angeles **2,276 mi**

11. Indianapolis to Denver **1,058 mi**

Use the timetable on page 4 to answer the following.   Pages 4–5

12. Suppose you board at Sunlawn and Miami at 1:42 P.M. When will you arrive at Starr and Third? **2:22 P.M.**

13. Suppose you board at Starr and Third at 11:22 A.M. When will you arrive at Sunlawn and Miami? **12:01 P.M.**

14. Suppose you board at Maple and Lenox at 10:24 A.M. When will you arrive at Sunlawn and Miami? **10:46 A.M.**

15. Suppose you board at Price and Lenox at 12:08 P.M. When will you arrive at Starr and Third? **12:37 P.M.**

Find the cost of sending each letter first class with the given weight.   Pages 6–7

16. 4 oz **$0.73**

17. $1\frac{3}{4}$ oz **$0.39**

18. 11 oz **$1.92**

19. $9\frac{1}{4}$ oz **$1.75**

20. 6 oz **$1.07**

21. $7\frac{1}{2}$ oz **$1.41**

22. 9 oz **$1.58**

23. $2\frac{1}{2}$ oz **$0.56**

24. 7 oz **$1.24**

25. $11\frac{1}{4}$ oz **$2.09**

Find the cost of sending each package first class with the given weight to the given zone.   Pages 6–7

26. 2.3 lb; 7 **$3.96**

27. 1 lb 2 oz; 1 **$2.40**

28. 5 lb; 3 **$3.61**

29. 3.8 lb; 5 **$4.13**

30. 10 lb; 4 **$7.39**

31. 4.7 lb; 8 **$6.37**

32. 6 lb 9 oz; 6 **$7.09**

33. 8 lb 4 oz; 2 **$5.43**

Find the cost of sending each package fourth class with the given weight to the given zone. Pages 6–7

34. 2 lb; local $1.35   **35.** 4.5 lb; 3 $1.92   **36.** 2 lb 4 oz; 7 $2.99   **37.** 1.6 lb; 5 $1.89

38. 3.8 lb; 2 $1.57   **39.** 4 lb; 6 $3.03   **40.** 5 lb; 8 $5.62   **41.** 2.9 lb; 4 $1.87

Use the chart on page 8 to find whether each call will be charged full rate, 40% discount, or 60% discount. Pages 8–9

42. 6:45 A.M.; Wed.
60% discount
43. 3:30 P.M.; Thurs.
full rate
44. 10:55 P.M.; Fri.
40% discount
45. 8:30 P.M.; Sun.
40% discount
46. 7:00 P.M.; Sat.
60% discount
47. 9:10 A.M.; Tues.
full rate

Use the table on page 8 to answer the following. Pages 8–9

48. What is the cost of a direct-dial one-minute call to Steubenville at 11:45 P.M.? What is the cost of each additional minute? $0.23, $0.16

49. What is the cost of a person-to-person one-minute call to Lancaster at 3:00 P.M.? What is the cost of each additional minute? $3.48, $0.28

Use the pay schedule on page 10 to find the amount earned. The hourly rate and number of hours worked are given. Pages 10–11

50. $4.20; 38 h $159.60   **51.** $4.50; 39 h $175.50   **52.** $4.00; 34 h $136.00

53. $4.60; 35 h $161.00   **54.** $4.10; 37 h $151.70   **55.** $4.30; 36 h $154.80

Use the tax table on page 10 to find the withholding tax. The weekly wage and the number of allowances are given. Pages 10–11

56. $290; 0 $43   **57.** $168; 3 $10   **58.** $127; 2 $7   **59.** $272; 1 $34

60. $175.18; 2 $14   **61.** $200.50; 4 $12   **62.** $289; 5 $21   **63.** $199.05; 2 $17

Use the federal income tax table on page 14 to find the tax for single(s), married filing jointly (mj), married filing separately (ms), or head of household (hh). Pages 14–15

64. $10,775; s $1,178   **65.** $10,362; hh $1,048   **66.** $10,526; mj $869

67. $10,049; ms $1,212   **68.** $10,437; mj $855   **69.** $10,601; s $1,154

Use the tax table on page 16 to find the sales tax on the following purchases. Page 16

70. $14.38 $0.80   **71.** $0.75 $0.05   **72.** $2.67 $0.15   **73.** $1.01 $0.06   **74.** $5.89 $0.33

75. $16.36 $0.90   **76.** $10.55 $0.59   **77.** $8.14 $0.45   **78.** $7.30 $0.41   **79.** $9.42 $0.52

Use Mickey Mantle's batting record on page 19 to answer the following. Pages 18–19

80. In what year did Mickey Mantle play in 153 games and have 163 hits? 1961

81. In what year did he have 40 runs and 23 home runs? 1966

CHAPTER 1 TEST

Use the mileage chart on page 3 to find each distance.

1. Dallas to Louisville **819 miles**

2. New Orleans to Boston **1,507 miles**

3. Seattle to Detroit **2,279 miles**

4. Salt Lake City to San Francisco **752 miles**

5. Philadelphia to Pittsburgh **288 miles**

6. San Francisco to Seattle **808 miles**

Use the timetable on page 4 to answer the following.

7. Suppose you board at Starr and Third at 12:37 P.M. When will you arrive at Sunlawn and Miami? **1:16 P.M.**

8. Suppose you board at Sunlawn and Miami at 11:27 A.M. When will you arrive at Starr and Third? **12:07 P.M.**

Use the chart on page 6 to find the cost of sending each package fourth class with the given weight to the given zone.

9. 4 lb; 3 **$1.78**

10. $2\frac{3}{4}$ lb; 2 **$1.49**

11. $3\frac{1}{4}$ lb; 7 **$3.57**

12. 1.8 oz; 1 **$1.41**

13. 5 lb; 6 **$3.47**

14. 2 lb 1 oz; 4 **$1.87**

15. 3.5 lb; 8 **$4.74**

16. 4 lb 8 oz; 5 **$2.86**

17. 1 lb 6 oz; 2 **$1.41**

Use the chart on page 8 to find whether each call will be charged full rate, 40% discount, or 60% discount.

18. 9:27 P.M.; Sat. **60% discount**

19. 7:01 P.M.; Wed. **40% discount**

20. 1:20 P.M.; Thurs. **full rate**

21. 11:45 A.M.; Sun. **60% discount**

22. 3:20 P.M.; Mon. **full rate**

23. 7:45 P.M.; Fri. **40% discount**

24. 2:15 A.M.; Tues. **60% discount**

25. 8:32 A.M.; Sat. **60% discount**

26. 10:30 P.M.; Sun. **40% discount**

Use the tax table on page 10 to find the withholding tax. The weekly wages and the number of allowances are given.

27. $256.90; 2 **$27**

28. $193.25; 1 **$20**

29. $210.15; 3 **$17**

30. $146.75; 0 **$16**

31. $178.18; 2 **$14**

32. $223.09; 1 **$25**

Use the federal tax table on page 14 to find the tax for single (s), married filing jointly (mj), married filing separately (ms), or head of household (hh).

33. $10,111; s **$1,074**

34. $10,249; hh **$1,023**

35. $10,701; mj **$897**

36. $10,550; ms **$1,313**

37. $10,478; s **$1,130**

38. $10,615; hh **$1,091**

Use the tax table on page 16 to find the sales tax on the following purchases.

39. $15.22 **$0.84**

40. $0.21 **$0.02**

41. $4.19 **$0.24**

42. $6.82 **$0.38**

43. $10.25 **$0.57**

44. $8.37 **$0.47**

45. $11.11 **$0.62**

46. $14.54 **$0.80**

47. $9.88 **$0.55**

48. $5.75 **$0.32**

Use Mickey Mantle's batting record on page 19 to answer the following.

49. In what years did Mickey Mantle play in less than 100 games? **1951, 1963**

50. How many years did he have an average below 0.300? **8 years**

CUMULATIVE REVIEW

FIRST-CLASS ZONE RATED (PRIORITY) MAIL

Weight over 12 ounces and not exceeding- pound(s)	Rate		
	Local zones 1, 2, and 3	Zone 4	Zone 5
1	$ 2.40	$ 2.40	$ 2.40
2	2.40	2.40	2.40
3	2.74	3.16	3.45
4	3.18	3.75	4.13
5	3.61	4.32	4.86

Find the cost of sending each package first class with the given weight to the given zone.   Pages 6–7

1. 4.2 lb; 4 $4.32
2. 14 oz; local $2.40
3. 3 lb; 5 $3.45
4. 2 lb 11 oz; 3 $2.74
5. 1.6 lb; 1 $2.40
6. 3.7 lb; 4 $3.75
7. 5 lb; 3 $3.61
8. 3 lb 8 oz; 5 $4.13

Use the tax table at the right to find the withholding tax. The monthly wage and the number of allowances are given. Pages 12–13

9. $595; 1 $49
10. $621; 0 $67
11. $541.25; 2 $31
12. $572.03; 3 $21
13. $536; 1 $40
14. $510.50; 2 $25
15. $640; 3 $33
16. $700.36; 0 $79
17. $756; 0 $86
18. $680.15; 3 $39

SINGLE Persons–MONTHLY Payroll Period

And the wages are–		And the number of withholding allowances claimed is–			
At least	But less than	0	1	2	3
		The amount of income tax to be withheld shall be–			
480	500	47	35	22	11
500	520	50	38	25	14
520	540	53	40	28	16
540	560	56	43	31	19
560	580	59	46	33	21
580	600	62	49	36	24
600	640	67	53	40	28
640	680	73	59	46	33
680	720	79	65	52	39
720	760	86	71	58	45

BRACKETED TAX COLLECTION SCHEDULE
SALES & USE TAX FOR STATE, COUNTY AND/OR TRANSIT TAX – TOTAL 5 1/2% TAX LEVY
SALES 15¢ AND UNDER – NO TAX

Each Sale		Tax	Each Sale		Tax
.16 to	.18	.01	8.19 to	8.36	.46
.19 to	.36	.02	8.37 to	8.54	.47
.37 to	.54	.03	8.55 to	8.72	.48
.55 to	.72	.04	8.73 to	8.90	.49
.73 to	.90	.05	8.91 to	9.09	.50
.91 to	1.09	.06	9.10 to	9.27	.51
1.10 to	1.27	.07	9.20 to	9.46	.52
1.28 to	1.46	.08	9.47 to	9.64	.53
1.47 to	1.64	.09	9.65 to	9.82	.54
1.65 to	1.82	.10	9.83 to	10.00	.55

Use the tax table to find the sales tax on the following purchases.   Page 16

19. $0.15 none
20. $1.38 $0.08
21. $9.04 $0.50
22. $8.34 $0.46
23. $9.46 $0.52
24. $1.28 $0.08
25. $0.72 $0.04
26. $1.80 $0.10
27. $8.56 $0.48
28. $9.13 $0.51
29. $1.07 $0.06
30. $1.62 $0.09
31. $10.00 $0.55
32. $2.54 $0.14
33. $3.64 $0.20

Solve. Make a table.   Pages 18–19

34. Duane, Doug, and Dugan have jobs as a farmer, florist, and forester (but not necessarily in that order). Duane lives 10 miles from the farmer. Doug and the forester both enjoy playing golf. Dugan is older than both the florist and the forester. Match the names with the jobs.

	Farmer	Florist	Forester
Duane	no	?	?
Doug	?	?	no
Dugan	?	?	?

Duane—forester, Doug—florist, Dugan—farmer

Everyday Statistics

2-1 Tallies

Objective: To gather and record data from a survey.

In some cases, data are collected by observation. When the data are organized, trends can be seen and logical conclusions made.

Statistics is the collection, analysis, and interpretation of information called data.
A simple way to count and record data is to use **tally marks.** A mark represents one unit. Marks are grouped by fives for easy counting.

Example

In a survey, 100 high-school students chose their favorite type of restaurant. Their responses were recorded on a tally sheet as shown at the right.

How many students chose Oriental restaurants as their favorite? The tally marks show that 12 students chose Oriental restaurants as their favorite.

Basic: 1–15; Average: 1–15; Enriched: 1–15

Favorite Type of Restaurant	Tally	
Sandwich	ⅡⅡ ⅡⅡ ⅡⅡ ⅡⅡ ⅡⅡ	25
Chicken & Ribs	ⅡⅡ ⅡⅡ ⅡⅡ ⅡⅡ Ⅰ	21
Seafood	ⅡⅡ ⅡⅡ Ⅲ	13
Steak	ⅡⅡ ⅡⅡ ⅢⅠ	14
Oriental	ⅡⅡ ⅡⅡ Ⅱ	12
Mexican	ⅡⅡ Ⅲ	8
Other	ⅡⅡ Ⅱ	7
Total		100

Exercises

State the number that each set of tally marks represents.

1. ⅡⅡ ⅡⅡ 10

2. ⅡⅡ ⅡⅡ ⅡⅡ Ⅲ 18

3. ⅡⅡ ⅡⅡ Ⅰ 11

4. ⅢⅠ 4

Use tally marks to represent each number.

5. 9 ⅡⅡ ⅢⅠ

6. 15 ⅡⅡ ⅡⅡ ⅡⅡ

7. 28 ⅡⅡ ⅡⅡ ⅡⅡ ⅡⅡ ⅡⅡ Ⅲ

8. 32 ⅡⅡ ⅡⅡ ⅡⅡ ⅡⅡ ⅡⅡ ⅡⅡ Ⅱ

9. 17 ⅡⅡ ⅡⅡ ⅡⅡ Ⅱ

Complete. Use the survey results shown above.

10. Find the number of students favoring each type of restaurant. What is the total? **See above.**

11. Which two types of restaurants together were chosen by 39 of the students? **sandwich and steak**

12. Which type of restaurant was chosen most often? **sandwich**

13. What age group was selected for this survey? **high-school age**

14. Do you think this survey tells where most people would prefer to dine out? Why or why not? **No, because the sample is not representative of the population.**

15. Conduct your own survey to find your classmates' favorite restaurants. Compare your results with the survey shown above. **See students' work.**

Teacher Resource Book, Page 69

2-2 Samples and Frequency Tables

Objective: To know what a sample is and to use data in a frequency table.

Cyndi Lewis is a marketing research assistant for a large advertising firm. She needs to find out the favorite types of radio stations for listeners in the Lyonsville area. Cyndi collects data by taking a survey in a shopping mall. Since every listener cannot be surveyed, she surveys a smaller group of people called a **sample.**

Example

A. The frequency table at the right shows the results of Cyndi's survey. How many people chose country as their favorite type of radio station?
29 people

Favorite Type of Station	Tally	Frequency
Adult Contemporary	卌 卌 卌 卌 卌 卌 卌 I	36
Popular Hits	卌 卌 卌 卌 卌 卌 卌 III	38
Easy Listening	卌 卌 I	11
Country	卌 卌 卌 卌 卌 IIII	29
Nostalgia	卌 卌 III	13
Rhythm and Blues	卌 卌 II	12
Other	卌 卌 卌 卌 卌 卌 卌 卌 卌 III	43

A *sample* is representative of a larger group called the **population.**

The following are characteristics of a good sample.

- A good sample is made randomly.
- A good sample is large enough to give accurate data.

Example

B. A survey was made to determine peoples' opinions of the 55 mile per hour speed limit.

Population Group	**Sample Group**
licensed drivers	drivers leaving parking lot

Basic: 1–12; Average: 1–19; Enriched: 1–10, 13–19

Exercises

Solve. Use the frequency table shown above.

1. Copy and complete the table.
See above.

2. How many people were surveyed?
182 people

3. Which type of station was chosen the most often? Least often? **popular hits; easy listening**

4. What two types of stations together were picked by 47 people? **adult contemporary and easy listening**

5. Explain why high-school students would not be a good sample. **not representative**

6. Describe a small group that would be a good sample. **Answers may vary.**

26 *Everyday Statistics*

Would the following locations be good for the kind of survey named? State why or why not.
For answers to 7–10, see Teacher Guide.

7. choose President, party headquarters

8. favorite actor, theater line

9. favorite detergent, laundromat

10. number of dogs, apartments

For answers to exercises 11 and 13 see Teacher Guide.

The incomes of 20 workers at a factory are listed below.

$14,500	19,400	13,000	14,500
11,300	28,600	14,500	11,300
13,000	14,500	16,000	19,400
13,000	11,300	13,000	14,500
16,000	14,500	16,000	13,000

11. Make a frequency table for the incomes listed above.

12. Use the frequency table to compute the total amount earned for each income. Find the total amount for all incomes. $301,300

The scores on a 25-point test are listed below.

22	15	18	12	17	16	14	15	20	14
20	15	12	22	14	25	18	24	18	13

13. Make a frequency table.

14. What is the lowest score? 12

15. What is the highest score? 25

16. Which scores occur most often? 14, 15, 18

17. How many scored less than 18? 11

18. How many scored 20 or more? 6

19. Why are the scores arranged from least to greatest in the table?
Easier to locate and analyze.

Mental Math

This feature promotes students' mental abilities in computation and reasonableness.

Numbers close in value may be clustered to estimate their sum.

$$42 + 38 + 44 + 36$$

Notice that each of these numbers is close to 40. To estimate their sum, think $4 \times 40 = 160$.

Estimate each sum using the clustering strategy. Answers may vary. Typical answers are given.

1. $73 + 70 + 68 + 71$ 280

2. $51 + 49 + 54 + 47$ 200

3. $36 + 43 + 44 + 35$ 160

4. $67 + 68 + 72 + 74$ 280

5. $27 + 43 + 31 + 32$ 120

6. $84 + 81 + 77 + 83$ 320

7. $95 + 102 + 104 + 97$ 400

8. $124 + 119 + 115 + 123 + 117$ 600

2-3 Using a Calculator

Objective: To become familiar with calculator functions.

There are many kinds of calculators, each slightly different. Take some time to get to know the calculator you are using.

You can see the *number* buttons on the calculator shown at the right. These will always be in the same order on any calculator. The *command* buttons can appear in various locations on different calculators. Locate the command buttons on your calculator.

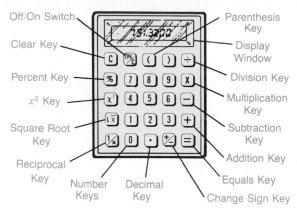

The flowchart below shows how a calculator can be used to perform any of the four basic operations.

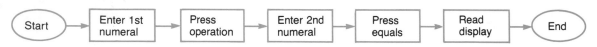

Start → Enter 1st numeral → Press operation → Enter 2nd numeral → Press equals → Read display → End

Examples

A. Find

$$\begin{array}{r} 121.5 \\ +\quad 3.06 \\ \hline \end{array}$$

Enter: 121.5 $+$ 3.06 $=$

Display: $121.5 \quad 121.5 \quad 3.06 \quad 124.56$

B. Find

$$\begin{array}{r} 121.5 \\ -\quad 3.06 \\ \hline \end{array}$$

Enter: 121.5 $-$ 3.06 $=$

Display: $121.5 \quad 121.5 \quad 3.06 \quad 118.44$

C. Find

$$\begin{array}{r} 121.5 \\ \times\quad 3.06 \\ \hline \end{array}$$

Enter: 121.5 $\times$ 3.06 $=$

Display: $121.5 \quad 121.5 \quad 3.06 \quad 371.79$

D. Find

$$121.5 \div 3.06$$

Enter: 121.5 $\div$ 3.06 $=$

Display: $121.5 \quad 121.5 \quad 3.06 \quad 39.7058823$

Most calculators can show numbers in decimal form only. The fraction $\frac{3}{8}$ can be entered into a calculator as follows.

Enter: 3 $\div$ 8 $=$

Display: $3 \quad 3 \quad 8 \quad 0.375$

Exercises

Use a calculator to compute the following.

1. $1,892.35 + 0.659$
1,893.009

2. $78,295.612 - 3,842.956$
74,452.656

3. $14,276 \div 83$
172

4. $3.024 \times 1,512$
4,572.288

5. $0.904 + 0.308 - 0.042$
1.17

6. $3.14 + 0.868 - 2.78$
1.228

7. $2.56 - 1.6 + 2.56$ **3.52**

8. 8.24×8.24 **67.8976**

9. $7.62 - 7.07$ **0.55**

10. $3.46 + 165 - 0.171$
168.289

11. $887.836 \div 1.73$ **513.2**

12. 0.779×0.612 **0.476748**

Use a calculator to change each fraction to a decimal.

13. $\frac{1}{4}$ 0.25

14. $\frac{1}{32}$ 0.03125

15. $\frac{3}{16}$ 0.1875

16. $\frac{5}{9}$ 0.5555556

17. $\frac{5}{33}$ 0.1515152

18. $\frac{136}{17}$ 8

19. $\frac{2.4}{8}$ 0.3

20. $\frac{7.29}{8.1}$ 0.9

21. $\frac{11}{17}$
0.64705882

22. $\frac{15,681}{324}$
48.398148

23. $1\frac{1}{4}$ 1.25

24. $2\frac{1}{32}$
2.03125

Solve.

25. A statute mile equals 1.1515 kilometers. How many kilometers are there in 17.9 statute miles to the nearest hundredth? **20.61 kilometers**

26. For 8 days, Kerry earns $26 per day. She wants to earn $500. How much more money does she need to earn? **$292**

27. Herman purchased the clothing shown at the right. How much change does he receive from a $60.00 gift certificate?
$6.98

$3.29

$42.75

$6.98

This feature incorporates the uses of a computer in mathematics.

Computer

Look at the following examples. Decide what each computer symbol means.

$3+5 = 8$ add | $9*8 = 72$ multiply | $3\uparrow2 = 9$ (Hint: $3 \times 3 = $ ▨) exponent

$12-7 = 5$ subtract | $36/4 = 9$ divide

Complete.

1. Which computer operation symbols are the same as those on a calculator? **+, =**

2. Which computer operation symbols are different from those on a calculator? ***, /, ↑**

Answer the following.

3. $178+122$
300

4. $906-287$
619

5. $41*12$
492

6. $912/6$
152

7. $4\uparrow3$
64

8. $304*15$
4560

9. $108/36$
3

10. $5\uparrow4$
625

2-4   Range and Mode

Objective: To determine the range and mode of a set of data.

Joe Kerr is a test driver for an auto manufacturer. He inspects and drives completed vehicles as they leave the assembly line. Joe makes a list of problems on a standardized inspection form.

Joe attended a vocational high school where he majored in auto mechanics. He also received on-the-job training.

In testing a series of 15 cars, Joe reported the number of problems as listed below.

6 3 3 4 9 4 2 3 1 6 6 0 3 4 5

One way to organize data is to arrange the numbers in increasing or decreasing order.

0 1 2 3 3 3 3 4 4 4 5 6 6 6 9

The **range** is the difference between the greatest and least numbers.

$$9 - 0 = 9$$

The range is 9.

The **mode** is the number that appears most often.

Cars having 3 problems appear most often. So, the mode is 3.

There can be more than one mode. However, if each number appears only once, there is no mode. **The mode can also be used for nonnumerical items.**

Basic Skills Appendix, Pages 422, 433
Basic: 1–10, 11–45 odd; Average: 1–46; Enriched: 11–18, 20–46 even

Exercises

Find the range and mode for each set of data.

1. 1, 4, 5, 5, 5, 6, 8, 9, 9, 9, 12
   11; 5, 9
2. 2.8, 2.8, 2.9, 3.5, 3.5, 3.5, 4.8, 4.9
   2.1; 3.5
3. 4, 6, 10, 3, 7, 6, 6, 8, 5, 9
   7; 6
4. 11, 17, 14, 15, 13, 19, 14, 19, 19
   8; 19
5. 0.6, 0.7, 0.7, 1.0, 0.9, 1.0, 1.2
   0.6; 0.7, 1.0
6. 1.4, 1.1, 1.2, 1.3, 1.4, 1.5, 1.6
   0.5; 1.4
7. 0.11, 0.12, 0.14, 0.13, 0.15, 0.1
   0.05; no mode
8. 143, 149, 156, 142, 149, 160, 161
   19; 149
9. 7.5, 8.3, 8.8, 8.3, 7.4, 8.3, 7.5, 8.1, 8.3, 7.6, 9.1, 8.8, 7.9, 6.5, 8.3
   2.6; 8.3
10. Name a situation where the mode is an item rather than a number. **Answers may vary.**

The table at the right lists the gallons of outdoor paint sold at a paint store.

Color	Tally
Green	IIII
Brown	IIII II
White	IIII IIII
Yellow	IIII II
Blue	III

11. What is the range of gallons sold? **7**

12. Which color is the mode? **white**

13. Would a numerical mode be of any value in this situation? **no**

For answers to exercises 14, 16, see Teacher Guide.

Use the telephone numbers listed at the right to complete the following.

14. Make a frequency table for the *last* digit of each number.

15. What is the range? The mode?
8, 3 and 4

16. Make a frequency table for the *first* digit.

17. What is the range? The mode?
7, 8

18. Explain why the ranges and modes differ in exercises 15 and 17. **The first digit cannot be 0 or 1 and the exchange (the 1st three digits) are limited to a few possibilities.**

Use the chart below to complete exercises 19–46.

```
SABO A 320 Diven Ct ------------------ 476-4210
     Alexander C 5703 Karl----------- 888-7944
     Amy 35 E 12 Av------------------ 291-2782
     B R 1546 Sandalwood Pl --------- 888-1444
     Chas 391 E Stewart-------------- 444-4634
     Chas J Sr 117 E Wilson Bridge -- 885-3843
     Chas L 503 Chateaugay SW------- 927-6085
     D 4603 Refugee ----------------- 864-1452
     D J 4380 Amalia Pl ------------- 235-8363
     Eugene L 3880 Grovprt ---------- 491-1508
     Eugene W 5517 Cedarbush -------- 885-0993
     Gary L 3714 Outville SW-------- 927-7555
     Geo A 1049 Harmon -------------- 443-2031
     Geo Edw 1102 Mulford ---------- 294-6584
     Geo H 3860 Ritamarie Dr ------- 451-5840
     Gregory & Robin
         1220 Chambers Rd -------- 486-2546
     Ilene G 2843 Northwest Bl ----- 486-6336
     Jim L 1350 Dyer --------------- 871-2645
         Children's Teleph
         1350 Dyer ---------------- 871-1123
     John 5265 Babbitt------------- 855-1792
```

INCHES OF RAINFALL											
	Jan.	Feb.	Mar.	Apr.	May	June	July	Aug.	Sept.	Oct.	Nov.	Dec.
Phoenix	0.1	1.4	1.7	0.1	0.1	0.05	0.05	0.05	0.05	0.05	1.4	0.05
Seattle	5.8	4.2	3.6	2.5	1.7	1.5	1.4	1.1	2.0	3.9	5.9	5.9
Newark	2.9	3.0	3.9	3.4	3.6	3.0	3.8	4.3	3.4	2.8	3.6	3.5
Jacksonville	2.8	3.6	3.6	3.1	3.2	6.3	6.9	7.9	7.8	4.5	1.8	3.6
Dodge City	0.5	0.6	1.1	1.7	3.1	3.3	3.0	2.6	1.7	1.7	0.6	8.5
Albany	2.2	2.1	2.6	2.7	3.3	3.0	2.9	2.9	3.1	2.6	2.8	2.9

Find the range for the rainfall in each month.

19. January 5.7 in.
20. March 2.8 in.
21. May 3.5 in.
22. June 6.25 in.
23. August 7.85 in.
24. September 7.75 in.
25. November 5.3 in.
26. December 8.45 in.

Find the range for the rainfall in each city.

27. Dodge City 8.0 in.
28. Albany 1.2 in.
29. Seattle 4.8 in.
30. Jacksonville 6.1 in.
31. Phoenix 1.65 in.
32. Newark 1.5 in.

Find the mode for the rainfall in each month.

33. January none
34. March 3.6 in.
35. May none
36. June 3.0 in.
37. August none
38. September none
39. November none
40. December none

Find the mode for the rainfall in each city.

41. Dodge City 1.7 in.
42. Albany 2.9 in.
43. Seattle 5.9 in.
44. Jacksonville 3.6 in.
45. Phoenix 0.05 in.
46. Newark 3.0 in., 3.6 in., 3.4 in.

2-5 Mean

Objective: To determine the mean of a set of data.

The table at the right shows the number of people who attended five home football games at Valley High School last season.

The Service Club members run the snack bar. To order food this season, the members need to know the mean of the number of people attending each game.

The **mean** of a set of data is the sum of the numbers divided by the number of addends. *The mean is also called the average or arithmetic mean.*

Opponents	Attendance
Hightown	832
Rigsby	1,028
Tech	1,256
Central	944
Finley	1,140

Example

Estimate: 800 + 1,000 + 1,300 + 900 + 1,000 = 5,100

Estimate: 5,000 ÷ 5 = 1,000

First, add the number of people attending the five games.

$$\begin{array}{r} 832 \\ 1,028 \\ 1,256 \\ 944 \\ + \ 1,140 \\ \hline 5,200 \ people \end{array}$$

Divide the sum by the number of games.

$$\begin{array}{r} 1,040 \ people \\ 5\overline{)5,200} \\ \underline{5} \\ 2 \\ \underline{-0} \\ 20 \\ \underline{-20} \\ 0 \\ \underline{-0} \\ 0 \end{array}$$

832 ⊞ 1028 ⊞ 1256 ⊞ 944 ⊞ 1140 ⊟ 5 ⊟ 1040

Is the answer reasonable? **yes**

The mean of the number of people attending each game is 1,040.

The Key Skills provides practice of skills needed in the exercises.

Key Skills

Round each number to the nearest tenth.

Round up if the digit to the right is 5 or greater.

To the nearest tenth, 174.6̲37 rounds to 174.6

The underlined digit remains the same if the digit to the right is 4 or less.

1. 118.706 **118.7**   **2.** 129.46 **129.5**   **3.** 84.68 **84.7**   **4.** 6.155 **6.2**   **5.** 47.48 **47.5**

6. 39.442 **39.4**   **7.** 53.21 **53.2**   **8.** 702.077 **702.1**   **9.** 60.625 **60.6**   **10.** 66.73 **66.7**

Basic Skills Appendix, Pages 421, 424, 428, 432, 434

Basic: 1–17 odd; Average: 1–17; Enriched: 2–16 even

Exercises

Find the mean for each set of data. Round decimal answers to the nearest tenth.

Encourage students to estimate first.

1. 7, 9 **8**   **2.** 3, 4, 5 **4**   **3.** 2, 4, 6, 8 **5**   **4.** 2, 3, 7, 8, 10 **6**

5. 5, 10, 15, 20, 25, 30, 35 **20**

6. 10, 40, 60, 80, 30, 50 **45**

7. 129, 215, 327, 242, 183 **219.2**

8. $1.10, $1.25, $1.34, $1.18, $3.13 **$1.60**

9. 0.98, 0.8, 0.75, 0.85 **0.8**

10. 68, 62, 78, 79, 83, 91, 70, 67 **74.8**

11. $4\frac{1}{2}$, $2\frac{1}{4}$, $3\frac{3}{4}$, 5, $3\frac{1}{2}$, 4 **3.8 or** $3\frac{5}{6}$

12. 4.8, 4.8, 6.4, 7.2, 3.2, 2.4, 4.5 **4.8**

Find the mean for each of the following.

13. Miguel's bowling scores are 84, 111, and 150. **115**

14. Sue buys 5 baseball tickets at $3.50 each, 4 tickets at $4.50, and 2 tickets at $5.50. **$4.23**

Solve. Round answers to the nearest tenth.

15. During this football season, Alonzo made the following punts (in yards): 32, 45, 50, 33, 36, 39, 27, 45, 10, 19, 20, 55, 32, 56, 43, 46, and 53. What is the average length of a punt? **37.7 yards per punt**

16. Last month Wilda paid $57.63 for gasoline, $6.10 for oil, $238.27 for a car payment, and $32.16 for car insurance. She drove 1,326 miles. What did it cost per mile for Wilda to drive her car? **$0.30 per mile**

17. Refer to the rainfall chart on page 31. What was the total rainfall in Jacksonville for the year? Find the mean of the monthly rainfall. **55.1 in., 4.6 in.**

This feature presents general topics of mathematics.

 ## Math Break

The **mean variation** is the average amount each measurement differs from the mean.

Find the mean variation of the temperatures (Celsius) 28°, 23°, 27°, 25°, 22°, and 24° as follows.

1. Find the mean of the temperatures (to the nearest tenth). **24.8°**

2. Find the difference between each number and the mean.
3.2°, 1.8°, 2.2°, 0.2°, 2.8°, 0.8°

3. Add the differences. **11°**

4. Then the mean variation is the sum in exercise 3 divided by the number of addends. **1.8°**

5. What kind of changes would greatly affect the mean variation?
very large or very small numbers

6. What kind would not? **numbers close to the mean, or group of numbers whose mean is close to the mean**

PRACTICE

State the number named by each digit in 29,736.

1. the 2
20,000

2. the 3
30

3. the 7
700

4. the 6
6

5. the 9
9,000

Round each number to the underlined place-value position.

6. 6<u>3</u>5 640

7. 6<u>1</u>2 610

8. 1<u>2</u>9 130

9. <u>9</u>9 100

10. 1,0<u>6</u>5 1,070

11. 7,<u>3</u>84 7,400

12. 3,<u>1</u>94 3,200

13. 2,<u>5</u>76 2,600

14. 12,<u>4</u>90 12,500

Estimate. Answers may vary. Typical answers are given.

15. 562
+ 254
900

16. 785
+ 239
1,000

17. 6,138
+ 776
6,800

18. 562
− 254
300

19. 7,204
− 658
6,500

Add or subtract.

20. 107
+ 78
185

21. 972
+ 376
1,348

22. 778
+ 975
1,753

23. 5,692
+ 760
6,452

24. 865
 422
+ 61
1,348

25. 404
+ 588
992

26. 4,042
+ 588
4,630

27. 4,042
+ 7,588
11,630

28. 1,000
 765
+ 671
2,436

29. 3,297
 794
+ 36
4,127

30. 159
− 78
81

31. 189
− 99
90

32. 659
− 237
422

33. 1,809
− 909
900

34. 4,237
− 2,459
1,778

35. 999
− 156
843

36. 1,000
− 156
844

37. 4,296
− 267
4,029

38. 6,904
− 5,877
1,027

39. 8,624
− 4,875
3,749

Multiply or divide.

40. 60
× 70
4,200

41. 700
× 6
4,200

42. 82
× 40
3,280

43. 90
× 76
6,840

44. 91
× 28
2,548

45. 181
× 29
5,249

46. 600
× 55
33,000

47. 607
× 85
51,595

48. 758
× 23
17,434

49. 3,000
× 55
165,000

50. 6)30 5

51. 6)36 6

52. 9)81 9

53. 6)306 51

54. 7)301 43

55. 10)440 44

56. 10)690 69

57. 20)800 40

58. 30)120 4

59. 50)250 5

60. 21)609 29

61. 31)837 27

62. 33)957 29

63. 47)799 17

64. 200)600 3

65. 37)9,398 254

66. 85)6,205 73

67. 54)4,698 87

68. 16)8,688 543

69. 79)5,293 67

State the number named by each digit in 35.748.

70. the 4 0.04   **71.** the 3 30   **72.** the 7 0.7   **73.** the 8 0.008   **74.** the 5 5

Express each of the following in standard form.

75. three hundredths 0.03

76. two and seven tenths 2.7

77. one hundred forty-five thousandths 0.145

78. ninety-three and six tenths 93.6

79. eight thousandths 0.008

80. twenty-five hundredths 0.25

Solve.

81. Yuri Miskin earns $652.75 a month. What are his yearly earnings? **$7,833.00**

82. Janet Thomas earns $8,478.08 in a year (52 weeks). What is her weekly wage? **$163.04**

83. Lew Weaver earns $192.35 a week. Bill Jako earns $4.90 an hour. Who earns more for a 40-hour week? **Bill Jako**

84. Cynthia Groza pays $24.90 withholding tax each week. How much tax is withheld in one year? **$1,294.80**

This feature presents useful ways of solving mathematical problems on a calculator.

Calculator

Calculators with memory keys can be used to solve multiple-step problems. Since calculators differ, check the instruction manual of the calculator for directions.

Memory Keys

    memory clear   add to memory   subtract from memory   memory recall

Compute. $(5,000 \times 0.005) + (9,278 - 5,000) \times 0.01$

 Press: 5000 0.005 9278 5000   0.01 **M+** **MR**

Display: *0. 5000   5000   0.005   25   9278   9278   5000   4278   4278   0.01   42.78   67.78*

Compute.

1. $(84 \div 6) + (3 \times 3)$ **23**

2. $(40 \div 5) \times (72 \div 8)$ **72**

3. $(7,050 \times 0.006) + (1,200 + 3,068) \times 0.04$ **213.02**

2-6 Median

Objective: To determine the median of a set of data.

Jim Brewster owns the Golden Moments jewelry store. He sells 14-karat gold jewelry. The price of an item is determined by its weight in grams and by the current market price of gold.

Jim wants to know the median weight of the gold he sells. The **median** of a set of data is the number in the middle when the data are organized from least to greatest. When there are two middle numbers, the median is their mean. **Point out that if there is an odd number of data, there is one middle number. If there is an even number of data, there are two middle numbers.**

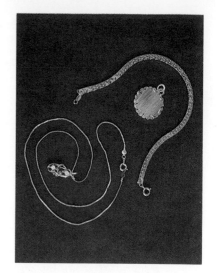

Example

Find the median weight of 1.5 g, 0.9 g, 3.7 g, 5.4 g, 2.9 g, 2.6 g, 4.6 g, and 3.3 g.

First, organize the data from least to greatest. Since there are two middle numbers, find the mean of the middle numbers.

0.9, 1.5, 2.6, 2.9, 3.3, 3.7, 4.6, 5.4
         └─┬─┘
      middle numbers

$$\begin{array}{r} 2.9 \text{ g} \\ + 3.3 \text{ g} \\ \hline 6.2 \text{ g} \end{array} \qquad \begin{array}{r} 3.1 \text{ g} \\ 2\overline{)6.2 \text{ g}} \end{array}$$

The median weight is 3.1 grams.

Basic Skills Appendix, Pages 435, 441

Basic: 1–9, 16–25; Average: 1–30; Enriched: 10–30

Exercises

Find the median for each set of data.

1. 15, 16, 19   **16**

2. 74, 83, 87, 92   **85**

3. 1.8, 2.1, 2.6   **2.1**

4. 0.9, 1.4, 1.9, 2.1   **1.65**

5. 83, 78, 97, 72, 84   **83**

6. 178, 149, 156, 160, 171, 166   **163**

7. 96.4, 95.8, 97.2, 96.6   **96.5**

8. 6.5, 4.53, 5.9, 6.04, 4.9, 5.15   **5.525**

9. How many numbers are greater than the median? How many are less?
The same number are greater than and less than the median.

Margie Feaser bought a 1.4-gram necklace, a 2.2-gram pair of earrings, and a 0.9-gram bracelet. Answer the following.

10. What was the median weight of the items Margie purchased? **1.4 g**

11. At $25 per gram, what was the total cost of the purchase above? **$112.50**

12. Find the mean weight. How much more or less than the median weight was the mean of the weights? **0.1 g more**

13. Include a 5.1-gram pendant in the purchase above. How does this affect the median? the mean? **median increases to 1.8 g; mean increases to 2.4 g.**

14. Suppose the current selling price of 14-karat gold jewelry is $25 per gram. What was the median price of the three items above? **$35**

15. Refer to exercise 11. Suppose the selling price of 14-karat gold jewelry increased by $0.35 per gram. What would be the cost of the three items above? **$114.08**

The miles per gallon (mpg) of the vehicles in a company fleet are listed at the right.

| 17 | 18 | 20 | 10 | 15 |
| 44 | 8 | 11 | 13 | 13 |

16. Find the median. **14**

17. Find the mean. **16.9 mpg**

18. Suppose the 44-mpg car is replaced by a 10-mpg truck. How is the median affected? **lowered to 13 mpg**

19. Suppose the 44-mpg car is replaced by a 10-mpg truck. How is the mean affected? **lowered to 13.5 mpg**

20. Suppose the 20-mpg truck is replaced by a 16-mpg truck. How is the median affected? **not affected**

21. Suppose the 20-mpg truck is replaced by a 15-mpg truck. How is the mean affected? **lowered to 16.4 mpg**

22. What kind of changes affect the median? **adding more numbers above or below the median**

23. What kind of changes greatly affect the mean? **very large or very small values**

24. What kind of changes do not affect the median? **not affected by adding large or small values**

25. What kind of changes do not greatly affect the mean? **adding or dropping values that are neither very large nor very small**

 The table at the right lists the salaries at a small business.

26. What is the range of salaries? **$22,000**

27. What is the mode of the salaries? **$8,000**

28. What is the median salary? **$10,000**

29. What is the mean salary? **$11,600**

30. Which *average* describes the salaries best: mode, median, or mean? **mean or median**

Salary	Employees
$30,000	1
20,000	1
15,000	2
12,000	3
10,000	6
8,000	7

This feature promotes students' mental abilities in computation and reasonableness.

Mental Math

Differences may be estimated by subtracting front end digits.
Compare the remaining digits to decide whether the actual difference is somewhat greater or less than the initial estimate.

$$\begin{array}{rcr} 331 & \longrightarrow & 300 \\ -\ 158 & \longrightarrow & -\ 100 \\ \hline & & 200 \end{array}$$

$$\begin{array}{rcr} 8{,}564 & \longrightarrow & 8{,}000 \\ -\ 3{,}446 & \longrightarrow & -\ 3{,}000 \\ \hline & & 5{,}000 \end{array}$$

Since 31 < 58, the actual difference is less than 200.

Since 564 > 446, the actual difference is greater than 5,000.

Estimate each difference using the strategy shown above.

1. $64 - 59$ **<10**
2. $66 - 27$ **<40**
3. $547 - 251$ **<300**
4. $682 - 304$ **>300**

5. $4{,}379 - 1{,}562$ **<3,000**
6. $5{,}627 - 1{,}297$ **>4,000**
7. $86{,}213 - 32{,}819$ **>50,000**

8. $80{,}468 - 55{,}464$ **<30,000**
9. $623{,}852 - 256{,}018$ **<400,000**
10. $389{,}035 - 146{,}498$ **>200,000**

11. $70{,}625 - 38{,}204$ **<40,000**
12. $856{,}291 - 507{,}268$ **>300,000**
13. $972{,}693 - 302{,}599$ **>600,000**

2-7 Using and Misusing Statistics

Objective: To determine whether the mean, median, or mode yields the desired result.

The average price of homes in a community is a concern to both buyers and sellers. The chart below shows the prices of homes listed by one realtor.

The average price of a home can be reported in three ways.

mode, median, mean
(to the nearest $10,000)

Price of Home	Number of Homes Listed
$ 40,000	1
50,000	6
60,000	4
70,000	2
80,000	2
90,000	3
110,000	1

Examples

A. mode: The mode, or most frequent price, is $50,000.

B. median: The median is the middle price. There are 19 homes advertised. The middle price or median is $60,000.

C. mean: $40,000 + 6(\$50,000) + 4(\$60,000) + 2(\$70,000) +$

$2(\$80,000) + 3(\$90,000) + \$110,000 = \frac{\$1,260,000}{19}$

or $70,000 to the nearest $10,000

MC 40000 M+ 6 X 50000 M+ 4 X 60000 M+ 2 X 70000 M+ 2 X 80000 M+

3 X 90000 M+ 110000 M+ MR 1260000 ÷ 19 = *66315.789*

The mean or average price is $70,000.

Basic Skills Appendix, Pages 426, 429

Basic: 1–24 even; Average: 1–24; Enriched: 1–24

Exercises

Use the chart above to answer the following.

1. The realtor wants to attract customers with lower incomes. Which average will be used? Why?
mode, Customers will expect to be able to afford lower priced homes.

A test was given to two groups of students. The results were as follows.

group A: 90, 88, 99, 87, 74,
　　　　 44, 80, 78, 94, 86

2. If the realtor wants to attract customers with higher incomes, which average will be used? Why?
mean, See Teacher Guide.

group B: 77, 81, 55, 57, 79,
　　　　 78, 60, 100, 81, 66

For group A, find the following.

3. range 55　　　　**4.** mode none

5. median 86.5　　**6.** mean 82

For group B, find the following.

7. range 45　　　　**8.** mode 81

9. median 77.5　　**10.** mean 73.4

11. Based on the averages, which group did better? Explain your answer. group A; see Teacher Guide.
Group A contains the lowest score. Group B contains the highest score.

Pam, Jim, and Kyo each weigh 3 specimens of a certain kind of beetle. The results are given below.

Pam: 8 g   11 g   38 g
Jim: 12 g   23 g   31 g
Kyo: 18 g   20 g   28 g

Find the median for each person's measurements.

12. Pam
11 g
13. Jim
23 g
14. Kyo
20 g

Find the mean for each person's measurements.

15. Pam
19 g
16. Jim
22 g
17. Kyo
22 g
18. Which average, median or mean, would be better to estimate the weight of the beetle? mean

Solve.

19. Kari Matsumara opened a savings account with $50. She made later deposits of $36, $22, $18, $29, and $24. Find the mean, median, and mode. Kari wants to deposit the same amount each time. She wants to deposit as much as she can afford. Which average should she use? $29.83, $26.50, no mode; median

20. Gary's baseball team scored 2 runs in its first game. In the games that followed, the team scored 7, 6, 9, 7, 10, 8, and 3 runs. What is the median? What is the mean? Which average would Gary want to have listed in the newspaper? 7 runs, 6.5 runs; median

21. Each of 6 employees earns $12,000, 3 employees each earns $15,000, and each of 2 employees earns $40,000. List the salaries of the employees. Find the median, mean, and mode. Which average would you use to attract new employees? $12,000, $17,909, $12,000; mean

22. You have scores of 80, 84, 81, 89, and 82 in golf. Find the mean, median, and mode. Which average would you use in talking with friends? 83.2, 82, no mode; median

23. Use the chart below to find the mean and the median for the number of times at bat. How does the mean compare with the median? 331 times at bat, 378 times at bat; 47 times at bat less

Batter	Times at Bat
Beniquez	316
Murray	445
Lacy	483
Lynn	378
Gerhart	32

24. Suppose that you wish to find the mean of several numbers. One of the numbers is quite large or quite small in value compared to the rest of the group. Which two numbers could you leave out in order to get a better average? largest and smallest

2-8 Problem Solving: Choosing the Best Average

Objective: To choose the best average for a given situation.

Averages have many uses in daily life. The mode, median, and mean are all kinds of averages.

It is important to know which average to use or which average is being used in a given situation.

The following information may help you choose the best average.

mode   It is the most frequent value.
           It applies to numbers as well as categories.

mean   There is one and only one mean.
           Very large or very small values greatly affect the mean.

median   It is the typical value.
           Very large or very small values have little effect.

Jill Tyo's lunch expenses last week were $2.47, $13.16, $4.26, $1.89, and $3.39. Find the average cost of her lunches.

 You need to find the average cost per lunch. You know the cost of each lunch and the number of lunches.

 Choose the average that best describes what Jill usually pays for lunch. The mode cannot be used because she never paid the same amount for any lunch. Since one lunch costs much more than the others, use the median. The more expensive meal will not affect the median as it would the mean. The mean would not give a good average of what she usually spends for lunch.

 List the lunch expenses from least to greatest.
$1.89, $2.47, $3.39, $4.26, $13.16
The middle number is $3.39.
Jill usually spends an average of $3.39 for lunch.

 Jill does not *usually* spend over $5 a day for lunch. The average of $3.39 is a reasonable solution.

Basic: 1–12, 22–25; Average: 1–25; Enriched: 7–25
Exercises

Which average—mode, mean, or median—would best describe each of the following?

1. favorite color mode

2. test scores mean

3. house prices median

4. bowling scores mean

5. average shoe size mode

6. family income median

40 *Everyday Statistics*

Solve. Name the average you used.

7. Find the average height. 172.4; mean

8. Find the average weight. 80.0; mean

9. Find the average eye color. brown; mode

10. Find the average favorite color. red; mode

11. Find the average favorite class. art; mode

12. Describe the "average" person in this group. He weighs about 80 kg, is 172 cm tall, has brown eyes, likes the color red, and likes art class.

Name	Height (cm)	Weight (kg)	Eyes	Favorite Color	Favorite Class
Tom	158	60	brown	red	math
Juan	165	80	brown	blue	art
Art	187	95	brown	white	art
Kuan	158	70	brown	red	math
Ben	190	95	blue	green	English
Tim	178	90	blue	yellow	science
Lee	170	75	blue	red	art
Zac	173	75	brown	green	science

The starters on the girls' basketball team have the following heights (in centimeters): 130, 154, 148, 155, and 172. Complete.

13. Find the median. 154 cm

14. Find the mean. 151.8 cm

15. Suppose a 184-cm player replaces the 155-cm player. What are the new median and mean? 154, 157.6 cm

16. Which average was affected more? Explain why. mean; Very large values affect the mean, but not the median.

Solve. Use the data at the right.

17. Make a frequency table for the set of data. For answer, see Teacher Guide.

18. Find the mean. 3.65 passengers

19. Find the median. 3 passengers

20. Find the mode. 3 passengers

21. Name the best average. Explain your answer. For answer, see Teacher Guide.

Passengers on Amusement Park Rides							
2	4	3	5	4	3	1	3
5	2	3	9	1	5	1	3
4	3	3	4	7	4	5	6
3	2	8	2	4	2	5	2
4	4	3	1	2	3	6	5

Find the mode, mean, and median for each of the following. Name the best average and explain why it is best.

22. The scores in a golf tournament are 95, 92, 88, 101, 101, 104, 109, 112, 125, 127, 130, and 132. 101, 109.7, 106.5; mean or median; no very high or very low scores

23. The salaries on a pro basketball team are as follows: 5 at $30,000; 5 at $100,000; and 1 at $820,000. $30,000 and $100,000, $133,636.37, $100,000; median; 1 high salary

24. Mrs. Friday sells televisions. She sells 3 at $190 each; 2 at $220 each; 4 at $280 each; and 1 at $325. $280, $245.50, $250; mean or median; no very high or very low values

25. The test scores in English class are 83, 91, 88, 82, 81, 84, 62, 93, 50, 63, 96, 68, 73, 80, 97, 95, 91, 38, 82, 72, 88, 83, 78, 93, and 91. 91, 80.1, 83; median; 2 very small values

CHAPTER 2 REVIEW

Vocabulary/Concepts

Choose the letter of the word or phrase at the right that best matches each description.

1. the collection, analysis, and interpretation of information called data **j**

2. a simple way to count and record observations **k**

3. used to record observations **b**

4. the difference between the greatest and least numbers **h**

5. the number or item in a set of data that appears most often **f**

6. find by first adding the numbers, and then dividing the sum by the number of addends **d**

7. the number in the middle when a set of data is organized from the least to the greatest **e**

8. representative of a population group **i**

a. data
b. frequency table
c. information
d. mean
e. median
f. mode
g. population
h. range
i. sample
j. statistics
k. tally marks

Exercises

State the number that each set of tally marks represents.   Page 25

9. 𝍪 ||| **8**

10. 𝍪 𝍪 𝍪 || **17**

11. 𝍪 𝍪 𝍪 𝍪 |||| **24**

Use tally marks to represent each number.   Page 25

12. 7 𝍪 ||

13. 29 𝍪 𝍪 𝍪 𝍪 𝍪 ||||

14. 16 𝍪 𝍪 𝍪 |

15. 41 𝍪 𝍪 𝍪 𝍪 𝍪 𝍪 𝍪 𝍪 |

Would the following locations be good for the kind of survey named? State why or why not.   Pages 26–27 For answers to exercises 16–19, see Teacher Guide.

16. favorite make of auto, dealership

17. favorite singer, concert

18. favorite sport, football game

19. favorite food, smorgasbord

Use a calculator to compute the following.   Pages 28–29

20. 17.6×1.85 **32.56**

21. $0.995 - 0.906$ **0.089**

22. $43.4 \div 7.773$ **5.5834298**

23. $73 + 50.6 - (50.6 \times 2.25)$ **9.75**

Change each fraction to a decimal.   Pages 28–29

24. $\frac{5}{16}$ **0.3125**

25. $\frac{7}{9}$ **0.7777778**

26. $\frac{2.4}{8}$ **0.3**

27. $5\frac{7}{8}$ **5.875**

Find the range and mode for each set of data. **Pages 30–31**

28. 3, 4, 4, 5, 5, 5, 7, 8, 13, 20
17, 5

29. 52, 53, 57, 64, 83, 85, 90
38, none

30. 7.3, 6.4, 5.24, 5, 6.4, 5, 6.4, 7.3
2.3, 6.4

31. c, a, b, c, d, b, a, c, b, b, a, d
no range, mode is b

Find the mean for each set of data. Round to the nearest tenth. **Pages 32–33**

32. 8.4, 8.4, 4.6, 2.7, 3.2, 4.2, 5.4 **5.3**

33. 3.02, 9.91, 1.22, 7.32, 2.12, 0.52, 1.12, 8.22, 1.82, 2.42, 9.12 **4.3**

Find the median for each set of the data. **Pages 36–37**

34. 0.8, 1.5, 1.9, 2.2, 6.8 **1.9**

35. 177, 148, 155, 159, 170, 165 **162**

36. 1.09, 0.99, 0.98, 1.11, 1.04, 1.14, 1.08, 1.25, 1.00, 1.14, 1.00 **1.08**

The scores on a 12-point quiz are listed below. **Pages 26–27, 30–33, 36–37**

37. Make a frequency table for the data shown at the right. **See Teacher Guide.**

8 6 9 10 10 12 5 8
12 8 7 9 8 10 7 7

38. What is the range? **7**

39. What is the mode? **8**

40. What is the mean? **8.5**

41. What is the median? **8**

The ages of the employees at a bookstore are listed at the right. **Pages 32–33, 36–37**

24 28 32
30 20 19
22 25 29

42. Find the median age. **25**

43. Find the mean age. **25.4**

44. Which average, median or mean, is most descriptive of the ages? **Since values of both are very close, either one could be used.**

45. Suppose the youngest had been 18 and the oldest 67. How would the median and mean be affected? **no effect on median; mean rises to 29.2**

Complete. Name the average you used. **Pages 40–41** **For answers to exercises 46–51, see Teacher Guide.**

46. Find the average height.

47. Find the average weight.

48. Find the average hair color.

49. Find the average favorite meat.

50. Find the average favorite sport.

Name	Height (cm)	Weight (kg)	Hair	Favorite meat	Favorite sport
Jana	163	58	Brown	Chicken	Basketball
Jane	149	48	Blonde	Beef	Football
Jean	156	62	Red	Pork	Swimming
Jill	178	65	Brown	Pork	Tennis
Joan	151	44	Blonde	Chicken	Basketball
Jodi	180	67	Black	Seafood	Football
Joni	168	56	Brown	Beef	Baseball
June	157	51	Black	Chicken	Basketball

51. Describe the "average" person in this group.

CHAPTER 2 TEST

Use tally marks to represent each number.

1. 5 ||||

2. 17 |||| |||| |||| ||

3. 27 |||| |||| |||| |||| |||| ||

4. 45 |||| |||| |||| |||| |||| |||| |||| |||| ||||

The number of people attending a science club per day is listed at the right. Round answers to the nearest whole number.

28	42	31	26
47	30	22	31
38	31	22	28
	36	40	

5. Make a frequency table for the data. Use tally marks. **For answer, see Teacher Guide.**

6. Find the range. 25

7. Find the mode. 31

8. Find the mean. 32

9. Find the median. 31

Which average—mode, mean, or median—would best describe each of the following?

10. miles driven per year mean

11. favorite color of art students mode

12. age of Americans median

13. grades on a test median or mean

The number of pushups each student did on a fitness test are listed at the right.

58	43	48	50	60
56	85	50	43	

14. Find the mode. 43, 50

15. Find the mean. 54.8

16. Find the median. 50

17. Which average—mode, mean, or median—best describes the test results? median

The heights (in centimeters) of the members of the chamber chorus are listed at the right.

157	154	157
169	168	155
162	155	165
173	155	

18. Find the range. 19 cm

19. Find the mode. 155 cm

20. Find the mean. 160.9 cm

21. Find the median. 157 cm

The ages of the members of a drama team are listed at the right.

23	27	31
29	21	19
23	26	30

22. Find the median age. 26 years

23. Find the mean age. 25.4 years

24. Which average, median or mean, is most descriptive of the ages? **Since the median and mean are quite close, either average is satisfactory.**

25. Suppose the youngest member was 18 and the oldest 64. How would the mean and median be affected? median—no change, mean becomes 29

44 *Everyday Statistics*

CUMULATIVE REVIEW

Use the timetable to answer the following. Pages 4–5

MON THROUGH FRI — WEST					
LEAVE	LEAVE	DUE	LEAVE	LEAVE	DUE
STARR AND THIRD	MAPLE AND LENOX	SUNLAWN AND MIAMI	STARR AND THIRD	MAPLE AND LENOX	SUNLAWN AND MIAMI
8:22	8:39	9:01	12:07	12:24	12:46
8:37	8:54	9:16	12:22	12:39	1:01
8:52	9:09	9:31	12:37	12:54	1:16
9:07	9:24	9:46	12:52	1:09	1:31
9:22	9:39	10:01	1:07	1:24	1:46

1. Suppose you board at Starr and Third at 12:37 P.M. When will you arrive at Sunlawn and Miami? 1:16 P.M.

2. Ms. Ho has a business appointment at Sunlawn and Miami at 10:00 A.M. What is the latest time she can board at Maple and Lenox? 9:24 A.M.

Use the chart on page 6 to find the cost of sending each letter first class with the given weight. Pages 6–7

3. 9 oz
$1.58

4. $3\frac{1}{2}$ oz
$0.73

5. $11\frac{1}{4}$ oz
$2.09

6. 8 oz
$1.41

7. $6\frac{3}{4}$ oz
$1.24

Use the chart on page 8 to find whether each call will be charged full rate, 40% discount, or 60% discount. Pages 8–9

8. 5:45 P.M.; Mon.
40% discount

9. 9:00 A.M.; Wed.
full rate

10. 11:05 P.M.; Fri.
60% discount

11. 2:20 P.M.; Tues.
full rate

12. 10:30 A.M.; Sun.
60% discount

13. 6:17 P.M.; Thurs.
40% discount

If line 37 (taxable income) is—		And you are—			
At least	But less than	Single	Married filing jointly *	Married filing separately	Head of a household
			Your tax is—		
8,000					
8,000	8,050	746	519	858	680
8,050	8,100	754	526	866	687
8,100	8,150	761	533	874	694
8,150	8,200	769	540	882	701

Solve. Use the federal income tax table. Pages 14–15

14. Juan Verdes is single. He earns $8,150 a year. His withholding tax is $825. Does he receive a refund or make an additional payment? refund

15. Karen Young is head of the household. She earned $8,127 last year. How much tax did she owe? $694

16. Chuck Rader is single. He earned $8,079 last year. How much tax did he owe? $754

The scores on a 100-point test are listed at the right. Pages 36–37

93, 37, 68, 59, 87, 86, 68, 75, 68, 75, 93, 100, 75, 83, 75, 77, 92, 81, 68, 72, 94, 100, 80

17. Make a frequency table for the set of data.
For answer, see Teacher Guide.

18. Find the range.
63

19. Find the mode.
68 and 75

20. Find the mean.
78.5

21. Find the median.
77

Which average—mode, mean, or median—would best describe each of the following? Why? Pages 40–41

22. brown, blue, blue, black, brown, blue, blue
mode; most frequent

23. 5, 7, 9, 11, 13, 15, 17, 50
median; one very large value affects mean

24. 21, 60, 85, 93, 97, 100
median; one very small value affects mean

25. 9, 47, 47, 47, 47, 60, 110 mode or median; most frequent value is also middle value

Ratio, Proportion, and Percent

3-1 Ratios

Objective: To use a ratio to compare two numbers and to write ratios as fractions.

A **ratio** is a comparison of two numbers. The ratio that compares the number of miles per gallon (mpg) for the Auto II to the number of miles per gallon for the Sporty may be written as follows:

	Sporty	Auto II
	$12,600	$15,400
	2 doors	4 doors
	4 passengers	5 passengers
	32 mpg	26 mpg
	4 cylinders	6 cylinders

26 out of 32, 26 to 32, 26:32, $\frac{26}{32}$

A ratio can be written as a fraction in simplest form.

Example

Write $\frac{26}{32}$ in simplest form.

Divide the numerator and denominator by their greatest common factor (GCF). The GCF of 26 and 32 is 2. The simplest form of $\frac{26}{32}$ is $\frac{13}{16}$.

$$\frac{26 \div 2}{32 \div 2} = \frac{13}{16}$$

Basic Skills Appendix, Pages 445, 446, 448, 449
Basic: 1–21; Average: 1–21; Enriched: 1–21

Exercises

Write a ratio that compares the following features of the Sporty to the same feature of the Auto II.

1. passengers $\frac{4}{5}$

2. doors $\frac{2}{4}$ or $\frac{1}{2}$

3. cylinders $\frac{4}{6}$ or $\frac{2}{3}$

4. price $\frac{12,600}{15,400}$ or $\frac{9}{11}$

Write each ratio as a fraction in simplest form.

5. 3 to 10 $\frac{3}{10}$

6. 5 out of 7 $\frac{5}{7}$

7. 7:4 $\frac{7}{4}$

8. 3 out of 9 $\frac{1}{3}$

9. 5 out of 25 $\frac{1}{5}$

10. 140 to 112 $\frac{5}{4}$

11. 16 to 18 $\frac{8}{9}$

12. 9:12 $\frac{3}{4}$

13. 21:60 $\frac{7}{20}$

14. 63 out of 105 $\frac{3}{5}$

15. 48 to 144 $\frac{1}{3}$

16. 90 out of 155 $\frac{18}{31}$

17. 14 to 98 $\frac{1}{7}$

18. 84:27 $\frac{28}{9}$

19. 33 out of 396 $\frac{1}{12}$

20. 462:770 $\frac{3}{5}$

Solve.

21. In a certain school, 328 students are female and 240 students are male. What is the ratio of females to males? What is the ratio of males to students? $\frac{328}{240}$ or $\frac{41}{30}$; $\frac{240}{568}$ or $\frac{30}{71}$

Teacher Resource Book, Page 89

47

3-2 Rate

Objective: To find unit rates.

A car being driven 55 miles per hour travels about 483 feet in 6 seconds. 483:6 compares feet to seconds.

A **rate** is a comparison of two measurements that have different units. $\frac{483\ feet}{6\ seconds}$ ▶ Rate

A rate with a denominator of 1 is called a **unit rate.** A unit rate can be found by dividing both the numerator and denominator of the rate by the number in the denominator.

$$\frac{483\ feet \div 6}{6\ seconds \div 6} = \frac{80.5\ feet}{1\ second}$$ ▶ Unit Rate

The car travels about 80.5 feet per second.

Unit rates can be used in solving problems.

Example

Beth Johnson paid $5.53 for 7 gallons of regular gasoline. At another station, Shelly Clark paid $4.86 for 6 gallons. Who paid the better rate? Find the unit rates and compare.

$\frac{\$5.53}{7}\ \frac{cost}{gallons}$ ▶ $\frac{\$5.53 \div 7}{7\ gallons \div 7} = \frac{\$0.79}{1\ gallon}$ **5.53** ⌹ **7** ⌹ *0.79*   Beth paid $0.79 for 1 gallon of gasoline.

$\frac{\$4.86}{6}\ \frac{cost}{gallons}$ ▶ $\frac{\$4.86 \div 6}{6\ gallons \div 6} = \frac{\$0.81}{1\ gallon}$ **4.86** ⌹ **6** ⌹ *0.81*   Shelly paid $0.81 for 1 gallon of gasoline.

Since $0.79 is less than $0.81, Beth paid the better rate.

Key Skills

The Key Skills provides practice of skills needed in the exercises.

Divide.

```
    1.59          3 5              2 3
5)7.95       3.2.)112.0.      4.8.)110.4.
 −5              −96              −96
  2 9            16 0            14 4
 −2 5           −16 0           −14 4
   45               0               0
  −45
    0
```

1. $\overset{1.72}{4)6.88}$ 2. $\overset{25}{4.2)105}$

3. $\overset{6}{2.2)13.2}$ 4. $\overset{20}{11.6)232}$

5. $5.61 \div 3$ **1.87**   6. $43.2 \div 1.8$ **24**

7. $169.4 \div 12.1$ **14**   8. $84 \div 5.25$ **16**

Exercises

Rates are listed below without units.

Write each of the following as a rate. Then write each rate as a unit rate.

1. 96 feet in 4 seconds $\frac{96}{4}, \frac{24}{1}$

2. 300 words typed in 5 minutes $\frac{300}{5}, \frac{60}{1}$

3. 8 quarts in 2 gallons $\frac{8}{2}, \frac{4}{1}$

4. 168 miles on 6 gallons of gas $\frac{168}{6}, \frac{28}{1}$

5. 300 bushels in 6 acres $\frac{300}{6}, \frac{50}{1}$

6. 96¢ for 8 oranges $\frac{0.96}{8}, \frac{0.12}{1}$

7. $40.00 for 4 hours $\frac{40}{4}, \frac{10}{1}$

8. 72 hours in 3 days $\frac{72}{3}, \frac{24}{1}$

9. 3,600 revolutions in 6 minutes $\frac{3,600}{6}, \frac{600}{1}$

10. $2.40 for 6 cans of soda $\frac{2.40}{6}, \frac{0.40}{1}$

11. 250 grams in 2.5 liters $\frac{250}{2.5}, \frac{100}{1}$

12. 140 kilometers in 2.5 hours $\frac{140}{2.5}, \frac{56}{1}$

13. $720 in 3 months $\frac{720}{3}, \frac{240}{1}$

14. $5.40 for 6 minutes $\frac{5.40}{6}, \frac{0.90}{1}$

15. 342 meters in 9 seconds $\frac{342}{9}, \frac{38}{1}$

16. 7,000 meters in 7 kilometers $\frac{7,000}{7}, \frac{1,000}{1}$

17. $3.95 for 5 heads of lettuce $\frac{3.95}{5}, \frac{0.79}{1}$

18. $10.15 for 7 gallons $\frac{10.15}{7}, \frac{1.45}{1}$

19. 9.6 meters in 0.4 seconds $\frac{9.6}{0.4}, \frac{24}{1}$

20. 495 miles in 11 hours $\frac{495}{11}, \frac{45}{1}$

21. 301 kilometers in 3.5 hours $\frac{301}{3.5}, \frac{86}{1}$

22. $6.32 for 8 pounds $\frac{6.32}{8}, \frac{0.79}{1}$

23. 58,080 feet in 11 miles $\frac{58,080}{11}, \frac{5,280}{1}$

24. 149.5 miles on 6.5 gallons $\frac{149.5}{6.5}, \frac{23}{1}$

Determine which size is the better buy.

25. Cereal 10 oz—71¢
    15 oz—99¢ **15 oz—99¢**

26. Mayonnaise 8 oz—89¢
    16 oz—$1.52 **16 oz—$1.52**

27. Detergent 49 oz—$2.57 **49 oz—$2.57**
    5 lb 4 oz—$5.13

28. Peaches 16 oz—46¢ **16 oz—46¢**
    29 oz—87¢

29. Milk 1 qt—72¢
    $\frac{1}{2}$ gal—$1.32 **$\frac{1}{2}$ gal—$1.32**

30. Toothpaste 7 oz—99¢ **7 oz—99¢**
    9 oz—$1.39

Solve.

31. Rick earns $36 in 8 hours. At that rate, how much does he earn working 1 hour? **$4.50**

32. Six cans of soda cost $2.28. At that rate, how much does one can of soda cost? **$0.38**

33. John can mow a $\frac{1}{2}$-acre yard in 50 minutes. At that rate, how much time will it take him to mow a 2-acre yard? **3 hours, 20 min.**

34. The Carsons travel 270 miles in 6 hours. At the same rate, how far do they travel in 1 hour? **45 miles**

35. Carey rides her bicycle at the rate of 14 miles per hour. At that rate, how much time will it take her to ride 49 miles? **3.5 hours**

36. One model train has a speed of 2 feet in 1 second. At that rate, how far does the model train travel in 40 seconds? **80 feet**

37. Marlene can type 56 words per minute. At that rate, how many words can she type in 5 minutes? **280 words**

38. Eight ounces of cheese cost $2.32. At that rate, how much does 1 ounce of cheese cost? **$0.29**

3-3 Proportion

Objective: To use cross products to solve proportions.

Kim Lee is an aerobics instructor. She checks her pulse rate during aerobics classes. During a class, she counts 14 heartbeats in 6 seconds. At this rate, how many times does Kim's heart beat in 60 seconds?

A proportion can be used to answer this question. A **proportion** states that two ratios are equivalent.

Two proportions are shown below.

$$\frac{15}{3} = \frac{5}{1} \qquad \frac{2}{3} = \frac{10}{15}$$

A proportion has two **cross products.** In the proportion $\frac{2}{3} = \frac{10}{15}$, the cross products are 2 × 15 and 3 × 10.

$$30 = \frac{2}{3} \bowtie \frac{10}{15} = 30$$

Two ratios form a proportion if and only if their cross products are equal.

Examples

Use cross products to determine whether each pair of ratios forms a proportion.

A. $\frac{3}{7} \stackrel{?}{=} \frac{9}{21}$

    3 × 21 = 63

    7 × 9 = 63 ▸ 63 = 63, so $\frac{3}{7} = \frac{9}{21}$

B. $\frac{1}{2} \stackrel{?}{=} \frac{3}{5}$

    1 × 5 = 5

    2 × 3 = 6 ▸ 5 ≠ 6, so $\frac{1}{2} \neq \frac{3}{5}$

    ≠ means is not equal to

C. Use this proportion to find Kim's heartbeat in 60 seconds.

  $\frac{14 \text{ heartbeats}}{6 \text{ seconds}} = \frac{n \text{ heartbeats}}{60 \text{ seconds}}$ *In this proportion, n represents the number of heartbeats in 60 seconds.*

  14 × 60 = 6 × n   *The cross products of a proportion are equal.*

    840 = 6 × n   *Multiply.*   14 ⊠ 60 ⊟ *840*

  $\frac{840}{6} = \frac{6 \times n}{6}$ *Divide each side by 6.*   840 ⊟ 6 ⊟ *140*

    140 = n   Kim's heart beats 140 times in 60 seconds.

Basic Skills Appendix, Pages 438, 439
Basic: 1–16, 17–65 odd; Average: 1–66; Enriched: 2–66 even

Exercises

Find the cross products.

1. $\frac{6}{1} = \frac{18}{3}$ 18 = 18   **2.** $\frac{3}{3} = \frac{25}{25}$ 75 = 75   **3.** $\frac{1}{3} = \frac{2}{6}$ 6 = 6   **4.** $\frac{5}{15} = \frac{1}{3}$ 15 = 15

5. $\frac{3}{9} = \frac{2}{6}$ **18 = 18**

6. $\frac{5}{6} = \frac{15}{18}$ **90 = 90**

7. $\frac{3}{12} = \frac{2}{8}$ **24 = 24**

8. $\frac{9}{24} = \frac{3}{8}$ **72 = 72**

9. $\frac{2}{12} = \frac{3}{18}$ **36 = 36**

10. $\frac{4}{5} = \frac{16}{20}$ **80 = 80**

11. $\frac{5}{10} = \frac{3}{6}$ **30 = 30**

12. $\frac{4}{7} = \frac{8}{14}$ **56 = 56**

13. $\frac{4}{10} = \frac{1}{2.5}$ **10 = 10**

14. $\frac{3}{40} = \frac{4.5}{60}$ **180 = 180**

15. $\frac{7.5}{25} = \frac{3}{10}$ **75 = 75**

16. $\frac{8.6}{25.8} = \frac{1}{3}$ **25.8 = 25.8**

Use cross products to determine whether each pair of ratios forms a proportion. Write yes or no.

17. $\frac{16}{8}$ and $\frac{8}{3}$ **no**

18. $\frac{3}{7}$ and $\frac{4}{9}$ **no**

19. $\frac{1.6}{2} = \frac{4}{5}$ **yes**

20. $\frac{8}{12}$ and $\frac{2}{3}$ **yes**

21. $\frac{4}{8}$ and $\frac{4}{16}$ **no**

22. $\frac{2.4}{3}$ and $\frac{4}{5}$ **yes**

23. $\frac{2}{3}$ and $\frac{6}{12}$ **no**

24. $\frac{6}{7}$ and $\frac{5}{8}$ **no**

25. $\frac{1}{2}$ and $\frac{5.6}{11.2}$ **yes**

26. $\frac{3}{4}$ and $\frac{2}{3}$ **no**

27. $\frac{1}{2}$ and $\frac{5}{10}$ **yes**

28. $\frac{3}{5}$ and $\frac{5}{9}$ **no**

29. $\frac{5}{8}$ and $\frac{10}{16}$ **yes**

30. $\frac{200}{120}$ and $\frac{2}{5}$ **no**

31. $\frac{1.3}{2}$ and $\frac{0.6}{0.1}$ **no**

32. $\frac{1.8}{0.9}$ and $\frac{0.6}{0.3}$ **yes**

Find the missing number.

33. $\frac{6}{12} = \frac{n}{50}$ **25**

34. $\frac{n}{5} = \frac{9}{15}$ **3**

35. $\frac{6}{9} = \frac{n}{15}$ **10**

36. $\frac{6}{21} = \frac{n}{70}$ **20**

37. $\frac{3.5}{7} = \frac{n}{4}$ **2**

38. $\frac{4}{7} = \frac{3}{n}$ **5.25**

39. $\frac{4}{n} = \frac{24}{60}$ **10**

40. $\frac{5}{2} = \frac{20}{n}$ **8**

41. $\frac{3}{n} = \frac{9}{15}$ **5**

42. $\frac{6}{1} = \frac{18}{n}$ **3**

43. $\frac{5}{n} = \frac{4}{1.6}$ **2**

44. $\frac{n}{9} = \frac{3}{2}$ **13.5**

45. $\frac{1}{10} = \frac{3}{m}$ **30**

46. $\frac{14}{16} = \frac{7}{c}$ **8**

47. $\frac{9}{10} = \frac{18}{n}$ **20**

48. $\frac{3}{5} = \frac{y}{42}$ **25.2**

49. $\frac{1}{2} = \frac{x}{15}$ **7.5**

50. $\frac{3}{2} = \frac{t}{10}$ **15**

51. $\frac{5}{4} = \frac{u}{100}$ **125**

52. $\frac{21}{49} = \frac{6}{x}$ **14**

53. $\frac{6}{33} = \frac{2}{a}$ **11**

54. $\frac{2}{3} = \frac{x}{100}$ **66$\frac{2}{3}$**

55. $\frac{1}{8} = \frac{n}{100}$ **12.5**

56. $\frac{5}{8} = \frac{g}{100}$ **62.5**

57. $\frac{8}{n} = \frac{1}{0.21}$ **1.68**

58. $\frac{3}{10} = \frac{7.5}{n}$ **25**

59. $\frac{8.6}{25.8} = \frac{1}{n}$ **3**

60. $\frac{12}{n} = \frac{1}{0.19}$ **2.28**

Solve.

61. One cup of ice cream contains 310 calories. How many calories are in $4\frac{1}{2}$ cups of ice cream? **1,395 calories**

62. Joan walks 5 miles in 1 hour. At that rate, how far can she walk in 36 minutes? **3 miles**

63. A recipe for party mix calls for 2 cups of corn cereal for 10 servings. How much corn cereal is needed for 15 servings? **3 cups**

64. Joel earns $90 in 4 days. At this rate, how many days will it take him to earn $315? **14 days**

65. Mike Johnson's car used 22 gallons of gasoline to travel 308 miles. At that rate, how much gasoline will he use to travel 420 miles? **30 gallons**

66. Becky's heart beats 12 times in 10 seconds. At that rate, how many times does her heart beat in 60 seconds? **72 times**

3-4 Scale Drawings

Objective: To learn how ratios are used in scale drawings.

An interior designer wants to know how furniture will fit into a model home. A scale drawing of the living room and furniture is shown below.

Scale drawings are used to picture things that are too large or too small to be drawn actual size. On the scale drawing below, 1 inch represents 48 inches.

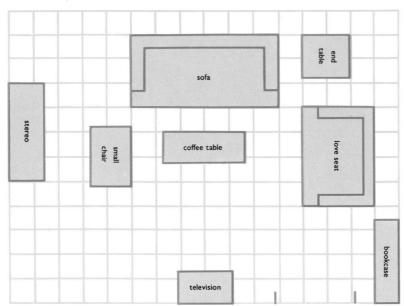

On the scale drawing, the sofa measures $1\frac{1}{2}$ in. What is the length of the actual sofa? Use a proportion to find the actual length, ℓ.

$$\frac{1}{48} = \frac{1\frac{1}{2}}{\ell}$$

$$1 \times \ell = 48 \times 1\frac{1}{2}$$

48 $\boxed{\text{X}}$ **1.5** $\boxed{=}$ **72**

$$\ell = 72$$

The actual length of the sofa is 72 inches.

Key Skills

The Key Skills provides practice of skills needed in the exercises.

$$4 \times \frac{3}{16} = \frac{4}{1} \times \frac{3}{16}$$

$$= \frac{4 \times 3}{1 \times 16}$$

$$= \frac{3}{4}$$

Multiply. Write each product in simplest form.

1. $2 \times \frac{5}{8}$ $1\frac{1}{4}$ **2.** $4 \times \frac{3}{8}$ $1\frac{1}{2}$ **3.** $7 \times \frac{3}{4}$ $5\frac{1}{4}$

4. $48 \times \frac{5}{16}$ 15 **5.** $48 \times \frac{3}{4}$ 36 **6.** $48 \times \frac{1}{32}$ $1\frac{1}{2}$

7. $7 \times \frac{3}{16}$ $1\frac{5}{16}$ **8.** $4 \times \frac{11}{32}$ $1\frac{3}{8}$ **9.** $48 \times 3\frac{5}{16}$ 159

Basic Skills Appendix, Pages 458, 459   Basic: 2–16 even; Average: 1–16; Enriched: 1–16

Exercises

Find the actual measurement of each of the following. The scale drawing measurement is given. Use the scale 1 inch represents 48 inches.

1. love seat, 1 in.   **48 in.**   **2.** width of the room, 3 in.   **144 in.**

3. length of the room, 4 in.   **192 in.**   **4.** bookcase, $\frac{3}{4}$ in.   **36 in.**

5. coffee table, $\frac{7}{8}$ in. **42 in.**

6. television, $\frac{9}{16}$ in. **27 in.**

7. end table, $\frac{7}{16}$ in. **21 in.**

8. small chair, $\frac{5}{8}$ in. **30 in.**

9. width of the doorway, $\frac{13}{16}$ in. **39 in.**

10. width of the coffee table, $\frac{11}{32}$ in. **16.5 in.**

Solve.

11. A photograph is 3 inches wide and 5 inches long. The photograph is enlarged to a width of 9 inches. What is the length of the enlarged photograph? **15 inches**

12. Make a scale drawing of a room in your house and the furniture in that room. Use the scale drawing to see how you could rearrange the furniture.
See students' work.

Mr. Baxter wishes to build a house. On the scale drawing of the house, 1 inch represents 3 feet.

13. If on the scale drawing the dimensions of the bathroom are 2 by 3 inches, what are the actual dimensions? **6 by 9 feet**

14. If the house is to be 57 feet long, what is the length on the scale drawing? **19 inches**

15. If the garage is to be 21 feet wide, what is the width on the scale drawing?
7 inches

16. If the dimensions of the kitchen measure 9 by 12 feet, what are the dimensions on the scale drawing?
3 by 4 inches

This feature presents general topics of mathematics.

Math Break

A turntable, speakers, and amplifier make up a stereo system. The money spent on these components should be in the ratio 1:2:3. The speakers should cost twice as much as the turntable, and the amplifier should cost three times as much as the turntable.

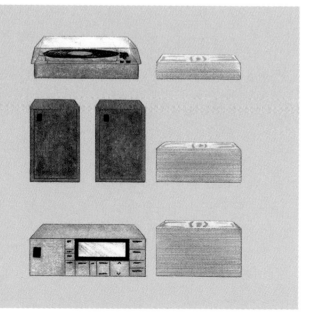

Solve.

1. If you spend $100 on the turntable, how much should you spend on the amplifier?
$300

2. If you have $1,200 to spend, how much should you spend on each of the components?
$200, $400, $600

PRACTICE

Express each of the following in standard form.

1. three hundred ninety **390**

2. forty-five thousand **45,000**

3. seven thousand fifty-one **7,051**

4. thirty-six thousand ten **36,010**

Write the number named by each digit in 53.216.

5. 5 **50**

6. 3 **3**

7. 2 **0.2**

8. 1 **0.01**

9. 6 **0.006**

Write each amount in words. (Example: $8.13 ▶ eight dollars and $\frac{13}{100}$)

10. $63.59 **Sixty-three dollars and $\frac{59}{100}$**

11. $21.08 **Twenty-one dollars and $\frac{08}{100}$**

12. $50.00 **Fifty dollars and $\frac{no}{100}$**

13. $809.46 **Eight hundred nine dollars and $\frac{46}{100}$**

14. $12.99 **Twelve dollars and $\frac{99}{100}$**

15. $7.65 **Seven dollars and $\frac{65}{100}$**

Round to the nearest cent.

16. $153.955 **$153.96**

17. $66.9375 **$66.94**

18. $162.504 **$162.50**

19. $170.505 **$170.51**

20. $121.905 **$121.91**

21. $84.4665 **$84.47**

Estimate. Answers may vary. Typical answers are given.

22. 329
+ 215
500

23. 727
− 249
500

24. 43
× 6
240

25. 592
× 6
3,600

26. 367
× 21
8,000

Add or subtract.

27. 379
+ 641
1,020

28. 561
+ 649
1,210

29. 921
+ 358
1,279

30. 5,768
+ 396
6,164

31. 1,784
+ 2,635
4,419

32. 802
− 45
757

33. 649
− 183
466

34. 810
− 264
546

35. 4,296
− 267
4,029

36. 2,408
− 2,403
5

37. 598
299
+ 37
934

38. 656
287
+ 59
1,002

39. 498
399
+ 62
959

40. 1,706
596
+ 35
2,337

41. 3,621
789
+ 99
4,509

42. 503
− 24
479

43. 503
− 124
379

44. 769
− 345
424

45. 7,621
− 569
7,052

46. 6,980
− 294
6,686

47. 4,621
+ 321
4,942

48. 2,431
+ 3,724
6,155

49. 8,038
+ 1,276
9,314

50. 7,047
+ 912
7,959

51. 8,263
+ 841
9,104

52. 736
124
+ 24
884

53. 9,721
368
+ 294
10,383

54. 7,000
− 2,000
5,000

55. 6,218
− 5,167
1,051

56. 3,624
− 1,612
2,012

Multiply or divide.

57.   725
  × 494
  358,150

58.   924
  × 214
  197,736

59.   6,450
  × 30
  193,500

60.   5,785
  × 56
  323,960

61.   5,600
  × 210
  1,176,000

62. 41)451 11

63. 37)777 21

64. 33)957 29

65. 169)845 5

66. 197)985 5

Add.

67.   4.09
  + 1.97
  6.06

68.   26.8
  + 49.5
  76.3

69.   4.79
  + 6.50
  11.29

70.   38.63
  + 24.59
  63.22

71.   4.989
  + 4.697
  9.686

72.   2.7
  + 2.3
  5.0

73.   2.79
  + 6.65
  9.44

74.   27.06
  + 7.06
  34.12

75.   59.65
  + 10.85
  70.50

76.   1.034
  + 60.08
  61.114

Subtract.

77.   1.7
  − 0.9
  0.8

78.   0.14
  − 0.09
  0.05

79.   2.11
  − 1.02
  1.09

80.   4.2
  − 1.4
  2.8

81.   0.21
  − 0.07
  0.14

82.   0.497
  − 0.168
  0.329

83.   4.063
  − 3.059
  1.004

84.   2.83
  − 0.95
  1.88

85.   4.824
  − 0.855
  3.969

86.   2.693
  − 1.487
  1.206

Solve.

87. Paige is saving to buy a car. The cost of the car is $4,876. She has $2,000 in the bank. How much more does she need to save? **$2,876.00**

88. Ricky wrote 135 checks last year and 200 checks this year. How many more checks did he write this year? **65 checks**

This feature presents general topics of mathematics.

Math Break

Most businesses consider payment within 30 days the same as cash. Therefore, it is important to make payments on time to avoid credit costs. What is the last day payment can be made for an item purchased on March 3?

  31 *days in March*
  − 3 *date of purchase*
  28 *remaining days of March*

  30 *total days*
  − 28 *remaining days of March*
  2 *days in April*

The payment must be made by April 2.

Find the 30-day deadline date for the purchase dates given.

1. October 5
   Nov. 4

2. September 9
   Oct. 9

3. November 17
   Dec. 17

4. May 21
   June 20

3-5 Percents

**Objective: To change a fraction, mixed numeral, or decimal to a percent.
To change a percent to a fraction, mixed numeral, or decimal.**

The Home City Stars made 53 out of 100, or 53%, of their free-throw attempts. **Percents** are ratios that compare numbers to one hundred. Percent means hundredths or per 100. The percent symbol (%) means that a number is being compared to 100.

53 out of 100 ▸ $\frac{53}{100}$ ▸ 0.53 ▸ 53%

In the figure at the right, 53% of the squares is shaded.

To change a fraction to a percent, set up a proportion. Use 100 as the denominator of one ratio. Then use cross products to solve the proportion.

Example

A. Change $\frac{2}{5}$ to a percent.

$\frac{2}{5} = \frac{n}{100}$ ▸ $2 \times 100 = 5 \times n$ *100 is the denominator of the second ratio.*

$200 = 5 \times n$

$\frac{200}{5} = \frac{5 \times n}{5}$

$40 = n$

So, $\frac{2}{5} = \frac{40}{100}$ or 40%.   *Since percent means hundredths, you can write $\frac{40}{100}$ as 40%.*

Mixed numerals can be changed to percents. Change the mixed numeral to an improper fraction. Then change the fraction to a percent.

Example

B. Change $1\frac{3}{4}$ to a percent.

$1\frac{3}{4} = \frac{7}{4}$

$\frac{7}{4} = \frac{n}{100}$ ▸ $7 \times 100 = 4 \times n$

$700 = 4 \times n$

$\frac{700}{4} = \frac{4 \times n}{4}$

700 ÷ 4 = 175

$175 = n$ *Fractions and decimals greater than one are expressed as percents greater than one hundred percent.*

So, $1\frac{3}{4} = 175\%$.

Percents can be changed to fractions. This is done by changing the percent to a fraction having a denominator of 100.

Examples

C. **Change 22% to a fraction.**

$$22\% = \frac{22}{100}$$

$$= \frac{\overset{11}{\cancel{22}}}{\underset{50}{\cancel{100}}}$$

$$= \frac{11}{50}$$

D. **Change $36\frac{2}{3}\%$ to a fraction.**

$$36\frac{2}{3}\% = \frac{36\frac{2}{3}}{100}$$

$$= 36\frac{2}{3} \div 100 \quad \textit{Change } 36\frac{2}{3} \textit{ to } \frac{110}{3}.$$

$$= \frac{\overset{11}{\cancel{110}}}{3} \times \frac{1}{\underset{10}{\cancel{100}}} \quad \textit{The reciprocal}$$
$$\textit{of 100 is } \frac{1}{100}.$$

$$= \frac{11}{30}$$

E. **Change 230% to a mixed numeral.**

$$230\% = \frac{230}{100}$$

$$= \frac{\overset{23}{\cancel{230}}}{\underset{10}{\cancel{100}}}$$

$$= \frac{23}{10}$$

$$= 2\frac{3}{10}$$

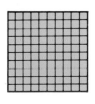 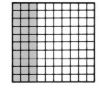

$$230\% = 2\frac{3}{10}$$

To change a decimal to a percent, multiply by 100. (This can be done by moving the decimal point two places to the right.) Attach the percent symbol.

Examples

F. **Change 0.17 to a percent.**

$$0.17 \times 100 = 17 \quad > \quad 17\%$$

G. **Change 3.0 to a percent.**

$$3.0 \times 100 = 300 \quad > \quad 300\%$$

To change a percent to a decimal, omit the percent symbol. Then divide by 100. (This can be done by moving the decimal point two places to the left.)

Examples

H. **Change 14.5% to a decimal.**

$$14.5\% \quad \rightarrow \quad 14.5 \div 100 = 0.145$$

14.5 ⌸ 100 🟰 *0.145*

I. **Change 7% to a decimal.**

$$7\% \quad \rightarrow \quad 7 \div 100 = 0.07$$

7 ⌸ 100 🟰 *0.07*

The Key Skills provides practice of skills needed in the exercises.

Key Skills

Change each mixed numeral to an improper fraction.

$$16\frac{3}{4} \quad \rightarrow \quad \frac{(16 \times 4) + 3}{4} = \frac{67}{4}$$

1. $4\frac{6}{7}$ $\frac{34}{7}$ **2.** $10\frac{16}{13}$ $\frac{146}{13}$ **3.** $14\frac{2}{3}$ $\frac{44}{3}$ **4.** $34\frac{4}{9}$ $\frac{310}{9}$

5. $19\frac{5}{8}$ $\frac{157}{8}$ **6.** $12\frac{3}{5}$ $\frac{63}{5}$ **7.** $27\frac{1}{9}$ $\frac{244}{9}$ **8.** $33\frac{5}{6}$ $\frac{203}{6}$

Change each improper fraction to a mixed numeral.

$$\frac{46}{5} \quad \rightarrow \quad 5\overline{)46} \quad \rightarrow \quad \frac{46}{5} = 9\frac{1}{5}$$
$$\underline{-45}$$
$$1$$

9. $\frac{15}{2}$ $7\frac{1}{2}$ **10.** $\frac{53}{10}$ $5\frac{3}{10}$ **11.** $\frac{42}{5}$ $8\frac{2}{5}$ **12.** $\frac{171}{20}$ $8\frac{11}{20}$

13. $\frac{79}{3}$ $26\frac{1}{3}$ **14.** $\frac{47}{4}$ $11\frac{3}{4}$ **15.** $\frac{55}{9}$ $6\frac{1}{9}$ **16.** $\frac{35}{6}$ $5\frac{5}{6}$

Basic Skills Appendix, Pages 451, 461
Basic: 2–56 even; Average: 1–57; Enriched: 1–57 odd

Exercises

Change each decimal, fraction, or mixed numeral to a percent.

1. $\frac{19}{100}$ **19%**   **2.** $\frac{7}{50}$ **14%**   **3.** 0.25 **25%**   **4.** 7.5 **750%**   **5.** 0.9 **90%**

6. $5\frac{1}{2}$ **550%**   **7.** $2\frac{1}{4}$ **225%**   **8.** $6\frac{2}{5}$ **640%**   **9.** $10\frac{1}{10}$ **1,010%**   **10.** $\frac{11}{20}$ **55%**

11. $\frac{9}{25}$ **36%**   **12.** $\frac{7}{8}$ **87.5%**   **13.** 0.015 **1.5%**   **14.** 2.0 **200%**   **15.** 0.092 **9.2%**

16. 0.1 **10%**   **17.** $\frac{3}{5}$ **60%**   **18.** $3\frac{3}{4}$ **375%**   **19.** $7\frac{6}{25}$ **724%**   **20.** 9.8 **980%**

21. $\frac{1}{5}$ **20%**   **22.** $\frac{4}{25}$ **16%**   **23.** 15.5 **1,550%**   **24.** $5\frac{5}{8}$ **562.5%**   **25.** 0.0005 **0.05%**

Change each percent to a decimal.

26. 65% **0.65**   **27.** 12% **0.12**   **28.** 100% **1.0**   **29.** 20% **0.2**   **30.** 4.75% **0.0475**

31. 304% **3.04**   **32.** 211% **2.11**   **33.** 157% **1.57**   **34.** 30.3% **0.303**   **35.** 3% **0.03**

36. 7% **0.07**   **37.** 50% **0.5**   **38.** 5% **0.05**   **39.** 0.5% **0.005**   **40.** 0.05% **0.0005**

Change each percent to a fraction or mixed numeral.

41. 70% $\frac{7}{10}$ **42.** 24% $\frac{6}{25}$ **43.** 3% $\frac{3}{100}$ **44.** 200% $\frac{2}{1}$ **45.** 116% $1\frac{4}{25}$

46. $37\frac{1}{2}$% $\frac{3}{8}$ **47.** $5\frac{1}{4}$% $\frac{21}{400}$ **48.** 93% $\frac{93}{100}$ **49.** 125% $1\frac{1}{4}$ **50.** 1% $\frac{1}{100}$

51. 450% $4\frac{1}{2}$ **52.** 42% $\frac{21}{50}$ **53.** $10\frac{3}{4}$% $\frac{43}{400}$ **54.** $63\frac{1}{2}$% $\frac{127}{200}$ **55.** $83\frac{1}{3}$% $\frac{5}{6}$

Solve.

56. There are 18 girls named Lisa out of a class with 150 girls. What percent of the girls are named Lisa? **12%**

57. Louis completed 24 passes out of 40 attempts. What percent of his passes did he complete? **60%**

3-6 Percent of a Number

Objective: To find the percent of a number.

The table below shows how 2,100 students responded to four statements about mathematics.

	A. I really want to do well in math.	B. Math is more for boys than girls.	C. I can get along well in everyday life without math.	D. I am taking math only because I have to.
Agree	84%	2%	10%	26%
Undecided	12%	7%	13%	11%
Disagree	4%	91%	77%	63%

Of the 2,100 students, 84% agree with statement A.
How many students agree with statement A?

You can use a proportion to answer this question.

$\dfrac{\text{Percentage}}{\text{Base}} = \text{Rate or } \dfrac{P}{B} = \dfrac{r}{100}$

The percentage (P) is compared to the total.
The base (B) is the total.
Percent means per one hundred.
Always compare r to 100.

Example

What number is 84% of 2,100?

$\dfrac{P}{B} = \dfrac{r}{100}$

$\dfrac{P}{2,100} = \dfrac{84}{100}$ *2,100 is the base. 84% or $\frac{84}{100}$ is the rate.*

$100 \times P = 176,400$ *Cross multiply. $100 \times P$; $84 \times 2,100 = 176,400$*

$\dfrac{100 \times P}{100} = \dfrac{176,400}{100}$ *Divide each side by 100.*

$P = 1,764$ Of the 2,100 students, 1,764 agree with statement A.

Basic Skills Appendix, Pages 427, 431
Basic: 1–23 odd; Average: 1–24; Enriched: 2–20 even, 21–24

Exercises

Use the table above to find the number of students for each situation.

1. agree with statement C **210 students**

2. undecided on statement A **252 students**

3. disagree with statement D **1,323 students**

4. undecided on statement B **147 students**

Solve.

5. What number is 30% of 150? **45**

6. 25% of 24 is what number? **6**

7. 18% of 25.5 is what number? **4.59**

8. What number is 10.5% of 36? **3.78**

9. What number is 45% of 36? **16.2**

10. 50% of 100.8 is what number? **50.4**

11. 120% of 60 is what number? **72**   **12.** What number is 0.8% of 15? **0.12**

13. 150% of 73 **109.5**   **14.** 0.1% of 300 **0.3**   **15.** 25% of 40.4 **10.1**   **16.** $37\frac{1}{2}$% of 320 **120**

17. $33\frac{1}{3}$% of 9.6 **3.2**   **18.** 35% of 35 **12.25**   **19.** 0.5% of 148 **0.74**   **20.** 8% of 4.5 **0.36**

Solve.

21. Mr. Graham's dinner came to $16.25. How much should he leave for a 20% tip? **$3.25**

22. Shannon earned 84% on a math test. If there were 50 questions, how many did she answer correctly? **42 questions**

23. Carl budgets 15% of his monthly income for groceries. If his monthly income is $840, what amount does he budget for groceries? **$126**

24. Of the light bulbs produced at Mann Lighting, 3% are defective. If 2,200 are produced each hour, how many are defective? **66 light bulbs**

This feature promotes students' mental abilities in computation and reasonableness.

Mental Math

Many percent problems can be solved mentally.

Find 50% of 300.
50% is $\frac{1}{2}$ of a number.
50% of 300 is 150.

Find 25% of 20.
25% is $\frac{1}{4}$ of a number.
25% of 20 is 5.

Find 40% of 110.
Express 40% as 4 × 10%. 10% is $\frac{1}{10}$ of a number. 10% of 110 is 11.
So, 40% of 110 is 4 × 11 or 44.

Find 15% of 240.
Express 15% as 10% + 5%. 10% of 240 is 24.
5% of 240 is 12.   *5% of 240 is $\frac{1}{2}$ of 10% of 240.*
So, 15% of 240 is 24 + 12 or 36.

Solve using the strategy shown above.

1. 50% of 80   **2.** 25% of 40   **3.** 40% of 60   **4.** 25% of 100

5. 10% of 200 **40**   **6.** 5% of 200 **10**   **7.** 15% of 200 **24**   **8.** 50% of 600 **25**

9. 20% of 450 **20**   **10.** 15% of 300 **10**   **11.** 25% of 400 **30**   **12.** 30% of 120 **300**

90   **45**   **100**   **36**

3-7 *What Percent One Number Is of Another*

Objective: To find the percent one number is of another.

Eve Cohan is an airlines reservation agent. Her responsibilities include answering customers' questions, calculating expenses, and using a computer terminal to book reservations. She also helps passengers plan their trips. The qualifications for Eve's job are a high school education, good communication skills, and problem-solving abilities. She must have a pleasant appearance and personality. For one month, Eve received formal classroom instruction. She then worked under a supervisor and experienced agents for several weeks.

From November 10 through March 10, the round-trip airfare from Detroit to Tampa is $500. From June 10 through September 10, there is a $170 discount. What is the percent of savings by going to Tampa in the summer?

Use $\frac{P}{B} = \frac{r}{100}$ to solve this problem.

Examples

A. Find what percent $170 is of $500.

$$\frac{P}{B} = \frac{r}{100}$$

$$\frac{\$170}{\$500} = \frac{r}{100} \quad \text{The percentage is \$170 and the base is 500.}$$

$$17,000 = 500 \times r$$

$$\frac{17,000}{500} = \frac{500 \times r}{500} \quad \text{Estimate: } 15,000 \div 500 = 30 \qquad 17000 \; \boxed{\div} \; 500 \; \boxed{=} \; 34$$

$$34 = r$$

The airfare from Detroit to Tampa is 34% less during the summer.

B. What percent of 21 is 63?

$$\frac{P}{B} = \frac{r}{100}$$

$$\frac{63}{21} = \frac{r}{100} \quad \text{63 is the percentage. 21 is the base.}$$

$$6,300 = 21 \times r$$

$$\frac{6,300}{21} = \frac{21 \times r}{21} \quad \text{Estimate: } 6,000 \div 20 \text{ is } 300 \qquad 6300 \; \boxed{\div} \; 21 \; \boxed{=} \; 300$$

$$300 = r$$

So, 63 is 300% of 21.

Exercises

Name the percentage, base, or rate.

1. 6 is what percent of 8? **P = 6, B = 8**
2. What percent of 40 is 25? **P = 25, B = 40**
3. 52% of 40 is what number? **B = 40, r = 52%**
4. What number is 110% of 80? **B = 80, r = 110%**
5. What percent of 24 is 18? **P = 18, B = 24**
6. What percent of 20 is 12? **P = 12, B = 20**
7. 24 is what percent of 16? **P = 24, B = 16**
8. What number is 37.5% of 16? **B = 16, r = 37.5%**
9. What number is 116% of 30? **B = 30, r = 116%**
10. What percent of 212 is 55? **P = 55, B = 212**

Solve.

11. What percent of 18 is 9? **50%**
12. What percent of 64 is 16? **25%**
13. 14 is what percent of 70? **20%**
14. 9 is what percent of 4? **225%**
15. What percent of 20 is 27? **135%**
16. $10\frac{1}{2}$ is what percent of 20? **$52\frac{1}{2}$%**
17. 63 is what percent of 42? **150%**
18. What percent of 260 is $58\frac{1}{2}$? **$22\frac{1}{2}$%**
19. 18 is what percent of 36? **50%**
20. What percent of 4 is 10? **250%**
21. What percent of 16 is 6? **37.5%**
22. 18.4 is what percent of 23? **80%**
23. What percent of 7.2 is 36? **500%**
24. 12 is what percent of 36? **$33\frac{1}{3}$%**
25. 148.2 is what percent of 190? **78%**
26. What percent of 54 is 24.3? **45%**
27. What percent of 32 is 40? **125%**
28. 8 is what percent of 32? **25%**
29. What percent of 16 is 5? **$31\frac{1}{4}$%**
30. What percent of 35 is 0.7? **2%**
31. 15 is what percent of 75? **20%**
32. What percent of 31 is 0.62? **2%**

33. Tom and Ellen purchase a new house for $63,000. Their down payment is $12,600. What percent of the total cost is the down payment? **20%**

34. Dorothy paid $32.30 for a model ship. This model usually sells for $38.00. What rate of discount did Dorothy receive on her purchase? **15%**

35. While on vacation, 9 people decide to go white-water rafting. They each pay $12 to have a guide take them downriver on a raft. The guide's total earnings are $54. What percent of the total amount paid does the guide receive? **50%**

62 *Ratio, Proportion, and Percent*

3-8 Finding a Number When a Percent of It Is Known

Objective: To find a number when a percent of it is known.

Matt Logan paid $3,240 for a used car. He paid 75% of the asking price. What was the asking price?

To find a number when a percent of it is known, use the proportion $\frac{P}{B} = \frac{r}{100}$.

Examples

A. **75% of what number is $3,240?**

$$\frac{P}{B} = \frac{r}{100}$$

$$\frac{\$3,240}{B} = \frac{75}{100} \quad \text{\$3,240 is the percentage. 75\% or } \tfrac{75}{100} \text{ is the rate.}$$

$$324,000 = B \times 75$$

$$\frac{324,000}{75} = \frac{B \times 75}{75} \quad \text{Estimate: } 320,000 \div 80 \text{ is } 4,000. \quad 324000 \;\div\; 75 \;=\; 4320$$

$$4,320 = B \quad \text{Is the answer reasonable?} \quad \textbf{Yes}$$

The asking price of the car was $4,320.

B. **$33\frac{1}{3}$% of what number is 9?**

$$\frac{P}{B} = \frac{r}{100}$$

$$\frac{9}{B} = \frac{33\frac{1}{3}}{100} \quad \text{9 is the percentage. } \tfrac{33\frac{1}{3}}{100} \text{ is the rate.}$$

$$900 = B \times 33\frac{1}{3} \quad \text{Find the cross products.}$$

$$900 \div 33\frac{1}{3} = B \times 33\frac{1}{3} \div 33\frac{1}{3} \quad \text{Divide each side by } 33\frac{1}{3} \text{ to find B.}$$

$$900 \div \frac{100}{3} = B \times \frac{100}{3} \div \frac{100}{3} \quad \text{Change } 33\frac{1}{3} \text{ to an improper fraction.} \quad 33 \;\times\; 3 \;+\; 1 \;=\; 100$$

$$900 \times \frac{3}{100} = B \quad \text{Multiply by the reciprocal of } \tfrac{100}{3}. \; \tfrac{100}{3} \div \tfrac{100}{3} = 1, B \times 1 = B$$

$$27 = B \quad 900 \;\times\; 3 \;\div\; 100 \;=\; 27$$

So, $33\frac{1}{3}$% of 27 is 9.

Basic Skills Appendix, Page 460

Basic: 1–20, 21–23 odd; Average: 1–24; Enriched: 2–20 even, 21–24

Exercises

Solve.

1. 20% of what number is 15? **75**

2. 42 is 25% of what number? **168**

3. 16 is 32% of what number? **50**

4. 50% of what number is 15.8? **31.6**

5. 64% of what number is 24? $37\frac{1}{2}$ **6.** 25 is 25% of what number? **100**

7. 84 is $33\frac{1}{3}$% of what number? **252**   **8.** $37\frac{1}{2}$% of what number is 9? **24**

Name the percentage, base, or rate. Then solve.

9. 3% of what number is 6?
$P = 6, r = 3\%; 200$

10. 86 is 43% of what number?
$P = 86, r = 43\%; 200$

11. 84 is what percent of 300?
$P = 84, B = 300; 28\%$

12. 78% of what number is 62.4?
$P = 62.4, r = 78\%; 80$

13. What number is 5% of 48?
$B = 48, r = 5\%; 2.4$

14. 608 is 95% of what number?
$P = 608, r = 98\%; 640$

15. 12.5% of what number is 6?
$P = 6, r = 12.5\%; 48$

16. 24 is 150% of what number?
$P = 24, r = 150\%; 16$

17. $33\frac{1}{3}$ of what number is 100? $P = 100, r = 33\frac{1}{3}\%;$ 300

18. 82 is what percent of 400?
$P = 82; B = 400; 20.5\%$

19. 37.5% of 80 is what number?
$B = 80, r = 37.5\%; 30$

20. $12\frac{1}{2}$% of what number is 91?
$P = 91, r = 12\frac{1}{2}\%; 728$

Solve.

21. In a class election, Mark received 55% of the votes. Mark received 77 votes. How many votes were cast? **140 votes**

22. Mia's soccer team won 75% of their games. If they won 12 games, how many games did they play? **16 games**

23. Annette received $2,100 as a 7% commission for selling merchandise at Hobby Town. What was the total amount of merchandise that Annette sold? **$30,000**

24. Four percent of the students enrolled at Lane High School live on Lane Avenue. If 14 students live on Lane Avenue, how many students attend Lane High School? **350 students**

This feature provides general topics about the uses of a computer.

 ## Computer

Victoria Thompson is a data entry operator. She enters the information on new employees in the computer. She enters the employee's name, address, telephone number, and other information. Some of the data she enters contain only numbers. These are **numeric** data. Other data may contain letters, numbers, and other symbols. These are **alphanumeric** data.

State whether the following information is numeric (numbers only) or is alphanumeric.

  1. employee's name **A**

  2. employee's street address **A**

  3. ZIP code **N**

  4. bank account number **N**

  5. nearest relative **A**

  6. number of children **N**

  7. Social Security number **A**

  8. age **N**

  9. hourly pay **N**

  10. job title **A**

3-9 Problem Solving: Using Ratios, Proportions, and Percents

Objective: To solve verbal problems involving ratios, proportions, and percents.

Like most wage earners, Ted Harris contributes to social security. The social security rate in 1986 is 7.15%. Find the weekly and yearly deductions if Ted's weekly wage is $235.64.

 Read

You must find the weekly and yearly deductions. You know the social security rate and Ted's weekly wage.

 Decide

To find the weekly deduction, multiply the rate by Ted's weekly wage.

Solve

Weekly Deduction

$$\frac{n}{235.64} = \frac{7.15}{100}$$

$$1{,}684.826 = n \times 100$$

$$\frac{1{,}684.826}{100} = \frac{n \times 100}{100}$$

$$16.84826 = n$$

235.64 $\boxed{X}$ 7.15 $\boxed{\div}$ 100 $\boxed{=}$ *16.84826*

Is the answer reasonable? **Yes**

To the nearest cent, Ted's weekly deduction is $16.85.

Yearly Deduction

Estimate: $17 × 50 = $850.

$$
\begin{array}{r r l}
\$\,16.85 & & \text{weekly deduction} \\
\times\quad 52 & & \text{weeks in year} \\
\hline
\$876.20 & & \text{deduction}
\end{array}
$$

16.85 $\boxed{X}$ 52 $\boxed{=}$ *876.2*

Is the answer reasonable? **Yes**

Ted's yearly deduction is $876.20.

 Examine

The answers are close to the estimates. So, the answers are reasonable.

Basic: 1–29 odd; Average: 1–29; Enriched: 2–28 even

Exercises

1. There are 4 bluegills for every 3 sunfish. Suppose 280 bluegills are put in the pond. How many sunfish should be stocked? **210 sunfish**

2. There are 16 girls and 12 boys in a math class. What is the ratio of girls to boys? What is the ratio of girls to the total number of students? $\frac{4}{3}, \frac{4}{7}$

3. Darlene walks at the rate of 6 kilometers per hour. At that rate, how far does she walk in 4 hours? **24 kilometers**

4. The Olson's bill for dinner is $30.56. *About* how much should they leave for a 15% tip? **$4.50**

5. Mr. Chandler weighed 160 pounds on his 35th birthday. He began gaining about $1\frac{1}{2}$ pounds every year. At this rate, how much will he weigh at age 45? **175 pounds**

6. Eli received 32% of the votes for class president. Eli received 40 votes. How many votes were cast? **125 votes**

7. A bookstore gives a 10% discount if over $20 of merchandise is bought. A person purchases items costing $6.40, $7.35, $2.86, and $3.59. How much is the person charged? **$18.18**

8. On a scale drawing of California, 1 cm represents 90 km. The map distance from Los Angeles to Eureka is 1.5 cm. What is the actual distance? **135 km**

9. An architect uses the scale $\frac{1}{4}$ inch = 1 foot. If a living room is 20 feet by 15 feet, what are the dimensions on the blueprint? **5 in. by $3\frac{3}{4}$ in.**

10. Lew has a photograph that measures 28 cm by 35 cm. He reduces the photo to 75% of its original dimensions. What are the new dimensions? **21 cm by 26.25 cm**

11. For a class of 25 students, the percentage of A's, B's, C's, D's, and F's are given in the table. Find the number of students who received each grade. **A—3 students; B—6 students; C—10 students; D—5 students; F—1 student**

Grade	Percent
A	12%
B	24%
C	40%
D	20%
F	4%

12. Renee works on her model ship from 5:00 P.M. to 7:00 P.M. What percent of the day is spent doing this? **$8\frac{1}{3}$%**

13. A 10-ounce box of crackers costs $1.35. A 16-ounce box of crackers costs $1.84. Which size is the better buy? **16 oz—$1.84**

14. Sara bought a television for 30% off of the regular price. If the regular price was $315, what was the sale price? **$220.50**

15. Anna Marie missed 3 out of 12 club meetings. What percent of meetings did she miss? **25%**

16. Terry earns $160 in 5 days. At that rate, how many days will it take him to earn $512? **16 days**

17. A model car costs $14. To put the model in layaway, Ted needs to make a 20% down payment. How much does he need? **$2.80**

18. A recipe calls for 3 cups of oatmeal for 48 cookies. How many cookies can be made with 2 cups of oatmeal? **32 cookies**

19. There are 220 females and 180 males in a certain school. What percent of the students are females? **55%**

20. Gary's shadow is 2.1 feet long. If his shadow is $\frac{1}{3}$ his actual height, what is Gary's actual height? **6.3 feet**

21. Iman types 55 words per minute. At that rate, how many words does he type in 15 minutes? **825 words**

2.1 ft

Solve. Use any strategy.

22. What is the distance between Boston and Cincinnati? **840 miles**

23. How many miles are covered traveling from Detroit to Atlanta and then to Houston? **1,488 miles**

24. What is the round-trip mileage from Dallas to Indianapolis? **1,730 miles**

25. The shadow of a building is 65 meters long at the same time that the shadow of a meter stick is 2.5 meters long. How tall is the building? **26 meters**

27. A firefighter earned $8,500 in 1967. In 1984, the same person earned $23,000. Due to inflation, a 1967 dollar was worth only $0.68 in 1984. What is the firefighter's 1984 salary in 1967 dollars? **$15,640**

29. On Monday, the morning paper has 132 pages. On Tuesday, there are 4 less pages than on Monday. On Wednesday, there are 8 more pages than on Tuesday. On Thursday, there are 4 more pages than on Monday. How many pages is Thursday's paper?
136 pages

	Atlanta	Boston	Cheyenne	Chicago	Cincinnati	Cleveland	Dallas	Denver	Des Moines	Detroit	Houston	Indianapolis	Kansas City	Los Angeles
Atlanta		1037	1442	674	440	672	795	1398	870	699	789	493	798	2182
Boston			1907	963	840	628	1748	1949	1280	695	1804	906	1391	2779
Cheyenne				954	1174	1279	869	100	627	1211	1107	1068	650	1137
Chicago					287	335	917	996	327	266	1067	181	499	2054
Cincinnati						244	920	1164	571	259	1029	106	591	2179
Cleveland							1159	1321	652	170	1273	294	779	2367
Dallas								781	684	1143	243	865	489	1387
Denver									669	1253	1019	1058	600	1059

26. On a map, 1 inch represents 20 miles. Cincinnati and Toledo are 190 miles apart. What is the map distance between the two cities? **9.5 in.**

28. On the first two Spanish quizzes, Chad scored 80% and 76%. What must he score on the third quiz so that his mean score is 82%? **90%**

This feature presents useful ways of solving mathematical problems on a calculator.

Calculator

When finding the percentage of a number on a calculator, the %️ key can be used.

Find 62% of 45.

Enter: 45 X️ 62 %️ *27.9*

Display: *45 45 62 27.9*

Find 15% of 3.28.

Enter: 3.28 X️ 15 %️ *0.492*

Display: *3.28 3.28 15 0.492*

Use a calculator to find the percentage.

1. 12% of 36 **4.32**

2. 20.5% of 40 **8.2**

3. 40% of 60 **24**

4. 25% of 200 **50**

5. 75% of 48 **36**

6. 82% of 65 **53.3**

7. 150% of 80 **120**

8. 0.5% of 16 **0.08**

CHAPTER 3 REVIEW

Vocabulary/Concepts

Choose a word from the list at the right that best completes each sentence.

1. Two equivalent ratios form a ___?___. **proportion**

2. A ___?___ is used to picture things that are too large to be drawn actual size. **scale drawing**

3. A comparison of two numbers is a ___?___. **ratio**

4. A rate with a denominator of 1 is a ___?___. **unit rate**

5. ___?___ means per one hundred. **percent**

6. The ___?___ of $\frac{4}{5} = \frac{8}{10}$ are 4×10 and 5×8. **cross products**

7. A comparison of two measurements that have different units is a ___?___. **rate**

base
cross products
equivalent
numerator
percent
proportion
rate
ratio
scale drawing
unit rate

Exercises

Write each ratio as a fraction in simplest form.   Page 47

8. 4 out of 7 $\frac{4}{7}$

9. 6 to 10 $\frac{3}{5}$

10. 50 : 100 $\frac{1}{2}$

11. 9 out of 12 $\frac{3}{4}$

12. 8 to 32 $\frac{1}{4}$

13. 25 : 40 $\frac{5}{8}$

14. 26 out of 65 $\frac{2}{5}$

15. 215 : 55 $\frac{43}{11}$

Write each of the following as a rate. Then write each rate as a unit rate.   Pages 48–49
Rates are listed below without units.

16. 400 meters in 50 seconds $\frac{400}{50}, \frac{8}{1}$

17. $1.20 for 5 tablets $\frac{1.20}{5}, \frac{0.24}{1}$

18. $32 for 2 shirts $\frac{32}{2}, \frac{16}{1}$

19. 276 miles on 12 gallons $\frac{276}{12}, \frac{23}{1}$

20. 96 hours in 4 days $\frac{96}{4}, \frac{24}{1}$

21. 2,500 revolutions in 5 minutes $\frac{2,500}{5}, \frac{500}{1}$

Find the cross products.   Pages 50–51

22. $\frac{2}{3} = \frac{10}{15}$ **30 = 30**

23. $\frac{4}{5} = \frac{32}{40}$ **160 = 160**

24. $\frac{17.5}{21} = \frac{5}{6}$ **105 = 105**

25. $\frac{1.5}{0.3} = \frac{40}{8}$ **12 = 12**

Use cross products to determine whether each pair of ratios forms a proportion. Write yes or no.   Pages 50–51

26. $\frac{3}{5}$ and $\frac{12}{20}$ **yes**

27. $\frac{2}{9}$ and $\frac{5}{23}$ **no**

28. $\frac{4}{15}$ and $\frac{3}{14}$ **no**

29. $\frac{6}{14}$ and $\frac{9}{21}$ **yes**

Find the missing number.   Pages 50–51

30. $\frac{3}{4} = \frac{a}{24}$ **18**

31. $\frac{b}{9} = \frac{49}{63}$ **7**

32. $\frac{5}{6} = \frac{c}{78}$ **65**

33. $\frac{9}{d} = \frac{3}{38}$ **114**

34. $\frac{6}{7} = \frac{54}{f}$ **63**

35. $\frac{q}{15} = \frac{7}{14}$ **7.5**

36. $\frac{h}{2.25} = \frac{15}{0.75}$ **45**

37. $\frac{0.04}{0.12} = \frac{0.6}{k}$ **1.8**

Refer to the scale drawing at the right. Find the actual measurement of each of the following. The scale drawing measurement is given. Use the scale 1 cm represents 46 cm.   Pages 52–53

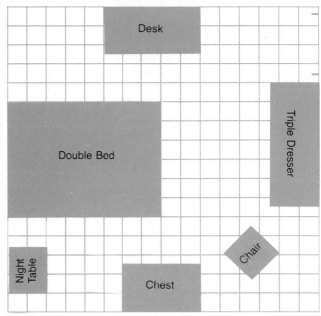

38. width of the chest, 2 cm **92 cm**

39. length of the bed, 4 cm **184 cm**

40. width of the room, 8 cm **368 cm**

41. width of the desk, $2\frac{1}{2}$ cm **115 cm**

42. width of the dresser, 3.25 cm **149.5 cm**

Change each decimal, fraction, or mixed numeral to a percent.   Pages 56–58

43. 0.36 **36%**   44. $\frac{3}{10}$ **30%**   45. $1\frac{2}{5}$ **140%**   46. 0.53 **53%**   47. 0.01 **1%**

48. 2.32 **232%**   49. $\frac{17}{20}$ **85%**   50. 1.5 **150%**   51. $\frac{3}{8}$ **37.5%**   52. $2\frac{2}{3}$ **$266\frac{2}{3}$%**

Change each percent to a decimal.   Pages 56–58

53. 42% **0.42**   54. 300% **3.0**   55. 0.3% **0.003**   56. $\frac{1}{2}$% **0.005**   57. $1\frac{1}{4}$% **0.0125**

Change each percent to a fraction or mixed numeral.   Pages 56–58

58. 50% **$\frac{1}{2}$**   59. 40% **$\frac{2}{5}$**   60. 130% **$1\frac{3}{10}$**   61. $\frac{1}{2}$% **$\frac{1}{200}$**   62. 8% **$\frac{2}{25}$**

Solve.   Pages 59–60

63. 70% of 120 **84**   64. 6% of 12.8 **0.768**   65. 15.5% of 112 **17.36**   66. $\frac{1}{4}$% of 68 **0.17**

Name the percentage, base, or rate. Then solve.   Pages 61–64

67. 50% of 8 is what number?
    B = 8, r = 50%; 4
69. What percent of 50 is 16?
    P = 16, B = 50; 32%

68. 3 is 10% of what number?
    P = 3, r = 10%; 30
70. 75% of 12 is what number?
    B = 12, r = 75%; 9

Solve.

71. Marge receives $264 commission on $2,200 of sales. At that rate, what is her commission on $4,000 of sales? **$480**

72. Carly's purchases total $54 and $2.97 is added for sales tax. What is the tax rate? **$5\frac{1}{2}$%**

CHAPTER 3 TEST

Write each ratio as a fraction in simplest form.

1. 4 out of 10 $\frac{2}{5}$ **2.** 15 to 20 $\frac{3}{4}$ **3.** 125 : 15 $\frac{25}{3}$ **4.** 64 to 28 $\frac{16}{7}$

Use cross products to determine whether each pair of ratios forms a proportion. Write yes or no.

5. $\frac{3}{7}$ and $\frac{5}{12}$ **no** **6.** $\frac{6}{24}$ and $\frac{2}{8}$ **yes** **7.** $\frac{1}{2}$ and $\frac{1.3}{2.6}$ **yes** **8.** $\frac{3}{9} = \frac{2.5}{8.5}$ **no**

Change each decimal, fraction, or mixed numeral to a percent.

9. $\frac{4}{5}$ **80%** **10.** 0.03 **3%** **11.** $4\frac{1}{4}$ **425%** **12.** $\frac{1}{3}$ **33$\frac{1}{3}$%** **13.** 1.75 **175%**

Change each percent to a decimal.

14. 1% **0.01** **15.** 25.5% **0.255** **16.** $10\frac{1}{4}$% **0.1025** **17.** $\frac{1}{2}$% **0.005** **18.** 200% **2.0**

Change each percent to a fraction or mixed numeral.

19. 75% $\frac{3}{4}$ **20.** 130% $1\frac{3}{10}$ **21.** $21\frac{1}{2}$% $\frac{43}{200}$ **22.** $66\frac{2}{3}$% $\frac{2}{3}$ **23.** 52.5% $\frac{21}{40}$

24. 120% $1\frac{1}{5}$ **25.** 25% $\frac{1}{4}$ **26.** 45% $\frac{9}{20}$ **27.** 225% $2\frac{1}{4}$ **28.** $3\frac{2}{3}$% $\frac{11}{300}$

Solve.

29. What number is 28% of 450? **126**

30. 112 is 28% of what number? **400**

31. 78% of what number is 50.7? **65**

32. What percent of 32 is 12? **37$\frac{1}{2}$%**

33. 3.5 is what percent of 14? **25%**

34. 6% of 120 is what number? **7.2**

35. A $10\frac{1}{2}$-ounce can of soup sells for 53¢ and a $12\frac{1}{4}$-ounce can sells for 75¢. Which is the better buy? **$10\frac{1}{2}$-oz at 53¢**

36. There are 14 girls and 11 boys in Mrs. Decker's math class. What percent of the students is boys? **44%**

37. The Martinos travel 50 miles on 2.5 gallons of gasoline. How far can they travel on 7.5 gallons? **150 miles**

38. A $40 lamp is sold at 175% of its wholesale cost. What is the selling price? **$70**

39. A photograph is 6 inches wide and 9 inches long. The photograph is reduced to a width of 4 inches. What is the length of the reduced photograph? **6 in.**

40. The original price of a table is $400. It is marked down 50%. The sales tax is 6%. What is the total cost of the table? **$212**

41. On a scale drawing of Indiana, 1 cm represents 35 km. The map distance from Evansville to Bloomington is 5.0 cm. What is the actual distance? **175 km**

42. Twenty-two pages in a certain book contain photographs. How many pages are in the book if 8% of them contain photographs? **275 pages**

CUMULATIVE REVIEW

Use the mileage chart at the left to find each distance. Page 3

1. Pittsburgh to Tulsa **984 mi**

2. Seattle to Toledo **2,245 mi**

3. Tulsa to San Francisco **1,760 mi**

4. Toledo to Pittsburgh **228 mi**

5. St. Louis to Salt Lake City **1,337 mi**

6. Philadelphia to Seattle **2,751 mi**

Would the following locations be good for the kind of survey named? Why or why not? Pages 26–27

7. favorite sport, baseball game **No, not a sample that represents all people**

8. choice for governor, grocery store **Yes, variety of people**

9. favorite magazine, newsstand **Yes, variety of people**

10. number of cats, apartment complex **No, most apartments do not allow pets**

Use a calculator to compute the following. Pages 28–29

11. $10,986 + 426$ **11,412**

12. $23.697 - 10.235$ **13.462**

13. $16,720 \div 45.026$ **371.341**

14. $15 \times 23 \div 40 + 26$ **34.625**

15. $(5.37 - 2.87) \times 5.4 \div 3.6$ **3.75**

16. $0.99 \div 1.5 + 0.89$ **1.55**

Find the range and mode of each set of data. Pages 30–31

17. 5, 5, 8, 9, 9, 9, 13, 13, 21, 28 **23; 9**

18. 47, 52, 56, 57, 59, 64, 71 **24; no mode**

19. 22, 18, 16, 22, 29, 32, 14, 23 **18; 22**

20. 4.5, 9.5, 3.5, 1.5, 2.5, 1.5, 1.5, 7.5 **8; 1.5**

Find the mean of each set of data. Round to the nearest hundredth. Pages 32–33

21. 6, 9, 21 **12**

22. 5, 7, 9, 11 **8**

23. 2, 3, 3, 4 **3**

24. 6, 7, 11, 25, 35, 43 **21.17**

25. 50, 47, 41, 54, 33 **45**

26. $1.60, $1.05, $1.25 **$1.30**

Write each ratio as a fraction in simplest form. Page 47

27. 7 to 10 $\frac{7}{10}$

28. 4 out of 8 $\frac{1}{2}$

29. 16 : 24 $\frac{2}{3}$

30. 3 out of 27 $\frac{1}{9}$

31. 15 : 65 $\frac{3}{13}$

32. 10 to 32 $\frac{5}{16}$

33. 49 out of 70 $\frac{7}{10}$

34. 12 : 60 $\frac{1}{5}$

Write each of the following as a rate. Then write each rate as a unit rate. Pages 48–49 Rates are listed below without units.

35. 460 miles on 20 gallons of gas $\frac{460}{20}, \frac{23}{1}$

36. 330 miles in 6 hours $\frac{330}{6}, \frac{55}{1}$

37. $5.25 for 5 pounds $\frac{5.25}{5}, \frac{1.05}{1}$

38. 192 inches in 16 feet $\frac{192}{16}, \frac{12}{1}$

39. 200 bushels in 5 acres $\frac{200}{5}, \frac{40}{1}$

40. $120 in 4 days $\frac{120}{4}, \frac{30}{1}$

Find the missing number. Pages 50–51

41. $\frac{3}{4} = \frac{n}{8}$ **6**

42. $\frac{n}{5} = \frac{16}{20}$ **4**

43. $\frac{17}{5} = \frac{68}{n}$ **20**

44. $\frac{24}{n} = \frac{4}{0.5}$ **3**

Graphs

4-1 Pictographs

Objectives: To interpret pictographs. To draw pictographs from data.

The frequency table at the right lists the number of FM radio stations in several cities.

This information can be shown on a pictograph. A **pictograph** is a graph that uses pictures to compare data.

City	FM Radio Stations
Austin	9
Boston	20
Honolulu	14
Miami	20
Oklahoma City	12
San Antonio	14

Draw a pictograph for FM radio stations in the six cities.

- Choose a title for the graph.
  FM Radio Stations

- Choose a picture and the number of stations it stands for.

  Each 📻 stands for 4 FM radio stations.

- Determine how many pictures will be used for each city.

  Austin: $9 \div 4 = 2\frac{1}{4}$ pictures.

FM Radio Stations	
Austin	📻📻
Boston	*You will*
Honolulu	*complete the*
Miami	*pictograph in*
Oklahoma City	*exercises 1–6.*
San Antonio	
Each 📻 stands for 4 stations.	

Basic: 1–14; Average: 1–14; Enriched: 1–14

Exercises

Find the number of pictures (📻) for each city.

1. Boston **5 pictures**　　　**2.** Honolulu $3\frac{1}{2}$ **pictures**　　　**3.** Miami **5 pictures**

4. Oklahoma City **3 pictures**　　　　**5.** San Antonio $3\frac{1}{2}$ **pictures**

6. Complete the pictograph for FM radio stations in the six cities.
　　For answers to exercise 6, see Teacher Guide.

Vehicles Passing by Each 15 Minutes	
Car	🚗🚗🚗🚗🚗🚗🚗🚗
Bus	🚗
Van	🚗🚗🚗
Pickup	🚗
Truck	🚗🚗
Each 🚗 stands for 10 vehicles	

Use the pictograph at the left. About how many vehicles of each kind passed by?

7. vans **28**　　**8.** trucks **19**　　**9.** cars **75**

10. pickups **12**　　　　**11.** buses **8**

How many 🚗 would be used to show each vehicle?

12. 20 bicycles **2**　　　　**13.** 35 motorcycles $3\frac{1}{2}$

14. Make a frequency table for the pictograph.
For answer to exercise 14, see Teacher Guide.

Teacher Resource Book, Page 111

73

4-2 Bar Graphs

Objectives: To interpret bar graphs. To draw bar graphs from data.

Donald Wofford is a technical artist for a daily newspaper. He draws many of the illustrations that appear in the newspaper.

One kind of illustration Donald draws is the bar graph. A **bar graph** uses bars to compare data. The length of each bar represents a number.

Favorite Car: Driver's Education Class	
Type of Car	Number of Votes
midsize	3
compact	6
luxury	1
sports	8
full size	3
other	4

Example

Make a horizontal bar graph for the data in the table above.

- Label the graph with a title.
  Favorite Car: Driver's Education Class

- Draw and label both axes.
  Horizontal: Number of Votes
  Vertical: Type of Car

- Mark off equal spaces on the horizontal axis and label it with the best scale to represent the data.
  Let each space represent 1 vote.

- Draw evenly spaced bars out from the vertical axis to show the quantities. Label each bar.

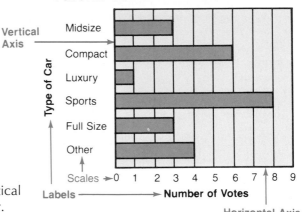

Basic: 1–53; Average: 1–53; Enriched: 1–53

Exercises

Use the horizontal bar graph above to answer each question.

This chart shows which letters of the alphabet are used most frequently in the English language.

1. What is the title? **Average Frequency of Letters—English Language**
2. What is the label for the vertical scale? **Letter**
3. What are the limits of the horizontal scale? **0 and 14.0**
4. What letters are listed on the vertical scale? **A, E, I, N, O, R, S, T**

Use the bar graph on page 74 to estimate to the nearest tenth the average frequency per 100 letters for each letter below. Answers may vary. Typical answers are given.

5. N **6.** S **7.** E **8.** R **9.** T **10.** I **11.** A **12.** O
7.1 6.1 13.1 6.8 10.5 6.3 8.2 8.0

13. Choose a short newspaper article. Count the first 100 letters. Then find the number of times each of the letters T, S, R, O, N, I, E, and A is used. How do your results compare with the graph? **See students' work.**

The vertical bar graph at the right compares the highest mountain on each of seven continents.

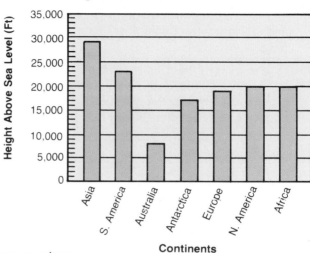

Highest Mountain on Each Continent

14. What is the title of the graph?
Highest Mountain on Each Continent

15. What numbers are listed along the vertical scale? **0 to 35,000**

16. What do the numbers on the vertical scale represent?
height above sea level in feet

17. Which continent has the highest mountain? **Asia**

18. Which continent's highest mountain is the lowest mountain? **Australia**

Estimate the height of the highest mountain on each continent. Answers may vary. Typical answers are given.

19. Asia **29,000 ft** **20.** Europe **19,000 ft** **21.** Africa **20,000 ft** **22.** Australia **8,000 ft**

23. South America **23,000 ft** **24.** Antarctica **17,000 ft** **25.** North America **20,000 ft**

Select the best scale for each range of data given below. The scale should always start at 0. Usually, 10 or fewer spaces along the scale is best.

26. The data goes from 0 to 10. **b or c**
   a. 0, 5, 10 **b.** 0, 2, 4, 6, 8, 10 **c.** 0, 1, 2, 3, 4, 5, 6, 7, 8, 9, 10

27. The data goes from 310 to 1,000. **d**
   a. 0, 10, 20, and so on to 1,000 **b.** 0, 1, 2, 3, 4, and so on to 1,000
   c. 0, 20, 40, 60, and so on to 1,000 **d.** 0, 100, 200, and so on to 1,000

River	Length
Mississippi	2,348 miles
Columbia	1,243 miles
Ohio	1,306 miles
Yukon	1,770 miles
Red	1,270 miles
Arkansas	1,459 miles
Wabash	529 miles
Snake	1,038 miles
Missouri	2,533 miles

The chart at the left shows the lengths of several rivers in the United States. Answer the following to make a vertical bar graph of the data.

28. Are all the lengths measured in the same units? **yes**

29. How many rivers are to be shown on the bar graph? **9**

30. What is the length of the longest river? **2,533 miles**

31. What is the length of the shortest river? **529 miles**

32. What is the range of the lengths? **2,004 miles**

33. Suppose 1 centimeter on the bar graph represents 1 mile. How long will the longest bar be? Is this scale reasonable? **2,533 cm; no**

34. Suppose 1 centimeter on the graph represents 10 miles. How long will the longest bar be? Is this scale reasonable? **253.3 cm; no**

35. Suppose 1 centimeter on the graph represents 100 miles. How long will the longest bar be? Is this scale reasonable? **25.33 cm; yes**

36. Suppose 1 centimeter on the graph represents 1,000 miles. Will there be much difference between the bars that represent the Ohio and Arkansas Rivers? **no**

37. Which scale will fit on your paper and still show the differences in length fairly well?
1 cm represents 100 mi

38. How many bars are needed to represent the rivers? **9 bars**

39. Suppose each bar is 1 centimeter wide and 1 centimeter apart. Allow 1 centimeter before the first bar and 1 centimeter after the last bar. How wide is the graph? **19 cm**

40. Draw the graph 26 centimeters high and 19 centimeters wide. **See students' work.**

41. Mark each centimeter on the vertical scale. Start with 100. Label each mark.
See students' work.

42. Mark each centimeter on the horizontal scale to allow for the bars. **See students' work.**

43. To the nearest tenth, how long should the bar for the Mississippi River be? **23.5 cm**

Find the length of the bar that represents each river. Round to the nearest tenth.

44. Columbia **12.4 cm**   **45.** Ohio **13.1 cm**   **46.** Yukon **17.7 cm**   **47.** Red **12.7 cm**

48. Arkansas **14.6 cm**   **49.** Wabash **5.3 cm**   **50.** Snake **10.4 cm**   **51.** Missouri **25.3 cm**

52. Label each bar with the name of the river it represents.
For answer to exercise 52, see Teacher Guide.

53. Give the bar graph a title. **Length of Rivers**

This feature presents general topics of mathematics.

 Math Break

The graph below is called a **100% bar graph.** The entire bar represents how Miko Sandy spends 100% or all of her time.

Miko's Time	sleep $33\frac{1}{3}\%$	school 25%	meals $12\frac{1}{2}\%$	study $8\frac{1}{3}\%$	sports $8\frac{1}{3}\%$	other $12\frac{1}{2}\%$

Find the hours spent on each of the following.

1. school **6 h**   **2.** sleep **8 h**   **3.** meals **3 h**   **4.** sports **2 h**

5. What is the sum of all the percents? **100%**

6. The bar is 10 cm long. How many millimeters long is each section?
sleep 33.3 mm, school 25 mm, meals 12.5 mm, study 8.3 mm, sports 8.3 mm, other 12.5 mm

4-3 Line Graphs

Objective: To interpret line graphs and to draw line graphs from data.

A **line graph** shows change and direction of change over a period
of time. The direction of change is called a **trend.**

Examples

A. The line graph below shows how
the price of CD Company Stock
changed in value during one week.

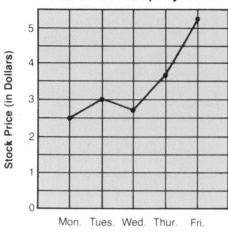

Price of CD Company Stock

The title of the graph is Price
of CD Company Stock. The
horizontal scale represents days
of the week. What does the
vertical scale represent?
stock price in dollars

B. The line graph below shows how
the Consumer Price Index (CPI)
changed from 1978 to 1984.

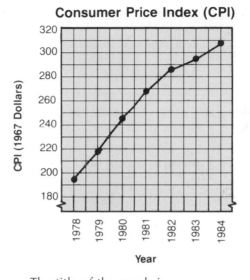

Consumer Price Index (CPI)

*The CPI is
the cost in
1967 dollars
of $100 worth
of goods.*

*The broken
line indicates
that the graph
does not begin
at zero.*

The title of the graph is
Consumer Price Index. The
horizontal scale represents
calendar years. What does the
vertical scale represent?
CPI in 1967 dollars

Basic: 1–17, 18–42 even; Average: 1–43; Enriched: 1–17, 19–43 odd

Exercises

Use the graph titled Price of CD Company Stock to answer each question.

1. What was the lowest price of the
stock for the week? $2\frac{1}{2}$

2. What was the highest price of the stock
for the week? $5\frac{1}{4}$

3. On what day did the price of the
stock decrease? **Wednesday**

4. What was the overall price trend for
the week? **upward**

Use the graph titled Consumer Price Index (CPI) to estimate the CPI for each year.
Answers may vary. Typical answers are given.

5. 1983 **$295**   **6.** 1980 **$245**   **7.** 1979 **$218**   **8.** 1984 **$308**   **9.** 1981 **$268**

10. Between which years did the CPI
increase least? **from 1982 to 1984**

11. Between which years did the CPI
increase most? **from 1978 to 1980**

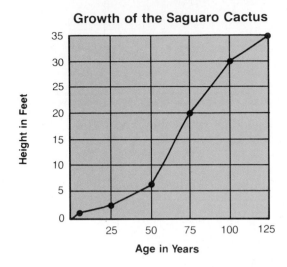

Growth of the Saguaro Cactus

Height in Feet / Age in Years

Use the graph at the left to answer each question.

12. What is the greatest height that can be shown on this graph? **35 feet**

13. What is the greatest age that can be shown on this graph? **125 years**

14. During which 25-year period does the height increase the most? **50–75 years**

15. During which 25-year period does the height increase the least? **0–25 years**

16. About how tall is the cactus after 50 years? **6 feet**

17. About how many years does it take the cactus to reach a height of 2 feet? **about 20 years**

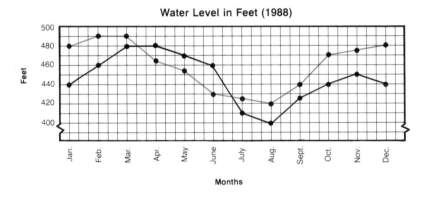

Water Level in Feet (1988)

Feet / Months

Use the line graph above to estimate the water level of Lake Anderson for each month.
Answers may vary. Typical answers are given.

18. January **440 ft**   **19.** March **480 ft**   **20.** June **460 ft**   **21.** July **410 ft**

22. August **400 ft**   **23.** October **440 ft**   **24.** November **450 ft**   **25.** September **425 ft**

Use the line graph to name the months in which Lake Thomas was at each level.

26. 480 feet **Jan., Dec.**

27. 430 feet **June, Aug.**

28. 420 feet **Aug.**

29. 440 feet **May, Sept.**

30. 470 feet **Mar., Oct.**

31. 425 feet **July, Aug.**

32. 475 feet **Mar., Nov.**

33. 465 feet **Apr., Sept.**

34. Between which two months was there no change in the water level of Lake Anderson? **Mar., Apr.**

35. Between which two months was there no change in the water level of Lake Thomas? **Feb., Mar.**

36. Between which two months did the water level of Lake Anderson decrease the most? **June, July**

37. Between which two months did the water level of Lake Thomas decrease the most? **Mar., Apr.; May, June**

38. Which lake had the greater increase in water level from January to February? **Lake Anderson**

39. Estimate the dates the lakes had the same water levels. **Mar. 10 and June 20; Answers may vary. Typical answers are given.**

For answers to exercises 40–42, see Teacher Guide.
Draw line graphs for each of the following.

40. Gail Derifield recorded her daily
jogging time for 6 days.
Mon., 32 min   Thur., 42 min
Tues., 36 min   Fri., 36 min
Wed., 29 min   Sat., 38 min

41. David Lawrence recorded his height on
his birthday for several years.
13th, 61 in.   16th, 69 in.
14th, 65 in.   17th, 70 in.
15th, $67\frac{1}{2}$ in.   18th, $70\frac{1}{2}$ in.

42. The production in a small gold mine was
22 kg in 1980, 30 kg in 1981, 40 kg in
1982, 45 kg in 1983, 35 kg in 1984, 20
kg in 1985, and 10 kg in 1986.

43. Describe the trends in exercises 40–42.
40, no trend; 41, increasing;
42, increasing then decreasing

This feature promotes students' mental abilities in computation and reasonableness.

Mental Math

You can estimate sums and differences by rounding numbers.

634	→	600	*634 rounds to 600*	78	→	80	*78 rounds to 80*
+ 279		+ 300	*279 rounds to 300*	− 23		− 20	*23 rounds to 20*
		900	*possible estimate*			60	*possible estimate*

3.2	3	$9.51 →	$10	$23.76 →	$20
2.7 →	3	− 6.39	− 6	48.61	50
+ 1.6	+ 2		$ 4	+ 9.26	+ 10
	8				$80

Answers may vary. Typical answers are given.

Estimate the sum or difference using this strategy.

1. 364
   + 118
   500

2. 32
   47
   + 28
   110

3. 523
   289
   + 676
   1,500

4. 53
   − 27
   20

5. $917
   − 609
   $300

6. 8,923
   − 2,450
   7,000

7. 4.5
   2.3
   + 1.9
   9

8. 6.78
   + 4.94
   12

9. $45.11
   32.33
   + 10.29
   $90

10. 78.1
   − 42.9
   40

11. 875 + 326 **1,200**

12. 529 − 201 **300**

13. 6.3 + 3.7 + 5.8 **16**

4-4 Reading Circle Graphs

Objective: To interpret circle graphs.

Ernie Sullivan is a financial counselor for a local tax firm. He helps his clients plan how their money should be spent. This is called a **budget**.

Ernie uses a circle graph to explain and plan budgets. A **circle graph** is used to compare parts of a whole. The entire graph represents 100% or the whole.

Examples

A. Julie Barnes earns $50 each week. How much does Julie budget each week for clothing?

The circle graph shows that 20% is budgeted for clothing.

$$\begin{array}{r} \$50 \\ \times\ 0.20 \\ \hline \$10.00 \end{array} \quad 20\% = 0.20$$

Julie budgets $10 each week for clothing.

Julie Barnes' Weekly Budget

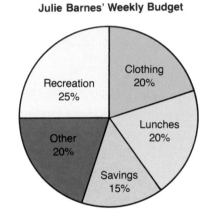

B. Paul, Julie's brother, earns $40 each week. He budgets $10 each week for clothing. Is this more or less than the percent that Julie budgets for clothing?

$$\underset{\text{total amount}}{\overset{\text{amount for clothing}}{\longrightarrow}} \frac{\$10}{\$40} = 0.25 \text{ or } 25\% \qquad 10 \boxdot 40 \boxminus \textit{0.25}$$

Paul budgets 25% each week for clothing. Julie budgets 20%.
So, Paul budgets more than the percent that Julie budgets.

The Key Skills provides practice of skills needed in the exercises.

Key Skills

Solve.

$$\boxed{15\% \text{ of } 45 \blacktriangleright 15 \times 45 \blacktriangleright 0.15 \times 45 = 6.75}$$

1. 35% of $360 **$126**

2. 80% of $275 **$220**

3. 7% of $192 **$13.44**

4. 2.75% of $150 **$4.13**

5. 12.8% of $245 **$31.36**

6. 7.15% of $215 **$15.37**

Basic Skills Appendix, Pages 432, 438, 461
Basic: 2–12 even, 14–21; Average: 1–21; Enriched: 1–11 odd, 12–21

Exercises

What percent of Julie's budget is for each item?

1. savings **15%**

2. lunches **20%**

3. recreation **25%**

4. other **20%**

Find the amount that Julie budgets for each item.

5. savings **$7.50**   **6.** lunches **$10**   **7.** recreation **$12.50**   **8.** other **$10**

The Spitzer family budgets the given amount for each item each month. If they earn $1,500 each month, find the percent that is budgeted for each item.

9. housing, $420 **28%**   **10.** food, $360 **24%**   **11.** transportation, $225 **15%**

Use the graph at the right to find the percent of the earth's land surface for each land area.

12. North America **16%**   **13.** Islands **2%**

14. Europe **6%**   **15.** Africa **20%**

There are 575 billion square miles of land surface on Earth. Find the number of billions of square miles in each continent. Round to the nearest tenth.
Encourage students to estimate first.

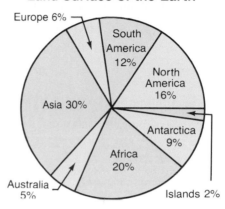

Land Surface of the Earth

16. Africa
115 billion mi²
17. Australia
28.8 billion mi²
18. Europe
34.5 billion mi²
19. Antarctica
51.8 billion mi²
20. South America
69 billion mi²
21. North America
92 billion mi²

This feature presents useful ways of solving mathematical problems on a calculator.

Calculator

A breakdown of the weekly sales at Buddy's Burgers is shown at the right.

Item	Sales
Sandwiches	$1,820.00
Drinks	873.60
Side Dishes	728.36
Desserts	582.40
Total Sales	$4,004.36

The amount of sales from desserts can be compared to the total sales by using percent.

582.40 ⌹ 4004.36 ⊟ *0.14544415* or 0.15

Thus, 15% of the total sales comes from the sale of desserts. A circle graph can be used to compare the sales of the various items to the whole.

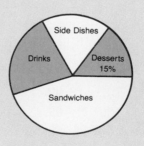

Find the percent of total sales for each item.

1. sandwiches **45%**   **2.** drinks **22%**   **3.** side dishes **18%**

4. Copy and complete the circle graph.
For answer to exercise 4, see the circle graph.

PRACTICE

What number is named by each digit in 425.683?

1. 5 5   2. 6 0.6   3. 2 20

4. 8 0.08   5. 4 400   6. 3 0.003

Express each of the following in decimal form.

7. eighty-three hundredths 0.83   8. nine and seven tenths 9.7

9. six and two hundredths 6.02   10. one hundred thirteen thousandths 0.113

11. seventy-five thousandths 0.075   12. four and forty-two thousandths 4.042

Write each number in words.

13. 0.6 six tenths   14. 0.11 eleven hundredths   15. 0.07 seven hundredths

16. 5.03 five and three hundredths   17. 12.5 twelve and five tenths   18. 0.005 five thousandths

Estimate. Answers may vary. Typical answers are given.

19. 2.11 + 1.02 = 3   20. 7.9 + 8.3 = 16   21. 75.7 + 8.13 = 84   22. 68.17 + 1.47 = 69   23. 42.04 + 18.94 = 60

24. 6.5 − 4.8 = 2   25. 8.00 − 1.63 = 6   26. 2.11 − 1.02 = 1   27. 86.1 − 29.81 = 60   28. 276.15 − 93.6 = 190

Add or subtract.

29. 528 + 73 = 601   30. 999 + 99 = 1,098   31. 429 + 573 = 1,002   32. 2,073 + 159 = 2,232   33. 6,521 + 1,879 = 8,400

34. 481 − 57 = 424   35. 903 − 56 = 847   36. 260 − 172 = 88   37. 1,200 − 248 = 952   38. 8,010 − 5,478 = 2,532

Multiply or divide.

39. 749 × 17 = 12,733   40. 624 × 34 = 21,216   41. 5,274 × 21 = 110,754   42. 2,765 × 69 = 190,785   43. 2,178 × 225 = 490,050

44. 14)154 = 11   45. 51)918 = 18   46. 16)912 = 57   47. 83)5,644 = 68   48. 42)8,862 = 211

49. 14 × 10 = 140   50. 14 × 0.1 = 1.4   51. 14 × 0.01 = 0.14   52. 14 × 0.001 = 0.014   53. 14 × 100 = 1,400

54. 32 × 0.1 = 3.2   55. 124 × 0.01 = 1.24   56. 65 × 0.001 = 0.065   57. 8 × 100 = 800   58. 9 × 0.001 = 0.009

59. 73 ÷ 10 = 7.3   60. 73 ÷ 0.1 = 730   61. 73 ÷ 0.01 = 7,300   62. 73 ÷ 0.001 = 73,000   63. 73 ÷ 100 = 0.73

64. 49 ÷ 100 = 0.49   65. 27 ÷ 0.01 = 2,700   66. 358 ÷ 0.001 = 358,000   67. 216 ÷ 0.1 = 2,160   68. 15 ÷ 10 = 1.5

69. 483 ÷ 0.01 = 48,300   70. 617 ÷ 0.1 = 6,170   71. 298 ÷ 10 = 29.8   72. 350 ÷ 0.001 = 350,000   73. 800 ÷ 100 = 8

74. 2.1 × 3 ‾‾‾‾ 6.3	**75.** 4.6 × 76 ‾‾‾‾ 349.6	**76.** 207 × 1.8 ‾‾‾‾ 372.6	**77.** 13.2 × 0.9 ‾‾‾‾ 11.88	**78.** 5.4 × 9.6 ‾‾‾‾ 51.84
79. 452.2 × 0.8 ‾‾‾‾ 361.76	**80.** 29.9 × 0.82 ‾‾‾‾ 24.518	**81.** 3.685 × 0.007 ‾‾‾‾ 0.025795	**82.** 0.75 × 0.013 ‾‾‾‾ 0.00975	**83.** 1.003 × 0.42 ‾‾‾‾ 0.42126

84. 3.50 ÷ 9)31.50 **85.** 9.3 ÷ 5)46.5 **86.** 0.41 ÷ 8)3.28 **87.** 0.08 ÷ 7)0.56 **88.** 0.007 ÷ 6)0.042

89. 1.3 ÷ 12)15.6 **90.** 8.4 ÷ 51)428.4 **91.** 0.58 ÷ 27)15.66 **92.** 0.035 ÷ 83)2.905 **93.** 0.007 ÷ 68)0.476

Solve.

94. There is a balance of $104.77 in Betsy Meyer's account. She writes checks for $23.40 and $18.60. What is the new balance? **$62.77**

95. Jerry Wu has checks of $40.95, $27.32, and $68.47 to deposit. He wants to receive $25 in cash. What is his total deposit? **$111.74**

96. Pam Hamilton has $123.85 to deposit. The checks total $115. How much of the deposit is currency and coin? **$8.85**

97. Don Ware has checks for $25.32, $14.98, and $3.50, and coins that total $2.85. What is his total deposit? **$46.65**

98. Sims Auto Sales had 314 vehicles in stock on November 1. During the month, they received 205 new vehicles and sold 184 vehicles. How many vehicles were in stock on December 1? **335 vehicles**

99. Westwood High School started the school year with 1,423 students. During the year 314 new students enrolled and 376 students withdrew. What was the enrollment at the end of the school year? **1,361 students**

100. Michael spent $19.28 for slacks, $14.57 for a shirt, and $2.49 for socks. How much change did Michael receive from $50.00? **$13.66**

101. Last week Michelle hiked 2.7 mi, 3.2 mi, 4.1 mi, 3.4 mi, and 4.8 mi. How far did Michelle hike in all? **18.2 mi**

This feature presents general topics of mathematics.

Math Break

Complete the following. Be sure to count all squares.

1. How many squares are in a 1 by 1 grid? **1**

2. How many are in a 2 by 2 grid? **4 + 1 = 5**

3. How many are in a 3 by 3 grid? A 4 by 4 grid? **1 + 4 + 9 = 14; 1 + 4 + 9 + 16 = 30**

4. Use the pattern to find the number of squares in the 10 by 10 grid. **1 + 4 + 9 + 16 + ... + 100 = 385**

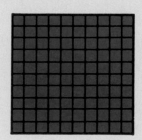

4-5 *Histograms*

Objective: To interpret histograms.

Lola Votaw is a licensed practical nurse, or LPN, in a care center. As an LPN, Lola takes and records blood pressures and temperatures. She gives prescribed medicines and helps patients with bathing.

Lola's training included one year of classroom instruction and clinical practice at a local hospital.

The chart below shows the room numbers and the ages of Lola's patients.

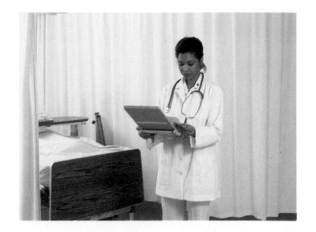

Room Numbers and Ages of Patients									
Room	L, R	Room	L, R	Room	L, R	Room	L, R	Room	L, R
A-1	74, 87	A-6	80, 97	B-1	86, 70	B-6	78, 70	C-1	88, 85
A-2	87, 91	A-7	86, 87	B-2	80, 75	B-7	82, 85	C-2	90, 91
A-3	84, 61	A-8	74, 84	B-3	80, 80	B-8	61, 77	C-3	89, 85
A-4	66, 74	A-9	59, 86	B-4	92, 93	B-9	90, 92	C-4	70, 78
A-5	81, 86	A-10	91, 79	B-5	77, 77	B-10	84, 86	C-5	85, 88

L, R means left side or right side of room.

A **histogram** is a bar graph with no spaces between the bars. All the bars are the same width. If a group has no members, then that space will be left empty. *The length of each bar represents a number.*

The histogram below compares the ages of Lola's patients.

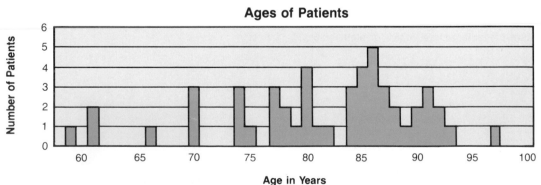

Ages of Patients

What is the age of the oldest patient? The histogram shows that the oldest patient is 97 years.

What 10-year span, 60–69, 70–79, 80–89, or 90–99 has the most patients?
80–89 year age span

84 *Graphs*

3. 57 yr, 58 yr, 60 yr, 62 yr, 63 yr, 64 yr, 65 yr, 67 yr, 68 yr, 69 yr, 71 yr, 72 yr, 73 yr, 76 yr, 83 yr, 94 yr, 95 yr, 96 yr, 98 yr, 99 yr, 100 yr

4. 59 yr, 66 yr, 75 yr, 79 yr, 81 yr, 82 yr, 89 yr, 93 yr, 97 yr

Basic: 1–13 odd; Average: 1–14; Enriched: 2–6 even, 8–14

Exercises

Use the chart or the histogram on page 84 to answer each question.

1. How many age groups have three members each? **6 age groups**

2. Which age groups have three members each? **70 yr, 74 yr, 77 yr, 84 yr, 87 yr, 91 yr**

3. Which age groups have no members?

4. Which age groups have only one member?

5. Lola is responsible for how many patients? **50 patients**

6. In how many rooms are the patients the same age? **2 rooms**

7. Could the histogram be drawn to also include the room number information?
No, histograms can show only two facts.

Use the histogram at the right to answer each question.

8. How many families were surveyed? **47 families**

9. How many families have 4 children? **6 families**

10. How many families have 1 child? **8 families**

11. How many families have 6 children? **none**

12. What is the mode? **2 children**

13. What type of families were surveyed?
families with children

14. Make a frequency table from the histogram.
For answers to exercise 14, see Teacher Guide.

This feature provides general topics about the uses of a computer.

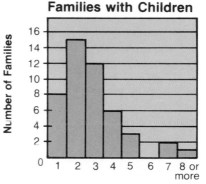

Families with Children

Number of Families

Number of Children

Computer

In a BASIC program, the computer follows the instructions in line number order. The output from the program is shown below.

```
20 PRINT "IS";
10 PRINT "TRUTH"!
40 END
30 PRINT "BEAUTY."
```

The computer rearranges the program.

```
10 PRINT "TRUTH";
20 PRINT "IS";
30 PRINT "BEAUTY."
40 END
```

The output of the program is TRUTH IS BEAUTY.

Show the output of each program.

```
1. 10 PRINT "YOU";
   30 PRINT "ONLY";
   40 PRINT "SUNSHINE."
   50 END
   20 PRINT "MY";
   15 PRINT "ARE";
```
YOU ARE MY ONLY SUNSHINE.

```
2. 20 PRINT "CAN'T";
   10 PRINT "COMPUTERS";
   40 END
   30 PRINT "THINK."
```
COMPUTERS CAN'T THINK.

4-6 Using and Misusing Graphs

OBJECTIVE: To determine what makes a graph misleading.

Graphs are often used to try to convince people that one product is better than another. In the example below, two bar graphs compare the sales of two makes of tape recorders.

Examples

Graph A: Sales of Recorders

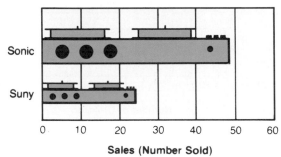

Sales (Number Sold)

According to graph A, 48 Sonics and 24 Sunys were sold.

Graph B: Sales of Recorders

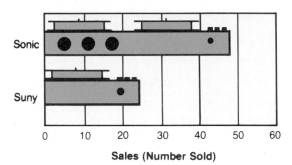

Sales (Number Sold)

According to graph B, 48 Sonics and 24 Sunys were sold.

Basic: 1–26; Average: 1–32; Enriched: 1–32

Exercises

Complete the following to discover which graph is misleading.

1. Do graphs A and B give the same information on sales? **yes**

2. Find the ratio of Sonics sold to Sunys sold. **2 to 1**

3. In graph A, the Sonic recorder is about 5 cm long and 1 cm wide. What is its area? The Suny recorder is about 2.5 cm by 0.5 cm. What is its area? (Hint: area = length × width.) **5 cm², 1.25 cm²**

4. In graph B, the Sonic recorder is about 5 cm by 1 cm. What is its area? The Suny recorder is about 2.5 cm by 1 cm. What is its area? **5 cm², 2.5 cm²**

5. Compute the following ratios.

graph A: $\dfrac{\text{area of Sonic}}{\text{area of Suny}}$ $\dfrac{5}{1.25}$ **or 4 to 1**

graph B: $\dfrac{\text{area of Sonic}}{\text{area of Suny}}$ $\dfrac{5}{2.5}$ **or 2 to 1**

6. Compare the results of exercises 2 and 5. Which graph is misleading? Why?
graph A; area should show same ratio

Graph C: Monthly Sales

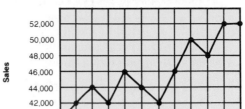

Graph D: Monthly Sales

Find the amount of sales for each month.

7. April $42,000

8. August $46,000

9. July $42,000

10. October $48,000

11. January $40,000

12. December $52,000

Compare graphs C and D to answer each question.

13. Which graph is easier to read? D

14. Compare the vertical scales. How do they differ? **Graph D expands part of Graph C's vertical scale.**

15. Do both graphs display the same data? **yes**

16. Compare the impressions given by the two graphs. **Graph D implies faster growth than Graph C.**

17. Which graph would you show to someone who wants to buy the business? Why? **D gives impression that the business is growing rapidly**

18. Which graph would you show an employee who asks for a big raise? Why? **C gives impression that the business is not growing rapidly**

Graph E: Favorite Restaurant

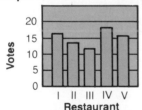

Find the number of votes for each restaurant in graph E.

19. V 16   **20.** II 14   **21.** III 12   **22.** IV 18

Find the number of votes for each restaurant in graph F.

23. V 16   **24.** II 14   **25.** III 12   **26.** IV 18

Graph F: Favorite Restaurant

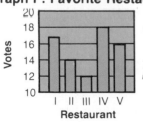

Compare graphs E and F to answer each question.

27. In graph F, the bar for restaurant II is twice the length of the bar for restaurant III. Does this mean there are twice the votes? **no, only 2 more**

28. What causes the difference in voting to be magnified in graph F? **part of vertical scale is expanded**

29. Do graphs E and F display the same data? **yes**

30. Why would restaurant III prefer graph E? **gives more realistic comparisons**

31. Why would restaurant IV prefer graph F? **gives impression that more people prefer restaurant IV**

32. Which graph better represents the results? **graph E**

4-7 Problem Solving: Using Graphs to Predict

Objective: To use graphs to predict and estimate the solutions to word problems.

Sometimes graphs are used to predict or estimate.
A track and field magazine is preparing a prediction
for the women's Olympic javelin throw.

The table below gives the winning distance in
four Olympics.

Year	1948	1952	1956	1960
Distance (m)	46	50	54	56

**Use the information in the table to predict the winning
distance in the javelin throw for the 1964 Olympics.**

Read

You must predict the 1964 winning distance.
You know the distances for 1948, 1952, 1956, and 1960.

Decide

Draw a line graph for the distances in 1948, 1952, 1956,
and 1960. Then extend the line to predict the 1964 distance.

Solve

Try to draw a straight line
as close to all the points
as possible.

Such a line is shown in color.
This line crosses the 1964
column at 60 meters.

The prediction for the 1964
winning distance is 60 meters.

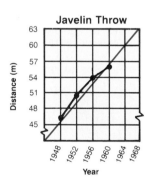

Examine

The actual winning distance in 1964 was 61 meters.
The estimate of 60 meters is reasonable.

Basic: 1–10; Average: 1–18; Enriched: 1–18

Exercises

1. How does the winning distance in
1960 compare to the winning distance
in 1948? **10 m longer**

2. Use the graph above to predict the
winning distance for 1968. How does
the prediction compare to the actual
winning distance of 60 meters?
63 m; too high

3. Graph all distances from 1948 through
1976. Predict the winning distance
for 1980, 1984, and 1988. Additional
data are: 1972, 64 m and 1976, 66 m.
See students' work. Answers may vary. 1980, 65 m; 1984, 67 m

4. How do your predictions for 1980 and
1984 compare to the actual results?
See students' work. Answers may vary.

The chart and graph below show how postal rates for a first-class letter have changed.

Year	1963	1968	1971	1974	1977	1978
Cents	5	6	8	10	13	15

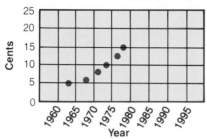

Rate for First-Class Letter

Use the graph to predict the following. Answers may vary. Typical answers are given.

5. when the cost reaches 20¢ **1983**

6. when the cost reaches 25¢ **1986**

7. the cost in 1985 **23¢**   **8.** the cost in 1990 **over 25¢**   **9.** the cost in 1995 **over 25¢**
The cost reached 20¢ in 1981. The next rate increase was to 22¢ in 1985.
10. What are some factors that could affect your prediction? **inflation, better mail handling technology, images of postal workers**

The graph at the right shows how the population of the United States changed from 1940 to 1980. Use the graph to complete the following.
Answers may vary. Typical answers are given.

11. Estimate the year when the population reached 200 million. (Hint: Use the blue lines.) **1968**

12. Estimate the year when the population reached 140 million. **1943**

13. Estimate the year when the population reached 220 million. **1978**

14. Predict the population in 1990. **240 million**

15. Predict the population in 1985. **230 million**

16. Estimate the year when the population reached 230 million. **1985**

17. Predict the year when the population will reach 240 million.
1990

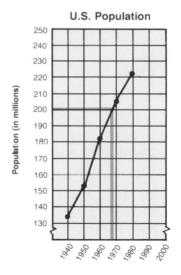

U.S. Population

18. Predict the 1980 population from the graph up to 1970. How does your prediction compare to the actual population?
225 million; a little high

CHAPTER 4 REVIEW

Vocabulary/Concepts

Choose the letter of the word or phrase that best matches each description.

1. a graph used to compare parts of a whole **b**

2. a graph used to show change and direction of change over a period of time **d**

3. a bar graph used to draw frequencies **c**

4. the direction of change shown by a graph **h**

5. a graph that uses bars to compare data **a or c**

6. a graph that uses pictures to compare data **e**

a. bar graph   **e.** pictograph

b. circle graph   **f.** range

c. histogram   **g.** scale

d. line graph   **h.** trend

Exercises

Use the pictograph at the right to answer the following.   Page 73

7. the number of votes for Sobel **45 votes**

8. the total number of votes **135 votes**

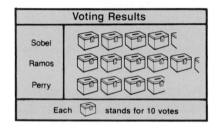

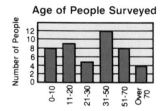

Use the bar graph at the left to answer each question.   Pages 74–76

9. How many people were in the 31–50 year age group? **12 people**

10. How many people were in the 11–20 year age group? **9 people**

Use the bar graph at the right to find the following.   Pages 74–76

11. the number of calls made by family D **15 calls**

12. the difference between the number of calls made by family A and family E **2 calls**

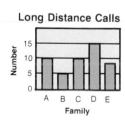

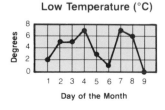

Use the line graph at the left to answer each question.   Pages 77–79

13. Which day(s) had the highest temperature? **day 7**

14. In which two days was the drop the greatest? **days 5 and 9**

Use the line graph at the right to answer each question.   Pages 77–79

15. Which month has the greatest high temperature? **Aug.**

16. Which month has the least high temperature? **Jan.**

17. Which month shows the greatest increase in high temperature? **May**

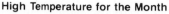
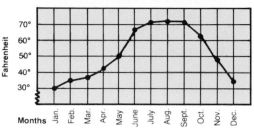

High Temperature for the Month

Use the circle graph at the right to answer the following.   Pages 80–81

18. What is the largest ocean?
Pacific Ocean
19. What is the smallest ocean?
Arctic Ocean
20. The area of the earth's water is 139 million square miles. What is the area of the Atlantic Ocean?
32 million mi²

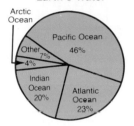

Earth's Water

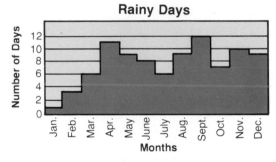

Rainy Days

Use the histogram at the left to answer each question.   Pages 84–85

21. Which month has the greatest number of rainy days? **Sept.**

22. Which month has the least number of rainy days? **Jan.**

23. What is the range in the number of rainy days? **11 days**

Use the bar graph at the right to answer the following.   Pages 86–87

24. Why is the graph misleading?
scale does not start at zero
25. Suppose you start the scale at zero. How will the graph change? **bars will be more nearly the same length**

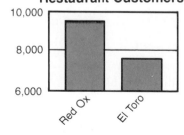

Restaurant Customers

Pay Scale

Use the line graph at the left.   Pages 88–89

26. Predict a person's earnings if he or she works 14 hours. **$56**

27. How much does he or she earn per hour? **$4 per hour**

CHAPTER 4 TEST

Use the pictograph at the right to answer each question.

Recorders Sold

Week 1	(9 recorders)
Week 2	(6 recorders)
Week 3	(7 recorders)
Week 4	(6 recorders)

Each (recorder) stands for 20 recorders.

1. How many recorders were sold during week 1? **90 recorders**

2. How many more were sold in week 3 than week 2? **15 recorders more**

3. How many were sold in the four weeks? **310 recorders**

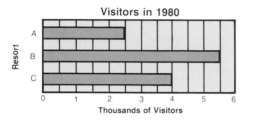

Visitors in 1980

Resort: A, B, C — Thousands of Visitors (0 to 6)

Use the bar graph at the left to answer each question.

4. Which resort had more visitors in 1980, A or C? **C**

5. Which resort had the most visitors in 1980? **B**

Suppose a family's income is $20,000. Use the circle graph at the right to answer each question.

6. What percent of money is spent on taxes? **19%**

7. What is the sum of the percents? **100%**

8. How much is spent on food? **$5,000**

Family Spending

- Transportation 8%
- Medical 5%
- Other 10%
- Clothing and Personal Care 10%
- Housing 23%
- Food 25%
- Taxes 19%

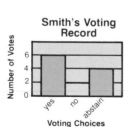

Smith's Voting Record

Number of Votes (0 to 6) — Voting Choices: yes, no, abstain

The histogram at the left shows how Representative Smith voted for one month.

9. How many chances did Smith have to vote? **12 chances**

10. How many times did Smith vote yes? **6 times**

11. The graph below shows Lindy's progress in the high jump. Predict Lindy's best jump for the next week. **5 ft $7\frac{1}{2}$ in.**

Best High Jump

Height: 5'8", 5'7", 5'6", 5'5", 5'4" — Week: 1 2 3 4 5

12. Explain why the bar graph below could be misleading. **horizontal scale starts at 100 instead of zero**

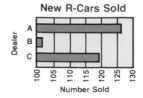

New R-Cars Sold

Dealer: A, B, C — Number Sold: 100 105 110 115 120 125 130

This page provides extra practice of the skills and applications presented thus far in the text.

CUMULATIVE REVIEW

Use the table on page 8 to answer each question. Pages 8–9

1. What is the most expensive type of long distance call? **operator assisted person-to-person**

2. Which cities are the least expensive to call? **Lancaster, Washington C.H., and Zanesville**

3. What is the cost of a direct-dial one-minute call to Marietta at 9:30 A.M.? **57¢**

4. What is the cost of a direct-dial one-minute call to Zanesville at 7:00 P.M.? **28¢**

Use the table on page 16 to find the sales tax on the following purchases. Page 16

5. $0.36 **$0.02**   **6.** $0.73 **$0.05**   **7.** $2.15 **$0.12**   **8.** $8.04 **$0.45**   **9.** $15.60 **$0.86**

State the number that each set of tally marks represents. Page 25

10. ⫼⫼⫼ **15**   **11.** ⫼||| **8**   **12.** ⫼⫼⫼|||| **19**

A survey was conducted of twenty families in a parking lot before a football game. They were asked how many children were in the family. The following numbers are their responses: 5, 3, 2, 4, 0, 1, 0, 3, 2, 2, 3, 2, 4, 0, 1, 3, 2, 2, 4, 0. Answer the following. Pages 38–39

13. Find the range. **5**

14. Find the median. **2**

15. Find the mode. **2**

16. Find the mean. **2.15**

Solve. Pages 61–62

17. What percent of 26 is 13? **50%**

18. What percent of 80 is 20.4? $25\frac{1}{2}$%

19. $40\frac{1}{2}$% of 120 is what number? **48.6**

20. 16.2 is what percent of 54? **30%**

Use the pictograph at the right. About how many of each vehicle passed by? Page 73

21. buses **10**   **22.** vans **45**   **23.** cars **55**

24. pickups **13**   **25.** trucks **28**

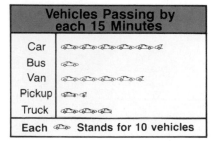

How many **would be used to show each vehicle?** Page 73

26. 30 vans **3**

27. 65 bicycles $6\frac{1}{2}$

28. 22 motorcycles **about** $2\frac{1}{5}$

Solve.

29. A photograph is 5 inches wide and 7 inches long. The photograph is enlarged to a width of 8 inches. What is the length of the enlarged photograph? **11.2 inches**

30. The following cars are in a parking lot: 10 sedans, 3 convertibles, 6 two-doors, and 8 hatchbacks. Draw a vertical bar graph to show the data. **For answer to exercise 30, see Teacher Guide.**

Probability

5-1 Counting Using Lists

Objective: To determine all the possible outcomes.

Mr. and Mrs. Cotter made a list showing all the possible ways they could make a round trip from their home to Denver.

Each of the round trips is called an **outcome.** There are 9 possibilities or 9 outcomes.

The outcome *bus, air* means the Cotters could travel to Denver by *bus,* and return home by *air.*

Basic: 1–13; Average: 1–13; Enriched: 1–13

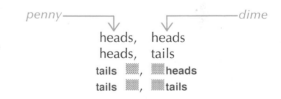

trip to Denver   *return trip home*

bus, bus
bus, air
bus, rail
rail, bus
rail, air
rail, rail
air, bus
air, air
air, rail

Exercises

Explain the meaning of each outcome. For answers to exercises 1–4, see Teacher Guide.

1. bus, bus   2. rail, air   3. bus, rail   4. air, bus

5. How many outcomes use the same method of transportation to and from Denver? **3 outcomes**

Suppose you toss a penny and a dime.

6. Complete the list at the right.

7. How many different outcomes are possible? **4**

8. How many outcomes show both tails? **1**

9. How many outcomes show a head on one coin and a tail on the other? **2**

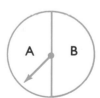

penny   *dime*

heads, heads
heads, tails
tails ▦, ▦heads
tails ▦, ▦tails

Suppose each spinner is spun once.

10. List all possible outcomes. One such outcome is 2A. **1A, 1B, 2A, 2B, 3A, 3B**

11. How many different outcomes are possible? **6**

List all possible outcomes. Then tell how many outcomes are possible.

12. This spinner is spun twice. (One possible outcome is AB.) **AA, AB, AC, BA, BB, BC, CA, CB, CC; 9**

Teacher Resource Book, Page 129

13. All 3-digit numerals using the digits 1, 2, and 3. **123, 321, 312, 231, 132, 213; 6**

5-2 Tree Diagrams

Objective: To use a tree diagram to determine all possible outcomes of a given situation.

John Bryant and his friends want to order
a pizza. They have the following
choices. They decide to have only one meat
on the pizza.

Size	Crust	Meat
Medium	Regular	Sausage
Large	Thick	Pepperoni
		Hamburger

One way to find the possible choices
(outcomes) for their pizza is to make a
tree diagram like the one shown below.

Examples

A.

Size	Crust	Meat	Outcomes
		S	MRS
	R	P	MRP
		H	MRH
M		S	MTS
	T	P	MTP
		H	MTH
		S	LRS
	R	P	LRP
		H	LRH
L		S	LTS
	T	P	LTP
		H	LTH

The red branch shows
the outcome of a *M*edium
pizza, with a *R*egular
crust and *S*ausage
topping. This is
symbolized *MRS*.
How many possible
outcomes are there? 12 outcomes

B. A penny, a nickel, and a dime are tossed
at the same time. The outcome shown
at the right can be symbolized as follows.

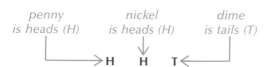

penny   *nickel*   *dime*
is heads (H)   *is heads (H)*   *is tails (T)*

H   H   T

Basic: 1–13 odd, 14–18, 19–27 odd; Average: 1–28; Enriched: 2–12 even, 14–18, 20–28 even

Exercises

Use the choices for pizza. State the outcome indicated by each of the following.

1. MRP **medium, regular crust, pepperoni**

2. LRH **large, regular crust, hamburger**

3. MTH **medium, thick crust, hamburger**

4. LTS **large, thick crust, sausage**

Find the number of outcomes for pizzas with the following.

5. Medium **6**

6. Thick crust **6**

7. Pepperoni **4**

8. Medium, Thick, Pepperoni **1**

9. Large and Sausage **2**

10. Regular crust, Hamburger **2**

11. *no* Hamburger **8**

12. *no* Pepperoni **8**

13. Thick crust, *no* Pepperoni **4**

Suppose a penny, a nickel, and a dime are tossed at the same time.
Copy and complete the tree diagram to answer the following.

14. How many possible outcomes are there? **8**

15. List the possible outcomes. **HHH, HHT, HTH, HTT, THH, THT, TTH, TTT**

16. What does TTT mean? **All three coins landed tails up.**

17. What does HHT mean? **The penny and nickel landed heads up. The dime landed tails up.**

18. How do HHT and THH differ? **HHT has heads on the penny and nickel while THH has heads on the nickel and dime.**

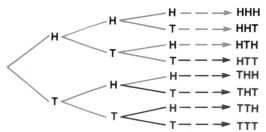

A penny, a nickel, and a dime are tossed. Find the number of outcomes.

19. THT **1**

20. TTH or TTT **2**

21. exactly one tail **3**

22. no tails **1**

23. tails on the dime **4**

24. at least two heads **4**

For answers to exercises 25–28, see Teacher Guide.

Draw a tree diagram. Then tell how many outcomes are possible.

25. Each spinner is spun once.

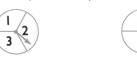

26. This spinner is spun twice.

27. This spinner is spun three times.

28. Each spinner is spun once.

This feature presents general topics.

Math Break

A square office contains 9 desks as shown at the right. Trace the office. Then draw two squares so that each desk is separated from the others.

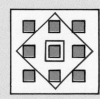

5-3 Problem Solving: Using Alternate Methods

Objective: To use more than one method to solve word problems.

Miko Ho is going on vacation with her family. She packs the following articles of clothing.

Tops	Shorts	Shoes
Pink	Gray	Tennis Shoes
White	Navy	Sandals
Red		

Example

A. How many possible outfits (outcomes) does Miko have?

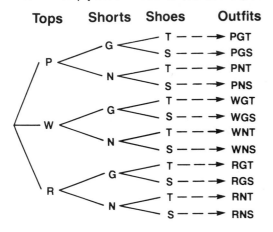

The tree diagram shows that Miko has 12 possible outfits. One possible outfit is WNS. This means a white top with navy shorts and sandals. What are the 12 possible outfits Miko has? **See outfits listed in the tree diagram.**

Here is a way to solve the problem using multiplication.

 Read

You know the number of tops, shorts, and shoes. You are asked to find the number of possible outfits.

 Decide

You could list the possible choices or draw a tree diagram. However, another way to find the number of possible outcomes is to multiply the number of choices of each type of clothing.

Solve

tops		shorts		shoes		possible outfits
3	×	2	×	2	=	12

There are 12 possible outfits.

 Examine

The tree diagram shows that there are 12 possible outfits. Multiplication gives the same answer. The answer is correct.

Two dice are shown at the right.
When one is rolled, there are six possible
outcomes; namely, 1, 2, 3, 4, 5, and 6.

Example

B. **Suppose you roll both dice. One outcome is 5, 1. This means
a 5 appears on the red die and a 1 on the blue die. How
many outcomes are possible?**

ways the red   *ways the blue*
die can come up   *die can come up*

    6   ×   6   =   36

There are 36 possible outcomes. *Does this answer seem
reasonable? How can you check the answer?* **Yes; list them or make a tree diagram.**

Basic Skills Appendix, Page 425
Basic: 1–10; Average: 1–10; Enriched: 1–10

Exercises

1. Craig can wear an outfit chosen from
4 shirts and 2 ties. How many outfits
are possible? **8 outfits**

choices for   *choices for*
shirt   *tie*

  4   ×   2

2. Three people sit in 3 seats in a row
on an airplane. How many ways can
the 3 persons be seated? **6 ways**

choices for   *choices for*   *choices for*
1st seat   *2nd seat*   *3rd seat*

  3 × 2 × 1

3. For dinner, you have 7 choices for
the main dish, 4 choices for vegetable,
3 for fruit, and 3 for beverage.
How many different dinner choices
are possible? **252 choices**

4. An ice cream store offers a choice
of 20 ice cream flavors and 15
toppings. How many sundae combinations
with one type of ice cream and topping
each are possible? **300 combinations**

5. Refer to page 98. Miko Ho decides to
take her yellow top and brown shorts
also. How many possible outfits does
she have now? **24 outfits**

6. In a certain state, license plates have
three digits followed by three letters.
How many different license plates are
possible? (Hint: Any of the 26 letters
and the digits 0, 1, 2, 3, 4, 5, 6, 7, 8,
and 9 can be used.) **17,576,000 plates**

7. This spinner is
spun twice. How
many outcomes
are possible?
16 outcomes

8. A multiple-choice test has four
questions. Each question is
answered a, b, c, or d. How many
sets of answers are possible?
256 sets of answers

9. How many outcomes are possible if
three dice are rolled? **216 outcomes**

10. How many different arrangements
of the digits 7, 4, 8, and 3
are possible? **24 arrangements**

5-4 Probability

Objective: To find the probability of an outcome and to express a probability as a fraction.

Jerry Baldwin is a radio service technician. He repairs radios after locating the source of trouble. He uses testing equipment to check the circuits. To qualify for the job, Jerry attended a vocational school for 2 years.

Jerry is repairing a radio. He must determine which circuit, A, B, or C, is faulty.

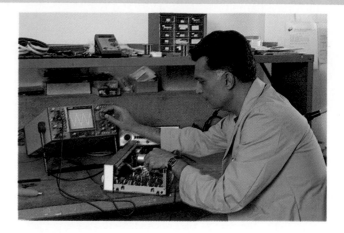

His choice of one of the three circuits to test is made at random. That is, each choice or outcome, A, B, or C, is **equally likely.**

Selecting the faulty circuit on his first try is the **favorable outcome.** An outcome is favorable if it is the one that is preferred.

Example

What are the chances that Jerry will select the faulty circuit on his first try?

There are 3 possible outcomes. Each one is equally likely. Only 1 circuit is faulty. So, there is 1 chance in 3 that Jerry will select the faulty circuit on his first try.

$\dfrac{1}{3}$ ← *number of favorable outcomes*
← *number of possible outcomes*

The chance, or **probability,** of selecting the faulty circuit on the first try is $\frac{1}{3}$.

The probability of a favorable outcome is the ratio of the number of favorable outcomes to the total number of outcomes. Remember, each outcome *must* be equally likely.

$$\textbf{probability} = \frac{\text{number of favorable outcomes}}{\text{number of possible outcomes}}$$

Basic Skills Appendix, Pages 421, 449
Basic: 2–36 even; Average: 1–37; Enriched: 1–37 odd

Exercises

Suppose the radio contained the number of circuits shown below, and one circuit is faulty. What is the probability of Jerry selecting the faulty circuit on his first choice?

1. $4 \frac{1}{4}$ **2.** $7 \frac{1}{7}$ **3.** $9 \frac{1}{9}$ **4.** $10 \frac{1}{10}$ **5.** $13 \frac{1}{13}$

6. As the number of possible outcomes increases, does the probability of selecting the faulty circuit on the first choice increase or decrease? **decrease**

A date is chosen at random from the month of June. Find the probability of the following.

7. the eleventh $\frac{1}{30}$

8. a Thursday $\frac{4}{30}$ or $\frac{2}{15}$

9. after the twentieth $\frac{10}{30}$ or $\frac{1}{3}$

10. before the sixth $\frac{5}{30}$ or $\frac{1}{6}$

11. a week day $\frac{21}{30}$ or $\frac{7}{10}$

12. a Sunday $\frac{5}{30}$ or $\frac{1}{6}$

13. an odd-numbered date $\frac{15}{30}$ or $\frac{1}{2}$

14. a Monday, Wednesday, or Friday $\frac{13}{20}$

June

S	M	T	W	T	F	S
1	2	3	4	5	6	7
8	9	10	11	12	13	14
15	16	17	18	19	20	21
22	23	24	25	26	27	28
29	30					

A die is rolled. Find the probability of the following.

15. a four $\frac{1}{6}$

16. a one $\frac{1}{6}$

17. a two or a six $\frac{2}{6}$ or $\frac{1}{3}$

18. an even number $\frac{3}{6}$ or $\frac{1}{2}$

19. a number less than five $\frac{4}{6}$ or $\frac{2}{3}$

20. a number greater than six **0**

21. a number no greater than four $\frac{4}{6}$ or $\frac{2}{3}$

The list at the right shows the possible outcomes when two dice are rolled. Note that the sum for 3, 1 is 3 + 1 or 4.

1, 6	*2, 6*	*3, 6*	*4, 6*	*5, 6*	*6, 6*
1, 5	*2, 5*	*3, 5*	*4, 5*	*5, 5*	*6, 5*
1, 4	*2, 4*	*3, 4*	*4, 4*	*5, 4*	*6, 4*
1, 3	*2, 3*	*3, 3*	*4, 3*	*5, 3*	*6, 3*
1, 2	*2, 2*	*3, 2*	*4, 2*	*5, 2*	*6, 2*
1, 1	*2, 1*	*3, 1*	*4, 1*	*5, 1*	*6, 1*

22. How many outcomes are possible? **36**

23. Does this agree with Example B on page 99? **yes**

24. How does 3, 1 differ from 1, 3? **3, 1 means 3 on 1st die, 1 on 2nd; 1, 3 means 1 on 1st die, 3 on 2nd**

25. What are the greatest and least sums? **greatest = 12; least = 2**

Two dice are rolled. Find each probability.

26. 6, 6 $\frac{1}{36}$

27. 3, 4 or 4, 3 $\frac{2}{36}$ or $\frac{1}{18}$

28. not 5, 2 or 2, 5 $\frac{34}{36}$ or $\frac{17}{18}$

29. a sum of 7 $\frac{6}{36}$ or $\frac{1}{6}$

30. a sum of 6 or 8 $\frac{10}{36}$ or $\frac{5}{18}$

31. a *product* of 6 $\frac{4}{36}$ or $\frac{1}{9}$

32. the same number on both dice $\frac{6}{36}$ or $\frac{1}{6}$

33. not a *product* of 9 $\frac{35}{36}$

Explain the meaning of the following.

34. a probability of 0
The event cannot happen.

35. a probability of 1
The event will happen.

Solve.

36. This spinner is spun once. What is the probability of landing on red? $\frac{2}{6}$ or $\frac{1}{3}$

37. A gumball machine has 33 red, 28 blue, and 32 white gumballs. Kris wants one gumball. What is the probability that Kris gets a red gumball? $\frac{11}{31}$

PRACTICE

Round each number to the underlined place-value position.

1. 0.6<u>1</u> 0.6   **2.** 8.2<u>5</u> 8.3   **3.** 0.1<u>0</u>8 0.11   **4.** 1<u>6</u>.08 16   **5.** <u>2</u>3.26 20

6. 0.0<u>4</u>8 0.05   **7.** 1.40<u>3</u>5 1.404   **8.** 0.<u>4</u>7 0.5   **9.** 10.1<u>0</u>6 10.11   **10.** <u>5</u>.82 6

Replace each ▓ with <, > or = to make a true statement.

11. 27.1 ▓ 32.5 <   **12.** 0.20 ▓ 0.200 =   **13.** 0.104 ▓ 0.006 >

14. 6 ▓ 6.1 <   **15.** 9.04 ▓ 9.4 <   **16.** 4.0 ▓ 4.00 =

17. 3.17 ▓ 31.7 <   **18.** 0.516 ▓ 0.515 >   **19.** 7.25 ▓ 7.2 >

Estimate. Answers may vary. Typical answers are given.

20. 2,397
     + 3,764
     ‾‾‾‾‾‾‾
      6,000

21. 864
     − 223
     ‾‾‾‾‾
      700

22. 423
     × 26
     ‾‾‾‾‾
     12,000

23. 29)928   30

24. 53)826   16

25. 82.56
     + 9.48
     ‾‾‾‾‾‾
       92

26. 7.382
     − 4.816
     ‾‾‾‾‾‾
       2.0

27. 5.17
     × 0.19
     ‾‾‾‾‾
       1.0

28. 43.6
     × 2.7
     ‾‾‾‾‾
      120

29. 1.7)5.89   3.0

Add or subtract.

30. 3,684
     + 2,768
     ‾‾‾‾‾‾
      6,452

31. 4,372
     + 7,294
     ‾‾‾‾‾‾
     11,666

32. 801
     − 247
     ‾‾‾‾‾
      554

33. 2,006
     − 214
     ‾‾‾‾‾
      1,792

34. 6,904
     − 5,877
     ‾‾‾‾‾‾
      1,027

Multiply or divide.

35. 4,610
     × 5
     ‾‾‾‾‾
     23,050

36. 7,654
     × 32
     ‾‾‾‾‾
     244,928

37. 629
     × 421
     ‾‾‾‾‾
     264,809

38. 872
     × 398
     ‾‾‾‾‾
     347,056

39. 5,324
     × 625
     ‾‾‾‾‾
     3,327,500

40. 9)6,642   738

41. 59)7,316   124

42. 116)928   8

43. 874)5,244   6

44. 712)6,408   9

Add or subtract.

45. 74.68
     + 49.23
     ‾‾‾‾‾‾
     123.91

46. 8.39
     + 15.99
     ‾‾‾‾‾‾
      24.38

47. 17.15
     + 7.6
     ‾‾‾‾‾
      24.75

48. 54
     + 3.85
     ‾‾‾‾‾
      57.85

49. 32.46
     + 10.9
     ‾‾‾‾‾
      43.36

50. 69.04
     − 58.77
     ‾‾‾‾‾‾
      10.27

51. 32.50
     − 21.63
     ‾‾‾‾‾‾
      10.87

52. 9.86
     − 0.78
     ‾‾‾‾‾
       9.08

53. 4.704
     − 2.583
     ‾‾‾‾‾‾
       2.121

54. 0.850
     − 0.294
     ‾‾‾‾‾‾
       0.556

Multiply or divide.

55. 3.21
     × 7
     ‾‾‾‾‾
     22.47

56. 79.52
     × 1.2
     ‾‾‾‾‾
     95.424

57. 53.07
     × 0.13
     ‾‾‾‾‾
     6.8991

58. 6.245
     × 0.82
     ‾‾‾‾‾
     5.1209

59. 0.179
     × 0.245
     ‾‾‾‾‾
     0.043855

60. 7)95.2   13.6

61. 0.4)57.2   143

62. 8.5)11.22   1.32

63. 0.28)4.312   15.4

64. 0.57)0.2622   0.46

Write the greatest common factor (GCF) of the numerator and denominator in each fraction.

65. $\frac{5}{15}$ 5 **66.** $\frac{4}{9}$ 1 **67.** $\frac{4}{10}$ 2 **68.** $\frac{12}{15}$ 3 **69.** $\frac{16}{24}$ 8

Write each fraction in simplest form.

70. $\frac{2}{8}$ $\frac{1}{4}$ **71.** $\frac{4}{12}$ $\frac{1}{3}$ **72.** $\frac{6}{8}$ $\frac{3}{4}$ **73.** $\frac{12}{15}$ $\frac{4}{5}$ **74.** $\frac{8}{12}$ $\frac{2}{3}$

Add or subtract. Write the sum or difference in simplest form.

75. $\frac{1}{5} + \frac{1}{5}$ $\frac{2}{5}$ **76.** $\frac{2}{8} + \frac{3}{8}$ $\frac{5}{8}$ **77.** $\frac{1}{12} + \frac{6}{12}$ $\frac{7}{12}$ **78.** $\frac{7}{8} + \frac{1}{8}$ 1 **79.** $\frac{1}{6} + \frac{4}{6}$ $\frac{5}{6}$

80. $\frac{2}{3} + \frac{1}{6}$ $\frac{5}{6}$ **81.** $\frac{3}{5} + \frac{3}{10}$ $\frac{9}{10}$ **82.** $\frac{1}{2} + \frac{3}{8}$ $\frac{7}{8}$ **83.** $\frac{1}{2} + \frac{1}{5}$ $\frac{7}{10}$ **84.** $\frac{1}{3} + \frac{1}{4}$ $\frac{7}{12}$

85. $\frac{7}{8} - \frac{2}{8}$ $\frac{5}{8}$ **86.** $\frac{5}{6} - \frac{3}{6}$ $\frac{1}{3}$ **87.** $\frac{6}{10} - \frac{1}{10}$ $\frac{1}{2}$ **88.** $\frac{7}{12} - \frac{5}{12}$ $\frac{1}{6}$ **89.** $\frac{9}{16} - \frac{3}{16}$ $\frac{3}{8}$

90. $\frac{1}{2} - \frac{1}{4}$ $\frac{1}{4}$ **91.** $\frac{3}{4} - \frac{3}{8}$ $\frac{3}{8}$ **92.** $\frac{5}{6} - \frac{2}{3}$ $\frac{1}{6}$ **93.** $\frac{3}{4} - \frac{1}{3}$ $\frac{5}{12}$ **94.** $\frac{4}{5} \quad \frac{1}{4}$ $\frac{11}{20}$

Solve.

95. Geoff charges purchases of $32.73, $4.87, $20.34, and $18.02 during the month. What are his total purchases for the month? **$75.96**

96. Kathy wants to buy a sewing machine on credit. The payments are $30.18 a month for 12 months. What is the total cost of the sewing machine? **$362.16**

This feature presents general topics of mathematics.

Math Break

Each graph at the right compares the number of guests that stayed at two desert resorts in a recent year.

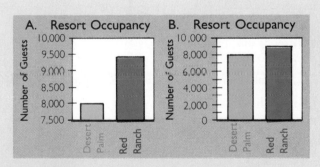

Answer the following.

1. Refer to graph **A**. About how many guests stayed at the Desert Palm? About how many guests stayed at the Red Ranch? **8,000 guests; 9,500 guests**

2. Refer to graph **B**. About how many guests stayed at the Desert Palm? About how many guests stayed at the Red Ranch? **8,000 guests; 9,500 guests**

3. Which graph is misleading? What makes it misleading? **Graph A.**
Starting the vertical scale at 7,500 magnifies the difference.

5-5 Probability of Independent Events

Objective: To find the probability of independent events.

Jerry Baldwin knows that 1 out of 3 circuits in the Tunit radio is faulty and that 2 out of 5 circuits in the Soundright radio are faulty.

The two sets of outcomes for choosing circuits in the radios are **independent** events. That is, the choice of a circuit in the Tunit radio does not affect what circuit will be chosen in the Soundright radio.

Example

What is the probability of locating faulty circuits on the first try in both radios? Show the tree diagram. See Teacher Guide.

The probability of locating the faulty circuit in the Tunit radio is $\frac{1}{3}$.

The probability of locating one of the two faulty circuits in the Soundright radio is $\frac{2}{5}$.

$\frac{1}{3} \times \frac{2}{5} = \frac{2}{15}$ Multiply the probabilities of the two events.

The probability of locating faulty circuits on the first try in both radios is $\frac{2}{15}$.

You can find the number of outcomes: $3 \times 5 = 15$. Find the number of correct outcomes: $1 \times 2 = 2$. Probability $= \frac{2}{15}$

$\left(\frac{\text{favorable}}{\text{total}}\right)$

The Key Skills provides practice of skills needed in the exercises.

Key Skills

Multiply. Write the product in simplest form.

 $\dfrac{7}{8} \times \dfrac{3}{5} = \dfrac{7 \times 3}{8 \times 5} = \dfrac{21}{40}$

1. $\dfrac{3}{4} \times \dfrac{1}{2}$ $\dfrac{3}{8}$

2. $\dfrac{2}{5} \times \dfrac{6}{7}$ $\dfrac{12}{35}$

3. $\dfrac{9}{11} \times \dfrac{3}{7}$ $\dfrac{27}{77}$

4. $\dfrac{7}{8} \times \dfrac{8}{9}$ $\dfrac{7}{9}$

5. $\dfrac{2}{3} \times \dfrac{6}{11}$ $\dfrac{4}{11}$

6. $\dfrac{5}{6} \times \dfrac{9}{14}$ $\dfrac{15}{28}$

Basic Skills Appendix, Pages 447, 449, 458
Basic: 1–6, 8–16 even; Average: 1–17; Enriched: 1–6, 7–17 odd

Exercises

Each spinner shown at the right is spun once. Find each probability.

1. two A's $\dfrac{1}{12}$

2. two B's $\dfrac{6}{12}$ or $\dfrac{1}{2}$

3. An A on spinner I and a B on spinner II $\dfrac{3}{12}$ or $\dfrac{1}{4}$

4. a B on spinner I and an A on spinner II $\dfrac{2}{12}$ or $\dfrac{1}{6}$

5. Add the probabilities in exercises 1–4. Explain why the sum is one. Sum is all possible outcomes.

Spinner I

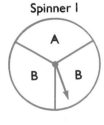

Spinner II

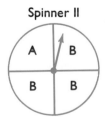

6. The top branch of the tree diagram for exercises 1–5 is shown. Complete the tree diagram on your paper. How can the tree diagram be used to find probabilities?
Multiply along the branches.

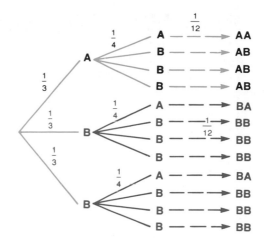

The probability given above each set of branches of the tree diagram is the probability for each branch.

A card is drawn from each of the three groups at the right. Find each probability.

7. all cards are numbered 2 $\frac{1}{60}$

8. all cards are odd-numbered $\frac{1}{5}$

9. all cards are even-numbered $\frac{1}{15}$

10. All cards are numbered 2 or less. $\frac{2}{15}$

11. the first card is a 1, the second is even, the third is 4 or 5 $\frac{1}{15}$

12. the first card is odd, the second is prime, the third is less than 4 $\frac{1}{5}$

Solve.

13. Four coins are tossed. Find the probability that all four come up heads. $\frac{1}{16}$

14. Two dice are rolled. Find the probability that both dice show a four. $\frac{1}{36}$

15. Two out of 4 circuits in a black and white television are faulty and 3 out of 7 circuits in a color television are faulty. What is the probability of locating faulty circuits on the first try in both televisions? $\frac{3}{14}$

16. The probability that a boy is born is about $\frac{1}{2}$. If a family has 3 children, what is the probability that all of them are boys? $\frac{1}{8}$

17. A history class has 25 students of which 9 are girls. Each day one student is chosen at random. If a student can be chosen more than once, find the probability that a girl is chosen two days in a row. $\frac{81}{625}$

5-6 *Probability of Dependent Events*

Objective: To find the probability of dependent events.

Green Room   **Blue Room**

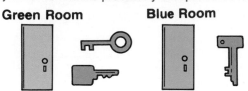

A hotel desk clerk has three different unlabeled keys and two rooms. Each room can be opened by one of the keys. The third key will open neither.

Since the selection of the first key will affect the selection of the second key, the events are **dependent**. For example, after the correct key is found for the green room, there are only two choices for the blue room.

Example

What is the probability that the first key chosen will open the green room and the second key chosen will open the blue room? Each key chosen is not replaced. Find the probability that the first key chosen opens the green room.

$$P(\text{Green}) = \frac{\textit{number of keys that will open the green room}}{\textit{total number of keys}} \quad \rightarrow \quad \frac{1}{3}$$

Find the probability that the second key chosen opens the blue room given that the first key opened the green room.

$$P(\text{Blue}) = \frac{\textit{number of keys that will open the blue room}}{\textit{total number of keys remaining}} \quad \rightarrow \quad \frac{1}{2}$$

Multiply the above probabilities. $\quad \frac{1}{3} \times \frac{1}{2} = \frac{1}{6}$

The probability that the first key chosen opens the green room and the second key chosen opens the blue room is $\frac{1}{6}$.

$$P(\text{Green and Blue}) = P(\text{Green}) \times P(\text{Blue})$$

Basic Skills Appendix, Pages 449, 458
Basic: 1–15; Average: 1–15; Enriched: 1–15

Exercises

Find the probability that the first key chosen opens the green room and the second key chosen opens the blue room. Each key chosen is not replaced.

1. two rooms, four keys $\quad \frac{1}{12}$ \qquad **2.** two rooms, five keys $\quad \frac{1}{20}$

3. two rooms, two keys (Hint: The probability of choosing a key from one key is 1.) $\quad \frac{1}{2}$

Suppose you choose three coins from those shown below. Each coin chosen is not replaced.

4. Find the number of possible outcomes.

   1st coin   *2nd coin*   *3rd coin*

   $\boxed{9}$ $\times$ $\boxed{8}$ $\times$ $\boxed{7}$ $=$ $\boxed{504}$

5. In how many outcomes are all three coins nickels? $3 \times 2 \times 1 = 6$

6. In how many outcomes are all three coins dimes? $4 \times 3 \times 2 = 24$

7. In how many outcomes are all three coins pennies? $2 \times 1 \times 0 = 0$

Use the results of exercises 4–7 to find each probability.

8. all three coins are nickels $\frac{6}{504}$ or $\frac{1}{84}$

9. all three coins are dimes $\frac{24}{504}$ or $\frac{1}{21}$

10. all three coins are pennies $\frac{0}{504}$ or 0

11. the coins are chosen, in order, penny, nickel, dime $\frac{24}{504}$ or $\frac{1}{21}$

Solve.

12. Adlai's drawer contains 6 brown socks and 5 black socks. He chooses two socks at random. Each sock chosen is not replaced. What is the probability that the first sock chosen is brown and the second is black? $\frac{3}{11}$

13. A box contains 8 orange, 10 yellow, and 4 blue marbles. Each marble drawn is not replaced. What is the probability of drawing three yellow marbles? $\frac{6}{77}$

14. Ginny's wallet contains nine $1 bills and four $5 bills. She chooses two bills at random. Each bill chosen is not replaced. What is the probability that she chooses two $5 bills? $\frac{1}{13}$

15. In a certain state, license plates have two digits followed by three letters. How many license plates are possible if the letters must be different? (Any of the 26 letters and 10 digits can be used.)
    1,560,000 license plates

This feature presents useful ways of solving mathematical problems on a calculator.

 Calculator

Probabilities can be expressed as percents.

Express $\frac{1}{8}$ as a percent. $\frac{1}{8}$ $\longrightarrow$ 1 $\boxed{\div}$ 8 $\boxed{=}$ *0.125* or 12.5%

Use a calculator to change each probability to a percent.

1. $\frac{5}{8}$ 62.5%   2. $\frac{2}{25}$ 8%   3. $\frac{6}{25}$ 24%   4. $\frac{3}{8}$ 37.5%   5. $\frac{9}{25}$ 36%

6. $\frac{3}{125}$ 2.4%   7. $\frac{17}{500}$ 3.4%   8. $\frac{113}{250}$ 45.2%   9. $\frac{327}{500}$ 65.4%   10. $\frac{84}{125}$ 67.2%

5-7 Adding Probabilities

Objective: To find the probability of an event using addition.

A bag contains 9 red tulip bulbs and 6 yellow tulip bulbs. Mr. Harmon chooses two bulbs at random. What is the probability that Mr. Harmon chooses two bulbs of the same color?

To answer this question, find the probability of choosing two red bulbs. Find the probability of choosing two yellow bulbs. Then add these probabilities.

Example

Find the probability of choosing two red bulbs. P(red, red)

number of red bulbs for the first choice — *number of red bulbs for the second choice*

$$\frac{\overset{3}{\cancel{9}}}{\underset{5}{\cancel{15}}} \times \frac{\overset{4}{\cancel{8}}}{\underset{7}{\cancel{14}}} = \frac{12}{35} \quad P(red, red) = \frac{12}{35}$$

total number of bulbs for the first choice — *total number of bulbs for the second choice*

Find the probability of choosing two yellow bulbs. P(yellow, yellow)

number of yellow bulbs for the first choice — *number of yellow bulbs for the second choice*

$$\frac{\overset{1}{\underset{13}{\cancel{6}}}}{\underset{13}{\cancel{15}}} \times \frac{\overset{1}{\cancel{5}}}{\underset{7}{\cancel{14}}} = \frac{1}{7} \quad P(yellow, yellow) = \frac{1}{7}$$

total number of bulbs for the first choice — *total number of bulbs for the second choice*

Add. P(red, red) + P(yellow, yellow)

$$\frac{12}{35} + \frac{1}{7} = \frac{12}{35} + \frac{5}{35} = \frac{17}{35}$$

The probability that Mr. Harmon chooses two bulbs of the same color is $\frac{17}{35}$.

The Key Skills provides practice of skills needed in the exercises.

Key Skills

Add. Write the sum in simplest form.

$\frac{1}{2}$	$\frac{5}{10}$
$+\ \frac{1}{5}$	$+\ \frac{2}{10}$
	$\frac{7}{10}$

1. $\frac{1}{15} + \frac{7}{15}$ **8/15**

2. $\frac{3}{4} + \frac{1}{2}$ $\frac{5}{4} = 1\frac{1}{4}$

3. $\frac{3}{4} + \frac{1}{7}$ **25/28**

4. $\frac{9}{10} + \frac{2}{5}$ **13/10**

5. $\frac{2}{5} + \frac{3}{7}$ **29/35**

6. $\frac{13}{15} + \frac{7}{10}$ $\frac{47}{30} = 1\frac{17}{30}$

7. $\frac{3}{8} + \frac{7}{12}$ **23/24**

8. $\frac{8}{9} + \frac{11}{15}$ $\frac{73}{45} = 1\frac{28}{45}$

9. $\frac{5}{6} + \frac{17}{24}$ $\frac{37}{24} = 1\frac{13}{24}$

Exercises

Suppose a marble is chosen at random
from those shown at the right. A second
marble is chosen without replacing the
first one. Find each probability.

1. both blue $\frac{7}{10} \times \frac{6}{9} = \frac{42}{90}$ or $\frac{7}{15}$ 2. both red $\frac{3}{10} \times \frac{2}{9} = \frac{6}{90}$ or $\frac{1}{15}$

3. a red, then a blue $\frac{7}{30}$ 4. a blue, then a red $\frac{7}{30}$

5. both the same color (Hint: Use addition.) $\frac{8}{15}$

6. one of each color (Hint: Use addition.) $\frac{7}{15}$

7. Find the sum of the probabilities for exercises 5 and 6.
   Is the sum what you would expect? 1; **Yes, since the four**
   possibilities account for all possible outcomes.

Solve.

8. Three coins are tossed. What is the
   probability of getting two tails and
   one head in any order? $\frac{3}{8}$

9. Four coins are tossed. What is the
   probability of getting three tails and
   one head in any order? $\frac{4}{16}$ or $\frac{1}{4}$

10. Refer to the previous page. What
    is the probability that Mr. Harmon
    chooses two bulbs that differ
    in color? $\frac{18}{35}$

11. Melva's drawer contains 8 blue socks
    and 3 brown socks. She chooses two
    socks at random. Each sock chosen is
    not replaced. Find the probability
    that she chooses a matching pair. $\frac{31}{55}$

This feature provides general topics about the uses of a computer.

Computer

Microcomputers contain two types of internal memory. One is the
Read-Only Memory. **Read-Only Memory** (ROM) may be thought of as
the "factory-installed brains" of the computer. ROM chips are
used to store programs that do not change. A program such as
the disk operating system might be stored in ROM.

Random Access Memory (RAM) chips are used to store programs
entered by the user. These programs can be entered from the
keyboard or from another input device. RAM is a **volatile** type of
memory. This means that information stored in RAM is lost if
the computer loses power.

State whether each type of information would be stored in ROM or RAM.

1. a program written by your teacher **RAM**

2. a game program read in from a disk **RAM**

3. a built-in word processing program **ROM**

4. a built-in paint program **ROM**

5. Give an example of a program that you have used. State
   whether it was stored in ROM or RAM. **Answers may vary.**

5-8 Estimating Probabilities

Objective: To find the probability of an event using estimation.

A quality-control inspector made a list of
the number of radios made and the number
of defective radios. He can use the
list to determine the probability that a
certain type of radio is defective.

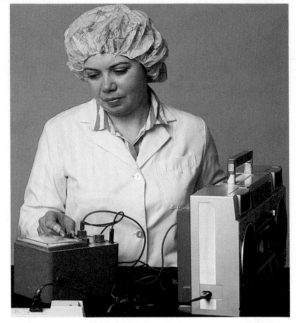

Radio	Units Made	Defective Units
SoundMaster AM	1,127	23
SoundMaster AM/FM	1,493	27
AudioTech AM	2,395	37
AudioTech AM/FM	2,772	32
MusicMaker AM	5,378	56
MusicMaker AM/FM	6,732	67
Total	19,897	242

Example

If a SoundMaster AM radio is chosen at random, about what is the probability that it is defective?

probability of defective radio $= \dfrac{23}{1,127}$ ← *number of defective units*
                                              ← *number of units made*

Estimate: $\dfrac{23}{1,127}$ → $\dfrac{20}{1,000}$ or $\dfrac{1}{50}$

The probability that a SoundMaster AM radio is defective is about
$\dfrac{1}{50}$. In other words, for about every 50 SoundMaster AM radios
made, one will be defective.

Basic Skills Appendix, Page 449
Basic: 2–24 even; Average: 1–25; Enriched: 1–25 odd

Exercises

Answers may vary. Typical answers are given.

Estimate the probability of choosing a defective radio for each type of radio.

1. SoundMaster AM/FM radio $\dfrac{3}{150}$ 2. AudioTech AM radio $\dfrac{1}{60}$

3. AudioTech AM/FM radio $\dfrac{1}{100}$ 4. MusicMaker AM radio $\dfrac{1}{90}$

5. MusicMaker AM/FM radio $\dfrac{1}{100}$ 6. AM radios $\dfrac{1}{90}$

7. AM/FM radios $\dfrac{1}{100}$ 8. SoundMaster radios $\dfrac{1}{60}$

9. AudioTech radios $\dfrac{7}{500}$ 10. MusicMaker radios $\dfrac{1}{100}$

Complete the chart below by estimating the probability of forest fires for each month. Answers may vary. Typical answers are given.

Month	Number of Fires	Probability of Fires
January	33	11. $\frac{3}{200}$
February	28	12. $\frac{3}{200}$
March	45	13. $\frac{1}{40}$
April	74	14. $\frac{7}{200}$
May	151	15. $\frac{1}{10}$
June	219	16. $\frac{1}{10}$
July	331	17. $\frac{3}{20}$
August	475	18. $\frac{1}{4}$
September	436	19. $\frac{1}{10}$
October	342	20. $\frac{3}{20}$
November	190	21. $\frac{1}{10}$
December	83	22. $\frac{1}{20}$
Total	2,407	

Solve. Answers may vary. Typical answers are given.

23. Molly has made 28 out of her last 43 free throws. Estimate the probability that she will make her next free throw. $\frac{3}{4}$

24. There are 18 green grapes and 12 red grapes in a bowl. Tyler chooses one grape at random without looking in the bowl. Estimate the probability that he chooses a red grape. $\frac{2}{5}$

25. There are 27 defective light bulbs out of 2,143 light bulbs produced. One light bulb is chosen at random to be tested. Estimate the probability of choosing a defective light bulb. $\frac{1}{70}$

This feature promotes students' mental abilities in computation and reasonableness.

Mental Math

Probabilities may be expressed as unit fractions. A **unit fraction** is a fraction with one as the numerator.

Answers may vary. Typical answers are given.

Estimate the unit fraction closest to the given probability.

1. $\frac{23}{570}$ a. $\frac{1}{10}$ b. $\frac{1}{17}$ c. $\frac{1}{25}$ **c**

2. $\frac{17}{320}$ a. $\frac{1}{30}$ b. $\frac{1}{11}$ c. $\frac{1}{20}$ **c**

3. $\frac{3}{10}$ a. $\frac{1}{29}$ b. $\frac{1}{7}$ c. $\frac{1}{3}$ **c**

4. $\frac{7}{90}$ a. $\frac{1}{15}$ b. $\frac{1}{13}$ c. $\frac{1}{6}$ **b**

5. $\frac{10}{141}$ a. $\frac{1}{9}$ b. $\frac{1}{31}$ c. $\frac{1}{14}$ **c**

6. $\frac{34}{880}$ a. $\frac{1}{28}$ b. $\frac{1}{2}$ c. $\frac{1}{16}$ **a**

7. $\frac{49}{1,560}$ a. $\frac{1}{32}$ b. $\frac{1}{23}$ c. $\frac{1}{12}$ **a**

8. $\frac{4}{31}$ a. $\frac{1}{15}$ b. $\frac{1}{8}$ c. $\frac{1}{33}$ **b**

CHAPTER 5 REVIEW

Vocabulary/Concepts

Choose a word from the list at the right that best completes each sentence.

1. When each outcome has the same probability, the outcomes are ___?___. **equally likely**

2. If one event is affected by the occurrence of another event, the events are ___?___. **dependent**

3. An ___?___ is a possible result. **outcome**

4. A ___?___ is a way of listing outcomes. **tree diagram**

5. Two events are ___?___ if the occurrence of one event does not affect the occurrence of another event. **independent**

6. ___?___ means a way of choosing things without any particular method. **random**

7. A ___?___ is the outcome that is preferred. **favorable outcome**

8. ___?___ is the number of favorable outcomes divided by the number of possible outcomes. **probability**

> chance
> dependent
> equally likely
> favorable outcome
> independent
> odds
> outcome
> probability
> random
> tree diagram
> unit fraction

Exercises

A penny and a nickel are tossed. Find the number of outcomes for the following.   Pages 95–97

9. two heads **1**

10. no heads **1**

11. one head **2**

12. one tail **2**

13. at least one tail **3**

14. no more than one head **3**

Use the lunch menu at the right to complete the following.   Pages 96–97

Sandwich	Potato	Drink
Hamburger, H	Baked, B	Tea, T
Egg Salad, E	Fries, F	Water, W
Grilled Cheese, G		

15. Draw a tree diagram for the lunch menu. **See students' work.**

16. How many outcomes are possible? **12 outcomes**

17. List the possible outcomes.
HBT, HBW, HFT, HFW, EBT, EBW, EFT, EFW, GBT, GBW, GFT, GFW

18. One possible outcome is EBW. What does EBW mean? **egg salad, baked potato, water**

The spinner at the right is spun once. Find each probability.   Pages 100–101

19. a four $\frac{1}{6}$

20. a one or a two $\frac{2}{6}$ or $\frac{1}{3}$

21. an even number $\frac{3}{6}$ or $\frac{1}{2}$

22. a number less than 6 $\frac{5}{6}$

112   *Probability*

Two dice are rolled. Find each probability. Pages 100–101

23. 3, 1 or 1, 3 $\frac{1}{18}$ **24.** a sum of 6 $\frac{5}{36}$ **25.** a product of 1 $\frac{1}{36}$

26. not a sum of 4 or 5 $\frac{29}{36}$ **27.** not the same number on both dice $\frac{5}{6}$

A box contains 6 red, 8 green, and 2 blue marbles. One is chosen, replaced, and a second marble is chosen. Find each probability. Pages 104–105

28. both green $\frac{1}{4}$ **29.** both blue $\frac{1}{64}$

30. a red, then a blue $\frac{3}{64}$ **31.** a green, then a red $\frac{3}{16}$

Refer to the cards at the right. Two cards are chosen at random without replacement. Find each probability. Pages 106–107

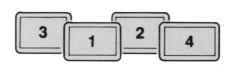

32. both odd-numbered $\frac{1}{6}$

33. both 3 or less $\frac{1}{2}$

Eleven students want to be prompters for a school play. Two will be chosen at random. The table at the right describes the eleven students. Find each probability. Pages 106–109

	Sophomores	Juniors	Seniors
girls	4	0	1
boys	1	3	2

34. both seniors $\frac{6}{110}$ or $\frac{3}{55}$ **35.** a girl, then a boy $\frac{30}{110}$ or $\frac{3}{11}$

36. both from the same class (Hint: You must add *three* probabilities.) $\frac{32}{110}$ or $\frac{16}{55}$

Use the chart at the right to estimate the probability of choosing a defective battery for each type of battery. Pages 110–111

Battery	Size	Units Made	Defective Units
Power Life	AAA	1,243	28
Power Life	C	1,486	21
Power Life	D	2,124	32
Super Tough	AAA	2,537	46
Super Tough	C	3,186	22
Super Tough	D	2,794	43
Total		13,370	192

37. Power Life AAA $\frac{3}{100}$ **38.** Super Tough AAA $\frac{1}{60}$

39. Super Tough C $\frac{1}{150}$ **40.** Power Life D $\frac{1}{70}$

41. Size D batteries $\frac{1}{60}$ **42.** Power Life batteries $\frac{1}{60}$

Solve.

43. Samuel has 3 ties he can wear with any of his 6 shirts. How many outfits are possible? **18 outfits**

44. This spinner is spun twice. How many outcomes are possible? **36 outcomes**

45. How many outcomes are possible of all 3-digit numerals using the digits 7, 8, and 9? **6 outcomes**

CHAPTER 5 TEST

Tell how many outcomes are possible for the following.

1. all different arrangements of the letters X, Y, and Z **6 outcomes**

2. spinning this spinner twice **16 outcomes**

Suppose a penny, a dime, and a quarter are tossed at the same time. Complete the following.

3. Draw the tree diagram. **See Teacher Guide.**

4. How many outcomes are possible? **8 outcomes**

5. How do HTH and HHT differ? **HTH has heads on the penny and quarter while HHT has heads on the penny and dime.**

6. How many outcomes have tails on the penny? **4 outcomes**

This spinner is spun once. Find each probability.

7. red $\frac{1}{6}$

8. not blue $\frac{4}{6}$ or $\frac{2}{3}$

9. white or blue $\frac{5}{6}$

A box contains 9 green, 5 blue, and 2 red marbles. One is chosen, replaced, and a second marble is chosen. Find each probability.

10. both marbles are red $\frac{1}{64}$

11. a red marble, then a blue one $\frac{5}{128}$

Suppose two coins are chosen at random from those shown at the right. Each coin chosen is not replaced. Find each probability.

12. both pennies $\frac{1}{36}$

13. a dime, then a nickel $\frac{1}{6}$

14. a penny, then a dime $\frac{1}{9}$

15. both the same $\frac{5}{18}$

Solve.

16. For dinner, you have 5 choices for a main dish, 4 choices for a vegetable, 2 for a fruit, and 2 for a beverage. How many different dinner combinations are possible? **80 choices**

17. A bag contains 4 red, 3 orange, and 3 yellow marbles. Three marbles are selected at random. They are not replaced. What is the probability of selecting a red, orange, and yellow marble in that order? $\frac{1}{20}$

CUMULATIVE REVIEW

Change each decimal, fraction, or mixed numeral to a percent. Pages 56–58

1. $\frac{16}{100}$ 16%   2. $3\frac{3}{4}$ 375%   3. 0.6 60%   4. $\frac{12}{25}$ 48%   5. $\frac{3}{8}$ $37\frac{1}{2}$%

Change each percent to a decimal. Pages 56–58

6. 35% 0.35   7. 215% 2.15   8. 4.9% 0.049   9. 8% 0.08   10. 0.7% 0.007

Use the circle graph at the right to answer each question. Pages 80–81

11. What section of the graph is smallest? health

12. What percent of time is spent on math? 30%

13. What percent of time is spent on science? 18%

14. Jack spent 100 minutes on homework. How many minutes did he spend on English? 22 min.

15. Carole spent 150 minutes on homework. How many minutes did she spend on history? 30 min.

Time Spent on Homework

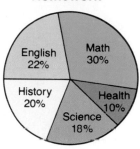

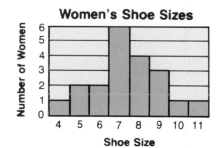
Women's Shoe Sizes

Use the histogram at the left to answer each question. Pages 84–85

16. How many women were surveyed? 20 women

17. What is the most common shoe size? size 7

18. How many of the women wear size 8 shoes? 4

19. How many of the women wear size 10 shoes? 1

20. Which shoe size is worn by three of the women? size 9

List all possible outcomes. Then tell how many outcomes are possible. Page 95

21. All different arrangements of the letters x, y, and z. xyz, xzy, yxz, yzx, zxy, zyx; 6

22. This spinner is spun three times. (One possible outcome is ABB.) AAA, AAB, ABA, ABB, BAA, BAB, BBA, BBB; 8

A penny, a nickel, and a dime are tossed. Find the number of outcomes. Pages 96–97

23. TTH 1   24. exactly one head 3   25. at least two tails 4

Solve.

26. Mr. Lee's purchases total $52 and $2.86 is added for sales tax. What is the tax rate? $5\frac{1}{2}$%

27. A multiple choice test has five questions. Each question is answered a, b, c, or d. How many sets of answers are possible? 1,024 sets of answers

Using Probability and Statistics

6-1 Odds

Objective: To find the odds, given the probability.

Test results show that the probability of a successful launch of the Orion Satellite is $\frac{5}{7}$. The probability of an unsuccessful launch is $\frac{2}{7}$. The **odds** for an event is the ratio of the number of successes to the number of failures for a given number of tries. *Note that $\frac{5}{7} + \frac{2}{7} = 1$.*

Example

What are the odds for successfully launching the Orion Satellite?

odds for success $= \frac{5}{2}$ ←   *probable number of successes out of 7 tries*
                        ←   *probable number of failures out of 7 tries*

The odds for successfully launching the Orion Satellite is 5 to 2.

Basic: 1–23 odd; Average: 1–23; Enriched: 2–22 even

Exercises

The probability that the Mayville Tigers will win is $\frac{7}{12}$. The probability that the Harding Blue Sox will win is $\frac{5}{12}$. Find the odds for the following.

1. Tigers win
7 to 5

2. Blue Sox win
5 to 7

3. Blue Sox lose
7 to 5

4. Tigers lose
5 to 7

A die is rolled. Find the odds for each roll.

5. a 2 1 to 5

6. not a 1 5 to 1

7. a 3 or a 4 2 to 4

8. a 2, 3, or 5 3 to 3

9. an odd number 3 to 3

10. an even number 3 to 3

11. a number greater than 4 2 to 4

12. a 4 or an odd number 4 to 2

13. a number greater than 3 and less than 5 1 to 5

Two dice are rolled. Find the odds for each roll.
You may wish to refer students to the list of outcomes on page 101.

14. a sum of 6 5 to 31

15. a sum of 8 5 to 31

16. not a sum of 5 32 to 4

17. an odd sum 18 to 18

18. a sum of 12 or 9 5 to 31

19. both dice the same 6 to 30

20. a sum of 6 and a 2 on one die
2 to 34

21. a sum of 10 and a 6 on one die
2 to 34

Solve.

22. In a contest, five price tags are posted. One is correct. If one price tag is chosen at random, what are the odds for choosing the correct one? 1 to 4

23. Two coins are tossed. What are the odds for tossing exactly one head? What are the odds for tossing at least one head? 2 to 2, 3 to 1

Teacher Resource Book, Page 149

6-2 Percents and Probability

Objective: To change chance to probability and vice versa.

Jim Bishop and his friends are going on a ski trip. A 70% **chance** of snow is predicted. The chance of an event occurring is the probability of the event's happening expressed as a percent.

Examples

A. What is the probability of snow?

$$70\% = \frac{70}{100} = \frac{7}{10}$$

The probability of snow is $\frac{7}{10}$.

B. Suppose the probability of snow is $\frac{2}{5}$. What is the chance of snow?

$$\frac{2}{5} = 2 \div 5 \quad \blacktriangleright \quad 5\overline{)2.0}^{\ 0.4} \text{ or } 40\% \quad 2 \boxed{\div} 5 \boxed{=} \ 0.4$$

The chance of snow is 40%.

Key Skills

The Key Skills provides practice of skills needed in the exercises.

Change each percent to a fraction in simplest form.

$$18\% = \frac{18}{100}$$
$$= \frac{9}{50}$$

$$14.5\% = \frac{14.5}{100}$$
$$= \frac{14.5 \times 10}{100 \times 10}$$
$$= \frac{145}{1,000}$$
$$= \frac{29}{200}$$

$$66\tfrac{2}{3}\% = \frac{66\tfrac{2}{3}}{100}$$
$$= 66\tfrac{2}{3} \div 100$$
$$= \frac{\overset{2}{\cancel{200}}}{3} \times \frac{1}{\cancel{100}}$$
$$= \frac{2}{3}$$

1. 8% $\frac{2}{25}$ **2.** 24% $\frac{6}{25}$ **3.** 6% $\frac{3}{50}$ **4.** 65% $\frac{13}{20}$

5. 0.5% $\frac{1}{200}$ **6.** $2\tfrac{1}{2}$% $\frac{1}{40}$ **7.** 87.5% $\frac{7}{8}$ **8.** $33\tfrac{1}{3}$% $\frac{1}{3}$

Basic Skills Appendix, Pages 428, 449, 460
Basic: 2–48 even; Average: 1–49; Enriched: 1–49 odd

Exercises

Write each chance as a probability in simplest form.

1. 10% $\frac{1}{10}$ **2.** 5% $\frac{1}{20}$ **3.** 1% $\frac{1}{100}$ **4.** 100% 1

5. 80% $\frac{4}{5}$ **6.** 90% $\frac{9}{10}$ **7.** 25% $\frac{1}{4}$ **8.** 20% $\frac{1}{5}$

9. $8\tfrac{1}{3}$% $\frac{1}{12}$ **10.** $33\tfrac{1}{3}$% $\frac{1}{3}$ **11.** 7.5% $\frac{3}{40}$ **12.** $16\tfrac{2}{3}$% $\frac{1}{6}$

13. There is a 50% chance of rain. $\frac{1}{2}$

14. The chance of snow is 60%. $\frac{3}{5}$

15. A 15% chance of showers. $\frac{3}{20}$

16. It will rain $62\tfrac{1}{2}$% of the days. $\frac{5}{8}$

Write each probability as a chance.

17. $\frac{1}{2}$ 50%   **18.** $\frac{3}{5}$ 60%   **19.** $\frac{7}{10}$ 70%   **20.** 1 100%   **21.** $\frac{17}{20}$ 85%   **22.** $\frac{7}{25}$ 28%

23. 0 0%   **24.** $\frac{1}{8}$ 12$\frac{1}{2}$%   **25.** $\frac{1}{40}$ 2$\frac{1}{2}$%   **26.** $\frac{7}{8}$ 87$\frac{1}{2}$%   **27.** $\frac{1}{6}$ 16$\frac{2}{3}$%   **28.** $\frac{2}{3}$ 66$\frac{2}{3}$%

29. The probability of rain is $\frac{1}{4}$. 25%   **30.** There is a $\frac{1}{10}$ probability of showers. 10%

31. The probability of snow is $\frac{1}{3}$. 33$\frac{1}{3}$%   **32.** The probability of frost is $\frac{5}{6}$. 83$\frac{1}{3}$%

Suppose you draw one of the cards shown at the right. Find the chance of drawing each of the following.

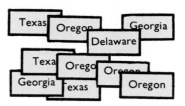

33. Oregon 40% **34.** Texas 30%   **35.** Georgia 20%

36. Delaware   **37.** not Georgia   **38.** Texas or Oregon 70%
10%   80%

Suppose you choose one letter from each city named below. Find the chance that the letter is a vowel. (a, e, i, o, or u)

39. Los Angeles   **40.** Omaha 60%   **41.** El Paso 50%
40%
42. Boston 33$\frac{1}{3}$% **43.** Columbus 37$\frac{1}{2}$%**44.** Milwaukee 55$\frac{5}{9}$%

Answer the following.

45. Naomi's chance of winning a cake raffle is 1%. What is the probability that Naomi wins the raffle? $\frac{1}{100}$

46. This spinner is spun once. What is the chance of red? 37$\frac{1}{2}$%

47. A die is rolled once. What is the chance of rolling an even number? 50%

48. A coin is tossed three times. What is the chance of tossing at least two tails? 50%

49. There is a 75% chance that a storm will pass over the city. The storm pattern suggests that 40% of the city will get at least 0.01 inch of rain. Find the chance that any given area in the city will receive at least 0.01 inch of rain. 30%

This feature presents general topics of mathematics.

Math Break

See Teacher Guide for more information.

Percentile is a number that indicates the percent of scores equal to or below it. For example, a score in the 70th percentile means that 70% of the scores are equal to or less than the given score.

Determine whether each statement is true or false.

1. A 10th percentile score is better than or equal to 10% of the scores. true

2. The 50th percentile includes the median score. true

6-3 More on Odds

Objective: To change odds to probability and vice versa.

The odds that the governor will be reelected are 5 to 3. The odds for an event compare the number of successes to the number of failures for a given number of tries.

$$5 \quad \text{to} \quad 3$$
successes   *failures*

You can use the odds for an event to find the probability of the event.

Examples

A. What is the probability that the governor is reelected?

The probability of an event compares the number of successes to the total number of tries.

$$\begin{array}{r} 5 \; successes \\ + \; 3 \; failures \\ \hline 8 \; \text{total tries} \end{array} \qquad \text{probability} = \frac{5}{8} \quad \begin{array}{l} \leftarrow \; successes \\ \leftarrow \; total \; tries \end{array}$$

The probability that the governor is reelected is $\frac{5}{8}$.

B. A senator has a 30% chance of being reelected. What are the odds that the senator is reelected?

To find the number of successes, express a 30% chance as a probability.

$$30\% = \frac{30}{100} = \frac{3}{10} \quad \begin{array}{l} \leftarrow \; successes \\ \leftarrow \; total \; tries \end{array}$$

Find the number of failures.
$$\begin{array}{r} 10 \; total \; tries \\ - \; 3 \; successes \\ \hline 7 \; \text{failures} \end{array}$$

Find the odds.

$$3 \quad \text{to} \quad 7$$
successes   *failures*   The odds that the senator is reelected are 3 to 7.

Exercises

Find the probability of an event given its odds. Express the probability as a fraction in simplest form and as a percent.

1. 1 to 9 $\frac{1}{10}$, 10%

2. 1 to 3 $\frac{1}{4}$, 25%

3. 3 to 7 $\frac{3}{10}$, 30%

4. 2 to 3 $\frac{2}{5}$, 40%

5. 1 to 1 $\frac{1}{2}$, 50%

6. 3 to 9 $\frac{1}{4}$, 25%

7. 3 to 17 $\frac{3}{20}$, 15%

8. 6 to 4 $\frac{3}{5}$, 60%

9. 8 to 12 $\frac{2}{5}$, 40%

10. 14 to 2 $\frac{7}{8}$, $87\frac{1}{2}$%

11. 2 to 1 $\frac{2}{3}$, $66\frac{2}{3}$%

12. 3 to 5 $\frac{3}{8}$, $37\frac{1}{2}$%

13. The odds on that horse are 6 to 4. $\frac{3}{5}$, 60%

14. The odds against rain are 4 to 1. $\frac{4}{5}$, 80%

15. The odds for a trial are 1 to 2. $\frac{1}{3}$, $33\frac{1}{3}$%

16. The odds for snow are 7 to 1. $\frac{7}{8}$, $87\frac{1}{2}$%

Find the odds for an event given its probability or chance.

17. $\frac{1}{10}$ 1 to 9

18. 90% 9 to 1

19. 30% 3 to 7

20. $\frac{1}{4}$ 1 to 3

21. 5% 1 to 19

22. $\frac{1}{6}$ 1 to 5

23. 95% 19 to 1

24. $\frac{5}{9}$ 5 to 4

25. $\frac{7}{11}$ 7 to 4

26. 85% 17 to 3

27. $\frac{2}{3}$ 2 to 1

28. $33\frac{1}{3}$% 1 to 2

29. The probability of a loss is $\frac{4}{5}$. 4 to 1

30. We have a 15% chance of winning. 3 to 17

31. It will rain 5 out of 6 days. 5 to 1

32. There is a 65% chance of showers. 13 to 7

Answer the following.

33. The odds that Mayor Cotter is reelected are 5 to 4. What is the probability that she is reelected? $\frac{5}{9}$

34. The odds that Martin will be elected as student council president are 3 to 2. What is the chance that he will be elected? 60%

This feature provides general topics about the uses of a computer.

Computer

Computers *speak* different languages. The names of these languages are usually derived in one of two ways. Names such as **BASIC** and **FORTRAN** are made up of letters from words that name the languages. BASIC stands for **B**eginner's **A**ll-Purpose **S**ymbolic **I**nstruction **C**ode. FORTRAN stands for **FOR**mula **TRAN**slation.

Other languages are named using words that refer to someone or something else. Logo comes from the Greek word *logos*, which means knowledge or reason. Ada is named to honor Lady Ada Lovelace who is given credit for being the first programmer.

Using library resources, find the origin of the name of each of these programming languages.

1. Common Business-Oriented Language   3. Program Language 1

2. Named for Blaise Pascal, French philosopher and mathematician

4. Algorithmic Language or Algebraic Oriented Language

1. COBOL   **2.** Pascal   **3.** PL/1   **4.** Algol

6-4   Probability and Predictions

Objective: To compare probabilities and expected values.

A weekly magazine included a multiple choice quiz on definitions of uncommon words. A sample question is shown below.

---

jink
- ○ a broad leap in ballet
- ○ an American wildcat
- ● a quick turn   *The correct answer is a quick turn.*
- ○ to throw out of joint

Examples

A. **Charlene Turner does not know the answer so she guesses. What is the probability that she guesses the correct answer?**

$\dfrac{1}{4}$ ← *number of correct answers*
   ← *number of possible answers*

The probability that Charlene guesses the correct answer is $\frac{1}{4}$.

B. **The quiz has 20 questions. Each question has four choices. Suppose Charlene guesses each answer. How many questions can she expect to guess correctly?**

This value is the **expected value**.

probability of a   number of   expected
correct answer   questions   value

$$\frac{1}{4} \quad \times \quad 20 \quad = \quad 5$$

Charlene can expect to guess 5 answers correctly.

Basic Skills Appendix, Page 458
Basic: 1–22; Average: 1–22; Enriched: 1–22

Exercises

Complete.

1. Find the probability you will guess the correct answer to a question with five choices. $\frac{1}{5}$

2. Find the probability you will guess the incorrect answer to a question with five choices. $\frac{4}{5}$

3. Find the probability you can guess the correct answer to a true-false question. $\frac{1}{2}$

4. On a 10-item true-false test, how many can you expect to guess correctly? **5**

Suppose all the answers are guesses. Find the expected score for each test.

5. 25 questions, 5 choices for each **5**

6. 50 true-false questions **25**

7. 100 questions, 4 choices for each **25**

8. 75 questions, 3 choices for each **25**

9. 10 true-false questions; 20 multiple choice, 5 choices each **9**

10. 20 true-false questions; 15 questions, 3 choices each; 15 questions, 5 choices each **18**

A coin is tossed. Predict the number of tails for each of the following.

11. 8 tosses **4**

12. 100 tosses **50**

13. 612 tosses **306**

14. 884 tosses **442**

Suppose you roll a die 60 times. Find how many times you would expect each to occur.

15. a three **10**

16. a one or a two **20**

17. not a six **50**

18. an even number **30**

19. a prime number **30**

20. a four or less **40**

Solve.

21. This spinner is separated so that it is $\frac{1}{8}$ green, $\frac{1}{4}$ white, $\frac{1}{3}$ red, and $\frac{1}{6}$ blue. The remainder is yellow. In 24 spins, how many are expected to be yellow? **3 spins**

22. Gabe took a multiple-choice science test. There were 30 questions and each had 5 choices. How many answers could he expect to guess correctly? **6 correct answers**

This feature presents general topics of mathematics.

Math Break

The **expected value** of a roll of a die can be found as follows. **Have students explain why.**

$$\text{expected value} = \left(\frac{1}{6} \times 1\right) + \left(\frac{1}{6} \times 2\right) + \left(\frac{1}{6} \times 3\right) + \left(\frac{1}{6} \times 4\right) + \left(\frac{1}{6} \times 5\right) + \left(\frac{1}{6} \times 6\right)$$

$$= \frac{1}{6} + \frac{2}{6} + \frac{3}{6} + \frac{4}{6} + \frac{5}{6} + \frac{6}{6}$$

$$= \frac{1 + 2 + 3 + 4 + 5 + 6}{6}$$

$$= \frac{21}{6} \text{ or } 3\frac{1}{2}$$

The expected value of a roll of a die is $3\frac{1}{2}$.

Find the expected value for throwing a dart at each target.

1. **5**

2. $2\frac{1}{3}$

3. $3\frac{1}{2}$

4. $8\frac{3}{4}$

This page provides an aid for maintaining skills.

PRACTICE

Estimate. Answers may vary. Typical answers are given.

1. $\begin{array}{r} 452 \\ +\ 87 \\ \hline 540 \end{array}$

2. $\begin{array}{r} 8,642 \\ -\ 3,295 \\ \hline 6,000 \end{array}$

3. $\begin{array}{r} 927 \\ \times\ 48 \\ \hline 45,000 \end{array}$

4. $\begin{array}{r} 2,864 \\ \times\ 22 \\ \hline 60,000 \end{array}$

5. $17\overline{)4,128}$ 200

6. $\begin{array}{r} 3.21 \\ +\ 6.84 \\ \hline 10.00 \end{array}$

7. $\begin{array}{r} 6.74 \\ +\ 2.98 \\ \hline 10.00 \end{array}$

8. $\begin{array}{r} 8.17 \\ -\ 2.26 \\ \hline 6.00 \end{array}$

9. $\begin{array}{r} 8.40 \\ \times\ 0.75 \\ \hline 6.4 \end{array}$

10. $4.4\overline{)15.5}$ 4

Add or subtract.

11. $\begin{array}{r} 2,789 \\ 3,241 \\ +\ 873 \\ \hline 6,903 \end{array}$

12. $\begin{array}{r} 16,728 \\ 7,651 \\ +\ 5,184 \\ \hline 29,563 \end{array}$

13. $\begin{array}{r} 36,294 \\ 2,764 \\ +\ 48,153 \\ \hline 87,211 \end{array}$

14. $\begin{array}{r} 3,624 \\ -\ 1,628 \\ \hline 1,996 \end{array}$

15. $\begin{array}{r} 5,136 \\ -\ 2,716 \\ \hline 2,420 \end{array}$

16. $\begin{array}{r} 8.407 \\ 0.78 \\ +\ 6.5 \\ \hline 15.687 \end{array}$

17. $\begin{array}{r} 52.93 \\ 7.406 \\ +\ 3.8 \\ \hline 64.136 \end{array}$

18. $\begin{array}{r} 72.83 \\ -\ 17.46 \\ \hline 55.37 \end{array}$

19. $\begin{array}{r} 5.307 \\ -\ 2.143 \\ \hline 3.164 \end{array}$

20. $\begin{array}{r} 8.2 \\ -\ 6.95 \\ \hline 1.25 \end{array}$

Multiply or divide.

21. $\begin{array}{r} 681 \\ \times\ 12 \\ \hline 8,172 \end{array}$

22. $\begin{array}{r} 814 \\ \times\ 453 \\ \hline 368,742 \end{array}$

23. $\begin{array}{r} 2,576 \\ \times\ 278 \\ \hline 716,128 \end{array}$

24. $94\overline{)3,760}$ 40

25. $83\overline{)5,644}$ 68

26. $\begin{array}{r} 3.78 \\ \times\ 16 \\ \hline 60.48 \end{array}$

27. $\begin{array}{r} 24.5 \\ \times\ 3.7 \\ \hline 90.65 \end{array}$

28. $\begin{array}{r} 6.032 \\ \times\ 0.59 \\ \hline 3.55888 \end{array}$

29. $37\overline{)8.399}$ 0.227

30. $7.4\overline{)0.4366}$ 0.059

Write the following as a decimal. Then write its equivalent fraction or mixed numeral.

31. 4 tenths $0.4, \frac{4}{10}$

32. 1 hundredth $0.01, \frac{1}{100}$

33. 1 thousandth $0.001, \frac{1}{1,000}$

34. 15 hundredths $0.15, \frac{15}{100}$

35. 207 thousandths $0.207, \frac{207}{1,000}$

36. 40 hundredths $0.40, \frac{40}{100}$

37. 1 and 2 tenths $1.2, 1\frac{2}{10}$

38. 4 and 52 hundredths $4.52, 4\frac{52}{100}$

39. 8 and 6 hundredths $8.06, 8\frac{6}{100}$

40. 3 and 175 thousandths $3.175, 3\frac{175}{1,000}$

41. 52 and 8 tenths $52.8, 52\frac{8}{10}$

42. 7 and 27 thousandths $7.027, 7\frac{27}{1,000}$

Find the GCF of each pair of numbers.

43. 5 and 25   5

44. 3 and 9   3

45. 6 and 8   2

46. 4 and 16   4

47. 10 and 4   2

48. 12 and 16   4

49. 9 and 15   3

50. 8 and 12   4

Express each fraction in simplest form.

51. $\frac{2}{4}$ $\frac{1}{2}$

52. $\frac{3}{9}$ $\frac{1}{3}$

53. $\frac{6}{10}$ $\frac{3}{5}$

54. $\frac{10}{12}$ $\frac{5}{6}$

55. $\frac{12}{15}$ $\frac{4}{5}$

56. $\frac{5}{4}$ $1\frac{1}{4}$

57. $\frac{6}{3}$ 2

58. $\frac{12}{5}$ $2\frac{2}{5}$

59. $\frac{12}{8}$ $1\frac{1}{2}$

60. $\frac{16}{6}$ $2\frac{2}{3}$

Complete.

61. $\frac{2}{3} = \frac{\blacksquare}{12}$ 8

62. $\frac{3}{4} = \frac{\blacksquare}{8}$ 6

63. $\frac{1}{2} = \frac{\blacksquare}{6}$ 3

64. $\frac{5}{6} = \frac{\blacksquare}{12}$ 10

65. $\frac{7}{8} = \frac{14}{\blacksquare}$ 16

66. $\frac{5}{12} = \frac{\blacksquare}{24}$ 10

67. $\frac{2}{5} = \frac{\blacksquare}{30}$ 12

68. $\frac{3}{4} = \frac{12}{\blacksquare}$ 16

Add or subtract. Write the sum or difference in simplest form.

69. $\frac{1}{4} + \frac{2}{4}$ $\frac{3}{4}$

70. $\frac{1}{3} + \frac{2}{6}$ $\frac{2}{3}$

71. $\frac{1}{2} + \frac{1}{8}$ $\frac{5}{8}$

72. $\frac{3}{10} + \frac{1}{5}$ $\frac{1}{2}$

73. $\frac{1}{4} + \frac{3}{8}$ $\frac{5}{8}$

74. $\frac{2}{3} + \frac{1}{6}$ $\frac{5}{6}$

75. $\frac{3}{4} + \frac{5}{12}$ $1\frac{1}{6}$

76. $\frac{1}{2} + \frac{3}{4}$ $1\frac{1}{4}$

77. $\frac{1}{2} + \frac{2}{5}$ $\frac{9}{10}$

78. $\frac{5}{6} + \frac{1}{4}$ $1\frac{1}{12}$

79. $\frac{2}{3} + \frac{7}{8}$ $1\frac{13}{24}$

80. $\frac{3}{4} + \frac{4}{5}$ $1\frac{11}{20}$

81. $\frac{3}{4} - \frac{1}{4}$ $\frac{1}{2}$

82. $\frac{5}{8} - \frac{2}{8}$ $\frac{3}{8}$

83. $\frac{6}{10} - \frac{1}{10}$ $\frac{1}{2}$

84. $\frac{7}{12} - \frac{3}{12}$ $\frac{1}{3}$

85. $\frac{3}{10} - \frac{1}{5}$ $\frac{1}{10}$

86. $\frac{2}{3} - \frac{1}{6}$ $\frac{1}{2}$

87. $\frac{5}{12} - \frac{1}{4}$ $\frac{1}{6}$

88. $\frac{3}{5} - \frac{1}{10}$ $\frac{1}{2}$

89. $\frac{3}{4} - \frac{1}{3}$ $\frac{5}{12}$

90. $\frac{4}{5} - \frac{1}{2}$ $\frac{3}{10}$

91. $\frac{5}{6} - \frac{3}{8}$ $\frac{11}{24}$

92. $\frac{3}{4} - \frac{1}{6}$ $\frac{7}{12}$

Answer the following.

93. Sam Spode earned $9,487 in wages and $5,862 in tips. What is his total earned income? **$15,349**

94. Sylvia Sanchez earns $5.65 an hour. She works 37 hours a week. How much does she earn in one week? **$209.05**

95. Joe Wesniewski earns $624 every two weeks. He works 40 hours a week. What is Joe's hourly wage? **$7.80**

96. Willa Brady's total payroll deductions are $214. Suppose 8¢ of each dollar goes to her retirement savings. How much of her total deductions goes to her retirement savings? **$17.12**

This feature promotes students' mental abilities in computation and reasonableness.

Mental Math

A company conducts a taste test. Eighty people compare Stardust pudding to Brand X. Both brands are the same. Forty-one people prefer Stardust. Which statements are true?

1. "More people prefer Stardust." **true**

2. "Consumers prefer Stardust 2 to 1." **false**

3. "Over 50% of the people surveyed prefer Stardust." **true**

4. "Forty people would have chosen Stardust by chance." **true**

5. "There is little difference between the number choosing Stardust and the number choosing Brand X." **true**

6-5   Statistics and Estimation

Objective: To use statistics to make predictions.

George Cleo is a stock clerk for an electrical company. He received on-the-job training for his job. George counts items on hand and makes a report showing the number of items in stock and the number that have been taken out of stock.

The electricians in Mr. Cleo's company use SureLife transistors. In each of the last six weeks, the following numbers of transistors were used.

35   62   44   73   36   68

Examples

A. **There are 238 transistors in stock. Estimate how long the supply will last.**

First, find the average number of transistors used per week.

$$\frac{35 + 62 + 44 + 73 + 36 + 68}{6} = \frac{318}{6}$$

$$= 53$$

$$35 \boxed{+} 62 \boxed{+} 44 \boxed{+} 73 \boxed{+} 36 \boxed{+} 68 \boxed{=} \; \textit{318}$$

About 53 transistors are used per week.

$$318 \boxed{\div} 6 \boxed{=} \; \textit{53}$$

Then, divide to find how many weeks the present supply of transistors will last if 53 are used each week.

transistors used per week $\rightarrow$ $53\overline{)238}^{\;4\frac{26}{53}}$ $\leftarrow$ *transistors in stock*

$$\underline{-212}$$
$$26$$

The supply of transistors should last about $4\frac{1}{2}$ weeks.

B. **Suppose a poll of 50 people is taken regarding the election for mayor. Twenty-eight people support Arum and 22 people support Savik. If 110,000 people vote in the election, about how many people will support each candidate?**

$\dfrac{28}{50} = \dfrac{14}{25}$ $\leftarrow$ *fraction supporting Arum* $\dfrac{22}{50} = \dfrac{11}{25}$ $\leftarrow$ *fraction supporting Savik*

number of people voting   *fraction supporting Arum*

$$110,000 \quad \times \quad \frac{14}{25} \quad = \quad 61,600 \quad \leftarrow \text{\textit{number of people expected to support Arum}}$$

$$110000 \boxed{\times} 14 \boxed{\div} 25 \boxed{=} \; \textit{61600}$$

	number of people voting	fraction supporting Savik		
.	110,000	$\times$	$\frac{11}{25}$	$= 48,400$ ← number of people expected to support Savik

110000 $\boxed{\times}$ 11 $\boxed{\div}$ 25 $\boxed{=}$ *48400*

About 61,600 people will support Arum and about 48,400 people will continue support Savik.

Basic Skills Appendix, Pages 421, 430, 431, 458
Basic: 1–13; Average: 1–13; Enriched: 1–13

Exercises

Estimate the number of weeks (to the nearest $\frac{1}{2}$ week) the following supply of parts will last. Answers may vary. Typical answers are given.

	Part	Number in Stock	Usage—Each of Last Six Weeks					
1.	heat sink	82	1	0	0	4	0	4 $54\frac{1}{2}$
2.	capacitor	26	3	3	1	6	3	4 8
3.	resistor	112	10	?	6	5	0	14 18
4.	potentiometer	19	3	1	4	0	5	2 $7\frac{1}{2}$
5.	fuse	18	2	6	1	0	4	4 $6\frac{1}{2}$
6.	diode	814	15	46	10	38	74	51 21
7.	connector	220	3	12	2	17	19	8 $21\frac{1}{2}$

Use the poll results at the right to complete the following.

State Issue 2	
Support	60
Oppose	64
Undecided	26

8. How many people were polled? 150 people

9. What fraction opposes Issue 2? $\frac{64}{150}$ or $\frac{32}{75}$

10. What fraction is undecided on Issue 2? $\frac{26}{150}$ or $\frac{13}{75}$

11. Suppose 1,500,000 people vote on Issue 2. Predict how many support Issue 2. 600,000 people

Answer the following.

12. A store advertises that they had fewer returns. Only 6 of their lawn mowers had been returned as defective. A large department store, they stated, had 28 mowers returned. The stores sold 40 mowers and 196 respectively. Which store actually had the better return rate? Use percents. $\frac{6}{40} = 15\%$, $\frac{28}{196} = 14\frac{2}{7}\%$; the store that sold 196 mowers

Teacher Resource Book, Page 153

13. Twenty freshmen were absent on Tuesday at Weston High School. Eighteen sophomores were absent on the same day. There are 125 freshmen and 105 sophomores enrolled at Weston High School. Did the freshmen class or the sophomore class have a higher rate of absent students? Use percents. $\frac{20}{125} = 16\%$; $\frac{18}{105} = 17\frac{1}{7}\%$; the sophomore class

6-6 Expected Winnings

Objective: To find the expected winnings.

Many states conduct state lotteries. A portion of the sales goes to schools. Another portion of the sales goes toward prizes.

Suppose a state lottery awards prizes as follows for each 1,000,000 lottery tickets.

1	$100,000 prize
9	$10,000 prizes
90	$1,000 prizes
900	$100 prizes

The probability of winning each prize is shown at the right. The **expected winnings** is the amount that a single ticket would win.

Prize	Probability
$100,000	$\frac{1}{1,000,000}$
$ 10,000	$\frac{9}{1,000,000}$
$ 1,000	$\frac{90}{1,000,000}$
$ 100	$\frac{900}{1,000,000}$

Example

What are the expected winnings in the lottery described above?

Divide the total prize money by the number of tickets sold.

$$\frac{(\$100,000 \times 1) + (\$10,000 \times 9) + (\$1,000 \times 90) + (\$100 \times 900)}{1,000,000}$$

$$= \frac{\$100,000 + \$90,000 + \$90,000 + \$90,000}{1,000,000}$$

$$= \frac{\$370,000}{1,000,000} \text{ or } \$0.37$$

[MC] 100000 [X] 1 [M+] 10000 [X] 9 [M+] 1000 [X] 90 [M+] 100 [X] 900 [M+] [MR] [÷] 1000000 [=] *0.37*

The expected winnings are $0.37. Therefore, you pay $1 for a ticket and expect to win only 37¢.

Does anyone actually win 37¢? Suppose a ticket costs $1. Is it wise to buy lottery tickets with money you cannot afford to lose? **no, no**

Basic Skills Appendix, Pages 421, 442, 449
Basic: 1–14; Average: 1–14; Enriched: 1–14

Exercises

Find the expected winnings for the following.

1. 1,000 tickets sold at $1 each

1	$200 prize
5	$50 prizes **45¢**

2. 500 tickets sold at 50¢ each

2	$30 prizes
3	$20 prizes **24¢**

3. For the lotteries described in exercises 1 and 2, find the probability of winning a prize. $\frac{6}{1,000}$ or $\frac{3}{500}$, $\frac{5}{500}$ or $\frac{1}{100}$

4. For the lotteries described in exercises 1 and 2, what is the average loss on 1 ticket? **55¢, 26¢**

A bakery ran a contest with prizes listed at the right. This contest was free. About 85,000,000 entries were made.

10	$5,000 prizes
50	$1,000 prizes
500	$100 prizes
10,000	$5 prizes

5. How many prizes were given away? **10,560 prizes**

6. Find the total prize money. **$200,000**

7. Find the probability of one entry winning a prize as a fraction in simplest form. $\frac{33}{265,625}$

8. Find the expected winnings for one entry. **little more than 0.2¢**

Many states have a lottery like the following. You can choose any one of the three-digit numbers from 000 to 999, such as 014. A lottery ticket costs $1. Each day one number is chosen. A winning number gets a $400 prize.

9. How many 3-digit numbers can be chosen? **1,000 numbers**

10. Find the probability that a given number will be a winner. $\frac{1}{1,000}$

11. Find the expected winnings for each number bet. **40¢**

12. Find the total payoff if ten persons bet the winning number. **$4,000**

Solve.

13. The prize for a lottery is $1,500. What are the expected winnings if 2,000 tickets are sold? **75¢**

14. Refer to exercise 13. What is the expected loss if Connie buys one ticket for $2? **$1.25**

This feature presents useful ways of solving mathematical problems on a calculator.

 Calculator

Numerals that read the same forward and backward are called **palindromes.** For example, 252, 66, and 416,614 are palindromes. You can use a calculator to form a palindrome.

Enter any whole number.	895
Reverse its digits and add the	+ 598 = *1493*
result to the original number.	+ 3941 = *5434*
Repeat this process until the	+ 4345 = *9779*
sum is a palindrome.	

Form a palindrome starting with each of the following numerals.

1. 524 **949**   **2.** 86 **1,111**   **3.** 268 **1,441**   **4.** 194 **2,992**   **5.** 792 **79,497**

6-7 Problem Solving: Using Venn Diagrams

Objective: To solve problems using Venn diagrams.

Communications satellites beam down
television programs to different regions
of the United States. The area covered
by a satellite's beam forms a circle.
The two circles on the map at the right
form a **Venn diagram.** A Venn diagram is
used to illustrate data.

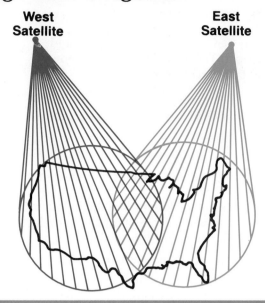

West Satellite

East Satellite

The two circles separate the United
States into three regions as shown below.

West Beam
Only

West and
East Beams

East Beam
Only

Example

The numbers in the Venn diagram at the
right represent the television viewers
in each region. How many television
viewers does the West Satellite reach?

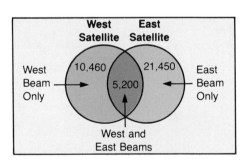

West
Satellite

East
Satellite

West
Beam
Only

10,460 5,200 21,450

East
Beam
Only

West and
East Beams

Read

You know the number of television
viewers in the two regions covered
by the West Satellite. You are
asked to find how many television
viewers the West Satellite reaches.

**Point out that the
rectangle in a Venn
diagram represents a
universal set.**

Decide

Add the number of television viewers in the
two regions covered by the West Satellite.

Solve

West Beam Only		West and East Beam		viewers covered by West Satellite
10,460	+	5,200	=	15,660

The West Satellite reaches 15,660 television viewers.

Examine

Since the number of television viewers covered
by the West Satellite is more than the number
covered by the West Beam only or the West and
East Beam, the answer is reasonable.

Exercises

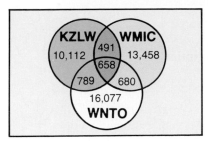

The Venn diagram at the left illustrates the broadcasting area (in square miles) of three radio stations. Find the broadcasting area for each of the following.

1. KZLW **12,050 mi²**
2. WMIC **15,287 mi²**
3. WNTO **18,204 mi²**
4. KZLW and WMIC **1,149 mi²**
5. KZLW and WNTO **1,447 mi²**
6. WMIC and WNTO **1,338 mi²**
7. KZLW, WMIC, and WNTO **658 mi²**

For each problem, draw and label a Venn diagram like the one above. Shade the region(s) covered for the given information.
For answers to exercises 8–11, see Teacher Guide.

8. receives only one station, KZLW
9. receives all three stations
10. receives both stations, WNTO and KZLW, but not station WMIC
11. receives at least one of the three stations

The ages of students in a math class are given in the chart at right. Complete the following.

age	boys	girls
15	5	8
16	8	9

12. What does the shaded area below represent? **16 year old girls**

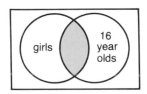

13. How many students are girls? **17 students**
14. How many students are 16 years old? **17 students**
15. How many students are girls or 16 years old? **25 students**

16. Draw a Venn diagram to represent 15-year-old boys. **See Teacher Guide.**
17. If one student is selected, what is the probability of choosing a boy? $\frac{13}{30}$

18. If one student is selected, what is the probability of choosing a 15 year old? $\frac{13}{30}$
19. If one student is selected, what is the probability of choosing a 15 year old boy? $\frac{5}{30}$ or $\frac{1}{6}$

Solve. Use a Venn diagram.

20. At Thorton High School, 32 freshmen take drafting, 28 take cooking, and 7 take both courses. There are 142 students in the freshmen class. How many freshmen take neither drafting nor cooking? **89 freshmen**

21. At a buffet, 32 people chose beef and 28 people chose chicken. Twelve people chose both beef and chicken. Each person at the buffet chose at least one of the two meats. How many people were served at the buffet? **48 people**

22. Out of 125 families polled, 86 families receive a daily newspaper, 53 families receive a Sunday newspaper, and 47 families receive both a daily and a Sunday newspaper. How many families receive neither a daily nor a Sunday newspaper? **33 families**

CHAPTER 6 REVIEW

Vocabulary/Concepts

Write the letter of the word or phrase that best matches each description.

1. a value that can be predicted before an event occurs **b**

2. used to illustrate data **h**

3. $\dfrac{\text{probability of success}}{\text{probability of failure}}$ **d**

4. the probability of an event expressed as a percent **a**

5. amount that a single ticket would win **c**

a. chance
b. expected value
c. expected winnings
d. odds
e. percentile
f. probability
g. statistics
h. Venn diagram

Exercises

A die is rolled. Find the odds for the following. Page 117

6. for a 6 **1 to 5**

7. for an odd number **3 to 3**

8. for at least a 3 **4 to 2**

Write each percent as a probability in simplest form. Pages 118–119

9. 40% $\frac{2}{5}$

10. 85% $\frac{17}{20}$

11. $37\frac{1}{2}$% $\frac{3}{8}$

12. $66\frac{2}{3}$% $\frac{2}{3}$

13. 12.5% $\frac{1}{8}$

Write each probability as a percent. Pages 118–119

14. $\frac{9}{10}$ **90%**

15. $\frac{7}{20}$ **35%**

16. $\frac{9}{25}$ **36%**

17. $\frac{5}{6}$ **$83\frac{1}{3}$%**

18. $\frac{5}{8}$ **$62\frac{1}{2}$%**

Find the probability of an event given its odds. Express the probability as a fraction in simplest form and as a percent. Pages 120–121

19. 1 to 9 $\frac{1}{10}$; **10%**

20. 4 to 1 $\frac{4}{5}$; **80%**

21. 1 to 3 $\frac{1}{4}$; **25%**

22. 2 to 6 $\frac{1}{4}$; **25%**

23. 4 to 8 $\frac{1}{3}$; $33\frac{1}{3}$%

Find the odds for an event given its probability or chance. Pages 120–121

24. $\frac{5}{6}$ **5 to 1**

25. $\frac{7}{8}$ **7 to 1**

26. 60% **3 to 2**

27. 35% **7 to 13**

28. $\frac{3}{4}$ **3 to 1**

Suppose all the answers to a test are guesses. Find the expected score for the following tests. Pages 122–123

29. 100 questions, 4 choices for each question **25**

30. 20 true-false questions **10**

A die is rolled 120 times. How many times would you expect each of the following to occur? Pages 122–123

31. a four **20**

32. a five or a six **40**

33. a 4 or less **80**

34. a prime number **60**

Estimate the number of weeks (to the nearest $\frac{1}{2}$ week) each of the following supply of parts will last. Pages 126–127 Answers may vary. Typical answers are given.

Part	Number in Stock	Usage—Each of last four weeks
35. microchip	37	3 7 17 8 **4**
36. mother board	15	0 2 10 3 **4**

Find the expected winnings for the following. Pages 128–129

37. 100 tickets are sold
  1 $25 prize
  2 $10 prizes
  3 $5 prizes **60¢**

38. 300 tickets are sold
  2 $50 prizes
  4 $25 prizes
  8 $10 prizes **93¢**

Use the following Venn diagrams to find the missing numbers. Pages 130–131

39. Population of A is 674 **613**

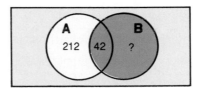

40. Population of B is 295 **253**

The numbers in the Venn diagram at the right represent the population in each region. Find the population in each region. Pages 130–131

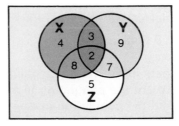

41. Region X **17**   **42.** Region Y **21**   **43.** Region Z **22**

Solve.

44. A box contains 4 yellow marbles, 3 red marbles, and 8 white marbles. One marble is chosen at random. What are the odds for choosing a yellow marble? **4 to 11**

45. A quiz has 15 questions with 5 choices for each question, and 10 true-false questions. Suppose all answers are guesses. What is the expected score? **8**

46. The odds that Jon's tennis team will win are 6 to 3. What is the chance that his team will win? **$66\frac{2}{3}$%**

47. The prize for a lottery is $10,000. What are the expected winnings if 200,000 tickets are sold? **5¢**

48. At Wilcox High School, 28 girls are on the volleyball team, 22 girls are on the basketball team, and 11 girls are on both teams. There are 215 girls in the school. How many girls are on neither the volleyball nor basketball teams?
176 girls

CHAPTER 6 TEST

Two coins are tossed. Find the odds for the following.

1. two heads 1 to 3

2. no heads 1 to 3

3. one head, one tail 2 to 2

Write each percent as a probability in simplest form.

4. 75% $\frac{3}{4}$

5. $33\frac{1}{3}$% $\frac{1}{3}$

6. The chance of rain is 40%. $\frac{2}{5}$

Find the probability of an event given its odds. Express the probability as a fraction in simplest form and as a percent.

7. 2 to 2 $\frac{1}{2}$; 50%

8. 2 to 3 $\frac{2}{5}$; 40%

9. 6 to 4 $\frac{3}{5}$; 60%

10. 1 to 2 $\frac{1}{3}$; $33\frac{1}{3}$%

Find the odds for an event given its probability or chance.

11. $\frac{1}{5}$ 1 to 4

12. 20% 1 to 4

13. 10% 1 to 9

14. $\frac{1}{8}$ 1 to 7

Use the poll results at the right to complete the following.

15. How many people were polled? 150 people

16. What fraction is against the increase? $\frac{115}{150}$ or $\frac{23}{30}$

17. Suppose another 2,500 people are polled. Predict how many would be against the increase. 1,916 or 1,917 people

Postal Rate Increase	
For	35
Against	115

If 2,000 tickets are sold, find the expected winnings for the following.

18. 1 $500 prize 25¢

19. 4 $100 prizes 20¢

20. 12 $50 prizes 30¢

The numbers in the Venn diagram at the right represent the population in each region. Find the population in each region if the population of A is 45.

21. Region A only 26

22. Region B 86

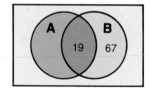

Answer the following.

23. Three coins are tossed. What are the odds for tossing at least two heads? 4 to 4

24. A die is rolled once. What are the chances of rolling a two or a four? $33\frac{1}{3}$%

25. A test has 36 questions each having 4 choices. Suppose all answers are guesses. Find the expected score. 9

26. A die is rolled 1,200 times. How many times would you expect an odd number? 600 times

27. Out of 40 people polled, 16 people were tennis players, 12 people were racquetball players, and 7 people were both tennis players and racquetball players. How many people were neither tennis players nor racquetball players? 19 people

CUMULATIVE REVIEW

Solve. Pages 59–60

1. 10% of 820 **82**

2. 25% of 640 **160**

3. 35% of 400 **140**

4. 28% of 600 **168**

5. 3% of 45 **1.35**

6. 150% of 90 **135**

7. 0.1% of 250 **0.25**

8. $42\frac{1}{2}$% of 120 **51**

Draw a line graph for the following. Pages 77–79 **See Teacher Guide.**

9. Mary Daniel's long jumping distances are:
April 7, 12ft 11in.   April 14, 13ft 2in.   April 21, 13ft 8in.
April 28, 12ft 7in.   May 5, 13ft 7in.   May 12, 14ft 5in.

The line graphs below show monthly sales for a small business. Answer each question. Pages 86–87

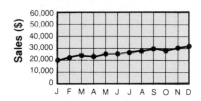

Graph A: Monthly Sales

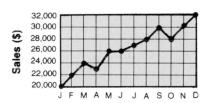

Graph B: Monthly Sales

10. What are the sales for November? **$30,500**

11. What are the sales for March? **$24,000**

12. Which graph is easier to read? **B**

13. Do both graphs display the same data? **Yes**

14. Which graph would you show to someone who wants to buy the business? **B**

15. Which graph would you show an employee who asked for a big raise? **A**

Use the U.S. Population graph on page 89 to answer each question. Pages 88–89

16. Estimate the year when the population reached 150 million. **1947**

17. Estimate the year when the population reached 180 million. **1959**

18. Predict the population in 1987.
235 million

19. Predict the population in 1995.
245 million

Suppose a marble is chosen at random from those shown at the right. A second marble is chosen without replacing the first one. Find each probability. Pages 108–109

20. both blue $\frac{3}{28}$

21. both red $\frac{5}{14}$

22. a red, then a blue $\frac{15}{56}$

23. a blue, then a red $\frac{15}{56}$

24. both the same color $\frac{13}{28}$

25. one of each color $\frac{15}{28}$

Suppose you choose one letter from each state named below. Find the chance that the letter is a vowel. (a, e, i, o, or u) Pages 118–119

26. California **50%**

27. Maine **60%**

28. Ohio **75%**

29. Arkansas $37\frac{1}{2}$%

Length

7-1 Nonstandard Units of Measure

Objective: To recognize and use nonstandard units of measure.

Standard units of measure help insure that car parts will fit together and work properly. Metric and customary units of measure are used in the auto industry.

Hundreds of years ago people used their fingers, hands, arms, and feet as measuring tools. Since they differ from person to person these units are called **nonstandard.** Nonstandard units are still useful in estimating length.

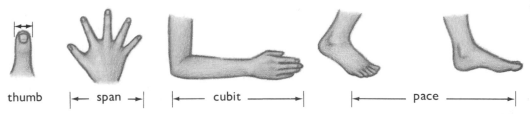

thumb　|← span →|　|← cubit →|　　|← pace →|

Basic: 1–24; Average: 1–24; Enriched: 1–24
Exercises

Name the best unit for measuring each of the following. Use thumb, span, cubit, or pace.

1. length of a van cubit or pace

2. thickness of a book thumb

3. width of a car tire thumb

4. length of a soccer field pace

5. length of a pin thumb

6. width of a magazine thumb or span

7. distance around a room pace

8. height of a person span or cubit

Choose the best estimate.

9. length of a house   **a.** 10 thumbs   **b.** 10 cubits   **c.** <u>10 paces</u>

10. height of a basketball hoop   **a.** 8 spans   **b.** <u>8 cubits</u>   **c.** 8 paces

11. thickness of a picture frame   **a.** <u>1 thumb</u>   **b.** 1 span   **c.** 1 cubit

12. diameter of a pizza   **a.** 2 thumbs   **b.** <u>2 spans</u>   **c.** 2 cubits

Name the larger unit.

13. <u>1 pace</u> or 1 span

14. 1 thumb or <u>1 cubit</u>

15. 1 span or <u>1 cubit</u>

16. <u>1 span</u> or 1 thumb

17. 1 cubit or <u>1 pace</u>

18. <u>1 pace</u> or 1 thumb

19. Anita's span is about 8 inches wide. Her desk measures 6 spans wide. About how many inches wide is Anita's desk? **48 inches**

20. Two of Tom's cubits are equal to 1 pace. His room is 12 cubits long. How many paces long is Tom's room?
6 paces

21. Eric's kitchen counter is 2 cubits high. Eric's cubit is about 16 inches long. About how many inches high is Eric's kitchen counter?
32 inches

22. Renee's span is equal in length to 10 thumbs. Her photo album is $2\frac{1}{2}$ spans wide. How many thumbs wide is Renee's photo album?
25 thumbs

23. Measure the length of your math book in thumbs. Compare your results with your classmates. Are the measurements the same?
Answers may vary.

24. Measure the height of a doorknob in spans. Compare your results with your classmates. Are the measurements the same?
Answers may vary.

This feature provides general topics about the computer.

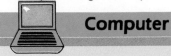

Computer

In 1946, **ENIAC** (**E**lectronic **N**umerical **I**ntegrator **A**nd **C**alculator) went into operation. It was a huge electronic computer using *vacuum tubes*. ENIAC weighed about 60,000 pounds and took up about 1,500 square feet of floor space. ENIAC could do about 5,000 additions per second.

In the 1950s, *transistors* made computers much smaller and faster.

The new breed of "supercomputers" use *integrated circuits (chips)*. The computers are much smaller and faster than ENIAC. The Cray-2 computer takes up about 18 square feet of floor space. It can do about 1.2 billion additions per second. That means that what used to take a year to compute, scientists can now do in a matter of seconds.

In the 1970s, *large-scale integration* (LSI) circuits and *very large-scale integrated* (VLSI) circuits were developed. From this came the *microprocessor*. Some uses of the microprocessor are in microwave ovens, thermostats, and microcomputers.

First Generation—1946
Vacuum Tubes

Second Generation—1959
Transistors

Third Generation—1965
Integrated Circuits

Fourth Generation—1971
LSI and Microprocessor

7-2 Metric Units of Length

Objective: To identify and use metric units of length.

A good system of measurement is one in which the units are well defined. One such system used in the auto industry is the *metric system*.

The **meter** is the basic unit of length in the metric system. *Prefixes* relate all other metric units to the meter. The chart shows how each prefix is related to a place value.

Other commonly used metric units are described below.

Place Values

Metric Units

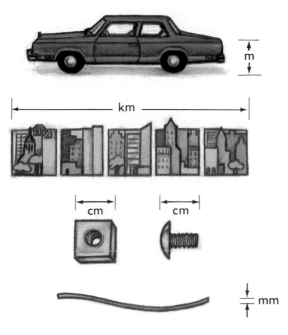

A car fender is about one **meter** (m) high.

Five city blocks are about one **kilometer** (km) long.

Small nuts and bolts used in cars are about one **centimeter** (cm) long.

The wires used in the electrical system of a car are about one **millimeter** (mm) wide.

Centimeter rulers and meter sticks can be used to measure length.

Examples

A. Find the length of each object.

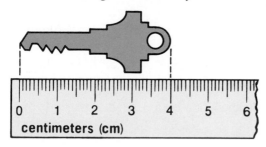

The key is 4 centimeters long. Since each centimeter is 10 millimeters, the key is also 40 millimeters long. So, 4 cm = 40 mm.

B.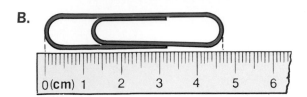

The paper clip is between 4 and 5 centimeters or 40 and 50 millimeters long. Since each small unit represents 1 millimeter, the paper clip is about 47 millimeters long. It is about 4.7 centimeters long.

Basic: 2–46 even; Average: 1–46; Enriched: 1–45 odd

Exercises

Name the larger unit.

1. kilometer or centimeter

2. millimeter or <u>centimeter</u>

3. centimeter or <u>meter</u>

4. <u>kilometer</u> or meter

5. millimeter or <u>kilometer</u>

6. <u>meter</u> or millimeter

Name the metric unit each symbol represents.

7. cm **centimeter**

8. mm **millimeter**

9. m **meter**

10. km **kilometer**

Name the best unit for measuring each of the following. Use km, m, cm, or mm.

11. thickness of a car window **mm**

12. distance between two factories **km**

13. length of a parking lot **m**

14. length of a pin **mm**

15. length of a sheet of paper **cm**

16. length of a river **km**

17. distance traveled in 2 hours **km**

18. length of a baseball bat **cm**

19. height of a building **m**

20. length of an athletic field **m**

Choose the best estimate.

21. your height   **a.** 2 cm   <u>**b.** 2 m</u>

22. width of a book   **a.** 20 km   <u>**b.** 20 cm</u>

23. thickness of a dime   <u>**a.** 1 mm</u>   **b.** 1 m

24. width of a door   <u>**a.** 1 m</u>   **b.** 1 km

25. height of a door   **a.** 2 km   <u>**b.** 2 m</u>

26. thickness of a button   **a.** 3 m   <u>**b.** 3 mm</u>

27. length of a pencil   <u>**a.** 15 cm</u>   **b.** 15 m

28. width of a staple   <u>**a.** 1 cm</u>   **b.** 1 m

Find the distance each letter on the arrow is from 0. Give the measurement in centimeters and then in millimeters.

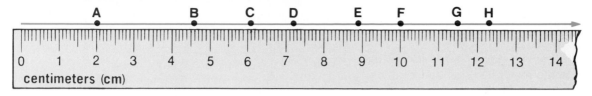

29. A
2 cm, 20 mm

30. B
4.6 cm, 46 mm

31. C
6.1 cm, 61 mm

32. D
7.2 cm, 72 mm

33. E
8.9 cm, 89 mm

34. F
10 cm, 100 mm

35. G
11.5 cm, 115 mm

36. H
12.3 cm, 123 mm

37. from point A to point F 8 cm, 80 mm

38. from point A to point E 6.9 cm, 69 mm

39. from point F to point G 1.5 cm, 15 mm

40. from point B to point H 7.7 cm, 77 mm

Measure the length of each object or line segment. Give the measurement in centimeters and then in millimeters.

41. 5.6 cm, 56 mm
42. 6.5 cm, 65 mm

41.

42.

43.
3.9 cm, 39 mm

44.
4.7 cm, 47 mm

Answer the following questions.

45. Which is longer—843 meters or 843 kilometers? **843 kilometers**

46. Which is shorter—57 millimeters or 57 centimeters? **57 millimeters**

This feature presents general topics of mathematics.

 Math Break

The chart below lists other metric units used to name very large or very small lengths.

Unit	Value
gigameter (Gm)	1,000,000,000 meters
megameter (Mm)	1,000,000 meters
micrometer (μm)	0.0000001 meter
nanometer (nm)	0.000000001 meter

Complete.

1. Earth is 150 Gm from the sun. Give this distance in meters.
150,000,000,000 meters

2. Which is longer—999,999 meters or one megameter?
1 megameter

3. Find the unit that is the name for one trillion meters.
terameter

4. Find the unit that is the name for one trillionth meter.
picometer

7-3 Changing Metric Units

Objective: To change from one metric unit of length to another.

The wheel base of a new car measures 275 centimeters. How many meters is 275 centimeters?

The chart shows how other units of length relate to the meter. To change metric units, multiply or divide by powers of ten.

| 1 millimeter = 0.001 meter |
| 1 centimeter = 0.01 meter |
| 1 kilometer = 1,000 meters |

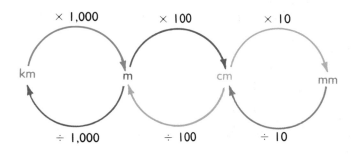

MULTIPLY *to change larger units to smaller units.*

DIVIDE *to change smaller units to larger units.*

Examples

A. Change 275 centimeters to meters.

275 cm = ▦ m   *You are changing from smaller to larger units.*

275 cm = ▦ m   *There will be fewer of these units after the*
  ↘ ÷ 100   *change, so DIVIDE.*

                   There are 100 centimeters in a meter. So,
275 cm = 2.75 m   *divide by 100. 275 ÷ 100 = 2.75*

B. Change 5.2 kilometers to meters.

5.2 km = ▦ m   *You are changing from larger to smaller units.*

5.2 km = ▦ m   *There will be more of these units after the*
  ↘ × 1,000   *change, so MULTIPLY.*

                   There are 1,000 meters in a kilometer. So,
5.2 km = 5,200 m   *multiply by 1,000. 5.2 × 1,000 = 5,200*

The Key Skills provides practice of skills needed in the exercises.

Key Skills

Multiply or divide.

| 45.3 × 100 = 4530   *To multiply by 100, move the decimal 2 places to the right.* |
| 45.3 ÷ 10 = 4.53   *To divide by 10, move the decimal 1 place to the left.* |

1. 56 × 10 **560**   **2.** 3.4 × 10 **34**   **3.** 0.43 × 100 **43**   **4.** 32.3 × 100 **3,230**

5. 14 ÷ 10 **1.4**   **6.** 6.5 ÷ 10 **0.65**   **7.** 230 ÷ 100 **2.3**   **8.** 27.9 ÷ 100 **0.279**

Exercises

Tell whether you would multiply or divide to complete the following.

1. 3 m = ▒ cm ×

2. 6 km = ▒ m ×

3. 38 mm = ▒ cm ÷

4. 4,000 mm = ▒ m ÷

5. 8 m = ▒ cm ×

6. 12 m = ▒ mm ×

7. 128 km = ▒ m ×

8. 2,700 m = ▒ km ÷

9. 536 cm = ▒ m ÷

Answer each of the following to complete 7,000 cm = ▒ m.

10. Which unit is larger, cm or m? m

11. Do you multiply or divide? ÷

12. How many cm in one m? 100

13. Would you use 10, 100, or 1,000? 100

14. 7,000 cm = ▒ m 70

Answer each of the following to complete 5 km = ▒ m.

15. Which unit is larger, km or m? km

16. Do you multiply or divide? ×

17. How many m in one km? 1,000

18. Would you use 10, 100, or 1,000? 1,000

19. 5 km = ▒ m 5,000

Complete.

20. 1 km = ▒ m 1,000

21. 1 cm = ▒ mm 10

22. 1 m = ▒ cm 100

23. 3 m = ▒ cm 300

24. 20 mm = ▒ cm 2

25. 8 km = ▒ m 8,000

26. 1,000 m = ▒ km 1

27. 400 cm = ▒ m 4

28. 4 m = ▒ cm 400

29. 100 cm = ▒ m 1

30. 4,000 mm = ▒ m 4

31. 40 mm = ▒ cm 4

32. 2 cm = ▒ mm 20

33. 8 m = ▒ mm 8,000

34. 100 mm = ▒ cm 10

35. 500 mm = ▒ cm 50

36. 1.2 m = ▒ cm 120

37. 0.2 cm = ▒ mm 2

38. 13.5 m = ▒ cm 1,350

39. 4.6 m = ▒ km 0.0046

40. 8.2 cm = ▒ mm 82

41. 1 km = ▒ cm 100,000

42. 1 km = ▒ mm 1,000,000

43. 9.78 m = ▒ km 0.00978

Answer the following.

44. The bicycle path at Mayberry Park is 7.8 kilometers long. How many meters is this? 7,800 meters

45. Hank is 180 cm tall. Paco is 1.75 m tall. How much taller is Hank than Paco? 5 cm or 0.05 m

46. There are 4 runners on a relay team. Each runner runs 1,500 meters. How many kilometers does each team run? 6 km

47. A picture measures 78 cm in width and 1.2 m in length. How much longer is the picture than it is wide? 42 cm

48. One lap in the swimming pool is 50 meters. Janice swims 1 kilometer. How many laps is this? 20 laps

7-4 Customary Units of Length

Objective: To identify and use customary units of length.
Each new design for a car is tested. Engines are run
thousands of test miles under different driving conditions.

The **mile** is a unit of length commonly used in the United
States. Other such units of length are inches, feet, and yards.

> 1 foot (ft) = 12 inches (in.)
> 1 yard (yd) = 3 feet (ft) or 36 inches (in.)
> 1 mile (mi) = 5,280 feet (ft)

A ruler can be used to measure inches.

Examples

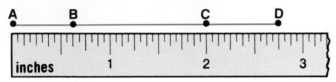

Each numbered space stands for 1 inch.
Each small space stands for $\frac{1}{16}$ inch.

A. The distance from A to C (AC) is 2 inches.

B. The distance from A to B (AB) is $\frac{10}{16}$ or $\frac{5}{8}$ inch.

C. The distance from A to D (AD) is $2\frac{12}{16}$ or $2\frac{3}{4}$ inches.

Basic: 2–42 even; Average: 1–42; Enriched: 1–37 odd, 39–42

Exercises

Name the larger unit.

1. foot or yard yard

2. inch or foot foot

3. mile or foot mile

4. mile or yard mile

5. yard or inch yard

6. inch or mile mile

**Name the best unit for measuring each of the following.
Use inch, foot, yard, or mile.**

7. width of a postage stamp inch

8. depth of a swimming pool foot

9. your height inch or foot

10. diameter of a pizza inch

11. length of a river mile

12. length of a football field foot or yard

13. height of a tree foot

14. distance from home to school yard or mile

15. length of tennis court foot or yard

16. length of a key inch

Choose the best estimate.

17. height of a piano

    a. 4 in.   **b.** 4 ft   **c.** 4 yd

18. width of a sidewalk

    a. 1 ft   **b.** 1 yd   **c.** 1 mi

19. length of a book   **a.** <u>10 in.</u>   **b.** 10 ft   **c.** 10 yd

20. length of a car   **a.** <u>12 ft</u>   **b.** 12 yd   **c.** 12 mi

21. your height   **a.** 5 in.   **b.** <u>5 ft</u>   **c.** 5 yd

22. distance from Chicago to New York   **a.** 800 ft   **b.** 800 yd   **c.** <u>800 mi</u>

23. length of a pencil   **a.** <u>7 in.</u>   **b.** 7 ft   **c.** 7 yd

24. length of a race   **a.** 26 ft   **b.** 26 yd   **c.** <u>26 mi</u>

Find each measurement in inches.

25. MN 1 in.   **26.** MO $1\frac{3}{4}$ in.   **27.** MP $2\frac{1}{8}$ in.   **28.** MQ $3\frac{1}{16}$ in.

29. MR $3\frac{7}{8}$ in.   **30.** MS $4\frac{7}{16}$ in.   **31.** MT $4\frac{15}{16}$ in.   **32.** MU $5\frac{9}{16}$ in.

Measure each line segment. Give the measurement in inches.

33. ▬▬▬▬▬▬ $1\frac{7}{16}$ in.   **34.** ▬▬▬▬▬▬▬ $1\frac{11}{16}$ in.

35. ▬▬▬▬▬▬ $1\frac{3}{4}$ in.   **36.** ▬▬▬▬ $\frac{7}{8}$ in.

Answer the following.

37. Which is longer—28 feet or 28 yards? **28 yards**

38. Which is shorter—$3\frac{1}{2}$ inches or $3\frac{1}{2}$ feet? **$3\frac{1}{2}$ inches**

39. Which is shorter—1 yard or 38 inches? **1 yard**

40. Which is longer—2 miles or 4,000 yards? **4,000 yards**

41. In 8 minutes Tonia runs 1 mile and Bill runs 5,000 feet. Who runs faster? **Tonia**

42. Leon is 2 yards tall. Anton is 5 feet tall. How much taller than Anton is Leon? **1 foot**

PRACTICE

Replace each ▓ with <, >, or = to make a true sentence.

1. 3.7 ▓ 0.37 **>**
2. 0.24 ▓ 0.214 **>**
3. 6.91 ▓ 6.910 **=**
4. 5.84 ▓ 5.94 **<**

5. $\frac{6}{16}$ ▓ $\frac{3}{8}$ **=**
6. $\frac{7}{8}$ ▓ $\frac{5}{8}$ **>**
7. $\frac{2}{3}$ ▓ $\frac{9}{12}$ **<**
8. $\frac{4}{7}$ ▓ $\frac{5}{8}$ **<**

9. $\frac{5}{6}$ ▓ $\frac{11}{12}$ **<**
10. $\frac{3}{6}$ ▓ $\frac{7}{15}$ **>**
11. $\frac{5}{9}$ ▓ $\frac{7}{12}$ **<**
12. $\frac{11}{15}$ ▓ $\frac{14}{25}$ **>**

Estimate. Answers may vary. Typical answers are given.

13.
$$\begin{array}{r} 7.61 \\ +\ 8.37 \\ \hline 16 \end{array}$$

14.
$$\begin{array}{r} 22.36 \\ -\ 10.81 \\ \hline 11 \end{array}$$

15.
$$\begin{array}{r} 6.07 \\ \times\ 3.80 \\ \hline 24 \end{array}$$

16. $5.8\overline{)41.79}$ **7**

17. $0.9\overline{)8.26}$ **9**

Add or subtract.

18.
$$\begin{array}{r} 79.39 \\ -\ 49.49 \\ \hline 29.90 \end{array}$$

19.
$$\begin{array}{r} 37.421 \\ +\ 6.58 \\ \hline 44.001 \end{array}$$

20.
$$\begin{array}{r} 40.06 \\ -\ 39.97 \\ \hline 0.09 \end{array}$$

21.
$$\begin{array}{r} 13.768 \\ +\ 18.512 \\ \hline 32.280 \end{array}$$

22.
$$\begin{array}{r} 36 \\ -\ 29.7 \\ \hline 6.3 \end{array}$$

23.
$$\begin{array}{r} 2.43 \\ -\ 1.8 \\ \hline 0.63 \end{array}$$

24.
$$\begin{array}{r} 6.51 \\ -\ 0.432 \\ \hline 6.078 \end{array}$$

25.
$$\begin{array}{r} 4 \\ -\ 0.98 \\ \hline 3.02 \end{array}$$

26.
$$\begin{array}{r} 12 \\ -\ 4.061 \\ \hline 7.939 \end{array}$$

27.
$$\begin{array}{r} 9.076 \\ +\ 0.841 \\ \hline 9.917 \end{array}$$

28. $12.69 + 3.7 + 42$ **58.39**

29. $16.9 - 13.46$ **3.44**

30. $53.7 + 21.309 + 16.95$ **91.959**

31. $227.18 - 88.96$ **138.22**

Multiply or divide.

32.
$$\begin{array}{r} 62.4 \\ \times\ 3.3 \\ \hline 205.92 \end{array}$$

33.
$$\begin{array}{r} 8.69 \\ \times\ 400 \\ \hline 3,476 \end{array}$$

34.
$$\begin{array}{r} 2.67 \\ \times\ 49 \\ \hline 130.83 \end{array}$$

35.
$$\begin{array}{r} 38.4 \\ \times\ 0.04 \\ \hline 1.536 \end{array}$$

36.
$$\begin{array}{r} 55.5 \\ \times\ 1.1 \\ \hline 61.05 \end{array}$$

37. $13\overline{)182}$ **14**

38. $7\overline{)45.5}$ **6.5**

39. $8\overline{)60.8}$ **7.6**

40. $8\overline{)5}$ **0.625**

41. $2.5\overline{)75}$ **30**

42. $4\overline{)66.0}$ **16.5**

43. $6\overline{)0.282}$ **0.047**

44. $8\overline{)16.6}$ **2.075**

45. $56\overline{)180.32}$ **3.22**

46. $64\overline{)48}$ **0.75**

Write the decimal named below and its equivalent fraction in simplest terms.

47. 8 tenths $0.8, \frac{4}{5}$
48. 26 hundredths $0.26, \frac{13}{50}$

49. 16 thousandths $0.016, \frac{2}{125}$
50. 1 hundredth $0.01, \frac{1}{100}$

51. 1 thousandth $0.001, \frac{1}{1,000}$
52. 60 hundredths $0.60, \frac{3}{5}$

53. 3 hundredths $0.03, \frac{3}{100}$
54. 82 thousandths $0.082, \frac{41}{500}$

Find the number named by each digit in 120,643.79.

55. the 6 **600**
56. the 2 **20,000**
57. the 7 **0.7**

58. the 1 **100,000**
59. the 9 **0.09**
60. the 0 **thousands**

Add. Write each sum in simplest form.

61. $\frac{1}{6} + \frac{1}{6}$ **$\frac{1}{3}$** 62. $\frac{1}{2} + \frac{1}{4}$ **$\frac{3}{4}$** 63. $\frac{1}{10} + \frac{1}{2}$ **$\frac{3}{5}$** 64. $\frac{1}{3} + \frac{1}{6}$ **$\frac{1}{2}$** 65. $\frac{3}{8} + \frac{1}{4}$ **$\frac{5}{8}$**

66. $\frac{2}{3} + \frac{1}{4}$ **$\frac{11}{12}$** 67. $\frac{3}{4} + \frac{1}{6}$ **$\frac{11}{12}$** 68. $\frac{3}{4} + \frac{7}{8}$ **$1\frac{5}{8}$** 69. $\frac{1}{2} + \frac{5}{8}$ **$1\frac{1}{8}$** 70. $\frac{2}{3} + \frac{1}{2}$ **$1\frac{1}{6}$**

71. $\frac{7}{12} + \frac{2}{3}$ **$1\frac{1}{4}$** 72. $\frac{3}{4} + \frac{7}{12}$ **$1\frac{1}{3}$** 73. $\frac{5}{6} + \frac{11}{12}$ **$1\frac{3}{4}$** 74. $\frac{11}{12} + \frac{11}{24}$ **$1\frac{3}{8}$** 75. $\frac{1}{10} + \frac{1}{15}$ **$\frac{1}{6}$**

Subtract. Write each difference in simplest form.

76. $\frac{5}{6} - \frac{1}{6}$ **$\frac{2}{3}$** 77. $\frac{1}{2} - \frac{1}{4}$ **$\frac{1}{4}$** 78. $\frac{3}{8} - \frac{1}{4}$ **$\frac{1}{8}$** 79. $\frac{7}{8} - \frac{1}{2}$ **$\frac{3}{8}$** 80. $\frac{5}{6} - \frac{1}{3}$ **$\frac{1}{2}$**

81. $\frac{3}{5} - \frac{1}{10}$ **$\frac{1}{2}$** 82. $\frac{1}{2} - \frac{1}{3}$ **$\frac{1}{6}$** 83. $\frac{7}{8} - \frac{1}{4}$ **$\frac{5}{8}$** 84. $\frac{4}{5} - \frac{1}{3}$ **$\frac{7}{15}$** 85. $\frac{1}{5} - \frac{1}{10}$ **$\frac{1}{10}$**

86. $\frac{7}{12} - \frac{1}{6}$ **$\frac{5}{12}$** 87. $\frac{7}{8} - \frac{2}{3}$ **$\frac{5}{24}$** 88. $\frac{2}{3} - \frac{1}{7}$ **$\frac{11}{21}$** 89. $\frac{9}{10} - \frac{1}{4}$ **$\frac{13}{20}$** 90. $\frac{3}{16} - \frac{1}{12}$ **$\frac{5}{48}$**

Multiply. Write each product in simplest form.

91. $\frac{1}{3} \times 2$ **$\frac{2}{3}$** 92. $\frac{2}{5} \times 4$ **$1\frac{3}{5}$** 93. $24 \times \frac{3}{8}$ **9** 94. $\frac{4}{5} \times 10$ **8** 95. $\frac{1}{2} \times \frac{1}{3}$ **$\frac{1}{6}$**

96. $\frac{3}{4} \times \frac{1}{6}$ **$\frac{1}{8}$** 97. $\frac{2}{3} \times \frac{3}{5}$ **$\frac{2}{5}$** 98. $\frac{7}{8} \times \frac{1}{2}$ **$\frac{7}{16}$** 99. $\frac{4}{15} \times \frac{5}{8}$ **$\frac{1}{6}$** 100. $\frac{3}{4} \times \frac{2}{5}$ **$\frac{3}{10}$**

101. $\frac{1}{3} \times \frac{8}{7}$ **$\frac{8}{21}$** 102. $\frac{5}{8} \times \frac{2}{5}$ **$\frac{1}{4}$** 103. $\frac{7}{11} \times 44$ **28** 104. $\frac{5}{9} \times \frac{3}{8}$ **$\frac{5}{24}$** 105. $\frac{5}{6} \times \frac{7}{9}$ **$\frac{35}{54}$**

Divide. Write each quotient in simplest form.

106. $4 \div \frac{1}{2}$ **8** 107. $5 \div \frac{1}{3}$ **15** 108. $\frac{3}{5} \div 6$ **$\frac{1}{10}$** 109. $\frac{3}{8} \div \frac{3}{4}$ **$\frac{1}{2}$** 110. $\frac{2}{3} \div \frac{5}{6}$ **$\frac{4}{5}$**

111. $\frac{1}{2} \div \frac{3}{4}$ **$\frac{2}{3}$** 112. $\frac{2}{3} \div \frac{1}{6}$ **4** 113. $\frac{5}{8} \div \frac{2}{3}$ **$\frac{15}{16}$** 114. $\frac{1}{6} \div \frac{4}{7}$ **$\frac{7}{24}$** 115. $\frac{7}{8} \div \frac{1}{6}$ **$5\frac{1}{4}$**

116. $\frac{4}{7} \div \frac{3}{8}$ **$1\frac{11}{21}$** 117. $\frac{4}{9} \div \frac{2}{7}$ **$1\frac{5}{9}$** 118. $\frac{5}{6} \div \frac{3}{10}$ **$2\frac{7}{9}$** 119. $\frac{8}{9} \div \frac{7}{18}$ **$2\frac{2}{7}$** 120. $\frac{7}{12} \div \frac{5}{14}$ **$1\frac{19}{30}$**

Solve.

121. One bolt measures 5.3 cm. Another bolt measures 54 mm. Which is the longer bolt? **54 mm**

122. Sam is 2 meters tall. Rich is 194 centimeters tall. How much taller is Sam than Rich? **6 cm**

123. Anthony rides his bicycle to school and back. The distance from home to school is 1,150 m. How many kilometers is it round trip? **2.3 km**

124. Marie has 2 meters of ribbon. If she cuts the ribbon into pieces that measure 1 cm in length, how many pieces does she have? **200 pieces**

7-5 Changing Customary Units

Objective: To change from one customary unit of length to another.

In football, a team must gain 10 yards to get a first down. How many feet are in 10 yards?

1 foot = 12 inches
1 yard = 3 feet or 36 inches
1 mile = 5,280 feet or 1,760 yards

To change customary units, multiply or divide by the appropriate number.

Examples

A. Change 10 yards to feet.

10 yds = ▨ ft   *You are changing from a larger to a smaller unit.*

10 yds = ▨ ft   *There will be more of these units after the change, so MULTIPLY.*
　　⤻
　× 3
　　　　　There are 3 feet in a yard. So, multiply by 3.
10 yds = 30 ft   *$10 \times 3 = 30$*

B. Change 48 inches to feet.

48 in. = ▨ ft   *You are changing from a smaller to a larger unit.*

48 in. = ▨ ft   *There will be fewer of these units after the change, so DIVIDE.*
　⤻
　÷ 12
　　　　There are 12 inches in a foot. So, divide by 12.
48 in. = 4 ft   *$48 \div 12 = 4$*

C. $\frac{1}{2}$ **mi** = ▨ **ft** $\frac{1}{2} \times \frac{5,280}{1} =$
　⤻
　× 5,280 $\frac{5,280}{2} = 2,640$

$\frac{1}{2}$ mi = 2,640 ft

D. **108 in.** = ▨ **yd**
　⤻
　÷ 36

108 in. = 3 yd

E. **40 in.** = ▨ **ft** ▨ **in.**
　⤻
　÷ 12   *$40 \div 12 = 3R4$*

40 in. = 3 ft 4 in.

Basic Skills Appendix, Pages 427, 430
Basic: 1–16, 17–35 odd; Average: 1–36; Enriched: 18–34 even, 35–36

Exercises

Tell whether you would multiply or divide to complete the following.

1. 2 ft = ▨ in. ×

2. 2 yd = ▨ ft ×

3. 72 in. = ▨ yd ÷

4. 24 in. = ▨ ft ÷

5. 2 mi = ▨ yd ×

6. 24 ft = ▨ yd ÷

7. 15,840 ft = ▨ mi ÷

8. 6 ft = ▨ in. ×

148 *Length*

Answer each of the following to complete 5 ft = ▨ in.

9. Which unit is larger, ft or in.? **ft**

10. Do you multiply or divide? **×**

11. How many in. in one ft? **12**

12. 5 ft = ▨ in. **60**

Answer each of the following to complete 180 in. = ▨ yd.

13. Which unit is larger, in. or yd? **yd**

14. Do you multiply or divide? **÷**

15. How many in. in one yard? **36**

16. 180 in. = ▨ yd **5**

Complete.

17. 10 ft = ▨ in. **120**

18. 3 yd = ▨ ft **9**

19. 144 in. = ▨ yd **4**

20. 10,560 ft = ▨ mi **2**

21. 72 in. = ▨ ft **6**

22. 8 mi = ▨ ft **42,240**

23. 36 ft = ▨ yd **12**

24. 4 mi = ▨ yd **7,040**

25. 5 yd = ▨ in. **180**

26. 3,520 yd = ▨ mi **2**

27. $\frac{1}{2}$ mi = ▨ yd **880**

28. $1\frac{1}{2}$ ft = ▨ in. **18**

29. $2\frac{1}{4}$ yd = ▨ in. **81**

30. 18 in. = ▨ ft $1\frac{1}{2}$

31. 54 in. = ▨ yd $1\frac{1}{2}$

32. 65 in. = ▨ ft ▨ in.
    5, 5

33. 96 in. = ▨ yd ▨ ft
    2, 2

34. 6,000 ft = ▨ mi ▨ ft
    1, 720

Answer the following.

35. A room is 12 ft long and 138 in. wide. Will a piece of carpet 12 ft by 11 ft be large enough to cover the entire floor? **no**

36. Connie buys 2 yards of ribbon for $1.38. Maria buys 80 in. of ribbon for $1.38. Who gets the better buy? **Maria**

 This feature presents useful ways of solving mathematical problems on a calculator.

Calculator

Kelly drove 830 miles in 15 hours 17 minutes. You can use a calculator to find her average rate in miles per hour.

$$\text{Rate} = \frac{\text{distance}}{\text{time}} \quad \Longrightarrow \quad \text{Rate} = \frac{830 \ miles}{15 \ hours \ 17 \ minutes}$$

Express the time as a single unit (a number of hours).

15 hours + 17 minutes = 15 + $\frac{17}{60}$ Change $\frac{17}{60}$ to a decimal first.

17 ÷ 60 + 15 M+ 830 ÷ MR = 54.307525

Kelly averaged about 54.31 mph.

Use this technique to find the average rate of speed. Round to the nearest hundredth.

1. Yoki drove 245 miles in 17 hours 13 minutes. **14.23 mph**

2. Susan ran a 26-mile marathon in 3 hours 35 minutes. **7.26 mph**

7-6 Using Customary Measures of Length

Objective: To add, subtract, multiply, and divide customary units of length.

Rose is making a skirt and a blouse. She needs 2 feet 8 inches of ribbon for the skirt and 3 feet 7 inches of ribbon for the blouse. How much ribbon does she need?

When you add, subtract, multiply, or divide measurements, you may need to rename some of the units.

Examples

A. Add.

$$\begin{array}{r} 2 \text{ ft } 8 \text{ in.} \\ + \underline{3 \text{ ft } 7 \text{ in.}} \\ 5 \text{ ft } 15 \text{ in.} \end{array}$$ *Add the inches, then the feet.*

Rename the sum. *15 in. = 1 ft 3 in.*

5 ft 15 in. = 6 ft 3 in.

B. Subtract.

$$\begin{array}{r} 9 \text{ ft } 4 \text{ in.} \\ - 3 \text{ ft } 7 \text{ in.} \end{array} \rightarrow \textit{Rename.} \rightarrow \begin{array}{r} \overset{8}{\cancel{9}} \text{ ft } \overset{16}{\cancel{4}} \text{ in.} \\ - \underline{3 \text{ ft } 7 \text{ in.}} \\ 5 \text{ ft } 9 \text{ in.} \end{array}$$

C. Multiply.

$$\begin{array}{r} 3 \text{ yd } 1 \text{ ft} \\ \times \underline{\qquad 4} \\ 12 \text{ yd } 4 \text{ ft} \end{array}$$ *Multiply the units separately.*

Rename the product. *4 ft = 1 yd 1 ft*

12 yd 4 ft = 13 yd 1 ft

D. Divide.

$$\begin{array}{r} \qquad \qquad \quad \frac{3 \text{ yd } 2 \text{ ft}}{} \\ 2\overline{)7 \text{ yd } 1 \text{ ft}} \qquad 2\overline{)6 \text{ yd } 4 \text{ ft}} \end{array}$$

Rename.

Basic: 2–22 even; Average: 1–22; Enriched: 1–15 odd, 17–22

Exercises

Add, subtract, multiply, or divide.

1.	$\begin{array}{r} 2 \text{ ft } 9 \text{ in.} \\ + \underline{11 \text{ ft } 2 \text{ in.}} \\ \mathbf{13 \text{ ft } 11 \text{ in.}} \end{array}$	**2.**	$\begin{array}{r} 6 \text{ ft } 8 \text{ in.} \\ + \underline{3 \text{ ft } 6 \text{ in.}} \\ \mathbf{10 \text{ ft } 2 \text{ in.}} \end{array}$
3.	$\begin{array}{r} 3 \text{ yd } 24 \text{ in.} \\ + \underline{4 \text{ yd } 22 \text{ in.}} \\ \mathbf{8 \text{ yd } 10 \text{ in.}} \end{array}$	**4.**	$\begin{array}{r} 4 \text{ mi } 900 \text{ yd} \\ + \underline{7 \text{ mi } 900 \text{ yd}} \\ \mathbf{12 \text{ mi } 40 \text{ yd}} \end{array}$
5.	$\begin{array}{r} 8 \text{ ft } 11 \text{ in.} \\ - \underline{3 \text{ ft } \;\; 6 \text{ in.}} \\ \mathbf{5 \text{ ft } 5 \text{ in.}} \end{array}$	**6.**	$\begin{array}{r} 13 \text{ ft} \\ - \underline{\;\; 6 \text{ ft } 8 \text{ in.}} \\ \mathbf{6 \text{ ft } 4 \text{ in.}} \end{array}$
7.	$\begin{array}{r} 7 \text{ yd } 1 \text{ ft} \\ - \underline{5 \text{ yd } 2 \text{ ft}} \\ \mathbf{1 \text{ yd } 2 \text{ ft}} \end{array}$	**8.**	$\begin{array}{r} 6 \text{ mi } 1{,}200 \text{ ft} \\ - \underline{3 \text{ mi } 4{,}700 \text{ ft}} \\ \mathbf{2 \text{ mi } 1{,}780 \text{ ft}} \end{array}$
9.	$\begin{array}{r} 4 \text{ ft } 4 \text{ in.} \\ \times \underline{\qquad 2} \\ \mathbf{8 \text{ ft } 8 \text{ in.}} \end{array}$	**10.**	$\begin{array}{r} 6 \text{ ft } 8 \text{ in.} \\ \times \underline{\qquad 3} \\ \mathbf{20 \text{ ft}} \end{array}$
11.	$\begin{array}{r} 13 \text{ yd } 2 \text{ ft} \\ \times \underline{\qquad \;\; 3} \\ \mathbf{41 \text{ yd}} \end{array}$	**12.**	$\begin{array}{r} 2 \text{ mi } 500 \text{ yd} \\ \times \underline{\qquad \;\; 5} \\ \mathbf{11 \text{ mi } 740 \text{ yd}} \end{array}$

13. $6\overline{)19\text{ mi }640\text{ yd}}$ **3 mi 400 yd**

14. $2\overline{)10\text{ ft }8\text{ in.}}$ **5 ft 4 in.**

15. $8\overline{)17\text{ yd }4\text{ in.}}$ **2 yd 5 in.**

16. $5\overline{)11\text{ mi }100\text{ ft}}$ **2 mi 1,076 ft**

Solve.

17. One board is 5 feet 3 inches long. Another is 3 feet 9 inches long. How much longer is one board than the other? **1 ft 6 in.**

18. A section of fence is 8 feet 8 inches long. Aaron needs six sections of fence. How many feet of fence is this? **52 ft**

19. Mount Everest is 29,028 feet above sea level. How many feet less than 6 miles is this? **2,652 feet**

20. Floor boards are each 3 inches wide. How many floor boards are needed to cover a floor 16 feet wide? **64 floor boards**

21. It takes 2 feet 2 inches of ribbon to make one hat. How many feet of ribbon are needed for six hats? **13 feet**

22. The heights of five ball players are 5 ft 11 in., 6 ft 6 in., 7 ft 2 in., 6 ft 8 in., and 6 ft 5 in. What is the difference in height between the tallest and shortest players? **1 ft 3 in.**

This feature promotes students' mental abilities in computation and reasonableness.

Mental Math

Sums may be estimated by adding front-end digits and then making an adjustment.

468	$\longrightarrow$	400
173	$\longrightarrow$	100
+ 219	$\longrightarrow$	+ 200
		700

68 and 73 are each more than half of 100. 19 is less than half of 100. Their sum is about 200.

700	
+ 200	adjustment
900	estimate

1,281	$\longrightarrow$	1,000
5,633	$\longrightarrow$	5,000
+ 7,227	$\longrightarrow$	+ 7,000
		13,000

633 is more than half of 1,000. 281 and 227 are each less than half of 1,000. Their sum is about 1,000.

13,000	
+ 1,000	adjustment
14,000	estimate

Estimate each sum using this strategy. Answers may vary. Typical answers are given.

1. 324 + 147 + 422 **900**

2. 286 + 328 + 215 **800**

3. 635 + 481 + 567 **1,700**

4. 145 + 497 + 364 **1,000**

5. 514 + 274 + 659 **1,500**

6. 87 + 922 + 376 **1,400**

7. 8,361 + 9,593 + 1,597 **20,000**

8. 7,574 + 8,615 + 8,110 **25,000**

9. 1,097 + 5,782 + 2,051 **9,000**

10. 3,169 + 2,813 + 7,035 **13,000**

11. 41,106 + 88,052 + 74,969 **200,000**

12. 48,199 + 87,210 + 69,922 **210,000**

13. 51,012 + 38,957 + 60,019 **150,000**

14. 443,781 + 288,782 + 426,823 **1,100,000**

7-7 Accuracy and Significant Digits

Objectives: To determine the more accurate of two measurements.
To determine the number of significant digits in a given measurement.

Frank Stamm is a tool-and-die maker. He constructs metal forms
(dies) into which molten metal is forced. Frank learned his
trade informally on the job. He also took classroom training
in industrial math and blueprint reading.

Tool-and-die makers must meet high standards. A measurement is
only as **accurate** as the measuring tool used. A ruler marked in
millimeters gives a more accurate measurement than a ruler
marked in centimeters. The smaller the unit, the more accurate
is the measurement.

Examples

Determine which measurement is more accurate.

A. $1\frac{7}{16}$ inch or $1\frac{1}{2}$ inch

$1\frac{7}{16}$ inch is more accurate than $1\frac{1}{2}$ inch.

   Smaller units are more accurate.

B. 12.32 m or 12.3 m   → *This measurement is given to tenths of a meter.*

12.32 m is more accurate than 12.3 m.

   → *This measurement is given to hundredths of a meter.*

C. 5.932 mm or 0.593 cm

5.932 mm is more accurate than 0.593 cm.

   Change to the same unit to compare. 0.593 cm = 5.93 mm
   So, 5.932 mm is more precise than 5.93 mm.

The accuracy of a measurement is determined by the number of
significant digits. In a measurement, all digits required to tell
how many units it took to make the measurement are significant.

Examples

Determine the number of significant digits in each measurement.

D. 3.98 m, 273 km, and 34.5 mm each have three significant digits.

   All nonzero digits are significant.

E. 6.0351 m, 900.28 mm, and 0.050796 m each have five significant digits.

   All zeros between nonzero digits are significant. Zeros used to show
   only the place value of the decimal are not counted as significant digits.

F. 150.0 mm, 13.00 m, and 1.160 m each have four significant digits.

All final zeros after a decimal point are significant.

G. 51,0̲0̲0̲ km and 3,20̲0̲ m each have four significant digits.

Specified (underscored) zeros are significant.

Basic: 2–42 even; Average: 1–42; Enriched: 1–39 odd, 41–42

Exercises

Name the more accurate measurement.

1. $3\frac{1}{4}$ in. or $3\frac{5}{16}$ in.   **2.** $12\frac{3}{8}$ in. or $12\frac{1}{2}$ in.   **3.** $9\frac{3}{19}$ in. or $9\frac{1}{4}$ in.

4. 43 m or 43.2 m   **5.** 56.5 km or 56 km   **6.** 24.3 mi or 24.28 mi

7. 390.4 cm or 3.9 m   **8.** 4.76 mm or 0.4762 cm   **9.** 0.5 m or 50.1 cm

10. 42 mm or 4.22 cm   **11.** 3.738 km or 3,738.3 m   **12.** 1.1 m or 0.001 km

Give the number of significant digits in each measurement.

13. 72 m **2**   **14.** 30.24 mm **4**   **15.** 84.0 cm **3**   **16.** 5,008 mi **4**

17. 53.005 m **5**   **18.** 4.5 cm **2**   **19.** 506.9 m **4**   **20.** 64 yd **2**

21. 1,284 mi **4**   **22.** 600 ft **1**   **23.** 4.0 mm **2**   **24.** 0.0593 m **3**

25. 58,005 km **5**   **26.** 0.008 cm **1**   **27.** 23 in. **2**   **28.** 8.090 cm **4**

29. 15 ft **2**   **30.** 87.496 m **5**   **31.** 24,000 mi **2**   **32.** 350̲,000 mi **3**

33. 4.0060 m **5**   **34.** 40,00̲0̲ cm **5**   **35.** 0.013 m **2**   **36.** 0.7060 cm **4**

37. 0.080 m **2**   **38.** 36,0̲0̲0 km **4**   **39.** 0.05900 cm **4**   **40.** 0.000050 m **2**

Solve.

41. A metal ruler is marked in thousandths of a meter. A plastic ruler is marked in centimeters. Which ruler should be used to make a more accurate measurement? **the metal ruler**

42. Chelsea and Jill both measure the same piece of wood. Chelsea says the length is 12.3 cm. Jill says the length is 123.4 mm. Which is the more accurate measurement? **123.4 mm**

7-8 Problem Solving: Comparing Systems of Measurement

Objective: To compare units of length in the metric and customary systems.

A road sign says that the Kwans are 134 kilometers from home. Is that more or less than 100 miles?

Sometimes you need to compare metric and customary measurements. The table at the right shows how the two systems of measurement compare.

> 1 inch = 2.54 centimeters
> 1 meter ≈ 39.37 inches
> 1 mile ≈ 1.6 kilometers
> 1 kilometer ≈ 0.62 mile
> ≈ *means "is approximately"*

Use estimation to solve the problem.

Read

The Kwans are 134 kilometers from home. You need to determine whether this is more or less than 100 miles.

Decide

Use the table to help compare measurements.

Solve

1 mi ≈ 1.6 km, so 100 mi ≈ 160 km *1.6 × 100 = 160*

Since 100 miles is about 160 kilometers, 134 kilometers is less than 100 miles.

Examine

You can use another comparison to check your answer. Since 1 kilometer is about 0.62 miles, multiply to find about how many miles 134 kilometers is.

134 ⓧ 0.62 ⊟ *83.08*

134 kilometers is about 83 miles. So, 134 kilometers is less than 100 miles.

Basic: 1–25 odd; Average: 1–25; Enriched: 2–14 even, 16–25

Exercises

Replace each ⬤ with <, >, or ≈ to compare.

1. 2.54 cm ⬤ 1 in. =

2. 1.6 km ⬤ 1 mi ≈

3. 0.62 mi ⬤ 1 km ≈

4. 1 m ⬤ 1 yd >

5. 1 mi ⬤ 1 km >

6. 1 in. ⬤ 1 cm >

7. 3 ft ⬤ 1 m <

8. 2 km ⬤ 1 mi >

9. 2 mi ⬤ 1 km >

10. 10 m ⬤ 393.7 in. ≈

11. 10 in. ⬤ 25.4 cm ≈

12. 1,500 m ⬤ 1 mi <

13. 2 in. ⬤ 1 m <

14. 2 yd ⬤ 2 m <

15. 3 cm ⬤ 3 in. <

Solve.

16. Calvin Smith ran the 100-meter dash in 9.93 seconds. At the same rate, would it take him more or less time to run a 100-yard dash? **less**

17. Jean Crane ran one mile in 5 minutes 46.31 seconds. At the same rate, would her time for a 1,500-meter race be more or less? **less**

18. The running track at the high school is $\frac{1}{4}$ mile long. About how many meters is this? **about 400 meters**

19. On the highway a speed limit of 55 miles per hour is posted. About how many kilometers per hour is this? **about 88 kph**

20. There are 10 meters of ribbon on a roll. How many pieces of ribbon 20 centimeters long can be cut from a roll? **50 pieces**

21. Ralph buys 8.5 meters of wood molding for $24.58. Rocio buys 850 centimeters of molding for $22.99. Who gets the better buy? **Rocio**

22. A desk is 1,200 millimeters long and 768 millimeters wide. Will this desk fit through a door that is 1 meter wide? **yes**

23. Jansen is 6 feet 3 inches tall. His brother is 5 feet 11 inches tall. How much taller is Jansen than his brother? **4 inches**

24. On his first try, Joe long jumped 19 feet 2 inches. His second try was 6 yards 3 inches. How much longer was Joe's first long jump? **11 inches**

25. One lap on the running track is 440 meters. Elena runs 2 laps every day. How many kilometers does she run in one week? **6.16 kilometers**

CHAPTER 7 REVIEW

Vocabulary/Concepts

Choose a word or numeral from the list at the right to complete each sentence.

1. The ___?___ is a nonstandard unit of length. **span**
2. The ___?___ is the basic unit of length in the metric system. **meter**
3. There are 1,000 meters in one ___?___. **kilometer**
4. One hundred ___?___ (s) equals one meter. **centimeter**
5. The most commonly used ___?___ units of length are the inch, foot, yard, and mile. **customary**
6. There are ___?___ feet in one mile. **5,280**
7. Thirty-six inches equals one ___?___. **yard**
8. The measurement 2.7380 meters has ___?___ significant digits. **5**

4
5
1,760
5,280
centimeter
customary
foot
kilometer
meter
metric
millimeter
span
yard

Exercises

Name the larger unit.   Pages 137–138

9. <u>pace</u> or span

10. <u>cubit</u> or span

11. thumb or <u>pace</u>

Name the larger unit. Pages 139–141

12. centimeter or <u>meter</u>

13. <u>kilometer</u> or meter

14. millimeter or <u>centimeter</u>

15. <u>meter</u> or millimeter

Measure the length of each line segment. Give the measurement in centimeters and then in millimeters.   Pages 139–141

16. ▬▬▬▬▬▬   **4.7 cm, 47 mm**

17. ▬▬▬▬▬▬   **3.9 cm, 39 mm**

18. ▬▬▬▬▬▬   **5.2 cm, 52 mm**

19. ▬▬▬▬▬▬▬   **6.0 cm, 60 mm**

Tell whether you would multiply or divide to complete the following.   Pages 142–143

20. 2 m = ▦ mm   **×**

21. 450 cm = ▦ m   **÷**

22. 5 km = ▦ m   **×**

23. 2.4 cm = ▦ mm   **×**

24. 1,300 mm = ▦ m   **÷**

25. 85 mm = ▦ cm   **÷**

26. 1,250 m = ▦ km   **÷**

27. 5 m = ▦ cm   **×**

28. 300 mm = ▦ m   **÷**

Complete.   Pages 142–143

29. 7 m = ▦ cm **700**

30. 4,200 mm = ▦ m **4.2**

31. 200 m = ▦ km **0.200**

32. 56 cm = ▦ m **0.56**

33. 51 cm = ▦ mm **510**

34. 163.2 cm = ▦ m **1.632**

35. 1,700 m = ▦ km **1.7**

36. 1.4 m = ▦ cm **140**

37. 3.3 cm = ▦ mm **33**

Name the larger unit.   Pages 144–145

38. <u>mile</u> or inch **39.** inch or <u>yard</u> **40.** yard or <u>mile</u>

41. foot or <u>mile</u> **42.** <u>foot</u> or inch **43.** <u>yard</u> or foot

Choose the best estimate.   Pages 144–145

44. length of a ball point pen | **a.** <u>6 in.</u> | **b.** 6 ft | **c.** 6 mi

45. width of a door | **a.** <u>3 ft</u> | **b.** 3 yd | **c.** 3 mi

46. length of a house | **a.** 50 in. | **b.** <u>50 ft</u> | **c.** 50 mi

47. a basketball player's height | **a.** 7 in. | **b.** <u>7 ft</u> | **c.** 7 mi

48. distance from Los Angeles, CA, to Miami, FL | **a.** 2,700 ft | **b.** 2,700 yd | **c.** <u>2,700 mi</u>

Complete.   Pages 148–149

49. 48 in. = ▨ ft **4** **50.** 3 yd = ▨ ft **9** **51.** 6 mi = ▨ ft **31,680**

52. 7 yd = ▨ in. **252** **53.** 4 mi = ▨ ft **21,120** **54.** 108 in. = ▨ yd **3**

55. 36 ft = ▨ yd **12** **56.** 72 in. = ▨ yd **2** **57.** 3,520 yd = ▨ mi **2**

Add, subtract, multiply, or divide.   Pages 150–151

58.   6 ft 7 in.
    + 1 ft 6 in.
    8 ft 1 in.

59.   12 ft
    − 5 ft 7 in.
    6 ft 5 in.

60.   3 yd 11 in.
    ×   4
    13 yd 8 in.

61. 4)9 yd 4 in.   **2 yd 10 in.**

Name the more accurate measurement.   Pages 152–153

62. $1\frac{1}{4}$ in. or <u>$1\frac{3}{16}$ in.</u> **63.** 72.3 m or <u>72.34 m</u> **64.** 53 mm or <u>5.33 cm</u>

Give the number of significant digits in each measurement.   Pages 152–153

65. 684 ft **3** **66.** 5,006 mi **4** **67.** 51,000 ft **2**

68. 0.003 m **1** **69.** 0.0070 m **2** **70.** 32,0<u>0</u>0 cm **4**

Solve.

71. Two pipes and a muffler form an exhaust system. The two pipes measure 30 cm and 72 cm. The muffler measures 0.75 m. What is the total length? **177 cm or 1.77 m**

72. A finished car off the assembly line measures 508 centimeters. Another car measures 5.2 meters. What is the difference in length? **12 cm or 0.12 m**

73. A road sign says it is 100 miles to Niagara Falls. Is this more or less than 100 kilometers? **more**

74. One lap in the swimming pool is 50 meters. Jan swims 10 laps a day. How many kilometers does she swim in one week? **3.5 km**

CHAPTER 7 TEST

Name the larger unit.

1. mm or <u>m</u>

2. yd or <u>mi</u>

3. <u>km</u> or m

4. in. or <u>ft</u>

5. cm or <u>m</u>

6. <u>mi</u> or ft

7. mm or <u>km</u>

8. <u>mi</u> or in.

9. <u>cm</u> or mm

10. <u>yd</u> or ft

11. cm or <u>km</u>

12. in. or <u>yd</u>

Measure each line segment. Give the measurement in inches.

13. _____ 2 in.

14. _____ $1\frac{13}{16}$ in.

15. _____ $1\frac{5}{8}$ in.

16. _____ $2\frac{1}{4}$ in.

Choose the best estimate.

17. thickness of a button

a. <u>6 mm</u>
b. 6 cm
c. 6 m

18. height of a woman

a. 160 mm
b. <u>160 cm</u>
c. 160 m

19. length of a river

a. 50 cm
b. 50 m
c. <u>50 km</u>

20. length of a tennis racket

a. 68 mm
b. <u>68 cm</u>
c. 68 m

21. distance from New York to Boston

a. 350 cm
b. 350 m
c. <u>350 km</u>

Complete.

22. 38 km = ▦ m **38,000**

23. 65 cm = ▦ m **0.65**

24. 4 m = ▦ cm **400**

25. 758 mm = ▦ m **0.758**

26. 8.5 m = ▦ mm **8,500**

27. 7 km = ▦ m **7,000**

28. 155 cm = ▦ m **1.55**

29. 1,245 m = ▦ km **1.245**

30. 16.5 m = ▦ cm **1,650**

31. 7 ft = ▦ in. **84**

32. 36 in. = ▦ ft **3**

33. 5 yd = ▦ in. **180**

34. 5 mi = ▦ yd **8,800**

35. 96 in. = ▦ ft **8**

36. 31,680 ft = ▦ mi **6**

37. 69 in. = ▦ ft ▦ in. **5, 9**

38. 8 mi = ▦ ft **42,240**

39. 7,040 yd = ▦ mi **4**

Add, subtract, multiply, or divide.

40.   3 ft 4 in.
    + 6 ft 9 in.
    10 ft 1 in.

41.   10 ft 3 in.
    − 4 ft 5 in.
    5 ft 10 in.

42.   5 ft 5 in.
    ×   4
    21 ft 8 in.

43. $\overset{\text{2 ft 3 in.}}{6\overline{)13\text{ ft 6 in.}}}$

Give the number of significant digits in each measurement.

44. 2,543 m **4**

45. 4,006 cm **4**

46. 0.007 m **1**

47. 24.050 mm **5**

Solve.

48. There are 4 runners on a team. Each runner runs 880 meters. How many kilometers does each team run?
3.2 kilometers

49. Inga is 5 feet 4 inches tall. Her sister is 4 feet 11 inches tall. How much taller than her sister is Inga?
5 inches

This page provides extra practice of the skills and
applications presented thus far in the text.

CUMULATIVE REVIEW

Two dice are rolled. Find each probability.   Pages 100–101

1. 5,5 $\frac{1}{36}$

2. not 2,4 $\frac{35}{36}$

3. 4,6 or 6,4 $\frac{2}{36}$ or $\frac{1}{18}$

4. not 1,2 or 2,1 $\frac{34}{36}$ or $\frac{17}{18}$

5. a sum of 10 $\frac{3}{36}$ or $\frac{1}{12}$

6. a product of 10 $\frac{2}{36}$ or $\frac{1}{18}$

**The spinner at the right is spun twice.
Find each probability.   Pages 104–105**

7. two B's $\frac{1}{16}$

8. an A, then a D $\frac{1}{16}$

9. two consonants $\frac{9}{16}$

10. an A, then a consonant $\frac{3}{16}$

**Find the probability for the following odds. Express the probability
as a fraction in simplest form and as a percent.   Pages 120–121**

11. 3 to 7 $\frac{3}{10}$; 30%

12. 2 to 3 $\frac{2}{5}$; 40%

13. 3 to 12 $\frac{1}{5}$; 20%

14. 2 to 14 $\frac{1}{8}$; $12\frac{1}{2}$%

15. 8 to 24 $\frac{1}{4}$; 25%

16. 11 to 9 $\frac{11}{20}$; 55%

17. 1 to 1 $\frac{1}{2}$; 50%

18. 4 to 2 $\frac{2}{3}$; $66\frac{2}{3}$%

Find the odds for each probability or chance.   Pages 120–121

19. $\frac{7}{10}$ 7 to 3

20. $\frac{1}{3}$ 1 to 2

21. 60% 3 to 2

22. $66\frac{2}{3}$% 2 to 1

**Suppose all the answers are guesses. Find the expected
score for each test.   Pages 122–123**

23. 100 questions, 4 choices for each 25

24. 100 true-false questions 50

**Name the best unit for measuring each of the following. Use thumb,
span, cubit, or pace.   Pages 137–138**

25. width of your math book
thumb or span

26. distance between bases on a
baseball field **pace**

27. length of a car
cubit or pace

28. length of a paper clip **thumb**

Name the larger unit.   Pages 139–141

29. 1 centimeter or 1 millimeter

30. 1 centimeter or <u>1 kilometer</u>

31. 1 meter or <u>1 kilometer</u>

32. <u>1 meter</u> or 1 millimeter

Solve.

33. Karen has a photograph that measures
30 cm by 36 cm. She reduces the
photo to 60% of the original size.
What are the new dimensions?
18 cm by 21.6 cm

34. A box contains 6 red, 5 yellow, and 4
blue marbles. Each marble drawn is not
replaced. What is the probability of
drawing three blue marbles in a row? $\frac{4}{455}$

35. There are 9 yellow tennis balls and 18 orange tennis balls in a bag.
Matt chooses one ball at random. Estimate the probability that he
chooses an orange tennis ball. $\frac{2}{3}$

Other Common Measurements

8-1 Mass

Objective: To familiarize students with the different metric units for weight.

The most commonly used units of mass in the metric system are the kilogram, gram, and milligram.

> 1 kilogram (kg) = 1,000 grams (g)
> 1 gram (g) = 1,000 milligrams (mg)

Mass is the amount of matter in an object. Weight is the measure of the pull of gravity on the object. In everyday language people talk about *weighing* the mass of an object. Mass remains constant. Weight changes from place to place on, within, or above the earth.

The kilogram, gram, and milligram are described below.

A textbook has a mass of about 1 kilogram (kg).

A paper clip has a mass of about 1 gram (g).

An ant has a mass of about 1 milligram (mg).

The terms mass and weight are often used interchangeably.
Basic: 1–22; Average: 1–22; Enriched: 1–22

Exercises

Name the best unit for measuring the mass of each item. Use kg, g, or mg.

1. set of lifting weights **kg**
2. sack of potatoes **kg**
3. box of cereal **g**
4. can of soup **g**
5. pinch of salt **mg**
6. an egg **g**
7. a jump rope **g**
8. a bicycle **kg**
9. a car **kg**
10. an apple **g**
11. a slice of bread **g**
12. a grain of sand **mg**

Choose the better estimate for the mass of each item.

13. one carrot **a.** 50 mg **b.** 50 g
14. box of cereal **a.** 424 mg **b.** 424 g
15. a motorcycle **a.** 250 kg **b.** 250 g
16. sack of flour **a.** 2.26 kg **b.** 2.26 g
17. loaf of bread **a.** 450 mg **b.** 450 g
18. your weight **a.** 60 kg **b.** 60 g
19. a feather **a.** 17 mg **b.** 17 g
20. a box of chocolates **a.** 2.5 kg **b.** 2.5 g

Solve.

21. A grain of rice has a mass of 10 milligrams. What is the mass of 5 grains of rice? **50 mg**

22. A basketball weighs about 0.6 kg. What is the weight of one dozen basketballs? **7.2 kg**

Teacher Resource Book, Page 187

8-2 Capacity

Objective: To identify the appropriate metric unit for measuring capacity in a given situation.

Ginger Scoles is a medical technologist at a local hospital. Ginger uses containers with many different capacities.

Capacity is the amount of liquid or gas a container can hold.

The most commonly used metric units of capacity are kiloliter, liter, and milliliter.

1 kiloliter (kL) = 1,000 liters (L)
1 liter (L) = 1,000 milliliters (mL)

The liter is the base unit of capacity in the metric system. 1 liter (L) = 1 cubic decimeter (dm³)

The capacity of five oil drums is about 1 kiloliter (kL).

The capacity of the bottle is 1 liter (L).

The capacity of the eyedropper is about 1 milliliter (mL).

Basic: 2–30 even; Average: 1–32; Enriched: 1–32

Exercises

Name the best unit for measuring the capacity of each item. Use kL, L, or mL.

1. a cup of soup **mL**
2. ear drops **mL**
3. water in a swimming pool **kL**
4. glass of orange juice **mL**
5. food coloring **mL**
6. bottle of perfume **mL**
7. cough syrup **mL**
8. gasoline **L**
9. jug of water **L**
10. hot air balloon **kL**
11. oxygen tank **L**
12. water in a lake **kL**

Name the larger unit.

13. milliliter or <u>liter</u>
14. <u>kiloliter</u> or milliliter
15. <u>kiloliter</u> or liter

Name the unit of capacity each symbol represents.

16. kL **kiloliter**

17. mL **milliliter**

18. L **liter**

Choose the best estimate for the capacity of each item.

19. swimming pool   **a.** 10 kL   **b.** 10 mL

21. bathtub   **a.** 300 L   **b.** 300 kL

23. ketchup bottle   **a.** 500 mL   **b.** 500 kL

25. house paint can   **a.** 4 L   **b.** 4 mL

20. medicine bottle   **a.** 150 mL   **b.** 150 L

22. gasoline tank in car   **a.** 50 mL   **b.** 50 L

24. soda bottle   **a.** 1 mL   **b.** 1 L

26. drinking glass   **a.** 250 mL   **b.** 250 L

Answer the following.

27. a milk carton holds 2 liters. How many milliliters is this? **2,000 mL**

28. A carton holds 1,000 milliliters of juice. How many liters is this? **1 L**

29. A soft drink bottle is labeled one-half liter. How many milliliters is this? **500 mL**

30. A water container holds 750 milliliters. What part of a liter is this? **0.750 L**

31. A gasoline tank has a capacity of 100 liters. Seventy-two liters of gasoline are needed to fill the tank. How much gasoline is in the tank? **28 L**

32. A propane delivery truck contains 10 kL of propane. How many 0.5 kL tanks can be filled from the truck? **20 tanks**

This feature presents general topics of mathematics.

 Math Break

A box that measures 10 centimeters on all edges filled with water holds 1 liter and weighs 1 kilogram.

A box that measures 1 centimeter on all edges filled with water holds 1 milliliter and weighs 1 gram.

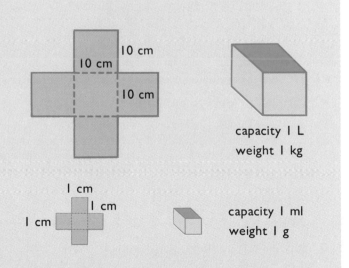

10 cm   10 cm   10 cm   capacity 1 L   weight 1 kg

1 cm   1 cm   1 cm   capacity 1 ml   weight 1 g

Solve.

1. How many kilograms does 5 liters of water weigh? **5 kg**

2. How many milliliters of water weigh 75 grams? **75 mL**

3. How many liters of water are in a container if the water weighs 825 grams? **0.825 L**

8-3   *Changing Metric Units*

Objective: To change from one metric unit to another.

Willie Spencer is a machinist for a company that makes transmission gears. In his work, Willie must be able to change from one unit of measure to another. Willie completed a four-year apprenticeship program. This included on-the-job training and classroom instruction.

The metric system is a decimal (base 10) system. To change metric units, multiply or divide by the appropriate power of ten.

MULTIPLY to change larger units to smaller units.

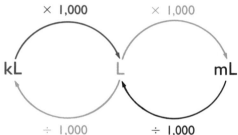

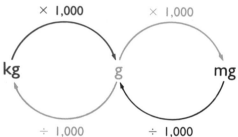

DIVIDE to change smaller units to larger units.

Examples

A. Change 20 liters to milliliters.

20 L = ▓ mL

    You are changing from a larger to a smaller unit. There will be more of these units after the change, so MULTIPLY.

20 L = ▓ mL
   ⤸
   × 1,000

20 L = 20,000 mL

    There are 1,000 milliliters in a liter. So, multiply by 1,000. 20 × 1,000 = 20,000

B. Change 325 milligrams to grams.

325 mg = ▓ g

    You are changing from a smaller to a larger unit. There will be fewer of these units after the change, so DIVIDE.

325 mg = ▓ g
   ⤸
   ÷ 1,000

325 mg = 0.325 g

    There are 1,000 milligrams in 1 gram. So, divide by 1,000. 325 ÷ 1,000 = 0.325

The Key Skills provides practice of skills needed in the exercises.

Key Skills

$7.2 \times 1,000 = 7200$ *Move the decimal point three places to the right.*
$7.2 \div 1,000 = 0.0072$ *Move the decimal point three places to the left.*

Multiply or divide.

1. $1,287 \div 1,000$ **1.287**

2. $72.6 \div 1,000$ **0.0726**

3. $6.156 \times 1,000$ **6,156**

4. $0.002 \times 1,000$ **2**

5. $480.2 \div 1,000$ **0.4802**

6. $1,000 \times 1,000$ **1,000,000**

Basic Skills Appendix, Pages 426, 442
Basic: 1–14, even; Average: 1–36; Enriched: 1–14, 15–33 odd, 35–36

Exercises

Use the diagrams on page 164 to complete each statement.

1. To change kilograms to grams, multiply by _____?_____ . **1,000**

2. To change kiloliters to liters, _____?_____ by 1,000. **multiply**

3. To change grams to kilograms, _____?_____ by 1,000. **divide**

4. To change liters to kiloliters, divide by _____?_____ . **1,000**

Answer each of the following to complete 7 L = ▧ mL.

5. Which unit is larger, L or mL? **L**

6. Do you multiply or divide? **multiply**

7. How many mL in one L? **1,000**

8. Which power of 10 do you use? **1,000**

9. $7 L = ▧ mL$ **7,000**

Answer each of the following to complete 200 g = ▧ kg.

10. Which unit is larger, g or kg? **kg**

11. Do you multiply or divide? **divide**

12. How many g in one kg? **1,000**

13. Which power of 10 do you use? **1,000**

14. $200 g = ▧ kg$ **0.2**

Complete.

15. $4 kg = ▧ g$ **4,000**

16. $2,000 mg = ▧ g$ **2**

17. $6 L = ▧ mL$ **6,000**

18. $127 g = ▧ kg$ **0.127**

19. $2.8L = ▧ mL$ **2,800**

20. $234 mL = ▧ L$ **0.234**

21. $5.72 kL = ▧ L$ **5,720**

22. $10,000 mg = ▧ g$ **10**

23. $7 kg = ▧ g$ **7,000**

24. $0.003 L = ▧ mL$ **3**

25. $34.2L = ▧ mL$ **34,200**

26. $8.75 kg = ▧ g$ **8,750**

27. $3 kL = ▧ mL$ **3,000,000**

28. $787 kg = ▧ mg$ **787,000,000**

29. $2.3 g = ▧ mg$ **2,300**

30. $37,600 mL = ▧ L$ **37.6**

Tell whether the measurements are equivalent. Write yes or no.

31. 1.65 kg, 165 g **no**

32. 950 mL, 0.95 L **yes**

33. 0.05 g, 50 mg **yes**

34. 0.001 L, 1 mL **yes**

Answer the following.

35. A basketball weighs 0.598 kg. How many grams does the basketball weigh? **598 g**

36. A milk carton contains 3.89 L of milk. How many milliliters of milk are in the carton? **3,890 mL**

8-4 Customary Units of Weight and Capacity

Objective: To change from one customary unit of weight or capacity to another.

Customary units of weight are **tons, pounds,** and **ounces.**

1 ton (T) = 2,000 pounds (lb)
1 pound (lb) = 16 ounces (oz)

A small car weighs about one ton (T).

A hammer weighs about one pound (lb).

A small bag of peanuts weighs about one ounce (oz).

To change customary units of weight, multiply or divide by the appropriate number.

$\times$ 2,000 $\times$ 16

T   lb   oz

$\div$ 2,000 $\div$ 16

Examples

A. Change $2\frac{5}{8}$ pounds to ounces.

$2\frac{5}{8}$ lb = ▧ oz   *You are changing from larger to smaller units.*

$2\frac{5}{8}$ lb = ▧ oz   *There will be more of these units after the change,*
$\quad\quad\quad\quad\quad\quad$ *so MULTIPLY.*
$\quad\quad\times 16$ *There are 16 ounces in a pound. So, multiply by 16.*
$2\frac{5}{8}$ lb = 42 oz $2\frac{5}{8} \times 16 = 42$ oz

B. Change 9,500 pounds to tons.

9,500 lb = ▧ T   *You are changing from smaller to larger units.*

9,500 lb = ▧ T   *There will be fewer of these units after the*
$\quad\quad\quad\quad\quad$ *change, so DIVIDE.*
$\quad\quad\div 2,000$ *There are 2,000 pounds in a ton. So, divide by 2,000.*
9,500 lb = $4\frac{3}{4}$ T $9,500 \div 2,000 = 4\frac{3}{4}$

Customary units of capacity are **fluid ounce, cup, pint, quart,** and **gallon.**

1 gallon (gal) = 4 quarts (qt)
1 quart (qt) = 2 pints (pt)
1 pint (pt) = 2 cups (c)
1 cup (c) = 8 fluid ounces (fl oz)

To change customary units of capacity, multiply or divide by
the appropriate number.

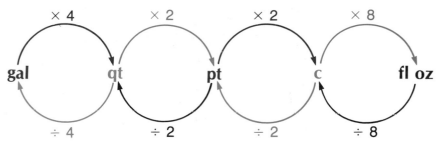

Examples

C. Change 3 pints to cups.

3 pt = ▒ c   *You are changing from a larger to a smaller unit.*

3 pt = ▒ c   *There will be* more *of these units after the change,*
⌣_____   *so MULTIPLY.*
× 2

                    There are 2 cups in a pint. So, multiply by 2.
3 pt = 6 c   *3 × 2 = 6*

D. Change 8 quarts to gallons.

8 qt = ▒ gal   *You are changing from a smaller to a larger unit.*

8 qt = ▒ gal   *There will be* fewer *of these units after the change,*
⌣_____   *so DIVIDE.*
÷ 4

                    There are 4 quarts in a gallon. So, divide by 4.
8 qt = 2 gal   *8 ÷ 4 = 2*

The Key Skills provides practice of skills needed in the exercises.

Key Skills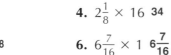

$$16 \times \frac{3}{8} = \frac{16}{1} \times \frac{3}{8}$$

$$2\frac{1}{4} \times 16 = \frac{9}{4} \times \frac{16}{1}$$

$$= \frac{\overset{2}{\cancel{16}} \times 3}{1 \times \cancel{8}}$$

$$= \frac{9 \times \overset{4}{\cancel{16}}}{\cancel{4} \times 1}$$

$$= 6$$

$$= 36$$

Multiply.

1. $16 \times \frac{1}{4}$ **4**

2. $16 \times \frac{1}{8}$ **2**

3. $16 \times \frac{3}{4}$ **12**

4. $2\frac{1}{8} \times 16$ **34**

5. $5\frac{1}{2} \times 16$ **88**

6. $6\frac{7}{16} \times 1$ **$6\frac{7}{16}$**

7. $2\frac{5}{8} \times 3\frac{1}{4}$ **$8\frac{17}{32}$**

8. $3\frac{1}{8} \times 4\frac{1}{2}$ **$14\frac{1}{16}$**

Exercises

Complete.

1. 2 lb = ▨ oz **32**

2. $11\frac{1}{2}$ lb = ▨ oz **184**

3. 7 T = ▨ lb **14,000**

4. $20\frac{3}{4}$ lb = ▨ oz **332**

5. 2,000 lb = ▨ T **1**

6. $\frac{1}{2}$ T = ▨ lb **1,000**

7. 40 lb 4 oz = ▨ oz **644**

8. $\frac{3}{4}$ T = ▨ lb **1,500**

9. $\frac{5}{8}$ lb = ▨ oz **10**

10. 256 oz = ▨ lb **16**

11. $3\frac{1}{4}$ T = ▨ lb **6,500**

12. 1 T = ▨ lb **2,000**

Choose the best estimate for the weight of each item.

13. a pork roast   **a.** 4 oz   **b.** 4 lb   **c.** 4 T

14. an orange   **a.** 8 lb   **b.** 8 oz   **c.** 8 T

15. a truck   **a.** 2 T   **b.** 2 lb   **c.** 2 oz

16. a bag of sugar   **a.** 5 oz   **b.** 5 T   **c.** 5 lb

Complete.

17. 2 pt = ▨ c **4**

18. 3 gal = ▨ qt **12**

19. 16 c = ▨ pt **8**

20. 4 pt = ▨ c **8**

21. 4 qt = ▨ gal **1**

22. 1 gal = ▨ pt **8**

23. 3 qt = ▨ c **12**

24. 8 pt = ▨ qt **4**

25. 12 qt = ▨ gal **3**

26. 1 pt = ▨ fl oz **16**

27. 4 fl oz = ▨ c $\frac{1}{2}$

28. 1 qt = ▨ fl oz **32**

29. 46 fl oz = ▨ c $5\frac{3}{4}$

30. 32 fl oz = ▨ pt **2**

31. 1 gal = ▨ fl oz **128**

32. 12 c = ▨ qt **3**

33. 6 qt = ▨ gal $1\frac{1}{2}$

34. 4 gal = ▨ c **64**

35. 16 c = ▨ gal **1**

36. 8 qt = ▨ c **32**

37. $3\frac{1}{2}$ gal = ▨ qt **14**

Choose the best estimate for the capacity of each item.

38. a bathtub   **a.** 40 cups   **b.** 40 gallons   **c.** 40 fluid ounces

39. a drinking glass   **a.** 2 quarts   **b.** 2 pints   **c.** 2 cups

40. a large can for fruits   **a.** 2 cups   **b.** 2 pints   **c.** 2 gallons

41. a large juice can   **a.** 3 pints   **b.** 3 gallons   **c.** 3 quarts

Solve.

42. How many ounces are in 2 tons? **64,000 ounces**

43. How many pints of water are needed to fill a 10-gallon aquarium? **80 pints**

44. How many 4-ounce boxes of cookies can be made from a 6-pound container of cookies? **24 boxes**

45. Ground beef sells for $1.44 per pound. How much does one ounce cost? **9¢**

46. A 46-fluid ounce can of juice sells for 97¢. Find the cost of one ounce to the nearest tenth of a cent. **2.1¢**

47. Milk is purchased in quarts at 79¢ each. How much will it cost for 9 one-cup servings? **$2.37**

This feature provides general topics about the computer.

The emphasis here should be twofold. One is the international character of the development; the other is the mechanical nature of early calculating devices.

Computer

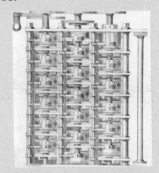

The first calculating devices were very simple.

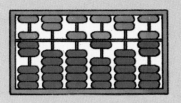

The Chinese developed the abacus around 3000 B.C.

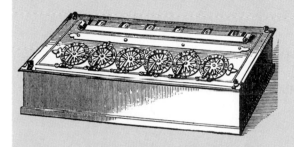

Blaise Pascal's gear-driven adding machine was patented in 1642 in France.

In 1801, Joseph Marie Jacquard of France invented a mechanical loom that was controlled by punch cards.

In England, (1834) Charles Babbage designed a steam-driven calculating device. It was never built because the tiny parts needed could not be manufactured. Lady Ada Lovelace wrote operating instructions for this device.

Processing the information collected in the 1880 census took seven years. The United States Census Office needed help for the 1890 census. Herman Hollerith designed a tabulating machine that used punched cards. The information in 1890 was processed in two and one-half years.

PRACTICE

Estimate. Answers may vary. Typical answers are given.

1. 745
    + 57
    810

2. 16.77
    − 4.21
    13

3. 326
    − 173
    100

4. 12.73
    + 6.79
    20

5. 0.16
    + 1.06
    1.2

6. 189
    × 19
    4,000

7. 81
    × 38
    3,200

8. 0.504
    × 0.042
    0.0200

9. 29)243 8

10. 0.08)7.32 90

Replace each ● with <, >, or = to make a true sentence.

11. 3.750 ● 3.75   =

12. 0.02 ● 0.2   <

13. 1.7 ● 1.07   >

14. $\frac{4}{5}$ ● $\frac{16}{20}$ =

15. $\frac{5}{8}$ ● $\frac{2}{3}$ <

16. $\frac{7}{8}$ ● $\frac{9}{10}$ <

17. $\frac{3}{4}$ ● $\frac{2}{3}$ >

18. $6\frac{1}{4}$ ● 6.25   =

19. 0.75 ● $\frac{4}{5}$ <

Add, subtract, multiply, or divide.

20. 4.07
    + 0.36
    4.43

21. 13.634
    + 6.366
    20.000

22. 279
    − 239
    40

23. 1,500
    − 101
    1,399

24. 6.004
    − 0.005
    5.999

25. 17.2
    × 1.11
    19.092

26. 59
    × 27
    1,593

27. 607
    × 1.52
    922.64

28. 11.54
    × 4.3
    49.622

29. 27.7
    × 0.82
    22.714

30. 11)253   23

31. 18)765   42.5

32. 24)612   25.5

33. 300)99   0.33

34. 0.09)45   500

Add. Write each sum in simplest form.

35. $\frac{1}{2} + \frac{1}{5}$ $\frac{7}{10}$

36. $\frac{1}{2} + 1\frac{1}{8}$ $1\frac{5}{8}$

37. $1\frac{2}{3} + \frac{1}{3}$ 2

38. $1\frac{3}{4} + \frac{1}{2}$ $2\frac{1}{4}$

39. $\frac{1}{4} + \frac{1}{3}$ $\frac{7}{12}$

40. $\frac{5}{8} + \frac{3}{4}$ $1\frac{3}{8}$

41. $\frac{2}{3} + \frac{1}{2}$ $1\frac{1}{6}$

42. $2\frac{1}{6} + \frac{4}{5}$ $2\frac{29}{30}$

43. $\frac{3}{5} + \frac{2}{3}$ $1\frac{4}{15}$

44. $\frac{3}{8} + \frac{5}{6}$ $1\frac{5}{24}$

45. $1\frac{2}{15} + 3\frac{2}{3}$ $4\frac{4}{5}$

46. $4\frac{8}{9} + 5\frac{1}{2}$ $10\frac{7}{18}$

Subtract. Write each difference in simplest form.

47. $\frac{3}{10} - \frac{1}{5}$ $\frac{1}{10}$

48. $\frac{5}{6} - \frac{1}{3}$ $\frac{1}{2}$

49. $1\frac{1}{2} - \frac{7}{8}$ $\frac{5}{8}$

50. $1\frac{1}{2} - \frac{2}{3}$ $\frac{5}{6}$

51. $\frac{1}{3} - \frac{1}{4}$ $\frac{1}{12}$

52. $\frac{7}{8} - \frac{5}{6}$ $\frac{1}{24}$

53. $\frac{6}{7} - \frac{1}{2}$ $\frac{5}{14}$

54. $1\frac{1}{3} - \frac{5}{8}$ $\frac{17}{24}$

55. $\frac{1}{3} - \frac{1}{8}$ $\frac{5}{24}$

56. $1\frac{1}{2} - \frac{4}{5}$ $\frac{7}{10}$

57. $5\frac{2}{5} - \frac{1}{2}$ $4\frac{9}{10}$

58. $3\frac{1}{3} - \frac{4}{5}$ $2\frac{8}{15}$

Multiply. Write each product in simplest form.

59. $2\frac{2}{3} \times 2$ $5\frac{1}{3}$ **60.** $12 \times \frac{5}{6}$ 10   **61.** $2\frac{1}{6} \times 42$ 91   **62.** $30 \times \frac{7}{10}$ 21

63. $11 \times 1\frac{1}{3}$ $14\frac{2}{3}$ **64.** $2\frac{1}{2} \times 1\frac{1}{4}$ $3\frac{1}{8}$ **65.** $\frac{3}{4} \times \frac{1}{3}$ $\frac{1}{4}$ **66.** $2\frac{5}{9} \times \frac{3}{5}$ $1\frac{8}{15}$

67. $\frac{2}{5} \times \frac{2}{3}$ $\frac{4}{15}$ **68.** $\frac{3}{4} \times \frac{3}{8}$ $\frac{9}{32}$ **69.** $1\frac{7}{9} \times 5\frac{3}{4}$ $10\frac{2}{9}$ **70.** $3\frac{1}{5} \times 2\frac{1}{12}$ $6\frac{2}{3}$

Divide. Write each quotient in simplest form.

71. $4 \div \frac{1}{3}$ 12   **72.** $3 \div 1\frac{1}{4}$ $2\frac{2}{5}$ **73.** $2\frac{4}{5} \div 8$ $\frac{7}{20}$ **74.** $1\frac{1}{8} \div \frac{1}{3}$ $3\frac{3}{8}$

75. $1\frac{3}{4} \div \frac{3}{8}$ $4\frac{2}{3}$ **76.** $\frac{5}{8} \div \frac{5}{7}$ $\frac{7}{8}$ **77.** $\frac{1}{6} \div \frac{2}{3}$ $\frac{1}{4}$ **78.** $\frac{5}{8} \div \frac{2}{7}$ $2\frac{3}{16}$

79. $\frac{5}{8} \div \frac{1}{3}$ $1\frac{7}{8}$ **80.** $\frac{1}{6} \div \frac{3}{7}$ $\frac{7}{18}$ **81.** $4\frac{1}{6} \div 7\frac{1}{2}$ $\frac{5}{9}$ **82.** $1\frac{7}{8} \div 1\frac{2}{3}$ $1\frac{1}{8}$

Multiply.

83. 10×14.6 146   **84.** 0.09×10 0.9   **85.** 2.73×100 273

86. 100×32 3,200   **87.** $1,000 \times 1.064$ 1,064   **88.** $43.1 \times 1,000$ 43,100

89. $738.1 \times 1,000$ 738,100   **90.** 100×8.6 860   **91.** $1,000 \times 0.9$ 900

92. 1.6×100 160   **93.** 0.78×100 78   **94.** 0.08×10 0.8

Divide.

95. $84 \div 10$ 8.4   **96.** $427 \div 10$ 42.7   **97.** $6.91 \div 10$ 0.691

98. $76 \div 100$ 0.76   **99.** $596 \div 100$ 5.96   **100.** $29 \div 1,000$ 0.029

101. $63.34 \div 10$ 6.334   **102.** $480.45 \div 100$ 4.8045   **103.** $801.6 \div 100$ 8.016

104. $194.3 \div 1,000$ 0.1943   **105.** $935.2 \div 100$ 9.352   **106.** $67,801.2 \div 100$ 678.012

Complete.

107. 21 cm = ▨ mm 210   **108.** 4 km = ▨ m 4,000   **109.** 38 mm = ▨ cm 3.8

110. 16 m = ▨ cm 1,600   **111.** 279 mm = ▨ m 0.279   **112.** 426 m = ▨ km 0.426

113. 38 km = ▨ m 38,000   **114.** 8.5 m = ▨ mm 8,500   **115.** 155 cm = ▨ m 1.55

116. 1,245 m = ▨ km 1.245   **117.** 247 cm = ▨ mm 2,470   **118.** 16.5 m = ▨ cm 1,650

Solve.

119. Sean has 1,500 milliliters of grape juice to take to a picnic. Will a 2-liter container hold all the juice? **yes**

120. A box of rice weighs 40,000 mg. What is the weight of the box of rice in grams? **40 g**

8-5 Temperature

Objective: To identify the appropriate Celsius temperature for a given situation. To change Fahrenheit to Celsius, and Celsius to Fahrenheit.

The customary unit for the measure of temperature is degrees **Fahrenheit (°F).** The metric unit for the measure of temperature is degrees **Celsius (°C).** The Fahrenheit and Celsius scales are shown together on the thermometer at the left. Normal body temperature in humans is 98.6°F. What is normal human body temperature in degrees Celsius? **37°C**

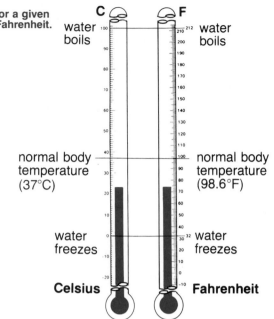

The formulas below show how the two temperature scales are related.

Fahrenheit to Celsius: $C = \frac{5}{9} \times (F - 32)$

Celsius to Fahrenheit: $F = \left(\frac{9}{5} \times C\right) + 32$

Examples

A. Change 86°F to degrees Celsius.

Use the formula $C = \frac{5}{9} \times (F - 32)$.

Estimate: $\frac{1}{2} \times (90 - 30) = \frac{1}{2} \times 60$ or 30   *Round $\frac{5}{9}$ to $\frac{1}{2}$.*

$C = \frac{5}{9} \times (86 - 32)$ *Replace F with 86.*

$C = \frac{5}{\overset{}{\underset{1}{9}}} \times \overset{6}{\cancel{54}}$

$C = 30$ 86 ⊖ 32 ⊜ 54 ⊠ 5 ⊝ 9 ⊜ *30*

$86°F = 30°C$ *Is the answer reasonable?* **Yes**

B. Change 20°C to degrees Fahrenheit.

Use the formula $F = \left(\frac{9}{5} \times C\right) + 32$.

Estimate: $(2 \times 20) + 30 = 40 + 30$ or 70   *Round $\frac{9}{5}$ to 2.*

$F = \left(\frac{9}{\underset{1}{\cancel{5}}} \times \overset{4}{\cancel{20}}\right) + 32$ *Replace C with 20.*

$F = 36 + 32$

$F = 68$ 9 ⊝ 5 ⊠ 20 ⊕ 32 ⊜ *68*

$20°C = 68°F$ *Is the answer reasonable?* **Yes**

172   *Other Common Measurements*

Exercises

Use the thermometers shown above to answer the following.

1. Find the boiling and freezing temperatures for water in degrees Celsius. **100°C, 0°C**

2. Find the boiling and freezing temperatures for water in degrees Fahrenheit. **212°F, 32°F**

Choose the better temperature for the following.

3. mowing, <u>25°C</u> or 35°C

4. ice cubes, <u>⁻5°C</u> or 10°C

5. bath water, <u>30°C</u> or 20°C

6. camping, <u>20°C</u> or 45°C

7. swimming, 10°C or <u>30°C</u>

8. skiing, <u>⁻10°C</u> or ⁻20°C

Change each Fahrenheit reading to a Celsius reading.

9. 212°F **100°C**   **10.** 32°F **0°C**   **11.** 41°F **5°C**   **12.** 77°F **25°C**   **13.** 176°F **80°C**

14. 68°F **20°C**   **15.** 86°F **30°C**   **16.** 140°F **60°C**   **17.** 50°F **10°C**   **18.** 284°F **140°C**

Change each Celsius reading to a Fahrenheit reading.

19. 70°C **158°F**   **20.** 15°C **59°F**   **21.** 40°C **104°F**   **22.** 55°C **131°F**   **23.** 0°C **32°F**

24. 115°C **239°F**   **25.** 75°C **167°F**   **26.** 45°C **113°F**   **27.** 85°C **185°F**   **28.** 340°C **644°F**

Solve.

29. Would you need to wear a coat if the temperature was 35°C? Why or why not?
95°F, too warm

30. Would you need to use a fan if the temperature was 22°C? Why or why not?
no, not hot enough, 71.6°F

31. The 6:00 P.M. weather report gave the current temperature at 78°F. The temperature was expected to drop 26°F before morning. What was the expected low temperature in degrees Celsius? **15°C**

This feature promotes student's mental abilities in computation and reasonableness.

Mental Math

A fraction of a whole number can often be calculated mentally.
Find $\frac{3}{5}$ of 350.

$\frac{1}{5}$ of 350 $\rightarrow$ 350 ÷ 5 or 70

$\frac{3}{5}$ of 350 is 3 times $\frac{1}{5}$ of 350.

So, $\frac{3}{5}$ of 350 is 3 × 70 or 210.

Multiply, using the strategy above.

1. $\frac{1}{8}$ of 48 **6**

2. $\frac{2}{5}$ of 25 **10**

3. $\frac{7}{8}$ of 56 **49**

4. $\frac{2}{3}$ of $720 **$480**

5. $\frac{5}{6}$ of 42 **35**

6. $\frac{5}{8}$ of 24 **15**

7. $\frac{4}{9}$ of 63 **28**

8. $\frac{4}{5}$ of $60,000 **$48,000**

8-6 Time

Objective: To familiarize students with time measurement and to change units of time.

Time is measured the same way in both the customary and metric systems.

Common units of time are shown below.

60 seconds(s) = 1 minute (min)
60 minutes(min) = 1 hour (h)
24 hour(h) = 1 day (d)
7 days(d) = 1 week (wk)
52 weeks(wk) = 1 year (yr)
365 days(d) = 1 year (yr)

366 days (d) = 1 leap year

To change units of time, multiply or divide by the appropriate number.

Examples

A. Change 20 minutes to seconds.

20 min = ▓ s   *minutes → seconds*

20 min = ▓ s   *larger → smaller*

$\times$ 60   *Multiply by 60.*

20 min = 1,200   20 × 60 = 1,200

B. Change 37 days to weeks.

37 d = ▓ wk   *days → weeks*

37 d = ▓ wk   *smaller → larger*

$\div$ 7   *Divide by 7.*

37 d = 5 wk 2 d   37 ÷ 7 = 5 R 2

Units of time can be added or subtracted.

Examples

C. Add.

$$\begin{array}{r} 9 \text{ h } 16 \text{ min} \\ +\ 15 \text{ h } 55 \text{ min} \\ \hline 24 \text{ h } 71 \text{ min} \\ +\ 1 \text{ h } 11 \text{ min} \\ \hline 25 \text{ h } 11 \text{ min} \end{array}$$

Rename 71 min as 1 h and 11 min and add to 24 h.

D. Subtract.

$$\begin{array}{r} \overset{4}{5} \text{ h } \overset{64}{4} \text{ min } 13 \text{ s} \\ -\ 3 \text{ h } 22 \text{ min }\ 7 \text{ s} \\ \hline 1 \text{ h } 42 \text{ min }\ 6 \text{ s} \end{array}$$

Rename 5 h 4 min as 4 h 64 min.

Basic: 2–32 even; Average: 1–32; Enriched: 1–29 odd, 31–32

Exercises

Complete.

1. 5 min = ▓ s **300**   **2.** 3 d = ▓ h **72**   **3.** 48 h = ▓ d **2**   **4.** 10 d = ▓ h **240**

5. 3 yr = ▓ d **1,095**   **6.** 2 wk = ▓ d **14**   **7.** 104 wk = ▓ yr **2**   **8.** 1 wk = ▓ h **168**

9. 90 min = ▓ h ▓ min **1, 30**   **10.** 12 d = ▓ wk ▓ d **1, 5**   **11.** 60 h = ▓ d ▓ h **2, 12**

12. 400 d = ▓ yr ▓ d **1, 35**   **13.** 210 wk = ▓ yr ▓ wk **4, 2**   **14.** ▓ s = 1 min 25 s **85**

Name the larger measurement.

15. 60 min or <u>1 h 5 min</u>

16. <u>3 d</u> or 60 h

17. <u>110 wk</u> or 2 yr

18. 365 d or <u>54 wk</u>

Add or subtract.

19.
$$
\begin{array}{r}
4\text{ h }\ \ 7\text{ min }30\text{ s}\\
+\ 3\text{ h }17\text{ min }58\text{ s}\\
\hline
7\text{ h }25\text{ min }28\text{ s}
\end{array}
$$

20.
$$
\begin{array}{r}
8\text{ min}\ \ \ \ \ \ \ \\
-\ 6\text{ min }45\text{ s}\\
\hline
1\text{ min }15\text{ s}
\end{array}
$$

21.
$$
\begin{array}{r}
3\text{ d }17\text{ h }50\text{ min}\\
+\ 2\text{ d }12\text{ h }\ \ 6\text{ min}\\
\hline
6\text{d }\ \ 5\text{ h }56\text{ min}
\end{array}
$$

22.
$$
\begin{array}{r}
3\text{ d }\ \ \ \ \ \ 16\text{ min}\\
-\ 1\text{ d }4\text{ h }\ \ 9\text{ min}\\
\hline
1\text{ d }20\text{ h }\ \ 7\text{ min}
\end{array}
$$

23.
$$
\begin{array}{r}
7\text{ wk }1\text{ d}\\
-\ 3\text{ wk }5\text{ d}\\
\hline
3\text{ wk }3\text{ d}
\end{array}
$$

24.
$$
\begin{array}{r}
36\text{ wk }6\text{ d }14\text{ h}\\
+\ 10\text{ wk }3\text{ d }18\text{ h}\\
\hline
47\text{ wk }3\text{ d }\ \ 8\text{ h}
\end{array}
$$

The bus schedule shown at the right gives the times buses leave Mick's hometown of Newark.

Find the time spent traveling from Newark to each town.

Hour of Departure	Location	Hour of Arrival
8:00 A.M.	Grand Falls	8:51 A.M.
9:30 A.M.	South Lake	10:50 A.M.
1:25 P.M.	Lancaster	2:19 P.M.
4:33 P.M.	Worthington	5:19 P.M.
9:30 A.M.	Centerville	11:29 A.M.
11:25 A.M.	Lima	12:45 P.M.
12:25 P.M.	Albany	1:19 P.M.

25. Grand Falls 51 min

26. Centerville 1 h 59 min

27. Worthington 46 min

28. Albany 54 min

29. Lima 1 h 20 min

30. Lancaster 54 min

Solve.

31. The hands of a clock are together at 12 noon. When are they next together?
at about 1:05 P.M.

32. Edna Watkins was born on May 23, 1973. How old will she be on her next birthday? **Answers may vary**

This feature presents useful ways of solving mathematical problems on a calculator.

Calculator

There are calculators that can add, subtract, multiply, and divide with fractions or mixed numerals. The problem, $3\frac{1}{8} + 2\frac{2}{3}$, would be done on one such calculator as shown below.

$$3\frac{1}{8} \qquad + \qquad 2\frac{2}{3} \qquad = \qquad 5\frac{19}{24}$$

$$3\lrcorner1\lrcorner8\ \boxed{+}\ 2\lrcorner2\lrcorner3\ \boxed{=}\ 5\lrcorner19\lrcorner24$$

Solve. Write your answers as they would appear on a fraction calculator.

1. $2\frac{1}{7} + 1\frac{3}{14}$
3 ⌐5 ⌐14

2. $7\frac{1}{5} - 6\frac{7}{10}$ 1 ⌐2

3. $7\frac{1}{9} \times 2\frac{1}{6}$
15 ⌐11 ⌐27

4. $1\frac{3}{5} \div 2\frac{2}{5}$
2 ⌐3

8-7 *Problem Solving: Using Measurements*

Objective: To solve multi-step word problems involving measurements.

Many problems are solved by using more than one computation.
Nancy drinks one cup of milk with each of her three daily
meals. How many quarts of milk does she drink in 4 weeks?

Read

You must find how many quarts of milk Nancy drinks in 4
weeks. You know Nancy drinks 3 cups each day for 4 weeks.

Decide

Find the number of days in 4 weeks. Then find the number
of cups of milk Nancy drinks in 4 weeks. Finally, find the
number of quarts equivalent to this number of cups.

Solve

weeks →   4 × 7 *days in each week* = 28 days
days   →   28 × 3 *cups each day*   = 84 cups
cups   →   84 ÷ 4 *cups in each quart* = 21 quarts

4 ⊠ 7 ⊠ 3 ⊟ 4 ⊟ *21*

Nancy drinks 21 quarts of milk in 4 weeks.

Examine

Use the following steps to check the solution.
quarts →   21 × 4 *cups in each quart* = 84 cups
cups   →   84 ÷ 3 *cups each day*   = 28 days
days   →   28 ÷ 7 *days in each week* =   4 weeks

The answer 21 quarts is correct.

Basic: 1–15 odd; Average: 1–16; Enriched: 1–16

Exercises

1. Yoki Sun drinks 2 cups of milk, 1 cup
   of water, and 5 cups of juice. How
   many quarts of liquid is this?
   2 quarts

2. Freda weighs 57 kilograms. If she
   loses 250 grams of weight a week,
   how many days until Freda weighs
   55 kilograms? **56 days**

3. The United States Department of
   Agriculture recommends that you
   eat 6 ounces of meat each day. In
   two weeks how many pounds of meat
   is this? $5\frac{1}{4}$ **pounds**

4. The temperature outside increased
   3°F every hour. At 12:00 P.M. the
   temperature was 72°F. What was the
   temperature at 4:00 P.M.? **84°F**

5. Eric begins fixing dinner at 5:23 P.M.
   and finishes at 6:07 P.M. How
   many minutes does it take Eric to
   prepare dinner? **44 minutes**

6. Mick Micone swims in an outdoor
   pool if the temperature is between
   20°C and 35°C. Does he swim if the
   temperature is 70°F? **yes**

7. Jacque's heart beats 72 times per minute. How many times does his heart beat in one day? **103,680 times**

8. The water temperature in the pool is 68°F. What is the temperature of the water in degrees Celsius? **20°C**

9. Inez begins doing sit-ups at 2:09 P.M. She finishes at 2:21 P.M. How many minutes is this? What part of an hour is this? **12 minutes, $\frac{1}{5}$ hour**

10. Jogging for 15 minutes burns 150 calories. How many calories do you burn while jogging 1 hour? **600 calories**

11. During exercise, Sam's lungs take in 100 liters of air per minute. How many kiloliters of air will Sam's lungs take in during 15 minutes of exercise? **1.5 kiloliters**

12. During a basketball game each of the twelve players drinks 1 quart of water. How many gallons of water does the team drink? **3 gallons**

13. Paula exercises 40 minutes three times a week. In one year, how many hours does Paula exercise? **104 hours**

14. The girls on a basketball team weigh 57 kg, 63 kg, 52 kg, 60 kg, and 54 kg. What is their total weight in grams? **286,000 grams**

15. Tyrone takes a 20-minute walk three times each week. How many hours will he walk in 32 weeks? **32 h**

16. Last week Tanya worked 3 h 15 min, 6 h 20 min, 7 h 30 min, 9 h, and 7 h 35 min. What was Tanya's total work time? **33 h 40 min**

CHAPTER 8 REVIEW

Vocabulary/Concepts

Choose the letter of the word, phrase, or numeral that best matches each description.

1. the customary unit of temperature measure **f**
2. object used to measure temperature **l**
3. the metric unit of temperature measure **e**
4. amount of liquid or gas a container can hold **d**
5. prefix that means 1,000 **g**
6. metric unit of measure of capacity **h**
7. meters in a kilometer **b**
8. customary and metric systems use same units **m**
9. pounds in one ton **c**
10. prefix milli means **a**

a. 0.001
b. 1,000
c. 2,000
d. Capacity
e. Celsius
f. Fahrenheit
g. kilo
h. liter
i. meter
j. metric
k. milli
l. thermometer
m. time

Exercises

Name the best unit for measuring the mass of each item.
Use kg, g, or mg.   Page 161

11. a bag of apples **kg**
12. a teabag **g**
13. a grain of sugar **mg**
14. a pencil **g**
15. a mosquito **mg**
16. a bicycle **kg**

Choose the best estimate for the mass of each item.   Page 161

17. a roll of nickels   a. 200 mg   **b. 200 g**   c. 200 kg
18. a package of ground beef   a. 0.5 mg   b. 0.5 g   **c. 0.5 kg**

Name the best unit for measuring the capacity of each item.
Use kL, L, or mL.   Pages 162–163

19. motor oil can **L**
20. blimp **kL**
21. coffee cup **mL**
22. railway tank car **kL**
23. baby's bottle **mL**
24. pitcher **L**

Choose the best estimate for the capacity of each item.   Pages 162–163

25. fuel oil tank   a. 500 kL   **b. 500 L**   c. 500 mL
26. medicine bottle   **a. 40 mL**   b. 40 kL   c. 40 L

Complete.   Pages 164–165

27. 9.42 g = ▨ mg **9,420**
28. 5 kL = ▨ L **5,000**
29. 1 g = ▨ kg **0.001**
30. 438 mg = ▨ g **0.438**
31. 4,300 L = ▨ kL **4.3**
32. 0.67 kg = ▨ mg **670,000**

Complete.   Pages 166–168

33. 2 pt = ▨ qt 1

34. 4,000 lb = ▨ T 2

35. 4 lb = ▨ oz 64

36. 32 fl oz = ▨ qt 1

37. 3 gal = ▨ qt 12

38. 1 pt = ▨ fl oz 16

39. 8 qt = ▨ gal 2

40. 4 c = ▨ pt 2

41. 1 gal = ▨ fl oz 128

42. 60 oz = ▨ lb $3\frac{3}{4}$

43. 7 qt = ▨ c 28

44. 12 fl oz = ▨ c $1\frac{1}{2}$

Use C = $\frac{5}{9}$ × (F − 32) or F = ($\frac{9}{5}$ × C) + 32 to change the following to degrees Celsius or degrees Fahrenheit.   Pages 172–173

45. 55°C = ▨°F 131

46. 85°C = ▨°F 185

47. 77°F = ▨°C 25

48. 41°F = ▨°C 5

49. 50°F = ▨°C 10

50. 28°C = ▨°F 82.4

Complete.   Pages 174–175

51. 4 d = ▨ hr 96

52. 2 wk = ▨ hr 336

53. 3 yr = ▨ d 1,095

54. 1 h ▨ min = 75 min 15

55. ▨ d = 4 wk 6 d 34

56. 600 d = ▨ yr ▨ d 1, 235

Name the larger measurement.   Pages 174–175

57. <u>90 min</u> or 1 hr 20 min

58. <u>6 yr</u> or 2,000 d

59. 6 wk or <u>43 d</u>

60. 4,330 s or <u>1 hr 12 min 11 s</u>

61. <u>30 d</u> or 500 h 200 min 17 s

Add or subtract.   Pages 174–175

62.   3 h 27 min 26 s
   + 5 h 11 min 41 s
        8 h 39 min 7 s

63.   6 h
   − 3 h 26 min
        2 h 34 min

64.   5 d 18 h 40 min
   − 1 d 15 h 16 min
        4 d 3 h 24 min

Solve.

65. How many one-ounce servings can be made from a $2\frac{1}{2}$-pound cheese? 40 servings

66. A window washer used a 10-gallon pail. How many cups is this? 160 cups

67. At a grocery store, milk is sold only in quarts. Nine one-cup servings of milk are needed. How many quarts are needed? 3 qt

68. Mary Robins' temperature was 99.2°F. Her temperature rose 1.9°F. What was Mary's temperature after it rose? 101.1°F

69. Stacy Coles drinks 1.9 quarts of liquid each day. How much liquid does he drink in one week? 13.3 quarts

70. An automobile crank case holds 5 quarts of oil. How many gallons is this? $1\frac{1}{4}$ gal

71. A box of spaghetti has a mass of 434,000 mg. How many grams are in this box of spaghetti? 434 g

72. A ten-quart pail contains 37 cups of water. How many more cups will the pail hold? 3 cups

73. Barry Case gets on a bus at 3:15 P.M. His trip takes 2 hours and 50 minutes. What time will it be then? 6:05 P.M.

74. Ana Garcia's heart beats 72 times in one minute. About how many times will her heart beat in one year? about 38 million

CHAPTER 8 TEST

Complete.

1. 7 kg = ▒ g **7,000**   2. 1.4 kg = ▒ g **1,400**   3. 850 mg = ▒ g **0.85**

4. 9.28 kg = ▒ g **9,280**   5. 1,650 mg = ▒ g **1.65**   6. 50 g = ▒ kg **0.05**

7. 2,500 mL = ▒ L **2.5**   8. 5.35 L = ▒ mL **5,350**   9. 12 L = ▒ mL **12,000**

10. 6 L = ▒ mL **6,000**   11. 250 mL = ▒ L **0.250**   12. 9.324 kL = ▒ L **9,324**

13. 5 gal = ▒ qt **20**   14. 6 c = ▒ pt **3**   15. 4 tons = ▒ lb **8,000**

16. 12 qt = ▒ gal **3**   17. 48 oz = ▒ lb **3**   18. 5,000 lb = ▒ tons $2\frac{1}{2}$

Replace each ▒ with >, <, or = to make a true sentence.

19. 3 g ▒ 300 mg **>**   20. 4.62 L ▒ 4,620 mL **=**   21. 500 mg ▒ 0.5 g **=**

22. 7.2 kL ▒ 7,200 L **=**   23. 700 kg ▒ 0.7 g **>**   24. 0.001 L ▒ 1 mL **=**

25. 3 lb ▒ 40 oz **>**   26. 8 gal ▒ 32 qt **=**   27. 2,000 lb ▒ 1 ton **=**

28. 32 oz ▒ 2 lb **=**   29. 8 c ▒ 4 qt **<**   30. 10 c ▒ 5 pt **=**

31. 1,200 lb ▒ 12 tons **<** 32. 1,000,000 mL ▒ 1 kL **=**   33. 10 mg ▒ 0.1 g **<**

Add or subtract.

34.　　2 wk 3 d
　　+ 3 wk 4 d
　　　　6 wk

35.　　3 h 20 min
　　− 1 h 50 min
　　1 h 30 min

36.　　1 d 17 h
　　+ 4 d 19 h
　　　6 d 12 h

37.　　5 wk 4 d 20 h
　　− 2 wk 6 d 14 h
　　2 wk 5 d 6 h

38.　　12 h 50 min 59 s
　　+ 9 h 23 min 14 s
　　22 h 14 min 13 s

39.　　6 d 12 h 20 min
　　− 4 d 18 h 42 min
　　1 d 17 h 38 min

Change each Fahrenheit reading to a Celsius reading.

40. 212°F **100°C**   41. 239°F **115°C**   42. 113°F **45°C**   43. 41°F **5°C**

Change each Celsius reading to a Fahrenheit reading.

44. 70°C **158°F**   45. 35°C **95°F**   46. 95°C **203°F**   47. 40°C **104°F**

Choose the better temperature for the following.

48. room temperature, <u>20°C</u> or 40°C

49. shower water, 60°C or <u>27°C</u>

Solve.

50. Steve wants to triple a recipe that calls for 2 cups of milk. How many pints of milk does he need?
3 pints

51. Susan weighs 120 pounds. She gains $2\frac{1}{2}$ pounds in one week. How many ounces does she gain?
40 ounces

52. The temperature in New York is 86°F. The temperature in Chicago is 30°C. Which city has the warmer temperature?
same temperature

53. Nancy's heart pumps 20 liters of blood in one minute. How many kiloliters is this in one hour?
1.2 kiloliters

CUMULATIVE REVIEW

Change each percent to a fraction or mixed numeral. Pages 56–58

1. 60% $\frac{3}{5}$ **2.** 25% $\frac{1}{4}$ **3.** 55% $\frac{11}{20}$ **4.** 64% $\frac{16}{25}$ **5.** 2% $\frac{1}{50}$

6. 300% 3 **7.** 450% $4\frac{1}{2}$ **8.** 115% $1\frac{3}{20}$ **9.** $65\frac{1}{2}$% $\frac{131}{200}$ **10.** $20\frac{3}{4}$% $\frac{83}{400}$

Use the poll results at the right to complete the following. Pages 126–127

State Issue 14
Support 70
Oppose 45
Undecided 35

11. How many people were polled? 150 people

12. What fraction is undecided on Issue 14? $\frac{7}{30}$

13. Suppose 150,000 people vote on Issue 14. Predict how many people support Issue 14. 70,000 people

Complete. Pages 142–143

14. 2 km = ▨ m 2,000 **15.** 3 m = ▨ cm 300 **16.** 10 mm = ▨ cm 1

17. 40 cm = ▨ mm 400 **18.** 0.5 km = ▨ cm 50,000 **19.** 6,230 m = ▨ km 6.23

Choose the best estimate. Pages 144–145

20. height of a table   **a.** 2 in.   **b.** 2 ft   **c.** 2 yd

21. distance from Boston to Los Angeles   **a.** 2,800 ft   **b.** 2,800 yd   **c.** 2,800 mi

22. length of a spoon   **a.** 6 in.   **b.** 6 ft   **c.** 6 yd

Complete. Pages 148–149

23. 20 ft = ▨ in. 240 **24.** 6 yd = ▨ ft 18 **25.** $2\frac{1}{2}$ ft = ▨ in. 30

26. 144 in. = ▨ yd 4 **27.** 10,560 ft = ▨ mi 2 **28.** $\frac{1}{2}$ mi = ▨ yd 880

Give the number of significant digits in each measurement. Pages 152–153

29. 365 m 3 **30.** 20.62 in. 4 **31.** 35,000 mi 2 **32.** 0.0060 cm 2

Name the best unit for measuring the mass of each item. Use kg, g, or mg. Page 161

33. an orange g **34.** a pinch of sugar mg **35.** a motorcycle kg

36. a raisin g **37.** a sofa kg **38.** a book g

Solve.

39. Cindy has 125 pennies, 46 nickels, and 59 dimes in her bank. She chooses one coin at random. Each coin chosen is not replaced. What is the probability that Cindy chooses a penny? $\frac{125}{230}$ or $\frac{25}{46}$

40. There are 22 students in Joe's class. Two representatives are chosen at random. What is the probability that Joe is chosen? $\frac{1}{11}$

Reading Measures

9-1 Odometers

Objective: To read an odometer and to use odometer readings to find the distance traveled.

Paco Gonzales works for Ace Truck Rental. When a truck is
rented, he records the beginning mileage from the odometer.
When it is returned, he records the ending mileage.
Paco subtracts the numbers that he recorded from the odometer
to find out how far the truck was driven.

Examples

A. Write the reading for each odometer.

Beginning Reading

4	3	9	7	5	2

Ending Reading

4	4	2	6	4	1

The number in the white box is read as tenths.

The odometer reading is
forty-three thousand, nine hundred
seventy-five *and* two tenths.

The odometer reading is
forty-four thousand, two hundred
sixty-four and one tenth.

And represents the decimal point.

B. Find out how far the truck with the
odometer readings in Example A was
driven. Subtract the odometer readings.
The truck was driven 288.9 miles.

$$\begin{array}{r} 44{,}264.1 \\ -\ 43{,}975.2 \\ \hline 288.9 \end{array}$$ *ending*
beginning
miles driven

Basic Skills Appendix, Pages 423, 436, 437

Basic: 1–9; Average: 1–9; Enriched: 1–9

Exercises

Write the reading for each odometer.

1.
5	5	6	2	4	8

55,624.8

2.
7	1	9	3	8	0

71,938.0

3.
3	1	3	9	6	2

31,396.2

Find the number of miles driven for each pair of odometer readings.

4. 36,751.3
36,826.5
75.2 mi

5. 32,644.7
34,823.1
2,178.4 mi

6. 72,634.5
77,326.2
4,691.7 mi

7. 10,403.8
10,641.9
238.1 mi

8. 98,326.1
99,702.4
1,376.3 mi

Solve.

9. Bev Ayers drove a car 146.7 miles. At the end of the trip, the odometer
reading was 14,302.6. What was the beginning reading? **14,155.9**

9-2 Reading Maps

Objective: To find routes, distances, and driving times on travel maps.

Mrs. Baker is an auto club counselor. She uses maps to help members plan trips.

Kelly and Josh Hogan are driving from Cheyenne, Wyoming, to New York City. The Hogans want to stop in Denver, Colorado; St. Louis, Missouri; and Columbus, Ohio. Mrs. Baker suggests the route shown in red on the highway map below. Kelly and Josh will take routes 25S to 70E to 76E to 78E.

Basic: 1–16, 18; Average: 1–19; Enriched: 1–19

Exercises

Use the map above to answer the following.

1. Name another possible interstate route you could take from Cheyenne, Wyoming to New York City, New York. **80E**

2. Name two possible routes from Chicago, Illinois, to St. Louis, Missouri. **55S to 70W, 57S to 70W**

3. What routes would you travel from Washington, D.C., to Dallas, Texas, with a stop in Nashville, Tennessee? **66W to 81S to 40W to 30W**

4. What routes would you travel from Washington, D.C., to Dallas, Texas, with a stop in Shreveport, Louisiana? **66W to 81S to 75S to 59S to 20W or 95S to 20W**

5. How many ways are there from Dallas, Texas, to Little Rock, Arkansas, using only routes 20, 30, 35, 40, and 55? **3 ways**

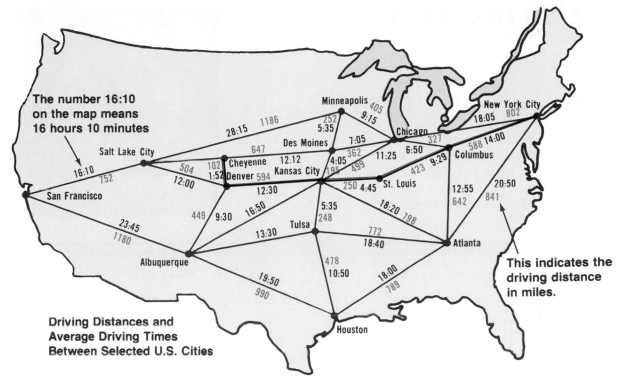

The number 16:10 on the map means 16 hours 10 minutes

This indicates the driving distance in miles.

Driving Distances and Average Driving Times Between Selected U.S. Cities

Exercises

Use the map above to find the distance and average driving time between the cities given.

6. Denver to Kansas City 594 mi, 12:30

7. Kansas City to St. Louis 250 mi, 4:45

8. St. Louis to Columbus 423 mi, 9:29

9. Columbus to New York City 588 mi, 14:00

10. Atlanta to Houston 789 mi, 18:00

11. San Francisco to Albuquerque 1,180 mi, 23:45

The Hogans' driving route is shown in red. Use the route to answer each question.

12. Between what cities is the driving time five hours or less?
Cheyenne and Denver, Kansas City and St. Louis

13. Between what cities is the driving time more than eight hours?

14. About how long will it take the Hogans to drive from Cheyenne to New York City? 42:36

15. How many miles will the Hogans drive from Cheyenne to New York City? 1,957 miles

13. Columbus and New York City, Denver and Kansas City, St. Louis and Columbus

Use the map above to answer the following.

16. What is the average driving time from Atlanta to Albuquerque going by way of Tulsa? 32:10

17. What is the average speed drivers are expected to drive going from Houston to Atlanta? 43.8 mph or 44 mph

18. What is the average speed drivers are expected to drive going from Columbus to New York City? 42 mph

19. What is the average speed drivers are expected to drive going from Salt Lake City to Kansas City going by way of Denver? 44.8 mph or 45 mph

9-3 24-Hour Clock

Objective: To tell time on a 24-hour clock.

Instead of using the standard 12-hour clock that is found in most public places and homes, the military uses a 24-hour clock. When using a 24-hour clock, there is no confusion about the time being A.M. or P.M.

When using a 24-hour clock, time is given without indicating A.M. or P.M. The A.M. times are 0001 hours to 1200 hours. The P.M. times are 1201 hours to 2400 hours. All 24-hour times are written with four digits.

Examples

Express the two possible times on each clock in 24-hour time and 12-hour time.

A.

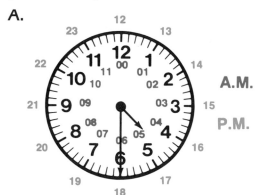

A.M.

P.M.

0430 ➡ oh four thirty
The time 0430 means 4 hours and thirty minutes after midnight, or 4:30 A.M.

1630 ➡ sixteen thirty
The time 1630 means 16 hours and thirty minutes after midnight, or 4:30 P.M.

B.

A.M.

P.M.

1040 ➡ ten forty
The time 1040 means 10 hours and forty minutes after midnight, or 10:40 A.M.

2240 ➡ twenty-two forty
The time 2240 means 22 hours and forty minutes after midnight, or 10:40 P.M.

Basic: 1–41 odd; Average: 1–41; Enriched: 2–32 even, 38–41

Exercises

Express each 24-hour time as a 12-hour time, using A.M. or P.M.

1. 0152 1:52 A.M.   **2.** 0928 9:28 A.M.   **3.** 1146 11:46 A.M.   **4.** 1530 3:30 P.M.

5. 2150 9:50 P.M.   **6.** 1211 12:11 P.M.   **7.** 0030 12:30 A.M.   **8.** 2010 8:10 P.M.

9. 1805 6:05 P.M.   **10.** 2400 12 midnight   **11.** 0650 6:50 A.M.   **12.** 1400 2:00 P.M.

Express each 12-hour time as a 24-hour time.

13. 3:00 P.M. **1500**   **14.** 1:45 P.M. **1345**   **15.** 5:30 A.M. **0530**   **16.** 12:15 A.M. **0015**

17. 7:30 P.M. **1930**   **18.** 9:45 A.M. **0945**   **19.** 11:30 P.M. **2330**   **20.** 10:20 P.M. **2220**

21. 4:16 A.M. **0416**   **22.** 12 noon **1200**   **23.** 8:47 P.M. **2047**   **24.** 2:16 A.M. **0216**

25. 5:52 P.M. **1752**   **26.** 7:32 P.M. **1932**   **27.** 9:27 P.M. **2127**   **28.** 6:14 A.M. **0614**

29. 8:30 P.M. **2030**   **30.** 11:00 A.M. **1100**   **31.** 10:00 P.M. **2200**   **32.** 12:26 P.M. **1226**

Express the two possible times on each clock in 24-hour time.

33.  **1030 2230**   **34.**  **0400 1600**   **35.**  **0912 2112**   **36.**  **0539 1739**   **37.**  **0015 1215**

Solve.

38. Rob eats a meal at 0630 hours. Using A.M. or P.M., what time does Rob eat the meal? **6:30 A.M.**

39. Rob reports for mail call at 1400 hours. Using A.M. or P.M., what time does Rob report for mail call? **2:00 P.M.**

40. Angie Miller eats a meal at 1730 hours. Using A.M. or P.M., what time does Angie eat the meal? **5:30 P.M.**

41. Angie reports for duty at 0715 hours. Using A.M. or P.M., what time does she report for duty? **7:15 A.M.**

This feature promotes student's mental abilities in computation and reasonableness.

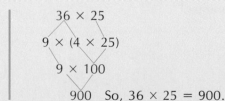

Mental Math

Use this method to help you multiply a two-digit number by a two-digit number mentally. Look for factors, from either of the two-digit numbers, that will make the multiplication easier. Then multiply.

35 × 18

(35 × 2) × 9

70 × 9

630   So, 35 × 18 = 630.

36 × 25

9 × (4 × 25)

9 × 100

900   So, 36 × 25 = 900.

Find each product using the strategy shown above.

1. 45 × 16 **720**
(45 × 2) × 8

2. 22 × 35 **770**
(22 × 5) × 7

3. 48 × 25 **1,200**
6 × (8 × 25)

4. 15 × 16 **240**
3 × (5 × 16)

5. 75 × 36 **2,700**
(75 × 4) × 9

6. 25 × 24 **600**
(25 × 4) × 6

7. 21 × 36 **756**
7 × (3 × 36)

8. 25 × 22 **550**
(25 × 2) × 11

9. 12 × 55 **660**
6 × (2 × 55)

10. 44 × 25 **1,100**
11 × (4 × 25)

9-4 Reading Measurement Instruments

Objective: To read a stopwatch and a graduated cylinder.

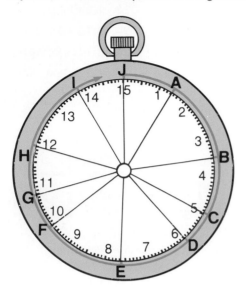

Time is usually measured with a clock or watch. Sporting events are timed by stopwatches. The **stopwatch** at the left measures time to the nearest one-tenth of a second.

Examples

A. How many seconds have passed if the hand is on its first revolution at letter A?

1.3 seconds have passed.

B. How many seconds have passed if the hand is on its second revolution at letter B?

18.5 seconds have passed.

The **graduated cylinder** shown at the right is used to measure milliliters of liquids. The cylinder measures liquids to the nearest one-tenth of a milliliter.

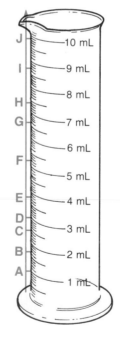

Examples

C. Name the measurement at letter A.

The measurement at letter A is 1 milliliter.

D. Name the measurement at letter B.

The measurement at letter B is 1.7 milliliters.

Basic: 1–23 odd; Average: 1–24; Enriched: 2–18 even, 19–24

Exercises

Find how many seconds have passed if the hand is at each letter. The hand is on its first revolution.

1. D 5.8 s   **2.** I 13.8 s   **3.** G 10.7 s   **4.** C 5 s   **5.** E 7.6 s   **6.** H 11.9 s

Suppose the hand is on its second revolution. Find how many seconds have passed if the hand is at each letter.

7. E 22.6 s   **8.** A 16.3 s   **9.** F 24.7 s   **10.** J 30 s   **11.** C 20 s   **12.** G 25.7 s

Name the measurement at each letter on the cylinder.

13. C 2.5 mL   **14.** F 5.2 mL   **15.** I 8.7 mL   **16.** D 3 mL   **17.** H 7.4 mL   **18.** G 6.6 mL

Solve.

19. How many graduated cylinders can be filled by a liter of water?
100 cylinders

20. Carl filled the cylinder to letter J. How much liquid did he put in the cylinder? **9.9 mL**

21. Mindy filled the cylinder to letter E. How much liquid did she put in the cylinder? **3.8 mL**

22. Jenny timed a commercial that was on the radio. The watch stopped at letter F on its first revolution. How long did the commercial last?
9.7 s

23. How much time did it take Alex to paint a board on a fence? The watch stopped at letter J on its third revolution. **45 s**

24. How long did it take Lisa to run $\frac{1}{4}$ of a mile on the school track? The watch stopped at letter D on its fifth revolution.
1 min 5.8 s

 This feature presents useful ways of solving mathematical problems on a calculator.

Calculator

On the map shown, one inch is equivalent to 50 miles (1 inch = 50 mi). If the map distance between two towns is $2\frac{1}{2}$ inches, what is the actual distance between the towns?

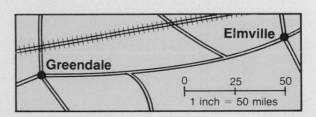

Greendale

Elmville

0   25   50

1 inch = 50 miles

Use the calculator to find the actual distance.

map distances
in inches   1 in. = 50 mi
2.5 $\boxed{X}$ 50 $\boxed{=}$ *125*

$2\frac{1}{2}$ = 2.5

The actual distance is 125 miles.

Use the calculator to find the actual distance for the following.

1. scale: 1 inch = 30 miles
map distance: 3.25 inches **97.5 mi**

2. scale: 1 inch = 12 miles
map distance: 9.125 inches **109.5 mi**

3. scale: $\frac{1}{2}$ inch = 25 miles
map distance: $5\frac{1}{2}$ inches **275 mi**

4. scale: $\frac{1}{2}$ inch = 50 miles
map distance: 3.75 inches **375 mi**

PRACTICE

Estimate. Answers may vary. Typical answers are given.

1.	2.	3.	4.	5.

1. $\$16.46$
$+\ \ 13.19$
$\$29.00$

2. $2{,}453$
$-\ 1{,}548$
$1{,}000$

3. 683
$\times\ \ 29$
$21{,}000$

4. $\$12.11$
$\times\ \ 0.72$
$\$8.40$

5. $38\overline{)476}$ → 12

Add or subtract.

6. 14.78
$-\ 11.79$
2.99

7. 379
$+\ 464$
843

8. $\$72.36$
$+\ \ \ 4.69$
$\$77.05$

9. 28.369
$-\ 28.342$
0.027

10. $1{,}063$
$-\ \ \ 974$
89

11. 760.41
$-\ \ 92.66$
667.75

12. 77.004
$-\ 24.52$
52.484

13. 52.8
$-\ 47.61$
5.19

14. 422
$-\ 193.4$
228.6

15. 26.3
$+\ \ 0.97$
27.27

Multiply or divide.

16. 3.6
$\times\ \ 14$
50.4

17. 41.32
$\times\ 0.231$
9.54492

18. 479
$\times\ \ 21$
$10{,}059$

19. 570
$\times\ 0.66$
376.2

20. 5.06
$\times\ 3.14$
15.8884

21. $45\overline{)2{,}025}$ → 45

22. $26\overline{)2{,}041}$ → 78.5

23. $3.8\overline{)6.27}$ → 1.65

24. $9.6\overline{)0.24}$ → 0.025

25. $5.6\overline{)4.76}$ → 0.85

Replace each ● with <, >, or = to make a true sentence.

26. $\frac{2}{7}$ ● $\frac{1}{5}$ >

27. $\frac{12}{20}$ ● $\frac{3}{5}$ =

28. $\frac{5}{9}$ ● $\frac{4}{7}$ <

29. 6.32 ● 6.23 >

30. 0.05 ● 0.5 <

31. 4.62 ● 4.620 =

Add or subtract. Write each sum or difference in simplest form.

32. $\frac{1}{2}+\frac{3}{4}$ $1\frac{1}{4}$

33. $\frac{2}{3}-\frac{1}{6}$ $\frac{1}{2}$

34. $2\frac{1}{3}-1\frac{1}{2}$ $\frac{5}{6}$

35. $\frac{7}{8}+\frac{5}{6}$ $1\frac{17}{24}$

36. $1\frac{1}{7}-\frac{3}{4}$ $\frac{11}{28}$

37. $\frac{3}{4}+\frac{1}{3}$ $1\frac{1}{12}$

38. $\frac{5}{7}-\frac{1}{2}$ $\frac{3}{14}$

39. $1\frac{2}{3}-\frac{7}{8}$ $\frac{19}{24}$

40. $\frac{14}{15}-\frac{2}{5}$ $\frac{8}{15}$

41. $1\frac{2}{3}-\frac{5}{6}$ $\frac{5}{6}$

42. $\frac{4}{15}+\frac{1}{6}$ $\frac{13}{30}$

43. $2\frac{2}{5}+6\frac{7}{10}$ $9\frac{1}{10}$

Multiply. Write each product in simplest form.

44. $\frac{2}{5}\times\frac{15}{16}$ $\frac{3}{8}$

45. $1\frac{1}{3}\times\frac{3}{4}$ 1

46. $\frac{3}{7}\times 21$ 9

47. $42\times\frac{5}{6}$ 35

48. $\frac{4}{5}\times\frac{10}{11}$ $\frac{8}{11}$

49. $10\times\frac{2}{3}$ $6\frac{2}{3}$

50. $\frac{2}{3}\times\frac{5}{8}$ $\frac{5}{12}$

51. $1\frac{1}{3}\times 1\frac{1}{5}$ 2

Divide. Write each quotient in simplest form.

52. $6\div\frac{1}{4}$ 24

53. $4\div 1\frac{1}{3}$ 3

54. $3\frac{1}{2}\div 7$ $\frac{1}{2}$

55. $1\frac{1}{8}\div\frac{1}{5}$ $5\frac{5}{8}$

56. $\frac{3}{4}\div\frac{4}{5}$ $\frac{15}{16}$

57. $2\frac{1}{3}\div 1\frac{1}{2}$ $1\frac{5}{9}$

58. $1\frac{1}{8}\div\frac{3}{7}$ $2\frac{5}{8}$

59. $16\div\frac{4}{5}$ 20

Multiply.

60. 4.2×10 42

61. 100×13 1,300

62. 10×39 390

63. 60×10 600

64. 0.75×100 75

65. $1,000 \times 4.361$ 4,361

66. 6.8×100 680

67. $34 \times 1,000$ 34,000

68. 6.72×10 67.2

Divide.

69. $56 \div 10$ 5.6

70. $2.6 \div 100$ 0.026

71. $529 \div 10$ 52.9

72. $39.4 \div 100$ 0.394

73. $641 \div 1,000$ 0.641

74. $0.14 \div 10$ 0.014

75. $71.97 \div 100$ 0.7197

76. $30 \div 100$ 0.3

77. $6.78 \div 1,000$ 0.00678

Complete.

78. 114 cm = ▦ m 1.14

79. 37 mm = ▦ cm 3.7

80. 4,329 m = ▦ km 4.329

81. 46 kg = ▦ g 46,000

82. 6.7 L = ▦ mL 6,700

83. 637 m = ▦ mm 637,000

84. 32 cm = ▦ mm 320

85. 2,763 g = ▦ kg 2.763

86. 29 L = ▦ mL 29,000

87. 1,463 mL = ▦ L 1.463

88. 16 km = ▦ m 16,000

89. 86 m = ▦ cm 8,600

90. 4 min = ▦ s 240

91. 6 h = ▦ min 360

92. 3 d = ▦ h 72

93. 2 d 4 h = ▦ h 52

94. 200 min = ▦ h $3\frac{1}{3}$

95. 300 s = ▦ min 5

96. 48 oz = ▦ lb 3

97. 2 qt = ▦ c 8

98. 3 pt = ▦ qt $1\frac{1}{2}$

99. $1\frac{1}{2}$ qt = ▦ c 6

100. 2 lb 4 oz = ▦ oz 36

101. 18 c = ▦ qt ▦ pt 4, 1

Find the greatest common factor (GCF) for each pair of numbers.

102. 6 and 20 2

103. 4 and 16 4

104. 27 and 15 3

105. 16 and 6 2

106. 18 and 4 2

107. 12 and 15 3

108. 12 and 4 4

109. 8 and 10 2

110. 7 and 3 1

Find the least common multiple (LCM) for each pair of numbers.

111. 3 and 5 15

112. 9 and 12 36

113. 6 and 9 18

114. 2 and 3 6

115. 5 and 4 20

116. 12 and 16 48

Write each fraction in simplest form.

117. $\frac{8}{24}$ $\frac{1}{3}$

118. $\frac{6}{16}$ $\frac{3}{8}$

119. $\frac{15}{24}$ $\frac{5}{8}$

120. $\frac{12}{54}$ $\frac{2}{9}$

121. $\frac{24}{36}$ $\frac{2}{3}$

Solve.

122. The Sloans travel 264 miles in 6 hours. At that rate, how far do they travel in 1 hour? 44 mi

123. Eric's model train completes 3 laps on the tracks in 27 seconds. At that rate, what is the time for 1 lap? 9 s

9-5 Reading Meters

Objective: To read electric, gas, and water meters.

Ben Duggan is an apartment manager. When renters move in, Ben asks them to contact the *electric, gas,* and *water* companies. After a renter calls each utility company the meters are read. These readings are the renter's beginning meter readings.

Electric meters measure the number of kilowatt hours (kWh) that are used. A 100-watt bulb burning for one hour uses 100-watt hours. The watt-hour is a very small unit to work with. Therefore, a kilowatt hour is used. A **kilowatt hour** is equal to one kilowatt (1,000 watts) of electricity being used for one hour.

Example

A. **Find the reading on the electric meter shown below.**

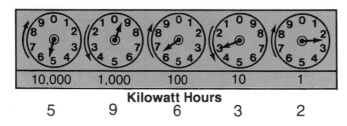

Kilowatt Hours

10,000	1,000	100	10	1
5	9	6	3	2

The electric meter shown is made up of five dials. To read the meter, find the last number passed on each dial as the arrow rotates from 0 through 9. This meter reads 59,632 kilowatt hours.

Notice the direction the arrow rotates on each dial.

Natural gas is measured in *hundreds of cubic feet* (ccf). You can read your own gas meter to see how many cubic feet of gas you have used.

Example

B. **Find the reading on the gas meter shown at the right.**

A gas meter is made up of four dials. To read the meter, find the number passed on each dial. This meter reads 2,540 hundreds of cubic feet.

To find the number of *cubic feet* (ft³), you must multiply by 100.

1,000,000	100,000	10,000	1,000

Hundreds of Cubic Feet

2	5	4	0

$$\begin{array}{r} 2,540 \\ \times\ \ \ 100 \\ \hline 254,000 \end{array}$$ *gas meter reading* *ccf* *cubic feet*   The reading 2,540 ccf is equal to 254,000 ft³.

Water is measured in cubic feet.

Example

C. Find the reading on the water meters shown below.

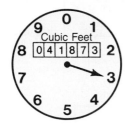

Newer meters measure water in cubic feet. You only need to read the numbers as shown.

The meter reading is 41,873 cubic feet.

Older meters measure water in gallons. You read each dial. Look at the last number passed on each dial. To find cubic feet, divide by 7.5.

The number of cubic feet is 129,163.

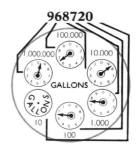

The Key Skills provides practice of skills needed in the exercises.

Key Skills

Subtract.

2,184	56,374	371,085
− 2,029	− 54,982	− 364,918
155	1,392	6,167

1. 3,360
− 3,242
118

2. 5,716
− 5,491
225

3. 21,804
− 20,436
1,368

4. 19,673
− 18,958
715

5. 326,459
− 317,832
8,627

Basic Skills Appendix, Page 422
Basic: 1–27 odd; Average: 1–28; Enriched: 2–22 even, 24–28

Exercises

How many kilowatt hours are shown on each electric meter below?

1.  15,825 kWh

2. 87,506 kWh

3. 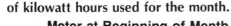 38,568 kWh

4.  42,382 kWh

For each set of electric meters, use subtraction to determine the number of kilowatt hours used for the month.

Meter at Beginning of Month | **Meter at End of Month**

5.   5,762 kWh

6.   5,540 kWh

Chapter 9 **193**

How many cubic feet of natural gas are shown on each gas meter below?

7.

238,700 ft³

8.
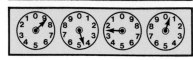
571,900 ft³

9.

620,100 ft³

10.

842,000 ft³

 For each set of gas meters, use subtraction to determine the number of cubic feet of natural gas used for the month.

Meter at Beginning of Month	Meter at End of Month
11. 	 129,800 ft³
12. 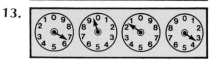	 144,900 ft³
13. 	12,400 ft³

How many cubic feet of water are shown on each water meter below?

14.
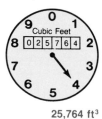
25,764 ft³

15.
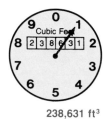
238,631 ft³

16.
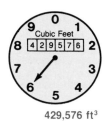
429,576 ft³

17.
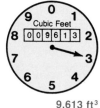
9,613 ft³

 For each set of water meters, use subtraction to determine the number of cubic feet of water used for the month.

	Beginning	Ending		Beginning	Ending
18.		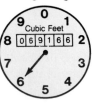 4,325 ft³	19.		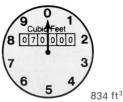 834 ft³
20.		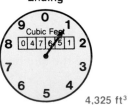 2,657 ft³	21.		3,162 ft³

22.

Beginning

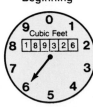
Cubic Feet
1 8 9 3 2 6

Ending

Cubic Feet
2 0 4 5 6 7

15,241 ft³

23.

Beginning

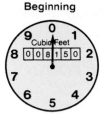
Cubic Feet
0 0 8 1 5 0

Ending

Cubic Feet
0 0 8 4 9 9

349 ft³

Solve.

24. Mr. Chin read the electric meter one month. The reading was 0,562 kWh. The following month the reading was 0,973 kWh. How many kilowatt hours of electricity did Mr. Chin use?
411 kWh

26. At the right is a chart of gas meter readings. The readings are given at the beginning of the month and at the end of the month. Find how many *hundreds of cubic feet* of gas are used for each month. **a. 283 ccf b. 180 ccf c. 78 ccf d. 22 ccf e. 24 ccf**

27. Use the chart to find the number of *cubic feet* of gas used for each month.

28. Much water is wasted because of leaky faucets. The chart at the right shows the amount of water wasted in 24 hours from leaks of different sizes.
How many ft³ of water are wasted in a week from each of these leaks? In a year? **21 ft³, 91 ft³, 371 ft³, 1,095 ft³, 4,745 ft³, 19,345 ft³**

25. Mrs. Alexander reads the water meter one month. The reading was 61,806 ft³. The next month's reading was 63,330 ft³. How many cubic feet of water did she use?
1,524 ft³

	Start of month	End of month
a.	9,406	9,689
b.	9,689	9,869
c.	9,869	9,947
d.	9,947	9,969
e.	9,969	9,993

27. a. 28,300 ft³
b. 18,000 ft³
c. 7,800 ft³
d. 2,200 ft³
e. 2,400 ft³

- $\frac{1}{32}$ in. leak wastes 3 ft³
- $\frac{1}{16}$ in. leak wastes 13 ft³
- $\frac{1}{8}$ in. leak wastes 53 ft³

This feature provides general topics about the uses of a computer.

Computer

Magnetic ink characters can be "read" by computers. These characters are used for high speed sorting.

ABCDEFGHIJKLMNOPQRSTUVWXYZ
0123456789

Numbers like these identify the account number, bank, and other special information along the bottom of checks. The checks are processed by computers that can sort up to 60,000 checks an hour.

9-6 Reading Protractors

Objective: To measure and draw angles using a protractor.

Paula Gardner works as a glazier. She cuts and installs all kinds and shapes of glass. To prepare the glass for cutting, she lays it on a flat table. Paula then measures and marks the glass. After using the cutter's wheel, she breaks the glass along the cut. To learn the trade, Paula was an apprentice for three years. As an apprentice she received classroom instruction and on-the-job training.

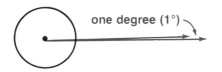

one degree (1°)

A unit for measuring angles is the **degree** (°). The angle at the left measures 1°. It takes 360 such angles to go around a circle.

A **protractor** can be used to measure angles.

Example

A. Measure ∠ABC. *The symbol for angle is ∠.*

- First, place the center of the protractor at the point where the sides of the angle meet (vertex).

- Then place the bottom edge of the protractor on ray *BC*.

- Use the scale that begins 0° on ray *BC*. Ray *BA* passes through the 30 degree mark. Angle *ABC* measures 30°.

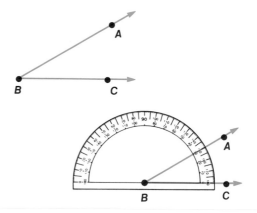

A protractor can be used to draw an angle with a given measurement.

Example

B. Draw a 65° angle.

- First, draw a ray such as ray *PQ*.

- Then, place the center of the protractor at *P*. Use the scale that begins with 0 on ray *PQ*.

- Find the 65 mark and draw point *R*. Draw ray *PR*. Angle *RPQ* measures 65°.

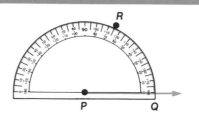

Exercises

Use the figure shown at the right to measure each angle.

1. ∠BZC 35°
2. ∠BZG 130°
3. ∠JZH 10°
4. ∠JZC 145°
5. ∠JZF 90°
6. ∠BZD 70°
7. ∠BZJ 180°
8. ∠BZF 90°
9. ∠HZG 40°
10. ∠GZD 60°
11. ∠FZD 20°
12. ∠JZB 180°
13. ∠CZH 135°
14. ∠GZC 95°

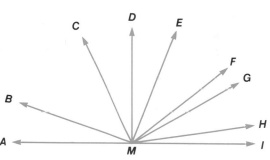

Use a protractor to measure each angle shown in the figure at the right.

15. ∠IMH 10°
16. ∠IMF 40°
17. ∠IMB 160°
18. ∠IMD 90°
19. ∠IMG 32°
20. ∠AMB 20°
21. ∠IMC 115°
22. ∠AMC 65°
23. ∠BMD 70°
24. ∠DME 22°

Use a protractor to measure each angle in circle A and circle B.

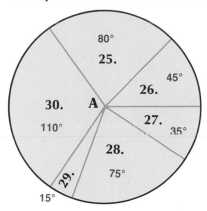

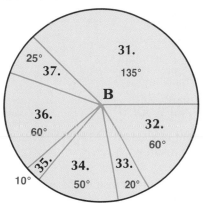

38. What is the sum of the measurements of the angles in circle A? **360°**
39. What is the sum of the measurements of the angles in circle B? **360°**
40. What is the sum of the measurements of the angles in *any* circle? **360°**

Use a protractor to draw angles having each measurement. See students' work.

41. 45°
42. 60°
43. 144°
44. 75°
45. 29°
46. 55°
47. 180°
48. 99°
49. 90°
50. 170°
51. 120°
52. 42°

9-7 Problem Solving: Extra Facts

Objective: To solve word problems that give too much information.

Sandi needs 2 snow tires, a gallon of antifreeze, and a new battery to winterize her Chevette. The tires cost $42 each, the antifreeze costs $5.20, and a new battery costs $48. Sandi also has a $139 monthly car payment and a $250 insurance bill due every 6 months. What does it cost to winterize her car?

Sometimes a problem contains more information than is needed to solve it. To solve the problem, choose from the facts given.

 You are asked to find the cost of winterizing Sandi's car. You are given the items needed to winterize the car and their costs. You are also given the monthly car payment and six-month insurance bill.

 Find the cost of 2 snow tires. Add it to the costs of the antifreeze and battery. The monthly car payment and six-month insurance bill are not needed.

Estimate: 40 × 2 = 80   *Estimate: 80 + 5 + 50 = 135*

$$\begin{array}{rl} \$42 & \textit{cost of a tire} \\ \times\ \ 2 & \textit{number of tires} \\ \hline \$84 & \textit{cost of 2 tires} \end{array}$$

$$\begin{array}{rl} \$84.00 & \textit{cost of 2 tires} \\ 5.20 & \textit{cost of antifreeze} \\ +\ \ 48.00 & \textit{cost of a battery} \\ \hline \$137.20 & \end{array}$$

42 Ⓧ 2 ⊟ *84*   84 ⊞ 5.20 ⊞ 48 ⊟ *137.2*

 It will cost Sandi $137.20 to winterize her car.

The answer is close to the estimate, so $137.20 is reasonable.

Basic: 1–10; Average: 1–10; Enriched: 1–10

Exercises

1. Sandi earns $80 a week. Suppose her first eight monthly gasoline bills are $25, $21, $28, $27, $30, $20, $25, and $32. What is her average monthly gasoline bill? **$26**

2. A 1988 Ford has power brakes, power windows, and an AM/FM stereo radio. It is red with black interior. The car gets 18 miles per gallon. What are the options on the car? **power brakes, power windows, AM/FM stereo**

3. Matt is buying a Dodge Colt for $3,200. The loan agency requires a minimum down payment of 20%. Matt has $650. What is the down payment required by the agency? **$640**

4. Bill's car has a 13.2-gallon gas tank. The car gets 33.5 miles per gallon. It costs Bill $16.50 for 11.3 gallons of gasoline. How much does one gallon of gasoline cost? **$1.46**

5. The odometer reading last week was 32,450.6 miles. Suppose the car was driven 246.1 miles before that reading and 263.8 miles after that reading. What is this week's odometer reading? **32,714.4 mi**

6. Kathy buys a used car for $4,000. She gives the owner a 20% down payment. Her payments are $115 a month for 36 months. How much will she pay each year? **$1,380**

7. Kathy is comparing the mileage her car gets with Bill's car in exercise **4.** Her car gets 28.6 miles per gallon and has a 15.8 gallon tank. At $1.45 a gallon, how much money does it take to fill the gasoline tank in her car? **$22.91**

8. Sandi's $1,000 down payment was more than one-third the amount of her car loan. At the rate of $35 per week, how long would it take Sandi to pay the remaining $1,000? **29 weeks**

9. A new car costs $6,250. The car dealership is asking for a $1,500 down payment and $170 each month for 36 months. Jodi has a 20% down payment saved. How much does she have saved? **$1,250**

10. Sandi sets up a budget allowing $25 for gasoline each month. Her car gets 26 miles per gallon. Suppose the gasoline tank holds 13.2 gallons. How far can she drive on one tank of gasoline? **343.2 mi**

This feature presents general topics of mathematics.

Math Break

A magic square is a number square whose rows, columns, and diagonals all have the same sum. Study the magic square at the right. What is the sum of each row, column, and diagonal?

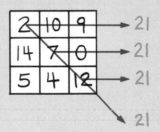

Copy and complete the magic squares.

1.

2	7	6
9	5	1
4	3	8

2.

16	2	3	13
5	11	10	8
9	7	6	12
4	14	15	1

3.

17	24	1	8	15
23	5	7	14	16
4	6	13	20	22
10	12	19	21	3
11	18	25	2	9

CHAPTER 9 REVIEW

Vocabulary/Concepts

Choose the word or phrase that best completes each statement.

1. Read the ___?___ to find the number of miles driven. **odometer**

2. A ___?___ is equal to one kilowatt of electricity being used for one hour. **kilowatt hour**

3. A unit for measuring angles is the ___?___ . **degree**

4. A ___?___ can be used to measure milliliters of liquids. **graduated cylinder**

5. To find the number of cubic feet of natural gas used, ___?___ by 100. **multiply**

6. A ___?___ can be used to measure time to the nearest one-tenth of a second. **stopwatch**

7. To measure an angle in degrees, a ___?___ is used. **protractor**

| 24-hour clock |
| add |
| degree |
| divide |
| graduated cylinder |
| kilowatt hour |
| multiply |
| odometer |
| protractor |
| ruler |
| speedometer |
| stopwatch |

Exercises

Find the number of miles driven for each pair of odometer readings. Page 183

8.
| 4 | 3 | 9 | 5 | 6 | 1 |

| 4 | 4 | 1 | 2 | 5 | 8 |
169.7 mi

9.
| 3 | 7 | 5 | 4 | 2 | 6 |

| 3 | 7 | 8 | 1 | 3 | 1 |
270.5 mi

10.
| 0 | 4 | 3 | 1 | 4 | 9 |

| 0 | 4 | 9 | 5 | 7 | 2 |
642.3 mi

Use the travel maps on pages 184 and 185 to answer the following. Pages 184–185

11. Name the route that is most direct from Atlanta to Jacksonville. **75S to 10E**

12. What is the distance and driving time between Atlanta and Kansas City? **798 mi, 18:20**

Express each 24-hour time as a 12-hour time, using A.M. or P.M. Pages 186–187

13. 1440 **2:40 P.M.**   14. 0700 **7:00 A.M.**   15. 2230 **10:30 P.M.**   16. 0315 **3:15 A.M.**   17. 2054 **8:54 P.M.**

Express each 12-hour time as a 24-hour time. Pages 186–187

18. 4:00 A.M. **0400**   19. 7:30 P.M. **1930**   20. 8:15 A.M. **0815**   21. 10:45 P.M. **2245**   22. 11:22 P.M. **2322**

Use the stopwatch or graduated cylinder on page 188 to answer the following. Pages 188–189

23. Alex stuffed 20 envelopes. The watch stopped at letter G on its fifth revolution. How long did it take him to stuff 20 envelopes? **1 min 10.7 s**

24. Alice filled a cylinder to letter J. How much liquid did she put in the cylinder? **9.9 milliliters**

How many kilowatt hours are shown on each electric meter below? Pages 192–195

25.

86,201 kWh

26.

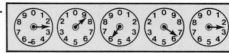

28,662 kWh

How many cubic feet of natural gas are shown on each gas meter below? Pages 192–195

27.

334,800 ft³

28.

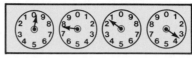

971,300 ft³

How many cubic feet of water are shown on each water meter below? Pages 192–195

29.

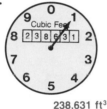

238,631 ft³

30.

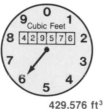

429,576 ft³

31.

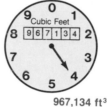

967,134 ft³

32.

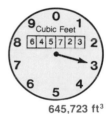

645,723 ft³

Use a protractor to measure each angle. Pages 196–197

33.

90°

34.

120°

35.

45°

36.

68°

Use a protractor to draw angles having each measurement. Pages 196–197

See students' work.

37. 60°   **38.** 85°   **39.** 38°   **40.** 150°   **41.** 145°   **42.** 172°

Solve.

43. A cook orders 50 pounds of meat a day, enough to feed about 100 people. How much does the meat cost at $3.25 a pound? **$162.50**

44. Suppose an odometer reading is now 48,924.2 miles. How many miles has the car been driven if the previous reading was 48,653.7 miles? **270.5 miles**

45. An electric meter reading is now 02,533 kWh. The previous reading was 02,307 kWh. How many kilowatt hours of electricity were used? **226 kWh**

46. Rudy sets 12 tables every hour. He begins work at 4:00 P.M. and works for 4 hours. How many tables does he set? **48 tables**

47. Lesley earns $78 in wages this week. She works 16 hours. Her tips amount to $40. What does she earn hourly in tips? **$2.50**

48. A gas meter reading is now 2,346 ccf. The previous reading was 1,938 ccf. How many cubic feet of natural gas were used? **40,800 ft³**

CHAPTER 9 TEST

Find the number of miles driven for each pair of odometer readings.

1.
```
1 6 9 2 3 4
1 7 3 1 6 9
```
393.5 mi

2.
```
2 4 3 7 6 1
2 4 3 8 5 7
```
9.6 mi

3.
```
7 2 8 6 4 8
7 2 9 7 5 9
```
111.1 mi

Use the travel maps on pages 184–185 to answer the following.

4. Name the route that is most direct from Nashville to Jackson.
40W to 55S or 65S to 20W

5. What is the distance and average driving time between Chicago and Tulsa going by way of Kansas City? 747 mi, 17 h

Express each 24-hour time as a 12-hour time, using A.M. or P.M.

6. 1320
1:20 P.M.

7. 1247
12:47 P.M.

8. 0008
12:08 A.M.

9. 0100
1:00 A.M.

10. 2156
9:56 P.M.

How many kilowatt hours are shown on each electric meter below?

11.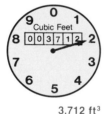
14,402 kWh

12.
96,136 kWh

How many cubic feet of water are shown on each water meter below?

13.
3,712 ft³

14.
564,214 ft³

15.
700,629 ft³

16.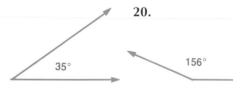
30,517 ft³

Use a protractor to measure each angle.

17. 125°

18. 82°

19. 35°

20. 156°

Use a protractor to draw angles having each measurement. See students' work.

21. 40°

22. 22°

23. 71°

24. 115°

25. 130°

26. 137°

Solve.

27. Adele works after school 3 days a week. She begins at 4:00 P.M. and finishes at 7:30 P.M. How many hours does she work each day? $3\frac{1}{2}$ h

28. A water-meter reading is now 002,432 ft³. The previous reading was 001,956 ft³. How many cubic feet of water were used? 476 ft³

CUMULATIVE REVIEW

Write each percent as a probability in simplest form. Pages 118–119

1. 30% $\frac{3}{10}$

2. 4% $\frac{1}{25}$

3. 200% 2

4. $22\frac{1}{2}$% $\frac{9}{40}$

Add, subtract, multiply or divide. Pages 150–151

5.
$$\begin{array}{r} 3\text{ ft }6\text{ in.} \\ +\ 12\text{ ft }4\text{ in.} \\ \hline \textbf{15 ft 10 in.} \end{array}$$

6.
$$\begin{array}{r} 13\text{ yd }1\text{ ft} \\ -\ \ 4\text{ yd }2\text{ ft} \\ \hline \textbf{8 yd 2 ft} \end{array}$$

7.
$$\begin{array}{r} 14\text{ ft }6\text{ in.} \\ \times\ \ \ \ \ \ \ 4 \\ \hline \textbf{58 ft} \end{array}$$

8. $\overset{\textbf{2 mi 2,128 ft}}{5\overline{)\,12\text{ mi }80\text{ ft}}}$

Name the more accurate measurement. Pages 152–153

9. $3\frac{3}{8}$ yd or $3\frac{1}{2}$ yd

10. $6\frac{1}{4}$ in. or $6\frac{5}{24}$ in.

11. 52 m or 52.1 m

12. 63.28 cm or 63.3 cm

13. 36 mm or 3.66 cm

14. 0.2 m or 20.5 cm

Replace each ▒ with >, <, =, or ≈ to compare. Pages 154–155

15. 1 ft ▒ 30.48 cm ≈

16. 2 m ▒ 2 yd >

17. 5 in. ▒ 5 cm >

18. 100 m ▒ 3,937 in. ≈

19. 3 km ▒ 3 mi <

20. 40 m ▒ 4,000 cm =

Name the most reasonable unit for measuring each item. Write milliliter, liter, or kiloliter. Pages 162–163

21. a glass of milk mL

22. eye drops mL

23. water in a pond kL

24. gasoline L

25. air in a classroom L or kL

26. a bottle of lemon extract mL

Complete. Pages 164–165

27. 3 kg = ▒ g 3,000

28. 20 mg = ▒ g 0.02

29. 3.5 L = ▒ mL 3,500

30. 65 g = ▒ mg 65,000

31. 510 g = ▒ kg 0.51

32. 4.79 kL = ▒ L 4,790

Complete. Pages 166–168

33. 4 lb = ▒ oz 64

34. 3 tons = ▒ lb 6,000

35. 2 lb 8 oz = ▒ oz 40

36. 80 oz = ▒ lb 5

37. $4\frac{1}{2}$ tons = ▒ lb 9,000

38. 4,000 lb – ▒ tons 2

Choose the better temperature for the following. Pages 172–173

39. water skiing, 35°C or 10°C

40. a picnic, 35°C or 25°C

41. a hamburger, 36°C or 48°C

42. ice cream, ⁻5°C or 15°C

Change the following Fahrenheit readings to Celsius readings. Pages 172–173

43. 113°F 45°C

44. 50°F 10°C

45. 122°F 50°C

46. 23°F ⁻5°C

Solve.

47. Two coins are tossed. What are the odds for tossing one tail? What are the odds for tossing at least one tail?
2 to 2; 3 to 1

Geometry

10-1 Basic Terms

Objective: To name and represent basic terms of geometry.

Each city shown on the map at the left is represented by a dot. A dot is used to represent an exact location, or **point.**

Each point shown on the map at the right is named by a capital letter. Just as the map at the left does not show all the cities in Colorado, the map at the right does not show all the possible points.

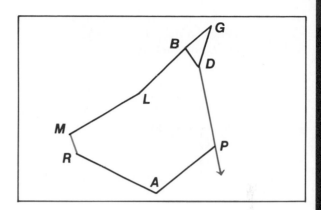

The shortest path from one point to another is called a **line segment.** The shortest path from Montrose to Ridgway may be thought of as a line segment. It is named line segment MR and is written $\overline{MR}$. Line segment MR is shown in blue on the map above.

MR *can also be written* RM.

In geometry, a never-ending straight path in one direction is called a **ray.** To name a ray, list the endpoint first. Then name another point on the ray. The path from Denver to Pueblo and beyond may be thought of as a ray. It is named ray DP and is written $\overrightarrow{DP}$. Ray DP is shown in red on the map above.

$\overrightarrow{DP}$ *cannot be written* PD. *Do you see why?* $\overrightarrow{DP}$ **begins at D and extends beyond P;** $\overrightarrow{PD}$ **begins at P and extends beyond D.**

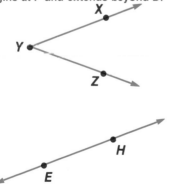

Two different rays that have a common endpoint form an **angle.** The common endpoint is called the **vertex.** The two rays are called the **sides.** In the drawing at the left, the angle shown is named angle XYZ and is written ∠ XYZ.

∠XYZ *can also be written* ∠ZYX. **The letter naming the vertex is between the other two letters.**

A **line** extends indefinitely in two directions. A line can be named by naming any two points that it contains. The line shown at the left is named line EH and is written $\overleftrightarrow{EH}$.

EH *can also be written* HE.

A **plane** is the set of all points on a never-ending flat surface. The part of Colorado that is flat can be thought of as part of a plane. A pane of glass and a sheet of paper are models of planes.

Exercises

Give two names for the line segment between each pair of cities.

1. Alamosa and Pueblo $\overline{AP}$ or $\overline{PA}$

2. Montrose and Leadville $\overline{ML}$ or $\overline{LM}$

3. Boulder and Denver $\overline{BD}$ or $\overline{DB}$

4. Ridgway and Alamosa $\overline{RA}$ or $\overline{AR}$

Complete. For exercises 5–9, answers may vary. See students' work.

5. A pin point is a model of a point. Name three other models.

6. A laser beam is a model of a ray. Name three other models.

7. A ruler's edge is a model of a line segment. Name three other models.

8. The end of a swing set is a model of an angle. Name three other models.

9. The ice on an ice rink is a model of a plane. Name three other models of planes.

10. From the symbol $\angle GEO$, how can you tell which point is the vertex?
The letter in the middle is the vertex.

Use the figure at the right to complete the following.

11. How does $\overrightarrow{XY}$ differ from $\overrightarrow{YX}$?

12. What is the endpoint of $\overrightarrow{YZ}$? Y

13. What is the endpoint of $\overrightarrow{ZY}$? Z

11. $\overrightarrow{XY}$ begins at X and extends beyond Y; $\overrightarrow{YX}$ begins at Y and extends beyond X.

Use symbols to name each figure.

14.  $\overrightarrow{AM}$

15. P ● —— ● U $\overline{PU}$ or $\overline{UP}$

16. T ● ← —— ● I $\overrightarrow{IT}$

17. $\angle CAT$ or $\angle TAC$

18. $\overleftrightarrow{ZW}$ or $\overleftrightarrow{WZ}$

19. $\angle YAM$ or $\angle MAY$

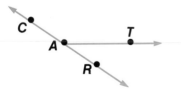

Use the figure at the left to find examples of the following.

20. a line $\overleftrightarrow{CA}$, $\overleftrightarrow{AR}$, or $\overleftrightarrow{CR}$

21. three rays $\overrightarrow{AC}$, $\overrightarrow{AR}$, $\overrightarrow{AT}$, $\overrightarrow{RC}$, or $\overrightarrow{Cr}$

22. two angles $\angle CAT$ or $\angle TAR$

23. the sides of $\angle CAT$ $\overrightarrow{AC}$, $\overrightarrow{AT}$

24. four line segments $\overline{CA}$, $\overline{AR}$, $\overline{CR}$, $\overline{AT}$

Answer the following.

25. How many lines can you draw through one point? an unlimited number

26. How many lines can you draw through two points? 1

27. How many points does a line contain? an unlimited number

28. How many rays can have the same endpoint? an unlimited number

29. Think of three points on one line through the binding of a book. Think of the pages as planes. How many planes can include the three points? an unlimited number

10-2 Right, Acute, and Obtuse Angles

Objective: To classify angles as acute, right, or obtuse.

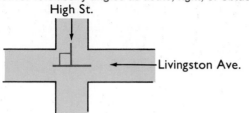
High St.

Livingston Ave.

In the figure at the left, High Street and Livingston Avenue intersect to form a 90° angle. An angle that measures 90° is called a **right angle.** The small square at the vertex indicates a right angle. Other angles can be classified by comparing them to a right angle.

An **acute angle** has a measure between 0° and 90°.

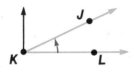

An **obtuse angle** has a measure between 90° and 180°.

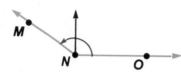

At this point, you may wish to review Lesson 9-6 on Reading Protractors.

Basic: 1–20; Average: 1–20; Enriched: 1–20

Exercises

Use the figure at the right to classify each angle as acute, right, or obtuse.

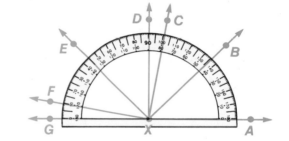

1. ∠ BXA acute
2. ∠ EXA obtuse
3. ∠ GXF acute
4. ∠ GXB obtuse
5. ∠ DXG right
6. ∠ AXC acute
7. ∠ BXE right
8. ∠ CXG obtuse
9. ∠ FXE acute
10. ∠ CXF right

Classify each angle as acute, right, or obtuse.

11. 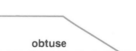 acute
12. obtuse
13. obtuse
14. right

15. acute
16. right
17. acute
18. obtuse

Answer the following.

19. In the picture at the right, do the cushions of the lounge chair form an acute, right, or obtuse angle?
    obtuse angle
20. Does each corner of this page represent an acute, right, or obtuse angle?
    right angle

10-3 Complementary and Supplementary Angles

Objective: To recognize and use complementary and supplementary angles.

In soccer, a throw-in is made from the sideline. The path of the ball and the sideline form two angles.

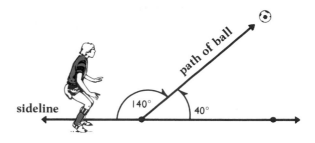

The angles above at the right show an important relationship. Two angles are **supplementary** if the sum of their degree measures is 180.

$$140° + 40° = 180°$$

Supplementary angles are called supplements of one another.

Two angles are **complementary** if the sum of their degree measures is 90.

$$30° + 60° = 90°$$

Complementary angles are called complements of one another.

Point out that a corner kick in soccer could be used to demonstrate complementary angles.

Pairs of angles that are supplementary or complementary need not have the same vertex or a common side.

These angles are supplementary.

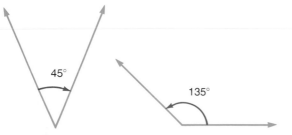

These angles are complementary.

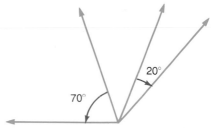

Basic: 2–30 even; Average: 1–31; Enriched: 1–31 odd

Exercises

Answer the following.

1. What is the sum of the degree measures of two complementary angles? **90**

2. What is the sum of the degree measures of two supplementary angles? **180**

Tell whether each pair of angles is complementary, supplementary, or neither.

3.

complementary (C)

4.

neither (N)

5.
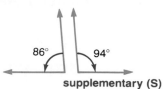
supplementary (S)

For each pair of angles whose degree measures are given below, tell whether the angles are complementary, supplementary, or neither.

6. 45°, 45° **C** 7. 130°, 50° **S** 8. 90°, 90° **S** 9. 127°, 43° **N** 10. 35°, 55° **C**

11. 63°, 127° **N** 12. 23°, 157° **S** 13. 121°, 59° **S** 14. 82°, 18° **N** 15. 15°, 75° **C**

For each angle whose degree measure is given below, find the degree measure of the complement and supplement.

16. 30° **60°, 150°** 17. 51° **39°, 129°** 18. 25° **65°, 155°** 19. 65° **25°, 115°** 20. 6° **84°, 174°**

21. 87° **3°, 93°** 22. 15° **75°, 165°** 23. 74° **16°, 106°** 24. 37° **53°, 143°** 25. 46° **44°, 134°**

Use the figure at the right to name the following.

26. the complement of ∠COD ∠BOC

27. a right angle ∠AOB or ∠DOB

28. two acute angles ∠BOC, ∠COD

29. two pairs of supplementary angles
    ∠AOB and ∠DOB, ∠AOC and ∠DOC

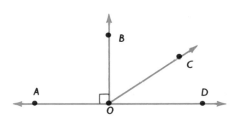

Answer the following.

30. What kind of angle is the complement of an acute angle? **acute angle**

31. What kind of angle is the supplement of a right angle? **right angle**

This feature promotes students' mental abilities in computation and reasonableness.

Mental Math

Sometimes it is easier to remember the results of a calculation if you add from left to right.

18		10	8		152		150	2	
+ 62		+ 60	+ 2		+ 28		+ 20	+ 8	
		70 +	10 = 80				170 +	10 =	180

You can use this method to determine if a pair of angles is complementary or supplementary.

The degree measures of pairs of angles are given below. Use mental calculation to determine whether each pair of angles is complementary, supplementary, or neither.

1. 18°, 122° **N** 2. 32°, 58° **C** 3. 61°, 49° **N** 4. 83°, 97° **S** 5. 25°, 65° **C**

10-4 Parallel and Perpendicular Lines and Vertical Angles

Objective: To recognize parallel and perpendicular lines and vertical angles.

Leo Dominguez is a tool programmer. To make a piece of metal into the desired shape and size, he must first determine the order of machine-cutting operations. Then he writes a set of instructions in the language of the machine's controller. Leo attended a vocational school for two years and received on-the-job training.

The machine tool Leo uses can make **parallel** grooves or shape a piece of metal so that its sides are **perpendicular.**

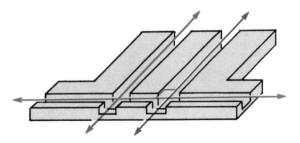

The red and green lines on this metal part do not meet. Lines in a plane that do not meet are called **parallel lines.**

Lines that meet are called **intersecting lines.** In a plane, lines either intersect or are parallel. **Point out that lines that are not in the same plane and do not intersect are called skew lines.**

The blue and red lines on the metal part form right angles. Lines that intersect to form right angles are called **perpendicular lines.**

When two lines intersect, they have one point in common. As shown at the right, four angles are formed. Two pairs of **vertical angles** are formed.

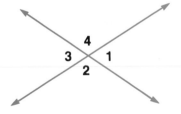

Angles may be named by numbers.

Angles 1 and 3 are vertical angles.
Angles 2 and 4 are also vertical angles.

Basic: 1–9, 11–33 odd; Average: 1–34; Enriched: 1–9, 10–34 even

Exercises

Use angles 1, 2, 3, and 4 above to complete the following.

1. Angles 1 and 4 are supplementary. Suppose ∠4 measures 110°. Find the degree measure of ∠1. **70°**

2. Use the results of exercise **1** to find the degree measures of ∠2 and ∠3. **∠2, 110°; ∠3, 70°**

3. Which pairs of angles have the same degree measure? **∠1 and ∠3, ∠2 and ∠4**

4. How do you think the degree measures of vertical angles are related? **They are equal.**

Match each letter with the appropriate exercise. Use the figure below.

5. ∠BGC and ∠AGB **c**   **a.** parallel lines

6. ∠FGB and ∠BGC **e**   **b.** vertical angles

7. $\overleftrightarrow{HC}$ and $\overleftrightarrow{AD}$ **a**   **c.** complementary angles

8. ∠AGB and ∠EGD **b**   **d.** perpendicular lines

9. $\overleftrightarrow{AD}$ and $\overleftrightarrow{FC}$ **d**   **e.** supplementary angles

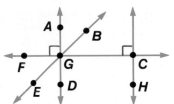

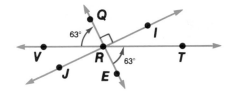

Use the figure at the left to complete the following.

10. Name three pairs of vertical angles.
∠VRQ, ∠TRE; ∠IRT, ∠VRJ; ∠QRI, ∠JRE

11. Are angles VRQ and IRT vertical angles? **no**

Find the degree measure of each angle shown above. Use your knowledge of right, vertical, supplementary, and complementary angles.

12. ∠IRQ **90°**   13. ∠VRQ **63°**   14. ∠VRE **117°**   15. ∠IRT **27°**

16. ∠JRE **90°**   17. ∠JRV **27°**   18. ∠QRJ **90°**   19. ∠VRI **153°**

Use the figure at the right to find the degree measure of each angle.

20. ∠AOC **90°**   21. ∠AOD **160°**

22. ∠COD **70°**   23. ∠AOB **70°**

24. ∠AOE **180°**   25. ∠BOD **90°**

Use the figure at the right to complete the following.

26. Name two pairs of perpendicular lines. $\overleftrightarrow{CR}$, $\overleftrightarrow{VG}$; $\overleftrightarrow{QS}$, $\overleftrightarrow{VG}$

27. Are ∠MRV and ∠ASG supplementary? Why or why not?
Yes, the sum of their measures is 180°.

28. Find the degree measures of ∠MAQ and ∠BAQ. How are these angles related?
75° and 105°, supplementary

29. Use a protractor to measure ∠JMC and ∠JMR. How are these angles related?
75° and 105°, supplementary

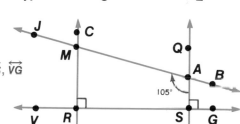

Answer the following.

31. What kind of lines are represented by the strings on a guitar?
parallel lines

33. What kind of lines are represented by rows of corn in a field?
parallel lines

30. Which two lines appear to be parallel? Explain why they must be parallel.
$\overleftrightarrow{CR}$ **and** $\overleftrightarrow{QS}$**; Two lines perpendicular to the same line in a plane are parallel.**

32. What kind of lines are represented by an artist's T-square?
perpendicular lines

34. What kind of lines are represented by the spokes on a wheel?
intersecting lines

10-5 Triangles and Circles

Objective: To identify the parts of triangles and circles.

The Very Large Array is a set of 27 radio dishes located on the flat desert of New Mexico. The radio dishes form a large radio telescope.

A single straight line cannot be used to connect the three outermost radio dishes. However, one **plane,** such as the flat desert of New Mexico does contain these three dishes.

Suppose you connect the three outermost radio dishes with line segments as shown at the right. These line segments form a **triangle.** The triangle formed here is named triangle *VLA* and is written △ *VLA*. △VLA *can also be written* △VAL, △ALV, △AVL, △LAV, *or* △LVA.

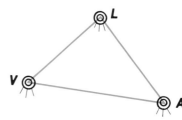

The line segments are called **sides.** The sides of △ *VLA* are $\overline{AV}$, $\overline{VL}$, and $\overline{LA}$.

The three angles of △ *VLA* are ∠ *VLA*, ∠ *LAV*, and ∠ *AVL*. The angles may also be named ∠ *L*, ∠ *A*, and ∠ *V*.

Suppose you draw a **circle** that contains the three outermost radio dishes as shown below. A circle is a path of points in a plane a given distance from a fixed point in the plane. The circle formed here is named circle C.

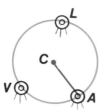

The fixed point is called the **center.** The given distance is called the **radius.**

The center of circle *C* is at point *C*. The radius is the distance from the center to a point on the circle. In circle *C*, the radius is the length of $\overline{CA}$.

Exercises

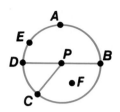

Use the figure at the left to answer the following.

1. Name the center of the circle. *P*

2. Name the circle. circle *P*

3. Name five points that lie on the circle. *A, B, C, D, E*

4. Is the center of the circle part of the circle? Explain. No. The circle is only those points in a plane a given distance from the center.

5. Name a segment that represents the radius of the circle. $\overline{PB}$, $\overline{PC}$, $\overline{PD}$, $\overline{PE}$, or $\overline{PA}$

The figure at the right represents a three-dimensional figure.
Use the figure to complete the following.
You may want to provide a three-dimensional model.

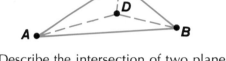

6. How many line segments make up the figure? Name them. 6: $\overline{AB}$, $\overline{AC}$, $\overline{BC}$, $\overline{AD}$, $\overline{DB}$, $\overline{DC}$ (or *BA, CA, CB, DA, BD, CD*)

7. Name the sides of $\triangle DCB$. *DC, DB, BC* (or *CD, BD, CB*)

8. Name the angles of $\triangle DCB$. $\angle CDB$, $\angle CBD$, $\angle DCB$ (or $\angle BDC$, $\angle DBC$, $\angle BCD$)

9. One plane is determined by points *A, B,* and *D.* How many other such planes are determined in the figure? 3 planes

10. Describe the intersection of two planes. a line

11. Describe the intersection of three planes. a point

Solve.

12. In your classroom, find three models of points. Be sure that the points are not in one line. Imagine a triangle formed by these points. How many planes contain the points of the triangle? 1 plane

13. Suppose you were to define a figure as the path of all points a given distance from a fixed point. What type of figure is this? How does this figure differ from a circle? a sphere, a circle is limited to a plane

14. Imagine four points not all in one plane. By choosing three points at a time, how many different planes can you find? 4 planes

This feature presents general topics of mathematics.

Math Break

Copy the letters below. Find and circle the words listed.

| H I S T O G R A M |
| T O C N D A T A E |
| A R E E O G S N D |
| M U T D M S I T I |
| P L A N E C M D A |
| B E R E T R O Y N |
| G R A P E N D A C |
| A B D E R F E R D |
| I O D D S M A C O |

add	math	odometer
data	mean	plane
dependent	median	rate
histogram	mode	ray
mass	odds	ruler

10-6 Classifying Triangles

Objective: To classify triangles by sides and by angles.

Triangles are often used in construction to provide extra strength. Notice how triangles are used in the supports for the bleachers.

The sides of a triangle are line segments. Line segments that are the same length are called **congruent** segments.

Triangles can be classified according to the number of congruent sides they have.

The red marks indicate congruent sides.

A **scalene triangle** has no sides congruent.

An **isosceles triangle** has at least two sides congruent.

An **equilateral triangle** has all sides congruent.

Triangles also can be classified according to their angles. Every triangle has at least two acute angles. First, find two acute angles in each triangle below. Then, classify the triangle according to its third angle.

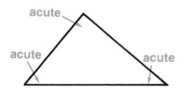
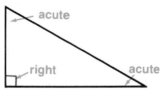
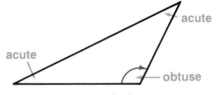

An **acute triangle** has all acute angles.

A **right triangle** has a right angle.

An **obtuse triangle** has an obtuse angle.

Basic: 1–25 odd; Average: 1–25; Enriched: 5–26

Exercises

Classify each triangle as scalene, isosceles, or equilateral.

1.

scalene

2.

equilateral

3.
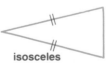
isosceles

4.
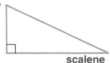
scalene

Classify each triangle as acute, right, or obtuse.

5.
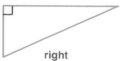
right

6.

acute

7.
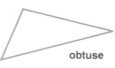
obtuse

8.
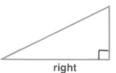
right

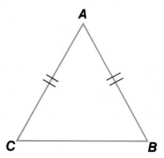

Use △ABC at the left to complete the following.

9. One side of △ABC is $\overline{AB}$. Name the other two sides.
   BC and CA

10. One angle of △ABC is ∠CAB. Angle CAB can also be symbolized as ∠A. Name the other two angles each in two ways. **∠ABC, ∠ACB, ∠B, ∠C**

11. What type of triangle is △ABC? Which sides are congruent? Do you think any angles have the same degree measure? **isosceles; $\overline{AC}$ and $\overline{AB}$ are congruent. Yes, ∠B and ∠C.**

Use the figure at the right to complete the following.

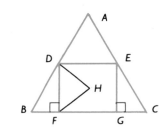

12. Carefully trace $\overline{AC}$. Also, mark point E on $\overline{AC}$. Lay the tracing over $\overline{AB}$. Is $\overline{AC}$ congruent to $\overline{AB}$? Is $\overline{AE}$ congruent to $\overline{AD}$? **yes, yes**

13. Name two isosceles triangles. **△ABC, △ADE**

14. Name two equilateral triangles. **△ABC, △ADE**

15. Name two right triangles. **△BDF, △CEG**

16. Name two acute triangles. **△ADE, △ABC, △DHF**

17. Name an obtuse triangle. **none**

18. Name two scalene triangles. **△BDF, △CEG**

Draw a triangle that satisfies the given conditions for the following. If no such triangle exists, write _none_. For answers to exercises 19–24, see Teacher Guide.

19. isosceles, right

20. scalene, obtuse

21. isosceles, obtuse

22. equilateral, right **none**

23. scalene, right

24. equilateral, acute

Answer the following.

25. Try to draw a triangle with two right angles. What do you find?
   not possible

26. Try to draw a triangle with two obtuse angles. What do you find?
   not possible

This feature presents general topics of mathematics.

 Math Break

Cut several long thin strips of paper. Then, do the following.
   A. Tear one strip into three pieces.
   B. If possible, form a triangle.
   C. Compare both shorter pieces to the longest one. What did you find?
   See below.

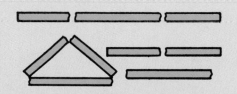

For each set of side measures, tell whether a triangle can be formed.

1. 3, 4, 5 **yes**

2. 13, 6, 9 **yes**

3. 30, 10, 19 **no**

4. 5, 3, 9 **no**

5. 1.4, 0.5, 1.2 **yes**

6. 0.11, 0.15, 0.2 **yes**

7. $\frac{1}{2}, \frac{1}{3}, 1$ **no**

8. $\frac{3}{7}, \frac{5}{8}, 1$ **yes**

A triangle can be formed when the sum of the lengths of the shorter sides is greater than the length of the longest side.

This page provides an aid for maintaining skills.

PRACTICE

Estimate. Answers may vary. Typical answers are given.

1.   379
     + 120
     500

2.   42.06
      − 21.98
      20

3.   384
      × 32
     12,000

4. $39.16
       × 19
     $800.00

5. 68)6,270 90

6.   751
     + 486
     1,300

7.   3.98
      − 1.45
      3.00

8.   297
      × 54
     15,000

9. $6.98
       × 30
     $210.00

10. 23)486 20

Add, subtract, multiply, or divide.

11.   7.56
      + 6.2
      13.76

12.   14.21
       × 0.03
      0.4263

13.   1,561
       − 562
       999

14. 126 ÷ 7 18

15.   303
       × 30
      9,090

16.   0.002
       × 36
      0.072

17. 22)319 14.5

18.   463
      + 537
      1,000

19. 17)952 56

20. $74.36
       − 27.61
      $46.75

21.   86.9
      + 27.1
      114.0

22.   37.8
       × 0.46
      17.388

23. 3.1)465 150

24.   86.9
       − 71.8
       15.1

25.   3.25
       + 1.98
       5.23

26. $\frac{1}{3} + \frac{5}{6}$ $1\frac{1}{6}$

27. $\frac{5}{7} + \frac{2}{5}$ $1\frac{4}{35}$

28. $\frac{3}{4} - \frac{3}{5}$ $\frac{3}{20}$

29. $\frac{2}{3} \div \frac{4}{15}$ $2\frac{1}{2}$

30. $\frac{3}{5} - \frac{1}{4}$ $\frac{7}{20}$

31. $1\frac{1}{2} \times 6$ 9

32. $6 \div 2\frac{1}{2}$ $2\frac{2}{5}$

33. $\frac{3}{5} \div \frac{5}{3}$ $\frac{9}{25}$

34. $1\frac{1}{3} + \frac{3}{4}$ $2\frac{1}{12}$

35. $4\frac{3}{4} - 2\frac{1}{3}$ $2\frac{5}{12}$

36. $\frac{3}{4} \div 1\frac{1}{3}$ $\frac{9}{16}$

37. $1\frac{1}{3} \times 1\frac{3}{5}$ $2\frac{2}{15}$

38. $3\frac{1}{2} + 2\frac{1}{4}$ $5\frac{3}{4}$

39. $6\frac{7}{8} + 3\frac{1}{8}$ 10

40. $6\frac{3}{4} - 3\frac{3}{8}$ $3\frac{3}{8}$

41. $10\frac{1}{3} \div 3\frac{1}{3}$ $3\frac{1}{10}$

42. $\frac{7}{8} - \frac{3}{4}$ $\frac{1}{8}$

43. $\frac{9}{10} + \frac{3}{5}$ $1\frac{1}{2}$

44. $1\frac{2}{3} \times \frac{1}{10}$ $\frac{1}{6}$

45. $3\frac{5}{6} \times 1\frac{2}{3}$ $6\frac{7}{18}$

46. 10 × 29 290

47. 4.2 × 10 42

48. 3.6 ÷ 10 0.36

49. 49 ÷ 100 0.49

50. 100 × 0.012 1.2

51. 46 × 1,000 46,000

52. 0.085 × 10 0.85

53. 100 × 46.8 4,680

54. 100 × 0.12 12

55. 36 ÷ 10 3.6

56. 3.9 × 100 390

57. 360 ÷ 10 36

58. 465 × 100 46,500

59. 0.88 × 10 8.8

60. 1,000 × 0.008 8

61. 3.45 ÷ 1,000 0.00345

62. 490 ÷ 100 4.9

63. 10 × 0.23 2.3

64. 4.9 ÷ 100 0.049

65. 0.42 × 100 42

Complete.

66. 69 min = ▨ h ▨ min 1, 9
67. 86 s = ▨ min ▨ s 1, 26
68. 2 h 45 min = ▨ min 165

69. 500 h = ▨ days ▨ h 20, 20
70. 2 qt 1 c = ▨ c 9
71. 1 h = ▨ s 3,600

72. 14 g = ▨ mg 14,000
73. 2.75 L = ▨ mL 2,750
74. 5 pt = ▨ qt $2\frac{1}{2}$

216   *Geometry*

75. 327 g = ▦ kg **0.327**   **76.** 3.5 m = ▦ mm **3,500**   **77.** 430 m = ▦ km **0.430**

78. 36 oz = ▦ lb $2\frac{1}{4}$ **79.** 4.5 kg = ▦ g **4,500**   **80.** 4.5 m = ▦ cm **450**

81. 50 h = ▦ min **3,000**   **82.** 80 oz = ▦ lb **5**   **83.** 120 s = ▦ min **2**

Add or subtract.

84.
$$3\text{ h }25\text{ min} + 1\text{ h }20\text{ min}$$
4 h 45 min

85.
$$4\text{ h }45\text{ min} - 2\text{ h }22\text{ min}$$
2 h 23 min

86.
$$2\text{ h }30\text{ min} + 1\text{ h }30\text{ min}$$
4 h

87.
$$4\text{ h }30\text{ min} - 1\text{ h }45\text{ min}$$
2 h 45 min

88.
$$1\text{ h }45\text{ min} + 1\text{ h }45\text{ min}$$
3 h 30 min

89.
$$2\text{ h }20\text{ min} - 1\text{ h }40\text{ min}$$
40 min

90.
$$6\text{ h }38\text{ min }27\text{ s} + 3\text{ h }25\text{ min }15\text{ s}$$
10 h 3 min 42 s

91.
$$2\text{ h }\qquad 48\text{ s} + 3\text{ h }15\text{ min }45\text{ s}$$
5 h 16 min 33 s

92.
$$8\text{ h }\qquad 16\text{ s} - 1\text{ h }45\text{ min }8\text{ s}$$
6 h 15 min 8 s

Change each percent to a decimal. Change each decimal to a percent.

93. 24% **0.24**   **94.** 0.51 **51%**   **95.** 81% **0.81**   **96.** 7% **0.07**   **97.** 15.34 **1,534%**

98. 0.4 **40%**   **99.** 135% **1.35**   **100.** 3.25 **325%**   **101.** 32.3% **0.323**   **102.** 5 **500%**

103. 51.8% **0.518**   **104.** 0.008 **0.8%**   **105.** 253% **2.53**   **106.** 0.032 **3.2%**   **107.** 0.06 **6%**

Solve.

108. 16% of 400 **64**   **109.** 6% of 72 **4.32**   **110.** 52% of 2.2 **1.144**   **111.** 19% of 130 **24.7**

112. 10.5% of $10 **$1.05**   **113.** 76% of 0.25 **0.19**   **114.** 6.2% of 20 **1.24**   **115.** 105% of 25 **26.25**

116. 300% of 10 **30**   **117.** 1% of 30 **0.3**   **118.** 250% of 4 **10**   **119.** $3\frac{1}{2}$% of 30 **1.05**

Use the proportion $\frac{P}{B} = \frac{r}{100}$ to solve each problem.

120. What percent of 80 is 20? **25%**

121. What number is 75% of 6.2? **4.65**

122. 4.5% of 60 is what number? **2.7**

123. 18 is 25% of what number? **72**

124. 25% of what number is 17? **68**

125. What percent of 120 is 45? **37.5%**

126. 16% of 85 is what number? **13.6**

127. What number is 300% of 1.5? **4.5**

Solve.

128. Danny's employer will pay 80% of his medical expenses. Suppose his medical expenses are $327. How much of the expenses will Danny pay? **$65.40**

129. Recall $50-deductible means you pay the first $50 of the expenses. Suppose the expenses are $250. What percent of the $250 does the $50 represent? **20%**

130. Suppose Danny's insurance pays for $270 of a year's medical expenses of $360. For what percent is the insurance company paying? **75%**

131. A van was rented to move furniture. The rent was $30 a day plus 30¢ a mile. Find the rent for one day and 88 miles driven.
$56.40

10-7 Squares, Square Roots, and the Pythagorean Theorem

Objectives: To find squares and square roots.
To find the hypotenuse of a right triangle.

Chet Solada and Tonya Holmes are collecting money for a charity. They have drawn a diagram of three regions of the city they will cover.

Chet will go to the houses in regions A and B. Tonya will cover region C. Notice the lengths of the sides of regions A, B, and C. Each region is a square.

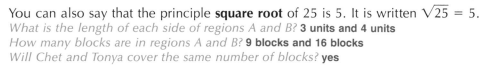

The length of each side of region C is 5 units. There are 25 blocks in region C. Notice that 25 is 5×5 or 5^2.

Read 5^2 as "5 to the second power" or "5 squared." Since 5^2 is 25, 25 is called the **square** of 5.

You can also say that the principle **square root** of 25 is 5. It is written $\sqrt{25} = 5$.

What is the length of each side of regions A and B? **3 units and 4 units**
How many blocks are in regions A and B? **9 blocks and 16 blocks**
Will Chet and Tonya cover the same number of blocks? **yes**

In the diagram above, the three regions form a right triangle around the fountain. The longest side of the triangle, the side opposite the right angle, is the **hypotenuse.** The other two sides are the **legs.**

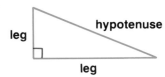

The example above illustrates a special relationship among the sides of a right triangle.

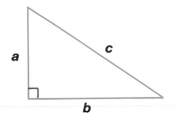

In a right triangle, the square of the length of the hypotenuse is equal to the sum of the squares of the lengths of the legs.

If c is the measure of the hypotenuse and a and b are the measures of the legs, then
$$a^2 + b^2 = c^2.$$

This relationship is called the **Pythagorean Theorem.**

Ask students to show how the Pythagorean Theorem works for the right triangle surrounding the fountain.

The square root table on page 419 can be used to find squares and square roots.

1955

Examples

A. Find the square of 62.

n	n^2	$\sqrt{n}$
62	3844	7.874

For $n = 62$, $n^2 = 3{,}844$ and $62^2 = 3{,}844$.

B. Find the square root of 1,089.

n	n^2	$\sqrt{n}$
33	1089	5.745

For $n = 33$, $n^2 = 1,089$
and $\sqrt{1,089} = 33$.

C. Find the length of the hypotenuse of the right triangle.

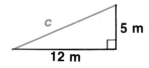

$a^2 + b^2 = c^2$	*Use the Pythagorean Theorem.*
$(5)^2 + (12)^2 = c^2$	*Replace a with 5 and b with 12.*
$25 + 144 = c^2$	*Square the numbers.*
$169 = c^2$	*Simplify the left side.*
$\sqrt{169} = \sqrt{c^2}$	*Find the square root of 169 and the square*
	root of c^2 to determine the value of c.
$13 = c$	*$169 = 13^2$, $c^2 = (c)^2$*

$5 \boxed{x^2} \boxed{+} 12 \boxed{x^2} \boxed{=} 169$

$169 \boxed{\sqrt{x}}$ 13

The length of the hypotenuse is 13 meters.

Basic Skills Appendix, Page 419
Basic: 2–76 even; Average: 2–74 even, 75–77; Enriched: 1–73 odd, 75–77

Exercises

Find the square of each number. Use the table
on page 419 if necessary for exercises 1–40.

1. 2 **4** 2. 10 **100** 3. 7 **49** 4. 6 **36** 5. 14 **196**

6. 11 **121** 7. 12 **144** 8. 17 **289** 9. 25 **625** 10. 50 **2,500**

11. 46 **2,116** 12. 39 **1,521** 13. 77 **5,929** 14. 53 **2,809** 15. 84 **7,056**

16. 28 **784** 17. 42 **1,764** 18. 15 **225** 19. 81 **6,561** 20. 65 **4,225**

Find each square root.

21. $\sqrt{4}$ **2** 22. $\sqrt{16}$ **4** 23. $\sqrt{36}$ **6** 24. $\sqrt{1}$ **1** 25. $\sqrt{64}$ **8**

26. $\sqrt{100}$ **10** 27. $\sqrt{144}$ **12** 28. $\sqrt{121}$ **11** 29. $\sqrt{49}$ **7** 30. $\sqrt{225}$ **15**

31. $\sqrt{400}$ **20** 32. $\sqrt{900}$ **30** 33. $\sqrt{256}$ **16** 34. $\sqrt{961}$ **31** 35. $\sqrt{196}$ **14**

36. $\sqrt{3,025}$ **55** 37. $\sqrt{1,764}$ **42** 38. $\sqrt{4,096}$ **64** 39. $\sqrt{6,724}$ **82** 40. $\sqrt{9,025}$ **95**

Identify the lengths of the legs and the hypotenuse in each right triangle.

41.

legs: 90 in.,120 in.
hypotenuse: 150 in.

42.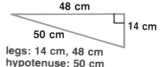

legs: 14 cm, 48 cm
hypotenuse: 50 cm

43.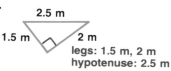

legs: 1.5 m, 2 m
hypotenuse: 2.5 m

The lengths of the sides of right triangles are given.
Identify the lengths of the legs and the hypotenuse.

44. 15 m, 36 m, 39 m **legs: 15 m, 36 m**
hypotenuse: 39 m

45. 85 cm, 13 cm, 84 cm **legs: 13 cm, 84 cm**
hypotenuse: 85 cm

46. 80 in., 39 in., 89 in. **legs: 39 in., 80 in.**
hypotenuse: 89 in.

47. 77 ft, 85 ft, 36 ft **legs: 36 ft, 77 ft**
hypotenuse: 85 ft

Use the Pythagorean Theorem to find the length of the hypotenuse in each right triangle.

48. 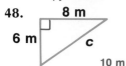 8 m, 6 m, c, 10 m

49. 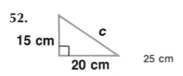 c, 16 km, 12 km, 20 km

50. 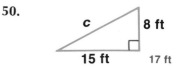 c, 8 ft, 15 ft, 17 ft

51. 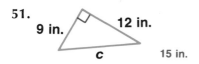 9 in., 12 in., c, 15 in.

52. 15 cm, c, 20 cm, 25 cm

53. 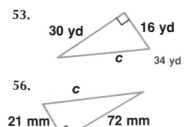 30 yd, 16 yd, c, 34 yd

54. 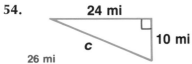 24 mi, c, 10 mi, 26 mi

55. 25 m, 60 m, c, 65 m

56. c, 21 mm, 72 mm, 75 mm

The lengths of the legs of right triangles are given below. Use the Pythagorean Theorem to find the length of each hypotenuse.

57. 30 mi, 40 mi 50 mi

58. 9 cm, 40 cm 41 cm

59. 7 ft, 24 ft 25 ft

60. 36 km, 77 km 85 km

61. 60 yd, 80 yd 100 yd

62. 11 in., 60 in. 61 in.

63. 14 cm, 48 cm 50 cm

64. 18 mm, 80 mm 82 mm

65. 32 mi, 60 mi 68 mi

Use the Pythagorean Theorem to tell whether triangles with sides having the following lengths are right triangles.

66. 6 ft, 7 ft, 8 ft no

67. 7 km, 24 km, 25 km yes

68. 24 cm, 26 cm, 10 cm yes

69. 10 mi, 10 mi, 13 mi no

70. 6 in., 20 in., 18 in. no

71. 20 yd, 48 yd, 52 yd yes

72. 24 m, 45 m, 51 m yes

73. 7 ft, 15 ft, 18 ft no

74. 16 mm, 20 mm, 28 mm no

Solve.

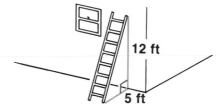

75. The bottom of a ladder is placed 5 feet from a building. The ladder reaches 12 feet high on the building. How long is the ladder? 13 feet

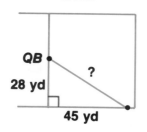

76. In a football game, the receiver runs 45 yards straight down the sideline. The quarterback is 28 yards from the sideline when he throws the ball to the receiver. How far is the ball thrown? 53 yards

77. A clock has a minute hand that is 3 inches long and an hour hand that is 4 inches long. What is the distance between the ends of the hands at 9 o'clock? 5 inches

10-8 Problem Solving: Organize Data: Look For a Pattern

Objective: To use number patterns and geometrical patterns to solve word problems.

To find the sum of the degree measures of the angles of a triangle, do the following.

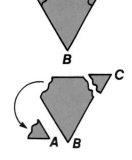

A. Cut out a triangle like △ABC.
B. Tear off ∠A and ∠C.
C. Place ∠A next to ∠B as shown.
D. Do the same for ∠C.
E. Use a protractor to measure the angle formed by ∠A, ∠B, and ∠C.

This experiment suggests that the sum of the measures of the angles of the triangle is 180°.
Have students repeat this activity using triangles with different shapes.

What is the sum of the degree measures of the angles of a 7-sided figure?

You know that the sum of the degree measures of the angles of a triangle is 180°. You want to find the sum of the degree measures of the angles of a 7-sided figure.

First, make drawings of other figures. Form triangles inside each figure. Use what you know about the angle sum of triangles to determine the angle sum of each figure you have drawn. Then, make a table to organize the data. Look for a pattern. Apply the pattern to find the angle sum of a 7-sided figure.

Solve

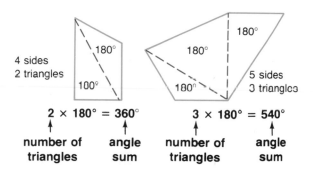

4 sides
2 triangles

2 × 180° = 360°
↑ ↑
number of   angle
triangles   sum

5 sides
3 triangles

3 × 180° = 540°
↑ ↑
number of   angle
triangles   sum

Separate each figure into triangles by drawing line segments from one vertex to each of the other vertices. Since the angle sum of a triangle is 180°, multiply the number of triangles in each figure by 180°. This will be the angle sum of each figure.

Organize the data in a table.

number of sides	number of triangles	number of triangles × 180°	angle sum
3	1	1 × 180°	180°
4	2	2 × 180°	360°
5	3	3 × 180°	540°

Notice that the number of triangles is two less than the number of sides in each figure.

A pattern can be found from the drawings and the data in the table. The angle sum of each of the figures on page 221 is two less than the number of sides multiplied by 180°.

$$\left(\begin{array}{c}\textbf{number of sides}\\ \textbf{of the figure}\end{array} - 2\right) \times \textbf{180° = angle sum}$$

Use the pattern to find the angle sum of a 7-sided figure.

$$\left(\begin{array}{c}\text{number of sides}\\ \text{of the figure}\end{array} - 2\right) \times 180° = \text{angle sum}$$
$$(7 - 2) \times 180° = 5 \times 180°$$
$$\underset{\textit{number of sides}}{\uparrow} \qquad\qquad = 900°$$

The angle sum of a 7-sided figure is 900°.

Examine

You can check the solution by extending the table to include a 7-sided figure.

number of sides	number of triangles	number of triangles × 180°	angle sum
6	4	4 × 180°	720°
7	5	5 × 180°	900°

The solution is correct.

Basic: 1–6, 8–14 even; Average: 9–15; Enriched: 1–6, 7–15 odd

Exercises

1. How many triangles will be formed when the figure has 12 sides?
10 triangles

3. A mosaic is made up of 8-sided figures and squares as shown at the right. What is the angle sum of an 8-sided figure? **1,080°**

4. Find the degree measure of the remaining angle in the following triangle. **27°**

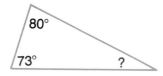

5. Find the degree measure of the remaining angle in the following figure. **138°**

2. What is the angle sum of a 12-sided figure? **1,800°**

6. Find the degree measure of the remaining angle in the following figure. **125°**

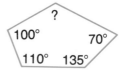

7. Eleven triangles are formed when the vertices of a figure are connected by line segments from one vertex. How many sides does the figure have? **13 sides**

8. A basketball team has 5 players. Suppose each player shakes hands with every other player. How many handshakes take place? **10 handshakes**

9. Nate begins a physical fitness program. On the first day of the program, he does 30 sit-ups. Every fifth day he plans to increase the number of sit-ups by 10. How many sit-ups should Nate be doing by day 20? **70 sit-ups**

10. Mrs. Hood buys numerals to put on the doors of each room in a 99-unit motel building. The rooms are numbered 1 through 99. How many of each digit 0, 1, 2, 3, 4, 5, 6, 7, 8, and 9 should Mrs. Hood buy? **9 zeros and 20 of every other digit**

11. Airfare rates change with the time of year. What do you expect the June-Sept. rates to be for this year if the same pattern continues? **$148**

Date	Oct.-May	June-Sept.
3 years ago	$160	$130
2 years ago	$171	$136
1 year ago	$182	$142
this year	$193	?

12. The map shows the streets between the Arma's house and the park. They are all one-way streets. How many different ways are there to go from the Arma's house to the park? **5 ways**

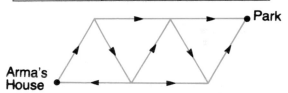

13. Carla mails a recipe to six friends. Each of the six friends mails the recipe to six of their friends and so on. What is the total number of recipes in the fifth mailing? **7,776 recipes**

14. The pages in a book are numbered starting with 1. To number all the pages, the printer uses a total of 534 digits. How many pages are in the book? **214 pages**

15. Forty-five percent of Mr. Chambers' math class are girls. If there are 20 students in his class, how many are boys? **11 boys**

This feature presents useful ways of solving mathematical problems on a calculator.

Calculator

Most calculators have a key labeled x^2. This key allows you to find the square of a number quickly. Suppose you want to find 36^2.

Enter 36. *36*

Press $\boxed{x^2}$ *1296*

The result appears immediately.

Use the $\boxed{x^2}$ key to find each square.

1. 17^2 **289**   **2.** 65^2 **4,225**   **3.** 99^2 **9,801**   **4.** 126^2 **15,876**   **5.** 173^2 **29,929**

6. 184^2 **33,856**   **7.** 207^2 **42,849**   **8.** $(6.5)^2$ **42.25**   **9.** $(11.8)^2$ **139.24**   **10.** $(0.46)^2$ **0.2116**

10-9 Conditional Statements

Objective: To identify the parts of a conditional statement, and to write the converse of a statement.

Annie Corbin is an illustrator. She is working on an advertising campaign for Gander Airlines. Their slogan is "When arriving on time is important, choose Gander."

The slogan can be rewritten using the words *if* and *then*. "If arriving on time is important, then you should choose Gander." A statement that can be written in *if-then* form is a **conditional statement.**

Conditional statements have two parts. The part following *if* is the **condition.** The part following *then* is the **conclusion.**

Example

A. Identify the condition and the conclusion in the slogan given above.

If arriving on time is important, then you should choose Gander.
    condition   *conclusion*

It is possible to interchange the condition and the conclusion of a conditional statement. The new statement is called the **converse** of the original statement.

Examples

B. Write the converse of the following statement.

Statement: If a triangle is obtuse, then the triangle has two acute angles.
Converse: If a triangle has two acute angles, then the triangle is obtuse.

C. Refer to example B. Is each statement true?

An obtuse triangle has two acute angles. The original statement is true. | A right triangle has two acute angles and it is *not* obtuse. The converse is false.

Basic: 1–17 odd, 18; Average: 1–18; Enriched: 2–16 even, 17–18

Exercises

Identify the condition and the conclusion in each sentence. The condition is underlined once and the conclusion is underlined twice.

1. If a number is even, then it is divisible by two.

2. If today is Tuesday, then today is a school day.

3. If the degree measure of an angle is 120, then it is an obtuse angle.

4. If an angle is an acute angle, then its degree measure is less than 90.

5. If the sum of the degree measures of two angles is 180, then they are supplementary angles.

6. When it rains, puddles form on the parking lot. (Hint: Write this in *if-then* form first.)

7. When we cook pizza, the smoke alarm goes off.

8. All great cooks make great pies.

Write the converse of each statement. Then determine whether each statement (original and converse) is true. For exercises 9–16, see Teacher Guide.

9. If an animal is a bear, then it is a mammal.

10. If the number is six, then it is divisible by three.

11. If a triangle has three congruent sides, then it is equilateral.

12. If a triangle is scalene, then it has no congruent sides.

13. If two angles are complementary, then the sum of their degree measures is 90.

14. If two lines form right angles, then they are perpendicular.

15. If a month is named May, then it has 31 days.

16. If today is Saturday, then I do not have to go to school.

Solve.

17. It is snowing. Yuri says that there must be clouds in the sky. Is her conclusion correct? Explain.
Yes. It cannot snow without clouds.

18. Robin lives in America. Carlos says that Robin lives in Maine. Is his conclusion correct? Explain.
No. Robin could live in a different state.

This feature provides general topics about the uses of a computer.

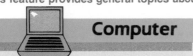

Computer

The computer uses the following inequality symbols.

< is less than   6<8

> is greater than   9>7

= is equal to   9=9

<= is less than or equal to   15<=15, 6<=12

>= is greater than or equal to   13>=13, 7>=5

<> is not equal to   7<>15

An **IF-THEN** statement is a conditional statement that can be read by the computer. If the condition is true, the computer follows the instructions given after the word THEN.

```
10 IF 7<9 THEN GOTO 40
```
The computer will go to line 40.

```
20 IF 8>10 THEN GOTO 40
```
The computer will not go to line 40.

Tell whether the computer will go to line 40 in each exercise below.

1. 10 IF 18.5<19 THEN GOTO 40 yes

2. 10 IF 7.8<>7.08 THEN GOTO 40 yes

3. 10 IF 18<>18 THEN GOTO 40 no

4. 10 IF 10.09>10.3 THEN GOTO 40 no

5. 10 IF 105<=105 THEN GOTO 40 yes

6. 10 IF 2.03>=2.3 THEN GOTO 40 no

7. Explain why <> is a logical symbol for "is not equal to." If a number is not equal to another number, then it is either less than or greater than the other number.

10-10 Deductive and Inductive Reasoning

Objective: To use and distinguish between deductive and inductive reasoning.

An art museum is having a special showing of a new exhibit for members only.

Bennie Fields is a guard at the museum. As visitors enter the museum, he checks for membership cards. If a visitor is a member of the museum, then the visitor may enter the exhibit. Theresa Osgood is a member of the museum. Bennie decides that Mrs. Osgood may enter the exhibit.

Bennie is using **deductive reasoning** to make his decision. He uses the general rule, "If you are a member of the museum, then you may enter the exhibit." Deductive reasoning is using a rule to make a decision.

Sometimes it is not possible to make a decision based on a rule.

Example

A. Rule: If it is Friday, then we will have a math quiz.
   Case: We are having a math quiz.

Does this mean that it is Friday?
No. There could be other reasons for having a math quiz.

So, no decision can be made from the rule.

Another kind of reasoning is **inductive reasoning.** Inductive reasoning is making a rule after seeing several examples.

Example

B. The lunchroom has run out of spoons every day for a week.

Paula concludes that the lunchroom does not have enough spoons.

Paula uses inductive reasoning to reach her conclusion. She bases her conclusion on what has happened in the past.

Basic: 1–18; Average: 1–18; Enriched: 1–18

Exercises

Use inductive reasoning to guess the next two numbers in each list of numbers.

1. 15, 20, 25, __?__, __?__ 30, 35
2. 18, 15, 12, __?__, __?__ 9, 6
3. 1, 4, 9, __?__, __?__ 16, 25
4. 10, 20, 40, 80, __?__, __?__ 160, 320
5. 1, 10, 100, __?__, __?__ 1,000; 10,000
6. 6, 7, 9, 12, 16, __?__, __?__ 21, 27

226 *Geometry*

If a decision is possible, write the decision for each case based on the given rule.

Rule: If you can swim a mile without stopping, then you may join the swim team.

7. **Case:** George cannot swim a mile without stopping.
no decision

9. **Case:** Chet is allowed to join the swim team.
no decision

8. **Case:** Nami can swim a mile without stopping.
Nami may join the swim team.

10. **Case:** Jillian is not allowed to join the swim team.
Jillian cannot swim a mile without stopping.

Determine whether each exercise is an example of deductive or inductive reasoning.

11. Even numbers are divisible by two. Eight is even. Eight is divisible by two. **deductive**

12. Isosceles triangles have two congruent sides. A certain triangle has no congruent sides. It is not isosceles. **deductive**

13. A child examines 12 tulips that are each red. The child concludes that all tulips must be red. **inductive**

14. Your French teacher has given a pop quiz every Monday. It is Monday. You say, "We'll have a quiz in French." **inductive**

15. If you are not passing English, then you will not be allowed to go on the field trip. You are not passing English. You are not allowed to go on the field trip. **deductive**

16. Lisa noticed that lasagna had been served in the school cafeteria for the past six Tuesdays. Lisa decides that the school always serves lasagna on Tuesday. **inductive**

Solve.

17. If you are accepted to Mr. Terrell's chorus, then you have an excellent voice. You are accepted to Mr. Terrell's chorus. What conclusion can be reached? **You have an excellent voice.**

18. If the team wins three more games, then they will make the playoffs. The team wins three more games. What conclusion can be reached? **They will make the playoffs.**

CHAPTER 10 REVIEW

Vocabulary/Concepts

Write the letter of the word or phrase that best matches each description.

1. two angles whose degree measures add up to 180° **k**
2. a never-ending straight path in one direction **j**
3. a statement that can be written in *if-then* form **c**
4. the longest side of a right triangle **e**
5. a triangle with at least two sides congruent **g**
6. an angle whose degree measure is between 0° and 90° **a**
7. lines in a plane that do not meet **h**
8. using a rule to make a decision **d**
9. the set of all points on a continuous flat surface **i**

a. acute angle
b. complementary angles
c. conditional statement
d. deductive reasoning
e. hypotenuse
f. inductive reasoning
g. isosceles triangle
h. parallel
i. plane
j. ray
k. supplementary angles

Exercises

Use the figure at the right to complete the following.   Pages 205–206

10. Name five points.   11. Name two lines.
   F, I, X, N, E
12. Name four rays.   13. Name four angles.
14. Name six line segments.
15. Name the sides of ∠FXN. $\overrightarrow{XF}, \overrightarrow{XN}$
16. How many planes contain the points *N, X,* and *E?* one

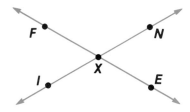

Classify each angle as acute, right, or obtuse.   Page 207

17.   18.   19.

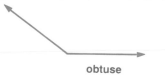
obtuse

acute

right

For each angle whose degree measure is given below, find the degree measure of the complement and the supplement.   Pages 208–209

20. 26° 64°, 154°   21. 81° 9°, 99°   22. 15° 75°, 165°   23. 43° 47°, 137°   24. 78° 12°, 102°

Use the figure at the right to complete the following.   Pages 210–211

25. Name a pair of parallel lines.
26. Name two pairs of perpendicular lines.
27. Name two pairs of vertical angles. ∠BCA (or ∠ACB)
   and ∠DCF (or ∠FCD); ∠BCD (or ∠DCB) and ∠ACF (or ∠FCA)

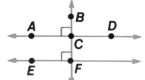

11. $\overleftrightarrow{FX}$ (or $\overleftrightarrow{XE}, \overleftrightarrow{FE}, \overleftrightarrow{XF}, \overleftrightarrow{EX}, \overleftrightarrow{EF}$); $\overleftrightarrow{NX}$ (or $\overleftrightarrow{NI}, \overleftrightarrow{XI}, \overleftrightarrow{XN}, \overleftrightarrow{IN}, \overleftrightarrow{IX}$)   12. $\overrightarrow{XF}, \overrightarrow{XI}, \overrightarrow{XE}, \overrightarrow{XN}$
13. ∠FXN, ∠FXI, ∠IXE, ∠EXN (or ∠NXF, ∠IXF, ∠EXI, ∠NXE)   14. $\overline{FX}, \overline{XE}, \overline{FE}, \overline{NX}, \overline{XI}, \overline{NI}$ (or $\overline{XF}, \overline{EX}, \overline{EF}, \overline{XN}, \overline{IX}, \overline{IN}$)

25. $\overleftrightarrow{AC}$ (or $\overleftrightarrow{AD}, \overleftrightarrow{CD}, \overleftrightarrow{CA}, \overleftrightarrow{DA}, \overleftrightarrow{DC}$) is parallel to $\overleftrightarrow{EF}$ (or $\overleftrightarrow{FE}$)
   26. $\overleftrightarrow{AC}$ is perpendicular to $\overleftrightarrow{BC}$; $\overleftrightarrow{EF}$ is perpendicular to $\overleftrightarrow{BC}$

Use the figure at the right to complete the following.   Pages 212–213

28. Name the circle. circle *M*

29. Name a segment that represents the
radius of the circle. $\overline{CM}$ or $\overline{MT}$ ($\overline{MC}$ or $\overline{TM}$)

30. Name the sides of △*CMT*. $\overline{CM}$, $\overline{MT}$, $\overline{CT}$ (or $\overline{TC}$)

31. Name the angles of △*CMT*. ∠*CMT* (or ∠*TMC*),
∠*MTC* (or ∠*CTM*), ∠*TCM* (or ∠*MCT*)

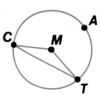

Classify each triangle as scalene, isosceles, or equilateral.   Pages 214–215

32.

equilateral

33.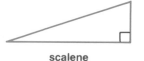

scalene

34.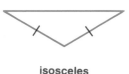

isosceles

**Use the Pythagorean Theorem to tell whether triangles with sides having the
following lengths are right triangles.   Pages 218–220**

35. 9 in., 40 in., 41 in. yes

36. 7 m, 25 m, 29 m no

37. 13 km, 84 km, 85 km yes

**Use the Pythagorean Theorem to find the length of the
hypotenuse in each right triangle.   Pages 218–220**

38.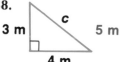

3 m   *c*   5 m
4 m

39.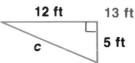

12 ft   13 ft
c   5 ft

40.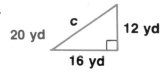

c   12 yd
20 yd
16 yd

42. true; If Mrs. Clark lives in a city, then Mrs. Clark lives in Boston. false
**Write the converse of each statement. Then determine whether each
statement (original and converse) is true.   Pages 224–225**

41. If an angle measures 90°, then it
is a right angle. true; If an angle is a
right angle, then it measures 90°. true

42. If Mrs. Clark lives in Boston, then
Mrs. Clark lives in a city.

**Determine whether each exercise is an example of
deductive or inductive reasoning.   Pages 226–227**

43. Your math teacher has given a pop quiz
every Friday. It is Friday. You say,
"We'll have a quiz in math."
inductive

44. A right triangle has one right angle.
A certain triangle has no right
angles. It is not a right triangle.
deductive

Solve.

45. A clock has a minute hand that is
6 cm long and an hour hand that is
8 cm long. What is the distance
between the ends of the hands at
3 o'clock? 10 cm

46. Mr. Morris plants seven strawberry
plants in his garden. The number of
plants triples every year. How many
strawberry plants will Mr. Morris have
in his garden in five years? 1,701 plants

CHAPTER 10 TEST

Use symbols to name each figure.

1.

$\overrightarrow{NX}$

2.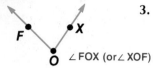

∠FOX (or∠XOF)

3.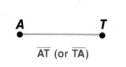

$\overline{AT}$ (or $\overline{TA}$)

4.

$\overleftrightarrow{JK}$ (or $\overleftrightarrow{KJ}$)

Use the figure at the right to complete the following.

5. Name two rays. $\overrightarrow{OB}$, $\overrightarrow{BO}$

6. Name three angles. ∠AOB (or ∠BOA), ∠OBA (or ∠ABO), ∠BAO (or ∠OAB)

7. Name a segment that represents the radius of the circle. $\overline{AO}$ or $\overline{OB}$

8. Name the sides of △AOB. $\overline{AO}$, $\overline{OB}$, $\overline{AB}$

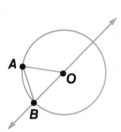

Classify each angle as acute, right, or obtuse.

9.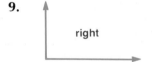

right

10.

obtuse

11.

acute

For each angle whose degree measure is given below, find the degree measure of the complement and supplement.

12. 40° 50°; 140°   13. 10° 80°; 170°   14. 65° 25°; 115°   15. 73° 17°; 107°   16. 88° 2°; 92°

Use the Pythagorean Theorem to find the length of the hypotenuse in each right triangle.

17.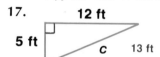

12 ft   5 ft   c   13 ft

18.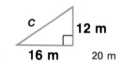

c   12 m   16 m   20 m

19.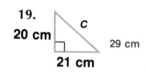

20 cm   c   29 cm   21 cm

Write the converse of the following statement. Then determine whether each statement (original and converse) is true.

20. If the sum of the measures of two angles is 180°, then the angles are supplementary. true; If two angles are supplementary, then the sum of the measures of the two angles is 180°. true

Determine whether the following is an example of deductive or inductive reasoning.

21. If you are a freshman, then you cannot attend the prom. Joni is a freshman. She is not allowed to attend the prom. deductive

Solve.

22. Kenji wants to save $20 for a gift. He begins by saving 20¢ the first week. Each week he saves twice as much as the week before. In how many weeks will he have saved at least $20? 7 weeks

CUMULATIVE REVIEW

Determine which size is the better buy.   Pages 48–49

1. cereal   12 oz – 78¢
              16 oz – 89¢

2. peanut butter   8 oz – $1.05
                      12 oz – $1.40

3. toothpaste   5 oz –   90¢
                   8 oz – $1.25

4. orange juice   16 oz –   75¢
                      48 oz – $2.60

**A coin is tossed. Predict the number of heads
for each of the following.**   Pages 122–123

5. 6 tosses **3**

6. 80 tosses **40**

7. 100 tosses **50**

8. 634 tosses **317**

Complete.   Pages 174–175

9. 3 min = ▨ sec **180**

10. 5 d = ▨ h **120**

11. 72 h = ▨ d **3**

12. 4 yr = ▨ d **1,460**

13. 208 wk = ▨ yr **4**

14. 18 d = ▨ wk ▨ d **2, 4**

15. 5 min = ▨ s **300**

16. 288 h = ▨ d **12**

17. 2 h 20 min = ▨ min **140**

Add or subtract.   Pages 174–175

18.   5 h 23 min 26 s
       + 8 h 20 min 45 s
       13 h 44 min 11 s

19.   9 min
       – 7 min 20 s
       1 min 40 s

20.   12 wk 4 d 13 h
       + 9 wk 2 d 15 h
       22 wk   4 h

Express each time as a 12-hour time, using A.M. or P.M.   Pages 186–187

21. 0243
       2:43 A.M.

22. 0845
       8:45 A.M.

23. 1050
       10:50 A.M.

24. 1325
       1:25 P.M.

25. 0020
       12:20 A.M.

26. 2310
       11:10 P.M.

27. 1715
       5:15 P.M.

28. 1200
       12:00 noon

29. 2400
       12:00 midnight

30. 0400
       4:00 A.M.

**Use the stopwatch shown on page 188 to name the time at each letter.
The hand of the watch is on its second revolution.**   Pages 188–189

31. A **16.3 s**

32. C **20 s**

33. E **22.6 s**

34. G **25.7 s**

35. D **20.8 s**

36. H **26.9 s**

Use symbols to name each figure.   Pages 205–206

37. $\overrightarrow{AB}$

38. $\overline{CD}$ or $\overline{DC}$

39. $\overleftrightarrow{HI}$ or $\overleftrightarrow{IH}$

40.   ∠JKL or ∠LKJ

41. $\overrightarrow{NM}$

42.   ∠FEG or ∠GEF

Answer the following.

43. Which is longer—38 meters or
38 kilometers? **38 kilometers**

44. Which is longer—65 feet or 65 yards?
65 yards

45. Which is shorter—20 inches or
2 feet? **20 inches**

46. Each corner of a stop sign represents
what kind of angle? **obtuse**

47. Gen Kim rented a car that had an odometer reading of 23,265.8
miles. When he returned the car, the odometer reading was
23,650.2 miles. How far did Gen drive? **384.4 miles**

Constructions

11-1 Congruent Figures

Objective: To identify congruent figures.

The roof rafters of a building may have the same size and shape.
Figures that have the same size and shape are **congruent.**

Examples

A. Two line segments with exactly
the same length are congruent.

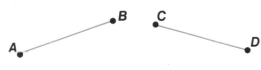

$\overline{AB}$ is congruent to $\overline{CD}$.
$$\overline{AB} \cong \overline{CD}$$

B. Two angles with exactly the same
measure are congruent.

$\angle EFG$ is congruent to $\angle HIJ$.
$$\angle EFG \cong \angle HIJ$$

To determine the congruency of figures an exact comparison must be made.

C. If the corresponding sides and angles of triangles
are congruent, the triangles are congruent.

$\triangle LMN$ is congruent to $\triangle PQR$.
$$\triangle LMN \cong \triangle PQR$$

Point out that vertices of congruent triangles are listed in order
of correspondence.

*Matching marks
show congruent
sides and angles.*

Basic: 1–7; Average: 1–7; Enriched: 1–7 .

Exercises

State whether each pair of figures is congruent.

1.

not congruent

2.

congruent

3.

not congruent

4.

congruent

5.

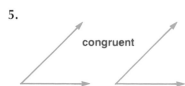

congruent

6.

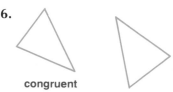

congruent

Use the figure at the right to complete the following.

7. How many triangles are shown? How many
sets of congruent triangles are shown? **27, 4**

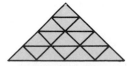

Teacher Resource Book, Page 245

11-2 *Constructing Congruent Segments and Circles*

Objective: To construct a line segment congruent to a given line segment. To construct a circle with a given radius.

Quan Sing is a drafter. She prepares drawings that show the exact dimensions and specifications of a building. These detailed drawings are taken from rough sketches made by an architect. Quan uses compasses, protractors, and other drafting tools to prepare her drawings.

After graduating from high school, Quan attended a technical school for 2 years. Other job qualifications included the ability to draw three-dimensional objects freehand, attention to detail, and neat work.

Quan must construct a line segment congruent to a given line segment. **Constructions** are made using only a compass and straightedge.

Examples

A. Construct a line segment congruent to a given line segment.

Given:

1. Draw a line segment longer than $\overline{AB}$. Choose some point C.

   After step 3, have students fold their paper so that $\overline{AB}$ and $\overline{CD}$ match end-to-end. Do they have the same length? yes

2. Open your compass to the length of $\overline{AB}$.

3. Place the compass point at C. Draw an arc to intersect the segment at point D, $\overline{AB} \cong \overline{CD}$.

B. Construct a circle with a given radius.

Given:

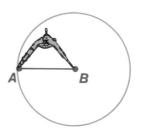

1. Open the compass to match $\overline{AB}$.

2. Use the same compass setting and draw a circle.

Exercises

Trace each line segment shown below. Construct a line segment congruent to each segment you traced. See students' work.

1.

2.

3.

4.

5.

6.

Trace each line segment shown below. Construct a circle with a radius the length of each segment. See students' work.

7.

8.

9.

10.

11.

12.

Complete.

13. Tess said that $\overline{MN}$ is congruent to $\overline{PQ}$ and $\overline{PQ}$ is congruent to $\overline{RS}$. If this is true, is $\overline{MN}$ congruent to $\overline{RS}$? **yes**

14. With the ruler Beth has, she cannot determine which line segment is longer. Trace each line segment. Use a compass to determine which segment is longer. $\overline{EF}$

This feature presents useful ways of solving mathematical problems on a calculator.

Calculator

Six numbers are shown below. Pick any two of them. Then divide the numbers in any order on a calculator.

2   4   5   20   25   80

Enter: 4 ÷ 20 =

Display: 4. 4. 20. 0.2

Find the number on the board. Then, pick other pairs of numbers to divide. Include your first guess to complete a vertical, horizontal, or diagonal line on the board.

Can you complete a line in 4 more guesses?
Answers may vary.

2	12.5	0.8	6.25	0.5
0.3125	0.2	40	0.16	20
0.05	0.4		2.5	1.25
16	0.25	3.2	0.0625	0.1
10	0.08	5	0.025	4

11-3 Constructing Congruent Angles

Objective: To construct an angle congruent to a given angle.

A ramp makes a certain angle with the floor. The angle is the same for all ramps in this building. You can use a compass and straightedge to construct congruent angles.

Example

Construct an angle congruent to a given angle.

Given:

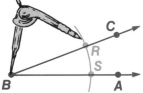

1. Place the compass point at *B* and draw an arc as shown in blue. Label points *R* and *S*.

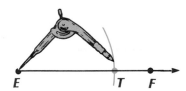

2. Draw $\overrightarrow{EF}$. With the same compass setting, draw an arc as shown in blue. Label the intersection *T*.

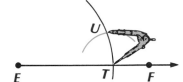

3. Open the compass to the length of $\overline{RS}$. Then with the compass point at *T*, draw an arc as shown. Label the intersection *U*.

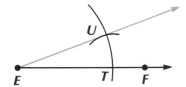

4. With a straightedge, draw $\overrightarrow{EU}$.

$\angle UEF \cong \angle ABC$

Use a protractor to check that ∠ABC and ∠UEF have the same measure.

Suppose an angle is traced twice and cut out. These angles can be arranged as shown below.

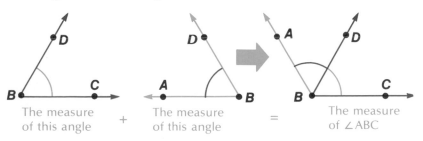

| The measure of this angle | + | The measure of this angle | = | The measure of ∠ABC |

Given the angles at the left, the angle at the right can be constructed. Can you explain how? **Construct an angle congruent to one of the angles. Then, using a common ray, construct an angle congruent to the second angle.**

Exercises

Trace each angle shown below. Construct an angle congruent to each angle you traced.
See students' work.

1. 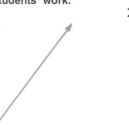 **2.** 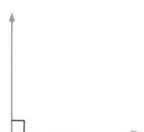  **3.**  **4.**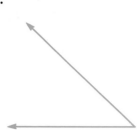

Draw an example of each angle. Construct an angle congruent to each angle you drew.
See students' work.

5. acute angle   **6.** right angle   **7.** obtuse angle

Trace each angle. Construct an angle whose measure is described below. See students' work.

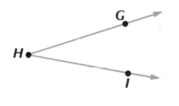

8. twice the measure of ∠GHI   **9.** twice the measure of ∠JKL

10. the measure of ∠GHI plus the measure of ∠MNO

11. the measure of ∠MNO plus the measure of ∠JKL

Study the diagram shown below. Then construct an angle having the measures described below. Refer to the angles used in exercises 8-11. See students' work.

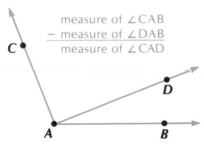

measure of ∠CAB
− measure of ∠DAB
measure of ∠CAD

12. the measure of ∠JKL minus the measure of ∠GHI

13. the measure of ∠MNO minus the measure of ∠JKL

14. the measure of ∠GHI plus the measure of ∠JKL.

Complete.

15. Using your paper, cut two congruent triangles, △ABC and △XYZ, so that ∠A ≅ ∠X, ∠B ≅ ∠Y, and ∠C ≅ ∠Z.
See students' work.

16. Trace the figure at the right. Then construct an angle that is congruent to ∠FGC.
See students' work.

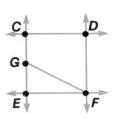

11-4 Bisecting Line Segments and Angles

Objective: To construct the bisector of a given line segment and a given angle.

In order to cut a board in half, a carpenter saws through the middle of the board. The resulting pieces are congruent.

Similarly, you can separate line segments and angles into two congruent parts. To **bisect** means to separate into two congruent parts.

Examples

A. Bisect a given line segment.

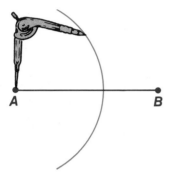

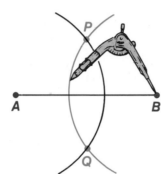

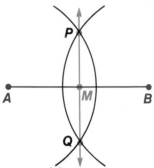

1. Open the compass to more than half the length of $\overline{AB}$. With compass point at A, draw an arc as shown in blue.

2. Use the same compass setting. With compass point at B, draw another arc. Label the intersection points P and Q.

3. Draw $\overleftrightarrow{PQ}$. Point M is the intersection of $\overleftrightarrow{PQ}$ and $\overline{AB}$ and bisects $\overline{AB}$. Point M is called the **midpoint** of $\overline{AB}$.
   $$\overline{AM} \cong \overline{MB}$$

After step 3, have students fold their paper, so that B aligns with A. Are $\overline{AM}$ and $\overline{MB}$ the same length? yes

B. Bisect a given angle.

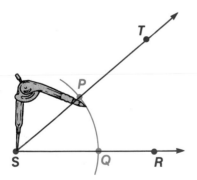

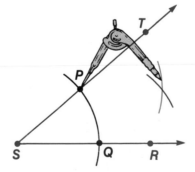

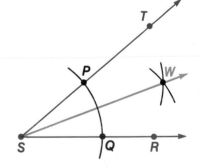

1. With compass point at S, draw an arc as shown above in blue. Label the intersection points P and Q.

2. With a convenient compass setting, place the compass point at P and draw an arc as shown in blue. Then, place the compass point at Q and draw an arc as shown in red.

3. Label intersection point W. Draw $\overrightarrow{SW}$. Ray SW bisects $\angle RST$. Ray SW is called the **bisector** of $\angle RST$.
   $$\angle TSW \cong \angle RSW$$

After step 3, have students fold their paper so that $\overrightarrow{ST}$ and $\overrightarrow{SR}$ align. Are $\angle TSW$ and $\angle WSR$ the same size? yes

238 *Constructions*

Exercises

Trace each line segment shown below. Bisect each line segment you traced. See students' work.

1.    2.    3.

4. 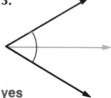   5. 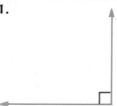   6.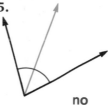

Trace each line segment shown below. Then, complete the following. See students' work.

7. Construct a segment whose length is half the length of $\overline{PQ}$.

8. Construct a segment whose length is equal to the length of $\overline{RS}$ plus half the length of $\overline{EF}$.

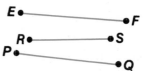

Trace each angle shown below. Bisect each angle you traced. See students' work.

9.   10.   11.   12.

Tell whether the ray shown in blue is the angle bisector. To check your answer, trace the angle and the ray. Fold your paper so that the sides of the angles line up.

13.   14.   15.   16.

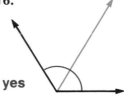

yes   no   no   yes

This feature promotes students' mental abilities in computation and reasonableness.

Mental Math

You can use compatible numbers to estimate a quotient. Round the divisor and dividend to numbers that are easy to divide.

$689 \div 12 \rightarrow 700 \div 10 = 70$ | $3,412 \div 42 \rightarrow 3,600 \div 40 = 90$

Find each quotient using the strategy shown above.

1. $740 \div 84$ 9   2. $523 \div 91$ 6   3. $9,511 \div 51$ 200

4. $2,448 \div 47$ 50   5. $29,000 \div 362$ 100   6. $881,397 \div 286$ 3,000

PRACTICE

Estimate. Answers may vary. Typical answers are given.

1. 673
    + 79
    750

2. 752
    − 69
    680

3. 392
    × 51
    20,000

4. $21\overline{)141}$ ⁷ 7

5. $28\overline{)242}$ ⁸ 8

Add, subtract, multiply, or divide.

6. 675
    + 27
    702

7. 753
    − 54
    699

8. 461
    + 439
    900

9. 7,085
    − 96
    6,989

10. 5,406
    + 651
    6,057

11. 2,361
    − 840
    1,521

12. 8,612
    − 4,221
    4,391

13. 9,400
    − 2,615
    6,785

14. 11,423
    − 6,594
    4,829

15. 25,493
    − 18,659
    6,834

16. 30
    × 65
    1,950

17. 205
    × 20
    4,100

18. 112
    × 100
    11,200

19. 115
    × 206
    23,690

20. 387
    × 296
    114,552

21. $13\overline{)195}$ 15

22. $37\overline{)555}$ 15

23. $65\overline{)1,755}$ 27

24. $50\overline{)261}$ 5.22

25. $18\overline{)297}$ 16.5

Add, subtract, multiply, or divide. Write each answer in simplest form.

26. $\frac{2}{5} + \frac{3}{4}$ $1\frac{3}{20}$

27. $\frac{9}{10} - \frac{3}{4}$ $\frac{3}{20}$

28. $\frac{5}{6} \times \frac{2}{5}$ $\frac{1}{3}$

29. $13 \div \frac{1}{4}$ 52

30. $2\frac{2}{3} + 1\frac{7}{15}$ $4\frac{2}{15}$

31. $2\frac{1}{4} - \frac{5}{6}$ $1\frac{5}{12}$

32. $1\frac{1}{5} \div \frac{1}{2}$ $2\frac{2}{5}$

33. $\frac{1}{2} + \frac{1}{3} + \frac{1}{4}$ $1\frac{1}{12}$

34. $2\frac{1}{4} \times 1\frac{3}{4}$ $3\frac{15}{16}$

35. $1\frac{5}{6} \div \frac{2}{3}$ $2\frac{3}{4}$

36. $15\frac{3}{8} - 7\frac{5}{6}$ $7\frac{13}{24}$

37. $3\frac{3}{5} \div 2\frac{7}{10}$ $1\frac{1}{3}$

Complete.

38. 6.5 m = ▨ cm 650

39. 10 km = ▨ m 10,000

40. 6.9 L = ▨ mL 6,900

41. 12 qt = ▨ gal 3

42. 7,420 mg = ▨ g 7.42

43. 2 lb = ▨ oz 32

44. 727 mL = ▨ L 0.727

45. 257 mm = ▨ cm 25.7

46. 468 g = ▨ kg 0.468

47. 27 g = ▨ mg 27,000

48. 8 pt = ▨ qt 4

49. 53 m = ▨ mm 53,000

50. 12 c = ▨ pt 6

51. 2,749 kL = ▨ L 2,749,000

52. 6,000 lb = ▨ ton 3

Add or subtract.

53.   2 h 40 min
    + 3 h 20 min
     6 h

54.   3 h 30 min
    − 1 h 45 min
     1 h 45 min

55.   2 d 17 h
    + 4 d 7 h
     7 d

Complete.

56. 2 wk = ▨ d 14

57. 4 d 3 h = ▨ h 99

58. 3 h = ▨ min 180

59. 5,400 s = ▨ min 90

60. 72 h = ▨ d 3

61. 3 h = ▨ s 10,800

Change each percent to a decimal.

62. 32% 0.32   **63.** 30.3% 0.303   **64.** 44% 0.44   **65.** 8.4% 0.084   **66.** 126% 1.26

67. 23.6% 0.236   **68.** 0.6% 0.006   **69.** 69.2% 0.692   **70.** 179% 1.79   **71.** 0.72% 0.0072

Change each decimal to a percent.

72. 0.36 36%   **73.** 0.55 55%   **74.** 0.64 64%   **75.** 0.03 3%   **76.** 0.09 9%

77. 0.1 10%   **78.** 0.415 41.5%   **79.** 0.327 32.7%   **80.** 1.23 123%   **81.** 0.002 0.2%

Solve using the proportion $\frac{P}{B} = \frac{r}{100}$.

82. 8 is __?__ % of 32 25   **83.** 9 is 20% of __?__ 45   **84.** 11 is __?__% of 22 50

85. 50% of __?__ is 6 12   **86.** 10% of 110 is __?__ 11   **87.** 20% of 30 is __?__ 6

88. __?__ is 50% of 142 71   **89.** 20 is 25% of __?__ 80   **90.** __?__ is 25% of 56 14

91. 140 is __?__% of 80 175   **92.** 98.1 is __?__% of 90 109   **93.** 80.5 is __?__% of 25 322

94. 5.6 is __?__% of 32 17.5   **95.** 20.4 is __?__% of 150 13.6   **96.** 4.24 is __?__% of 16 26.5

Use symbols to name each figure.

97.  $\overrightarrow{BA}$ **98.**  $\overline{CD}$ **99.**  ∠EFG   **100.**  $\overleftrightarrow{HK}$

101. Name the three sides and three angles of the triangle shown at the right.
$\overline{AB}$, $\overline{BC}$, $\overline{CA}$; ∠A, ∠B, ∠C

Use a protractor to measure each angle. Then, classify each angle as acute, right, or obtuse.

102.   **103.**   **104.**

22°, acute   180°, straight   100°, obtuse

Refer to the figure at the right to find the measure of each angle.

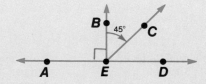

105. ∠AEB 90°   **106.** ∠CED 45°

107. ∠DEB 90°   **108.** ∠AEC 135°

Solve.

109. Construct an angle that has a degree measure of 45. See students' work.

11-5 Constructing Perpendicular Lines

Objective: To construct a line perpendicular to a given line.

A door will not close properly unless the door frame is **perpendicular** to the floor. The door frame and the floor must meet at right angles.

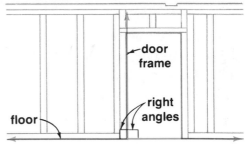

Examples

A. Construct a line perpendicular to a given line at a given point on the line.

Given:

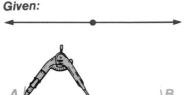

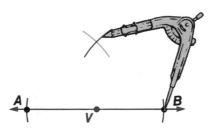

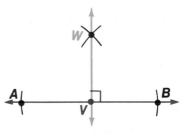

1. With a convenient compass setting, place the compass point at *V*. Draw two arcs that intersect the line. Label the points of intersection *A* and *B*.

2. Use a compass setting of more than half the length of $\overline{AB}$. Place the compass point at *A* and draw an arc as shown in blue. Then place the compass point at *B* and draw an arc that intersects the previous arc.

3. Label the intersection point *W*. Draw $\overleftrightarrow{WV}$. Line $\overleftrightarrow{WV}$ is perpendicular to $\overleftrightarrow{AB}$.
$$\overleftrightarrow{WV} \perp \overleftrightarrow{AB}$$

After step 3, have students fold their paper along $\overrightarrow{VW}$ so that $\overrightarrow{VA}$ matches $\overrightarrow{VB}$. Notice that $\angle WVA \cong \angle WVB$. They are both right angles.

B. Through a point not on a line, construct a line perpendicular to a given line.
Given: •*M*

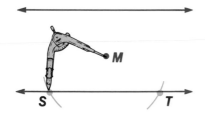

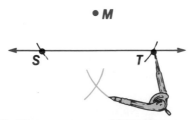

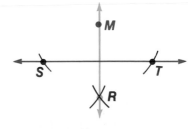

1. Open the compass to the distance from *S* to *M*. Draw two arcs that intersect the line. Label the points of intersection *S* and *T*.

2. Use a compass setting of more than half the length of $\overline{ST}$. Place the compass point at *S* and draw an arc as shown in blue. Then place the compass point at *T* and draw an arc that intersects the previous arc.

3. Label the intersection point *R*. Draw $\overleftrightarrow{MR}$. Line $\overleftrightarrow{MR}$ is perpendicular to $\overleftrightarrow{ST}$ and passes through point *M*.
$$\overleftrightarrow{MR} \perp \overleftrightarrow{ST}$$

After step 3, have students fold their paper to show that the angles formed are right angles.

A line perpendicular to a line segment that also bisects the line segment is called a **perpendicular bisector.**

The procedure used on page 238 to bisect a line segment is also used to construct the perpendicular bisector of a line segment.

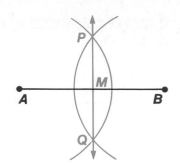

$\overline{PQ}$ is called the perpendicular bisector of $\overline{AB}$.

Basic: 1–13; Average: 1–15; Enriched: 1–11 odd, 12–15

Exercises

Trace each line and point. Construct a line perpendicular to the line you traced at the given point. **See students' work.**

1.

A

2.

B

3.

C

4.

D

Trace each line and point. Construct a line perpendicular to the line you traced through the point not on the line. **See students' work.**

5.

•*V*

6.

•*S*

7.

N•

Trace each line segment. Construct the perpendicular bisector of the line segment you traced. **See students' work.**

8.

9.

10.

11.

Complete. **For answers to exercises 14–15, see Teacher Guide.**

12. Draw $\overline{AB}$ and construct its bisector. Then fold your paper so that point B matches point A. What kind of angles were formed by the bisector? **right angles**

13. Explain why the line you constructed in exercise 12 is called the perpendicular bisector of $\overline{AB}$. **It forms two right angles and separates the line into two congruent parts.**

14. Construct a square with $\overline{EF}$ as one of its sides.

E   *F*

15. Construct a right triangle with $\overline{MN}$ as one of its legs.

M   *N*

11-6 Constructing Parallel Lines

Objective: To construct a line parallel to a given line through a point not on the line.

Some of the beams used in a building suggest parts of lines that do not intersect. Remember, lines in the same plane that do not intersect are **parallel**.

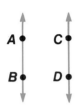

Line *AB* and line *CD*, shown at the left, are parallel.

$$\overleftrightarrow{AB} \parallel \overleftrightarrow{CD}$$

In a plane a **transversal** is a line that intersects two or more lines at different points. In the figure below, a transversal, shown in blue, intersects two parallel lines.

$$\overleftrightarrow{MN} \parallel \overleftrightarrow{OP}$$

Angles *A* and *E* are **corresponding angles.** When a transversal intersects parallel lines, corresponding angles are congruent; that is, $\angle A \cong \angle E$. Another pair of corresponding angles is $\angle C$ and $\angle G$. Name two other pairs.
$\angle B$ and $\angle F$, $\angle D$ and $\angle H$

The fact that corresponding angles are congruent justifies the following construction.

Example

Construct a line parallel to a given line through a point not on the line.

Given:

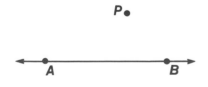

1. Draw $\overleftrightarrow{AP}$ as shown above in blue.

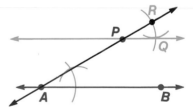

2. With *P* as the vertex, construct an angle congruent to $\angle BAP$. See page 238. Draw $\overleftrightarrow{PQ}$.
$$\overleftrightarrow{PQ} \parallel \overleftrightarrow{AB}$$

In step 3, $\angle BAP$ and $\angle RPQ$ are corresponding angles. Does this fact ensure that $\overleftrightarrow{PQ} \parallel \overleftrightarrow{AB}$? **yes**

Exercises

Use the figure at the right to name the corresponding angle for each of the following angles.

1. ∠1 ≅ ∠▦ **5**

2. ∠6 ≅ ∠▦ **2**

3. ∠▦ ≅ ∠3 **7**

4. ∠8 ≅ ∠▦ **4**

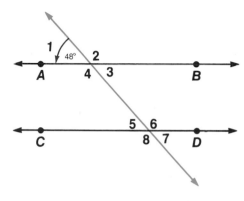

Use the figure at the left to find the measure of each angle. $\overleftrightarrow{AB} \parallel \overleftrightarrow{CD}$

5. ∠1 **48°**   **6.** ∠3 **48°**   **7.** ∠5 **48°**   **8.** ∠6 **132°**

9. ∠4 **132°**   **10.** ∠8 **132°**   **11.** ∠2 **132°**   **12.** ∠7 **48°**

Use the figure at the left to complete the following.

13. Name all the angles that have the same measure as ∠1. **∠3, ∠5, ∠7**

14. Name all the angles that have the same measure as ∠8. **∠2, ∠4, ∠6**

Trace each line and point shown below. Construct a line parallel to the line you traced through the point not on the line. **See students' work.**

15.   Z •

16.

• F

Construct and label a figure for each description below. **For answers to exercises 17–18, see Teacher Guide.**

17. $\overleftrightarrow{AB} \parallel \overleftrightarrow{JK}$ and both lines are intersected by $\overleftrightarrow{LM}$.

18. $\overleftrightarrow{CD}$ and $\overleftrightarrow{GH}$ are parallel lines. $\overleftrightarrow{XY}$ is perpendicular to both $\overleftrightarrow{CD}$ and $\overleftrightarrow{GH}$.

This feature presents general topics of mathematics.

Math Break

The screwdriver has **line symmetry**. That is, a line can be drawn so that the shape on one side of the line matches the shape on the other. The bolt has **point symmetry**. As you rotate the bolt about the point shown, there are six matching positions. Does this bolt also have line symmetry? **yes**

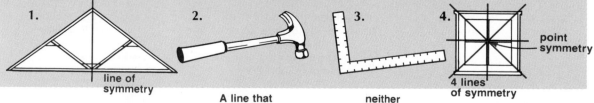

For each object, tell whether there is line symmetry, point symmetry, or neither.

1. line of symmetry

2. A line that would go through the claw.

3. neither

4. point symmetry — 4 lines of symmetry

11-7 Constructing Triangles

Objective: To construct a triangle congruent to a given triangle using the SSS, SAS, or ASA rule.

Max Krieger is a builder. He must follow blueprints that show exact dimensions of a project.

Triangles are used in structures because they provide support. Some examples are shown below.

Two triangles are congruent if the corresponding sides of the triangles are congruent. This is called the **SSS** (side-side-side) rule.

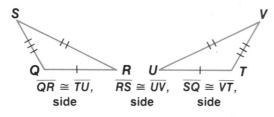

$\overline{QR} \cong \overline{TU}$, $\overline{RS} \cong \overline{UV}$, $\overline{SQ} \cong \overline{VT}$,
    side   side   side

In the figures at the left $\triangle QRS \cong \triangle TUV$ by the SSS rule.

Example

A. Construct a triangle congruent to a given triangle using the SSS rule.

Given:

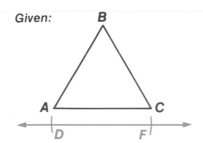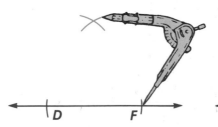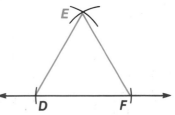

1. Draw a line. Construct a line segment congruent to $\overline{AC}$. Label it $\overline{DF}$. *(side)*

2. With compass open to the length of $\overline{AB}$, draw an arc from point *D*. With compass open to the length of $\overline{BC}$, draw an arc from point *F*.

3. Label the intersection of the arcs *E*. Draw $\overline{DE}$ and $\overline{EF}$. *(side, side)*
$\triangle DEF \cong \triangle ABC$

There are rules involving angles as well as sides that can be used to show that two triangles are congruent.

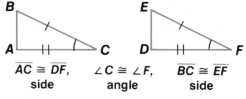

$\overline{AC} \cong \overline{DF}$, $\angle C \cong \angle F$, $\overline{BC} \cong \overline{EF}$
    side   angle   side

Two triangles are congruent if two sides and the included angle of one triangle are congruent to the corresponding parts of the other triangle. This is called the **SAS** (side-angle-side) rule.

$$\triangle ABC \cong \triangle DEF$$

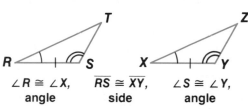

$\angle R \cong \angle X$, $\overline{RS} \cong \overline{XY}$, $\angle S \cong \angle Y$,
    angle   side   angle

Two triangles are congruent if two angles and the included side of one triangle are congruent to the corresponding parts of the other triangle. This is called the **ASA** (angle-side-angle) rule.

$$\triangle RST \cong \triangle XYZ$$

Examples

B. Construct a triangle congruent to a given triangle using the SAS rule.

Given:

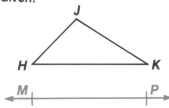

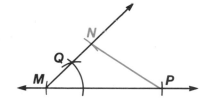

1. Draw a line. Construct a line segment congruent to $\overline{HK}$. Label it $\overline{MP}$. *(side)*

2. Construct an angle at *M* that is congruent to $\angle H$. *(angle)*

3. With compass open to the length of $\overline{HJ}$, draw an arc from point *M* that intersects $\overrightarrow{MQ}$. Label the intersection *N*. *(side)* Draw $\overline{NP}$.
       $\triangle MNP \cong \triangle HJK$

C. Construct a triangle congruent to a given triangle using the ASA rule.

Given:

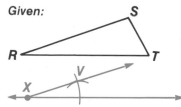

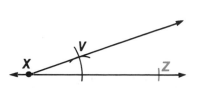

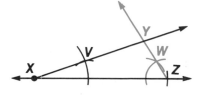

1. Draw a line. Label point *X*. Construct an angle at *X* that is congruent to $\angle R$. *(angle)*

2. Construct a line segment congruent to $\overline{RT}$ using *X* as one endpoint. Label it $\overline{XZ}$. *(side)*

3. Construct an angle at *Z* that is congruent to $\angle T$. *(angle)* Label the intersection of the rays *Y*.
       $\triangle XYZ \cong \triangle RST$

Exercises

Use the congruent triangles at the right
to complete the following.

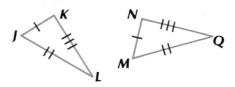

1. $\overline{JK} \cong$ ▨ $\overline{MN}$
2. $\overline{MQ} \cong$ ▨ $\overline{JL}$
3. $\overline{KL} \cong$ ▨ $\overline{NQ}$
4. $\triangle JKL \cong \triangle$ ▨ MNQ

Are the following pairs of triangles congruent by SSS, SAS, or ASA?

5.

6.

7.

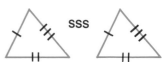

Trace each triangle. Construct a triangle congruent to the
triangle you traced. Use the SSS rule. **See students' work.**

8.

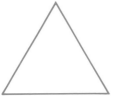

9.

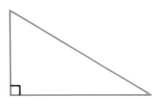

10.

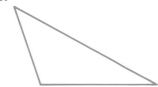

Trace each triangle. Construct a triangle congruent to the
triangle you traced. Use the SAS rule. **See students' work.**

11.

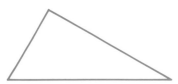

12.

13.

Trace each triangle. Construct a triangle congruent to the
triangle you traced. Use the ASA rule. **See students' work.**

14.

15.

16.

Trace each line segment. Construct a triangle with each side
congruent to the segment you traced. **See students' work. Each
triangle is equilateral.**

17.

18.

19.

Trace each set of line segments shown below. Construct a triangle with sides congruent to the segments you traced. See students' work.

20.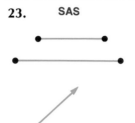

21.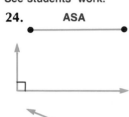

22.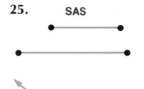

Trace each set of line segments and angles. Construct a triangle with sides and angles congruent to those you traced. Use either the SAS rule or the ASA rule. See students' work.

23. SAS

24. ASA

25. SAS

26. ASA

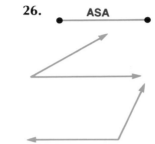

Refer to the segments at the right to complete the following.

27. Attempt to construct a triangle with sides congruent to the given segments. What happens? **No triangle is possible.**

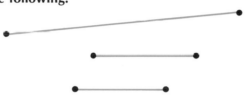

28. State a rule that describes the lengths of the segments in a triangle.
The length of the longest side must be less than the sum of the lengths of the shorter sides.

This feature provides general topics about the uses of a computer.

Computer

There are certain words in BASIC that can be used to give a computer instructions or commands. The computer will carry out the commands without using a program. When a computer is used this way it is said to be in **calculator mode**. In calculator mode, the computer prints answers to problems.

```
PRINT 9 * 8        PRINT (18 + 16) - 25
72                 9
```
The parentheses tell the computer which operation to do first.

Write the output for each PRINT statement.

1. PRINT 12 * 24 288
2. PRINT 326 - 149 177
3. PRINT 348/12 29
4. PRINT (56 + 18) * 16 1,184
5. PRINT (48/16) * 21 63
6. PRINT 378 + (2,016/36) 434
7. PRINT 1,895 - (631 + 768) 496

CHAPTER 11 REVIEW

Vocabulary/Concepts

Choose the word or phrase from the list at the right to complete each sentence.

1. Figures that have the same size and shape are ___?___. **congruent**

2. To ___?___ is to separate into two congruent parts. **bisect**

3. Two lines that intersect to form right angles are ___?___. **perpendicular**

4. Lines in the same plane that do not intersect are ___?___. **parallel**

5. In a plane, a ___?___ is a line that intersects two or more lines at different points. **transversal**

6. Two triangles are congruent if two corresponding sides and the included angle are congruent. This is called the ___?___ rule. **SAS**

ASA
acute
bisect
bisector
congruent
corresponding angles
midpoint
parallel
perpendicular
protractor
SAS
transversal

Exercises

State whether each pair of figures is congruent or not congruent.   Page 233

7.   **congruent**

8.   **not congruent**

9.

congruent

Trace each line segment. Construct a circle with each segment as a radius.   Pages 234–235
See students' work.

10.   11.   12.   13.

Trace each angle. Construct an angle congruent to each angle you traced.
Pages 236–237 See students' work.

14.   15.   16.   17.

Trace each line segment. Bisect each segment you traced.   Pages 238–239 See students' work.

   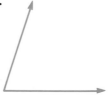

18.   19.   20.

Trace each angle. Bisect each angle you traced.   Pages 238–239 See students' work.

21.

22.

23.

Trace each line and point. Construct a line perpendicular to the line you traced
at the given point.   Pages 242–243 See students' work.

24.

G

25.

H

Use the figure at the right to find the measure of
each angle. $\overleftrightarrow{XY} \parallel \overleftrightarrow{FG}$ Pages 244–245

26. ∠3 **125°**   27. ∠6 **55°**   28. ∠5 **125°**   29. ∠4 **55°**

30. ∠2 **55°**   31. ∠8 **55°**   32. ∠1 **125°**   33. ∠7 **125°**

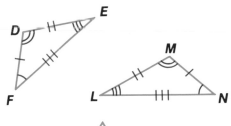

Trace each line and point. Construct a line parallel to the line you
traced through the point not on the line.   Pages 244–245 See students' work.

34.   • **D**

35.
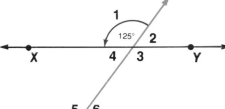

E •

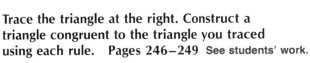

Use the congruent triangles at the right
to complete the following.   Pages 246–249

36. $\overline{DF} \cong$ ▨ $\overline{MN}$ 37. $\overline{LM} \cong$ ▨ $\overline{ED}$

38. ∠ $DEF \cong$ ▨ ∠MLN 39. ∠$LMN \cong$ ▨ ∠EDF

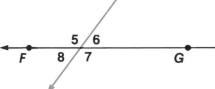

Trace the triangle at the right. Construct a
triangle congruent to the triangle you traced
using each rule.   Pages 246–249 See students' work.

40. SSS   41. SAS   42. ASA

CHAPTER 11 TEST

See students' work.

Trace each figure. Construct a figure congruent to the figure you traced.

1.

2.

Trace each figure. Then, bisect each line segment or angle you traced.

3.

4.

Trace each line and point. Construct a line perpendicular to the line you traced at the given point.

5.
G

6.
H

Trace each line segment. Construct the perpendicular bisector of the line segment you traced.

7.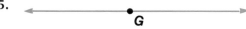

8.

Trace each line and point. Construct a line parallel to the line you traced through the point not on the line.

9. J •

10.

• K

Use the congruent triangles at the right to complete the following.

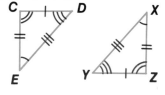

11. $\overline{XZ} \cong$ ▨ $\overline{EC}$

12. $\angle CED \cong$ ▨ $\angle ZXY$

13. $\angle XYZ \cong$ ▨ $\angle EDC$

14. $\overline{DE} \cong$ ▨ $\overline{YX}$

Trace the triangle at the right. Construct a triangle congruent to the triangle you traced using each rule. See students' work.

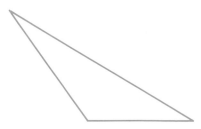

15. SSS   16. SAS   17. ASA

This page provides extra practice of the skills and applications presented thus far in the text.

CUMULATIVE REVIEW

Growth of the Poplar Tree

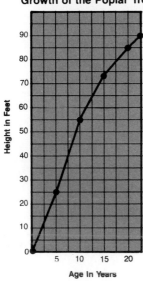

Use the graph at the left to answer the following questions. Pages 77–79

1. What is the greatest age that can be shown on this graph? **22.5 years**

2. What is the greatest height that can be shown on this graph? **100 feet**

3. During which 5-year period does the height increase the most? **5–10 years**

4. During which 5-year period does the height increase the least? **15–20 years**

5. About how tall is the Poplar after 15 years? **73 feet**

6. About how many years does it take the Poplar to reach a height of 10 feet? **2 years**

Terri Myers earns $275 each week. Use the graph on page 80 to find how much she budgets for each item. Pages 80–81

7. Lunches **$55.00**

8. Recreation **$68.75**

9. Clothing **$55.00**

10. Savings **$41.25**

For each angle whose measure is given below, find the measure of the complement and supplement. Pages 208–209

11. 48° **42°, 132°**   **12.** 67° **23°, 113°**   **13.** 32° **58°, 148°**   **14.** 53° **37°, 127°**   **15.** 17° **73°, 163°**

16. 61° **29°, 119°**   **17.** 24° **66°, 156°**   **18.** 87° **3°, 93°**   **19.** 75° **15°, 105°**   **20.** 8° **82°, 172°**

Use the figure at the right to complete the following. Pages 210–211

21. Name two pairs of perpendicular lines. $\overleftrightarrow{EA}$, $\overleftrightarrow{BI}$; $\overleftrightarrow{JH}$, $\overleftrightarrow{BI}$

22. Find the measures of ∠CDF and ∠EDF. How are these angles related? **120°, 60°; supplementary**

23. Are $\overleftrightarrow{EA}$ and $\overleftrightarrow{FH}$ parallel? Explain why.

24. Use a protractor to measure ∠KFJ and ∠KFI. How are these angles related? **60°, 120°; supplementary**

23. Yes. Both lines are perpendicular to the same line. Therefore, they are parallel.

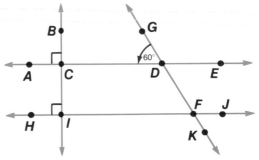

Trace each line segment. Construct a circle with each segment as a radius. Pages 234–235 See students' work.

25.   **26.**   **27.**   **28.**

Polygons and Circles

12-1 Polygons

Objective: To determine if a given figure is a polygon.

Some highway signs are shaped like polygons. A **polygon** is a
closed plane figure formed by line segments called **sides**.
The sides meet but do not cross. The point where two sides
meet is called a **vertex**.

The figures below are polygons.

*They are made up of line
segments that meet, but
do not cross.*

The figures below are *not* polygons.

open　　　**curves**　　　**crossed
lines**

Basic: 1–10; Average: 1–10; Enriched: 1–10

Exercises

Tell whether each figure is a polygon. Write yes or no.

1.   2.   3.   4.    5.

1. yes
2. no
3. yes
4. no
5. yes

Study the chart. Then answer each question.

6. What is true about the number
   of sides and the number of
   angles in a given polygon?
   they are the same

7. Are all triangles congruent? **no**

8. Are all quadrilaterals congruent? **no**

9. Are all pentagons congruent? **no**

10. Can a polygon have more than
    twelve sides? **yes**

Sides	Angles	Polygon
3	3	triangle
4	4	quadrilateral
5	5	pentagon
6	6	hexagon
7	7	heptagon
8	8	octagon
9	9	nonagon
10	10	decagon
12	12	dodecagon

Teacher Resource Book, Page 265

12-2 *Quadrilaterals*

Objective: To classify quadrilaterals.

Each highway sign shown here is a four-sided polygon.

Any four-sided polygon is a **quadrilateral.**

Quadrilaterals are classified according to their angles and sides.

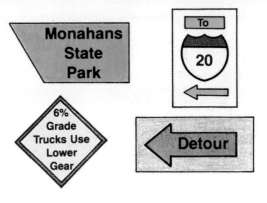

Name of Quadrilateral	Description	Illustration
trapezoid	exactly one pair of parallel sides	
parallelogram	two pairs of parallel sides	
rhombus	{ a parallelogram with four congruent sides	
rectangle	{ a parallelogram with four congruent angles	
square	{ a parallelogram with four congruent sides and four congruent angles	

Basic: 2–36 even; Average: 1–37; Enriched: 1–37 odd

Exercises

Use the lettered quadrilaterals to answer each question.

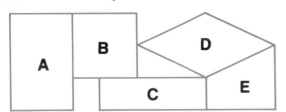

1. Which appear to be trapezoids? **E**
2. Which appear to be parallelograms? **A, B, C, D**
3. Which appear to be rectangles? **A, B, C**
4. Which appear to be rhombuses? **B, D**
5. Which appear to be squares? **B**

Complete the sentence with each word. Then, tell whether the sentence is true or false.

A square is also a ___?___ .

6. rectangle **true**   7. trapezoid **false**   8. rhombus **true**   9. polygon **true**

10. hexagon **false**   11. quadrilateral **true**   12. triangle **false**   13. parallelogram **true**

Classify each lettered quadrilateral as a trapezoid, parallelogram, rectangle, rhombus, or square. Use the word that best describes what each quadrilateral appears to be.

14. F trapezoid
15. G rhombus
16. H parallelogram
17. I parallelogram
18. J trapezoid
19. K rectangle
20. L square
21. M square
22. N rectangle
23. O trapezoid
24. P trapezoid
25. Q trapezoid

Is it possible to do the following? Write YES or NO.

26. Draw a square that is not a rhombus?
no
27. Draw a square that is not a rectangle?
no

28. Draw a rhombus that is neither a square nor a rectangle? **yes**
29. Draw a rectangle that is not a parallelogram? **no**

30. Draw a parallelogram that is not a rectangle? **yes**
31. Draw a parallelogram that is not a square? **yes**

32. Draw a parallelogram that is not a rhombus? **yes**
33. Draw a parallelogram that is not a quadrilateral? **no**

34. Draw a parallelogram that is not a trapezoid? **yes**
35. Draw a trapezoid that is not a quadrilateral? **no**

36. Draw a quadrilateral that is not a rectangle? **yes**
37. Draw a quadrilateral that is not a parallelogram? **yes**

▲ This feature presents general topics of mathematics.

Math Break

Use the following steps to construct a square.

- Draw a circle with diameter $\overline{AB}$.

- Construct the perpendicular bisector of $\overline{AB}$. Label the points where the bisector intersects the circle C and D.

- Draw four chords as shown in blue. Quadrilateral *ACBD* is a square.

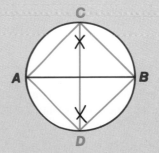

1. Construct a regular octagon by constructing the perpendicular bisector of each of the sides of a square.
See Teacher Guide.

2. Explain how you could construct a right triangle in a circle.
Construct a square in a circle. Any angle of the square is a right angle. Draw a diameter between a pair of opposite vertices.

12-3　Similar Figures

Objective: To use proportions to find missing lengths in similar figures.

Jean Bolen is an engineering technician. She assists engineers and scientists by setting up equipment, preparing experiments, and designing models. She also advises customers of manufacturers on the installation and operation of technical equipment. After

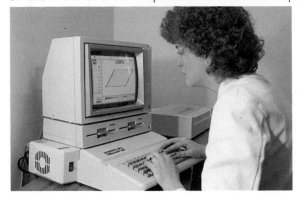

graduating from high school, Jean received technical training at a community college.

Jean used the computer to enlarge a parallelogram, as shown at the left. The new parallelogram is larger than the original parallelogram. The new parallelogram is similar to the original parallelogram.

Similar figures have the same shape but may differ in size.

If two figures are similar, the lengths of their corresponding sides are in proportion. **Point out that corresponding sides are opposite congruent angles.**

Examples

A. Triangle **ABC** is similar to triangle **DEF**. List the corresponding sides and find their ratios.

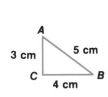

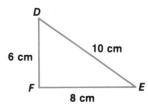

$\overline{AB}$ corresponds to $\overline{DE}$.　$\overline{AC}$ corresponds to $\overline{DF}$.　$\overline{BC}$ corresponds to $\overline{EF}$.

$\dfrac{5 \text{ cm}}{10 \text{ cm}} = \dfrac{1}{2}$ 　　　$\dfrac{3 \text{ cm}}{6 \text{ cm}} = \dfrac{1}{2}$ 　　　$\dfrac{4 \text{ cm}}{8 \text{ cm}} = \dfrac{1}{2}$

$$\frac{AB}{DE} = \frac{AC}{DF} = \frac{BC}{EF} \qquad \textit{AB means the length of } \overline{AB}.$$

B. The two rectangles shown below are similar. Set up a proportion to find the missing length.

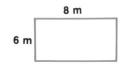

$\dfrac{8}{4} = \dfrac{6}{y}$

$8 \times y = 4 \times 6$ 　　*Cross products are equal.*

$8 \times y = 24$

$\dfrac{8 \times y}{8} = \dfrac{24}{8}$ 　　*Divide each side by 8.*

$y = 3$ 　　Side y is 3 m long.

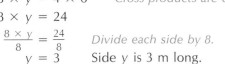

The Key Skills provides practice of skills needed in the exercises.

Key Skills

$$\frac{4}{5} = \frac{1.6}{h}$$

$4 \times h = 5 \times 1.6$

$4 \times h = 8$

$\frac{4 \times h}{4} = \frac{8}{4}$

$h = 2$

Solve each proportion.

1. $\frac{3}{4} = \frac{6}{x}$ **8**   2. $\frac{4}{5} = \frac{8}{n}$ **10**   3. $\frac{4}{c} = \frac{8}{16}$ **8**   4. $\frac{t}{5} = \frac{4}{10}$ **2**

5. $\frac{d}{15} = \frac{6}{5}$ **18**   6. $\frac{7}{8} = \frac{14}{r}$ **16**   7. $\frac{3}{6} = \frac{1.5}{a}$ **3**   8. $\frac{8}{y} = \frac{4}{13}$ **26**

9. $\frac{b}{7} = \frac{12}{21}$ **4**   10. $\frac{1.8}{8} = \frac{e}{4}$ **0.9** 11. $\frac{5}{12} = \frac{m}{3.6}$ **1.5** 12. $\frac{8}{z} = \frac{7.2}{9.9}$ **11**

Basic: 1–8; Average: 1–8; Enriched: 1–8

Exercises

Find the missing length for each pair of similar figures.

1.

8 mm 9 mm e 18 mm 16 mm

2.
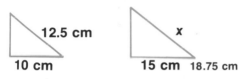
12.5 cm x 10 cm 15 cm 18.75 cm

3.
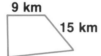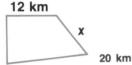
9 km 12 km 15 km x 20 km

4.

5 m 7.5 m 4 m x 6 m

5.
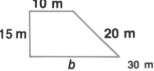
6 m 9 m 12 m 18 m 10 m 15 m 20 m b 30 m

6.

12 km 4 km c 7 km 21 km

Use a proportion to solve each problem.

7. An apple tree casts a shadow of 24 feet while a man casts a shadow of 8 feet. The man is 6 feet tall. How tall is the tree? **18 ft**

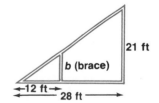
6 ft 8 ft 24 ft

8. Maureen cuts a piece of board to use as a vertical brace on a roof. How long should the board be? **9 ft**

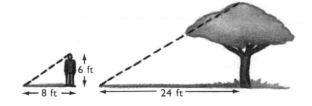
21 ft b (brace) 12 ft 28 ft

Teacher Resource Book, Page 267

12-4 Perimeter

Objective: To find the perimeter of a polygon.

Karl Shaw sells wood and chain link fence. To find how much fence
is needed, Karl finds the perimeter of the yard to be enclosed.
The **perimeter** (P) of a polygon is the distance around it.

A polygon in which all sides and all angles are congruent is
called a **regular polygon**.

Examples

A. Find the perimeter of the regular hexagon.

3.5 cm

$P = 3.5 + 3.5 + 3.5 + 3.5 + 3.5 + 3.5$ *Add the lengths of each side.*

3.5 ⊞ 3.5 ⊞ 3.5 ⊞ 3.5 ⊞ 3.5 ⊞ 3.5 ⊟ *21*

OR

$P = 3.5 \times 6$ *Multiply the length of one side times the number of sides.*

3.5 ⊠ 6 ⊟ *21*

The perimeter is 21 cm.

B. Find the perimeter of the rectangle.

109 m

73 m

$P = 109 + 73 + 109 + 73$ *The opposite sides have the same measure.*

109 ⊞ 73 ⊞ 109 ⊞ 73 ⊟ *364*

The perimeter is 364 m.

C. Find the perimeter of the pentagon.

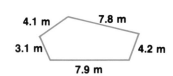

$P = 7.8 + 4.2 + 7.9 + 3.1 + 4.1$

7.8 ⊞ 4.2 ⊞ 7.9 ⊞ 3.1 ⊞ 4.1 ⊟ *27.1*

The perimeter is 27.1 m.

Basic Skills Appendix, Page 435
Basic: 2–26 even; Average: 1–26; Enriched: 1–25 odd

Exercises

Find the perimeter of each regular polygon.

1.

4 m

16 m

2.

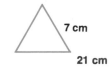

7 cm

21 cm

3.

3 in.

15 in.

4.

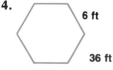

6 ft

36 ft

5.

12 cm

36 cm

6.

8 yd

48 yd

7.

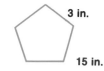

4.5 cm

36 cm

8.

3.25 m

13 m

Find the perimeter of each polygon.

9.

square

7 m

28 m

10.

rectangle

$3\frac{1}{2}$ in.

8 in.

23 in.

11.

5 cm

7.4 cm

rectangle

24.8 cm

12.

2 cm

3 cm

4 cm

2 cm

3 cm

14 cm

13.

1.5 cm

1.5 cm

1.5 cm

1.5 cm

1.5 cm

1.5 cm

9 cm

14.

1.75 cm

3 cm

1.25 cm

1.75 cm

2.5 cm

1 cm

11.25 cm

15.

1 cm

1 cm

1.75 cm

1.5 cm

3.25 cm

1 cm

9.5 cm

16.

1.25 cm

1 cm→

←1 cm

1.25 cm

1.25 cm

1 cm

1.2 cm

0.5 cm↘

2.3 cm

1.5 cm

12.25 cm

17.

4 cm

2 cm

3.75 cm

9.75 cm

The length of each side of a regular polygon is given. Find the perimeter.

18. square, 14 centimeters
  56 cm
20. triangle, 9 inches
  27 in.
22. pentagon, $7\frac{1}{2}$ feet
  $37\frac{1}{2}$ ft

19. hexagon, 10.5 meters
  63 m
21. octagon, 10 kilometers
  80 km
23. square, $4\frac{1}{4}$ yard
  17 yd

Solve.

24. A rectangular patio has sides of $8\frac{1}{4}$ feet and 12 feet. What is the perimeter of the patio? **$40\frac{1}{2}$ feet**

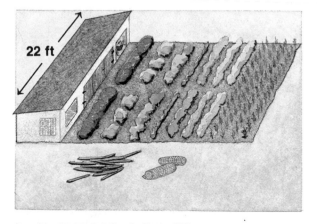

22 ft

25. Each side of a regular pentagon is 6.4 centimeters long. Each side of a square is 8.25 centimeters long. Which has the greater perimeter? **the square**

26. A rectangular garden is up against a shed that is 22 feet long. Kerri has 80 feet of fencing. How wide can she make the garden and have it all enclosed? **29 feet**

12-5 *Circumference*

Objective: To find the circumference of a circle.
The distance around a circle is called its
circumference. When a bicycle tire makes
one complete turn, the distance it travels
is the same as the circumference of
the tire.

June Heid's racing bicycle has tires with a 27-inch diameter.
The **diameter** of a circle is a line segment through the center
of a circle with both endpoints on the circle.

The circumference and diameter of three tires are given below.
What is the ratio of the circumference to the diameter ($\frac{C}{d}$) for
each tire? **about 3.14**

Circumference (C)	22	81.64	84.78
Diameter (d)	7	26	27
$\frac{C}{d}$	≈3.14	≈3.14	≈3.14

*Since measurements
are approximations,
the quotients may
vary slightly.*

The ratio of the circumference to the diameter is the same for
all circles. The Greek letter pi (π) stands for this number.

$$\frac{\text{Circumference } (C)}{\text{diameter } (d)} = \pi \quad \Longrightarrow \quad C = \pi \times d \text{ or } C = \pi d \qquad \pi \approx 3.14$$

The diameter of a circle is twice the length of
the **radius.** If you know the radius of a circle,
you can use the formula below to find circumference.

$$C = \pi \times 2r \quad 2r = d$$

or

$$C = 2\pi r$$

diameter

Examples

A. **A clock has a diameter of 15 cm. Find
its circumference. Use 3.14 for π.**

$C = \pi d$

$C \approx 3.14 \times 15$ *Replace d with 15.*

$C \approx 47.1$

3.14 $\boxed{×}$ 15 $\boxed{=}$ *47.1*

The circumference of the clock is about 47.1 cm.

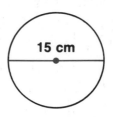

15 cm

262 *Polygons and Circles*

B. A circle has a radius of 6 inches. Find the circumference. Use 3.14 for π.

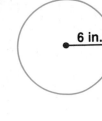

6 in.

$C = 2\pi r$

$C \approx 2 \times 3.14 \times 6$ *Replace r with 6.*

$C \approx 37.68$

2 ⊠ 3.14 ⊠ 6 ⊟ 37.68

The circumference is about 37.68 inches.

Basic Skills Appendix, Pages 425, 438, 439
Basic: 1–19 odd, 21, 22; Average: 1–22; Enriched: 2–20 even, 21, 22

Exercises

Find the circumference of each circle described below.
Use $C = \pi d$ or $C = 2\pi r$. Use 3.14 for π.

1.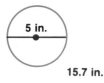

5 in.

15.7 in.

2.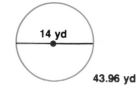

14 yd

43.96 yd

3.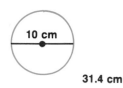

10 cm

31.4 cm

4.

13.4 mm

42.076 mm

5.

3 cm

18.84 cm

6.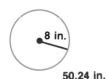

8 in.

50.24 in.

7.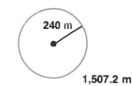

240 m

1,507.2 m

8.

6.2 m

38.936 m

9. d, 12 m **37.68 m**   **10.** d, 30 in. **94.2 in.**   **11.** d, 20 ft **62.8 ft**   **12.** d, 8.1 mm **25.434 mm**

13. d, 50 yd **157 yd**   **14.** d, 5.5 m **17.27 m**   **15.** r, 5 ft **31.4 ft**   **16.** r, 7 m **43.96 m**

17. r, 12 mm **75.36 mm**   **18.** r, 100 mm **628 mm**   **19.** r, 6.5 m **40.82 m**   **20.** r, 12.3 cm **77.244 cm**

Solve.

21. Yolanda puts lace around the edge of a circular tablecloth. The diameter of the tablecloth is 70 inches. How much lace should she buy?
about 220 inches

22. Keith plants flowers in a circular flower bed. The radius of the flower bed is 7.8 meters. What is the circumference of the flower bed?
48.984 meters

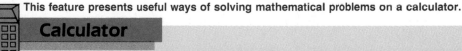

This feature presents useful ways of solving mathematical problems on a calculator.

Calculator

Some calculators have a key labeled π. If not, the fractions $\frac{22}{7}$ and $\frac{355}{113}$ provide a close approximation for π.

Use a calculator to find the following values to seven decimal places.

1. π 3.1415927

2. $\frac{22}{7}$ 3.1428571

3. $\frac{355}{113}$ 3.1415929

PRACTICE

Estimate. Answers may vary. Typical answers are given.

1. $\begin{array}{r} 63 \\ +\ 79 \\ \hline 140 \end{array}$	**2.** $\begin{array}{r} 8.74 \\ -\ 0.69 \\ \hline 8 \end{array}$	**3.** $\begin{array}{r} 42.7 \\ +\ 37.1 \\ \hline 80 \end{array}$	**4.** $\begin{array}{r} 67 \\ -\ 32 \\ \hline 40 \end{array}$	**5.** $\begin{array}{r} 80.6 \\ -\ 9.7 \\ \hline 71 \end{array}$
6. $\begin{array}{r} 82 \\ \times\ 12 \\ \hline 800 \end{array}$	**7.** $\begin{array}{r} 16.9 \\ \times\ 10.3 \\ \hline 170 \end{array}$	**8.** $52\overline{)296}$ 6	**9.** $19\overline{)238}$ 12	**10.** $39\overline{)358}$ 9

Add, subtract, multiply, or divide.

11. $\begin{array}{r} 5.76 \\ +\ 7.2 \\ \hline 12.96 \end{array}$	**12.** $\begin{array}{r} 46.7 \\ +\ 9.623 \\ \hline 56.323 \end{array}$	**13.** $\begin{array}{r} 2{,}473 \\ +\ 7{,}527 \\ \hline 10{,}000 \end{array}$	**14.** $\begin{array}{r} 0.684 \\ +\ 7.4 \\ \hline 8.084 \end{array}$	**15.** $\begin{array}{r} 87.6 \\ +\ 0.18 \\ \hline 87.78 \end{array}$
16. $\begin{array}{r} 39.7 \\ -\ 19.8 \\ \hline 19.9 \end{array}$	**17.** $\begin{array}{r} 3{,}650 \\ -\ 2{,}651 \\ \hline 999 \end{array}$	**18.** $\begin{array}{r} 4.062 \\ -\ 0.072 \\ \hline 3.990 \end{array}$	**19.** $\begin{array}{r} 57 \\ -\ 3.19 \\ \hline 53.81 \end{array}$	**20.** $\begin{array}{r} 6.209 \\ -\ 6.208 \\ \hline 0.001 \end{array}$
21. $\begin{array}{r} 6.1 \\ \times\ 7 \\ \hline 42.7 \end{array}$	**22.** $\begin{array}{r} 8.32 \\ \times\ 9 \\ \hline 74.88 \end{array}$	**23.** $\begin{array}{r} 9.76 \\ \times\ 10.1 \\ \hline 98.576 \end{array}$	**24.** $\begin{array}{r} 14.37 \\ \times\ 12.2 \\ \hline 175.314 \end{array}$	**25.** $\begin{array}{r} 18.9 \\ \times\ 14 \\ \hline 264.6 \end{array}$
26. $7\overline{)85}$ 12.142857	**27.** $10\overline{)112}$ 11.2	**28.** $12\overline{)273}$ 22.75	**29.** $15\overline{)405}$ 27	**30.** $27\overline{)609}$ 22.5

31. 10×37 370 **32.** 37×100 3,700 **33.** 370×10 3,700 **34.** 3.7×10 37 **35.** 100×3.7 370

36. $37 \div 100$ 0.37 **37.** $37 \div 10$ 3.7 **38.** $3.7 \div 100$ 0.037 **39.** $370 \div 10$ 37 **40.** $3.7 \div 10$ 0.37

Compute.

41. $(24 \div 3) + 9$ 17 **42.** $24 \div (3 + 9)$ 2 **43.** $24 \div (8 - 2)$ 4 **44.** $(24 \div 8) - 2$ 1

45. $18 - (6 + 3)$ 9 **46.** $(18 - 6) + 3$ 15 **47.** $(6 \times 3) + 18$ 36 **48.** $6 \times (3 + 18)$ 126

Complete.

49. $4.5 \text{ g} = $ ▨ mg 4,500 **50.** $39 \text{ in.} = $ ▨ ft $3\frac{1}{4}$ ft **51.** $437 \text{ cm} = $ ▨ m 4.37

52. $16.2 \text{ km} = $ ▨ m 16,200 **53.** $380 \text{ mm} = $ ▨ m 0.380 **54.** $7.8 \text{ L} = $ ▨ mL 7,800

55. $422 \text{ mL} = $ ▨ L 0.422 **56.** $3.5 \text{ kg} = $ ▨ g 3,500 **57.** $7 \text{ pt} = $ ▨ qt $3\frac{1}{2}$

58. $4\frac{1}{2} \text{ lb} = $ ▨ oz 72 **59.** $62 \text{ cm} = $ ▨ mm 620 **60.** $6\frac{1}{3} \text{ yd} = $ ▨ ft 19

Change each percent to a decimal. Change each decimal to a percent.

61. 14% 0.14 **62.** 0.36 36% **63.** 49% 0.49 **64.** 1.72 172% **65.** 137% 1.37

66. 0.07 7% **67.** 6% 0.06 **68.** 2.08 208% **69.** 6.4% 0.064 **70.** 0.004 0.4%

Solve.

71. 40% of 200 80 **72.** 65% of 320 208 **73.** 16% of 26 4.16 **74.** 3% of 47 1.41

75. 132% of 72 95.04 **76.** 5.2% of 19 0.988 **77.** 101% of 90 90.9 **78.** 23.9% of 5 1.195

Use the proportion $\frac{P}{B} = \frac{r}{100}$ to solve the following.

79. 108 is 60% of what number? **180**

80. What number is 19% of 86? **16.34**

81. What percent of 129 is 57? **44.2%**

82. 37.2% of 83 is what number? **30.876**

Find the greatest common factor (GCF) for each pair of numbers.

83. 4 and 6 **2**

84. 6 and 9 **3**

85. 9 and 12 **3**

86. 6 and 18 **6**

87. 14 and 21 **7**

88. 12 and 15 **3**

89. 12 and 18 **6**

90. 10 and 15 **5**

Change each fraction to simplest form.

91. $\frac{6}{8}$ $\frac{3}{4}$

92. $\frac{6}{12}$ $\frac{1}{2}$

93. $\frac{10}{15}$ $\frac{2}{3}$

94. $\frac{4}{16}$ $\frac{1}{4}$

95. $\frac{9}{15}$ $\frac{3}{5}$

96. $\frac{20}{25}$ $\frac{4}{5}$

97. $\frac{18}{24}$ $\frac{3}{4}$

98. $\frac{15}{18}$ $\frac{5}{6}$

99. $\frac{15}{24}$ $\frac{5}{8}$

100. $\frac{5}{30}$ $\frac{1}{6}$

Find the least common multiple (LCM) for each group of numbers.

101. 4 and 12 **12**

102. 10 and 15 **30**

103. 9 and 15 **45**

104. 6 and 8 **24**

105. 3, 4, and 5 **60**

106. 4 and 5 **20**

107. 6, 9, and 27 **54**

108. 8 and 28 **56**

Add, subtract, multiply, or divide. Write each answer in simplest form.

109. $\frac{2}{5} + \frac{2}{5}$ $\frac{4}{5}$

110. $\frac{3}{4} + \frac{3}{4}$ $1\frac{1}{2}$

111. $\frac{7}{8} + \frac{3}{8}$ $1\frac{1}{4}$

112. $\frac{2}{3} + \frac{3}{4}$ $1\frac{5}{12}$

113. $\frac{3}{8} + \frac{3}{4}$ $1\frac{1}{8}$

114. $\frac{6}{7} + \frac{1}{3}$ $1\frac{4}{21}$

115. $\frac{2}{5} + \frac{1}{4}$ $\frac{13}{20}$

116. $\frac{3}{4} - \frac{1}{4}$ $\frac{1}{2}$

117. $\frac{5}{6} - \frac{1}{6}$ $\frac{2}{3}$

118. $\frac{3}{4} - \frac{2}{3}$ $\frac{1}{12}$

119. $\frac{1}{4} \times \frac{1}{3}$ $\frac{1}{12}$

120. $\frac{1}{2} \times \frac{1}{5}$ $\frac{1}{10}$

121. $\frac{3}{4} \times \frac{2}{3}$ $\frac{1}{2}$

122. $\frac{4}{5} \times \frac{3}{4}$ $\frac{3}{5}$

123. $\frac{6}{7} \times \frac{5}{6}$ $\frac{5}{7}$

124. $\frac{1}{4} \div \frac{3}{8}$ $\frac{2}{3}$

125. $\frac{1}{3} \div \frac{5}{6}$ $\frac{2}{5}$

126. $\frac{2}{3} \times 7$ $4\frac{2}{3}$

127. $\frac{3}{8} \times \frac{4}{9}$ $\frac{1}{6}$

128. $\frac{8}{9} \times \frac{9}{16}$ $\frac{1}{2}$

Use $C = \frac{5}{9} \times (F - 32)$ or $F = \left(\frac{9}{5} \times C\right) + 32$ to change the following to degrees Celsius or degrees Fahrenheit.

129. 10°C **50°F**

130. 25°C **77°F**

131. 0°C **32°F**

132. 5°C **41°F**

133. 15°C **59°F**

134. 50°F **10°C**

135. 32°F **0°C**

136. 68°F **20°C**

137. 68°F **20°C**

138. 35°F **95°C**

Solve.

139. A picket fence is to have a gate 28 inches wide. The gate is 45 inches high. Find the length of a diagonal brace for the gate. Use the Pythagorean Theorem. **53 inches**

140. Two similar triangles have corresponding sides of 9 and 21 meters. A second set of corresponding sides are 6 meters and an unknown length, x. Find the unknown length. **14 m**

12-6 Area of Rectangles and Parallelograms

Objective: To find the area of rectangles and parallelograms.

The area of any rectangle can be found by multiplying the
measures of the length (ℓ) and width (w). The formula is
A = ℓ x w or A = ℓw. *The multiplication sign can be omitted in a formula.*

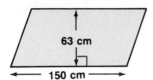

Lisa's counter, however, is shaped like a
parallelogram. To find how much tile is
needed to cover the top, Lisa finds
the area.

The area of a parallelogram can be found by
using the area of a rectangle.

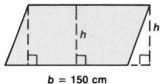 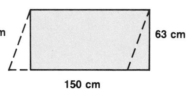 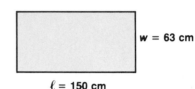

How does the length (ℓ) of the rectangle compare to the base (b)
of the parallelogram? **They are equal.**

How does the width (w) of the rectangle compare to the height
(h) of the parallelogram? **They are equal.**

● The height of a parallelogram is the length of a perpendicular
  line segment between the bases.

● The rectangle and the parallelogram have the same area.

● The formula for the area of a parallelogram is
  A = b × h or A = bh.

**Remind students that
a rectangle *is* a
parallelogram.**

Examples

A. **Find the area of a rectangle with a
length of 5 ft and a width of 3 ft.**

A = ℓw

A = 5 × 3   *Replace ℓ with 5 and w with 3.*

A = 15   The area is 15 square feet (ft²).

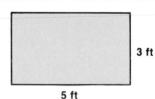

B. **Find the area of a parallelogram with a
base of 150 cm and a height of 63 cm.**

A = bh

A = 150 × 63   *Replace b with 150 and h with 63.*

A = 9,450

150 Ⓧ 63 🟰 *9450*

The area is 9,450 square centimeters (cm²).

Exercises

Find the area of each rectangle or parallelogram described below.

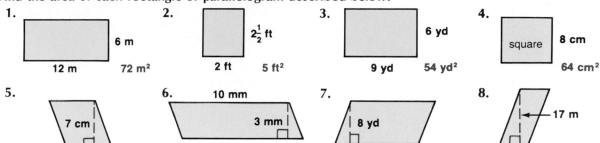

1. 6 m, 12 m, 72 m²
2. 2½ ft, 2 ft, 5 ft²
3. 6 yd, 9 yd, 54 yd²
4. square, 8 cm, 64 cm²
5. 7 cm, 6 cm, 42 cm²
6. 10 mm, 3 mm, 30 mm²
7. 8 yd, 15 yd, 120 yd²
8. 17 m, 8.5 m, 144.5 m²

9. length, 14 m; width, 12 m
   168 m²
10. base, 12 m; height, 7 m
    84 m²
11. length, 10 km; width, 11.5 km
    115 km²
12. base, 10 cm; height, 5.5 cm
    55 cm²
13. length, 15 cm; width, 13 cm
    195 cm²
14. base, 13 ft; height, 6 ft
    78 ft²
15. length, 7 ft; width, $7\frac{1}{2}$ ft
    52.5 ft²
16. base, 20 m; height, 6.5 m
    130 m²
17. length, 9 yd; width, 9 yd
    81 yd²
18. base, 4.1 cm; height, 9.3 cm
    38.13 cm²

Solve.

19. A rectangular living room measures 20
    feet by $18\frac{1}{2}$ feet. What is the area
    of the room? **370 ft²**

20. A gallon of paint covers 400 square
    feet. The floor is 32 feet long and
    24 feet wide. How many gallons of
    paint are needed? **2 gallons**

This feature presents general topics of mathematics.

Math Break

Complete.

1. Find the perimeter of rectangle R.
   24 m
2. Find the perimeter of square S. **24 m**

3. Find the area of rectangle R. **32 m²**

4. Find the area of square S. **36 m²**

5. Which polygon has a greater area
   for a given perimeter? **the square**

6. Find dimensions for three more
   rectangles that have a perimeter equal
   to the square. **Answers may vary.**

7. Find the areas of the figures in
   exercise 6. **Answers may vary.**

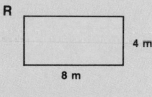

R, 4 m, 8 m

S, 6 m

8. What can you conclude about the areas
   of rectangles with the same perimeter?
   **The closer the length and width are in
   size, the greater the area of the
   rectangle.**

12-7 Area of Triangles

Objective: To find the area of a triangle.

Kip Shumaker designs quilts. One of his designs is a pattern of parallelograms and triangles.

The formula for the area of a triangle can be found by using the formula for the area of a parallelogram.

The formula for finding the area of a parallelogram is $A = bh$. The area of the parallelogram shown at the right is 8×5 or 40 square inches.

The diagonal separates the parallelogram into two congruent triangles. The area of each triangle is one half the area of the parallelogram. So, each triangle has an area of 20 square inches.

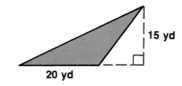

5 in.

8 in.

Since the formula for finding the area of a parallelogram is $A = bh$, the formula for finding the area of a triangle is $A = \frac{1}{2} \times b \times h$ or $A = \frac{1}{2} bh$.

Examples

A. **Find the area of the triangle shown at the right.**

$A = \frac{1}{2} bh$

$A = \frac{1}{2} \times 20 \times 15$ *Replace b with 20 and h with 15.*

$A = 150$ 0.5 ⓧ 20 ⓧ 15 ⊜ 150 $\frac{1}{2} = 0.5$

The area is 150 square yards (yd²).

15 yd

20 yd

B. **Find the area of the triangle shown at the right.**

$A = \frac{1}{2} bh$

$A = \frac{1}{2} \times 7.4 \times 6.7$ *Replace b with 7.4 and h with 6.7.*

$A = 24.79$ 0.5 ⓧ 7.4 ⓧ 6.7 ⊜ 24.79 $\frac{1}{2} = 0.5$

The area is 24.79 square meters (m²).

6.7 m

7.4 m

Exercises

Find the area of each triangle described below.

1.
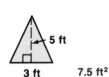
5 ft

3 ft   7.5 ft²

2.
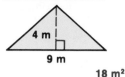
4 m

9 m   18 m²

3.
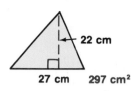
22 cm

27 cm   297 cm²

4.
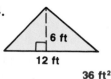
6 ft

12 ft   36 ft²

	base	height		base	height		base	height
5.	8 m	6 m **24 m²**	**6.**	7 in.	10 in. **35 in²**	**7.**	12 cm	9 cm **54 cm²**
8.	15 mm	4 mm **30 mm²**	**9.**	16 yd	3 yd **24 yd²**	**10.**	8 km	11 km **44 km²**

Solve.

11. The base of a triangular sign is 13 inches. The height of the sign is 22 inches. What is the area of the sign? **143 in²**

12. Part of a roof is shaped like a triangle. The base is 7 meters and the height is 3.4 meters. What is the area of part of the roof? **11.9 m²**

This feature provides general topics about the uses of a computer.

Computer

A **flow chart** is a graphic representation of a program or procedure. This flow chart shows the procedure of a computerized payroll system. Many businesses use such a system to compute and print paychecks.

Use the flow chart to answer these questions.

1. Each different shape represents a different type of instruction. How many shapes are there? **4**

2. What does the oval shape represent? **start and stop**

3. What shape represents something that is to be copied or recorded? **parallelogram**

4. What kind of instruction does the rectangle represent? **compute**

5. What shape shows that a question to be answered by yes or no is asked? **diamond or rhombus**

6. Why does this program ask a question about personal deductions?
Some employees have personal deductions, others do not.

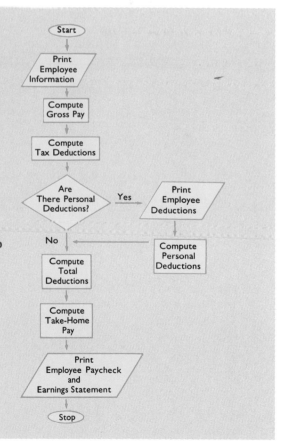

12-8 Area of Trapezoids

Objective: To find the area of a trapezoid.

Tyrone Crowder works for a lawn maintenance company. To compute
costs, Tyrone finds the area of the lawn that will be treated.
One lawn is shaped like a trapezoid. How can he find the area?

Two congruent trapezoids form a parallelogram. Find the area
of the parallelogram. The area of each trapezoid is one half
the area of the parallelogram.

base of the parallelogram: $a + b$

area of the parallelogram: $(a + b) \times h$ *base × height*

area of each trapezoid: $\frac{1}{2} \times (a + b) \times h$ or $\frac{1}{2}(a + b)h$

half the area of the parallelogram

Examples

A. **Find the area of the trapezoid at the right.**

$A = \frac{1}{2}(a + b)h$ *a and b are the bases.*

$A = \frac{1}{2} \times (12 + 5) \times 8$ *Replace a with 12, b with 5,*
and h with 8.

$A = \frac{1}{2} \times (17) \times 8$ *Do the addition first.*

$A = 68$ *Then multiply.*

0.5 Ⓧ Ⓒ 12 ⊕ 5 Ⓓ Ⓧ 8 ⊜ *68*

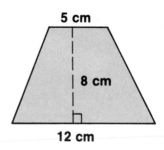

The area is 68 square centimeters (cm²).

B. **Find the area of the trapezoid at the right.**

$A = \frac{1}{2}(a + b)h$

$A = \frac{1}{2} \times (9.3 + 5.6) \times 4$ *Replace a with 9.3, b with*
5.6, and h with 4.

$A = \frac{1}{2} \times (14.9) \times 4$

$A = 29.8$

0.5 Ⓧ Ⓒ 9.3 ⊕ 5.6 Ⓓ Ⓧ 4 ⊜ *29.8*

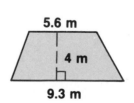

The area is 29.8 square meters (m²).

Exercises

Find the area of each trapezoid described below.

1.

81 m²

2.

24 cm²

3.
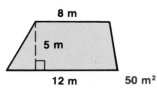
50 m²

4.
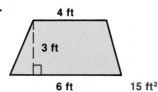
15 ft²

5.
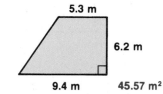
45.57 m²

6.
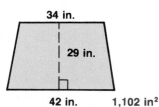
1,102 in²

	base (*a*)	base (*b*)	height (*h*)
7.	4 m	5 m	3 m 13.5 m²
9.	4 cm	5 cm	4 cm 18 cm²

	base (*a*)	base (*b*)	height (*h*)
8.	3 m	6 m	2 m 9 m²
10.	5 in.	6 in.	4 in. 22 in²

Solve.

11. The floor of the school stage needs to be painted. The floor is shaped like a trapezoid. The bases measure 32 feet and 48 feet. The floor measures 20 feet from front to back. What is its area? **800 ft²**

12. A garden is shaped like a trapezoid. The sum of the measures of the bases is 50 feet. The garden measures 30 feet from front to back. Will a bag of fertilizer that covers 1,000 square feet be enough for the garden? **yes**

This feature promotes students' mental abilities in computation and reasonableness.

Mental Math

The distributive property can be used to find products mentally.

$35 \times 22 = 35(20 + 2)$

    Rename 22 as 20 + 2.

  $= (35 \times 20) + (35 \times 2)$

  $= 700 + 70$

  $= 770$ *35 × 22 = 770*

$75 \times 2.6 = 75(3.0 - 0.4)$

    Rename 2.6 as 3.0 − 0.4.

  $= (75 \times 3.0) - 75(0.4)$

  $= 225 - 30$

  $= 195$ *75 × 2.6 = 195*

Find each product using the strategy shown above.

1. 7×14 **98**

2. 9×102 **918**

3. 42×18 **756**

4. 35×33 **1,155**

5. 2.4×27 **64.8**

6. 1.5×340 **510**

7. $3,000 \times 63$ **189,000**

8. $3\frac{1}{2} \times \$12.50$ **\$43.75**

12-9 Area of Circles

Objective: To find the area of a circle.

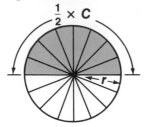

The placement of sprinklers in an automatic sprinkler system is shown at the left. A full-circle sprinkler throws water over a circular region. What area is watered by a full-circle sprinkler with a throw radius of 7 meters? To answer this question, you must know the formula for finding the area of a circle.

A circle can be separated into sections. The sections can be rearranged as shown.

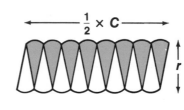

Figure II resembles a parallelogram. The formula for the area of a circle can be found by using the formula for the area of a parallelogram.

$A = b \times h$ *Use the formula for the area of a parallelogram.*

$A = \left(\frac{1}{2} \times C\right) \times r$ *Replace b with $\frac{1}{2} \times C$ and h with r.*

$A = \frac{1}{2} \times (2 \times \pi \times r) \times r$ *Remember, C = 2 × π × r.*

$A = \pi \times r \times r$ *$\frac{1}{2} \times 2 = 1$ and $1 \times \pi = \pi$.*

$A = \pi \times r^2$ *Write r × r as r².*

The formula for the area, A, of a circle with a radius of r units is $\boldsymbol{A = \pi r^2}$.

Example

What is the area of the region watered by a full-circle sprinkler with a throw radius of 7 meters? Use $\frac{22}{7}$ for π.

$A = \pi \times r^2$ *Use the formula for the area of a circle.*

$A \approx \frac{22}{7} \times 7^2$ *Replace π with $\frac{22}{7}$ and r with 7.*

$A \approx \frac{22}{7} \times 49$ *Compute 7².*

$A \approx \frac{22}{\cancel{7}_1} \times \cancel{49}^7$ *Multiply.*

$A \approx 154$

The area of the region watered is about 154 square meters (m²).

22 ÷ 7 × (7 x²) = 154

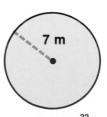

Point out that $\frac{22}{7}$ is easier to use than 3.14 for π when the radius is a multiple of 7.

Exercises

Find the area of each circle with the given radius. Remember that r^2 means $r \times r$.

Use 3.14 for π.

1. 3 cm **28.26 cm²**   2. 4 m **50.24 m²**

Use $\frac{22}{7}$ for π.

3. 14 km **616 km²**   4. 21 m **1,386 m²**

5. 5 in. **78.5 in²**   6. 0.1 ft **0.0314 ft²**

7. $3\frac{1}{2}$ ft **$38\frac{1}{2}$ ft²**   8. $1\frac{3}{4}$ in. **$9\frac{5}{8}$ in²**

9. 6 km **113.04 km²**   10. 8 mm **200.96 mm²**

11. 35 cm **3,850 cm²**   12. 28 cm **2,464 cm²**

13. Suppose the length of the diameter of a circle is known. How would you find the radius? **The radius is one-half of the diameter.**

14. Suppose the length of the diameter of a circle is known. How would you find the area of the circle? **Find one-half of the diameter, square it, and multiply by π.**

Find the area of each circle with the given diameter.

Use 3.14 for π.

15.

28.26 m²

16.

12.56 in²

Use $\frac{22}{7}$ for π.

17.

616 cm²

18.

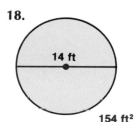

154 ft²

Solve.

19. A shrubbery sprinkler has a throw radius of 12 feet. What is the area of the region watered by a full-circle sprinkler? Use 3.14 for π. **≈452.16 ft²**

20. A full-circle sprinkler throws water over a region 13 meters in diameter. What is the area of the region watered? Use 3.14 for π. **132.67 m²**

21. A sprinkler has a throw radius of 9 meters. What is the area of a region watered by a half-circle sprinkler? Use 3.14 for π. **≈127.17 m²**

22. The wooden deck shown below is to be painted. The radius is 2.8 meters. Find the area of the surface to be painted. Use $\frac{22}{7}$ for π. **≈18.48 m²**

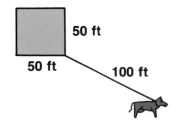

23. A cow is tethered to a corner of the building shown with a rope 100 feet long. What is the area of the region the cow can graze? Use 3.14 for π. **≈27,475 ft²**

12-10   Problem Solving: Find Composite Areas

Objective: To use diagrams and formulas to find composite areas.

The field shown at the right is to be
fertilized. What is the area of the field?

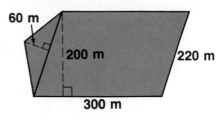

60 m

200 m · 220 m

300 m

Read

You must find the area of the field.
You know certain lengths.

Decide

The field has an irregular shape. There is no
formula for the area of such a figure.
Therefore, separate the figure into smaller,
more familiar shapes. Find the area of each
shape. Then, add to find the total area of
the field.

Separate the shape into a triangle
and a parallelogram.

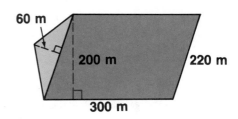

60 m

200 m   220 m

300 m

Solve

A. Find the area of the triangle.

$A = \frac{1}{2} bh$

$A = \frac{1}{2} \times 220 \times 60$ *Replace b with 220 and h with 60.*

$A = 6,600$ 0.5 ⊠ 220 ⊠ 60 🭮 *6600*

The area of the triangle is 6,600 square meters (m²).

B. Find the area of the parallelogram.

$A = bh$

$A = 300 \times 200$ *Replace b with 300 and h with 200.*

$A = 60,000$

**The height of the triangle is
different from the height of the
parallelogram.**

The area of the parallelogram is 60,000 square meters (m²).

Add the areas to find the total area of the field.

```
    6,600 m²   area of the triangle
+  60,000 m²   area of the parallelogram
   66,600 m²   area of the field
```

The area of the field is 66,600 m².

Examine

The area of the parallelogram is 60,000 m². Therefore,
the area of the field should be more than 60,000 m²
because of the extended region. The answer is reasonable.

Exercises

Find each composite area. Make a sketch on your paper to show how you separated each figure. You may need all or part of the area of a circle. Use 3.14 for π.

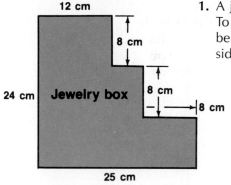

1. A jewelry box is damaged on one side. To refinish that side, its area must be found. What is the area of the side shown? **432 cm²**

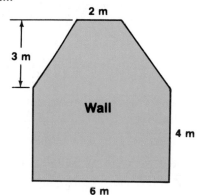

2. One wall of a room is to be wallpapered. What is the area of the wall shown? **36 m²**

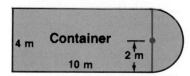

3. One side of a container will be covered with colorful tape. How much tape is needed to cover the side shown? **46.28 m²**

4. To carpet a hallway pictured at the right, the area must be found. What is the area of the hallway shown? **94.625 m²**

5. Fertilizer is bought according to the area needing treatment. If the entire garden pictured needs to be treated, how large an area Is that? **140 m²**

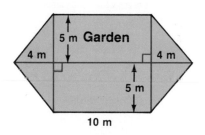

6. The wall shown at the right is to be painted, except for the window shown. What is the area to be painted? **96 ft²**

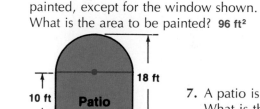

7. A patio is to be constructed of concrete. What is the area of the patio shown? **260.48 ft²**

CHAPTER 12 REVIEW

Vocabulary/Concepts

Write the letter of the word or phrase that best matches each description.

1. the distance around a circle **a**

2. figures with the same shape but may be different in size **r**

3. a polygon with 5 sides **j**

4. a closed plane figure formed by line segments **l**

5. a quadrilateral with exactly one pair of parallel sides **q**

6. a parallelogram with four congruent sides **p**

7. a point where two sides of a polygon meet **k**

8. a polygon with 6 sides **f**

9. a polygon with 8 sides **h**

10. a quadrilateral with two pairs of parallel sides **i**

11. a line segment through the center of a circle with both endpoints on the circle **c**

12. a polygon in which all sides and all angles are congruent **o**

a. circumference
b. decagon
c. diameter
d. dodecagon
e. heptagon
f. hexagon
g. nonagon
h. octagon
i. parallelogram
j. pentagon
k. vertex
l. polygon
m. quadrilateral
n. radius
o. regular polygon
p. rhombus
q. trapezoid
r. similar figures

Exercises

Tell whether each figure is a polygon. Write yes or no.   Page 255

13. no

14. yes

15.  yes

16. no

17. no

Classify each lettered quadrilateral as a trapezoid, parallelogram, rectangle, rhombus, or square. Use the word that best describes what each quadrilateral appears to be.   Pages 256–257

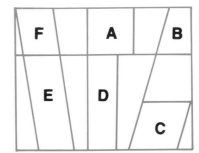

18. A **square**

19. B **trapezoid**

20. C **rhombus**

21. D **rectangle**

22. E **parallelogram**

23. F **parallelogram**

Find the missing length for each pair of similar figures. Pages 258–259

24. 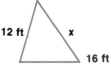   6 ft   8 ft   12 ft   x   16 ft

25. 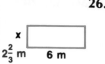   4 m   10 m   x $2\frac{2}{3}$ m   6 m

26. 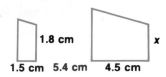   1.8 cm   x   1.5 cm   5.4 cm   4.5 cm

Find the perimeter of each polygon. Pages 260–261

27. rectangle   4 in.   6 in.   20 in.

28.    8 cm $7\frac{1}{2}$ cm   12 cm $27\frac{1}{2}$ cm

29. 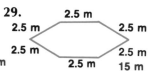   2.5 m   2.5 m   2.5 m   2.5 m   2.5 m   2.5 m   15 m

30. 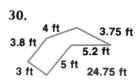   4 ft   3.8 ft   3.75 ft   5.2 ft   3 ft   5 ft   24.75 ft

Find the circumference of each circle. Use 3.14 for π. Pages 262–263

31. 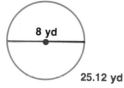   8 yd   25.12 yd

32. 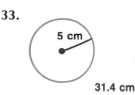   20 mm   62.8 mm

33.   5 cm   31.4 cm

34.   7.5 in.   47.1 in.

Find the area of each rectangle or parallelogram described below. Pages 266–267

35. length, 12 m; width, 15 m **180 m²**

36. length, 17 km; width, 8 km **136 km²**

37. base, 11 cm; height, 4.2 cm **46.2 cm²**

38. base, 3.2 ft; height, 16.3 ft **52.16 ft²**

Find the area of each triangle described below. Pages 268–269

base	height		base	height		base	height
39. 10 m	4 m **20 m²**		40. 8 in.	12 in. **48 in²**		41. 15 mm	6 mm **45 mm²**
42. 5 cm	11 cm **27.5 cm²**		43. 6 ft	$6\frac{1}{2}$ ft **$19\frac{1}{2}$ ft²**		44. 7.3 yd	4.2 yd **15.33 yd²**

Find the area of each trapezoid. Pages 270–271

45.   4 ft   6 ft   8 ft   36 ft²

46.   12 m   8 m   15 m   108 m²

47. 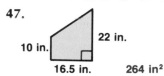   22 in.   10 in.   16.5 in.   264 in²

Find the area of each circle with the given radius. Use $\frac{22}{7}$ for π. Pages 272–273

48. 14 mm
616 mm²

49. 35 cm
3,850 cm²

50. 42 yd
5,544 yd²

51. 2.8 in.
24.64 in²

52. 5.6 ft
98.56 ft²

Solve.

53. A can of paint covers 300 square feet. A floor is in the shape of a right triangle. The sides of the floor that are perpendicular are 27 feet and 16 feet. How many cans of paint are needed? **2 cans**

CHAPTER 12 TEST

Find the missing length for each pair of similar figures.

1.
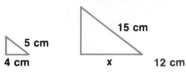
5 cm   15 cm
4 cm   x   12 cm

2.

x
16 m

7.5 m
12 m   10 m

3.
3.2 ft
6.5 ft
x
26 ft
12.8 ft

Find the perimeter of each polygon.

4.
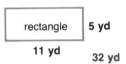
rectangle   5 yd
11 yd   32 yd

5.
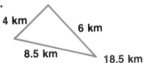
4 km   6 km
8.5 km   18.5 km

6.
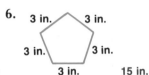
3 in.   3 in.
3 in.   3 in.
3 in.   15 in.

7.
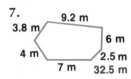
9.2 m
3.8 m   6 m
4 m   2.5 m
7 m   32.5 m

Find the circumference of each circle. Use 3.14 for π.

8.

16 m
50.24 m

9.

13 yd
40.82 yd

10.
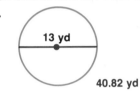
4 cm
25.12 cm

11.
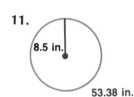
8.5 in.
53.38 in.

Find the area of each rectangle or parallelogram described below.

12. length, 13 km; width, 20 km **260 km²**

13. length, 4.5 cm; width, 8 cm **36 cm²**

14. base, 10 in.; height, 5.2 in. **52 in²**

15. base, 3.8 ft; height, 10.5 ft **39.9 ft²**

Find the area of each triangle described below.

base	height		base	height		base	height
16. 12 m	6 m **36 m²**		**17.** 22 in.	$4\frac{1}{2}$ in. **$49\frac{1}{2}$ in²**		**18.** 8.2 yd	15 yd **61.5 yd²**

Find the area of each trapezoid.

19.
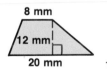
8 mm
12 mm
20 mm   168 mm²

20.
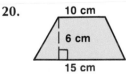
10 cm
6 cm
15 cm   75 cm²

21.
3 in.
5.5 in.
9 in.   33 in²

Find the area of each circle with the given radius. Use 3.14 for π.

22. 2 cm
12.56 cm²

23. 7 ft
153.86 ft²

24. 12 in.
452.16 in²

25. 15 km
706.5 km²

26. 3.5 m
38.465 m²

Solve.

27. The garden pathway shown at the right
is to be paved. What is its area?
68.13 m²

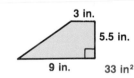
10 m
8 m
4 m   2 m

This page provides extra practice of the skills and applications presented thus far in the text.

CUMULATIVE REVIEW

Find the range and mode.   Pages 30–31

1. The city of Seattle had 3.6 in., 2.5 in., 1.7 in., and 1.5 in. of rainfall in four months. **2.1 in., no mode**

2. The low temperatures for a week are 12°, 16°, 10°, 12°, 13°, 11°, and 8°. **8°, 12°**

Find the mean.   Pages 32–33

3. January has 31 days, February has 28 days, March has 31 days, and April has 30 days. **30 days**

4. There are 20 students in class A, 19 in class B, 17 in class C, and 22 in class D. **19.5 students**

Trace each angle. Construct an angle whose measure is described below.   Pages 236–237
See students' work.

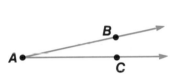
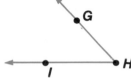

5. The measure of ∠ EDF plus the measure of ∠ BAC.

6. The measure of ∠ BAC plus the measure of ∠ GHI.

7. Three times the measure of ∠ BAC.

8. Twice the measure of ∠ GHI.

Trace each line segment shown below. Then, complete the following.   Pages 238–239
See students' work.

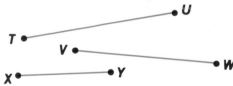

9. Construct a segment whose length is twice the length of $\overline{VW}$.

10. Construct a segment whose length is equal to the length of $\overline{TU}$ plus half the length of $\overline{XY}$.

Tell whether each figure is a polygon. Write yes or no.   Page 255

11. **no**

12. **yes**

13. **no**

14. **yes**

15. **no**

16. **yes**

The length of each side of a regular polygon is given. Find the perimeter.   Pages 260–261

17. hexagon, 9.2 cm **55.2 cm**

18. triangle, 10 in. **30 in.**

19. pentagon, $11\frac{1}{4}$ yd **56.25 yd**

20. square, 5 ft **20 ft**

21. octagon, $8\frac{1}{2}$ m **68 m**

22. decagon, 12.3 in. **123 in.**

23. pentagon, $16\frac{3}{4}$ yd **83.75 yd**

24. decagon, 63 cm **630 cm**

25. triangle, $10\frac{1}{5}$ m **30.6 m**

Surface Area and Volume

13-1 Surface Area of Rectangular Prisms

Objective: To find the surface area of rectangular prisms.

Rhonda is building a cage for small animals. She needs to cover the top, bottom, and sides of the cage with wire mesh.

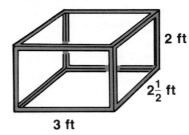
2 ft
$2\frac{1}{2}$ ft
3 ft

To know how much wire mesh she needs, Rhonda must find the **surface area** of the cage. The cage is shaped like a *rectangular prism*. The surface area of a rectangular prism is the sum of the areas of its surfaces. The cage is an example of a solid figure. It has three dimensions and encloses part of space. A solid figure with flat surfaces called faces is a polyhedron. A prism is a polyhedron with two parallel congruent faces called bases. A rectangular prism is a prism with rectangular bases.

Example

Find the surface area of the cage.

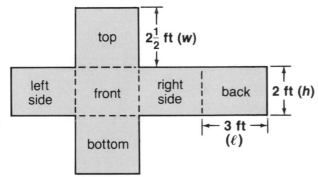

Surface	Dimensions		Area
top	$3 \times 2\frac{1}{2}$	=	$7\frac{1}{2}$ ft²
bottom	$3 \times 2\frac{1}{2}$	=	$7\frac{1}{2}$ ft²
front	3×2	=	6 ft²
back	3×2	=	6 ft²
left side	$2\frac{1}{2} \times 2$	=	5 ft²
right side	$2\frac{1}{2} \times 2$	=	5 ft²
	surface area (S.A.)	=	37 ft²

S.A. = 2($\ell w + \ell h + wh$)

Rhonda needs 37 ft² of wire mesh.

Basic: 1–7 odd; Average: 1–7; Enriched: 2–6 even

Exercises

Find the surface area of each rectangular prism described below.

1.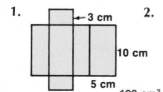
3 cm
10 cm
5 cm
190 cm²

2.
4 in.
4 in.
4 in.
96 in²

3.
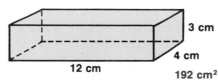
3 cm
4 cm
12 cm
192 cm²

4. ℓ = 10 cm, w = 3 cm, h = 4 cm
164 cm²

5. ℓ = 8 yd, w = 5 yd, h = 6.5 yd
249 yd²

Solve. For answers to exercises 6–7, see Teacher Guide.

6. Draw six connected squares that will form a cube when folded.

7. Draw five connected squares to make a cube with no top.

Teacher Resource Book, Page 287

13-2 Surface Area of Pyramids

Objective: To find the surface area of pyramids.

Chad Evans makes tents. He makes the sides and bottom of the tent out of canvas.

To know how much canvas to order, Chad must find the surface area of the tent. The tent is shaped like a *pyramid*.

A pyramid is a polyhedron with a base shaped like a polygon. The faces of a pyramid are triangular and meet at a point.

Face

Base

A pyramid is named by the shape of its base.
If the base is a regular polygon, the faces are the same size and shape.

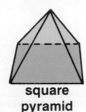

| triangular pyramid | square pyramid | pentagonal pyramid | hexagonal pyramid | octagonal pyramid |

To find the surface area of a pyramid, add the area of the base and the areas of the triangular faces.

Example

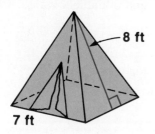

8 ft

7 ft

Find the surface area of the tent.

Surface	Dimensions		Area	
one face	$\frac{1}{2} \times 7 \times 8$	=	28 ft²	*Area (triangle) = $\frac{1}{2}$bh*
four faces	4×28	=	112 ft²	*The four faces are congruent.*
base	7×7	=	49 ft²	*Area (square) = s²*
			161 ft²	

Chad needs 161 ft² of canvas.

Basic: 1–8, 13–19 odd; Average: 1–22; Enriched: 1–4, 14–22 even

Exercises

Copy and complete the chart below to find the surface area of each square pyramid with the given dimensions.

length of side of square	height of triangular face	area of base	area of one triangular face	area of four triangular faces	surface area
4 m	2.8 m	**1.** 16 m²	**2.** 5.6 m²	**3.** 22.4 m²	**4.** 38.4 m²
12 cm	4.4 cm	**5.** 144 cm²	**6.** 26.4 cm²	**7.** 105.6 cm²	**8.** 249.6 cm²
10 in.	$10\frac{1}{2}$ in.	**9.** 100 in²	**10.** $52\frac{1}{2}$ in²	**11.** 210 in²	**12.** 310 in²

Find the surface area of each pyramid. Round decimal answers to the nearest tenth. (The base of each pyramid is a regular polygon.)

13.

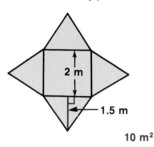

2 m

1.5 m

10 m²

14.

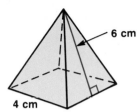

6 cm

4 cm

64 cm²

15.

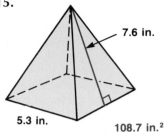

7.6 in.

5.3 in.

108.7 in.²

16.

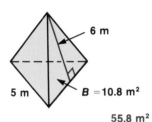

6 m

5 m $B = 10.8$ m²

55.8 m²

17.

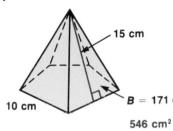

15 cm

10 cm $B = 171$ cm²

546 cm²

18.

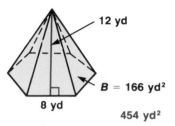

12 yd

$B = 166$ yd²

8 yd

454 yd²

Solve. Round decimal answers to the nearest tenth.

19. A tent shaped like a square pyramid measures 10 ft on each side. The height of each triangular wall is 8 ft. How many square feet of canvas are there in the floor and walls of the tent?
260 ft²

20. A tent is shaped like an octagonal pyramid. Each wall is a triangle measuring 15 ft wide and 20 ft high. Find the surface area of the tent walls.
1,200 ft²

21. Each side of a hexagonal steeple measures 6 ft wide and 18 ft high. How many square feet of roofing are needed to cover the steeple?
(Roofing is not put on the floor of the steeple.) 324 ft²

22. Chad is making a tent with a hexagonal base. Each wall is a triangle with a height of 2.8 m and a base of 3.3 m. Find the surface area of the walls of the tent.
27.7 m²

13-3 Surface Area of Cylinders

Objective: To find the surface area of a cylinder.

A **cylinder** has two parallel congruent circular *bases*. A common example of a cylinder is pictured at the right.

Imagine cutting out the top and bottom of the can. The top and bottom of the can are the circular bases of the cylinder.

Now think of cutting the wall of the can from top to bottom and unrolling it. This rectangular surface is the **lateral surface** of the cylinder.

The length of the lateral surface is the same as the circumference of each base. To find the length, use the formula for the circumference $C = 2 \times \pi \times r$.

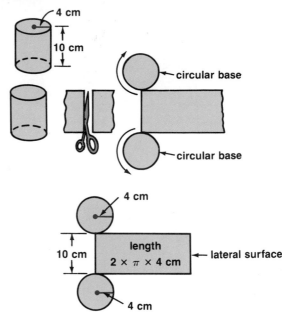

To find the area of each circular base, use the formula $A = \pi \times r^2$.
To find the area of each lateral surface, use the formula $A = \ell \times w$.
The **surface area** of a cylinder is the sum of the areas of the bases and the lateral surface area.
Only right circular cylinders will be considered in this book.

Example

Find the surface area of the cylinder shown above. Use 3.14 for π. Round the answer to the nearest tenth.

Base	**Lateral Surface**	**Sums of Areas**
$A = \pi r^2$	$A = \ell w$	50.24 *top base*
$A \approx 3.14 \times 4^2$	$A = 2\pi r h$	50.24 *bottom base*
$A \approx 3.14 \times 16$	$A \approx 2 \times 3.14 \times 4 \times 10$	$+\ \ 251.2$ *lateral surface*
$A \approx 50.24$ cm^2	$A \approx 251.2$ cm^2	351.68 *or 351.7 cm^2*

The width (w) of a rectangle is also the height (h).

The surface area is about 351.7 cm^2.

The Key Skills provides practice of skills needed in the exercises.

Key Skills

Multiply. Use 3.14 for π. Round decimal answers to the nearest tenth.

$$2 \times \pi \times 3 \approx 2 \times 3.14 \times 3 \approx 18.8$$

1. $\pi \times 4 \times 4$ **50.2**
2. $2 \times \pi \times 7$ **44.0**
3. $2 \times 2 \times \pi$ **12.6**
4. $\pi \times 3 \times 3$ **28.3**
5. $\pi \times 7 \times 10$ **219.8**
6. $\pi \times 3.4 \times 5$ **53.4**
7. $\pi \times 7 \times 2.3$ **50.6**
8. $2 \times \pi \times 5.5$ **34.5**
9. $\pi \times 6.28 \times 6$ **118.3**

Exercises

Copy and complete the chart below to find surface area of each cylinder described. Use 3.14 for π. Round decimal answers to the nearest tenth.

radius	height	area of two bases	area of lateral surface	surface area
r	h	$2 \times \pi \times r^2$	$2 \times \pi \times r \times h$	$2\pi r (r + h)$
10 cm	4 cm	**1.** 628 cm²	**2.** 251.2 cm²	**3.** 879.2 cm²
2 in.	5 in.	**4.** 25.1 in²	**5.** 62.8 in²	**6.** 87.9 in²
4 m	7 m	**7.** 100.5 m²	**8.** 175.8 m²	**9.** 276.3 m²
5 mm	10 mm	**10.** 157 mm²	**11.** 314 mm²	**12.** 471 mm²

Find the surface area of each cylinder. Use 3.14 for π. Round answers to the nearest tenth.

13.
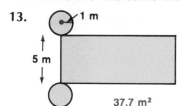
37.7 m²

14.
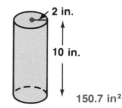
150.7 in²

15.
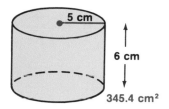
345.4 cm²

Solve. Use 3.14 for π. Round answers to the nearest tenth.

16. A can of vegetables has a 3-in. radius and a 7-in. height. What is the approximate area of the paper label that covers the side of the can?
131.9 in²

17. A juice can has a radius of 1.3 in. and a height of 4.9 in. What is its surface area?
50.6 in²

This feature presents useful ways of solving mathematical problems on a calculator.

Calculator

A calculator with a π key can be used to find the area of a circle as follows. Use the formula $A = \pi r^2$.

Find the area of a circle if the radius is 5 ft. long.

π X 5 X 5 = *78.539816*   *Round decimal answer to the nearest tenth.*

≈ 78.5 ft²

Use a calculator with a π key to find the area of each circle. Round answers to the nearest tenth.

1. $r = 11$ cm 380.1 cm²

2. $r = 12.4$ m 483.1 m²

3. $r = 8.34$ in. 218.5 in²

4. $r = 100$ yd 31,415.9 yd²

5. $d = 73$ ft 4,185.4 ft²

6. $d = 32$ mm 804.2 mm²

13-4 *Surface Area of Cones*

Objective: To find the surface area of a cone.

Alan Clay is a sheet-metal worker for a heating and air conditioning company. He makes and installs metal ductwork for heating and cooling systems. Alan's preparation for his job included an apprentice program with classroom instruction.

Alan needs to make a cone-shaped cap for a chimney.

A **cone** is a solid figure with a circular base and a curved surface that comes to a point. Only right circular cones will be considered in this book.

Two views of a cone are shown below.

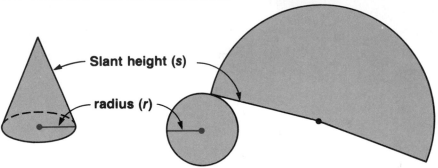

Slant height (s)

radius (r)

The formula for the surface area of a cone is given below.

surface area = $\pi \times r \times (r + s)$ r is the radius of the circular base.
     s is the slant height.

Example

Find the surface area of a cone with a radius of 4 inches and a slant height of 6 inches. Use 3.14 for π.

surface area $= \pi r(r + s)$

$\approx 3.14 \times 4 \times (4 + 6)$ *Estimate: 3 × 4 × (4 + 6) = 12 × 10 = 120*

$\approx 3.14 \times 40$

≈ 125.6

3.14 ⊠ 4 ⊠ 10 ⊟ *125.6*

6 in.

4 in.

The surface area of the cone is about 125.6 in².

Exercises

Copy and complete the charts below to find the surface area of each cone with the given dimensions. Use 3.14 for π. Round decimal answers to the nearest tenth.

Radius (r)	Slant height (s)	
1. 2 cm	5 cm	44.0 cm²
2. 3 in.	4 in.	65.9 in²
3. 1 ft	3 ft	12.6 ft²
4. 4 m	8 m	150.7 m²
5. 5 yd	3 yd	125.6 yd²
6. 7 mm	10 mm	373.7 mm²
7. 8 cm	9 cm	427.0 cm²
8. 4.5 in.	11.5 in.	226.1 in²
9. 7.1 cm	15.4 cm	501.6 cm²

Radius (r)	Slant height (s)	
10. 2 cm	10 cm	75.4 cm²
11. 3 cm	6 cm	84.8 cm²
12. 1 ft	6 ft	22.0 ft²
13. 5 m	5 m	157 m²
14. 7 in.	8 in.	329.7 in²
15. 4 mm	10 mm	175.8 mm²
16. 8 yd	5 yd	326.6 yd²
17. 6.3 in.	11.6 in.	354.1 in²
18. 12.6 ft	3.6 ft	640.9 ft²

Find the surface area of each cone. Use 3.14 for π.
Round decimal answers to the nearest tenth.

19.
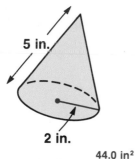
24 cm
3 cm
254.3 cm²

20.
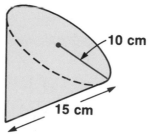
10 cm
15 cm
785 cm²

21.
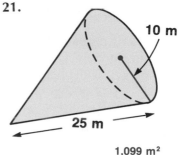
10 m
25 m
1,099 m²

22.
5 in.
2 in.
44.0 in²

23.
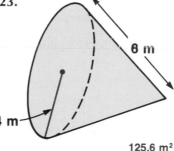
8 m
4 m
125.6 m²

24.
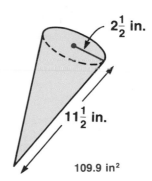
$2\frac{1}{2}$ in.
$11\frac{1}{2}$ in.
109.9 in²

Solve. Use 3.14 for π. Round answers to the nearest tenth.

25. A cone-shaped funnel has a radius of 7 cm and a slant height of 10 cm. What is the surface area of the funnel? 373.7 cm²

26. A cone has a radius of 10 in. and a slant height of 14 in. Find the surface area of the cone. 753.6 in²

13-5 Volume of Prisms

Objective: To find the volume of prisms.

Forms are built where concrete is to be poured. The amount of space the forms enclose is called the **volume.**

Volume is measured in cubic units. Cubic centimeters (cm³), cubic meters (m³), cubic yards (yd³), and cubic feet (ft³) are common units for measuring volume. **The surface area and the volume of a solid can be compared in this way: surface area—to cover a solid; volume—to fill a solid.**

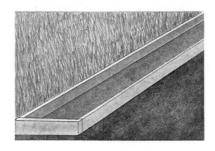

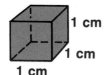

Each edge of this cube measures one centimeter. The volume is one cubic centimeter.

Cubes like the one above can be used to find the volume of a rectangular prism shown here.

You can find the volume of a rectangular prism by multiplying the measures of the length (ℓ), width (w), and height (h).

$$V = \ell \times w \times h$$

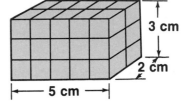

The volume of *any* prism can be found by multiplying the area of the base (B) by the height (h).

$$V = B \times h$$

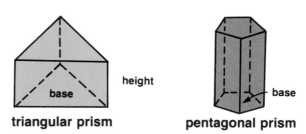

triangular prism　　　　　**pentagonal prism**

Examples

A. Find the volume of the rectangular prism shown above.

$V = \ell wh$

$V = 5 \times 2 \times 3$　*Replace ℓ with 5, w with 2, and h with 3.*

$V = 30$　*The volume is 30 cm³.*

B. Find the volume of the prism shown at the right.

$V = Bh$

$V = (\frac{1}{2} \times 4 \times 6) \times 10$　*The area of the triangular face is*

$V = 12 \times 10$　　　　　　　　$\frac{1}{2} \times b \times h.$

$V = 120$　　The volume is 120 cm³.

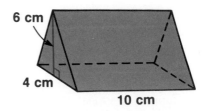

Exercises

Find the volume of each rectangular prism.

1.

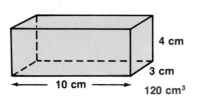

4 cm

3 cm

10 cm

120 cm³

2.

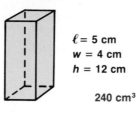

ℓ = 5 cm
w = 4 cm
h = 12 cm

240 cm³

3.

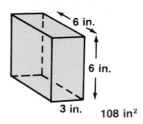

6 in.

6 in.

3 in.   **108 in²**

Find the volume of each rectangular prism described below.

	Length	Width	Height	
4.	10 cm	4 cm	8 cm	**320 cm³**
5.	12 in.	12 in.	4 in.	**576 in³**
6.	15 mm	10 mm	11 mm	**1,650 mm³**

	Length	Width	Height	
7.	2 ft	1 ft	4 ft	**8 ft³**
8.	20 cm	10 cm	16 cm	**3,200 cm³**
9.	3 in.	3 in.	3 in.	**27 in³**

Find the volume of each prism described below.

10.

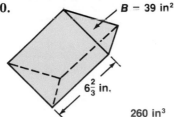

B = 39 in²

$6\frac{2}{3}$ in.

260 in³

11.

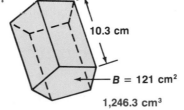

10.3 cm

B = 121 cm²

1,246.3 cm³

12. |←15.5 cm→|

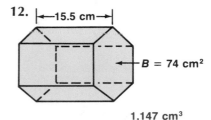

B = 74 cm²

1,147 cm³

Area of Base	Height
13. 55 in²	6.2 in.
14. 123.4 cm²	10 cm
15. 27.6 cm²	4.5 cm

Area of Base	Height
16. 37 m²	5.75 m
17. 80 ft²	$3\frac{1}{2}$ ft
18. 25 cm²	5 cm

Area of Base	Height
19. 100 cm²	19.4 cm
20. 36 in²	$4\frac{1}{2}$ in.
21. 96 cm²	7.1 cm

**13. 341 in³   14. 1,234 cm³   15. 124.2 cm³   16. 212.75 m³   17. 280 ft³   18. 125 cm³   19. 1,940 cm³   20. 162 in³
21. 681.6 cm³**

Solve.

22. The base of a concrete support column measures 1 foot by 1 foot. The column is 10 feet tall. How many cubic feet of concrete are in the column? **10 ft³**

23. A cord of wood measures 4 feet by 4 feet by 8 feet. How many cubic feet of space does it occupy? **128 ft³**

24. Rose Parker sells microwave ovens. If an oven is 1.3 ft long, 1.3 ft wide, and 0.8 ft high, what is the volume of the cooking space? **1.352 ft³**

25. A greenhouse is shaped like a triangular prism. Its base measures 64 square feet and its height is 8 feet. What is the volume of the greenhouse? **512 ft³**

26. A steel beam measures 1 ft by 1 ft by 10 ft. A cubic foot of steel weighs 490 pounds. How much does the steel beam weigh? **4,900 lb**

27. There are 231 cubic inches of water in one gallon. How many gallons does an aquarium 21 in. by 10 in. by 11 in. hold? **10 gal**

PRACTICE

Estimate. Answers may vary. Typical answers are given.

1. 695
$+\ 276$
1,000

2. 825
$-\ 386$
400

3. 590
$\times\ 62$
36,000

4. 61
$\times\ 45$
3,000

5. $27\overline{)307}$ **10**

Add, subtract, multiply, or divide.

6. 196
$+\ 452$
648

7. 42.68
$-\ 25.45$
17.23

8. 345
$\times\ 24$
8,280

9. 3.48
$\times\ 0.15$
0.522

10. $4.3\overline{)0.774}$ **0.18**

11. $49.6 + 2.53$ **52.13**   **12.** $318 - 159$ **159**   **13.** 1.9×13 **24.7**

14. $15.68 - 8.9$ **6.78**   **15.** $899 \div 29$ **31**   **16.** $2.25 \div 1.5$ **1.5**

17. $\frac{4}{9} - \frac{1}{9}$ $\frac{1}{3}$ **18.** $\frac{7}{8} + \frac{3}{4}$ $1\frac{5}{8}$ **19.** $\frac{4}{5} \times \frac{10}{11}$ $\frac{8}{11}$ **20.** $\frac{5}{6} \div \frac{1}{3}$ $2\frac{1}{2}$

21. $\frac{9}{10} - \frac{3}{8}$ $\frac{21}{40}$ **22.** $6 - 3\frac{3}{4}$ $2\frac{1}{4}$ **23.** $9 + 3\frac{7}{8}$ $12\frac{7}{8}$ **24.** $1\frac{5}{6} + 3\frac{5}{9}$ $5\frac{7}{18}$

25. $1\frac{1}{2} \times 2\frac{1}{4}$ $3\frac{3}{8}$ **26.** $3\frac{2}{3} \div 1\frac{1}{4}$ $2\frac{14}{15}$ **27.** $6\frac{1}{3} - 4\frac{4}{5}$ $1\frac{8}{15}$ **28.** $8 \div 2\frac{2}{3}$ **3**

29. $38.6 \div 100$ **0.386**   **30.** 10×0.0864 **0.864**   **31.** 100×43.7 **4,370**

32. $523 \div 10$ **52.3**   **33.** $1,000 \times 0.6$ **600**   **34.** $1.7 \div 1,000$ **0.0017**

Complete.

35. 46 cm = ▓ m **0.46**   **36.** 4,600 mg = ▓ g **4.6**   **37.** ▓ mL = 0.04 L **40**

38. ▓ km = 6,730 m **6.73**   **39.** ▓ g = 0.47 kg **470**   **40.** 14 cm = ▓ mm **140**

41. $2\frac{1}{2}$ lb = ▓ oz **40**   **42.** ▓ yd = 14 ft $4\frac{2}{3}$ **43.** 31 qt = ▓ gal $7\frac{3}{4}$

Add or subtract.

44.   6 h 14 min 25 s
$+\ 3$ h 37 min 53 s
9 h 52 min 18 s

45.   8 h 38 min
$-\ 3$ h 43 min
4 h 55 min

46.   10 h 33 min 14 s
$-\ 8$ h 42 min 39 s
1 h 50 min 35 s

47.   1 ft 7 in.
$+\ 2$ ft 9 in.
1 yd 1 ft 4 in.

48.   7 yd 2 ft 3 in.
$-\ 3$ yd 1 ft 5 in.
4 yd 0 ft 10 in.

49.   6 yd 2 ft 10 in.
$+\ 3$ yd 2 ft 8 in.
10 yd 2 ft 6 in.

Change each percent to a decimal. Change each decimal to a percent.

50. 57% **0.57**   **51.** 0.08 **8%**   **52.** 18% **0.18**   **53.** 4.65 **465%**   **54.** 70.5% **0.705**

55. 0.375 $37\frac{1}{2}$%   **56.** 123% **1.23**   **57.** 6.5% **0.065**   **58.** 0.008 **0.8%**   **59.** 0.0665 **6.65%**

Solve.

60. 10% of 42 **4.2**

61. 48% of 180 **86.4**

62. 4.1% of 15 **0.615**

63. 97% of 2,100 **2,037**

64. 6.5% of 128 **8.32**

65. 120% of 2 **2.4**

Use the proportion $\frac{P}{B} = \frac{r}{100}$ to solve each problem.

66. __?__% of 50 is 75 **150**

67. __?__ is 83% of 40 **33.2**

68. 0.5% of __?__ is 2.17 **434**

69. 155% of 6.4 is __?__ **9.92**

70. 16 is 40% of __?__ **40**

71. 12 is __?__% of 48 **25**

Find the perimeter of each figure.

72. a rectangle having a length of 8 in. and a width of 6 in. **28 in.**

73. a right triangle with a 13 cm hypotenuse and a 12 cm base. **30 cm**

Find the area of each figure. Use 3.14 for π. Round decimal answers to the nearest tenth.

74.
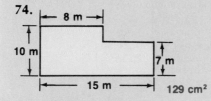
129 cm²

75.
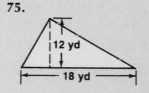
108 yd²

76.

28.26 in²

Find the surface area of each figure. Use 3.14 for π. Round decimal answers to the nearest tenth.

77.
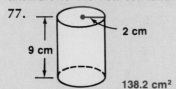
138.2 cm²

78.
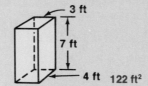
122 ft²

79.
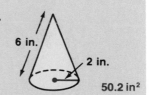
50.2 in²

Find the mode, median, and mean for each set of data.

80. 6, 8, 8, 9, 9, 9, 10, 11, 12, 12
9; 9; 9.4

81. 10, 12, 12, 13, 13, 14, 15, 16, 17, 17
12, 13 and 17; 13.5; 13.9

82. 12.3, 14.8, 12.3, 15.2, 11.8, 12.3, 15.2, 13.7, 14.0, 16, 13.2
12.3, 13.7; about 13.7

Solve.

83. Find the greatest area of a postcard whose perimeter must be 20 cm.
25 cm²

84. A long-distance telephone call costs $0.41 for the first minute. Each additional minute is $0.27. Find the cost of a 17-minute call. **$4.73**

85. A term paper has pages numbered from 1 to 26. How many digits are used in all the page numbers? **43**

86. In a paperback book, a total of 192 digits are used in the page numbers. How many pages are in the book? **100**

13-6 Volume of Cylinders

Objective: To find the volume of cylinders.

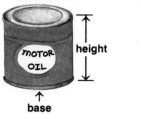 

Service stations sell motor oil, grease, and many other items that come in cylindrical containers.

A cylinder can be thought of as a prism with a circular base. The formula for the volume of a prism is $V = B \times h$ or $V = Bh$. The base of a cylinder is a circle. So, for a cylinder, B is equal to $\pi \times r^2$. Thus, the formula for the volume of a cylinder is as follows.

$$V = \pi \times r^2 \times h \text{ or } V = \pi r^2 h$$

Examples

A. Find the volume of the cylinder shown at the right. Use 3.14 for π.

$V = Bh$

$V = 25 \times 6$ *Replace B with 25 and h with 6.*

$V = 150$ 25 Ⓧ 6 🟰 *150*

The volume of the cylinder is 150 in³.

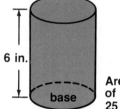

6 in.

Area of base 25 in²

base

B. Find the volume of the cylinder shown at the right. Use 3.14 for π.

Estimate: $3 \times 3^2 \times 10 = 27 \times 10 = 270$

$V = \pi r^2 h$

  $\approx 3.14 \times 3^2 \times 9$ *Replace π with 3.14, r with 3, and h with 9.*

  ≈ 254.34 3.14 Ⓧ 3 Ⓧ 3 Ⓧ 9 🟰 *254.34*

Is the answer reasonable? **yes**

The volume of the cylinder is about 254.34 cm³.

Basic: 1–25 odd; Average: 1–25; Enriched: 2–20 even; 21–25

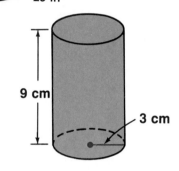

9 cm

3 cm

Exercises

Find the volume of each cylinder. Use 3.14 for π.
Round decimal answers to the nearest hundredth.

1.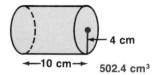
4 cm
←10 cm→   502.4 cm³

2. ← 3 ft →

1 ft
9.42 ft³

3. ← 8 cm →
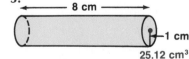
1 cm
25.12 cm³

4. ←—14 ft —→
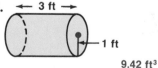
1.5 ft
98.91 ft³

5. 14 cm
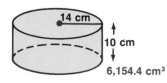
10 cm
6,154.4 cm³

6.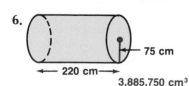
75 cm
← 220 cm →
3,885,750 cm³

292   *Surface Area and Volume*

Find the volume of each cylinder described below. Use 3.14 for π.
Round decimal answers to the nearest hundredth.

7. $B = 42$ cm^2, $h = 20$ cm
840 cm³
10. $r = 3$ m, $h = 12$ m
339.12 m³
13. $B = 100$ in., $h = 9.3$ in.
930 in³
16. $r = 4$ ft, $h = 4$ ft
200.96 ft³
19. $B = 31$ m^2, $h = 10.7$ m
331.7 m³

8. $r = 2$ in., $h = 10$ in.
125.6 in³
11. $B = 25$ ft^2, $h = 8\frac{1}{2}$ ft
212.5 ft³
14. $r = 3$ cm, $h = 8$ cm
226.08 cm³
17. $B = 52$ m^2, $h = 6.1$ m
317.2 m³
20. $r = 7$ cm, $h = 9$ cm
1,384.74 cm³

9. $B = 32$ in^2, $h = 6\frac{1}{2}$ in.
208 in³
12. $r = 2$ cm, $h = 15$ cm
188.4 cm³
15. $B = 16$ m^2, $h = 7.2$ m
115.2 m³
18. $r = 8$ yd, $h = 18$ yd
3,617.28 yd³
21. $B = 37$ ft^2, $h = 4\frac{1}{2}$ ft
166.5 ft³

Solve. Use 3.14 for π.

22. A cylindrical tank has a radius of 3 meters and a height of 4.5 meters. Find its volume. **127.17 m³**

23. A cylindrical silo for storing grain has a radius of 2 meters and a height of 10.5 meters. Find its volume. **131.88 m³**

24. A candle is 2 cm in radius and 10 cm tall. Find the amount of wax used in making it. **125.6 cm³**

25. An automobile cylinder has a radius of 6 cm and a height of 8 cm. Find its volume. **904.32 cm³**

This feature presents general topics of mathematics.

Math Break

Two wooden blocks that are the same size are placed in a container of water. One sinks and the other floats. Why?

Although the volume of the two blocks is the same, the density is different. The **density** of a substance is the mass per unit of volume.

$$\text{density} = \frac{\text{mass (g)}}{\text{volume (cm}^3)}$$

Suppose the blocks each have a volume of 120 cm^3. The mass of the first block is 150 g. The mass of the second block is 96 g. Find the density of each block.

first block **density $= \frac{150}{120}$ or 1.25**   *second block* **density $= \frac{96}{120}$ or 0.80**

The density of water is 1.00. The first block sinks because its density is greater than the density of water. The second block floats because its density is less than the density of water.

Find the density of each object. Then, tell whether the object would float or sink in water. Round decimal answers to the nearest hundredth.

1. chunk of ice: mass, 79 g; volume, 86 cm^3 **density 0.92; floats**

2. foam insulation: mass, 255 g; volume, 830 cm^3 **density 0.31; floats**

3. rocks: mass, 300 g; volume, 180 cm^3 **density 1.67; sinks**

4. glass: mass, 275 g; volume, 106 cm^3 **density 2.59; sinks**

13-7 Volume of Pyramids and Cones

Objective: To find the volume of pyramids and cones.

If a pyramid and a prism have the same base and height, then the
volume of the pyramid is one-third the volume of the prism.

The formula for the volume of a prism is
$V = B \times h$ or $V = \ell \times w \times h$.

The formula for the volume of a pyramid is
$V = \frac{1}{3} \times B \times h$ or $V = \frac{1}{3} \times \ell \times w \times h$.

Examples

A. Find the volume of the pyramid
shown at the right.

Estimate: 2 × 60 = 120

$V = \frac{1}{3} \ell wh$

$V = \frac{1}{3} \times 6 \times 7 \times 9$

$V = 126$

1 ÷ 3 ⊠ 6 ⊠ 7 ⊠ 9 = *126*

The volume of the pyramid is 126 ft³.

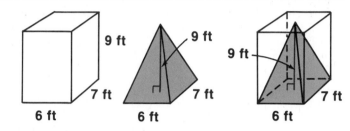

Is the answer reasonable? **yes**

If a cone and a cylinder have the same radius and height, then
the volume of the cone is one-third the volume of the cylinder.

The formula for the volume of a cylinder is
$V = B \times h$ or $V = \pi \times r^2 \times h$.

The formula for the volume of a cone is
$V = \frac{1}{3} \times B \times h$ or $V = \frac{1}{3} \times \pi \times r^2 \times h$.

B. Find the volume of the cone shown at
the right. Use 3.14 for π.

Estimate: 1 × 20 × 20 = 400

$V = \frac{1}{3} \pi r^2 h$

$V \approx \frac{1}{3} \times 3.14 \times 4^2 \times 18$

≈ 301.44 or 301.4

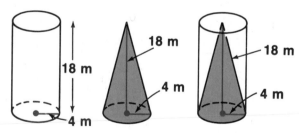

1 ÷ 3 ⊠ 3.14 ⊠ 16 ⊠ 18 = *301.44*

Is the answer reasonable? **yes**

The volume of the cone is about 301.4 m³.

Basic: 1–21 odd; Average: 1–24; Enriched: 2–20 even, 21–24

Exercises

Find the volume of each pyramid described below.
Round decimal answers to the nearest tenth.

1.
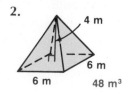

9 cm
8 cm
8 cm   192 cm³

2.
4 m
6 m
6 m   48 m³

3.
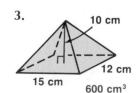

10 cm
12 cm
15 cm   600 cm³

4.
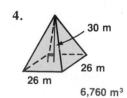

30 m
26 m
26 m
6,760 m³

Length	Width	Height
5. 24 cm	10 cm	7 cm
6. 5 cm	5 cm	5 cm
7. 20 cm	12 cm	6.5 cm

5. 560 cm³ 6. 41.7 cm³ 7. 520 cm³

Length	Width	Height
8. 37 m³	10 m	7 m
9. 17 cm	6 cm	8 cm
10. 10 ft	15 ft	5 ft

8. 863.3 m³   9. 272 cm³   10. 250 ft³

Find the volume of each cone described below. Use 3.14 for π.
Round decimal answers to the nearest tenth. Remember _d_ = 2_r_.

11.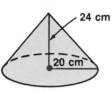

24 cm

20 cm

10,048 cm³

12.

9 m

4 m

150.7 m³

13.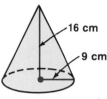

16 cm

9 cm

1,356.5 cm³

14.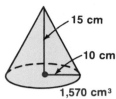

15 cm

10 cm

1,570 cm³

15. _r_ = 6 in., _h_ = 12 in.
452.2 in³

16. _r_ = 5 cm, _h_ = 6 cm
157 cm³

17. _d_ = 9 ft, _h_ = 15 ft
317.9 ft³

18. _d_ = 3.6 m, _h_ = 4.8 m
16.3 m³

19. _r_ = 12 mm, _h_ = 42 mm
6,330.2 mm³

20. _d_ = 12 cm, _h_ = 6.5 cm
244.9 cm³

24. 1,465.3 in³; 5,861.3 in³; 13,188 in³; The volume would be four times as large.
The volume would be nine times as large.

Solve.

21. A cone-shaped flour bin has a radius of 10 ft and a height of 18 ft. Find its volume. Use 3.14 for π.
1,884 ft³

22. The Great Pyramid in Egypt is about 755 ft on each side of the base, and about 480 ft high. What is its volume?
about 91,204,000 ft³

23. A cone-shaped funnel has a radius of 7 inches and a height of 10 inches. What is the volume of the funnel to the nearest tenth? 512.9 in³

24. A cone has a radius of 10 inches and a height of 14 inches. What happens to the volume of the cone if the radius is doubled? Tripled?

This feature promotes students' mental abilities in computation and reasonableness.

 Mental Math

Estimating the range of an answer helps to determine if your answer to a problem is reasonable.

18 ÷ 4   16 ÷ 4 = 4
              20 ÷ 4 = 5

The answer is between 4 and 5.

The range is 4 to 5.

4.3 × 5.6   4 × 5 = 20
                5 × 6 = 30

The answer is between 20 and 30.

The range is 20 to 30.

Find the range using the strategy above. Answers may vary. Typical answers are given.

1. 62 × 39 1,800—2,800

2. 41 × 96 3,600—5,000

3. 89.9 × 4.11 320—450

4. 2.41 × 5.41 10—18

5. 2.49 × 42.3 80—150

6. 259 × 616 120,000—210,000

7. 167 ÷ 69 2—3

8. 298 ÷ 78.1 3—4

9. 190 ÷ 8.4 20—30

13-8 Surface Area and Volume of Spheres

Objective: To find the surface area and volume of spheres.

Spherical tanks are often used to store liquids and gases because they require less building material for a given volume.

A **sphere** is a solid figure in which all points are the same distance from the center. The formulas for the surface area and volume of a sphere are based on the formula for the area of a circle ($A = \pi r^2$). The radius (r) of a sphere is the distance from any point on the sphere to its center.

To find the surface area of a sphere, use the following formula.

$$S.A. = 4 \times \pi \times r^2$$

Teacher Resource Book, Page 292

To find the volume of a sphere, use the following formula.

$$V = \frac{4}{3} \times \pi \times r^3$$

Examples

A. Find the surface area of a sphere with a radius of 2 meters. Use 3.14 for π. Round answer to the nearest tenth.

Estimate: 4 × 3 × 4 = 48

$S = 4 \times \pi \times r^2$

$S \approx 4 \times 3.14 \times 2^2$

$S \approx 50.24$

4 [X] 3.14 [X] 2 [X] 2 [=] 50.24

The answer is reasonable.

The surface area of the sphere is about 50.2 m².

B. Find the volume of a sphere with a radius of 2 meters. Use 3.14 for π. Round answer to the nearest tenth.

Estimate: 1 × 3 × 8 = 24

$V = \frac{4}{3} \times \pi \times r^3$

$V \approx \frac{4}{3} \times 3.14 \times 2^3$

$V \approx 33.49$

4 [÷] 3 [X] 3.14 [X] 2 [X] 2 [X] 2 [=] 33.49

The answer is reasonable.

The volume of the sphere is about 33.5 m³.

Basic: 1–17 odd; Average: 1–19; Enriched: 2–12 even, 13–19

Exercises

Find the surface area and the volume for each sphere described below. Use 3.14 for π. Round decimal answers to the nearest tenth.

1.

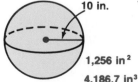

10 in.

1,256 in²

4,186.7 in³

2.

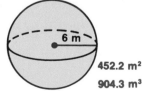

6 m

452.2 m²

904.3 m³

3.

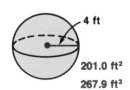

4 ft

201.0 ft²

267.9 ft³

4.

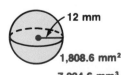

12 mm

1,808.6 mm²

7,234.6 mm³

5. 5,024 in²; 33,493.3 in³

5. radius, 20 in.

6. 7,850 ft²; 65,416.7 ft³
6. radius, 25 ft

7. diameter, 15.4 m
744.7 m², 1,911.4 m³

8. radius, 4.36 in.
238.8 in², 347.0 in³

9. radius, 2.4 in.
72.3 in²,
57.9 in³

10. radius, 4.2 ft
221.6 ft²,
310.2 ft³

11. radius, 7.8 ft
764.2 ft²,
1,986.8 ft³

12. diameter, 8.72 in.
238.8 in²,
347.0 in³

Solve. Use 3.14 for π. Round decimal answers to the nearest tenth.

13. A spherical water tank has a radius of 7.2 meters. What is the surface area of the tank?
651.1 m²

14. A spherical hot air balloon has a radius of 57.2 feet. Find the surface area of the balloon.
41,094.3 ft²

15. A bathysphere is a spherical structure used underwater. If it has a radius of 6 ft, what is its volume?
904.3 ft³

16. A marble has a radius of 0.3 in. Find the volume of the marble to the nearest hundredth of a cubic inch.
0.1 in³

17. The earth is almost a perfect sphere. The radius is about 4,000 mi. Find its surface area to the nearest million square miles.
201,000,000 mi²

18. The radius of the earth is about 6.4 megameters (million meters). Find the volume of the earth to the nearest cubic megameter.
1,098 cubic megameters

19. There are 231 cubic inches of water in one gallon. How many gallons of water can be stored in a spherical tank with radius of 10 inches? Round to the nearest gallon. 18 gal

This feature provides general topics about the uses of a computer.

Computer

Information, or data, can be transmitted in a computer system in two ways.

- **Digital:** This method is based on counting. Data jump from one number to the next in an off/on pulse. A car odometer is an example of a digital operation.

- **Analog:** This method is based on measuring. Data move gradually from one number to the next in a continuous manner. A car speedometer is an example of an analog operation.

4. Clock with sweep second hand; radio with moving marker on dial; scales with moving dial.

Find an example of each object that is digital.

1. clock **light emitting diode (LED) display**

2. radio **LED frequency display on dial**

3. bathroom scales **electronic digital readout**

4. Find an example of each object in exercises 1–3 that is analog.

5. Does a handheld calculator use digital or analog operation? **digital**

13-9 Problem Solving: Comparing Volumes

Objective: To compare volumes by subtraction and division.

Two numbers can be compared in the following ways.

Use subtraction to show:

A. how much greater the first number is than the second number.

B. how much less the first number is than the second number.

Use division to show:

C. that the first number is how many times as much as the second number.

D. what part the first number is of the second number.

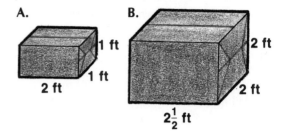

A. 1 ft / 1 ft / 2 ft

B. 2 ft / 2 ft / $2\frac{1}{2}$ ft

The dimensions of two rectangular packages are shown at the right. Find the volume of each package. Then compare the volumes in each of the ways given above.

Read

You know the dimensions of the two packages. You are to find the two volumes and compare them in four different ways.

Decide

Multiply length by width by height to find the volume of each package. Compare the volumes first by subtraction and then by division.

Solve

Find the volume of each package.

A. $V = \ell wh$
$\quad = 2 \times 1 \times 1$
$\quad = 2$

The volume is 2 ft³.

B. $V = \ell wh$
$\quad = 2\frac{1}{2} \times 2 \times 2$
$\quad = 10$

The volume is 10 ft³.

Use subtraction to compare.

A. 10 ft³ is how much more than 2 ft³?

$10 - 2 = 8$

10 ft³ is 8 ft³ more than 2 ft³.

B. 2 ft³ is how much less than 10 ft³?

$10 - 2 = 8$

2 ft³ is 8 ft³ less than 10 ft³.

Use division to compare.

C. 10 ft³ is how many times as much as 2 ft³?

$10 \div 2 = 5$

10 ft³ is 5 times as much as 2 ft³.

D. 2 ft³ is what part of 10 ft³?

$2 \div 10 = \frac{1}{5}$

2 ft³ is $\frac{1}{5}$ of 10 ft³.

Examine

To check the answers above, the inverse operations can be used.

A. $2 + 8 = 10$ **B.** $2 + 8 = 10$ **C.** $2 \times 5 = 10$ **D.** $\frac{1}{5} \times 10 = 2$

The answers are correct.

Exercises

Answer the questions about the containers shown at the right.

1. Which appears to hold more, A or B? **B**

2. What is the volume of container A? **343 cm³**

3. What is the volume of container B? **297 cm³**

4. Which holds more? How much more?
   A, 46 cm³ more

5. Which appears to hold less, C or D? **C**

6. What solid figure does C resemble?
   cylinder
7. What is the volume of C?
   401.9 cm³
8. What solid figure does D resemble?
   cone
9. What is the volume of D?
   392.5 cm³
10. Which holds less? How much less?
    cone, 9.4 cm³ less

A. **B.**

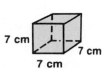

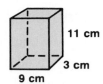
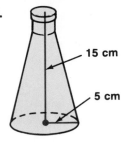

C. **D.**

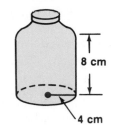

Solve.

E. **F.**

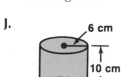
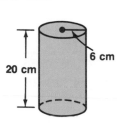

11. Juice can be purchased in the containers shown at the left. If the price of each is 50¢, which is the better buy? (Hint: First find the volume of each container.)
    neither, volumes are the same

12. Which of the two figures shown at the right has the greater volume? How much greater? **G, 20.9 ft³ more**

G. **H.**

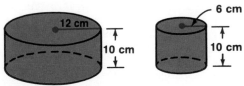

J. **K.**

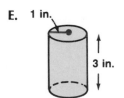
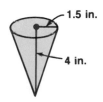

13. Cylinder K shown at the left has how many times the volume of cylinder J? **2 times as much**

L. **M.**

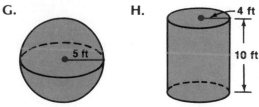

14. The volume of cylinder L shown at the right is how many times as great as the volume of cylinder M? **4 times as much**

N. **P.**

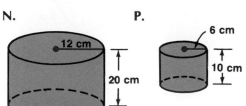

15. Cylinder P shown at the left has what part of the volume of cylinder N? **$\frac{1}{8}$**

CHAPTER 13 REVIEW

Vocabulary/Concepts

Use a word, phrase, or formula from the list at the right to complete each sentence.

1. The surface area of a ___?___ is the sum of the areas of its surfaces. **cylinder or rectangular prism**

2. The ___?___ of a cylinder is the rectangular surface formed when the cylinder is cut apart and unrolled. **lateral surface**

3. A ___?___ is a flat surface. **face**

4. The surface area of a ___?___ is the sum of the areas of the bases and the lateral surface area. **cylinder or rectangular prism**

5. The formula for the surface area of a cone is ___?___. **$\pi r (r + s)$**

6. A ___?___ is a solid figure with two parallel congruent circular bases. **cylinder**

7. The formula for the volume of any prism is ___?___. **Bh**

8. How much space an object contains is its ___?___. **volume**

9. The distance from any point on a sphere to its center is a ___?___. **radius**

10. The formula for the volume of a cylinder is ___?___. **$\pi r^2 h$**

11. The formula for the surface area of a sphere is ___?___. **$4\pi r^2$**

cone
cylinder
edge
face
lateral surface
prism
pyramid
radius
rectangular prism
sphere
volume
$\pi r^2 h$
$\pi r (r + s)$
Bh
$4\pi r^2$

Exercises

Find the surface areas of each figure described below.   Pages 281–283

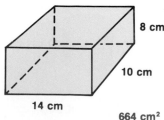

8 cm

10 cm

14 cm

664 cm²

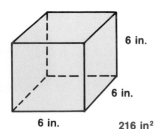

6 in.

6 in.

6 in.

216 in²

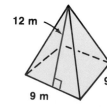

12 m

9 m

9 m

297 m²

15. rectangular prism
$\ell = 9$ cm, $w = 12$ cm,
$h = 8$ cm
552 cm²

16. square pyramid
$\ell = 10$ m, $h = 12.5$ m
350 m²

17. triangular pyramid
$B = 6.1$ ft², $\ell = 7$ ft,
$h = 9$ ft
100.6 ft²

Find the surface area of each solid described below. Use 3.14 for π. Round decimal answers to the nearest tenth.   Pages 284–287, 296–297

18.

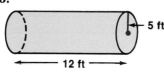

5 ft

12 ft

533.8 ft²

19.

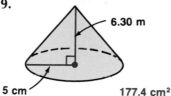

6.30 m

5 cm

177.4 cm²

20.

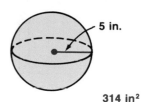

5 in.

314 in²

21. cylinder
$r = 5.2$ in.; $h = 26$ in.
1,018.9 in²

22. cone
$r = 8.4$ yd; $s = 11$ yd
511.7 yd²

23. sphere
$r = 25$ in.
7,850 in²

Find the volume of each solid described below.   Pages 288–289; 294–295

24.

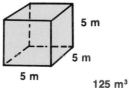

5 m

5 m

5 m

125 m³

25.

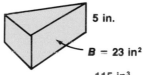

5 in.

$B = 23$ in²

115 in³

26.

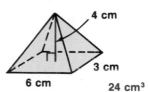

4 cm

3 cm

6 cm

24 cm³

27. rectangular prism
$\ell = 5$ in.; $w = 6$ in.;
$h = 4\frac{1}{2}$ in. **135 in³**

28. square pyramid
length of a side = 10 m;
$h = 9$ m **300 m³**

29. triangular pyramid
$B = 6.1$ ft²; $h = 9$ ft
18.3 ft³

Find the volume of each solid described below. Use 3.14 for π. Round answers to the nearest tenth.   Pages 292–297

30.

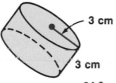

3 cm

3 cm

84.8 cm³

31.

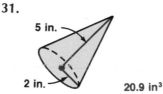

5 in.

2 in.

20.9 in³

32.

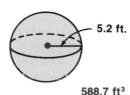

5.2 ft.

588.7 ft³

33. cylinder
$r = 2.6$ in.; $h = 26$ in.
551.9 in³

34. cone
$r = 8.4$ yd; $h = 12.7$ yd
937.9 yd³

35. sphere
$r = 25$ in.
65,416.7 in³

Solve. Use 3.14 for π. Round decimal answers to the nearest tenth.

36. A round of cheese is 2.5 ft thick. The radius is 1.3 ft. Find its surface area. **31 ft²**

37. The floor of a square pyramid tent is 12 feet on each side. The height of the tent is 11 feet. Find its volume. **528 ft³**

38. The radius of a spherical balloon is 4 meters. A second spherical balloon has a radius of 2 meters. The surface area of the first balloon is how many times as large as the surface area of the second balloon?
4 times as large

CHAPTER 13 TEST

Find the surface area of each figure. Use 3.14 for π.
Round decimal answers to the nearest tenth.

1.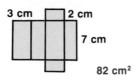
3 cm 2 cm
7 cm
82 cm²

2.
6 m
1 m
2 m
40 m²

3.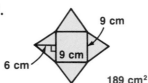
2 in.
10 in.
5 in.
160 in²

4.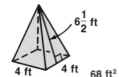
$6\frac{1}{2}$ ft
4 ft 4 ft
68 ft²

5.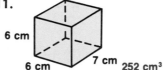
9 cm
9 cm
6 cm
189 cm²

6.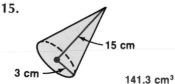
24 in.
3 in.
508.7 in²

7.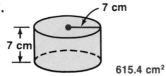
7 cm
7 cm
615.4 cm²

8.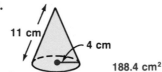
11 cm
4 cm
188.4 cm²

9.
5 cm 14 cm
298.3 cm²

Find the volume of each solid. Use 3.14 for π.
Round decimal answers to the nearest tenth.

10.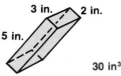
3 in. 2 in.
5 in.
30 in³

11.
6 cm
6 cm 7 cm 252 cm³

12.
4 cm
6 cm
301.4 cm³

13.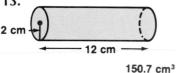
2 cm
12 cm
150.7 cm³

14.
16 in.
14 in. 14 in.
1,045.3 in³

15.
15 cm
3 cm
141.3 cm³

Solve. Use 3.14 for π. Round decimal answers to the nearest tenth.

16. A storage silo is cylindrical. Its radius is 2 meters and its height is 12 meters. Find its volume. **150.7 m³**

17. The base of a steel beam measures 0.5 meters by 0.2 meters. Its height is 7 meters. Find its volume. **0.7 m³**

18. A cone-shaped funnel has a radius of 21 centimeters and a slant height of 33 centimeters. Find its surface area. **3,560.8 cm²**

19. A cylindrical water tank has a radius of 2 meters and a height of 3.2 meters. Find the surface area of the tank. **65.3 m²**

20. Box A measures 14 in. long, 9 in. wide, and 11 in. high. Box B measures 17 in. long, 11 in. wide, and 7 in. high.
Which box has the greater volume? How much greater? **A; 77 in³ more**

This page provides extra practice of the skills and applications presented thus far in the text.

CUMULATIVE REVIEW

Answer each of the following to complete
600 mm = ▓ m.   Pages 142–143

1. Which unit is larger, mm or m?

2. Do you multiply or divide?

3. How many mm in one m? **1,000**

4. Would you use 10, 100, or 1,000?

5. 600 mm = ▓ m **0.6**

Answer each of the following to complete
15 km = ▓ m.

6. Which unit is larger, km or m?

7. Do you multiply or divide?

8. How many m in one km? **1,000**

9. Would you use 10, 100, or 1,000?

10. 15 km = ▓ m **15,000**

Add or subtract.   Pages 174–175

11. 　3 h 11 min 55 s
     − 1 h 13 min 58 s
     1 h 57 min 57 s

12. 　5 d 14 h 40 min
     + 2 d 6 h 52 min
     7 d 21 h 32 min

13. 　8 wk 3 d
     − 5 wk 5 d
     2 wk 5 d

For each set of gas meters, use subtraction to determine the number of cubic feet of
natural gas used for the month.   Pages 192–195

Meter at Beginning of Month	Meter at End of Month	

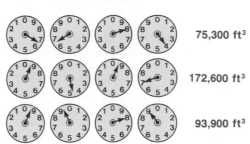

14. 75,300 ft³

15. 172,600 ft³

16. 93,900 ft³

Use a protractor to measure each angle shown
in the figure at the right.   Pages 196–197

17. WOV **27°**

18. WOQ **150°**

19. POS **80°**

20. SOT **10°**

21. POR **45°**

22. POU **117°**

23. UOS **40°**

24. WOS **100°**

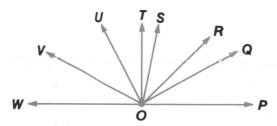

Find the surface area of each rectangular prism described below.   Page 281

25. ℓ = 11.5 cm, w = 5 cm,
    h = 4 cm **247 cm²**

26. ℓ = 8 m, w = 3 m,
    h = 7.5 m **213 m²**

27. ℓ = 4 yd, w = 3 yd,
    h = 5 yd **94 yd²**

Find the volume of each rectangular prism described below.   Pages 288–289

28. ℓ = 16 cm, w = 5 cm,
    h = 20 cm **1,600 cm³**

29. ℓ = 9 ft, w = 4 ft,
    h = 6 ft **216 ft³**

30. ℓ = 20 mm, w = 12 mm,
    h = 15 mm **3,600 mm³**

Rational Numbers

14-1 Integers and Opposites

Objective: To recognize integers and their opposites.

In one day, temperatures across the United States ranged from 80°
above zero to 40° below zero. Temperatures can be written as
positive or negative numbers called **integers**.

80° above zero ➡ 80°   40° below zero ➡ ⁻40°

Integers can be shown on a number line. Numbers to the left of
zero are less than zero. Numbers to the right of zero are
greater than zero. For example, ⁻3 < 0, 5 > 0, and so on.

The numbers, ⁻1, ⁻2, ⁻3, . . . ,
are called negative integers.
The number negative three is
written ⁻3.

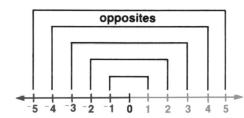

The numbers, 1, 2, 3, . . . ,
are called positive integers.
The number positive four is
written ⁺4 or 4.

Zero is neither positive nor negative.

Notice that every negative integer can be paired with a positive
integer so that their sum is zero. These pairs are called **opposites**.
For example, the opposite of 1 is ⁻1 and the opposite of ⁻4 is 4.   *The opposite of 0 is 0.*

Basic: 1–20; Average: 1–20; Enriched: 1–20

Exercises

Name the integer that corresponds to each letter on the number line.

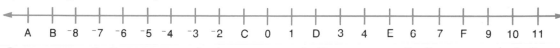

1. B ⁻9 **2.** F 8 **3.** A ⁻10 **4.** D 2 **5.** C ⁻1 **6.** E 5

Write an integer to describe each situation.

7. 12° above zero 12° **8.** 13° below zero ⁻13° **9.** $400 increase **400**

10. $300 decrease ⁻**300** **11.** 7-yard loss ⁻7 **12.** 10-yard gain **10**

Write the opposite of each integer.

13. 8 ⁻8 **14.** ⁻27 **27** **15.** ⁻42 **42** **16.** 0 **0** **17.** 36 ⁻**36** **18.** ⁻81 **81**

19. Find the opposite of the opposite
    of ⁻32. ⁻**32**

20. Find three examples of negative
    integers used in everyday living.
    Answers may vary.

14-2 Rational Numbers and Absolute Value

Objective: To recognize rational numbers, their opposites, and their absolute values.

Water in one end of a swimming pool is $3\frac{1}{2}$ feet deep. Suppose the top of the water is represented by 0. Then the bottom of the pool can be represented by the rational number $^-3\frac{1}{2}$ or $-\frac{7}{2}$. Any number that can be written as the ratio of two integers, $\frac{a}{b}$, where $b \neq 0$, is called a **rational number.** Several rational numbers are shown below.

$$^-4 = \frac{^-4}{1} \qquad \frac{2}{3} \qquad 4.2 = \frac{42}{10} \qquad 0 = \frac{0}{1} \qquad -\frac{7}{8}$$

Rational numbers can be compared on a number line. The greater of two numbers is always on the right.

Examples

A. Compare $^-1.5$ and $^-6$.

$^-1.5$ lies to the right of $^-6$.

$^-1.5 > ^-6$ $>$ *means is greater than*

B. Order $^-5, 5, ^-3\frac{1}{3}, 3\frac{1}{3}$, and 0 from least to greatest.

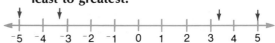

The order from least to greatest is

$^-5, ^-3\frac{1}{3}, 0, 3\frac{1}{3}$, and 5.

Rational numbers and their opposites can be shown on a number line. The opposite of 1.5 is $^-1.5$.

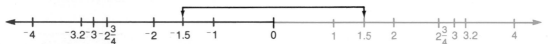

The distance a number is from zero is called its **absolute value.** A number and its opposite have the same absolute value. Since the absolute value of a number indicates distance, it is always positive or zero. The symbol $|\ \ |$ is used to indicate absolute value.

$|8| = 8$ *The absolute value of 8 is 8.* $|^-4| = 4$ *The absolute value of $^-4$ is 4.*

Example

C. Name the rational number that has the same absolute value as each given number.

7 has the same absolute value as $^-7$ *$^-5$ has the same absolute value as 5*

Basic Skills Appendix, Page 453
Basic: 1–49 odd; Average: 1–50; Enriched: 2–42 even, 43–50

Exercises

Write the opposite of each rational number.

1. $2\frac{1}{3}$ $^-2\frac{1}{3}$ 2. 12.6 $^-12.6$ 3. $-\frac{4}{5}$ $\frac{4}{5}$ 4. $^-4\frac{1}{4}$ $4\frac{1}{4}$ 5. $^-(^-5)$ $^-5$ 6. $|^-4|$ $^-4$

Write the letter that names each rational number on the number line below.

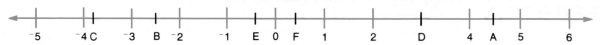

7. 0.4 **F**   8. 3 **D**   9. ⁻3.8 **C**   10. $4\frac{1}{2}$ **A**   11. ⁻0.4 **E**   12. ⁻$2\frac{1}{2}$ **B**

Replace each ▦ with <, >, or = to make a true sentence.

13. ⁻6 ▦ ⁻8 **>**   14. ⁻0.8 ▦ ⁻0.1 **<**   15. $\frac{4}{5}$ ▦ $\frac{3}{5}$ **>**   16. $\frac{3}{5}$ ▦ 0.6 **=**

17. 0 ▦ ⁻18 **>**   18. ⁻2.14 ▦ ⁻2.1 **<**   19. |7| ▦ |⁻7| **=**   20. |⁻5| ▦ |⁻4.5| **>**

Order each set of numbers from least to greatest. For answers to exercises 21–26, see Teacher Guide.

21. 5, 7, ⁻2, 0, 4

22. 12, ⁻7, 1, ⁻3, ⁻2

23. 7, 3, 6, ⁻15, ⁻8

24. 0, $\frac{-1}{2}$, 3, $\frac{2}{3}$, $\frac{-4}{2}$

25. 3.5, ⁻3, 0, ⁻3.5, 3

26. 8, |⁻6|, 5, |4|, 0

Write a rational number to describe each situation.

27. a loss of 0.75 kilograms **⁻0.75**

28. a gain of $2\frac{1}{2}$ pounds **$2\frac{1}{2}$**

29. 25 minutes before closing time **⁻25**

30. an increase of $3.16 **3.16**

Complete.

31. |9| = ▦ **9**   32. |⁻6| = ▦ **6**   33. |12| = ▦ **12**   34. |0| = ▦ **0**

35. |⁻4| = ▦ **4**   36. |⁻21| = ▦ **21**   37. |1.5| = ▦ **1.5**   38. $|\frac{1}{8}|$ = ▦ **$\frac{1}{8}$**

39. $|-\frac{2}{3}|$ = ▦ **$\frac{2}{3}$**   40. |⁻5.7| = ▦ **5.7**   41. |⁻9| − |6| = ▦ **3**   42. |⁻4| + |⁻9| = ▦ **13**

Complete.

43. If ⁻4 indicates a loss of 4 yards, what does 4 indicate? **gain of 4 yards**

44. If 12 indicates 12 seconds after takeoff, what does ⁻12 indicate?
12 seconds before takeoff

45. Acme stock lost $3\frac{1}{8}$ points on the market. Express this as a rational number **⁻$3\frac{1}{8}$**

46. An infant's weight increased $3\frac{1}{4}$ pounds in 16 weeks. Express this increase as a rational number. **$3\frac{1}{4}$**

Use the table at the right to answer the following.

47. What is the lowest elevation in North America? **⁻282**

48. Where is the lowest elevation in the world? **Asia**

49. What is the lowest elevation in the world? **⁻1,290 ft**

50. Order the lowest elevations of the continents, beginning with the lowest.
⁻1,290; ⁻571; ⁻282; ⁻131; ⁻38; 0; 0

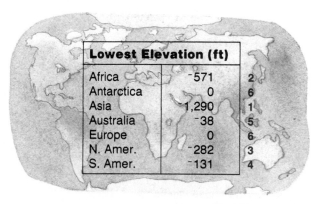

Lowest Elevation (ft)	
Africa	⁻571
Antarctica	0
Asia	⁻1,290
Australia	⁻38
Europe	0
N. Amer.	⁻282
S. Amer.	⁻131

14-3 Graphing Rational Numbers

Objective: To investigate patterns on number lines.

As water freezes, its volume expands. Most of this expansion happens
between the temperatures of 4°C and 0°C. You can show this
with the following number line graph.

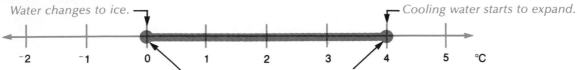

Water changes to ice.   *Cooling water starts to expand.*

These dots show that 0 and 4 are included in the set of members.

Other sets of numbers can be graphed on a number line.

Examples

Graph each set of numbers on a number line.
Point out that brackets { } are used when describing a set.

A. {0, 2, 4, 6, 8}

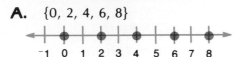

B. {⁻5, ⁻3, ⁻1, 1}

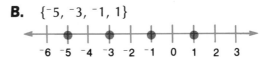

C. {4, 5, 6, 7, 8, . . .}
and so on

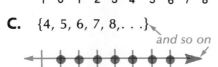

D. {all numbers < 4}
includes all numbers less than 4

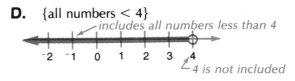

4 is not included

E. {all numbers ≥ 5}
≥ *means greater than or equal to*

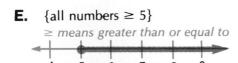

F. {all numbers > 4 and < 6}

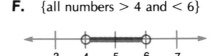

G. {all numbers ≥ ⁻3 and < 1}

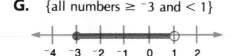

H. {all numbers ≥ ⁻3 and ≤ 3}

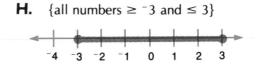

I. {all positive numbers < 0}
No points are graphed.

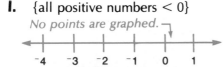

*There are no positive numbers less than zero,
so this set has no members. It is called the
empty set and is written as { } or Ø.*

Basic: 1–10, 12–38 even; Average: 1–38; Enriched: 1–10, 11–37 odd

Exercises

Refer to Example C to answer the following.

1. What do the three dots in
4, 5, 6, 7, 8, . . . indicate?
pattern continues indefinitely

2. How does the graph show that the
pattern continues?
a bold arrow pointing to the right

Refer to Example D to answer the following.

3. How does the graph show that 4 is *not* included? **circle at 4**

4. How does the graph show that numbers such as ⁻1, ½, and 3 *are* included? **solid line that continues indefinitely to the left**

Refer to Example E to answer the following.

5. How does the graph show that 5 is included? **a dot on the line at 5**

6. Does the graph show that 6½ is included? How? **yes; solid line**

Refer to Examples F, G, and H to answer the following.

7. What does the symbol ≥ mean? **greater than or equal to**

8. What does the symbol ≤ mean? **less than or equal to**

9. Which graph shows the numbers between 4 and 6? **F**

10. Which graph shows the numbers ⁻3 and 3 and all numbers between? **H**

11. Which graph shows all the numbers greater than or equal to ⁻3 and less than one? **G**

Graph each set of numbers on a number line. For answers to exercises 12–26, see Teacher Guide.

12. {0, 1, 2, 3, 4}

13. {⁻4, ⁻3, ⁻2, ⁻1, 0}

14. {0, 1, 2, 3, 4, . . .}

15. {4, 3, 2, 1, 0}

16. {0, ⁻1, ⁻2, ⁻3, ⁻4}

17. {4, 3, 2, 1, 0, . . .}

18. {3, 5, 7, 9}

19. {3, 5, 7, 9, . . .}

20. {1.7, 2.6, 3.5, . . .}

21. {all numbers less than ⁻2}

22. {all numbers greater than 9}

23. {all numbers 2 or greater}

24. {all numbers ⁻1 or less}

25. {all numbers > ⁻5}

26. {all numbers ≤ 15}

Name each set of numbers graphed below.

27.  {⁻1, 2, 3}

28. ∅ or { }

29. {4, 5, 6 . . .}

30. {. . . 0, 1, 2, 3}

31. {all numbers > 0}

32. {all numbers < ⁻2}

33. {all numbers ≥ 4}

34. {all numbers ≤ 3}

35. {all numbers between ⁻2 and 2}

36. {3 and all numbers between ⁻2 and 3}

Complete. For answers to 37 and 38, see Teacher Guide.

37. Tickets at a concert were priced at $6, $7, $9, and $11. Draw a number line and graph the numbers that represent the price of each ticket.

38. The lowest temperature on Tuesday was ⁻3°C. The highest temperature was 4°C. Draw a number line and graph the numbers that represent the range in temperature.

14-4 Adding Rational Numbers

Objective: To add rational numbers using rules for addition.

Marilyn Ramos works as a teller at a local bank. Marilyn is a high school graduate and received on-the-job training for her position. She cashes checks for her customers. She also handles deposits (positive numbers) and withdrawals (negative numbers) for customers.

The number line can be used to add rational numbers.

- Start at zero.
- Move right for positive numbers.
- Move left for negative numbers.

Example

A. Use a number line to find $2 + {}^-5$.

Start at zero.
Move right 2 units.
From there, move left 5 units.

$2 + {}^-5 = {}^-3$

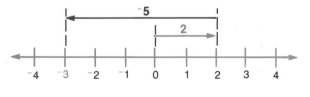

$2 + {}^-5 = {}^-3$

$|2| = 2 \quad |{}^-5| = 5$
$5 - 2 = 3$

Which number being added has the greater absolute value? **${}^-5$**
The sum has the same sign as this number.

This example suggests the following rule.

> **To add rational numbers with different signs, subtract their absolute values. Give the result the same sign as the number with the greater absolute value.**

Example

B. Use a number line to find ${}^-1 + {}^-4$.

Start at zero.
Move left 1 unit.
From there, move left 4 units.

${}^-1 + {}^-4 = {}^-5$

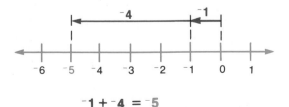

${}^-1 + {}^-4 = {}^-5$

$|{}^-1| = 1 \quad |{}^-4| = 4$
$1 + 4 = 5$

How does the sum of the absolute values of the addends compare to the sum of the addends?
It is the opposite.

The sum of two negative rational numbers is negative. You already know that the sum of two positive rational numbers is positive. This suggests the following rule.

Rules are used because graphing is not convenient.

> **To add rational numbers with the same sign, add their absolute values. Give the result the same sign as the numbers.**

Examples

Find each sum.

C. $^-13 + 8$ *The numbers have different signs.*

$|^-13| - |8| = 13 - 8$ *Subtract their absolute values.*
$= 5$

$^-13 + 8 = ^-5$ *Give the result a negative sign because the number with the greater absolute value, $^-13$, is negative.*

D. $^-9 + ^-16$ *Both numbers are negative.*

$|^-9| + |^-16| = 9 + 16$ *Add their absolute values.*
$= 25$

$^-9 + ^-16 = ^-25$ *Give the result a negative sign.*

E. $14 + ^-4$ *The numbers have different signs.*

$|14| - |^-4| = 14 - 4$ *Subtract their absolute values.*
$= 10$

$14 + ^-4 = 10$ *The sum is positive. Why?*

The number with the greater absolute value, 14, is positive.

The Key Skills provides practice of skills needed in the exercises.

Key Skills

Add or subtract. Write each answer in simplest form.

$$\frac{2}{3} \rightarrow \frac{6}{9}$$
$$\frac{3}{4} \rightarrow \frac{9}{12}$$
$$-\frac{4}{9} \rightarrow \frac{4}{9}$$
$$+\frac{1}{6} \rightarrow \frac{2}{12}$$
$$\frac{2}{9}$$
$$\frac{11}{12}$$

1. $\frac{2}{3} + \frac{3}{4}$ $1\frac{5}{12}$

2. $1\frac{3}{7} + \frac{6}{7}$ $2\frac{2}{7}$

3. $4\frac{4}{9} - 1\frac{1}{9}$ $3\frac{1}{3}$

4. $\frac{7}{8} - \frac{5}{6}$ $\frac{1}{24}$

5. $1\frac{1}{2} + 3\frac{7}{10}$ $5\frac{1}{5}$

6. $5\frac{1}{5} - 2\frac{2}{3}$ $2\frac{8}{15}$

Basic Skills Appendix, Pages 450, 452, 454, 455, 456, 457
Basic: 1–45 odd; Average: 1–45 odd; Enriched: 2–46 even

Exercises

Write an addition sentence for each diagram.

1.

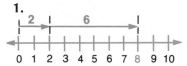

2.

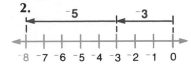

3.

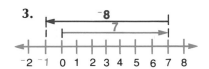

Add. Use a number line. For answers to exercises 4–11, see Teacher Guide.

4. $^-7 + 3$

5. $8 + ^-3$

6. $^-10 + 10$

7. $^-9 + ^-7$

8. $^-2 + 6 + ^-7$

Add.

9. $17 + 16$ **33**

10. $^-5 + 2$ **$^-3$**

11. $^-4 + 9$ **5**

12. $^-37 + ^-46$ **$^-83$**

13. $^-36 + 18$ **$^-18$**

14. $6 + ^-8$ **$^-2$**

15. $54 + ^-78$ **$^-24$**

16. $68 + ^-25$ **43**

17. $^-16 + ^-15$ **$^-31$**

18. $\frac{3}{4} + \left(-\frac{2}{3}\right)$ **$\frac{1}{12}$**

19. $-\frac{5}{6} + \frac{7}{8}$ **$\frac{1}{24}$**

20. $^-1\frac{2}{3} + \left(-\frac{5}{6}\right)$ **$^-2\frac{1}{2}$**

21. $\frac{33}{100} + \frac{49}{100}$ **$\frac{41}{50}$**

22. $^-1\frac{8}{10} + ^-3\frac{5}{10}$ **$^-5\frac{3}{10}$**

23. $\frac{2}{7} + \frac{3}{7}$ **$\frac{5}{7}$**

24. $-\frac{3}{7} + \left(-\frac{1}{7}\right)$ **$-\frac{4}{7}$**

25. $\frac{1}{3} + \frac{1}{2}$ **$\frac{5}{6}$**

26. $-\frac{1}{6} + \left(-\frac{3}{4}\right)$ **$-\frac{11}{12}$**

27. $^-4\frac{1}{4} + ^-3\frac{2}{4}$ **$^-7\frac{3}{4}$**

28. $3\frac{1}{8} + 4\frac{7}{8}$ **8**

29. $^-4\frac{1}{8} + ^-4\frac{1}{3}$ **$^-8\frac{11}{24}$**

30. $6\frac{2}{3} + 7\frac{1}{2}$ **$14\frac{1}{6}$**

31. $\frac{2}{10} + \left(-\frac{8}{10}\right)$ **$-\frac{3}{5}$**

32. $-\frac{1}{2} + \frac{1}{3}$ **$-\frac{1}{6}$**

33. $5\frac{7}{10} + ^-3\frac{4}{10}$ **$2\frac{3}{10}$**

34. $\frac{5}{7} + \left(-\frac{4}{7}\right)$ **$\frac{1}{7}$**

35. $-\frac{7}{8} + \frac{3}{4}$ **$-\frac{1}{8}$**

36. $-\frac{5}{9} + \left(-\frac{2}{9}\right)$ **$-\frac{7}{9}$**

37. $\frac{1}{2} + \left(-\frac{1}{3}\right)$ **$\frac{1}{6}$**

38. $\frac{5}{6} + \left(-\frac{7}{8}\right)$ **$-\frac{1}{24}$**

39. $-\frac{2}{3} + \left(-\frac{3}{4}\right)$ **$^-1\frac{5}{12}$**

40. $^-7\frac{3}{10} + 2\frac{1}{5}$ **$^-5\frac{1}{10}$**

Solve.

41. Wayne Purdue had $108 in his checking account. He wrote a check for $49. How much was left in his account? **$59**

42. A submarine is 128 feet below the surface. The submarine dives 286 feet. How far below the surface is the submarine now? **414 ft**

43. An elevator on the forty-fifth floor goes down 27 floors. What floor is it on then? **18th floor**

44. A scuba diver, 35 feet below the surface, moves up 21 feet. At what depth is the diver then?
14 ft below the surface

45. A football team has the ball on its own 20 yard line. After a 7 yard loss and a 16 yard gain, where is the football? **29 yard line**

46. A football team has the ball on its opponent's 20 yard line. The team gained 5 yards, lost 2 yards, and then gained 17 yards. Did the team score a touchdown? **yes**

This feature presents useful ways of solving mathematical problems on a calculator.

 Calculator

Many calculators have a plus/minus key. It can be useful when adding negative numbers. The display shows $100 + (^-23) = 77$

Add. Use the plus/minus key.

1. $1,842 + ^-6,584$ **$^-4,742$**

2. $^-22.91 + ^-42.4$ **$^-65.31$**

3. $64,296 + ^-22,050$ **42,246**

4. $\$100 + \$23.86 + ^-\$65.29$ **$58.57**

5. $\$243.25 + ^-\$200 + \$96.98$ **$140.23**

14-5 Subtracting Rational Numbers

Objective: To subtract rational numbers.

Mt. Whitney is 14,494 feet above sea level. Death Valley is 282 feet below sea level. Suppose you want to find the difference between these two elevations.

To find the difference, subtract ⁻282 from 14,296. **Distances above sea level are represented by positive numbers. Distances below sea level are represented by negative numbers.** For every subtraction sentence, there is a corresponding addition sentence. Study the following examples.

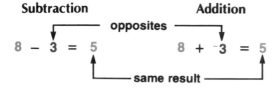

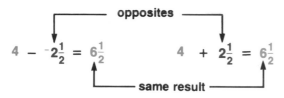

These examples suggest the following rule.

To subtract a rational number, add its opposite.

Examples

A. **What is the difference in elevation between Mt. Whitney and Death Valley?**

$$14{,}494 - {}^-282 - 14{,}494 + 282 \qquad \text{\textit{Use the rule above.}}$$
$$= 14{,}776$$

14494 ⊟ 292 ⊠ ⊟ *14776*   *Use the plus/minus key.*

The difference in elevation is 14,776 feet.

B. **A certain spot in a cave is 35 feet below sea level. Another spot in the cave is 45 feet below sea level. What is the difference in height between these two spots?**

$$^-35 - {}^-45 = {}^-35 + 45$$
$$= 10$$

⊟ 35 ⊟ 45 ⊠ ⊟ *10*

The difference in height is 10 feet.

Exercises

Copy and complete each pattern.

1. $4 - 2 = 2$ $4 + {}^-2 = 2$ **2.** ${}^-4 + 2 = {}^-2$ ${}^-4 - {}^-2 = {}^-2$
   $4 - 3 = 1$ $4 + {}^-3 = 1$ ${}^-4 + 3 = {}^-1$ ${}^-4 - {}^-3 = {}^-1$
   $4 - 4 = 0$ $4 + {}^-4 = 0$ ${}^-4 + 4 = 0$ ${}^-4 - {}^-4 = 0$
   $4 - 5 = \blacksquare$ **⁻1** $4 + {}^-5 = \blacksquare$ **⁻1** ${}^-4 + 5 = \blacksquare$ **1** ${}^-4 - {}^-5 = \blacksquare$ **1**
   $4 - 6 = \blacksquare$ **⁻2** $4 + {}^-6 = \blacksquare$ **⁻2** ${}^-4 + 6 = \blacksquare$ **2** ${}^-4 - {}^-6 = \blacksquare$ **2**

Complete.

3. $6 - 5 = 6 + {}^-5 = \blacksquare$ **1** **4.** ${}^-8 - 9 = {}^-8 + {}^-9 = \blacksquare$ **⁻17**

5. $4 - 11 = 4 + {}^-11 = \blacksquare$ **⁻7** **6.** ${}^-2 - {}^-5 = {}^-2 + 5 = \blacksquare$ **3**

7. ${}^-5 - 2 = {}^-5 + {}^-2 = \blacksquare$ **⁻7** **8.** ${}^-3 - {}^-1 = {}^-3 + 1 = \blacksquare$ **⁻2**

Write an addition expression for each of the following.

9. $5 - 2$ **10.** $8 - 9$ **11.** ${}^-16 - 16$ **12.** ${}^-3 - 5$
   5 + ⁻2   **8 + ⁻9**   **⁻16 + ⁻16**   **⁻3 + ⁻5**
13. $5 - {}^-4$ **5 + 4** **14.** $0 - 29$ **0 + ⁻29** **15.** $0.7 - 0.5$ **0.7 + ⁻0.5** **16.** ${}^-1.6 - {}^-1.9$
                        ⁻1.6 + 1.9
17. $-\frac{7}{10} - \frac{3}{10}$ **$-\frac{7}{10} + \left(-\frac{3}{10}\right)$** **18.** $\frac{7}{10} - \frac{5}{10}$ **$\frac{7}{10} + \left(-\frac{5}{10}\right)$** **19.** ${}^-3 - {}^-46$ **20.** $6.36 - 4.27$
                                    ⁻3 + 46   **6.36 + ⁻4.27**

Subtract.

21. $19 - 19$ **0** **22.** $13 - 15$ **⁻2** **23.** $61 - 98$ **⁻37** **24.** $7 - {}^-4$ **11**

25. $8 - {}^-8$ **16** **26.** $0 - {}^-16$ **16** **27.** ${}^-3 - 5$ **⁻8** **28.** ${}^-5 - 5$ **⁻10**

29. ${}^-13 - 13$ **⁻26** **30.** ${}^-25 - 69$ **⁻94** **31.** ${}^-3 - {}^-4$ **1** **32.** ${}^-8 - {}^-8$ **0**

33. ${}^-26 - {}^-21$ **⁻5** **34.** ${}^-48 - {}^-42$ **⁻6** **35.** $0 - 72$ **⁻72** **36.** ${}^-5 - 85$ **⁻90**

37. $27 - 48$ **⁻21** **38.** $2.7 - 4.8$ **⁻2.1** **39.** ${}^-54 - 21$ **⁻75** **40.** ${}^-5.4 - 2.1$ **⁻7.5**

41. $3.7 - 1.9$ **1.8** **42.** ${}^-8.3 - 5.6$ **⁻13.9** **43.** $4.7 - {}^-6.3$ **11** **44.** ${}^-1.9 - {}^-5.7$ **3.8**

45. $0 - 1.8$ **⁻1.8** **46.** ${}^-7.3 - 7.3$ **⁻14.6** **47.** $1.2 - {}^-1.5$ **2.7** **48.** ${}^-6.4 - {}^-5.8$ **⁻0.6**

49. $6.9 - 4.3$ **2.6** **50.** $6\frac{9}{10} - 4\frac{3}{10}$ **$2\frac{3}{5}$** **51.** ${}^-6.7 - 2.1$ **⁻8.8** **52.** ${}^-6\frac{7}{10} - 2\frac{1}{10}$ **$-8\frac{4}{5}$**

53. $\frac{9}{10} - \frac{7}{10}$ **$\frac{1}{5}$** **54.** $\frac{5}{7} - \frac{2}{7}$ **$\frac{3}{7}$** **55.** $\frac{3}{5} - \left(\frac{-1}{5}\right)$ **$\frac{4}{5}$** **56.** $\frac{-3}{5} + \frac{-1}{5}$ **$-\frac{4}{5}$**

57. $8\frac{3}{4} - 2\frac{1}{4}$ **$6\frac{1}{2}$** **58.** $1\frac{2}{5} - 3\frac{4}{5}$ **$-2\frac{2}{5}$** **59.** ${}^-9\frac{1}{2} - 8\frac{3}{4}$ **$-18\frac{1}{4}$** **60.** ${}^-1\frac{1}{4} - 5\frac{3}{4}$ **⁻7**

69. Years A.D. and B.C. can be placed on a number line, but exact answers are difficult to find because of calendar changes.

Solve.

61. Find the vertical distance between an airplane 25,000 ft above the ocean and a submarine 380 ft below. **25,380 ft**

62. In a mine, coal seams are located 88 ft and 165 ft below the surface. Find the distance between the seams. **77 ft**

63. A patient's temperature was 102.6°F and decreased to 99.8°F after an ice pack was applied. What was the decrease in temperature? **2.8°F**

64. The elevation of Denver is 5,280 feet. The elevation of San Francisco is 929 feet. What is the difference in elevation between the two cities? **4,351 ft**

65. In Spearfish, South Dakota, on January 22, 1943, the temperature was ⁻4°F at 7:30 A.M. and 45°F at 7:32 A.M. What was the increase in temperature? **49°F**

66. Katie Crosby had $508.42 in her bank account. She deposited a check for $236.78 and withdrew $75 in cash. How much did she then have in her account? **$670.20**

67. The air temperature decreases about 3.5°F for each 1,000 ft increase in altitude. Suppose that the surface air temperature is 66°F. What is the air temperature at 7,000 ft? **about 41.5°F**

68. The maximum rate your heart should beat is 220 beats per minute minus your age. What is the maximum heart-beat rate for a person 30 years old? Find your maximum rate. **190 beats per minute; Answers may vary.**

69. Algebraic symbols have been found on stone pillars that date back to around 240 B.C. About how old are the pillars? **about 2,227 years old**

70. The word algebra comes from the Arabic word al-jabr which was used by a Hindu mathematician around 825 A.D. How many centuries has this word been used? **about $11\frac{1}{2}$ centuries**

 This feature provides general topics about the ~~uses~~ of a computer.

Computer

An assignment statement is shown below.
It assigns the value of 5 to the variable *A*.

```
10 LET A = 5
20 LET B = -7
30 LET C = A*B
```

What value is assigned to C? *Remember ∗ means multiply.*
C has the value ⁻35.

Find the value of each variable in the following programs.

1. 10 LET C = 17   **17**
   20 LET A = ⁻3   **⁻3**
   30 LET T = A−C   **⁻20**

2. 10 LET K = ⁻2   **⁻2**
   20 LET I = K/2   **⁻1**
   30 LET N = I ∗ ⁻7   **7**

3. 10 LET A = ⁻5   **⁻5**
   20 LET N = A∗A   **25**
   30 LET D = 3∗N+1   **76**

4. 10 LET A = 100   **100**
   20 LET V = 85   **85**
   30 LET G = (A+V)/2
   92.5

5. 10 LET M = ⁻21   **⁻21**
   20 LET I = ⁻18   **⁻18**
   30 LET N = 52   **52**
   40 LET D = M−I−N
   ⁻55

6. 10 LET M = 48   **48**
   20 LET A = ⁻12   **⁻12**
   30 LET T = A/M − 1/M
   $\frac{-13}{48}$

PRACTICE

Estimate. Answers may vary. Typical answers are given.

1. 451 + 294 800	**2.** 831 − 499 300	**3.** 619 × 8 4,800	**4.** 88 × 41 3,600	**5.** $31\overline{)234}$ 7

Add, subtract, multiply, or divide.

6. $46.9 + 95.6$ **142.5**

7. $86.5 - 47.8$ **38.7**

8. 21.9×0.4 **8.76**

9. 0.009×1.6 **0.0144**

10. $810 \div 0.9$ **900**

11. $0.048 \div 1.2$ **0.04**

12. $6.104 - 5.7$ **0.404**

13. $60.8 - 0.806$ **59.994**

14. 0.15×804 **120.6**

15. $\frac{3}{4} + \frac{5}{16}$ $1\frac{1}{16}$

16. $\frac{1}{2} - \frac{1}{5}$ $\frac{3}{10}$

17. $\frac{3}{4} \times \frac{7}{8}$ $\frac{21}{32}$

18. $\frac{3}{5} \div 10$ $\frac{3}{50}$

19. $\frac{4}{5} \times \frac{9}{10}$ $\frac{18}{25}$

20. $6\frac{1}{2} - \frac{3}{4}$ $5\frac{3}{4}$

21. $2\frac{2}{3} + 3\frac{7}{8}$ $6\frac{13}{24}$

22. $4\frac{3}{4} \div 1\frac{3}{4}$ $2\frac{5}{7}$

23. $11\frac{1}{10} \div 6$ $1\frac{17}{20}$

24. $3\frac{7}{8} \times 8$ **31**

25. $6\frac{1}{4} - 3\frac{3}{5}$ $2\frac{13}{20}$

26. $6 \div 2\frac{1}{3}$ $2\frac{4}{7}$

Use the proportion $\frac{P}{B} = \frac{r}{100}$ to solve each problem.

27. ___?___% of 6 is 3   **50**

28. 25 is 40% of ___?___   **62.5**

29. ___?___ is 92% of 180   **165.6**

30. ___?___ is 6.5% of 20   **1.3**

31. 16% of ___?___ is 704   **4,400**

32. ___?___% of 50 is 10   **20**

33. 60% of 25 is ___?___   **15**

34. 3 is ___?___% of 9 $33\frac{1}{3}$

35. 108% of ___?___ is 54   **50**

Find the perimeter of each figure.

36.
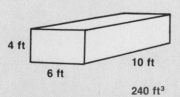
44 cm

37.
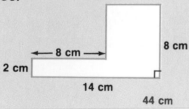
36 in.

38.
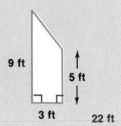
22 ft

Find the volume of each solid. Use 3.14 for π. Round decimal answers to the nearest tenth.

39.
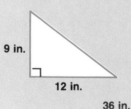
240 ft³

40.
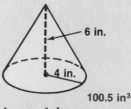
100.5 in³

41.
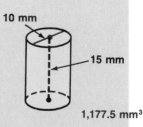
1,177.5 mm³

Find the mode, median, and mean for each set of data.

42. 30.1, 29.8, 31.2, 30.1, 30.3, 33
     30.1; 30.2; 30.75

43. 98.4, 100, 96, 95, 96, 98.3, 96
     96; 96; 97.1

Math Break

Kathy Steiner is opening a checking account with her weekly paycheck. She deposits all of the check but $50, which she wants in cash. The deposit slip at the right shows her deposit.

DEPOSIT TICKET

NAME   Kathy Steiner

CASH	CURRENCY		
	COIN		
	LIST CHECKS SINGLY	285	31

DATE   Sept. 16   19 88

Kathy Steiner

TOTAL FROM OTHER SIDE		
TOTAL	285	31
LESS CASH RECEIVED	50	00
NET DEPOSIT	235	31

25-7068/2440

USE OTHER SIDE FOR ADDITIONAL LISTING

BE SURE EACH ITEM IS PROPERLY ENDORSED

Mid★America Federal
SAVINGS & LOAN ASSOCIATION
COLUMBUS, OHIO 43215   FSLIC

⑆244070689⑆098 5000455⑈

The bank gives Kathy a check register. She uses it to record all deposits and checks. The register below shows her opening balance, two deposits, and four checks that she wrote.

		RECORD ALL CHARGES OR CREDITS THAT AFFECT YOUR ACCOUNT					BALANCE	
NUMBER	DATE	DESCRIPTION OF TRANSACTION	PAYMENT/DEBIT (−)	√ T	FEE (IF ANY) (−)	DEPOSIT/CREDIT (+)	$	O
	9/16	deposit weekly paycheck	$		$	$ 235 31	235 31 235 31	
101	9/18	Food Mart groceries	92 86				92 86	
102	9/21	Sights and Sounds tape	10 38				10 38	
103	9/21	Edison Power Co. electric bill	45 29				45 29	
	9/23	deposit weekly paycheck				235 31	235 31	
104	9/26	Creekside Properties rent	325 00				325 00	

REMEMBER TO RECORD AUTOMATIC PAYMENTS / DEPOSITS ON DATE AUTHORIZED.

202.45

192.07

146.78

382.09

57.09

Once each month the bank sends its checking account customers a statement showing the bank's record of the customer's deposits and withdrawals. Kathy must compare the bank statement to her own record to be sure that both are correct.

Use the check register above to answer each question.

1. What does the balance mean?
   amount left in checking account
3. Are deposit amounts added or subtracted? **added**

2. What is the opening balance?
   $235.31
4. Are check amounts added or subtracted? **subtracted**

Find the balance after each check or deposit.

5. check 101 **$202.45**   6. check 102 **$192.07**   7. check 103 **$146.78**

8. deposit on Sept. 23 **$382.09**   9. check 104 **$57.09**

14-6 Multiplying Rational Numbers

Objective: To multiply rational numbers.

Thad Byers works at a water treatment
plant. He is responsible for controlling
the amount of water in certain tanks. He
thinks of fill/empty rates and time changes
as follows.

Positive: filling, future time

Negative: emptying, past time

Examples

The tank is being filled or emptied at
a rate of 10 gallons per minute.

A. **The tank is being filled. How much**
more will the tank contain in 5 minutes?

future
time   *filling*

    5 × 10 = 50

In five minutes the tank will
contain 50 gallons more.

B. **The tank is being emptied. How much**
more did the tank contain 5 minutes ago?

past
time   *emptying*

   ⁻5 × ⁻10 = 50

Five minutes ago the tank contained
50 gallons more.

These examples suggest the following rule.

The product of two rational numbers with the same sign is positive.

C. **The tank is being filled. How much**
less did the tank contain 5 minutes ago?

past
time   *filling*

   ⁻5 × 10 = ⁻50

Five minutes ago the tank contained
50 gallons less.

D. **The tank is being emptied. How much**
less will the tank contain in 5 minutes?

future
time   *emptying*

    5 × ⁻10 = ⁻50

In 5 minutes the tank will contain
50 gallons less.

These examples suggest the following rule.

The product of two rational numbers with different signs is negative.

Basic Skills Appendix, Page 459
Basic: 2–52 odd; Average: 1–52; Enriched: 13–48 even, 49–52

Exercises

Copy and complete each pattern.

1. $2 \times 4 = $ ▨ **8**
   $1 \times 4 = $ ▨ **4**
   $0 \times 4 = $ ▨ **0**
   $^-1 \times 4 = $ ▨ **-4**
   $^-2 \times 4 = $ ▨ **-8**

2. $^-7 \times 2 = $ ▨ **-14**
   $^-7 \times 1 = $ ▨ **-7**
   $^-7 \times 0 = $ ▨ **0**
   $^-7 \times {}^-1 = $ ▨ **7**
   $^-7 \times {}^-2 = $ ▨ **14**

3. $9 \times 2 = $ ▨ **18**
   $9 \times 1 = $ ▨ **9**
   $9 \times 0 = $ ▨ **0**
   $9 \times {}^-1 = $ ▨ **-9**
   $9 \times {}^-2 = $ ▨ **-18**

4. $2 \times {}^-6 = $ ▨ **-12**
   $1 \times {}^-6 = $ ▨ **-6**
   $0 \times {}^-6 = $ ▨ **0**
   $^-1 \times {}^-6 = $ ▨ **6**
   $^-2 \times {}^-6 = $ ▨ **12**

State whether each product is positive or negative.

5. $7 \times {}^-8$ **negative**   **6.** 2×8 **positive**   **7.** ${}^-7 \times 5$ **negative**   **8.** ${}^-7 \times {}^-9$ **positive**

9. ${}^-4 \times {}^-9$ **positive**   **10.** ${}^-6 \times 5$ **negative**   **11.** 6×3 **positive**   **12.** $8 \times {}^-64$ **negative**

Multiply.

13. $6 \times {}^-3$ **-18**   **14.** $3 \times {}^-8$ **-24**   **15.** ${}^-5 \times {}^-1$ **5**   **16.** 3×9 **27**

17. ${}^-1 \times 0$ **0**   **18.** ${}^-8 \times {}^-2$ **16**   **19.** ${}^-5 \times 9$ **-45**   **20.** 4×10 **40**

21. 16×6 **96**   **22.** $32 \times {}^-5$ **-160**   **23.** ${}^-7 \times {}^-21$ **147**   **24.** ${}^-13 \times 5$ **-65**

25. $48 \times {}^-27$ **-1,296**   **26.** ${}^-21 \times 17$ **-357**   **27.** ${}^-83 \times {}^-28$ **2,324**   **28.** $42 \times {}^-63$ **-2,646**

29. $12 \times {}^-16$ **-192**   **30.** $1.2 \times {}^-1.6$ **-1.92**   **31.** ${}^-14 \times 8$ **-112**   **32.** ${}^-1.4 \times 0.8$ **-1.12**

33. ${}^-8 \times {}^-4$ **32**   **34.** ${}^-0.8 \times {}^-0.4$ **0.32**   **35.** 12×12 **144**   **36.** ${}^-1.2 \times {}^-1.2$ **1.44**

37. 0.1×0.3 **0.03**   **38.** ${}^-7.2 \times {}^-4.8$ **34.56**   **39.** 2.4×2.6 **6.24**   **40.** ${}^-1.7 \times {}^-1.17$ **1.989**

41. $\frac{1}{4} \times \left(-\frac{3}{8}\right)$ $-\frac{3}{32}$ **42.** $\frac{1}{10} \times \frac{3}{10}$ $\frac{3}{100}$ **43.** $\frac{-1}{3} \times \frac{3}{4}$ $\frac{-1}{4}$ **44.** $4\frac{1}{2} \times {}^-6$ **-27**

45. $3 \times 4\frac{1}{3}$ **13**   **46.** $2\frac{1}{2} \times {}^-4\frac{1}{2}$ **-11$\frac{1}{4}$**   **47.** $\frac{-7}{8} \times \left(\frac{-5}{9}\right)$ $\frac{35}{72}$ **48.** $\frac{-8}{9} \times {}^-1\frac{1}{2}$ **1$\frac{1}{3}$**

Solve.

49. A 5,600 gallon water tank is emptied at the rate of 600 gallons per hour. How much water is left after 6.4 hours? **1,760 gallons**

50. At 10:00 P.M. the temperature is 7°C. It drops 2° each hour. What is the temperature at 3:00 A.M.? **-3°C**

51. A football team received three 15-yard penalties in a game. Express the total penalty yardage as a rational number. **-45 yards**

52. A shoe store sold 386 pairs of shoes during a $19.95 sale. If 216 pairs of shoes were not sold, what was the total amount of sales? **$7,700.70**

This feature presents general topics of mathematics.

Math Break

Evaluate products such as ${}^-4 \times 5 \times {}^-2$ and ${}^-2 \times {}^-3 \times {}^-5$ as follows.

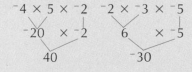

Multiply.

1. ${}^-3 \times 4 \times {}^-9$ **108**   **2.** ${}^-7 \times {}^-3 \times {}^-2$ **-42**   **3.** $5 \times 4 \times 2$ **40**

4. $5 \times {}^-3 \times 6$ **-90**   **5.** ${}^-8 \times 6 \times 1$ **-48**   **6.** ${}^-7 \times {}^-2 \times 9$ **126**

7. ${}^-8 \times 7 \times 4 \times {}^-6$ **1,344**   **8.** ${}^-7 \times 5 \times {}^-3 \times {}^-1$ **-105**   **9.** ${}^-4 \times {}^-6 \times {}^-3 \times {}^-5$ **360**

10. State a rule for determining the sign of a product.
positive product when the number of negative factors is even;
negative product when the number of negative factors is odd

14-7 Dividing Rational Numbers

Objective: To divide rational numbers.

As a person breathes, air is inhaled and then exhaled.
Exhaling reverses the action of inhaling.

Division reverses the operation of multiplication.
Study the following examples.

$$3 \times 4 = 12 \qquad 12 \div 4 = 3$$

$$3 \times {}^-4 = {}^-12 \qquad {}^-12 \div {}^-4 = 3$$

These examples suggest the following rule.

**The quotient of two rational numbers
with the same sign is positive.**

$$^-3 \times 4 = {}^-12 \qquad {}^-12 \div 4 = {}^-3$$

$$^-3 \times {}^-4 = 12 \qquad 12 \div {}^-4 = {}^-3$$

These examples suggest the following rule.

**The quotient of two rational numbers
with different signs is negative.**

Examples

A. Solve. 24 ÷ 8 = ▧

*Both numbers have the same sign.
So, the quotient is positive.*

$24 \div 8 = 3$

Check: $3 \times 8 = 24$

B. Solve. $^-27 \div {}^-4\frac{1}{2} = ▧$

*Both numbers have the same sign.
So, the quotient is positive.*

$^-27 \div {}^-4\frac{1}{2} = 6$

Check: $6 \times {}^-4\frac{1}{2} = {}^-27$

C. Solve. 35 ÷ $^-7$ = ▧

*The numbers have different signs.
So, the quotient is negative.*

$35 \div {}^-7 = {}^-5$

Check: $^-5 \times {}^-7 = 35$

D. Solve. $^-13 \div 5.2 = ▧$

*The numbers have different signs.
So, the quotient is negative.*

$^-13 \div 5.2 = {}^-2.5$

Check: $^-2.5 \times 5.2 = {}^-13$

Basic Skills Appendix, Pages 443, 444, 460
Basic: 1–57 odd; Average: 1–57; Enriched: 2–56 even, 57

Exercises

Study the examples above. Describe the following as positive or negative.

1. the quotient of two positive numbers
positive

2. the quotient of two negative numbers
positive

3. the quotient of one positive number and one negative number **negative**

State whether each quotient is positive or negative.

4. $42 \div {}^-7$ **negative**   **5.** $24 \div 4$ **positive**   **6.** ${}^-18 \div {}^-3$ **positive**   **7.** ${}^-20 \div 5$ **negative**

8. ${}^-84 \div {}^-12$ **positive**   **9.** ${}^-120 \div 5$ **negative**   **10.** ${}^-32 \div 2$ **negative**   **11.** $660 \div 15$ **positive**

Divide.

12. ${}^-27 \div {}^-9$ **3**   **13.** $18 \div {}^-2$ **${}^-9$**   **14.** ${}^-4 \div {}^-1$ **4**   **15.** ${}^-11 \div {}^-11$ **1**

16. $64 \div {}^-16$ **${}^-4$**   **17.** $0 \div 400$ **0**   **18.** ${}^-169 \div {}^-13$ **13**   **19.** $120 \div {}^-20$ **${}^-6$**

20. ${}^-576 \div 24$ **${}^-24$**   **21.** $630 \div {}^-15$ **${}^-42$**   **22.** ${}^-729 \div {}^-27$ **27**   **23.** $0 \div {}^-597$ **0**

24. $2.8 \div 4$ **0.7**   **25.** ${}^-2.8 \div 4$ **${}^-0.7$**   **26.** $56 \div 0.8$ **70**   **27.** $56 \div {}^-0.8$ **${}^-70$**

28. $8.4 \div 1.2$ **7**   **29.** ${}^-8.4 \div {}^-1.2$ **7**   **30.** $1.76 \div 2.2$ **0.8**   **31.** $1.76 \div {}^-2.2$ **${}^-0.8$**

32. $0.6 \div 0.2$ **3**   **33.** $\frac{6}{10} \div \frac{2}{10}$ **3**   **34.** $\frac{6}{10} \div \left(-\frac{2}{10}\right)$ **${}^-3$**   **35.** $-\frac{6}{10} \div \frac{2}{10}$ **${}^-3$**

36. $\frac{2}{3} \div \left(-\frac{3}{4}\right)$ **$-\frac{8}{9}$**   **37.** $-\frac{7}{8} \div \left(-\frac{1}{2}\right)$ **$1\frac{3}{4}$**   **38.** $-\frac{1}{2} \div \frac{2}{3}$ **$-\frac{3}{4}$**   **39.** $\frac{7}{8} \div \left(-\frac{1}{6}\right)$ **$-5\frac{1}{4}$**

40. $2\frac{1}{2} \div 1\frac{1}{4}$ **2**   **41.** ${}^-2\frac{1}{3} \div 1\frac{3}{4}$ **$-1\frac{1}{3}$**   **42.** ${}^-2\frac{1}{2} \div \frac{1}{3}$ **$-7\frac{1}{2}$**   **43.** ${}^-6\frac{1}{2} \div {}^-1\frac{1}{4}$ **$5\frac{1}{5}$**

Write each fraction in simplest form.

44. $\frac{84}{7}$ **12**   **45.** $\frac{{}^-9}{3}$ **${}^-3$**   **46.** $\frac{30}{{}^-5}$ **${}^-6$**   **47.** $\frac{{}^-45}{{}^-3}$ **15**   **48.** $\frac{176}{11}$ **16**   **49.** $\frac{0}{{}^-14}$ **0**

50. $\frac{78}{13}$ **6**   **51.** $\frac{{}^-85}{5}$ **${}^-17$**   **52.** $\frac{225}{{}^-75}$ **${}^-3$**   **53.** $\frac{{}^-144}{{}^-9}$ **16**   **54.** $\frac{{}^-72}{36}$ **${}^-2$**   **55.** $\frac{{}^-91}{{}^-13}$ **7**

Solve.

56. Ellen lost 27 pounds in 15 weeks. What was her average weight change per week? **${}^-1.8$ lb**

57. The population of Greensboro increased by 11,560 in ten years. What was the average increase per year?
1,156 people per year

This feature promotes students' mental abilities in computation and reasonableness.

Mental Math

You can find the answer to a division problem by mentally changing it to a multiplication problem.

$75 \div 25 = \blacksquare$ ➡ $25 \times \blacksquare = 75$
$$$25 \times 3 = 75$

$1 \div 2 = \blacksquare$ ➡ $2 \times \blacksquare = 1$
$$$2 \times \frac{1}{2} = 1$

Find each quotient by thinking of each division problem as a multiplication problem.

1. $90 \div 15$ **6**   **2.** $39 \div 13$ **3**   **3.** $\frac{2}{3} \div \frac{1}{3}$ **2**   **4.** $\frac{5}{8} \div \frac{1}{8}$ **5**

5. ${}^-60 \div 12$ **${}^-5$**   **6.** ${}^-64 \div 16$ **${}^-4$**   **7.** $10 \div 2.5$ **4**   **8.** $6 \div \frac{1}{2}$ **12**

9. $48 \div {}^-12$ **${}^-4$**   **10.** $120 \div 12$ **10**   **11.** $280 \div 70$ **4**   **12.** ${}^-900 \div 30$ **${}^-30$**

14-8 Order of Operations

Objective: To learn the order of operations.

A computer program is a set of coded instructions for a computer to follow. The instructions must be given in a specific order for the computer to follow them.

Mathematical expressions often contain more than one operation. An expression like $8 + 5 \times 7$ might be computed in two ways.

A. $8 + 5 \times 7 = 8 + 35$ *Multiply 5 and 7 first.*

$\quad\quad\quad\quad\quad = 43$ *Then add 8 and 35.*

B. $8 + 5 \times 7 = 13 \times 7$ *Add 8 and 5 first.*

$\quad\quad\quad\quad\quad = 91$ *Then multiply 13 and 7.*

To be sure an expression has only one value, there is a specific order in which operations are to be done.

- First, do all multiplications and/or divisions from left to right.
- Then, do all additions and/or subtractions from left to right.

Example

A. Compute $^-3 + 5 \times 7$.

$^-3 + 5 \times 7 = {}^-3 + 35$ *Multiply first.*

$\quad\quad\quad\quad\quad = 32$ *Then add.*

$^-3 + 5 \times 7 = 32$

B. Compute $10 \div 2 - 4 \times 3$.

$10 \div 2 - 4 \times 3 = 5 - 4 \times 3$ *Divide first.*

$\quad\quad\quad\quad\quad\quad = 5 - 12$ *Multiply.*

$\quad\quad\quad\quad\quad\quad = {}^-7$ *Then subtract.*

$10 \div 2 - 4 \times 3 = {}^-7$

The order of operations may be changed by using grouping symbols such as parentheses ( ) or brackets [ ].

If an expression contains grouping symbols, use the following order of operations.

- Do all operations within grouping symbols first; start with the innermost grouping symbols.
- Next, do all multiplications and/or divisions from left to right.
- Then, do all additions and/or subtractions from left to right.

Basic: 2–38 even; Average: 1–39; Enriched: 1–39

Example

C. Compute. $[36 - (3 \times 2)] \times 4$.

$[36 - (3 \times 2)] \times 4 = [36 - 6] \times 4$ *Do operations within the innermost grouping*

$\quad\quad\quad\quad\quad\quad\quad = 30 \times 4$ *symbols first. Do operations within the remaining*

$\quad\quad\quad\quad\quad\quad\quad = 120$ *grouping symbols. Multiply.*

$[36 - (3 \times 2)] \times 4 = 120$

Name the operation that should be done first.

1. $(^-3 + 5) \times 4$ **add**
2. $^-3 + 5 \times 4$ **multiply**
3. $(13 - 5) \div 4$ **subtract**
4. $28 \div 7 \times 2$ **divide**
5. $28 \div (7 \times 2)$ **multiply**
6. $(^-36 + 16) \div 4$ **add**
7. $[36 - (3 \times 2)] \times 4$ **multiply 3 × 2**
8. $[42 + (4 \times 3)] \div 6$ **multiply 4 × 3**

Compute.

9. $^-24 \times 4 \div 3$ **-32**
10. $^-16 \div 2 \times 3$ **-24**
11. $16 + 4 \div ^-2$ **14**
12. $5 + 8 \times 2 - 7$ **14**
13. $^-7 \times 3 - 5 + 4$ **-22**
14. $3 \times ^-7 - 5 + 4$ **-22**
15. $13 + 28 \div 4 - 5$ **15**
16. $^-42 \times 3 \div 14 - 6$ **-15**
17. $^-12 - 8 \div 4 + 6$ **-8**
18. $(64 - 8) \div 4$ **14**
19. $64 \div 8 \div 4$ **2**
20. $(243 \div 27) \div 9$ **1**
21. $243 \div 27 \times 9$ **81**
22. $(243 \div 27) \times 9$ **81**
23. $576 \div (24 \times 8)$ **3**
24. $84 - 28 \div 4 \times 7$ **35**
25. $(84 - 28) \div 4 \times 7$ **98**
26. $84 - (28 \div 4) \times 7$ **35**
27. $84 - 28 \div (4 \times 7)$ **83**
28. $^-92 - 46 \div ^-23 \times 2$ **-88**
29. $^-92 - (46 \div ^-23) \times 2$ **-88**
30. $^-92 - 46 \div (23 \times 2)$ **-93**
31. $(76 + ^-19) \times 3 \div 2$ **$85\frac{1}{2}$ or 85.5**
32. $[(36 - 3) \times 2] \times 4$ **264**
33. $36 - [(3 \times 2) \times 4]$ **12**
34. $[^-72 \div (4 \times 2)] + ^-16$ **-25**
35. $[(72 \div 4) \times 2] + 16$ **20**
36. $^-72 \div [4 \times (2 + ^-16)]$ **$1\frac{2}{7}$**
37. $^-72 \div [(4 \times 2) + ^-16]$ **9**

Solve.

38. Mark Stevens buys 3 pairs of socks at $1.89 per pair. How much change should he receive from a $10 bill? **$4.33**

39. Susan bought 6 cans of juice at $1.39 each, 2 loaves of bread at 89¢ each, and 4 pounds of bananas at 49¢ per pound. What was the total cost? **$12.08**

This feature presents useful ways of solving mathematical problems on a calculator.

 Calculator

Many calculators follow the order of operations. To see if a calculator follows the order of operations, enter a mixed numeral such as $3\frac{1}{8}$.

If the display reads 3.125, the calculator follows the order of operations. If the display reads 0.5, the calculator does all operations from left to right. How can $3\frac{1}{8}$ be entered into a calculator that does not follow the order of operations? **Enter $\frac{1}{8}$. Then, add 3.**

$3\frac{1}{8} = 3 + \frac{1}{8} = 3 + 1 \div 8$

Enter: $3\frac{1}{8}$

 Enter: $3 \; \boxed{+} \; 1 \; \boxed{\div} \; 8 \; \boxed{=}$

Display: $3 \; 3 \; 1 \; 1 \; 8 \; 3.125$

14-9 Problem Solving: Using Rational Numbers

Objective: To solve problems involving rational numbers.

The world's high temperature record was 136°F on September 13, 1922, at El Azizia, Africa. The low temperature record was ⁻127°F on August 24, 1960, at Vostok, Antarctica. What is the difference between the highest and lowest temperatures?

Read

You must find the difference in temperatures.
You know the highest and lowest temperatures.

Decide

The difference can be found by subtracting the lowest from the highest temperature.

Solve

136 − ⁻127 = 136 + 127   *To subtract a number,*
= 263   *add its opposite.*

The difference between the highest and lowest temperatures is 263°F.

Examine

To check your answer, reverse the order of the addends and add again. 127 + 136 = 263

Basic: 1–11 odd; Average: 1–12; Enriched: 1–12

Exercises

1. A traffic helicopter descended 500 feet to observe road conditions. It leveled off at 450 feet. What was its original altitude? **950 feet**

3. Nita's score at the end of a board game was 95. Halfway through the game her score was ⁻42. How many points did she score during the last half of the game? **137 points**

2. The sum of two numbers is ⁻25. One of the numbers is 9. What is the other number? **⁻34**

4. A passenger gets off an elevator at the tenth floor. Another passenger stays in the elevator and goes up 12 more floors. The elevator then goes down 14 floors. What floor is the elevator on? **8th floor**

Solve. Use any strategy.

5. Fritz spent $2.88 on supplies. Fred spent $3\frac{1}{2}$ times as much. How much did Fred spend? **$10.08**

7. Jerry lost 132 points in a game. Jill lost one-third as many points. Express Jill's loss as a rational number. **⁻44**

6. Golda bought a stereo for $287 including tax and interest. She has made 5 payments of $37 each. How much does she still owe? **$102**

8. How many 26-inch pieces of wood can Alex cut from a 10-foot board? How much wood will be left? **4 boards; 16 inches**

9. Ground meat costs $1.60 a pound. If Tom has $6.00, does he have enough to purchase $4\frac{1}{2}$ pounds of meat?
No

10. Stewart earns $97 in 4 days. At that rate, how many days will it take him to earn $485?
20 days

11. Sandy's garden has 120 square feet of planting space. She plants $\frac{1}{4}$ of her garden in flowers, $\frac{1}{3}$ in tomatoes, and the rest in beans. How many square feet are in beans?
50 ft²

12. You have a 5-liter container and a 2-liter container. You can fill and empty your containers with liquid as many times as you want. How can you end up with exactly one liter in a container? **See Teacher Guide.**

This feature presents general topics of mathematics.

Math Break

Nim is a strategy game played with 3 rows of circles as shown:

○ ○ ○
○ ○ ○ ○
○ ○ ○ ○ ○

Have students try to develop winning strategies.

Two people or two teams may play against each other. Each player or team is allowed to cross out any number of circles in exactly one row. At least one circle must be crossed out in each turn. The person or team who crosses out the last circle is the winner.

Nim can also be played with 3 rows using any number of circles in each row.

Sample play between red and blue.

Game ready to play:

○ ○ ○
○ ○ ○ ○
○ ○ ○ ○ ○

Red starts game.

○ ○ ⊘
○ ○ ○ ○
○ ○ ○ ○ ○

Blue:

⊘ ○ ⊘
⊘ ⊘ ⊘ ⊘
○ ○ ○ ○ ○

Red:

○ ○ ⊘
⊘ ⊘ ⊘ ⊘
○ ⊘ ⊘ ⊘ ⊘

Blue:

○ ⊘ ⊘
⊘ ⊘ ⊘ ⊘
○ ⊘ ⊘ ⊘ ⊘

Red:

⊘ ⊘ ⊘
⊘ ⊘ ⊘ ⊘
○ ⊘ ⊘ ⊘ ⊘

Blue wins the game.

⊘ ⊘ ⊘
⊘ ⊘ ⊘ ⊘
⊘ ⊘ ⊘ ⊘ ⊘

CHAPTER 14 REVIEW

Vocabulary/Concepts

Write the letter of the word or phrase that best matches each description.

1. two numbers that are the same distance from zero on the number line **h**

2. distance a number is from zero on the number line **a**

3. the set of whole numbers and their opposites **e**

4. a number that can be written as the ratio of two integers **l**

5. the same as subtracting a number **b**

6. the product of two numbers with the same sign **j**

7. the quotient of two numbers with different signs **f**

a. absolute value
b. adding its opposite
c. fractions
d. graph
e. integers
f. negative number
g. number line
h. opposites
i order of operations
j. positive number
k. ratio
l. rational number

Exercises

Write a rational number to describe each situation. Pages 305–307

8. a 14° temperature drop **-14°**

9. 37 minutes after lift-off **37**

10. a 7% decline in sales **-7%**

11. a $75 raise in salary **$75**

Replace each ▦ with <, >, or = to make a true sentence. Pages 305–307

12. $^-7$ ▦ 5 **<**

13. 32 ▦ $^-32$ **>**

14. 1.32 ▦ $1\frac{8}{25}$ **=**

15. $\frac{1}{5}$ ▦ $^-3$ **>**

16. $\frac{3}{4}$ ▦ 0.83 **<**

17. $^-3.4$ ▦ 2.9 **<**

18. 2.9 ▦ 2.87 **>**

19. $|6|$ ▦ $|^-7|$ **<**

Write the absolute value of each rational number. Pages 305–307

20. $|18| = $ ▦ **18**

21. $|^-11| = $ ▦ **11**

22. $|2.6| = $ ▦ **2.6**

23. $|^-3\frac{2}{3}| = $ ▦ **$3\frac{2}{3}$**

Graph each set of numbers on a number line. Pages 308–309

24. $\{^-3, 1, 2, 5\}$

25. $\{$all numbers $\geq {}^-2\}$

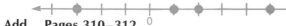

Add. Pages 310–312

26. $14 + 26$ **40**

27. $^-14 + 23$ **9**

28. $11 + {}^-36$ **-25**

29. $^-29 + {}^-42$ **-71**

30. $^-1.5 + {}^-1.3$ **-2.8**

31. $^-4.2 + 1.6$ **-2.6**

32. $2.5 + {}^-11.9$ **-9.4**

33. $3.41 + 5.82$ **9.23**

34. $\frac{^-1}{2} + \frac{1}{3}$ **$-\frac{1}{6}$**

35. $\frac{7}{8} + \left(-\frac{3}{4}\right)$ **$\frac{1}{8}$**

36. $\frac{5}{^-8} + \left(-\frac{5}{6}\right)$ **$-1\frac{11}{24}$**

37. $1\frac{1}{2} + 3\frac{1}{4}$ **$4\frac{3}{4}$**

Write an addition expression for each of the following. Pages 313–315

38. $6 - 3$ **$6 + {}^-3$**

39. $9 - 10$ **$9 + {}^-10$**

40. $^-1.7 - 2.1$
    $^-1.7 + {}^-2.1$

41. $6.36 - 4.37$
    $6.36 + {}^-4.37$

Subtract. Pages 313–315

42. $^-13 - 14$ **-27**
43. $^-23 - {}^-14$ **-9**
44. $22 - {}^-41$ **63**
45. $11 - 28$ **-17**

46. $2.3 - {}^-1.4$ **3.7**
47. $0 - 0.5$ **-0.5**
48. $^-6.1 - {}^-4.3$ **-1.8**
49. $^-5.1 - 5.1$ **-10.2**

50. $-\dfrac{7}{12} - \dfrac{3}{4}$ **-1$\frac{1}{3}$**
51. $-\dfrac{5}{8} - \left(-\dfrac{7}{8}\right)$ **$\frac{1}{4}$**
52. $\dfrac{5}{6} - \dfrac{11}{12}$ **-$\frac{1}{12}$**
53. $\dfrac{3}{5} - \left(-\dfrac{2}{3}\right)$ **1$\frac{4}{15}$**

State whether each product is positive or negative. Pages 318–319

54. $^-4 \times {}^-6$ **positive**
55. $5 \times {}^-6$ **negative**
56. 3×6 **positive**
57. $^-9 \times 7$ **negative**

Multiply. Pages 318–319

58. $8 \times {}^-7$ **-56**
59. $^-12 \times 8$ **-96**
60. $^-22 \times {}^-6$ **132**
61. 14×13 **182**

62. $^-0.6 \times {}^-1.5$ **0.9**
63. $0 \times {}^-0.9$ **0**
64. 2.1×0.8 **1.68**
65. $5.2 \times {}^-4$ **-20.8**

66. $\dfrac{3}{8} \times \left(-\dfrac{2}{3}\right)$ **-$\frac{1}{4}$**
67. $^-1\dfrac{1}{4} \times \left(-\dfrac{1}{5}\right)$ **$\frac{1}{4}$**
68. $-\dfrac{3}{7} \times \dfrac{14}{15}$ **-$\frac{2}{5}$**
69. $2\dfrac{1}{2} \times 3\dfrac{1}{4}$ **8$\frac{1}{8}$**

State whether each quotient is positive or negative.

70. $42 \div {}^-6$ **negative**
71. $28 \div 7$ **positive**
72. $^-21 \div {}^-3$ **positive**
73. $^-30 \div 6$ **negative**

Divide. Pages 320–321

74. $^-25 \div {}^-5$ **5**
75. $84 \div {}^-7$ **-12**
76. $56 \div 8$ **7**
77. $^-42 \div 3$ **-14**

78. $7.2 \div {}^-9$ **-0.8**
79. $^-6.3 \div 2.1$ **-3**
80. $^-4.8 \div {}^-1.2$ **4**
81. $3.9 \div 1.3$ **3**

82. $-\dfrac{4}{9} \div \dfrac{2}{3}$ **-$\frac{2}{3}$**
83. $\dfrac{4}{7} \div \left(-\dfrac{8}{9}\right)$ **-$\frac{9}{14}$**
84. $-\dfrac{4}{5} \div \left(-\dfrac{7}{10}\right)$ **1$\frac{1}{7}$**
85. $1\dfrac{1}{4} \div 2\dfrac{1}{2}$ **$\frac{1}{2}$**

Compute. Pages 322–323

86. $^-25 - 8 \div 4$ **-27**
87. $(6 + 7) \times 5$ **65**
88. $6 + 7 \times 5$ **41**
89. $6 \times (5 + 7)$ **72**

90. The water level in a reservoir was lowered 35 feet during repairs. Express this as an integer. **-35 ft**

91. An ant moved from $^-5$ to 8 on a number line. How many units did the ant move? **13 units**

92. At 8:00 A.M. the temperature was $^-8°$C. By 2:00 P.M., the temperature rose 18°C. By 10:00 P.M., it dropped 7°C. What was the temperature at 10:00 P.M.? **3°C**

93. A scuba diver swam to a depth of 53 meters. Then he saw a shark 10 meters above him. At what level was the shark? **a depth of 43 meters**

94. On January 23–24, 1916, at Browning, Montana, the temperature dropped from 44°F to $^-56°$F. What was the change in temperature? **-100°F**

95. The population of Augusta decreased from 59,864 to 47,534 in ten years. What was the average annual change in population? **-1,233 persons**

96. Jeri's highest weight last year was 102 pounds. Her lowest weight was 97 pounds. Graph the numbers representing her weight on a number line.

96.

97. Tanya made 7 deposits of $20 each to her bank account. She made 4 withdrawals of $40 each. What was the net change in her bank balance? **-$20**

‹——|———◆———|———|———|———◆———|———›
  96   97   98   99   100   101   102

CHAPTER 14 TEST

Replace each ● with <, >, or = to make a true sentence.

1. 15 ● ⁻2 **>**   **2.** 0 ● 4 **<**   **3.** ⁻6 ● ⁻5 **<**

Graph each set of numbers on a number line.

4. {0, 2, 4, 6, 8}   **5.** {all numbers ≤ 0}   **6.** {all numbers less than 3}

4.
5.
6.

Add.

7. 9 + 7 **16**   **8.** ⁻8 + 5 **⁻3**   **9.** ⁻3 + ⁻8 **⁻11**   **10.** 9 + ⁻7 **2**

11. 83 + 74 **157**   **12.** ⁻28 + 13 **⁻15**   **13.** ⁻47 + ⁻25 **⁻72**   **14.** 63 + ⁻84 **⁻21**

15. ⁻6.3 + 4.7 **⁻1.6**   **16.** ⁻41.9 + ⁻1.71 **⁻43.61**   **17.** $-\frac{3}{7} + \frac{2}{7}$ **$-\frac{1}{7}$**   **18.** $-\frac{7}{8} + \frac{1}{4}$ **$-\frac{5}{8}$**

Subtract.

19. 0 − 7 **⁻7**   **20.** ⁻8 − 7 **⁻15**   **21.** 8 − ⁻7 **15**   **22.** ⁻16 − ⁻7 **⁻9**

23. 16 − 48 **⁻32**   **24.** ⁻32 − ⁻18 **⁻14**   **25.** 18 − ⁻43 **61**   **26.** ⁻9 − 48 **⁻57**

27. ⁻8.6 − 4.1 **⁻12.7**   **28.** ⁻0.27 − 0.63 **⁻0.9**   **29.** $\frac{5}{7} - \frac{6}{7}$ **$-\frac{1}{7}$**   **30.** $-\frac{3}{8} - \frac{1}{2}$ **$-\frac{7}{8}$**

Multiply.

31. 7 × ⁻5 **⁻35**   **32.** ⁻3 × ⁻8 **24**   **33.** ⁻8 × 9 **⁻72**   **34.** 0 × ⁻7 **0**

35. 16 × ⁻37 **⁻592**   **36.** ⁻43 × 54 **⁻2,322**   **37.** ⁻18 × ⁻36 **648**   **38.** ⁻127 × 0 **0**

39. 8.4 × ⁻4.2 **⁻35.28**   **40.** ⁻1.9 × ⁻1.6 **3.04**   **41.** $-\frac{3}{4} × \frac{1}{5}$ **$-\frac{3}{20}$**   **42.** $\frac{3}{4} × \left(-\frac{2}{3}\right)$ **$-\frac{1}{2}$**

Divide.

43. 24 ÷ ⁻6 **⁻4**   **44.** ⁻72 ÷ 9 **⁻8**   **45.** ⁻56 ÷ ⁻8 **7**   **46.** 0 ÷ ⁻8 **0**

47. ⁻144 ÷ 12 **⁻12**   **48.** 576 ÷ ⁻24 **⁻24**   **49.** ⁻196 ÷ ⁻7 **28**   **50.** ⁻4,096 ÷ 32 **⁻128**

51. 9.6 ÷ ⁻1.2 **⁻8**   **52.** ⁻5.76 ÷ 0.8 **⁻7.2**   **53.** $-\frac{3}{10} ÷ \frac{1}{2}$ **$-\frac{3}{5}$**   **54.** $-\frac{8}{9} ÷ \frac{3}{4}$ **$-1\frac{5}{27}$**

Compute.

55. 6 × 3 + 5 **23**   **56.** 12 ÷ 4 × 3 **9**   **57.** ⁻48 + ⁻16 ÷ 8 **⁻50**

58. 64 + ⁻8 ÷ 4 **62**   **59.** 36 ÷ 4 + 2 **11**   **60.** 36 + 4 ÷ ⁻2 **34**

61. (72 + 18) ÷ 18 **5**   **62.** 72 + 18 ÷ 18 **73**   **63.** 576 + ⁻24 ÷ 8 + 4 **577**

Solve.

64. Ella is 5 years younger than Bernie. Bernie is 22. How old is Ella? **17 years old**

65. An airplane has an altitude of 6,000 feet. A helicopter has an altitude of 1,200 feet. The helicopter is how many feet lower than the airplane? **4,800 ft**

This page provides extra practice of the skills and applications presented thus far in the text.

CUMULATIVE REVIEW

Solve.   Pages 198–199

1. Mr. and Mrs. Champer are buying a $35,000 house. They have $9,000. The loan agency requires a 23% down payment. What is the down payment required by the agency?
$8,050

2. Nancy earns $5.00 an hour. She works 8 hours on Mondays, 7 hours on Tuesdays and Wednesdays, and 8.5 hours on Fridays. She spends $5 a week on gasoline. How much money does she make in a week?
$152.50

The figure below represents a rectangular prism. Use the figure to complete the following.   Pages 212–213

3. How many line segments make up the prism? Name them. 12; $\overline{AB}$, $\overline{AC}$, $\overline{BD}$, $\overline{CD}$, $\overline{EF}$, $\overline{EC}$, $\overline{EG}$, $\overline{AG}$, $\overline{DF}$, $\overline{FH}$, $\overline{BH}$, $\overline{HG}$

4. Name the angles of $\square GEFH$.
∠EGH, ∠EFH, ∠FEG, ∠FHG

5. One plane is determined by points A, B, and H. How many other such planes are determined in the prism? 5 planes

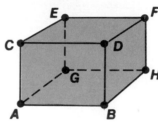

Find the surface area of each square pyramid shown below.   Pages 282–283

6. 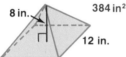 8 in.   12 in.   384 in²

7.  4 m   6 m   96 m²

8. 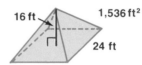 16 ft   24 ft   1,536 ft²

Find the surface area of each cylinder described below. Use 3.14 for π. Round answers to the nearest tenth.   Pages 284–285

9. 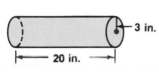 3 in.   20 in.
433.3 in²

10. 6 m $7\frac{1}{2}$ m
508.7 m²

11. 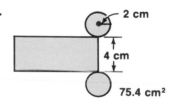 2 cm   4 cm
75.4 cm²

Replace each ▓ with <, >, or = to make a true sentence.   Pages 305–307

12. ⁻10 ▓ 10 <

13. $\frac{1}{20}$ ▓ $\frac{1}{30}$ >

14. |⁻3| ▓ |3| =

15. 110 ▓ |⁻115| <

16. |4| ▓ |⁻3.5| >

17. ⁻9 ▓ 9 <

18. ⁻4 ▓ ⁻3 <

19. $\frac{1}{2}$ ▓ |⁻$\frac{1}{2}$| =

20. ⁻$\frac{1}{4}$ ▓ $\frac{1}{4}$ <

21. $\frac{1}{4}$ ▓ 0.25 =

22. 0.67 ▓ 0.6 >

23. ⁻$\frac{1}{20}$ ▓ ⁻$\frac{1}{30}$ <

Graph each set of numbers on a number line.   Pages 308–309

24. {1.2, 1.9, 2.6, . . .}

25. {2, 4, 6, 8, . . .}

26. {0, ⁻1, ⁻2, ⁻3}

27. {all numbers ≤ 10}

28. {all numbers ≥ 0}

29. {all numbers ⁻2 or less}

For answers to exercises 24–29 see Teacher Guide.
Teacher Resource Book, Pages 319, 320

Solving Open Sentences

15-1 Open Sentences

Objective: To discover how placeholders are used in mathematics.

Suppose the following questions were on a true-false test.

(a) Marie Curie won 2 Nobel prizes.   **(b)** Uranium is radioactive.

(c) It is metal.   **(d)** She discovered polonium.

It is not possible to determine whether sentences **c** and **d** are true or false. That is because you do not know what the placeholders *it* and *she* stand for.

Placeholders can also be used in mathematical sentences. In mathematical sentences, placeholders are called **variables.** An **open sentence** contains one or more variables and is neither true nor false. The following are open sentences.

$3 \times a = 21$ ▨ $+ 2 > 7$ 19 $x < {}^-2$

A sentence with an equals sign (=) is called an **equation.**
A sentence with symbols such as $<$ or $>$ is called an **inequality.**
The sentence $18 < 54$ is read eighteen is less than fifty-four.
The sentence $26 > 14$ is read twenty-six is greater than fourteen.

Basic Skills Appendix, Page 453
Basic: 2–18 even, 19; Average: 1–19; Enriched: 1–19 odd

Exercises

Determine whether each sentence is true, false, or open.

1. Alaska is the largest state. **true**   **2.** Colorado is an eastern state. **false**

3. They are good athletes. **open**   **4.** Einstein wrote *Gone With the Wind*. **false**

5. It is the state capital. **open**   **6.** Hydrogen will burn. **true**

7. $7 + 9 - 15$ **false**   **8.** $38 - 15 = 13$ **false**   **9.** $m - 7 = 9$ **open**

10. $75 > 2 \times 37$ **true**   **11.** $96 < 10^2$ **true**   **12.** $3x - 4 = 41$ **open**

13. $42 \neq 48$ *(The symbol $\neq$ means is not equal to.)* **true**

14. $58 \geq 71$ *(The symbol $\geq$ means is greater than or equal to.)* **false**

15. $\frac{4}{9} \not< \frac{1}{3}$ *(The symbol $\not<$ means is not less than.)* **true**

16. $5.6 \neq 5.60$ **false**   **17.** $0.8 \leq 0.45 \times q$ **open**   **18.** $\frac{25}{8} \not> \frac{5}{8} + n$ **open**

Solve.

19. Sabrina owns 53 records and tapes. She owns 35 records.
Use t as a placeholder for the number of tapes Sabrina owns.
Write an open sentence for this situation.
$35 + t = 53$

15-2 Solving Open Sentences

Objective: To solve open sentences using a replacement set and the guess-and-check method.

Number of People	Year Reached
1 billion	1850
2 billion	1930
3 billion	1961
4 billion	1975
5 billion	1986

In 1986, the world's population reached 5 billion. The table at the left shows that the population has increased.

How many years did it take for the population to increase from 4 billion to 5 billion?

This question can be answered by **solving** the open sentence $1975 + n = 1986$. Solving an open sentence means to find a replacement for the variable that makes the sentence true.

One way to solve an open sentence is to try numbers until you find a solution or pattern. The numbers used to replace the variable come from a *replacement set*.

Examples

A. Solve $1975 + n = 1986$. Use {9, 10, 11, 12} as a replacement set.

$1975 + 9 \stackrel{?}{=} 1986$ false

$1975 + 10 \stackrel{?}{=} 1986$ false

$1975 + 11 \stackrel{?}{=} 1986$ true

$1975 + 12 \stackrel{?}{=} 1986$ false

The number 11 makes the sentence true. It took 11 years for the population to increase from 4 billion to 5 billion.

B. Solve $x + 2 < 5$. Use {1, 2, 3, 4, . . .} as a replacement set.

$1 + 2 \stackrel{?}{<} 5$ true

$2 + 2 \stackrel{?}{<} 5$ true

$3 + 2 \stackrel{?}{<} 5$ false

$4 + 2 \stackrel{?}{<} 5$ false

The numbers 1 and 2 make the sentence true. The solutions of $x + 2 < 5$ from the given replacement set are 1 and 2.

If a replacement set is not given, then you can assume that the replacement set is the set of all numbers. Since it is impossible to try all numbers, *guess* the solution or solutions. Then *check* to see if they are correct.

Examples

C. Solve $3 \times a = {}^-21$.

Guess $a = {}^-7$.

Check: Since $3 \times {}^-7 = {}^-21$, $a = {}^-7$.

D. Solve $\frac{n}{4} = 5$. $\frac{n}{4}$ means $n \div 4$

Guess $n = 20$.

Check: Since $20 \div 4 = 5$, $n = 20$.

Basic Skills Appendix, Pages 421, 422, 425, 428
Basic: 1–37 odd; Average: 2–34 even, 36–37; Enriched: 1–35 odd, 36–37

Exercises

Solve each open sentence using the given replacement set.

1. $3 + k = 7$, {0, 1, 2, 3, 4, 5} **4**

2. $m - 4 = 2$, {0, 2, 4, 6, 8} **6**

3. $3 \times w = 15$, {1, 2, 3, 4, 5, 6} **5**

4. $\frac{t}{4} = 3$, {6, 8, 10, 12, 14} **12**

5. $n + 2 = {}^{-}3$, {${}^{-}6, {}^{-}5, {}^{-}4, {}^{-}3$} **${}^{-}5$**

6. $n - 5 = {}^{-}2$, {0, 1, 2, 3, 4} **3**

7. $n + 5 > 7$, {0, 1, 2, 3, 4, 5, . . .} **3, 4, 5, . . .**

8. $4 \times a < 8$, {0, 1, 2, 3, 4} **0, 1**

9. $x - 8 > 2$, {8, 9, 10, 11, 12, . . .} **11, 12, 13, . . .**

10. $\frac{x}{3} < 5$, {0, 3, 6, 9, 12} **0, 3, 6, 9, 12**

Solve each equation using the guess-and-check method.

11. $n + 5 = 7$ **2**

12. $4 + x = 6$ **2**

13. $6 = t + 2$ **4**

14. $8 = 5 + r$ **3**

15. $n + {}^{-}8 = {}^{-}8$ **0**

16. ${}^{-}9 + k = {}^{-}9$ **0**

17. $k - 4 = 3$ **7**

18. $3 - a = 0$ **3**

19. $8 = b - 5$ **13**

20. $9 = 12 - c$ **3**

21. $r - 5 = {}^{-}6$ **${}^{-}1$**

22. $b - 5 = {}^{-}5$ **0**

23. $m \times 2 = 6$ **3**

24. $3 \times b = 15$ **5**

25. $16 = 2 \times k$ **8**

26. $8 = 2 \times k$ **4**

27. $3 \times t = 12$ **4**

28. $3 \times b = {}^{-}12$ **${}^{-}4$**

29. $m \div 3 = 2$ **6**

30. $k \div {}^{-}8 = 1$ **${}^{-}8$**

31. $m \div 7 = {}^{-}1$ **${}^{-}7$**

Translate each sentence into an equation. Then solve the equation and check your solution.

32. The sum of x and 5 is 18. **$x + 5 = 18$; 13**

33. Six more than t is 22. **$t + 6 = 22$; 16**

34. n decreased by 10 is ${}^{-}3$. **$n - 10 = {}^{-}3$; 7**

35. The product of n and 11 is 99. **$n \times 11 = 99$; 9**

Write an equation for each problem. Then solve using the guess-and-check method.

36. Kamie sold 215 tickets. She has 38 tickets left. How many tickets did Kamie have before she sold any? **$n - 215 = 38$; 253 tickets**

37. Lin is six years younger than his sister. Lin is 13 years old. How old is his sister? **$13 = n - 6$; 19 years old**

15-3 Equations Involving Addition

Objective: To solve equations by using subtraction.

Chemists use scales to obtain accurate measurements. Suppose a scale is balanced and a weight is removed from one side. The same amount must be removed from the other side to keep the scale balanced.

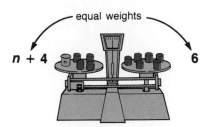

A balanced scale is like a mathematical equation. Suppose *n* represents the amount in the beaker. Then the scale above represents the equation $n + 4 = 6$.

scale—same amount on each side
equation—same number named on each side

To find the amount *n* or solve the equation, remove 4 weights from each side. This will isolate the unknown amount in the beaker, *n*.

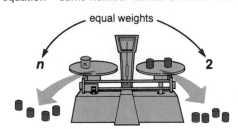

The new equation is $n = 2$.
Thus, the solution for $n + 4 = 6$ is 2.

Removing weights reminds us of subtraction.
Equations such as $n + 4 = 6$ can be solved by using subtraction.

Examples

A. Solve $n + 4 = 6$.

$n + 4 - 4 = 6 - 4$ *Subtract 4 from each side to isolate n.*

$n + 0 = 2$ $4 - 4 = 0$ *and* $6 - 4 = 2$

$n = 2$ $n + 0 = n$

Check: $n + 4 = 6$

$2 + 4 \overset{?}{=} 6$ *Replace n with 2.*

$6 = 6$ *It checks.*

The solution is 2.

B. Solve $^-5 = x + 7$.

$^-5 - 7 = x + 7 - 7$ *Subtract 7 from each side to isolate x.*

$^-12 = x + 0$ $^-5 - 7 = {^-12}$ *and*
$7 - 7 = 0$

$^-12 = x$ $x + 0 = x$

Check: $^-5 = x + 7$

$^-5 \overset{?}{=} {^-12} + 7$ *Replace x with $^-12$.*

$^-5 = {^-5}$ *It checks.*

The solution is $^-12$.

The Key Skills provides practice of skills needed in the exercises.

Key Skills

Find each difference.

$26 - {^-11}$ ▶ $26 + 11 = 37$ $\quad -\dfrac{1}{2} - 1\dfrac{3}{4}$ ▶ $-\dfrac{1}{2} + 1\dfrac{3}{4} = \dfrac{^-2}{4} + \dfrac{^-7}{4}$

$= \dfrac{^-9}{4} \text{ or } {^-2}\dfrac{1}{4}$

1. $^-8 - 7$ **$^-15$** **2.** $16 - {^-5}$ **21** **3.** $^-3 - {^-9}$ **6** **4.** $^-10 - 7$ **$^-17$** **5.** $2.5 - 1.9$ **0.6**

6. $^-6.4 - {^-3.8}$ **$^-2.6$** **7.** $6 - 2\dfrac{3}{4}$ **$3\dfrac{1}{4}$** **8.** $\dfrac{1}{3} - {^-1}\dfrac{1}{6}$ **$1\dfrac{1}{2}$** **9.** $\dfrac{^-5}{8} - \dfrac{1}{4}$ **$\dfrac{^-7}{8}$** **10.** $^-2\dfrac{1}{6} - {^-3}\dfrac{2}{3}$ **$1\dfrac{1}{2}$**

Exercises

Write an equation for each scale. Then state what you would do to find a new equation that gives the solution.

1.

$n + 2 = 6$; remove 2 from each side; $n = 4$

2.

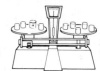

$x + 3 = 5$; remove 3 from each side; $x = 2$

3.

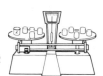

$t + 4 = 5$; remove 4 from each side; $t = 1$

State the number to subtract from each side to solve each equation. Then solve the equation and check your solution.

4. $n + 3 = 5$ **3, 2**　　**5.** $x + 2 = 8$ **2, 6**　　**6.** $z + 5 = 11$ **5, 6**　　**7.** $k + 6 = 13$ **6, 7**

8. $4 + k = 9$ **4, 5**　　**9.** $7 + t = 13$ **7, 6**　　**10.** $3 + m = 12$ **3, 9**　　**11.** $12 + y = 25$ **12, 13**

Solve each equation. Check your solution.

12. $n + 2 = 9$ **7**　　**13.** $3 + n = 14$ **11**　　**14.** $16 = b + 7$ **9**　　**15.** $k + {}^-5 = 6$ **11**

16. $83 = s + 110$ **-27**　　**17.** $n + {}^-45 = {}^-98$ **-53**　　**18.** $1.9 = b + 1.7$ **0.2**　　**19.** $g + 144 = {}^-302$ **-446**

20. $1.3 + t = 3.4$ **2.1**　　**21.** ${}^-0.3 + d = {}^-1.3$ **-1.0**　　**22.** $g + \frac{1}{4} = \frac{1}{2}$ **$\frac{1}{4}$**　　**23.** $2\frac{1}{6} + r = {}^-\frac{2}{3}$ **$-2\frac{5}{6}$**

24. $n + {}^-4 = {}^-16$ **-12**　　**25.** $0.11 = k + {}^-0.4$ **0.51**　　**26.** ${}^-133 = {}^-8 + m$ **-125**　　**27.** $x + 1.05 = {}^-3.08$ **2.03**

28. $y + {}^-82.6 = {}^-10$ **72.6**　　**29.** $x + {}^-18 = 37$ **55**　　**30.** $n + 2.5 = {}^-8.1$ **-10.6**　　**31.** ${}^-30 + b = 85.2$ **115.2**

Solve. Write an equation.

32. A number is increased by 14. The result is ${}^-45$. What is the number?
$x + 14 = {}^-45$; **-59**

33. Karen must travel 52 miles to reach her home. She has traveled 37.5 miles. How many miles more does Karen have to travel to reach her home?
$x + 37.5 = 52$; **14.5 miles**

34. There were 562 students enrolled at Crosby High School last year. This year, there are 581 students enrolled. How many new students have enrolled at Crosby High School? $562 + x = 581$; **19 students**

This feature presents general topics of mathematics.

Math Break

Charlie is thinking of two 2-digit numbers. They have the same digits, only reversed, like 23 and 32. The sum of the digits of each of Charlie's numbers is 10. The difference between the numbers is 36. Find Charlie's numbers. **73, 37**

15-4 Equations Involving Subtraction

Objective: To solve equations by using addition.

 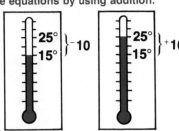

The temperature reading on a thermometer is 25 degrees. If the temperature goes down 10 degrees, the new reading will be 15 degrees. $25 - 10 = 15$

If the temperature then goes up 10 degrees, the reading will be 25 degrees. $15 + 10 = 25$

Adding 10 undoes *subtracting* 10. Thus, we say addition and subtraction are **inverse operations.**

The equation $m - 5 = 8$ involves subtraction. Since addition undoes subtraction, $m - 5 = 8$ can be solved by using addition.

Example

Solve $m - 5 = 8$.

$m - 5 + 5 = 8 + 5$ *Add 5 to each side to isolate m.*

$m + 0 = 13$

$m = 13$

Check: $m - 5 = 8$

$13 - 5 \stackrel{?}{=} 8$ *Replace m with 13.*

$8 = 8$ *It checks.*

The solution is 13.

Basic Skills Appendix, Pages 450, 454, 457
Basic: 2–60 even; Average: 1–61 odd; Enriched: 1–57 odd, 58–61

Exercises

Complete.

1. In $n - 4 = 6$, _____?_____ is being performed. **subtraction**

2. To undo the subtraction of 4, _____?_____ 4 to each side. **add**

3. In $k + 8 = 19$, _____?_____ is being performed. **addition**

4. To undo the addition of 8, _____?_____ 8 from each side. **subtract**

5. State a general rule for solving equations such as $n - 4 = 6$ and $k + 8 = 19$. Undo the indicated operation.

State the number to add to each side to solve each equation.
Then solve the equation and check your solution.

6. $m - 8 = 11$ **8, 19**

7. $t - 6 = 11$ **6, 17**

8. $r - 0.9 = 1.4$ **0.9, 2.3**

9. $3\frac{1}{2} = a - 1\frac{1}{2}$ **1$\frac{1}{2}$, 5**

10. $x - 12 = 16$ **12, 28**

11. $23 = y - 9$ **9, 32**

12. $a - 10 = 21$ **10, 31**

13. $12 = n - 12$ **12, 24**

14. $k - 3 = 9$ **3, 12**

15. $t - 0.08 = 1.8$ **0.08, 1.88**

16. $21 = m - 13$ **13, 34**

17. $r - 18 = 24$ **18, 42**

18. $35 = b - 17$ **17, 52**

19. $21 = m - 6$ **6, 27**

20. $23 = r - 5$ **5, 28**

21. $x - 1.2 = 1.8$ **1.2, 3**

Solve each equation. Check your solution.

22. $t - 4 = 16$ **20**   23. $x - 8 = 14$ **22**   24. $y - 0.9 = 2.0$ **2.9**   25. $n - 13 = 17$ **30**

26. $m - 13 = 26$ **39**   27. $k - 21 = 34$ **55**   28. $b + 1.8 = 4.3$ **2.5**   29. $8 + f = 11$ **3**

30. $15 = a + 9$ **6**   31. $14 = b - 3$ **17**   32. $3.7 = c + 1.2$ **2.5**   33. $w - 0.5 = 0.5$ **1**

34. $24 = h - 7$ **31**   35. $42 = j - 13$ **55**   36. $5.3 = k - 1.7$ **7.0**   37. $9 = m + 2$ **7**

38. $x - 4 = ^-9$ **-5**   39. $z - 3 = ^-7$ **-4**   40. $w - 4 = ^-1.8$ **2.2**   41. $k - 1.6 = 4.3$ **5.9**

42. $^-18 = y + 6$ **-24**   43. $^-21 = d - 8$ **-13**   44. $^-7.3 = f - 16$ **8.7**   45. $^-46 = x - 13$ **-33**

46. $^-18 = y - 9$ **-9**   47. $^-42 = m - 13$ **-29**   48. $^-35 = r - 3.7$ **-31.3**   49. $^-5.4 = b + 1.8$ **-7.2**

50. $x - 4 = ^-10$ **-6**   51. $r - \frac{1}{4} = \frac{5}{8}$ **$\frac{7}{8}$**   52. $b + \frac{2}{7} = 2$ **$1\frac{5}{7}$**   53. $n - \frac{2}{5} = \frac{2}{3}$ **$1\frac{1}{15}$**

54. $t - \frac{4}{9} = \frac{2}{9}$ **$\frac{2}{3}$**   55. $^-1\frac{1}{2} = c - \frac{3}{4}$ **$-\frac{3}{4}$**   56. $-\frac{7}{12} + p = ^-2\frac{2}{3}$ **$-2\frac{1}{12}$** 57. $2\frac{4}{5} = m - 1\frac{1}{10}$ **$3\frac{9}{10}$**

Choose the correct equation for each situation. Then solve.

58. The temperature went down 15 degrees. It is now 3 degrees below zero. What was the temperature before the decrease?
$t - 15 = ^-3$ $t - 15 = ^-3; 12°$
$t + 15 = ^-3$

59. When the wind is blowing, the temperature feels colder than it actually is. At 40°F with a wind of 10 mph, it feels 12° colder. How cold does it feel? $t = 40 - 12; 28°F$
$t = 40 - 12$
$t = 40 + 12$

Solve. Write an equation.

60. Rita boiled away 25 mL of her salt solution. She now has 43 mL of solution. How much did she have before boiling? $n - 25 = 43; 68$ mL

61. Jorge had 38 g of salt in solution before he added more. Now he has 62 g in solution. How many grams did he add? $38 + n = 62; 24$ grams

This feature presents useful ways of solving mathematical problems on a calculator.

 Calculator

Perform the following operations on a calculator using the left and right parentheses keys. **The order of operations is built into some calculators, so the answers may vary.**

4 ⊞ 3 ☒ 6 ÷ 2 ⊟ 21 or 13   4 ⊞ ⦅ 3 ☒ 6 ⦆ ÷ 2 ⊟ 13

⦅ 4 ⊞ 3 ⦆ ☒ ⦅ 6 ÷ 2 ⦆ ⊟ 21   ⦅ 4 ⊞ ⦅ 3 ☒ 6 ⦆ ⦆ ÷ 2 ⊟ 11

4 ⊞ ⦅ ⦅ 3 ☒ 6 ⦆ ÷ 2 ⦆ ⊟ 13   4 ⊞ ⦅ 3 ☒ ⦅ 6 ÷ 2 ⦆ ⦆ ⊟ 13

Notice that the use of parentheses significantly affects the results.

Insert parentheses in each mathematical statement to obtain the given result.

1. $10 - 6 \times 8 + 1$; 36
   $(10 - 6) \times (8 + 1)$

2. $6 + 8 \times 3 \div 3$; 10
   $(6 + (8 \times 3)) \div 3$

3. $20 \div 9 + 4 - 3$; 2
   $20 \div ((9 + 4) - 3)$

15-5 Equations Involving Multiplication

Objective: To solve equations by using division.

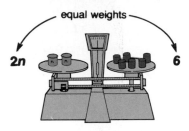

equal weights

2n   **6**

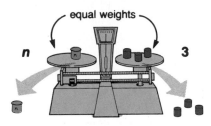

equal weights

n   **3**

The scale shown at the left is balanced. Suppose *n* represents the amount in each of the two beakers on one side of the scale. Then the scale represents the equation $2 \times n = 6$. *2 × n can also be written as 2n.*

To find the amount *n* or solve the equation, count the number of beakers on one side of the scale. Since there are two beakers, separate the weights into two equal-sized groups. Remove a beaker from one side and a group of three weights from the other side. This will determine the unknown amount in each beaker, *n*.

The new·equation is $n = 3$.
Thus, the solution for $2n = 6$ is 3.

Separating into equal-sized groups reminds us of division.
Equations such as $2n = 6$ can be solved by using division.

Example

Solve 2*n* = 6.

$$\frac{2n}{2} = \frac{6}{2} \quad \textit{Divide each side by 2.}$$

$1 \times n = 3 \quad 2 \div 2 = 1 \text{ and } 6 \div 2 = 3$

$n = 3 \quad 1 \times n = n$

Check: $2n = 6$

$2 \times 3 \stackrel{?}{=} 6 \quad \textit{Replace n with 3.}$

$6 = 6 \quad \textit{It checks.}$

The solution is 3.

The Key Skills provides practice of skills needed in the exercises.

Key Skills

Divide.

$$^-4 \div \frac{4}{5} \quad \blacktriangleright \quad \frac{^-\overset{1}{\cancel{4}}}{1} \times \frac{5}{\underset{1}{\cancel{4}}} = {}^-5 \qquad {}^-2\frac{1}{2} \div \frac{^-5}{9} \quad \blacktriangleright \quad \frac{^-\overset{1}{\cancel{5}}}{2} \times \frac{^-9}{\underset{1}{\cancel{5}}} = \frac{9}{2} \text{ or } 4\frac{1}{2}$$

1. $\dfrac{^-14}{^-7}$ **2**

2. $\dfrac{^-56}{7}$ **-8**

3. $\dfrac{28}{-4}$ **-7**

4. $\dfrac{^-8.4}{^-1.2}$ **7**

5. $\dfrac{56}{^-0.8}$ **-70**

6. $^-1.76 \div 2.2$ **-0.8**

7. $^-2 \div \dfrac{4}{5}$ **-2$\frac{1}{2}$**

8. $\dfrac{^-2}{3} \div {}^-6$ **$\frac{1}{9}$**

9. $\dfrac{^-7}{8} \div \dfrac{^-1}{2}$ **1$\frac{3}{4}$**

10. $^-6\frac{1}{2} \div 1\frac{1}{4}$ **-5$\frac{1}{5}$**

Basic Skills Appendix, Pages 443, 444, 460
Basic: 2–28 even; Average: 1–28; Enriched: 1–27 odd, 28

Exercises

Write an equation for each scale. Then state what you would do to find a new equation that gives the solution.

1.

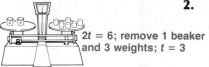

$2t = 6$; remove 1 beaker and 3 weights; $t = 3$

2.

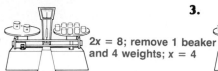

$2x = 8$; remove 1 beaker and 4 weights; $x = 4$

3.

$3n = 9$; remove 2 beakers and 6 weights; $n = 3$

State the number to divide each side by to solve each equation. Then solve each equation and check your solution.

4. $3y = 12$ **3, 4**   **5.** $4x = 20$ **4, 5**   **6.** $2a = 16$ **2, 8**   **7.** $7m = 21$ **7, 3**

8. $56 = 8q$ **8, 7**   **9.** $^-14 = 2t$ **2, -7**   **10.** $32 = ^-4r$ **-4, -8**   **11.** $^-48 = ^-6y$ **-6, 8**

Solve each equation. Check your solution.

12. $2n = 18$ **9**   **13.** $5a = 95$ **19**   **14.** $96 = 8t$ **12**   **15.** $^-4m = 72$ **-18**

16. $^-7m = ^-21$ **3**   **17.** $^-63 = ^-9n$ **7**   **18.** $^-55 = ^-11t$ **5**   **19.** $5z = ^-32$ $^-6\frac{2}{5}$

20. $^-8p = 4.8$ **-0.6** **21.** $^-7.29 = 27d$ **-0.27** **22.** $^-3b = 1.8$ **-0.6** **23.** $2.16 = 3.6b$ **0.6**

24. $4t = \frac{4}{5}$ $\frac{1}{5}$ **25.** $6y = \frac{3}{5}$ $\frac{1}{10}$ **26.** $^-21z = \frac{7}{9}$ $^-\frac{1}{27}$ **27.** $\frac{2}{3}d = ^-\frac{4}{9}$ $^-\frac{2}{3}$

Solve. Write an equation.

28. Angela weighs 3.5 times what her sister weighs. Angela weighs 112 pounds. How much does her sister weigh? **$112 = 3.5n$; 32 pounds**

This feature promotes students' mental abilities in computation and reasonableness.

Mental Math

Fractions may be rounded by comparing the numerator with the denominator. If both numbers have about the same value, then the value of the fraction is about one. ($\frac{5}{6} \approx 1$)
If the numerator is about half the denominator, then the value of the fraction is about one-half. ($\frac{3}{5} \approx \frac{1}{2}$)
If the numerator is much less than the denominator, then the value of the fraction is about zero. ($\frac{2}{7} \approx 0$)

You can use the guidelines given above to estimate sums and differences of fractions.

$$\frac{7}{8} \approx 1$$
$$+\ \frac{7}{12} \approx\ \frac{1}{2}$$
$$1\frac{1}{2}$$

Estimate. Answers may vary. Typical answers are given.

1. $\frac{3}{5} + \frac{7}{8}$ $1\frac{1}{2}$ **2.** $\frac{1}{6} + \frac{3}{8}$ $\frac{1}{2}$ **3.** $\frac{6}{7} + \frac{7}{8}$ **2**

4. $\frac{7}{8} - \frac{1}{15}$ **1**   **5.** $\frac{6}{11} - \frac{8}{14}$ **0**   **6.** $3\frac{2}{3} + 8\frac{4}{5} - 11\frac{1}{10}$ **2**

PRACTICE

Estimate. Answers may vary. Typical answers are given.

1. $\begin{array}{r} 1,256 \\ -\ \ 663 \\ \hline 600 \end{array}$

2. $\begin{array}{r} 189 \\ \times\ \ 80 \\ \hline 16,000 \end{array}$

3. $\begin{array}{r} 923 \\ +\ 547 \\ \hline 1,400 \end{array}$

4. $\begin{array}{r} 52 \\ \times\ 43 \\ \hline 2,000 \end{array}$

5. $19\overline{)458}$ **23**

Add, subtract, multiply, or divide.

6. $\begin{array}{r} 438 \\ +\ 341 \\ \hline 779 \end{array}$

7. $\begin{array}{r} 7.35 \\ -\ 0.95 \\ \hline 6.40 \end{array}$

8. $\begin{array}{r} 123 \\ \times\ \ 45 \\ \hline 5,535 \end{array}$

9. $\begin{array}{r} 0.99 \\ \times\ \ 2.2 \\ \hline 2.178 \end{array}$

10. $4.2\overline{)18.9}$ **4.5**

11. $\frac{7}{8} + \frac{3}{8}$ $1\frac{1}{4}$

12. $\frac{7}{9} + 2\frac{2}{3}$ $3\frac{4}{9}$

13. $1\frac{3}{4} \times 5$ $8\frac{3}{4}$

14. $3\frac{1}{2} \div 7$ $\frac{1}{2}$

15. $\frac{2}{3} \times \frac{7}{9}$ $\frac{14}{27}$

16. $5\frac{3}{4} - 4\frac{7}{8}$ $\frac{7}{8}$

17. $10 \div 2\frac{1}{2}$ **4**

18. $6 - 3\frac{5}{8}$ $2\frac{3}{8}$

19. $9\frac{3}{5} - 4$ $5\frac{3}{5}$

20. $\frac{2}{3} + 3\frac{4}{5}$ $4\frac{7}{15}$

21. $6\frac{1}{2} \div \frac{1}{8}$ **52**

22. $4\frac{1}{5} - 1\frac{3}{4}$ $2\frac{9}{20}$

23. $0.464 \times 1,000$ **464**

24. $56.3 \div 100$ **0.563**

25. 0.09×10 **0.9**

26. $4 \div 10$ **0.4**

27. $6.4 \div 1,000$ **0.0064**

28. 21×100 **2,100**

Complete.

29. 64 in. = ▨ ft $5\frac{1}{3}$

30. ▨ cm = 63 m **6,300**

31. 4 kg = ▨ g **4,000**

32. ▨ gal = 6 qt $1\frac{1}{2}$

33. 14 lb = ▨ oz **224**

34. 0.75 km = ▨ m **750**

35. 2.4 L = ▨ mL **2,400**

36. 5.6 cm = ▨ mm **56**

37. ▨ L = 425 mL **0.425**

Add or subtract.

38. $\begin{array}{l} 6\ h\ 45\ min\ \ 8\ s \\ +\ 3\ h\ 14\ min\ 52\ s \\ \hline 10\ h \end{array}$

39. $\begin{array}{l} 6\ h\ 43\ min \\ -\ 5\ h\ 27\ min \\ \hline 1\ h\ 16\ min \end{array}$

40. $\begin{array}{l} 9\ h\ 53\ min\ 23\ s \\ -\ 7\ h\ 49\ min\ 40\ s \\ \hline 2\ h\ \ 3\ min\ 43\ s \end{array}$

41. $\begin{array}{l} 2\ h\ 22\ min\ \ 9\ s \\ +\ 9\ h\ 14\ min\ 52\ s \\ \hline 11\ h\ 37\ min\ \ 1\ s \end{array}$

42. $\begin{array}{l} 8\ h\ 48\ min\ 33\ s \\ +\ 6\ h\ 27\ min\ 12\ s \\ \hline 15\ h\ 15\ min\ 45\ s \end{array}$

43. $\begin{array}{l} 14\ h\ 56\ min\ 14\ s \\ -\ \ 5\ h\ 55\ min\ 22\ s \\ \hline 9\ h\ \ \ \ \ \ \ \ \ \ 52\ s \end{array}$

Change each percent to a decimal. Change each decimal to a percent.

44. 42% **0.42**

45. 0.01 **1%**

46. 7% **0.07**

47. 1.56 **156%**

48. 0.2 **20%**

49. 163% **1.63**

50. 1.5% **0.015**

51. 0.005 **0.5%**

52. 0.45 **45%**

53. 0.45% **0.0045**

54. 64% **0.64**

55. 216% **2.16**

56. 0.235 **23.5%**

57. 0.1% **0.001**

58. 0.004 **0.4%**

Solve.

59. 20% of 200 **40**

60. 21% of 93 **19.53**

61. 3% of 75 **2.25**

62. 99% of 6,500 **6,435**

63. 35% of 12 **4.2**

64. 50% of 8.6 **4.3**

65. 245% of 50 **122.5**

66. 12% of 0.12 **0.0144**

67. 1% of 52,000 **520**

68. 15% of 70 **10.5**

69. 0.5% of 25 **0.125**

70. 2.1% of 135 **2.835**

Use the proportion $\frac{P}{B} = \frac{r}{100}$ to solve each problem.

71. __?__ % of 12 is 9 75

72. 15 is 25% of __?__ 60

73. 12 is __?__ % of 8 150

74. __?__ is 6% of 50 3

75. __?__ is 150% of 12 18

76. 5.12 is 16% of __?__ 32

77. 4 is __?__ % of 800 0.5

78. 7.5% of __?__ is 2.1 28

79. 14% of 23 is __?__ 3.22

80. 137.5 is __?__ % of 250
55

81. 0.172 is 0.2% of __?__
86

82. 325 is __?__ % of 130
250

Find the perimeter of each figure.

83. a square $3\frac{1}{2}$ inches on a side
14 in.

84. a rectangle 3 yd by 4 yd
14 yd

Find the area of each figure. Use 3.14 for π.

85.

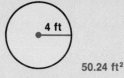

50.24 ft²

86.

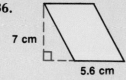

7 cm

5.6 cm   39.2 cm²

87.

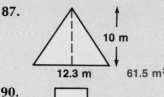

10 m

12.3 m   61.5 m²

88.

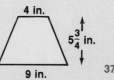

4 in.

$5\frac{3}{4}$ in.

9 in. $37\frac{3}{8}$ in²

89.

7 yd

7 yd   49 yd²

90.

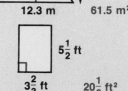

$5\frac{1}{2}$ ft

$3\frac{2}{3}$ ft $20\frac{1}{6}$ ft²

Find the volume of each solid. Use 3.14 for π.

91.

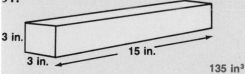

3 in.

3 in.   15 in.   135 in³

92.

14 cm

6 cm   527.52 cm³

Find the mode, median, and mean for the following set of data.

93. 3.0, 2.9, 4, 3.6, 3.8, 3.8, 2.9, 3.6, 4, 3.2, 3.5, 3.8, 2.9, 3.2
3.8; 3.6; 3.5

Solve. Use the pattern of numbers given below.

94. Each number is the sum of the two numbers above it in the previous row. For example, 2 = 1 + 1 and 6 = 3 + 3. Use this pattern to find the next two rows. See the pattern.

```
                    1
                 1     1
              1     2     1
           1     3     3     1
        1     4     6     4     1
     1     5    10    10     5     1
  1     6    15    20    15     6     1
```

95. The sums of the numbers in the first three rows are 1, 1 + 1 or 2, and 1 + 2 + 1 or 4. Find the sums for the next four rows. Describe the pattern.
8; 16; 32; 64 Each row is twice the row above it.

15-6 Equations Involving Division

Objective: To solve equations by using multiplication.

Mrs. Collins is a biologist. She has been feeding a group of
plants 80 grams of plant food each month. As an experiment,
she decides to divide the amount of plant food she feeds the
plants by two. The plants will then receive half the amount
of food, or 40 grams, for 6 months. *80 ÷ 2 = 40*
After six months, she will double the amount of plant food. The
plants will once again be fed 80 grams of plant food. *40 × 2 = 80*

Multiplying by 2 undoes *dividing* by 2. Thus, we say multiplication
and division are **inverse operations.**

The equation $\frac{m}{7} = 12$ involves division. Since multiplication
undoes division, $\frac{m}{7} = 12$ can be solved by using multiplication.

Example

Solve $\frac{m}{7} = 12$.

$\frac{m}{7} \times 7 = 12 \times 7$ *Multiply each side by 7 to undo dividing by 7.*

$\frac{7m}{7} = 84$ *m × 7 = 7m and 12 × 7 = 84*

$m = 84$

Check: $\frac{m}{7} = 12$

$\frac{84}{7} \stackrel{?}{=} 12$ *Replace m with 84.*

$12 = 12$ *It checks.*

The solution is 84.

Exercises

Complete.

1. In $5x = 65$, ___?___ is being performed. **multiplication**

2. To undo the multiplication by 5, ___?___ each side by 5. **divide**

3. In $\frac{k}{6} = {}^-13$, ___?___ is being performed. **division**

4. To undo the division by 6, ___?___ each side by 6. **multiply**

5. State a general rule for solving equations such as $5x = 65$ and $\frac{k}{6} = {}^-13$. **Undo the indicated operation.**

State the number to multiply each side by to solve each equation. Then solve the equation and check your solution.

6. $\frac{n}{5} = 7$ **5; 35**

7. $\frac{x}{7} = 12$ **7; 84**

8. $\frac{a}{6} = {}^-14$ **6; ${}^-84$**

9. $\frac{k}{8} = 11$ **8; 88**

10. $-\frac{i}{10} = 32$ **${}^-10$; ${}^-320$**

11. $\frac{g}{12} = 11$ **12; 132**

12. ${}^-4 = \frac{m}{6}$ **6; ${}^-24$**

13. $8 = \frac{k}{6}$ **6; 48**

 Solve each equation. Check your solution.

14. $\frac{k}{7} = 9$ **63**

15. $\frac{a}{9} = 13$ **117**

16. $8 = \frac{b}{6}$ **48**

17. $\frac{n}{6} = 7$ **42**

18. $52 = \frac{k}{10}$ **520**

19. $85 = \frac{f}{12}$ **1,020**

20. $27 = \frac{g}{14}$ **378**

21. $\frac{s}{15} = 47$ **705**

22. $-\frac{z}{7} = 12$ **${}^-84$**

23. ${}^-6 = -\frac{b}{5}$ **30**

24. ${}^-8 = \frac{c}{18}$ **${}^-144$**

25. $-\frac{y}{6} = 13$ **${}^-78$**

26. $\frac{r}{3} = 27$ **81**

27. $\frac{y}{5} = 12$ **60**

28. $\frac{n}{7} = 1.4$ **9.8**

29. $\frac{t}{1.9} = 1.8$ **3.42**

Solve. Write an equation.

30. Three friends share the cost of a pizza equally. Each person pays $3.15. What is the cost of the pizza? $\frac{c}{3} = 3.15$; **$9.45**

This feature provides general topics about the uses of a computer.

Computer

```
10 LET A = 5+7*3
```
This **assignment statement** uses the order of operations that you have learned. The value assigned to A would be 26.

```
10 LET A = (5+7)*3
```
The value assigned to A in this expression would be 36.

Find the value assigned to A in each assignment statement.

1. LET A = 8+4-3 **9**

2. LET A = ${}^-4*6+5$ **${}^-19$**

3. LET A = 144-12*4+1 **97**

4. LET A = (144-12)/4+1 **34**

5. LET A = (-36-4)/(-6+1) **8**

6. LET A = -42/3-14+6 **${}^-22$**

15-7 *Two-Step Equations*

Objective: To solve equations that involve two operations.

David Stover is a real estate agent. He talks with possible home buyers and shows them homes that appear to meet their needs. David also obtains listings for his real estate firm from home owners who want to sell their homes. After graduating from high school, David received 30 hours of classroom instruction on real estate law. Then he had to pass a written test to receive his real estate license.

In 1987, David sold three more than twice as many homes as he sold in 1977. David sold 15 homes in 1987. How many homes did he sell in 1977?

Let *n* represent the number of homes David sold in 1977. Then translate the problem into an equation.

number sold in 1987	is	three	more than	twice as	many sold in 1977
15	=	3	+	2 ×	n

There are two operations, multiplication and additon, involved in the equation $15 = 3 + 2n$. To solve equations with two operations, undo the given operations one step at a time. Use the order of operations in the reverse order to undo the operations. **You may wish to review the order of operations.**

Example

Solve $15 = 3 + 2n$.

$15 - 3 = 3 - 3 + 2n$ *Subtract 3 from each side to undo adding 3.*

$\quad 12 = 2n$

$\quad \dfrac{12}{2} = \dfrac{2n}{2}$ *Divide each side by 2 to undo multiplying by 2.*

$\quad 6 = n$

Check: $15 = 3 + 2n$

$\qquad 15 \overset{?}{=} 3 + 2 \times 6$ *Replace n with 6.*

$\qquad 15 \overset{?}{=} 3 + 12$ *Use the order of operations to simplify the right—hand side.*

$\qquad 15 = 15$ *It checks.*

The solution to $15 = 3 + 2n$ is 6. David sold 6 homes in 1977.

344 *Solving Open Sentences*

Basic Skills Appendix, Pages 435, 436, 456
Basic: 1–51 odd; Average: 1–49 odd, 50–51; Enriched: 2–48 even, 50–51

Exercises

**State the steps you would use to solve each equation.
Then solve the equation and check your solution.**

1. $3x + 5 = 23$ $-, \div; 6$

2. $2r - 8 = 24$ $+, \div; 16$

3. $48 = 4k + 8$ $-, \div; 10$

4. $\frac{m}{2} - 9 = 11$ $+, \times; 40$

5. $\frac{n}{8} + 5 = 7$ $-, \times; 16$

6. $2 = \frac{t}{4} - 6$ $+, \times; 32$

7. $2 + 3a = 8$ $-, \div; 2$

8. $8x + 5 = {}^-45$ $-, \div; {}^-6\frac{1}{4}$

9. $\frac{c}{5} + 1 = {}^-1$ $-, \times; {}^-10$

Solve each equation. Check your solution.

10. $2x + 5 = 13$ 4

11. $3r - 6 = 18$ 8

12. $3a - 9 = {}^-15$ ${}^-2$

13. $2y + 5 = 7$ 1

14. $4a - 6 = 2$ 2

15. $5n + 7 = {}^-8$ ${}^-3$

16. $20 = 4m + 8$ 3

17. $34 = 5n - 6$ 8

18. ${}^-2b + 6 = 14$ ${}^-4$

19. $5 = \frac{m}{6} + 3$ 12

20. $2 = \frac{d}{9} - 5$ 63

21. ${}^-\frac{k}{5} - 4 = 6$ ${}^-50$

22. $6 + 2n = 16$ 5

23. $49 = 9 + 4b$ 10

24. ${}^-5c - 8 = {}^-28$ 4

25. $4 + \frac{b}{2} = 8$ 8

26. $16 = \frac{x}{5} - 4$ 100

27. ${}^-\frac{b}{5} + 3 = 2$ 5

28. ${}^-3m - 2 = {}^-11$ 3

29. $8p - 16 = 0$ 2

30. ${}^-3.5x - 2 = {}^-9$ 2

31. ${}^-1.2y + 3.7 = {}^-3.5$ 6

32. $0.5 = 4x - 1.5$ 0.5

33. ${}^-3.2 = 6t - 4.2$ $\frac{1}{6}$

34. $2x - 1\frac{1}{2} = 2\frac{1}{4}$ $1\frac{7}{8}$

35. $3b + 1\frac{5}{6} = 2\frac{3}{4}$ $\frac{11}{36}$

36. ${}^-2x + 1\frac{1}{2} = 4\frac{1}{3}$ ${}^-1\frac{5}{12}$

37. $\frac{n}{3} + \frac{2}{3} = 1\frac{1}{2}$ $2\frac{1}{2}$

38. $\frac{n}{5} - \frac{2}{3} = \frac{3}{4}$ $7\frac{1}{12}$

39. ${}^-\frac{k}{8} - \frac{1}{2} = \frac{2}{3}$ ${}^-9\frac{1}{3}$

**Translate each sentence into an equation. Then solve
the equation and check your solution.**

40. The sum of $3m$ and 15 is 45.
$3m + 15 = 45$, 10

41. The sum of $5t$ and 11 is 56.
$5t + 11 = 56$; 9

42. Four more than $8m$ is ${}^-92$.
$8m + 4 = {}^-92$; ${}^-12$

43. Ten increased by $6r$ is ${}^-14$.
$10 + 6r = {}^-14$; ${}^-4$

44. Five decreased by $6n$ is ${}^-4$. $5 - 6n = {}^-4$; $1\frac{1}{2}$

45. Eight more than $\frac{t}{2}$ is 11. $\frac{t}{2} + 8 = 11$; 6

46. Sixteen decreased by $4z$ is 22. $16 - 4z = 22$; ${}^-1\frac{1}{2}$

47. Twenty increased by $\frac{y}{3}$ is 25. $20 + \frac{y}{3} = 25$; 15

48. Twelve less than $\frac{k}{4}$ is ${}^-12\frac{1}{2}$. $\frac{k}{4} - 12 = {}^-12\frac{1}{2}$; ${}^-2$

49. Six more than twice n is 22.
$2n + 6 = 22$; 8

Solve. Write an equation.

50. Ray has 2 more than 4 times the
number of coins in his collection
as Amy has in her collection. Ray
has 162 coins. How many coins does
Amy have? (Hint: Let c represent the
number of coins that Amy has.)
$162 = 4c + 2$; 40 coins

51. Mr. Grover's age is 4 less than 3
times his daughter's age. Mr. Grover
is 38 years old. How old is his
daughter? (Hint: Let d represent his
daughter's age.) $38 = 3d - 4$; 14 years old

15-8 Solving Inequalities

Objective: To solve inequalities.

Bart weighs 136 pounds and Shawna weighs 121 pounds. If they both sit the same distance from each end of a seesaw, they will not be able to balance the seesaw.

Just as a seesaw may not be balanced, a mathematical sentence may not be balanced. In such cases, the symbols, $<$ and $>$, are used.

$<$ **means** **is less than** $>$ **means** **is greater than**

Sentences such as $7 > 5$, $8 - 6 < 3$, and $n + 3 > 7$ are called **inequalities.**

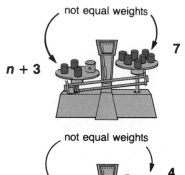

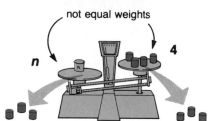

The scale at the left is not balanced. Suppose n represents the amount in the beaker. Then the scale represents the inequality $n + 3 > 7$. *Since n + 3 is heavier, it names the greater number.*

To find the amount n or find solutions to the inequality, remove 3 weights from each side. This will isolate the unknown amount in the beaker, n. *You must not change the way the scale is unbalanced.*

The new inequality is $n > 4$. Thus, $n > 4$ indicates that the solution set for $n + 3 > 7$ is the set of all numbers greater than 4.

Inequalities such as $n + 3 > 7$ can be solved by using the same methods as those used for solving equations.

Example

Solve $n + 3 > 7$.

$n + 3 - 3 > 7 - 3$ *Subtract 3 from each side.*

$n + 0 > 4$

$n > 4$

Check: $n + 3 > 7$ *Replace n with a number that is*
$5 + 3 \overset{?}{>} 7$ *greater than 4. You may use 5.*
$8 > 7$ *It checks.*

The solution is $n > 4$ (all numbers greater than 4).

The solution set can be graphed on a number line.

Put an open circle on 4. Since all numbers greater than 4 lie to the right of 4 on a number line, draw the arrow pointing to the right.

The Key Skills provides practice of skills needed in the exercises.

Draw a graph for each set of numbers.

all numbers less than 2	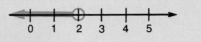

For answers to Key Skills, see Teacher Guide.

1. all numbers less than 4

2. all numbers greater than 8

3. all numbers greater than ⁻3

4. all numbers less than ⁻5

5. all numbers less than $2\frac{1}{2}$

6. all numbers greater than ⁻4.5

Basic Skills Appendix, Pages 435, 457, 458
Basic: 2–36 even; Average: 2–34 even, 36–37; Enriched: 1–35 odd, 36–37

Exercises

Write an inequality for each scale.

1.
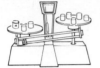
$x + 2 > 5$

2.

$k + 3 < 8$

3.
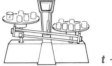
$t + 4 < 7$

State how to solve each inequality. Then solve the inequality and check your solutions.

4. $13 < y - 7 + 7$;
$20 < y$ or $y > 20$

5. $\frac{t}{8} < 9$
$\times 8; t < 72$

6. $m + 2 > 7$
$-2; m > 5$

7. $9 > a + 4 - 4$;
$5 > a$ or $a < 5$

8. $\frac{k}{6} < 12$
$\times 6; k < 72$

9. $7 > \frac{c}{8} \times 8$;
$56 > c$ or $c < 56$

10. $8z > 96$
$\div 8; z > 12$

11. $y - 6 < 24$
$+ 6; y < 30$

Solve each inequality and check your solutions. Then graph each solution set on a number line. For answers to exercises 12–23, see Teacher Guide.

12. $2 + b < 9$ $b < 7$

13. $x - 8 > 15$ $x > 23$

14. $3b < 24$ $b < 8$

15. $\frac{w}{3} < 5$ $w < 15$

16. $3b > 78$ $b > 26$

17. $r + 7 < 15$ $r < 8$

18. $m - 9 > 64$ $m > 73$

19. $\frac{t}{18} < 24$ $t < 432$

20. $2b > ⁻14$ $b > ⁻7$

21. $18m < 324$ $m < 18$

22. $6y > ⁻120$ $y > ⁻20$

23. $⁻40 + m < 53$ $m < 93$

Solve each inequality. Check your solutions.

24. $\frac{h}{6} < ⁻11$ $h < ⁻66$

25. $f - 15 < ⁻25$
$f < ⁻10$

26. $\frac{x}{3} > ⁻9$ $x > ⁻27$

27. $14z > ⁻28$ $z > ⁻2$

28. $m + 1.5 < 2.3$
$m < 0.8$

29. $n - 1.9 > 4.7$
$n > 6.6$

30. $5r < 1.75$
$r < 0.35$

31. $\frac{t}{1.5} > 3.2$ $t > 4.8$

32. $z - 6.8 > 10.5$
$z > 17.3$

33. $3m > ⁻6.3$ $m > ⁻2.1$

34. $8t > 1\frac{1}{3}$ $t > \frac{1}{6}$

35. $p + \frac{3}{4} > 1\frac{1}{2}$ $p > \frac{3}{4}$

Answer the following.

36. Norma has less than 22 pages left to read in her book. Let p represent the number of pages she has left to read. Write an inequality for this situation. $p < 22$

37. Together, a stove and freezer weigh more than 270 kg. The stove weighs 120 kg. Let f represent the weight of the freezer. Write an inequality for this situation. $120 + f > 270$

15-9 Problem Solving: Using Equations and Inequalities

Objective: To solve verbal problems using equations and inequalities.

Study the inequalities that correspond to the following word statements.

The number x is greater than or equal to 5.　　$x \geq 5$

The number y is less than or equal to 7.　　$y \leq 7$

Inequalities involving *greater than or equal to* and *less than or equal to* can be used to solve problems.

Yolanda Ramos wishes to spend no more than $300 on a new camera and camera accessories. She has chosen a camera that costs $210. How much can she spend on camera accessories?

 Read

You need to find how much money Yolanda can spend on camera accessories. You know that she wishes to spend no more than $300. You know that the camera costs $210.

 Decide

Choose a variable to represent the amount of money that Yolanda can spend on camera accessories. Translate the problem into an inequality.

Let *x* represent the amount of money Yolanda can spend on camera accessories. Write an inequality.

| amount to spend on accessories | cost of camera | *Since Yolanda wishes to spend no more than $300 in all, use $\leq$ in the inequality.* |

$$x \quad + \quad 210 \leq 300$$

 Solve

Solve the inequality.

$$x + 210 \leq 300$$
$$x + 210 - 210 \leq 300 - 210 \quad \textit{Subtract 210 from each side.}$$
$$x \leq 90$$

Yolanda can spend no more than $90 on camera accessories.

 Examine

Suppose Yolanda spends $89 on camera accessories. Since $89 + $210 = $299 and $299 is not more than $300, the answer is reasonable.

Exercises

1. Judy wishes to save at least $30 to buy a gift. She has saved $7.50. How much more must she save? **$22.50 or more**

2. John and his father spent more than $120.00 while shopping. John spent $42.30. How much did his father spend? **$77.70 or more**

3. Hoshiko ran a half-mile in 142 seconds. This was 14 seconds faster than her mother. What was her mother's time? **156 seconds**

4. Missy plans to spend no more than $75 for jeans and shirts. She bought 2 shirts for $14.20 each. How much can she spend on jeans? **$46.60 or less**

5. Kevin plans to spend at most $10.00 on art supplies. He buys 2 brushes for $4.15 each. How much will he have left for other supplies? **$1.70 or less**

6. Jim plans to spend at most $40 for records and tapes. He bought 3 records for $7.95 each. How much can he spend on tapes? **$16.15 or less**

7. Two times a number increased by 10 is 34. What is the number? **12**

8. Eight times a number decreased by 5 is ⁻21. What is the number? **-2**

9. Four times a number increased by 10 is at least 30. What is the number? **5 or more**

10. Six times a number decreased by 3 is no more than 15. What is the number? **3 or less**

11. After diving 30 meters, a submarine leveled off at a depth of 305 meters. What was the depth before the last dive? **275 meters**

12. At 9:00 A.M. the temperature is 14°F. It rises 3°F each hour. What is the temperature at 2:00 P.M.? **29°F**

13. The temperature in Newport rose 2°F every hour for 6 hours. The low temperature was ⁻5°F. What was the temperature after 6 hours? **7°F**

14. The Three Rivers Gazette pays 8¢ per paper to the carrier. How many papers must the carrier deliver to earn $6 per day? **75 papers**

15. Mr. Cross bought 40 shares of stock at $24 per share. Then the value of each share fell $2.50. What was the total value of the 40 shares after the price fell? **$860**

16. Carol weighs 125 pounds. She loses 2 pounds each week for 6 weeks, then gains 1 pound each week for 3 weeks. How much does she weigh after 9 weeks? **116 pounds**

17. Alonso sells his stereo for $160. This is $8 more than half what he paid for it. How much did he pay for his stereo? **$304**

This feature presents general topics of mathematics.

 Math Break

Find the sum for each addition shown at the right. Study the pattern of the sums.

$$\frac{1}{2} = \frac{1}{1 \times 2}$$

$$\frac{2}{3} = \frac{1}{1 \times 2} + \frac{1}{2 \times 3}$$

$$\frac{3}{4} =$$

Use the pattern to predict each sum.

1. $\frac{1}{1 \times 2} + \frac{1}{2 \times 3} + \cdots + \frac{1}{19 \times 20}$ $\frac{19}{20}$

2. $\frac{1}{1 \times 2} + \frac{1}{2 \times 3} + \cdots + \frac{1}{n(n + 1)}$ $\frac{n}{n + 1}$

CHAPTER 15 REVIEW

Vocabulary/Concepts

Choose a word from the list at the right that best completes each sentence.

1. ___?___ an open sentence means to find a replacement for the variable that makes the sentence true. **solving**

2. Place holders in mathematical sentences are called ___?___. **variables**

3. A sentence with symbols such as $<$ or $>$ is a(n) ___?___. **inequality**

4. Operations that undo one another are called ___?___. **inverse operations**

5. A(n) ___?___ is a mathematical sentence with one or more variables and is neither true nor false. **open sentence**

6. A sentence with an equal sign ($=$) is a(n) ___?___. **equation**

equation
inequality
inverse operations
open sentence
order of operations
replacement set
simplifying
solving
variables

Exercises

Determine whether each sentence is true, false, or open.   Page 331

7. Thanksgiving Day is in November. **true**

8. He likes pizza. **open**

9. Oregon is a southern state. **false**

10. $6z + 2 = 14$ **open**

11. $4 + 6 < 11 - 1$ **false**

12. $3 \times 5 \not< 12$ **true**

Translate each sentence into an equation. Then solve the equation and check your solution.   Pages 332–333

13. The sum of 8 and m is 40.
$8 + m = 40; 32$

14. y decreased by 12 is 35.
$y - 12 = 35; 47$

15. The product of $^-3$ and h is 21.
$^-3h = 21; ^-7$

16. t divided by 4 is 3. $\frac{t}{4} = 3; 12$

Solve each equation. Check your solution.   Pages 334–339, 342–345

17. $a + 6 = 9$ **3**

18. $8 + k = 24$ **16**

19. $82 = 63 + f$ **19**

20. $r + 6 = 3$ **$^-3$**

21. $d + 1.5 = 2.7$ **1.2**

22. $5.5 = b + {}^-2.2$ **7.7**

23. $\frac{3}{4} + c = 1\frac{1}{2}$ **$\frac{3}{4}$**

24. $y + -\frac{2}{3} = -1\frac{1}{6}$ **$-\frac{1}{2}$**

25. $y - 4 = 8$ **12**

26. $8 = b - 9$ **17**

27. $m - 24 = 6$ **30**

28. $^-5 = d - {}^-3$ **$^-8$**

29. $k - \frac{7}{8} = \frac{3}{4}$ **$1\frac{5}{8}$**

30. $\frac{4}{5} = x - \frac{1}{5}$ **1**

31. $t - 4.2 = {}^-3.5$ **0.7**

32. $0.65 = a - 0.35$ **1**

33. $8x = 24$ **3**

34. $42 = 14g$ **3**

35. $^-5t = 95$ **$^-19$**

36. $^-6q = {}^-36$ **6**

37. $18 = {}^-4x$ **$^-4\frac{1}{2}$**

38. $2z = \frac{8}{9}$ **$\frac{4}{9}$**

39. $\frac{2}{3}y = \frac{5}{12}$ **$\frac{5}{8}$**

40. $1\frac{1}{2}r = 1\frac{1}{4}$ **$\frac{5}{6}$**

41. $\frac{h}{7} = 4$ **28** **42.** $9 = \frac{w}{9}$ **81** **43.** $\frac{d}{7} = {}^-9$ **‑63** **44.** $-\frac{h}{4} = {}^-8$ **32**

45. $5 = -\frac{c}{6}$ **‑30** **46.** $\frac{x}{1.8} = {}^-0.5$ **‑0.9** **47.** $-\frac{z}{2.1} = {}^-0.4$ **0.84** **48.** $\frac{y}{9} = 4\frac{1}{2}$ **$40\frac{1}{2}$**

49. $2y + 4 = 18$ **7** **50.** $6a - 3 = 33$ **6** **51.** $3z - 4 = {}^-28$ **‑8**

52. $\frac{a}{7} + 2 = 3$ **7** **53.** $30 = 3p - 6$ **12** **54.** $\frac{p}{4} - 6 = {}^-1$ **20**

55. $6x + 3.8 = 6.8$ **0.5** **56.** $3 = \frac{c}{1.5} + 4$ **‑1.5** **57.** $\frac{m}{2.5} - 5 = {}^-1$ **10**

Translate each sentence into an equation. Then solve the equation and check your solution.   Pages 344–345

58. The sum of 3 and $4m$ is 19.
 $3 + 4m = 19;\ 4$
59. Five more than $3z$ is 35.
 $3z + 5 = 35;\ 10$
60. Twelve decreased by $2n$ is 18.
 $12 - 2n = 18;\ {}^-3$
61. Two more than $\frac{x}{5}$ is 6. $\frac{x}{5} + 2 = 6;\ 20$
62. Thirteen increased by $4t$ is 9.
 $13 + 4t = 9;\ {}^-1$
63. $\frac{k}{2}$ decreased by 6 is 1. $\frac{k}{2} - 6 = 1;\ 14$
64. Fifteen less than $\frac{y}{3}$ is $^-30$. $\frac{y}{3} - 15 = {}^-30;\ {}^-45$
65. Ten less than twice n is 28.
 $2n - 10 = 28;\ 19$

Solve each inequality and check your solutions. Then graph each solution set on a number line.   Pages 346–347 For answers to exercises 66–67, see Teacher Guide.

66. $3t > 15$ $t > 5$ **67.** $y - 4 > 7$ $y > 11$ **68.** $2b < 8$ $b < 4$ **69.** $\frac{j}{4} < 6$ $j < 24$

70. $16 < 4n$
 $4 < n$ or $n > 4$
71. $^-11 < z - 5$
 $^-6 < z$ or $z > {}^-6$
72. $\frac{h}{6} > 1.5$ $h > 9$
73. $7t < {}^-3.5$
 $t < {}^-0.5$

74. $a + 6 > 2\frac{1}{2}$
 $a > {}^-3\frac{1}{2}$
75. $b - 16 < 43$
 $b < 59$
76. $x - 4.3 > {}^-2.8$
 $x > 1.5$
77. $^-8 < \frac{m}{3}$
 $^-24 < m$ or $m > {}^-24$

Solve. Use an equation or an inequality.

78. There were 28 girls on Nadia's drill team last year. This year, there are 34 girls on her team. How many new girls are on Nadia's drill team?
 $28 + x = 34;\ 6$ **girls**

79. Lou has four times as many coins as Jerry has. Lou has 348 coins. How many coins does Jerry have?
 $348 = 4x;\ 87$ **coins**

80. Denise is five years younger than her brother. Denise is 14 years old. How old is her brother?
 $14 = x - 5;\ 19$ **years old**

81. Pedro boiled away 20 mL of his salt solution. He now has 52 mL of solution. How much did he have before boiling? $x - 20 = 52;\ 72$ **mL**

82. Casie weighs $2\frac{1}{2}$ times what her sister weighs. Casie weighs 125 pounds. How much does her sister weigh? $125 = 2\frac{1}{2}x;\ 50$ **pounds**

83. Mrs. Hudson's age is 8 more than twice her son's age. Mrs. Hudson is 40 years old. How old is her son?
 $40 = 2x + 8;\ 16$ **years old**

84. Tina studied more than $5\frac{1}{2}$ hours for her math and history tests. She studied math for $3\frac{1}{2}$ hours. How long did she study history?
 $3\frac{1}{2} + x > 5\frac{1}{2};$ **more than 2 hours**

85. Jason wishes to spend at most $30 for new stamps for his collection. He has selected a new stamp that costs $3.75. How much can he spend on other stamps?
 $x + 3.75 \leq 30;\ \$26.25$ **or less**

CHAPTER 15 TEST

Determine whether each sentence is true, false, or open.

1. Texas is the smallest state. **false**

2. They like to play tennis. **open**

3. $5 + n = 22$ **open**

4. $16 \times 2 > 3^2$ **true**

Translate each sentence into an equation. Then solve the equation and check your solution.

5. The product of k and $^-4$ is 28.
$k \times {^-4} = 28; \; ^-7$

6. t decreased by 14 is 35.
$t - 14 = 35; \; 49$

7. Six increased by $3b$ is 18.
$6 + 3b = 18; \; 4$

8. a divided by 5 is $^-6$.
$\frac{a}{5} = {^-6}; \; ^-30$

Solve each equation. Check your solution.

9. $m + 3 = 9$ **6**

10. $13 = t + 8$ **5**

11. $46 = 19 + b$ **27**

12. $r + 8 = 5$ **$^-3$**

13. $m + 12 = {^-19}$ **$^-31$**

14. $n + \frac{3}{4} = 2\frac{1}{3}$ **$1\frac{7}{12}$**

15. $x - 5 = 7$ **12**

16. $y - 14 = 29$ **43**

17. $31 = y - 17$ **48**

18. $x - 8 = {^-7}$ **1**

19. $n - {^-5} = {^-13}$ **$^-18$**

20. $j - 1.3 = 2.8$ **4.1**

21. $13m = 156$ **12**

22. $27 = 3b$ **9**

23. $729 = 81t$ **9**

24. $3y = {^-12}$ **$^-4$**

25. $^-3b = {^-48}$ **16**

26. $6m = 4\frac{1}{2}$ **$\frac{3}{4}$**

27. $\frac{x}{6} = 9$ **54**

28. $\frac{y}{8} = 63$ **504**

29. $3x + 5 = 23$ **6**

30. $5y - 8 = 32$ **8**

31. $\frac{m}{6} + 5 = 12$ **42**

32. $\frac{c}{2} - 8 = {^-12}$ **$^-8$**

33. $\frac{t}{3} + 5 = {^-21}$ **$^-78$**

34. $2x + 2\frac{1}{2} = 4\frac{1}{2}$ **1**

Solve each inequality and check your solutions. Then graph each solution set on a number line. For answers to exercises 35–42, see Teacher Guide.

35. $5m > 15$ **$m > 3$**

36. $w + 5 > 13$ **$w > 8$**

37. $x - 3 > 6$ **$x > 9$**

38. $t + 5 < 16$ **$t < 11$**

39. $\frac{x}{5} > 13$ **$x > 65$**

40. $2x > 8$ **$x > 4$**

41. $4x < 16$ **$x < 4$**

42. $\frac{t}{7} < 13$ **$t < 91$**

Solve. Write an equation or inequality.

43. Mrs. Lugo had 7 scarves. She received some new scarves as gifts. Mrs. Lugo now has a total of 11 scarves. How many scarves did she receive as gifts?
$7 + x = 11; \; 4$ **scarves**

44. Mr. Dalton is saving to renew his auto club membership for four years. How much money must he save if the yearly membership is \$13.50? $\frac{x}{4} = \$13.50; \; \$54$

45. Melissa has 3 times as many stamps as Steve has. Melissa has 255 stamps. How many stamps does Steve have?
$3x = 225; \; 75$ **stamps**

46. Five times a number is decreased by 12. The result is 28. What is the number? $5x - 12 = 28; \; 8$

47. Eduardo weighs 165 pounds. He loses 2 pounds each week for 8 weeks, then gains 1 pound each week for 3 weeks. How much does he weigh after 11 weeks?
$165 - (2 \times 8) + (1 \times 3) = w; \; 152$ **pounds**

48. Yokiko wishes to spend at most \$80 for jeans and shirts. She bought 2 pairs of jeans for \$22.50 each. How much can she spend on shirts?
$(2 \times 22.50) + x \leq 80; \; \$35$ **or less**

CUMULATIVE REVIEW

Use △MNP at the right to complete the following. Pages 214–215

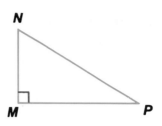

1. One angle of △MNP is ∠NMP. Name the other two angles.
   ∠PNM and ∠MPN
2. One side of △MNP is $\overline{MP}$. Name the other two sides. $\overline{MN}$ and $\overline{NP}$

3. What type of triangle is △MNP? right

Trace each line segment. Construct the perpendicular bisector of the line segment you traced. Pages 242–243 See students' work.

4. 5. 6.

7. 8. 9.

Classify each lettered quadrilateral as a trapezoid, parallelogram, rectangle, rhombus, or square. Use the word that best describes what each quadrilateral appears to be. Pages 256–257

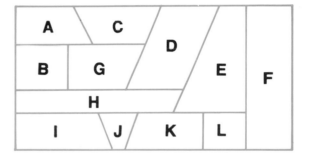

10. G trapezoid
11. A trapezoid
12. L square
13. F rectangle
14. D parallelogram
15. C trapezoid

Write an addition sentence for each diagram. Pages 310–312

16.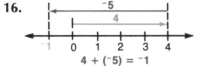
$4 + (^-5) = ^-1$

17.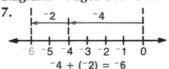
$^-4 + (^-2) = ^-6$

18.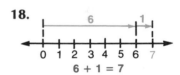
$6 + 1 = 7$

Determine whether each sentence is true, false, or open. Page 331

19. $4 \times 3 = 3 \times 4$ true

20. $^-161 > 1 - 61$ false

21. $3a + 2 = 7$ open

22. She studies music. open

Translate each sentence into an equation. Then solve the equation and check your solution. Pages 332–333

23. The product of y and 3 is 27. $3y = 27; 9$

24. Twelve less than a is 11.
   $a - 12 = 11; 23$

25. Thirty divided by x is 5.
   $\frac{30}{x} = 5; 6$

26. Fifteen increased by k is 24.
   $15 + k = 24; 9$

Solve. Write an equation or inequality.

27. A group of people are planning a trip to Europe. They need a minimum of 30 people, and only 21 have signed up. How many more people have to sign up?
   $x + 21 \geq 30$; at least 9 more people

Teacher Resource Book, Pages 340, 341

Using Formulas

16-1 Exponents

Objective: To write powers as a product of the same factor and vice versa, and to evaluate powers.

A seismograph measures ground motion caused by an earthquake. The Richter Magnitude Scale is then used to express the strength of the earthquake. Each number of the Richter Scale represents an earthquake 10 times as strong as an earthquake of the next lower magnitude.

Magnitude	Number of Times More Intense than a Magnitude of 2
2	
3	10
4	$10 \times 10 = 10^2$ or 100
5	$10 \times 10 \times 10 = 10^3$ or 1,000

The expression 10^3 is read *ten to the third power* or *ten cubed*. The number 10 is the **base.** The number 3 is the **exponent.** The exponent is the number of times the base is used as a factor.

exponent $\longrightarrow$ $10^3 = 10 \times 10 \times 10 = 1,000$ Numbers such as 10^3 are called **powers.**

$\uparrow$

base   3 factors

exponent $\longrightarrow$ $a^5 = a \cdot a \cdot a \cdot a \cdot a$ This is read *a to the fifth power.*

$\uparrow$ *Multiplication can also be indicated by a raised dot.*

base

Explain that using x for multiplication can sometimes be confused with the variable x.
Basic: 1–15 odd; Average: 2–14 even, 15; Enriched: 1–13 odd, 15

Exercises

Write each product using exponents.

1. 3×3 3^2

2. $4 \times 4 \times 4 \times 4 \times 4$ 4^5

3. $p \cdot p \cdot p$ p^3

4. $r \cdot r \cdot r \cdot r$ r^4

5. $m \cdot m \cdot m$ m^3

6. $5 \cdot y \cdot y$ $5y^2$

7. $2 \cdot 2 \cdot w \cdot w$ 2^2w^2

8. $y \cdot y \cdot z \cdot z \cdot z$ y^2z^3

Find the number named by each of the following.

9. 4^2 16

10. 5^2 25

11. 2^3 8

12. 2^4 16

13. 1^2 1

14. 1^3 1

Solve.

15. In 1981, Dodson Inc. used two suites of Stockdale Towers. Each year after 1981, they used twice as many suites as the year before. Express the number of suites used in 1986 as a power. 2^6 or 64

Teacher Resource Book, Page 351

16-2 Evaluating Expressions

Objective: To use the order of operations to evaluate expressions.

Karen and Gregg are performing an experiment in their chemistry class. All of the steps must be performed in a particular order for the experiment to be successful.

The operations in a mathematical expression are performed in a particular order. The order for performing the operations is summarized as follows.

1. Do all operations within grouping symbols first; start with the parentheses.

2. Find the value of each power.

3. Do all multiplications and divisions in order from left to right.

4. Do all additions and subtractions in order from left to right.

Examples

A. $(4 + 8) \div (5 - 2) = 12 \div 3$ *Do all operations in parentheses first.*
$\qquad\qquad\qquad\quad = 4$ *The value of $(4 + 8) \div (5 - 2)$ is 4.*

B. $[(3 + 4^2) - 3] \times 7 = [(3 + 16) - 3] \times 7$ *Find 4^2.*
$\qquad\qquad\qquad\quad = [19 - 3] \times 7$ *Add 3 and 16.*
$\qquad\qquad\qquad\quad = 16 \times 7$ *Subtract 3 from 19.*
$\qquad\qquad\qquad\quad = 112$ *Multiply. The value of $[(3 + 4^2) - 3] \times 7$ is 112.*

Once the operations within parentheses and brackets are completed, the symbols ( ) and [ ] do not have to be used.

The value of an expression containing variables varies depending on the numbers that replace the variables. **Emphasize that finding the value of an expression is different from solving an equation.**

Examples

C. **Find the value of $2(x + y^3)$ if $x = 5$ and $y = 2$.**

$2(x + y^3) \longrightarrow \quad 2(5 + 2^3)$ *Replace x with 5 and y with 2.*
$\qquad\qquad\qquad = 2(5 + 8)$ *Find 2^3.*
$\qquad\qquad\qquad = 2(13)$ *Add 5 and 8.*
$\qquad\qquad\qquad = 26$ *Multiply. The value of $2(5 + 2^3)$ is 26.*

D. **Find the value of k^3 if $k = {}^-2$.**

$k^3 \longrightarrow \quad ({}^-2)^3$ *Replace k with ${}^-2$.*
$\qquad\quad = ({}^-2)({}^-2)({}^-2)$
$\qquad\quad = {}^-8$ *Multiply. The value of $({}^-2)^3$ is ${}^-8$.*

The Key Skills provides practice of skills needed in the exercises.

Key Skills

Find each product.

$$^-3 \times {}^-3 \times {}^-3 = {}^-27 \qquad {}^-2 \times {}^-2 \times {}^-2 \times {}^-2 = 16$$

1. $^-4 \times {}^-4$ **16**

2. $^-5 \times {}^-5 \times {}^-5$ **-125**

3. $^-7 \times {}^-7$ **49**

4. $^-2 \times {}^-2 \times {}^-2$ **-8**

5. $^-3 \times {}^-3$ **9**

6. $^-1 \times {}^-1 \times {}^-1 \times {}^-1 \times {}^-1$ **-1**

7. $^-3 \times {}^-3 \times {}^-3 \times {}^-3$ **81**

Basic: 1–41 odd; Average: 1–39 odd, 41–44; Enriched: 2–40 even, 41–44

Exercises

Find the value of each expression.

1. $15 - 6 + 1$ **10**

2. $5 + 6 \times 3 - 3$ **20**

3. $36 \div 3^2$ **4**

4. $20 \div 4 + 8 \times 9$ **77**

5. $3 \times (34 - 19)$ **45**

6. $(5 \times 6^2) \div 15$ **12**

7. $4^3 \div (8 + 2^3)$ **4**

8. $5 \times (4 + 6) - 3$ **47**

Find the value of each expression if $a = 5$.

9. $8a$ **40**

10. $^-5(7 - a)$ **-10**

11. $2a - 30$ **-20**

12. $3a^2$ **75**

13. $16.4 - 2a$ **6.4**

14. $\frac{a}{2}$ $2\frac{1}{2}$

15. $\frac{3a}{5}$ **3**

16. $\frac{a^2 + 3}{7}$ **4**

Find the value of each expression if $x = 3$, $y = 6$, and $z = 4$.

17. $2x - 3y$ **-12**

18. $3(x + z)$ **21**

19. $y^2 + y$ **42**

20. $\frac{1}{2}z(x + 2)$ **10**

21. $2x - (y - z)$ **4**

22. $x^2 - (y^2 + 1)$ **-28**

23. $2xy - 3yz$ **-36**

24. $2y^2 - 4z$ **56**

25. $z + 12x + 7$ **47**

26. $\frac{2}{3}(z - {}^-5)$ **6**

27. $\frac{xy}{3}$ **6**

28. $\frac{x + y - z}{15}$ $\frac{1}{3}$

Find the value of each expression if $k = 3$, $n = 2$, and $t = {}^-2$.

29. n^3 **8**

30. $k^3 + 1^2$ **28**

31. t^3 **-8**

32. $t - 4^2$ **-18**

33. $4k^2$ **36**

34. $(4k)^2$ **144**

35. $(n + k)^3$ **125**

36. $n^2 + t^2$ **8**

37. $t^3 - k^3$ **-35**

38. $k^3 - t^3$ **35**

39. k^4 **81**

40. $\left(\frac{t}{n}\right)^6$ **1**

Solve.

41. Hope's patio is in the shape of a square. The length of each side, s, is 4 yards. Use $A = s^2$ to find the area of Hope's patio. **16 yd²**

42. Mr. Kim's garden is in the shape of a rectangle. The length, ℓ, is 38 feet. The width, w, is 16 feet. Use $P = 2(\ell + w)$ to find the perimeter of Mr. Kim's garden. **108 feet**

43. Write a formula to find the perimeter of your bedroom. Then find the perimeter. **Answers may vary.**

44. Carmen mails a recipe to four friends. Each of the four friends mails the recipe to four more friends and so on. Express the total number of recipes in the fifth mailing as a power. **4^5 or 1,024**

16-3 Formulas

Objective: To solve problems using formulas.

Mr. Antonio builds and repairs boats. The caulking on the seams on the bottom of a boat needs to be repaired. How much work is needed to lift the 200-pound boat 5 feet?

The relationship between work, force, and distance can be written as a **formula.** A formula shows how certain quantities are related. **The first letter of a key word is often used to represent a quantity.**

$$\text{work} = \text{force} \times \text{distance}$$

$$W = F \times d$$

work (W) = units of work needed

force (F) = units of weight to be moved

distance (d) = number of units the object is moved

Note that force and distance are not numbers, but measurements.

Example

A. **Find the amount of work needed to lift the 200-pound boat 5 feet.**

$W = F \times d$ *Write the formula.*

$W = 200 \times 5$ *The force is 200 pounds. The distance is 5 feet.*

$W = 1,000$

The amount of work needed is 1,000 foot-pounds.

There are two formulas for the circumference of a circle. The formula that relates the circumference (C) to the diameter (d) is $C = \pi d.$ The formula that relates the circumference (C) to the radius (r) is $C = 2\pi r.$

Example

B. **Find the circumference of a circle whose radius is 98 cm long. Use $\frac{22}{7}$ for π.**

$C = 2\pi r$ *Write the correct formula.*

$C \approx 2 \times \frac{22}{7} \times 98$ *Replace π with $\frac{22}{7}$ and r with 98.*

$C \approx 616$

The circumference is about 616 cm.

Remind students that $\frac{22}{7}$ and 3.14 are approximations for π.

Exercises

Use the formula $W = F \times d$ to find the amount of work needed.

1. $F = 15$ lb; $d = 3$ ft
   45 ft-lb

2. $F = 87$ lb; $d = 9$ ft
   783 ft-lb

3. $F = 162$ lb; $d = 4.5$ ft
   729 ft-lb

4. $F = 286$ lb; $d = 27.5$ ft
   7,865 ft-lb

5. $F = 86.8$ lb; $d = 35$ ft
   3,038 ft-lb

6. $F = 147$ lb; $d = 12.5$ ft
   1,837.5 ft-lb

**Find the circumference of each circle with the given diameter or radius.
Use $C = \pi d$ or $C = 2\pi r$. Use $\frac{22}{7}$ for π.**

7. $d = 21$ ft **66 ft**
   8. $r = 35$ in. **220 in.**
   9. $r = 28$ km **176 km**
   10. $d = 2\frac{1}{2}$ m $7\frac{6}{7}$ **m**

**Find the circumference of each circle with the given diameter or radius.
Use $C = \pi d$ or $C = 2\pi r$. Use 3.14 for π.**

11. $d = 10$ yd **31.4 yd**
   12. $r = 10$ m **62.8 m**
   13. $d = 6.5$ ft **20.41 ft**
   14. $r = 5\frac{1}{2}$ m **34.54 m**

**A formula for determining a normal blood pressure reading (B.P.) is B.P. $= 110 + \frac{A}{2}$.
The A stands for age in years. Find the normal blood pressure reading for each age.**
This formula is used to calculate the systolic pressure.

15. 18 **119**
   16. 30 **125**
   17. 58 **139**
   18. 36 **128**
   19. 24 **122**

20. 70 **145**
   21. 62 **141**
   22. 9 **114.5**
   23. 13 **116.5**
   24. 33 **126.5**

**The charts below compare customary units of measure with metric units of measure.
Use the charts to complete the following.**

Mass
1 oz $\approx$ 28 g
1 lb $\approx$ 0.45 kg

Length
1 in. $=$ 2.54 cm
1 ft $\approx$ 30.48 cm
1 yd $\approx$ 0.9 m
1 mi $\approx$ 1.6 km

Capacity
1 tsp $\approx$ 5 mL
1 Tbsp $\approx$ 15 mL
1 fl oz $\approx$ 30 mL
1 c $\approx$ 0.24 L
1 pt $\approx$ 0.47 L
1 qt $\approx$ 0.95 L
1 gal $\approx$ 3.8 L

25. 22 pt $\approx$ ▨ L **10.34**

26. 85 oz $\approx$ ▨ g **2,380**

27. 4 in. $\approx$ ▨ cm **10.16**
   28. 12 ft $\approx$ ▨ cm **365.76**

29. 3 mi $\approx$ ▨ km **4.8**
   30. 2 tsp $\approx$ ▨ mL **10**

31. 8 Tbsp $\approx$ ▨ mL **120**
   32. 130 lb $\approx$ ▨ kg **58.5**

33. 20 qt $\approx$ ▨ L **19**
   34. 1.5 fl oz $\approx$ ▨ mL **45**
   35. 2.4 yd $\approx$ ▨ m **2.16**

36. 1.8 pt $\approx$ ▨ L **0.846**
   37. $\frac{5}{9}$ yd $\approx$ ▨ m $\frac{1}{2}$
   38. $\frac{2}{3}$ Tbsp $\approx$ ▨ mL **10**

39. $2\frac{1}{2}$ gal $\approx$ ▨ L $9\frac{1}{2}$
   40. $2\frac{1}{5}$ tsp $\approx$ ▨ mL **11**
   41. 28 g $\approx$ ▨ oz **1**

42. 5 mL $\approx$ ▨ Tbsp $\frac{1}{3}$
   43. 20 mL $\approx$ ▨ tsp **4**
   44. 36 L $\approx$ ▨ c **150**

Write a formula for each sentence.

45. A baseball player's batting average (B) is the ratio of the player's number of hits (h) to the player's number of times at bat (a). $B = \dfrac{h}{a}$

46. The volume (V) of a cube is the length of the edge (e) cubed.
$V = e^3$

47. The temperature in Fahrenheit (F) degrees is $\frac{9}{5}$ times the temperature in Celsius (C) degrees, plus 32.

$F = \frac{9}{5} C + 32$

48. A person's maximum desirable pulse rate (p) is 176 minus 80 percent of the person's age (A).

$p = 176 - 0.8A$

Use a formula to solve the following.

49. Use the formula on page 359 for normal blood pressure to find your normal blood pressure reading.
Answers may vary.

50. Mrs. Valentine drove her car 347.9 miles on 9.8 gallons of gasoline. What is the gas mileage?
35.5 mpg

This feature provides general topics about the uses of a computer.

Computer

Computer systems are classified as microcomputers, minicomputers, or mainframe computers based on their physical size and their internal memory.

Each character of information is stored in a computer as a **byte.**

A microcomputer might be able to store 64 kilobytes, or 64k, of information. (1 kilobyte = 1,024 bytes) Only one person at a time can use a microcomputer.

A minicomputer, like the one shown at the left, might be able to store 512k of information. Three people can use a minicomputer at the same time.

A mainframe computer, like the one shown at the right, might be able to store 16 megabytes of information.

(1 megabyte = 1,048,576 bytes)

Twenty-four people can use a mainframe computer at the same time.

Answer the following.

1. How many bytes of information might be stored in a microcomputer?
65,536 bytes

2. How many bytes of information might be stored in a minicomputer?
524,288 bytes

3. How many bytes of information might be stored in a mainframe computer? **16,777,216 bytes**

16-4 More Formulas

Objective: To practice using formulas.

Light travels at the rate of 186,000 miles per second. How long does it take light from the sun to reach the earth 93,000,000 miles away?

The relationship between rate (r), time (t), and distance (d), can be written as a formula. $rt = d$

If any two of the values, rate, time, and distance, are known, the third value can be found by using the methods for solving equations.

Emphasize that the time is the amount of time it takes to travel a certain distance, and not a time such as 1:15.

Example

$rt = d$ *Write the formula.*

$186{,}000 \times t = 93{,}000{,}000$ *The rate of light is 186,000 miles per second. The distance it travels is 93,000,000 miles.*

$\dfrac{186{,}000 \times t}{186{,}000} = \dfrac{93{,}000{,}000}{186{,}000}$ *To solve the equation for t, divide each side by 186,000.*

$t = 500$ seconds or 8.3 minutes

93000000 ÷ 186000 = *500*

500 ÷ 60 = *8.3333333*

seconds   number of seconds in one minute
↓   ↓
$500 \div 60 \approx 8.3$ ⟵ minutes

It takes about 8.3 minutes for light from the sun to reach the earth.

Basic Skills Appendix, Pages 425, 428, 438, 443
Basic: 1–45 odd; Average: 1–45 odd; Enriched: 2–46 even

Exercises

Use the formula $rt = d$ to solve for the missing value.

1. $r = 30$ mph, $t = 2$ hours
   $d = 60$ mi
2. $r = 47$ mph, $t = 5$ hours
   $d = 235$ mi
3. $d = 241.8$ miles, $t = 6$ hours
   $r = 40.3$ mph
4. $d = 40$ miles, $t = 2.5$ hours
   $r = 16$ mph
5. $d = 408$ miles, $r = 51$ mph
   $t = 8$ hours
6. $d = 55.5$ miles, $r = 37$ mph
   $t = 1.5$ hours
7. $r = 4$ mph, $t = 0.75$ hours
   $d = 3$ mi
8. $d = 3$ miles, $r = 12$ mph
   $t = 0.25$ hours
9. $d = 85$ miles, $t = 30$ minutes
   $r = 170$ mph
10. $r = 25$ mph, $t = 15$ minutes
    $d = 6.25$ mi
11. $d = 118.75$ miles, $r = 95$ mph
    $t = 1.25$ hours
12. $d = 12$ miles, $t = 45$ minutes
    $r = 16$ mph

Use the gas mileage formula, $s = \dfrac{m}{g}$, to solve for the missing value.

13. $m = 200$, $g = 8$
    $s = 25$
14. $m = 201.5$, $g = 6.5$
    $s = 31$
15. $m = 291.6$, $g = 9$
    $s = 32.4$
16. $s = 20$, $g = 5$
    $m = 100$
17. $s = 38$, $g = 8.5$
    $m = 323$
18. $s = 26.4$, $g = 5$
    $m = 132$
19. $s = 17$, $m = 187$
    $g = 11$
20. $s = 22$, $m = 167.2$
    $g = 7.6$
21. $s = 29.5$, $m = 271.4$
    $g = 9.2$
22. $s = 33.6$, $g = 5.5$
    $m = 184.8$
23. $m = 316.8$, $g = 7.2$
    $s = 44$
24. $s = 41.2$, $m = 473.8$
    $g = 11.5$

Use the formulas for circumference, $C = \pi d$ and $C = 2\pi r$, to solve for the indicated variable. Use 3.14 for π.

25. $d = 4$ m, $C \approx$ ▒ m
    12.56
26. $d = 10$ mi, $C \approx$ ▒ mi
    31.4
27. $d = 6.5$ ft, $C \approx$ ▒ ft
    20.41

28. $r = 3$ yd, $C \approx$ ▒ yd
    18.84
29. $r = 8.5$ cm, $C \approx$ ▒ cm
    53.38
30. $r = 10$ km, $C \approx$ ▒ km
    62.8

31. $C = 31.4$ m, $d \approx$ ▒ m
    10
32. $C = 15.7$ in., $d \approx$ ▒ in.
    5
33. $C = 21.98$ mi, $d \approx$ ▒ mi
    7

34. $C = 62.8$ ft, $r \approx$ ▒ ft
    10
35. $C = 37.68$ cm, $r \approx$ ▒ cm
    6
36. $C = 18.84$ m, $r \approx$ ▒ m
    3

37. $C = 7.85$ cm, $d \approx$ ▒ cm
    2.5
38. $C = 21.98$ yd, $r \approx$ ▒ yd
    3.5
39. $r = 7.5$ km, $C \approx$ ▒ km
    47.1

Use a formula to solve the following.

40. Kenji runs an average of 10 miles per hour. How far does he run in $1\frac{1}{2}$ hours? **15 miles**

41. A circular field is fenced with 172.7 meters of fencing. What is the diameter of the field? **≈ 55 meters**

42. Sherry drives 222.6 miles on 8.4 gallons of gasoline. What is the gas mileage? **26.5 mpg**

43. A driver covers 327.25 kilometers in 3 hours, 30 minutes. What is the average speed? **93.5 km/h**

44. The circumference of a circle is 18.84 kilometers. What is the radius of the circle? **≈3 km**

45. The radius of the moon is approximately 1,080 miles. What is its circumference? **≈ 6,782.4 miles**

46. A blackpoll warbler, a bird no bigger than a sparrow, migrates 2,500 miles nonstop from North America to South America every year. The trip takes about 90 hours. How fast does the bird fly? **about 27.8 mph**

This feature presents useful ways of solving mathematical problems on a calculator.

Calculator

Light travels through air almost a million times faster than sound. That is why you see lightning before you hear thunder. The speed of sound varies according to the substance through which it is traveling. Use your calculator to find the missing values in the chart below.

Speed of Sound				
Substance	d(in meters)	r(in m/sec)	t(in sec)	
air (0°C)	1. ___?___	331	8	2,648
aluminum	2. ___?___	5,000	0.01	50
brick	109.5	3. ___?___	0.03	3,650
seawater	8,267.4	1,531	4. ___?___	5.4
steel	5. ___?___	5,200	0.02	104
wood	1,644	4,110	6. ___?___	0.4
glass	317.8	7. ___?___	0.07	4,540

PRACTICE

Estimate. Answers may vary. Typical answers are given.

1. $\begin{array}{r} 85 \\ \times\ 33 \\ \hline 2,700 \end{array}$ **2.** $\begin{array}{r} 329 \\ \times\ 59 \\ \hline 18,000 \end{array}$ **3.** $\begin{array}{r} 458 \\ +\ 313 \\ \hline 800 \end{array}$ **4.** $\begin{array}{r} 881 \\ -\ 465 \\ \hline 400 \end{array}$ **5.** $38\overline{)499}^{\ \ 12}$

Add, subtract, multiply, or divide.

6. $\begin{array}{r} 1.25 \\ \times\ 0.09 \\ \hline 0.1125 \end{array}$ **7.** $\begin{array}{r} 2.56 \\ \times\ 0.4 \\ \hline 1.024 \end{array}$ **8.** $\begin{array}{r} 486 \\ -\ 197 \\ \hline 289 \end{array}$ **9.** $3.2\overline{)0.9664}^{\ 0.302}$ **10.** $\begin{array}{r} 238 \\ \times\ 96 \\ \hline 22,848 \end{array}$

11. $2.48 + 69.5$ **71.98**

12. $83.14 - 0.695$ **82.445**

13. 23×0.44 **10.12**

14. 6.32×1.5 **9.48**

15. $21.07 - 4.9$ **16.17**

16. 9×0.035 **0.315**

17. $1\frac{3}{4} + 6\frac{1}{2}$ $8\frac{1}{4}$

18. $3\frac{3}{10} - 1\frac{1}{5}$ $2\frac{1}{10}$

19. $4\frac{3}{5} \times 1\frac{1}{3}$ $6\frac{2}{15}$

20. $\frac{7}{8} \div \frac{1}{4}$ $3\frac{1}{2}$

21. $\frac{3}{8} \times \frac{9}{10}$ $\frac{27}{80}$

22. $8 \times \frac{7}{8}$ **7**

23. $6 - 4\frac{3}{13}$ $1\frac{10}{13}$

24. $7\frac{1}{2} \div 1\frac{1}{2}$ **5**

25. $6\frac{7}{12} + 3\frac{7}{12}$ $10\frac{1}{6}$

26. 14×10 **140**

27. $38.3 \div 100$ **0.383**

28. $1.85 \div 10$ **0.185**

29. 0.008×100 **0.8**

30. $1,000 \times 4.8$ **4,800**

31. $28 \div 1,000$ **0.028**

Complete.

32. $1.5 \text{ m} = $ ▨ cm **150**

33. $10 \text{ km} = $ ▨ m **10,000**

34. ▨ $\text{kg} = 4,200 \text{ g}$ **4.2**

35. $6,450 \text{ mL} = $ ▨ L **6.45**

36. $61 \text{ mm} = $ ▨ cm **6.1**

37. $4.01 \text{ L} = $ ▨ mL **4,010**

38. $6\frac{1}{2} \text{ ft} = $ ▨ in. **78**

39. $192 \text{ oz} = $ ▨ lb **12**

40. ▨ $\text{qt} = 6.5 \text{ gal}$ **26**

Add or subtract.

41. $\begin{array}{r} 6 \text{ h } 43 \text{ min } 15 \text{ s} \\ +\ 3 \text{ h } 37 \text{ min } 19 \text{ s} \\ \hline 10 \text{ h } 20 \text{ min } 34 \text{ s} \end{array}$

42. $\begin{array}{r} 11 \text{ h } 58 \text{ min } 58 \text{ s} \\ +\ 3 \text{ h } \ 3 \text{ min } \ 3 \text{ s} \\ \hline 15 \text{ h } 2 \text{ min } 1 \text{ s} \end{array}$

43. $\begin{array}{r} 8 \text{ h } 30 \text{ min } 30 \text{ s} \\ -\ 7 \text{ h } 30 \text{ min } 35 \text{ s} \\ \hline 59 \text{ min } 55 \text{ s} \end{array}$

44. $\begin{array}{r} 10 \text{ h } 25 \text{ min } 16 \text{ s} \\ -\ 4 \text{ h } 16 \text{ min } 14 \text{ s} \\ \hline 6 \text{ h } 9 \text{ min } 2 \text{ s} \end{array}$

45. $\begin{array}{r} 9 \text{ h } 35 \text{ min } 22 \text{ s} \\ +\ 2 \text{ h } 26 \text{ min } 39 \text{ s} \\ \hline 12 \text{ h } 2 \text{ min } 1 \text{ s} \end{array}$

46. $\begin{array}{r} 12 \text{ h } 59 \text{ min } 13 \text{ s} \\ -\ 5 \text{ h } 33 \text{ min } 20 \text{ s} \\ \hline 7 \text{ h } 25 \text{ min } 53 \text{ s} \end{array}$

Change each percent to a decimal. Change each decimal to a percent.

47. 43% **0.43**

48. 1.08 **108%**

49. 0.9 **90%**

50. 0.75% **0.0075**

51. 1.51 **151%**

52. $6\frac{1}{2}\%$ **0.065**

53. 0.05 **5%**

54. 1 **100%**

55. 0.083 **8.3%**

56. 3.2% **0.032**

Solve.

57. 36% of 50 **18**

58. 95% of 300 **285**

59. 150% of 14 **21**

60. 62% of 40 **24.8**

61. 1.3% of 50 **0.65**

62. 0.8% of 200 **1.6**

63. 200% of 35 **70**

64. 100% of 0.16 **0.16**

65. 22% of 0.051 **0.01122**

Solve each problem using the proportion $\frac{P}{B} = \frac{r}{100}$.

66. 12 is ___?___ % of 20 **60**   **67.** ___?___ is 62% of 50 **31**   **68.** 45% of ___?___ is 27 **60**

69. 5 is ___?___ % of 6 **83$\frac{1}{3}$**   **70.** 150% of ___?___ is 30 **20**   **71.** 0.5% of 6,100 is ___?___ **30.5**

Find the perimeter of each figure.

72. A square which is $1\frac{3}{4}$
inches on a side. **7 in.**

73. A right triangle with legs of
5 feet and 12 feet. **30 ft**

Find the area of the shaded parts of each figure.

74.

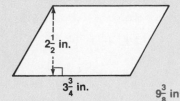

$2\frac{1}{2}$ in.

$3\frac{3}{4}$ in.

9$\frac{3}{8}$ in²

75.

10 in.

39.25 in²

76.

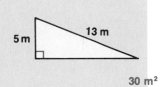

5 m   13 m

30 m²

Find the volume of each solid.

77.

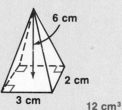

6 cm

2 cm

3 cm

12 cm³

78.

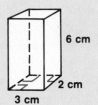

6 cm

2 cm

3 cm

36 cm³

Find the mode, median, and mean for the following set of data.

79. 60, 50, 40, 50, 50, 50, 70, 60, 50, 40, 75, 65, 85 **50; 50; 57$\frac{4}{13}$ ≈ 57.3**

The chart at the right lists temperatures at
noon on the first day of each month.

Date	Temperature
Jan.	⁻10°C
Feb.	⁻5°C
March	8°C
April	14°C
May	19°C
June	23°C
July	37°C
Aug.	24°C
Sept.	16°C
Oct.	5°C
Nov.	⁻4°C
Dec.	⁻7°C

Find the change from Jan. 1 to Feb. 1.
⁻5 − ⁻10 = ⁻5 + 10
    = 5   *The change is 5°C.*

80. Find the change from June 1 to July 1. **14°C**

81. Find the change from February 1 to March 1. **13°C**

82. How much colder was it on December 1
than on March 1? **15°C**

83. Find the difference between the highest and
lowest temperature reading. **47°C**

84. Find the average temperature on the first of the month. **10°C**

16-5 Squares and Square Roots

Objective: To compute squares and square roots, and to use a square root table.

The formula for finding the area (A) of a square is $A = s^2$, where s is the length of one side.

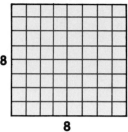

8

8

s^2 represents a number with two equal factors. s^2 is called a **perfect square.** Sixty-four is a perfect square because $64 = 8^2$ or 8×8.

A **square root** of 64 is 8. The symbol used is $\sqrt{}$. $\sqrt{64} = 8$ is read *the positive square root of 64 is 8.*

Most practical applications with square roots involve the positive square root. It is also true that $^-8 \times {}^-8 = 64$. A negative sign is used in front of the square root symbol to indicate the negative square root of a number.

$^-\sqrt{64} = {}^-8$ is read *the negative square root of 64 is negative 8.* In general, if no sign is given, the positive square root is meant.

The following whole numbers are perfect squares.

1, 4, 9, 16, 25, 36, 49, 64, . . .

The square root of a whole number that is a perfect square is a whole number.

$\sqrt{1} = 1$, $\sqrt{4} = 2$, $\sqrt{9} = 3$, $\sqrt{16} = 4$, . . . **Point out the relationship these numbers have to square figures.**

The square root of a whole number that is not a perfect square is not a whole number. Since 18 is not a perfect square, $\sqrt{18}$ is not a whole number.

Example

A. Between what two whole numbers is $\sqrt{18}$?

It is true that $16 < 18 < 25$.   *18 lies between the perfect squares 16 and 25.*

Therefore, $\sqrt{16} < \sqrt{18} < \sqrt{25}$.   **Point out that 16 is the greatest perfect square less than 18 and that 25 is the least perfect square greater than 18.**

Then $4 < \sqrt{18} < 5$.

So, $\sqrt{18}$ is between 4 and 5.

This can be checked on a calculator by using the square root key, $\boxed{\sqrt{x}}$.

18 $\boxed{\sqrt{x}}$ `4.2426406` ≈ 4.243   *The answer is correct.*

The table of square roots on page 419 can also be used to approximate square roots.

Example

B. Use the table to approximate $\sqrt{12}$.

For $n = 12$, $\sqrt{n} \approx 3.464$.

n	n^2	$\sqrt{n}$
12	144	3.464

Exercises

Find the square of each number.

1. 2 **4** 2. 5 **25** 3. 10 **100** 4. 7 **49** 5. 20 **400**

6. 13 **169** 7. 50 **2,500** 8. 15 **225** 9. 11 **121** 10. 12 **144**

Find each square root.

11. $\sqrt{4}$ **2** 12. $\sqrt{25}$ **5** 13. $\sqrt{36}$ **6** 14. $\sqrt{16}$ **4** 15. $\sqrt{900}$ **30**

16. $^-\sqrt{9}$ **-3** 17. $^-\sqrt{81}$ **-9** 18. $^-\sqrt{64}$ **-8** 19. $^-\sqrt{1}$ **-1** 20. $^-\sqrt{400}$ **-20**

Find each square root. Use the table on page 419 for exercises 21–40.

21. $\sqrt{169}$ **13** 22. $\sqrt{196}$ **14** 23. $^-\sqrt{289}$ **-17** 24. $^-\sqrt{5,329}$ **-73** 25. $\sqrt{441}$ **21**

26. $^-\sqrt{961}$ **-31** 27. $\sqrt{7,569}$ **87** 28. $\sqrt{256}$ **16** 29. $^-\sqrt{676}$ **-26** 30. $^-\sqrt{324}$ **-18**

Find the square of each number.

31. 19 **361** 32. 35 **1,225** 33. 29 **841** 34. 37 **1,369** 35. 59 **3,481**

36. $^-$63 **3,969** 37. $^-$83 **6,889** 38. $^-$91 **8,281** 39. $^-$42 **1,764** 40. $^-$38 **1,444**

Determine between which two whole numbers each square root lies.

41. $\sqrt{8}$ **2, 3** 42. $\sqrt{20}$ **4, 5** 43. $\sqrt{44}$ **6, 7** 44. $\sqrt{27}$ **5, 6** 45. $\sqrt{69}$ **8, 9**

46. $\sqrt{32}$ **5, 6** 47. $\sqrt{112}$ **10, 11** 48. $\sqrt{86}$ **9, 10** 49. $\sqrt{73}$ **8, 9** 50. $\sqrt{140}$ **11, 12**

Use the table on page 419 or a calculator to approximate each square root.

51. $\sqrt{10}$ **3.162** 52. $^-\sqrt{15}$ **-3.873** 53. $^-\sqrt{24}$ **-4.899** 54. $\sqrt{37}$ **6.083** 55. $\sqrt{42}$ **6.481**

56. $^-\sqrt{56}$ **-7.483** 57. $^-\sqrt{68}$ **-8.246** 58. $\sqrt{72}$ **8.485** 59. $^-\sqrt{46}$ **-6.782** 60. $\sqrt{99}$ **9.950**

61. $^-\sqrt{21}$ **-4.583** 62. $\sqrt{51}$ **7.141** 63. $\sqrt{30}$ **5.477** 64. $^-\sqrt{92}$ **-9.592** 65. $\sqrt{85}$ **9.220**

Solve.

66. The radius of a circle is 7 cm. Use the formula $A = \pi r^2$ to find the area of the circle. Use $\frac{22}{7}$ for π. **154 cm²**

67. The area of a square is 25 yd². What is the length of each side of the square? **5 yd**

▲ This feature presents general topics of mathematics.

Math Break

1. One-fifth of a number plus 5 times that number is equal to 7 times the number less 18. What is the number? **10**

2. Two people play chess. The winner of each game receives 75 chips from the loser. When they finish, one player has won 3 games, and the other has received 525 chips. How many games did they play? **10 games**

16-6 *Using the Pythagorean Theorem*

Objective: To use the Pythagorean Theorem to find unknown lengths.

Marge Broderick is a landscaper for a small landscaping company. She plans lawns and decides on the location of shrubs, trees, and flowers. She also mows, trims, and fertilizes lawns. After graduating from high school, Marge took classes on landscape design and landscape installation at a two-year college. She received on-the-job training from her employer.

Marge is planning a flower bed for a customer. The flower bed will be in the shape of a right triangle. The hypotenuse will be 13 feet long. One leg will be 5 feet long. What will the length of the third side of the flower bed be?

This question can be answered by using the Pythagorean Theorem. If c is the measure of the hypotenuse and a and b are the measures of the legs, then $a^2 + b^2 = c^2$.

Review with students the terms legs and hypotenuse.

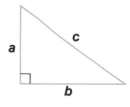

Example

Find the length of the third side of the flower bed.

$a^2 + b^2 = c^2$ *Write the Pythagorean Theorem.*

$5^2 + b^2 = 13^2$ *Replace a with 5 and c with 13.*

$25 + b^2 = 169$ *Find 5^2 and 13^2.*

$25 - 25 + b^2 = 169 - 25$ *Subtract 25 from each side.*

$b^2 = 144$

$\sqrt{b^2} = \sqrt{144}$ *Find the square root of each side.*

$b = 12$ $(b)^2 = b^2, 12^2 = 144$

144 ⏺√x⏺ *12*

Check: $a^2 + b^2 = c^2$

$5^2 + 12^2 \stackrel{?}{=} 13^2$ *Replace a with 5, b with 12, and c with 13.*

$25 + 144 \stackrel{?}{=} 169$

$169 = 169$ *It checks.*

The third side of the flower bed will be 12 feet long.

Exercises

Use the Pythagorean Theorem to find the third side of each triangle if *a* and *b* are legs and *c* is the hypotenuse.

1. $a = 3, b = 4$
$c = 5$

2. $c = 10, a = 6$
$b = 8$

3. $b = 24, c = 26$
$a = 10$

4. $a = 7, b = 24$
$c = 15$

5. $c = 34, b = 30$
$a = 16$

6. $a = 9, b = 40$
$c = 41$

7. $b = 21, c = 29$
$a = 20$

8. $a = 12, b = 35$
$c = 37$

9. $b = 60, c = 61$
$a = 11$

10. $a = 8, b = 15$
$c = 17$

11. $a = 5, b = 6$
$c \approx 7.810$

12. $a = 8, c = 12$
$b \approx 8.944$

13. $a = 6, b = 7$
$c \approx 9.220$

14. $b = 12, c = 15$
$a = 9$

15. $a = 5, c = 10$
$b \approx 8.660$

16. $b = 16, c = 18$
$a \approx 8.246$

Solve.

17.

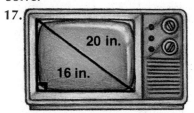

How high is the television screen? **12 in.**

18.

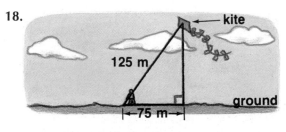

How far above the ground is the kite? **100 m**

19.

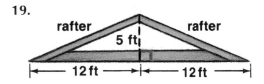

How long is each rafter? **13 ft**

20.

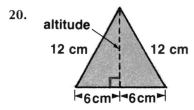

What is the altitude of the equilateral triangle? **≈ 10.392 cm**

21. The anchor of a boat is 60 ft right below its stern. The distance from the anchor to the bow of the boat is 61 ft. What is the length of the deck from bow to stern?
11 ft

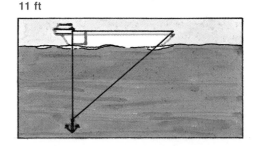

22. One end of a rope is attached to the top of a sailboat mast. It is drawn tightly and attached 9 feet from the base of the mast. The rope is 41 feet long. How high is the mast?
40 ft

23. The diagonal brace on a gate is 2 meters long. The height of the gate is 1 meter. How wide is the gate?
≈ 1.732 m

24. Lucas walked 62 yards due north, then 30 yards due east. How far is Lucas from his starting point?
≈ 68.877 yards

16-7 Problem Solving: Using Formulas

Objective: To use formulas to solve problems.

Rick Romero has $100 to open a savings account. The bank will pay an annual *interest rate* of 6% on the amount of money, or **principal,** he has in the account. The interest will be computed quarterly (four times a year). The interest earned each quarter will be added to the account. At the end of each quarter, interest is paid on the balance, which includes the previous interest. Interest computed on interest is called **compound interest.**

If Rick does not deposit or withdraw any money, what will be Rick's savings total at the end of one year?

To calculate the interest, the formula $I = prt$, is used. The I stands for the interest, p for the principal, r for the interest rate, and t for the time in years.

Read

You need to find the total amount of money in Rick's account at the end of one year. You know the principal, the interest rate, and how often the interest is compounded.

Decide

Use the formula $I = prt$ to find the interest earned each quarter. Add the interest earned each quarter to the previous principal. This will be the new principal.

Solve

You can approximate Rick's savings total for one year by computing the *simple interest.*
Explain the difference between simple and compound interest.

   $I = prt$ *Write the formula.*

   $I = \$100 \times 0.06 \times 1$ *Replace p with 100, r with 0.06 (6%), and t with 1.*

   $I = \$6$

Rick's savings total at the end of one year will be approximately $100 + $6 or $106.

Find the compound interest.

Quarter	$prt = I$	New Principal
first	$100 × 0.06 × 0.25 = \$1.50$	$100 + \$1.50 = \$101.50$

↑

Each quarter is 0.25 of a year.

second	$101.50 × 0.06 × 0.25 ≈ \$1.52$	$101.50 + \$1.52 = \$103.02$
third	$103.02 × 0.06 × 0.25 ≈ \$1.55$	$103.02 + \$1.55 = \$104.57$
fourth	$104.57 × 0.06 × 0.25 ≈ \$1.57$	$104.57 + \$1.57 = \$106.14$

Rick's savings total for one year will be $106.14.

Since the approximate savings total is close to the
actual savings total, the answer is reasonable.

Notice the amount compounded quarterly is greater than the amount from simple interest.
Basic Skills Appendix, Pages 435, 439
Basic: 1–21 odd; Average: 1–23 odd; Enriched: 2–22 even

Exercises

Find the savings total for each account. Use the formula $I = prt$. (Semi-annually means twice a year.)

1. principal: $100
annual rate: 6%
compounded semi-annually
time: 1 year **$106.09**

2. principal: $250
annual rate: 5%
compounded semi-annually
time: 1 year **$262.66**

3. principal: $250
annual rate: $6\frac{1}{2}$%
compounded semi-annually
time: 1 year **$266.52**

4. principal: $1,000
annual rate: 6%
compounded quarterly
time: 1 year **$1,061.37**

5. principal: $500
annual rate: 5%
compounded quarterly
time: 1 year **$525.48**

6. principal: $500
annual rate: $5\frac{1}{2}$%
compounded quarterly
time: 1 year **$528.08**

The total cost of an item, including the sales tax, can be found by using the formula $T = C(1 + r)$. The T stands for the total cost, C stands for the cost of the item, and r stands for the sales tax rate. Use the formula to solve each problem.
You may also use $T = C + Cr$.

7. Cost: $10
tax rate: 6%
What is the total cost?
$10.60

8. Total cost: $84.40
tax rate: $5\frac{1}{2}$%
What is the cost?
$80

9. Cost: $20
Total cost: $21.20
What is the tax rate?
6%

The sale price of an item, not including the sales tax, can be found by using the formula $S = P(1 - r)$. The S stands for the sale price, P stands for the original price, and r stands for the rate of the discount. Use the formula to solve each problem. You may also use $S = P - Pr$.

10. Price: $63
Discount rate: 25%
What is the sale price? **$47.25**

11. Price: $42
Discount rate: 15%
What is the sale price? **$35.70**

12. Sale price: $114
Discount rate: $\frac{1}{4}$
What is the original price?
$152

13. Price: $95
Sale price: $52.25
What is the discount rate?
45%

370 *Using Formulas*

Solve.

14. Use the formula $I = prt$ to find the interest owed on a loan of $400 for 1 year at an annual rate of 15%.
$60

15. The top of Karen's kitchen table is in the shape of a square. The length of each side, s, is 92 cm. Use $A = s^2$ to find the area of the top of Karen's table.
8,464 cm²

16. Use the formula $W = F \times d$ to find the amount of work needed to lift a 450-pound barrel 20 feet.
9,000 ft-lbs

17. Use the formula $C = \pi d$ to find the circumference of a circle whose diameter is 15 cm. Use 3.14 for π.
≈ 47.1 cm

18. Use the formula $C = 2\pi r$ to find the radius of a circle whose circumference is 43.96 yd. Use 3.14 for π.
≈ 7 yd

19. Juan is 22 years old. Use the formula B.P. $= 110 + \frac{A}{2}$ to find his normal blood pressure reading.
121

20. Kristen drove her car 99.45 miles on 4.5 gallons of gasoline. Use the formula $S = \frac{m}{g}$ to find the gas mileage.
22.1 mpg

21. The Turi family traveled 312 miles in $6\frac{1}{2}$ hours. Use the formula $rt = d$ to find their average rate.
48 mph

22. The diameter of a circle is 14 m long. Use the formula $A = \pi r^2$ to find the area of the circle. Use $\frac{22}{7}$ for π.
≈ 154 m²

23. Yang walked 45 feet due west, then 15 feet due south. How far is Yang from his starting point?
≈ 47.434 ft

This feature promotes students' mental abilities in computation and reasonableness.

Mental Math

Study the following list of squares.

$15^2 = 225$ $25^2 = 625$ $35^2 = 1{,}225$

Notice that each square ends in 25 (5^2). Notice that the numbers preceding 25 in each square follow a pattern.

1 × 2 ⟵ *1 more than 1*   *2 × 3* ⟵ *1 more than 2*   *3 × 4* ⟵ *1 more than 3*

↓   ↓   ↓

$15^2 = 225$ $25^2 = 625$ $35^2 = 1{,}225$

This pattern can be used mentally to square a number that ends in five.

Find 65^2.

The square will end in 25.   __25

Multiply 6 by the next larger   42 25

whole number.   6 × 7 = 42

So $65^2 = 4{,}225$.

Use the above strategy to find each square.

1. 45^2 2,025   **2.** 55^2 3,025   **3.** 75^2 5,625   **4.** 85^2 7,225   **5.** 95^2 9,025   **6.** 105^2 11,025

CHAPTER 16 REVIEW

Vocabulary/Concepts

Write the letter of the word, phrase, or number that best matches each description.

1. numerals that contain exponents **h**
2. the square root of 81 **e**
3. interest computed on interest **b**
4. an equation that shows how certain quantities are related **c**
5. the base in 4^3 **d**
6. the exponent in 4^3 **j**
7. a number with two equal factors **g**

a. brackets
b. compound interest
c. formula
d. 4
e. 9
f. parentheses
g. perfect square
h. powers
i. simple interest
j. 3

Exercises

Find the number named by each of the following. Page 355

8. 5^2 25
9. 3^3 27
10. 2^5 32
11. 7^2 49
12. 2^3 8
13. 1^3 1
14. 1^7 1
15. 4^3 64
16. 10^2 100
17. 10^5 100,000

Find the value of each expression. Pages 356–357

18. $10 - 5 + 3$ 8
19. $4 + 6 \times 2 - 7$ 9
20. $24 \div 2^2$ 6
21. $(3^2 + 5^2) - 8$ 26
22. $(30 \times 2) - (15 \times 3)$ 15
23. $2 \times [5 \times (20 - 8)]$ 120
24. $[3 \times (2 + 6)] \div 12$ 2
25. $(5 + 3^2) \div 2$ 7

Find the value of each expression if $a = 3$, $b = 4$, and $c = {}^-2$. Pages 356–357

26. $a + 10$ 13
27. $6b$ 24
28. $3a - 2$ 7
29. $3b - 2a$ 6
30. $a + b^2$ 19
31. c^2 4
32. $5a^2 + c^2$ 49
33. $\dfrac{2b}{c}$ $^-4$
34. $\dfrac{ab}{c}$ $^-6$
35. $(b + c)^2$ 4
36. $a^3 - b^3$ $^-37$
37. $\left(\dfrac{b}{c}\right)^3$ $^-8$

Use the charts on page 359 to complete the following. Pages 358–360

38. 5 in. ≈ ▓ cm 12.7
39. 25 mi ≈ ▓ km 40
40. 40 oz ≈ ▓ g 1,120
41. 4 Tbsp ≈ ▓ mL 60
42. 6 c ≈ ▓ L 1.44
43. 15 mL ≈ ▓ fl oz 0.5

Use the formula $rt = d$ to solve for the missing value. Pages 361–362

44. $r = 25$ mph, $t = 3$ hours
    $d = 75$ miles
45. $d = 256$ miles, $t = 8$ hours
    $r = 32$ mph
46. $d = 110$ miles, $t = 2.5$ hours
    $r = 44$ mph
47. $d = 76.5$ miles, $r = 25.5$ mph
    $t = 3$ hours

372 *Using Formulas*

Use the gas mileage formula, $s = \frac{m}{g}$, to solve for the missing value. Pages 361–362

48. $m = 150$, $g = 15$
$s = 10$

49. $m = 128$, $s = 16$
$g = 8$

50. $s = 25$, $g = 6$
$m = 150$

51. $s = 40$, $g = 4.8$
$m = 192$

52. $m = 290.5$, $g = 8.3$
$s = 35$

53. $m = 256.5$, $s = 28.5$
$g = 9$

Use the formulas for circumference, $C = \pi d$ and $C = 2\pi r$, to solve for the indicated variable. Use 3.14 for π. Pages 361–362

54. $d = 5$ m, $C \approx$ ▨ m
15.7

55. $r = 10$ yd, $C \approx$ ▨ yd
62.8

56. $C = 25.12$ cm, $d \approx$ ▨ cm
8

57. $C = 94.2$ ft, $r \approx$ ▨ ft
15

58. $d = 2.5$ km, $C \approx$ ▨ km
7.85

59. $C = 47.1$ in., $r \approx$ ▨ in.
7.5

Find the square of each number. Pages 365–366

60. 6 36 **61.** 9 81 **62.** ⁻11 121 **63.** ⁻15 225 **64.** 25 625

Find each square root. Pages 365–366

65. $\sqrt{1}$ 1 **66.** $^-\sqrt{4}$ ⁻2 **67.** $^-\sqrt{49}$ ⁻7 **68.** $\sqrt{100}$ 10 **69.** $\sqrt{16}$ 4

70. $^-\sqrt{400}$ ⁻20 **71.** $\sqrt{144}$ 12 **72.** $^-\sqrt{121}$ ⁻11 **73.** $^-\sqrt{196}$ ⁻14 **74.** $\sqrt{900}$ 30

Use the table on page 419 to find the square of each number. Pages 365–366

75. 21 441 **76.** 28 784 **77.** 36 1,296 **78.** ⁻42 1,764 **79.** ⁻81 6,561

80. 78 6,084 **81.** ⁻26 676 **82.** ⁻63 3,969 **83.** 74 5,476 **84.** 88 7,744

Use the Pythagorean Theorem to find the third side of each triangle if a and b are legs and c is the hypotenuse. Round decimal answers to the nearest thousandth. Pages 367–368

85. $a = 5$, $b = 12$
$c = 13$

86. $a = 9$, $c = 15$
$b = 12$

87. $a = 15$, $c = 25$
$b = 20$

88. $a = 6$, $b = 8$
$c = 10$

89. $a = 4$, $b = 7$
$c \approx 8.062$

90. $b = 10$, $c = 12$
$a \approx 6.633$

91. $b = 20$, $c = 22$
$a \approx 9.165$

92. $a = 7$, $c = 11$
$b \approx 8.485$

Find the savings total for each account. Pages 369–371

93. principal: $150
annual rate: 5%
compounded semi-annually
time: 1 year $157.59

94. principal: $500
annual rate: $5\frac{1}{2}$%
compounded semi-annually
time: 1 year $527.88

95. principal: $1,200
annual rate: 6%
compounded quarterly
time: 1 year $1,273.63

Solve.

96. The radius of a circle is 14 cm. Use the formula $A = \pi r^2$ to find the area of the circle. Use $\frac{22}{7}$ for π.
≈ 616 cm^2

97. The area of a square is 42 m^2. Use the formula $A = s^2$ to approximate the length of each side of the square.
≈ 6.481 m

98. Carl traveled 325.5 miles in 7 hours. Use the formula $rt = d$ to find his average rate. 46.5 mph

99. The diagonal brace on a gate is 5 feet long. The height of the gate is 3 feet. How wide is the gate?
4 ft

100. Use the formula $I = prt$ to find the interest owed for a loan of $1,500 for 1 year at an annual rate of 12%. $180

101. The original price of a sweater is $24. It is on sale for $20.40. Use the formula $S = P(1 - r)$ to find the discount rate. 15%

CHAPTER 16 TEST

Find the number named by each of the following.

1. 1^6 1   **2.** 2^3 8   **3.** 3^2 9   **4.** 2^4 16   **5.** 4^3 64

Find the value of each expression.

6. $3 + 4 \times 2 - 6$ 5   **7.** $28 \div 2^2$ 7   **8.** $(4 + 4^2) \div 5$ 4   **9.** $6 + [4 \times (8 \div 2)]$ 22

Find the value of each expression if $x = 4$, $y = 6$, and $z = {}^-3$.

10. $4x + 7$ 23   **11.** $x - 2y$ ⁻8   **12.** xy 24   **13.** $x^2 + z^2$ 25

14. $(x + y)^2$ 100   **15.** $\frac{2y}{3}$ 4   **16.** $\left(\frac{y}{z}\right)^2$ 4   **17.** z^3 ⁻27

Use the formula $rt = d$ to solve for the missing value.

18. $r = 40$ mph, $t = 5$ hours
$d = 200$ miles

19. $r = 125$ mph, $t = 2.5$ hours
$d = 312.5$ miles

20. $d = 344$ miles, $t = 4$ hours
$r = 86$ mph

21. $d = 5.25$ miles, $r = 3.5$ mph
$t = 1.5$ hours

Use the gas mileage formula, $s = \frac{m}{g}$, to solve for the missing value.

22. $m = 135$, $g = 9$ s = 15   **23.** $m = 340$, $s = 42.5$ g = 8   **24.** $s = 32$, $g = 7.3$ m = 233.6

Use the formulas for circumference, $C = \pi d$ and $C = 2\pi r$, to solve for the indicated variable. Use 3.14 for π.

25. $d = 9$ ft, $C \approx$ ▓ ft
28.26

26. $C = 34.54$ cm, $d \approx$ ▓ cm
11

27. $C = 50.24$ m, $r \approx$ ▓ m
8

Find each square root.

28. $\sqrt{36}$ 6   **29.** $\sqrt{81}$ 9   **30.** $^-\sqrt{100}$ ⁻10   **31.** $^-\sqrt{144}$ ⁻12   **32.** $\sqrt{225}$ 15

Use the table on page 419 or a calculator to approximate each square root. Round answers to the nearest thousandth.

33. $\sqrt{7}$ 2.646   **34.** $\sqrt{12}$ 3.464   **35.** $\sqrt{33}$ 5.745   **36.** $^-\sqrt{60}$ ⁻7.746   **37.** $^-\sqrt{72}$ ⁻8.485

Use the Pythagorean Theorem to find the third side of each triangle.

38. $a = 6$, $b = 8$
$c = 10$

39. $a = 12$, $c = 20$
$b = 16$

40. $b = 20$, $c = 25$
$a = 15$

41. $a = 3$, $b = 9$
$c \approx 9.487$

Solve.

42. Use the formula $I = prt$ to find the interest owed for a loan of $800 for 1 year at an annual rate of 13%. **$104**

43. The area of a square is 625 ft². Use the formula $A = s^2$ to find the length of each side of the square. **25 ft**

44. Mary traveled 135 miles at an average rate of 45 mph. Use the formula $rt = d$ to find how many hours Mary traveled. **3 hours**

45. The hypotenuse of a right triangle is 26 cm. One leg is 10 cm. Find the length of the third side of the right triangle. **24 cm**

CUMULATIVE REVIEW

The lengths of the legs of right triangles are given below. Use the Pythagorean Theorem to find the length of each hypotenuse.   Pages 218–220

1. 12 in., 16 in. **20 in.**

2. 6 cm, 8 cm **10 cm**

3. 24 ft, 32 ft **40 ft**

4. 20 m, 48 m **52 m**

5. 39 mm, 80 mm **89 mm**

6. 15 yd, 20 yd **25 yd**

Use a proportion to solve the following.   Pages 258–259

7. A tall building casts a shadow 79 feet long. An 8-foot pole near the building casts a shadow 12 feet long. How tall is the building? **52.7 ft**

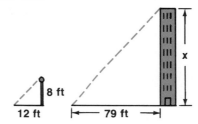

Find the circumference of each circle described below. Use $C = \pi d$ or $C = 2\pi r$. Use 3.14 for π. Round answers to the nearest tenth.   Pages 262–263

8. r, 11 cm
69.1 cm

9. d, 22 m
69.1 mm

10. d, 7.9 m
24.8 m

11. r, 13.2 in.
82.9 in.

12. d, 44 ft
138.2 ft

13. r, 81 yd
508.7 yd

14. r, 16.3 mm
102.4 mm

15. d, 15.17 cm
47.6 cm

Find the area of each rectangle or parallelogram described below.   Pages 266–267

16. length, 12 m; width, 8 m **96 m²**

17. base, 31.2 cm; height, 34 cm **1060.8 cm²**

18. base, 6 in.; height, 15 in. **90 in²**

19. length, 13.4 ft; width, 4 ft **53.6 ft²**

20. base, 66.3 km; height, 10 km **663 km²**

21. length, 11.5 yd; width, 25 yd **287.5 yd²**

Subtract.   Pages 313–315

22. $^-14 - 1$ **$^-15$**

23. $8.9 - 3.3$ **5.6**

24. $\frac{6}{5} - \frac{1}{5}$ **1**

25. $^-9 - 11$ **$^-20$**

26. $3\frac{9}{4} - 2\frac{3}{8}$ **$2\frac{7}{8}$**

27. $23 - 17$ **6**

28. $16.2 - 18.1$ **$^-1.9$**

29. $^-51 - 49$ **$^-100$**

30. $5 - (^-4)$ **9**

31. $0 - 4.7$ **$^-4.7$**

32. $1.5 - 1.3$ **0.2**

33. $^-8\frac{4}{3} - 10\frac{1}{3}$ **$^-19\frac{2}{3}$**

Solve.

34. Peggy and Mark need to make hamburgers for 12 people. If each person eats 2 hamburgers, how many hamburgers do they need to make? **24 hamburgers**

35. Hector works 8 hours a day, 5 days a week. He makes $4.90 per hour. How much money does he make in a week? **$196**

36. A pyramid's length is 91 ft, its width is 80 ft, and its height is 110 ft. What is its volume? **266,933.3 ft³**

37. A cone-shaped paper cup has a radius of 1.5 in. and a height of 4 in. What is the volume of the cup? Use 3.14 for π. **9.42 in³**

Patterns and Functions

17-1 Expressions and Tables

Objective: To write expressions and to organize information in a table.

Tables are very helpful in mathematics. They are often used to organize information. The table below shows several fractions and their equivalent percents.

To add more values to the table, you must know the relationship between each fraction and its percent.

Study the following pattern.

$\frac{1}{2} \times 100 = 50$ $\frac{1}{3} \times 100 = 33\frac{1}{3}$

$\frac{1}{4} \times 100 = 25$ $\frac{2}{3} \times 100 = 66\frac{2}{3}$

$\frac{3}{4} \times 100 = 75$

Fraction	$\frac{1}{2}$	$\frac{1}{4}$	$\frac{3}{4}$	$\frac{1}{3}$	$\frac{2}{3}$
Percent	50%	25%	75%	$33\frac{1}{3}\%$	$66\frac{2}{3}\%$

To change a fraction to a percent, multiply the fraction by 100. Let n stand for the fraction value. Let p stand for the percent. Then $n \times 100 = p$.

Basic: 1–15 odd; Average: 1–15; Enriched: 2–14 even, 15

Exercises

Use $n \times 100 = p$ to change each fraction to a percent.

1. $\frac{9}{10}$ 90%

2. $\frac{1}{5}$ 20%

3. $\frac{2}{5}$ 40%

4. $\frac{3}{8}$ $37\frac{1}{2}\%$

5. $\frac{7}{8}$ $87\frac{1}{2}\%$

Write a mathematical expression for each verbal expression.

6. 6 more than a number x + 6

7. 3 less than a number x − 3

8. twice a number 2x

9. the product of 6 and a number increased by 2 6x + 2

10. the quotient of a number and 4 decreased by 1 $\frac{x}{4}$ 1

Copy and complete each table.

11.

x	x + 4
5	9
12	▨
23	▨

16
27

12.

n	$\frac{1}{2}n$
6	▨
22	▨
35	▨

3
11
$17\frac{1}{2}$

13.

a	1 − a
$\frac{1}{4}$	▨
$\frac{4}{5}$	▨
$\frac{3}{7}$	▨

$\frac{3}{4}$
$\frac{1}{5}$
$\frac{4}{7}$

14.

y	3y − 2
5	13
▨	28
▨	49

10
17

15. Make a table to organize the following fractions and their equivalent decimals. $\frac{1}{2}$, $\frac{3}{4}$, $\frac{4}{5}$, $1\frac{1}{4}$, $3\frac{5}{8}$ **See Teacher Guide.**

Teacher Resource Book, Page 369

17-2 Functions and Tables

Objective: To complete a function table given a function rule.

The distance a car travels before it stops depends upon the speed of the car when the brakes are applied. **Assume that the brakes are applied with equal force.** The table at the right shows this relationship. The relationship between the speed of the car and the braking distance is a **function**.

Speed (mph)	Braking Distance (feet)
5	4
15	13
25	28
35	52
45	92
55	148

A function pairs two sets so that each member of the first set corresponds to exactly one member of the second set. One way to represent a function is with a table.

A function can also be described with a rule.

Example

The distance (d) a car travels at a constant rate of 55 mph depends on the traveling time (t). The rule, $d = 55 \times t$, is used to complete the table.

Rule: $d = 55 \times t$ Table:

t	$55 \times t$	d
1	55×1	55
2	55×2	110
4	55×4	220
4.2	55×4.2	231
6.4	55×6.4	352

Basic Skills Appendix, Pages 431, 439
Basic: 1–9 odd; Average: 1–10; Enriched: 2–10 even

Exercises

Use the given function rule to complete each table.

1. hours = $\frac{\text{minutes}}{60}$

$h = \frac{m}{60}$

m	$\frac{m}{60}$	h
60	$\frac{60}{60}$	1
90	$\frac{90}{60}$	$1\frac{1}{2}$
240	$\frac{240}{60}$	4
300	$\frac{300}{60}$	5

2. area of a square = side squared

$A = s^2$

s	s^2	A
1	1^2	1
9	9^2	81
13	13^2	169
24	24^2	576
35	35^2	1,225
$\frac{1}{2}$	$\left(\frac{1}{2}\right)^2$	$\frac{1}{4}$

Remind students that $s^2 = s \times s$.

3. maximum heart rate = 220 − age

$h = 220 - a$

a (years)	$220 - a$	$h\left(\frac{\text{beats}}{\text{min}}\right)$
15	$220 - 15$	205
24	$220 - 24$	196
39	$220 - 39$	181
42	$220 - 42$	178
56	$220 - 56$	164
65	$220 - 65$	155

4. The amount of sales tax (t) at 5% depends on the cost (c) of an item.
$$t = 0.05 \times c$$

c	0.05 × c	t
$2.40	0.05 × $2.40	$0.12
$3.00	0.05 × $3.00	$0.15
$9.60	0.05 × $9.60	$0.48

5. The number (n) of times that a cricket chirps per minute depends on the temperature (t) in degrees Fahrenheit.
$$n = 4(t - 40)$$

t	4(t − 40)	n
42	4(42 − 40)	8
54	4(54 − 40)	56

Copy and complete each table.

6.

Month	Number of Days
Jan.	31
March	31
April	30
Sept.	30

7.

Word	Number of Letters in Word
function	8
algebra	7
mathematician	13

Solve. Answers may vary. See students' work.

8. Make a table to represent the shoe sizes of five people in your math class.

9. Make a table to represent the height of each person in your family.

10. Make a table to represent the classes you attend during each period of the school day.

This feature promotes students' mental abilities in computation and reasonableness.

 Mental Math

Products and quotients involving fractions and mixed numerals can be easily estimated.

$$\frac{7}{16} \times \frac{2}{5} \approx \frac{1}{2} \times \frac{1}{2} \qquad \frac{7}{16} \approx \frac{1}{2} \quad \frac{2}{5} \approx \frac{1}{2},$$
$$\approx \frac{1}{4}$$

$$3\frac{13}{16} \div 2\frac{1}{8} \approx 4 \div 2 \qquad 3\frac{13}{16} \approx 4, \ 2\frac{1}{8} \approx 2$$
$$\approx 2$$

Answers may vary. Typical answers are given.
Estimate each product or quotient using the strategy above.

1. $\frac{7}{8} \times 9$ 9

2. $2\frac{1}{8} \times 3\frac{4}{5}$ 8

3. $2\frac{1}{2} \times \frac{4}{5}$ $2\frac{1}{2}$

4. $\frac{3}{8} \times \frac{9}{16}$ $\frac{1}{4}$

5. $9 \div 2\frac{3}{4}$ 3

6. $\frac{5}{6} \div 7\frac{1}{7}$

7. $2 \div \frac{5}{8}$ 4

8. $\frac{13}{16} \div \frac{5}{9}$ 2

17-3 Finding the Function Rule

Objective: To find a rule for a function given a table.

A function rule is helpful in determining the values in a function table. Likewise, a function table can be used to determine the function rule.

Examples

A.

number correct	grade
20	80
21	84
16	64
25	100
23	92

A teacher made the table at the left to show the grades on a test. The number (n) of correct problems determines the grade (g). Find the rule that the teacher used.

$$80 = 4 \times 20$$
$$84 = 4 \times 21$$
$$64 = 4 \times 16$$
$$100 = 4 \times 25$$
$$92 = 4 \times 23$$
$$\text{grade} = 4 \times \text{number correct}$$
$$g = 4 \times n$$

The teacher used the rule $g = 4n$.

B. Use the values in the table to find the function rule.

x	y
2	3
3	5
7	13
12	23

$2(2) - 1 = 3$
$2(3) - 1 = 5$
$2(7) - 1 = 13$
$2(12) - 1 = 23$

rule: $2x - 1 = y$ or $y = 2x - 1$

Encourage students to use the guess-and-check method to find the function rule.
Basic: 1–9 odd; Average: 1–9; Enriched: 2–8 even, 9

Exercises

Use the values in each table to find the function rule.

1.

x	y
15	20
9	14
4	9
27	32

rule: $y = $ ▨

$x + 5$

2.

x	y
2	0.02
14	0.14
236	2.36
189	1.89

rule: $y = $ ▨

$\dfrac{x}{100}$

3.

x	y
$\frac{1}{5}$	1
$\frac{1}{10}$	$\frac{1}{2}$
5	25

rule: $y = $ ▨

$5x$

380 *Patterns and Functions*

Use the figures in each problem to complete the following.

4. Write a rule to express the relationship between the number of sides (*s*) and the number of angles (*a*) in a polygon.
s = a

5. Write a rule to express the relationship between the number of sides (*s*) of a polygon and the number of non-overlapping triangles (*t*) in the polygon. *t = s − 2*

6. Find the sum of the measures of the angles in each triangle. Then state a rule about the angles of a triangle.
The sum of the measures of the angles of a triangle is 180°.

7. Find the sum of the measures of the angles of each quadrilateral. Then state a rule about the angles of a quadrilateral. **The sum of the measures of the angles of a quadrilateral is 360°.**

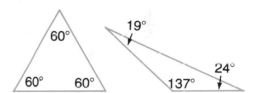

Solve.

8. The perimeter (*p*) of a rectangle whose length is 4 cm depends on its width (*w*). Write a rule for this function. *p = 2w + 8*

9. Jamie received $50 as his first week's salary. He then received weekly raises of $1. The number of weeks (*w*) Jamie works determines the amount of his weekly salary (*s*). Copy and complete the table at the left. Then write a rule for this function. *s = (w − 1) + 50*

w	s
1	$50
2	$51
3	$52
4	$53
10	$59

17-4 *Arithmetic Sequences*

Objective: To find the terms in an arithmetic sequence.

Sharon Perez is a postal clerk. Her responsibilities include selling stamps, weighing packages, and sorting and preparing mail for delivery. Sharon qualified for the job by being a United States citizen and having a high school diploma. She also had to pass a physical exam, a written exam, and a mechanical aptitude exam. Sharon then received on-the-job training.

If the cost of mailing a letter first class is 22 cents for the first ounce and 17 cents for each additional ounce, how much would it cost to mail a 5-ounce letter first class?

22,	**39,**	**56,**	**73,** . . .
1 oz	2 oz	3 oz	4 oz

The pairs of numbers form a function. This special function is called a *sequence*.

The difference in cost between postage for a 1-oz letter and postage for a 2-oz letter is 17 cents. The difference in cost between postage for a 2-oz letter and postage for a 3-oz letter is also 17 cents.

$$22 \underset{+17}{\frown} 39 \underset{+17}{\frown} 56 \underset{+17}{\frown} 73 \quad \underset{+17}{\frown} \ldots$$

This sequence is called an **arithmetic sequence**. Each term of the sequence can be found by adding the same number to the term before it.

Example

What is the cost of mailing a 5-oz letter first class? The next number in the arithmetic sequence shown above would be the cost of mailing a 5-oz letter first class.

$$22 \underset{+17}{\frown} 39 \underset{+17}{\frown} 56 \underset{+17}{\frown} 73 \underset{+17}{\frown} 90$$

So, the cost of mailing a 5-oz letter first class is 90 cents.

The Key Skills provides practice of skills needed in the exercises.

Key Skills

Add.

$^-2 + {}^-6 = {}^-8$ $^-6 + 8 = 2$ $5 + {}^-9 = {}^-4$

1. $^-4 + {}^-5$ **-9**

2. $^-12 + {}^-9$ **-21**

3. $^-5 + {}^-17$ **-22**

4. $^-11 + {}^-25$ **-36**

9. $^-13 + 1$ **-12**

10. $17 + {}^-44$ **-27**

11. $\frac{-2}{3} + \frac{-1}{3}$ **-1**

12. $\frac{-3}{4} + \frac{1}{4}$ **$\frac{-1}{2}$**

Basic Skills Appendix, Pages 435, 436, 450

Basic: 2–18 even; Average: 1–17 odd, 19–22; Enriched: 2–18 even, 19–22

Exercises

Find the number that is being added to each term in each arithmetic sequence.

1. 1.1, 1.2, 1.3, 1.4, 1.5, . . . **0.1**

2. $1, 1\frac{1}{2}, 2, 2\frac{1}{2}, 3 \dots$ **$\frac{1}{2}$**

3. 40, 37, 34, 31, 28, . . . **-3**

4. 85, 79, 73, 67, 61, . . . **-6**

Find the next three terms in each arithmetic sequence.

5. 2, 8, 14, 20, ▦, ▦, ▦ **26, 32, 38**

6. 18, 23, 28, 33, ▦, ▦, ▦ **38, 43, 48**

7. 13, 27, 41, 55, ▦, ▦, ▦ **69, 83, 97**

8. 253, 270, 287, 304, ▦, ▦, ▦ **321, 338, 355**

9. $^-185, {}^-205, {}^-225, {}^-245,$ ▦, ▦, ▦ **-265, -285, -305**

10. 85, 48, 11, $^-26$, ▦, ▦, ▦ **-63, -100, -137**

11. $\frac{-3}{4}, \frac{-2}{4}, \frac{-1}{4}, 0,$ ▦, ▦, ▦ **$\frac{1}{4}, \frac{1}{2}, \frac{3}{4}$**

12. $\frac{3}{5}, \frac{2}{5}, \frac{1}{5}, 0,$ ▦, ▦, ▦ **$\frac{-1}{5}, \frac{-2}{5}, \frac{-3}{5}$**

13. $^-1\frac{1}{2}, {}^-1, {}^-\frac{1}{2}, 0,$ ▦, ▦, ▦ **$\frac{1}{2}, 1, 1\frac{1}{2}$**

14. $2\frac{1}{2}, 1\frac{1}{2}, \frac{1}{2}, {}^-\frac{1}{2},$ ▦, ▦, ▦ **$^-1\frac{1}{2}, {}^-2\frac{1}{2}, {}^-3\frac{1}{2}$**

15. 30, 22, 14, 6, ▦, ▦, ▦ **-2, -10, -18**

16. 3.0, 2.2, 1.4, 0.6, ▦, ▦, ▦ **-0.2, -1.0, -1.8**

17. $^-1.9, {}^-1.6, {}^-1.3, {}^-1.0,$ ▦, ▦, ▦ **-0.7, -0.4, -0.1**

18. 2.9, 1.8, 0.7, $^-0.4$, ▦, ▦, ▦ **-1.5, -2.6, -3.7**

Complete.

19. Draw the next figure in this sequence. Then write a number sequence for these figures.

1, 3, 5, 7, . . .

20. Draw the next figure in this sequence. Then write a number sequence for these figures.

4, 8, 12, 16, . . .

Solve.

21. An apartment rents for $360. Each year the monthly rent increases $15. What will be the monthly rent in 5 years? **$435**

22. Dawn is saving money to buy a stereo. She saves $2 the first week, $4 the second week, $6 the third week, and so on. How much does she save in the tenth week? **$20**

PRACTICE

Estimate. Answers may vary. Typical answers are given.

1.	486	2.	721	3.	993	4.	88	5. $42\overline{)768}$
	$\times$ 38		$+$ 386		$-$ 379		$\times$ 33	20
	20,000		1,100		600		2,700	

Add, subtract, multiply, or divide.

6. $48.6 + 9.69$ **58.29**   **7.** $356 - 29.5$ **326.5**   **8.** 38.1×36 **1,371.6**

9. $46.08 - 1.8$ **44.28**   **10.** 56×0.09 **5.04**   **11.** $451.05 - 1.5$ **449.55**

12. $9\frac{2}{3} - 3\frac{1}{3}$ $6\frac{1}{3}$ **13.** $8 + 3\frac{3}{5}$ $11\frac{3}{5}$ **14.** $1\frac{2}{4} + 3\frac{1}{4}$ $4\frac{3}{4}$

15. $1\frac{9}{10} - \frac{2}{5}$ $1\frac{1}{2}$ **16.** $4\frac{1}{8} - 2\frac{4}{5}$ $1\frac{13}{40}$ **17.** $16\frac{1}{2} \times \frac{3}{11}$ $4\frac{1}{2}$

18. $\frac{3}{4} - \frac{2}{3}$ $\frac{1}{12}$ **19.** $1\frac{9}{10} \times \frac{1}{2}$ $\frac{19}{20}$ **20.** $13\frac{3}{4} - 6\frac{1}{2}$ $7\frac{1}{4}$

21. $456 \times 1,000$ **456,000**   **22.** 100×4.8 **480**   **23.** $0.8 \div 100$ **0.008**

24. 561×10 **5,610**   **25.** $96.5 \div 10$ **9.65**   **26.** $0.41 \times 1,000$ **410**

Complete.

27. 456 cm = ▓ m **4.56**   **28.** 20 g = ▓ mg **20,000**   **29.** 7.8 m = ▓ cm **780**

30. 4.6 L = ▓ mL **4,600**   **31.** 0.6 m = ▓ mm **600**   **32.** ▓ km = 28 m **0.028**

33. 108 in. = ▓ ft **9**   **34.** 80 oz = ▓ lb **5**   **35.** ▓ gal = 42 qt **10.5**

Add or subtract.

36.	3 h 14 min 9 s	37.	5 h 16 min	38.	8 h 3 min 14 s
	$+$ 2 h 43 min 29 s		$+$ 4 h 48 min		$-$ 2 h 9 min 15 s
	5 h 57 min 38 s		10 h 4 min		5 h 53 min 59 s

Change each percent to a decimal. Change each decimal to a percent.

39. 120% **1.2**   **40.** 0.51 **51%**   **41.** 0.006 **0.6%**   **42.** 1.5% **0.015**   **43.** 2.5 **250%**

44. 37% **0.37**   **45.** 2% **0.02**   **46.** 3.14 **314%**   **47.** 7 **700%**   **48.** 62.5% **0.625**

Solve.

49. 4% of 1,000 **40**   **50.** 39% of 75 **29.25**   **51.** 225% of 20 **45**

52. 83% of 200 **166**   **53.** 5% of 125 **6.25**   **54.** 10% of 550 **55**

55. 90% of 300 **270**   **56.** 50% of 12.5 **6.25**   **57.** 2% of 0.8 **0.016**

Solve each problem using the proportion $\frac{P}{B} = \frac{r}{100}$.

58. 15 is __?__% of 45 $33\frac{1}{3}$ **59.** __?__% of 60 is 48 **80**   **60.** __?__ is 75% of 50 **37.5**

61. 6% of __?__ is 12 **200**   **62.** __?__ is 70% of 9.5 **6.65**   **63.** 82 is 200% of __?__ **41**

64. 24 is __?__% of 60 **40**   **65.** 48 is __?__% of 72 $66\frac{2}{3}$ **66.** __?__ is 48% of 50 **24**

Find the perimeter of each figure described below.

67. a square whose area is 25 square inches 20 in.

68. a triangle whose sides are $3\frac{1}{2}$ feet, $2\frac{1}{4}$ feet, and 3 feet $8\frac{3}{4}$ ft

Find the area of each figure described below. Use 3.14 for π.

69. rectangle: length, 6.9 m; width, 3.7 m 25.53 m²

70. circle: radius, 3.2 m 32.1536 m²

71. square: perimeter, 28 in. 49 in.²

72. a rectangle whose length is twice its width, which is 6 ft 72 ft²

73. a circle whose diameter is 20 cm 314 cm²

Find the volume of each solid described below. Use 3.14 for π.

74. rectangular prism: base, 4 ft by $3\frac{1}{2}$ ft; height, 6 ft 84 ft³

75. cone: diameter, 6 in.; height, 22 in. 207.24 in.³

Find the mode, median, and mean for each set of data.

76. 3.2, 4.0, 3.5, 3.3, 4.0, 3.6, 3.5, 3.2, 4.0, 3.8 4.0; 3.55; 3.61

77. 50, 97, 3, 50, 34, 66, 50, 50, 50

Add, subtract, multiply, or divide.

78. $9 + {}^-3$ 6

79. ${}^-8 \times 9$ -72

80. ${}^-56 \div 7$ -8

81. ${}^-3 \times {}^-5$ 15

82. $28 \div {}^-4$ -7

83. ${}^-8 - {}^-4$ -4

84. ${}^-12 \div 4$ -3

85. ${}^-3 + {}^-8$ -11

86. $(4 + {}^-6) - 2$ -4

87. ${}^-18 - 9 + 3$ -24

88. ${}^-6 \times 4 + 6 - 5$ -23

Find the value of each expression if $x = 5$ and $y = {}^-2$.

89. $x + 6$ 11

90. $10 - x$ 5

91. $3x$ 15

92. $2x + y$ 8

93. $x - y$ 7

94. xy -10

95. $4xy$ -40

96. $3x - xy$ 25

97. x^2 25

98. $x^2 + 9$ 34

99. $x^2 - y^2$ 21

100. y^3 -8

101. $\frac{x}{15}$ $\frac{1}{3}$

102. $\frac{6}{y}$ -3

103. $\frac{xy}{2}$ -5

104. $\frac{2x^2}{5}$ 10

Solve.

105. The weight of one rock is 7.4 kg. Another weighs 1,300 g. Find the total weight in kilograms. weight is 8.7 kg

106. Michelle worked for 36 hours at the local bakery owned by her uncle. He paid her $4.95 an hour. How much money did she earn? $178.20

107. Out of 32 students, 20 earned a B on the science test. What percent of the students earned a B? $62\frac{1}{2}$% earned a B

108. Bob measured the circumference of a tree as 471 centimeters. Find the radius of the tree trunk. Use 3.14 for π. radius is 75 cm

17-5 Other Sequences

Objective: To find the terms in other kinds of sequences.

The Paxton Skateboard Company employed 42 people in 1960, 84 people in 1970, and 168 people in 1980.

42,   84,   168, . . .
1960   1970   1980

The numbers shown in bold above form a new kind of sequence.

The number of employees in 1970 is two times the number of employees in 1960. The number of employees in 1980 is two times the number of employees in 1970.

42   84   168 . . .
  ×2   ×2   ×2

This sequence is called a **geometric sequence**. Each term of the sequence can be found by multiplying the same number by the term before it.

Example

If the Paxton Skateboard Company continues to double the number of people they employ every 10 years, how many employees can they expect to have in the year 2000?

The number of employees in the year 2000 would be the fifth term in the geometric sequence.

1960   1970   1980   1990   2000
42   84   168   336   672
  ×2   ×2   ×2   ×2

So, the Paxton Skateboard Company can expect to have 672 employees in the year 2000.

Sometimes sequences involve powers or alternating patterns.   The following are not geometric sequences.

1, 4, 9, 16, 25, . . .   1   4   2   5   3   6 . . .
1^2 2^2 3^2 4^2 5^2 +3 −2 +3 −2 +3

Exercises

Find the number each term is multiplied by in each geometric sequence.

1. 3, 6, 12, 24, 48, . . . **2**

2. 5, 15, 45, 135, 405, . . . **3**

3. 2, ⁻8, 32, ⁻128, 512, . . . **⁻4**

4. 200, ⁻100, 50, ⁻25, $12\frac{1}{2}$, . . . $-\frac{1}{2}$

Find the next three terms in each geometric sequence.

5. 4, 8, 16, 32, ▨, ▨, ▨ **64, 128, 256**

6. 1, 3, 9, 27, ▨, ▨, ▨ **81, 243, 729**

7. 1, 5, 25, 125, ▨, ▨, ▨ **625; 3,125; 15,625**

8. 64, 32, 16, 8, ▨, ▨, ▨ **4, 2, 1**

9. 224, 112, 56, 28, ▨, ▨, ▨ **14, 7, $3\frac{1}{2}$**

10. 729, 243, 81, 27, ▨, ▨, ▨ **9, 3, 1**

11. 6, ⁻18, 54, ⁻162, ▨, ▨, ▨
486; ⁻1,458; 4,374

12. ⁻2, ⁻10, ⁻50, ⁻250, ▨, ▨, ▨
⁻1,250; ⁻6,250; ⁻31,250

13. ⁻2, 12, ⁻72, 432, ▨, ▨, ▨
⁻2,592; 15,552; ⁻93,312

14. 800, ⁻400, 200, ⁻100, ▨, ▨,▨ **50, ⁻25, $12\frac{1}{2}$**

15. 400, 100, 25, $6\frac{1}{4}$, ▨, ▨, ▨ $1\frac{9}{16}, \frac{25}{64}, \frac{25}{256}$

16. 450, 150, 50, $16\frac{2}{3}$, ▨, ▨, ▨ $5\frac{5}{9}, 1\frac{23}{27}, \frac{50}{81}$

Determine the pattern in each sequence to find the next three terms.

17. 3, 4, 5, 7, 9, ▨, ▨, ▨ **12, 15, 19**

18. 16, 15, 14, 12, 10, ▨, ▨, ▨ **7, 4, 0**

19. 15, 17, 16, 18, 17, ▨, ▨, ▨ **19, 18, 20**

20. 4, 7, 5, 8, 6, ▨, ▨, ▨ **9, 7, 10**

21. $1\frac{1}{4}, 1\frac{1}{2}, 1\frac{3}{4}, 2, 2\frac{1}{4}$, ▨, ▨, ▨ $2\frac{1}{2}, 2\frac{3}{4}, 3$

22. $2\frac{2}{3}, 2\frac{5}{6}, 3, 3\frac{1}{6}, 3\frac{1}{3}$, ▨, ▨, ▨ $3\frac{1}{2}, 3\frac{2}{3}, 3\frac{5}{6}$

23. 23, 32, 25, 52, 27, ▨, ▨, ▨ **72, 29, 92**

24. 209, 198, 187, 176, 165, ▨, ▨, ▨
154, 143, 132

Solve.

25. The number of bacteria in a culture triples every hour. There are 300 bacteria in the culture. How many bacteria will be in the culture 4 hours later? **24,300 bacteria**

26. A ball dropped 40 cm bounces $\frac{1}{2}$ of the height from which it fell on each bounce. How far does the ball travel after the third bounce? **5 cm**

This feature presents general topics of mathematics.

Math Break

The sequence 1, 1, 2, 3, 5, 8, 13, . . . is called a **Fibonacci Sequence.** These numbers seem to be closely related to events in nature. They can be found when the number of leaves on a branch are counted, the number of petals on a flower are counted, and in the spiral arrangement of a pine cone.

1. Find the next three terms of the Fibonacci Sequence above. **21, 34, 55**

2. How are the Fibonacci numbers used to create this new sequence?
$1, \frac{1}{2}, \frac{2}{3}, \frac{3}{5}, \frac{5}{8}, \frac{8}{13}, \cdots$ $\frac{1st}{2nd}, \frac{2nd}{3rd}, \frac{3rd}{4th}, \frac{4th}{5th}, \cdots$

3. Use a calculator to change each fraction to a decimal. Round to the nearest hundredth. Describe these quotients. **They approach 0.62.**

17-6   Scientific Notation

Objective: To change numbers in standard notation to scientific notation, and vice versa.

The earth is approximately 93,000,000 miles from the sun.
Neptune is approximately 2,794,000,000 miles from the sun.
Numbers such as these are difficult to read without counting
each place value. Therefore, large numbers are often written
in **scientific notation.**

A number expressed in scientific notation
is written as a product. One factor is
a number that is at least 1 but less than
10. The other factor is a power of 10.
**For a number to be at least 1 but less
than 10, there is only one digit to the
left of the decimal point.**

standard notation		scientific notation
$93,000,000 =$	9.3	$\times \quad 10^7$

at least 1   power
but less   of 10
than 10

$$2,794,000,000 = 2.794 \times 10^9$$

Some powers of 10 are listed below.

$10^0 = 1$	$10^5 = 100,000$
$10^1 = 10$	$10^6 = 1,000,000$
$10^2 = 100$	$10^7 = 10,000,000$
$10^3 = 1,000$	$10^8 = 100,000,000$
$10^4 = 10,000$	$10^9 = 1,000,000,000$

**For the powers
of 10, the
exponent equals
the number of
zeros**

Examples

A. Express 520,000 in scientific notation.

520,000   *5.2 is at least 1 but less than 10.*
The decimal point was moved 5 places to the left.

So, $520,000 = 5.2 \times 10^5$.

B. Express 2.3×10^6 in standard notation.

2.300000   *Move the decimal point 6 places to
the right. Attach 5 zeros.*

so, $2.3 \times 10^6 = 2,300,000$. **It is also convenient to write very small numbers in scientific notation
using negative exponents. You may wish to challenge more able
students with this topic.**

388 *Patterns and Functions*

Exercises

Determine how many places the decimal point should be moved to find a number that is at least 1 but less than 10.

1. 12 **1**   **2.** 316 **2**   **3.** 1,200 **3**   **4.** 36,500 **4**

5. 469,000 **5**   **6.** 7,820 **3**   **7.** 620 **2**   **8.** 935,100,000 **8**

9. 306.5 **2**   **10.** 23.45 **1**   **11.** 14.502 **1**   **12.** 7 **0**

Express each number in scientific notation.

13. 530
5.3×10^2

14. 3,840
3.84×10^3

15. 642
6.42×10^2

16. 42,000
4.2×10^4

17. 927
9.27×10^2

18. 961,000
9.61×10^5

19. 1,200
1.2×10^3

20. 8,260
8.26×10^3

21. 36,500
3.65×10^4

22. 2,060,000
2.06×10^6

23. 925,000,000
9.25×10^8

24. 1,000,000,000
1×10^9

25. The early horse is believed to have lived 40,000,000 years ago.
4×10^7

26. Uranus is approximately 2 billion miles from the sun.
2×10^9

Express each number in standard notation.

27. 1.3×10^3
1,300

28. 4.6×10^8
460,000,000

29. 1.66×10^4
16,600

30. 4.7×10^1
47

31. 3.71×10^3
3,710

32. 5.8×10^5
580,000

33. 8.93×10^3
8,930

34. 9.99×10^6
9,990,000

35. Mars is approximately 1.42×10^8 miles from the sun. **142,000,000**

36. There are more than 2×10^{20} stars in the universe. **200,000,000,000,000,000,000**

Solve. Express each answer in scientific notation and then in standard notation.

37. Find a number 10 times larger than 3.2×10^4. **3.2×10^5; 320,000**

38. Find a number 100 times greater than 6.45×10^5. **6.45×10^7; 64,500,000**

39. Each year, over 50 billion cans are discarded in the United States. How many cans are discarded in 10 years? **5×10^{11} cans; 500,000,000,000 cans**

40. There are 9.07×10^4 days in one year on Pluto. How many days are there in 10 years on Pluto? **9.07×10^5 days; 907,000 days**

This feature provides general topics about the uses of a computer.

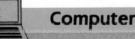

Computer

Mark I was an electromechanical computer developed by the scientists at Harvard University in 1944. Many of its parts were relays that opened and closed. Once when the computer would not operate properly, the scientists found that a moth was trapped in one of the relays. They removed the moth and said that they were "debugging" their computer. Today, debug means to find an error in a program.

17-7 Problem Solving: Look For a Pattern

Objective: To use geometrical patterns and numerical patterns to solve word problems.

Wilma Crawford is a member of the bowling team. In bowling, the pins are arranged as shown. The 10 pins are in the shape of a triangle.

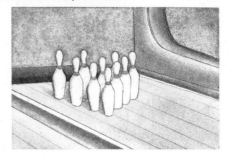

Numbers, such as 10, are called **triangular numbers.** The first four triangular numbers are shown below.

Find the next triangular number.

Read

You must find the fifth triangular number. You know that the first four triangular numbers are 1, 3, 6, and 10.

Decide

Use the patterns of the triangular arrangements of dots to find a solution.

Solve

Add the number of dots as follows.

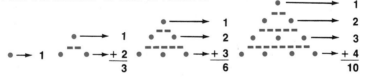

Now, study the addition patterns at the right.

$$1 = 1$$
$$3 = 1 + 2$$
$$6 = 1 + 2 + 3$$
$$10 = 1 + 2 + 3 + 4$$

What is the pattern of the sums?

To find the fifth triangular number, add $1 + 2 + 3 + 4 + 5$.

$$1 + 2 + 3 + 4 + 5 = 15$$

The fifth triangular number is 15.

Examine

Use a triangular arrangement of dots to represent the fifth triangular number. Since there are 15 dots in this diagram, the answer is correct.

Exercises

1. Find the sixth triangular number. **21**

2. Find the eighth triangular number. **36**

3. Which triangular number is the sum of the numbers 1 through 20? **twentieth (210)**

4. Explain how to find any triangular number using addition. **Add all the counting numbers up to and including the triangular number.**

Another type of number is called a square number. The first four square numbers are shown below. Study the following addition patterns.

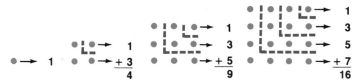

5. Use the above pattern to find the fifth square number as a sum.
$1 + 3 + 5 + 7 + 9 = 25$

6. Which square number is the sum $1 + 3 + 5 + 7 + 9 + 11 + 13$? **seventh (49)**

7. Which square number is the sum $1 + 3 + 5 + 7 + 9 + 11 + 13 + 15 + 17 + 19 + 21$? **eleventh (121)**

8. Explain how to find any square number using addition. **To find the nth square number, add the first n odd numbers.**

9. The first square number is 1×1 or 1. The second square number is 2×2 or 4. Use this pattern to find the third and tenth square numbers.
$3 \times 3 = 9$; $10 \times 10 = 100$

The first four triangular numbers are 1, 3, 6, and 10. Study the following addition patterns.

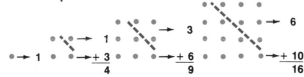

10. The second square number is $1 + 3$ or 4. The third is $3 + 6$ or 9. The fourth is $6 + 10$ or 16. Describe this pattern.
The sum of adjacent triangular numbers is a square number.
1 3 6 10 15 21

1 4 9 16 25 36

This feature presents useful ways of solving mathematical problems on a calculator.

Calculator

Use the given function rule to complete each table. Notice the patterns in the values of *y* in each table.

1. rule: $y = 9x$

x	y
3	27
33	297
333	2,997
3,333	29,997

2. rule: $y = 11x$

x	y
12	132
13	143
14	154
15	165

3. rule: $y = 101x$

x	y
111	11,211
222	22,422
333	33,633
444	44,844

CHAPTER 17 REVIEW

Vocabulary/Concepts

Choose a word from the list at the right that best completes each sentence.

1. The numbers 1, 4, 9, and 16 are __?__ .
   square numbers
2. In a(n) __?__ sequence, each term in the sequence can be found by adding the same number to the term before it.
   arithmetic
3. A(n) __?__ pairs two sets so that each member of the first set corresponds to exactly one member of the second set.
   function
4. The numbers 1, 3, 6, and 10 are __?__ .
   triangular numbers
5. A number that is written in __?__ is written as a product of a number that is at least 1 but less than 10 and a power of 10.
   scientific notation
6. In a(n) __?__ sequence, each term in the sequence can be found by multiplying the same number by the term before it. **geometric**

arithmetic
Fibonacci
function
geometric
rule
scientific notation
sequence
square numbers
standard notation
triangular numbers

Exercises

Use $n \times 100 = p$ to change each fraction to a percent. Page 377

7. $\frac{7}{10}$ **70%**   8. $\frac{3}{5}$ **60%**   9. $\frac{4}{5}$ **80%**   10. $\frac{5}{8}$ **62.5%**   11. $\frac{1}{8}$ **12.5%**

Write a mathematical expression for each verbal expression. Page 377

12. 4 more than a number **x + 4**

13. 10 less than a number **x − 10**

14. 3 times a number **3x**

15. a number divided by 5 **$\frac{x}{5}$**

Write a verbal expression for each mathematical expression. Page 377

16. $x + 2$
   2 more than a number

17. $n - 9$
   9 less than a number

18. $5p$
   5 times a number

19. $\frac{t}{3} - 10$

20. y^3
   cube a number

Use the given function rule to complete each table. Pages 378–379

21. rule: $y = \frac{x}{10}$

x	$\frac{x}{10}$	y
30	$\frac{30}{10}$	3
60	$\frac{60}{10}$	6
75	$\frac{75}{10}$	$7\frac{1}{2}$
110	$\frac{110}{10}$	11

22. rule: $y = x + 5$

x	x + 5	y
14	14 + 5	19
5	5 + 5	10
−5	−5 + 5	0
−20	−20 + 5	−15

23. rule: $y = x^2 + 1$

x	$x^2 + 1$	y
4	$(4)^2 + 1$	17
10	$(10)^2 + 1$	101
12	$(12)^2 + 1$	145
$\frac{1}{2}$	$\left(\frac{1}{2}\right)^2 + 1$	$1\frac{1}{4}$

19. **10 less than $\frac{1}{3}$ of a number**

Use the values in each table to find the function rule. Pages 380–381

24.

x	y
2	4
5	25
7	49

rule: y = ▨▨
x^2

25.

x	y
3	1
16	14
25	23

rule: y = ▨▨
$x - 2$

26.

x	y
⁻2	⁻8
7	28
12	48

rule: y = ▨▨
$4x$

Find the next three terms in each arithmetic sequence. Pages 382–383

27. 7, 10, 13, 16, ▨, ▨, ▨ **19, 22, 25**

28. 8, 4, 0, ⁻4, ▨, ▨, ▨ **⁻8, ⁻12, ⁻16**

29. $10\frac{1}{2}, 9\frac{1}{2}, 8\frac{1}{2}, 7\frac{1}{2}$, ▨, ▨, ▨ $6\frac{1}{2}, 5\frac{1}{2}, 4\frac{1}{2}$

30. 2.5, 3, 3.5, 4, ▨, ▨, ▨ **4.5, 5, 5.5**

Find the next three terms in each geometric sequence. Pages 386–387

31. 2, 8, 32, 128, ▨, ▨, ▨ **512; 2,048; 8,192**

32. 400, 200, 100, 50, ▨, ▨, ▨ $25, 12\frac{1}{2}, 6\frac{1}{4}$

33. ⁻3, ⁻6, ⁻12, ⁻24, ▨, ▨, ▨ **⁻48, ⁻96, ⁻192**

34. 1, ⁻3, 9, ⁻27, ▨, ▨, ▨ **81, ⁻243, 729**

Determine the pattern in each sequence to find the next three terms. Pages 386–387

35. 2, 6, 3, 7, 4, ▨, ▨, ▨ **8, 5, 9**

36. 5, 6, 7, 9, 11, ▨, ▨ ▨ **14, 17, 21**

37. 20, 19, 17, 14, 10, ▨, ▨, ▨ **5, ⁻1, ⁻8**

38. 1, 2, 7, 14, 19, ▨, ▨, ▨ **38, 43, 86**

Express each number in scientific notation. Pages 388–389

39. 260 **2.6 × 10²** 40. 3,500 **3.5 × 10³** 41. 756,000
7.56 × 10⁵ 42. 82,000,000
8.2 × 10⁷

43. 6,000 **6 × 10³** 44. 28,500 **2.85 × 10⁴** 45. 46,000 **4.6 × 10⁴** 46. 99,000,000,000
9.9 × 10¹⁰

Express each number in standard notation. Pages 388–389

47. 2.6 × 10³ **2,600** 48. 5.1 × 10² **510** 49. 8.2 × 10⁶
8,200,000 50. 7.25 × 10⁴
72,500

51. 8.94 × 10⁷
89,400,000 52. 5 × 10³ **5,000** 53. 1.3 × 10⁵
130,000 54. 9.6 × 10⁸
960,000,000

Solve.

55. Make a table to represent the heights of the members of your family.
Answers may vary.

56. Which square number is the sum 1 + 3 + 5 + 7 + 9 + 11 + 13 + 15?
eighth (64)

57. The perimeter (p) of a triangle with sides 8 ft and 10 ft depends on the length of the third side (s). Write a rule for this function.
p = 18 + s

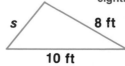
s / 8 ft / 10 ft

58. The number of bacteria in a culture doubles every hour. There are 150 bacteria in the culture. How many bacteria will there be in 5 hours?
4,800 bacteria

59. The speed of light in a vacuum is approximately 30,000,000,000 cm per second. Express this number in scientific notation.
3 × 10¹⁰

CHAPTER 17 TEST

Use $n \times 100 = p$ to change each fraction to a percent.

1. $\frac{3}{10}$ **30%** **2.** $\frac{1}{5}$ **20%** **3.** $\frac{3}{4}$ **75%** **4.** $\frac{1}{4}$ **25%** **5.** $\frac{2}{3}$ **66$\frac{2}{3}$%**

Write a mathematical expression for each verbal expression.

6. 5 less than a number **x – 5**

7. 4 more than a number **x + 4**

8. a number divided by 8 **$\frac{x}{8}$**

9. 6 times a number **6x**

Use the values in each table to find the function rule.

10.

x	y
4	9
8	13
10	15
15	20

rule: y = ▩
x + 5

11.

x	y
10	2
25	5
40	8
100	20

rule: y = ▩
$\frac{x}{5}$

12.

x	y
4	12
1	3
⁻2	⁻6
⁻5	⁻15

rule: y = ▩
3x

Find the next three terms in each arithmetic sequence.

13. 5, 7, 9, 11, ▩, ▩, ▩ **13, 15, 17**

14. 15, 25, 35, 45, ▩, ▩, ▩ **55, 65, 75**

15. $12\frac{1}{2}$, $10\frac{1}{2}$, $8\frac{1}{2}$, $6\frac{1}{2}$, ▩, ▩, ▩ **$4\frac{1}{2}$, $2\frac{1}{2}$, $\frac{1}{2}$**

16. 1, 1.25, 1.5, 1.75, ▩, ▩, ▩ **2, 2.25, 2.5**

Find the next three terms in each geometric sequence.

17. 7, 14, 28, 56, ▩, ▩, ▩
112, 224, 448

18. 3, 12, 48, 192, ▩, ▩, ▩
768; 3,072; 12,288

19. 160, 80, 40, 20, ▩, ▩, ▩
10, 5, $2\frac{1}{2}$

20. 2, ⁻6, 18, ⁻54, ▩, ▩, ▩
162; ⁻486; 1,458

Determine the pattern in each sequence to find the next three terms.

21. 16, 25, 36, 49, ▩, ▩, ▩
64, 81, 100

22. 5, 6, 8, 11, 15, ▩, ▩, ▩
20, 26, 33

Express each number in scientific notation.

23. 3,200 **3.2×10^3**

24. 76,000 **7.6×10^4**

25. 865,000,000
8.65×10^8

26. 425 **4.25×10^2**

Express each number in standard notation.

27. 6.4×10^4 **64,000**

28. 3.2×10^3 **3,200**

29. 5.25×10^2 **525**

30. 6.35×10^6 **6,350,000**

Solve.

31. Pedro is saving money to buy a bicycle. He saves $4 the first week, $8 the second week, $12 the third week, and so on. How much does he save the eighth week? **$32**

32. The number of bacteria in a culture triples every hour. There are 200 bacteria in the culture. How many bacteria will be in the culture in 4 hours? **16,200 bacteria**

CUMULATIVE REVIEW

Write the converse of each statement. Then determine whether each statement (original and converse) is true. Pages 224–225 For answers to exercises 1–4, see Teacher Guide.

1. If two angles are supplementary, then the sum of their measures is 180°.

2. If you have $10,000, then you can buy a car.

3. If two lines in a plane are perpendicular to the same line, then they are parallel.

4. If a polygon is a trapezoid, then it has 2 parallel sides.

If a decision is possible, write the decision for each case based on the given rule. Pages 226–227

Rule: If it is Sunday, then we will go to the park.

5. Case: We are not going to the park.
We will go to the park.

6. Case: We are going to the park.
no decision

7. Case: It is Sunday.
It is not Sunday.

8. Case: It is not Sunday.
no decision

State the number to add to each side to solve each equation. Then solve the equation and check your solution. Pages 336–337

9. $x - 9 = 27$
9, 36

10. $b - 3\frac{1}{4} = 6\frac{1}{4}$ $3\frac{1}{4}, 9\frac{1}{2}$

11. $n - 1 = 5$
1, 6

12. $y - 10 = 19$
10, 29

13. $m - 0.02 = 1.82$
0.02, 1.84

14. $f - 0.8 = 3.1$
0.8, 3.9

15. $a - 1\frac{1}{2} = 2\frac{1}{2}$
$1\frac{1}{2}, 4$

16. $z - 4 = 10$
4, 14

Find the value of each expression if $x = 2$, $y = 5$, and $z = 6$. Pages 356–357

17. $\frac{^-x + y + z}{18}$ $\frac{1}{2}$

18. $\frac{3y}{z}$ $2\frac{1}{2}$

19. $\frac{xy}{z}$ $1\frac{2}{3}$

20. $z^2 - 2x + y$ 37

21. $z^2 + y \div 5$ 37

Use the formula $V = \frac{d}{t}$ to find the velocity. (V – velocity, d – distance, t – time) Round decimal answers to the nearest tenth. Pages 358–360

22. $d = 27$ km; $t = \frac{1}{2}$ h $54\frac{km}{h}$

23. $d = 200.1$ cm; $t = 3$ s $66.7\frac{cm}{s}$

24. $d = 84$ mi; $t = 3\frac{1}{4}$ h $25.8\frac{mi}{h}$

Use the given function rule to complete each table. Round decimal answers to the nearest tenth. Pages 378–379

25. complement of an angle = 90° – angle

angle	90° – angle	complement
32	90 – 32	58
48	90 – 48	42
51	90 – 51	39
11	90 – 11	79
9	90 – 9	81
3	90 – 3	87

26. days $- \frac{hours}{24}$; $d = \frac{h}{24}$

h	$\frac{h}{24}$	d
48	$\frac{48}{24}$	2
52	$\frac{52}{24}$	2.2
60	$\frac{60}{24}$	2.5

Find the number that is being added to each term in each arithmetic sequence. Pages 382–383

27. 1.3, 1.5, 1.7, 1.9, . . .
0.2

28. 55, 47, 39, 31, 23, . . .
⁻8

29. 1.5, 1.4, 1.3, 1.2, . . .
⁻0.1

The Coordinate Plane

18-1 Ordered Pairs

Objective: To locate and name points by using ordered pairs.

An **ordered pair** can be used to name the location of a point on a grid. The first number represents the number of horizontal units the point is from zero. The second number represents the number of vertical units the point is from zero. The two numbers separated by a comma and surrounded by parentheses represent an ordered pair.

Example

Graph the ordered pair (5, 6).

Start at the origin label O.

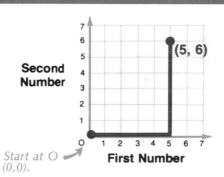

The dot at (5, 6) is the **graph** of the point.

Basic: 1–28; Average: 1–28; Enriched: 1–28

Exercises

Use the grid at the right to find the letter for each ordered pair.

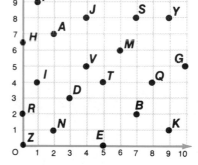

1. (0, 0) Z   **2.** (6, 6) M   **3.** (2, 1) N

4. (10, 5) G   **5.** (4, 8) J   **6.** (8, 4) Q

7. (1, 4) I   **8.** (9, 8) Y   **9.** (3, 3) D

10. (0, 2) R   **11.** (2, 7) A   **12.** (1, 9) P

Use the grid to find the ordered pair for each letter.

13. V (4, 5)   **14.** T (5, 4)   **15.** B (7, 2)   **16.** K (9, 1)

17. L (10, 10)   **18.** W (3, 10)   **19.** E (5, 0)   **20.** H (0, 6.5)

Graph each ordered pair on graph paper. Label each point with the given letter.
For answers to exercises 21–28, see Teacher Guide.

21. A (1, 5)   **22.** B (5, 1)   **23.** C (4, 4)   **24.** D (0,4)

25. E (4,0)   **26.** F (3, 2)   **27.** G $(8\frac{1}{2}, 6\frac{1}{4})$ **28.** H (5.5, 9.3)

18-2 The Coordinate System

Objective: To learn more about the coordinate system.

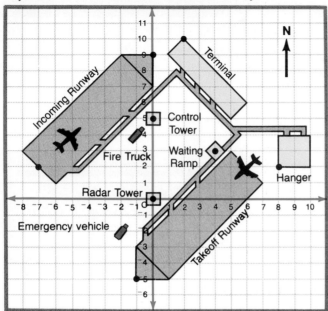

Betty Osborn is an air traffic controller at a local airport. Betty had to pass a Federal Civil Service examination. She received classroom and on-the-job training. As an air traffic controller, Betty directs pilots as they taxi, take off, and land their aircraft. She is part of a team that is responsible for keeping air traffic moving smoothly and safely.

Along with radar, air traffic controllers use ordered pairs to keep track of aircraft. The location of the waiting ramp can be indicated by the ordered pair (4, 3). What ordered pair indicates the location of the emergency vehicle? **(⁻2, ⁻2)**

In mathematics, ordered pairs are used to locate points in a plane. A horizontal number line and a vertical number line intersect at their zero points to form a **coordinate system** for the plane. The horizontal number line is called the **x-axis.** The vertical number line is called the **y-axis.** The point where the two lines intersect is called the **origin.** The number lines separate the plane into four **quadrants.**

The plural of axis is axes.

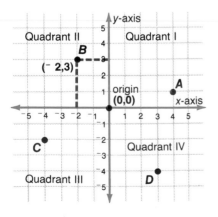

The *x-coordinate* of the ordered pair (⁻2, 3) is ⁻2 and the *y-coordinate* is 3. The dot at (⁻2, 3) is the **graph** of point B.

What are the coordinates of point A? **4 and 1**
What are the coordinates of the points labeled in quadrants III and IV? **⁻4 and ⁻2, 3 and ⁻4**
What are the coordinates of the origin? **0 and 0**

The origin and the x- and y-axes are not in any quadrant.

Exercises

Name the *x*-coordinate and the *y*-coordinate of each ordered pair.

1. A (1, 1)
$x = 1, y = 1$

2. B ($^-$4, 7)
$x = ^-4, y = 7$

3. C ($^-$8, 0)
$x = ^-8, y = 0$

4. D (5, 4)
$x = 5, y = 4$

5. E ($^-$3, $^-$6)
$x = ^-3, y = ^-6$

Name the quadrant that contains the graph of each ordered pair.

6. A (1, 1)
I

7. B ($^-$4, 7)
II

8. C ($^-$8, 0)
none

9. D (5, 4)
I

10. E ($^-$3, $^-$6)
III

11. F (0, $^-$2)
none

12. G ($^-$2, 8)
II

13. H (2, $^-$3)
IV

14. J ($^-$8, $^-$3)
III

15. K (2, $^-$7)
IV

Name the ordered pair that indicates the location of each of the following. Refer to the map on page 398.

16. end of take-off runway ($^-$1, $^-$5)

17. start of take-off runway (6, 2)

18. fire truck ($^-$1, 4)

19. plane on incoming runway ($^-$5, 4)

20. start of incoming runway ($^-$7, 2)

21. northernmost corner of terminal (2, 10)

22. southwest corner of hanger (8, 2)

23. control tower (0, 5)

24. radar tower (0, 0)

25. northwest boundary corner of airport ($^-$9, 11)

Tell how a coordinate system can be used in each occupation.

26. forest ranger
location of fires

27. city planner
location of streets

28. naval commander
location of ships

Draw coordinate axes on graph paper. Then graph each ordered pair. Label each point with the given letter. For answers to exercises 29–44, see Teacher Guide.

29. A (0, 6)

30. B (0, 3)

31. C (4, 3)

32. D (6, 6)

33. E ($^-$1, 0)

34. F ($^-$4, 5)

35. G ($^-$3, $^-$7)

36. H ($^-$3, $^-$3)

37. I (5, $^-$2)

38. J (0, $^-$4)

39. K ($^-$7, $^-$3)

40. L ($^-$5, $^-$5)

41. M ($2\frac{1}{2}$, $^-$1)

42. N ($^-3\frac{1}{3}$, 0)

43. P ($\frac{1}{4}$, $\frac{1}{4}$)

44. Q ($7\frac{3}{4}$, $^-4\frac{1}{2}$)

For answers to exercises 45–53, see Teacher Guide.

Draw coordinate axes on graph paper. Locate these features on the map.

45. control tower (8, 0)

46. radar tower (0, 0)

47. incoming runway; starts at (5, $^-$1); stops at ($^-$1, 7)

48. outgoing runway; starts at ($^-$5, $^-$1); stops at ($^-$5, 9)

49. boundary corners of airport (10, 10), (10, $^-$10), ($^-$10, 10), ($^-$10, $^-$10)

50. emergency equipment station; 8 units north of radar tower

51. hangers; between (8, 0) and (8, $^-$3)

52. terminal; between ($^-$2, 2) and ($^-$2, $^-$2)

53. emergency equipment station; 5 units south of control tower

54. Draw coordinate axes on graph paper. Show a design or plan for one of the following. See students' work.
shopping center   basketball court   park

18-3 Solving for y

Objective: Select values for x and find the corresponding values for y from a linear equation in x and y.

Miriam earns $3.50 per hour making pizzas after school. She works 2, 3, or 4 hours each weekday. On Saturdays, she works 8 hours. The amount of money she earns each day depends on the number of hours worked.

Exercises

A. Make a chart that shows how much Miriam earns for each number of hours worked.

Let x = hours worked

Let y = dollars earned

Then, $y = 3.5x$

y = 3.5x		
x	**3.5x**	**y**
2	3.5(2)	7.0
3	3.5(3)	10.5
4	3.5(4)	14.0
8	3.5(8)	28.0

B. Choose four values for x and find the corresponding values for y in the equation $y = x - 4$.

x	x − 4	y
⁻1	⁻1 − 4	⁻5
0	0 − 4	⁻4
3	3 − 4	⁻1
5	5 − 4	1

C. Choose four values for x and find the corresponding values for y in the equation $y = 2.5x - 3$.

x	2.5x − 3	y	Calculator
0	2.5(0) − 3	⁻3	2.5 ⊠ 0 − 3 ⊟ ⁻3
2	2.5(2) − 3	2	2.5 ⊠ 2 − 3 ⊟ 2
4	2.5(4) − 3	7	2.5 ⊠ 4 − 3 ⊟ 7
⁻2	2.5 (⁻2) − 3	⁻8	2.5 ⊠ 2 ⊘ − 3 ⊟ ⁻8

Basic: 1–10, 12–32 even; Average: 1–34; Enriched: 1–29 odd, 31–34

Exercises

Copy and complete each chart for the given equation.

1. $y = x + 3$

x	x + 3	y
⁻4	⁻4 + 3	⁻1
⁻2	⁻2 + 3	1
0	0 + 3	3
3	3 + 3	6

2. $y = x - 8$

x	x − 8	y
⁻1	⁻1 − 8	⁻9
2	2 − 8	⁻6
4	▩ − 8	⁻4
8	▩ − 8	0

3. $y = 3x - 4$

x	3x − 4	y
⁻2	3(▩) − 4	⁻10
0	3(▩) − 4	⁻4
2	3(▩) − 4	2
3	3(▩) − 4	5

4. $y = \frac{1}{2}x + 1$

x	$\frac{1}{2}x + 1$	y
$^-2$	$\frac{1}{2}(^-2) + 1$	0
0	$\frac{1}{2}(0) + 1$	1
2	$\frac{1}{2}(2) + 1$	2
4	$\frac{1}{2}(4) + 1$	3

5. $y = {}^-2x$

x	^-2x	y
$^-3$	$^-2(^-3)$	6
$^-1$	$^-2(^-1)$	2
0	$^-2(0)$	0
2	$^-2(2)$	$^-4$

6. $y = x - \frac{3}{4}$

x	$x - \frac{3}{4}$	y
$\frac{3}{4}$	$\frac{3}{4} - \frac{3}{4}$	0
1	$1 - \frac{3}{4}$	$\frac{1}{4}$
$\frac{6}{4}$	$\frac{6}{4} - \frac{3}{4}$	$\frac{3}{4}$
2	$2 - \frac{3}{4}$	$1\frac{1}{4}$

For answers to exercises 7–30, see Teacher Guide.

Choose four values for x and find the corresponding values for y in each equation. Write your answers in chart form.

7. $y = 2x$

8. $y = 3x$

9. $y = 5x$

10. $y = {}^-4x$

11. $y = {}^-6x$

12. $y = {}^-x$

13. $y = 3x + 1$

14. $y = 2x - 4$

15. $y = 5x + 5$

16. $y = {}^-x - 1$

17. $y = {}^-4x + 3$

18. $y = {}^-3x - 2$

19. $y = \frac{1}{2}x$

20. $y = \frac{2}{3}x$

21. $y = \frac{3}{4}x$

22. $y = \frac{1}{4}x + 1$

23. $y = \frac{1}{3}x - 2$

24. $y = \frac{4}{3}x - 1$

25. $y = {}^-2x + 3$

26. $y = {}^-4x + 5$

27. $y = {}^-x + 7$

28. $y = -\frac{2}{3}x + 3$

29. $y = {}^-5x + 6$

30. $y = \frac{3}{5}x - 2$

For answers to exercises 31–34, see Teacher Guide.

Write an equation for each situation. Then choose four values for x and find the corresponding values for y in each equation. Write your answers in chart form.

31. Phil's brother is 3 years younger than Phil.
Let x = Phil's age.
Let y = brother's age. $y = x - 3$

32. Molly has 3 dollars more than twice as much money as her sister.
Let x = sister's money.
Let y = Molly's money. $y = 2x + 3$

33. A car rental agency charges $100 per week plus $0.10 per mile. How much would it cost to rent a car for one week?
Let x = miles driven.
Let y = rental cost. $y = 0.1x + 100$

34. Mia earns $4.75 per hour. The amount Mia earns depends on the number of hours worked.
Let x = hours worked.
Let y = dollars earned. $y = 4.75x$

This feature presents general topics of mathematics.

Math Break

A photographer stepped out of a building and walked one mile south, turned and walked one mile east. He took a picture of a bear, turned again and walked one mile north. He then opened a door and stepped back into the same building he had just left. Draw a picture of the path the photographer followed. Where was the photographer? **North Pole**

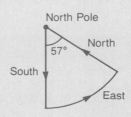

18-4 Graphing Linear Equations

Objective: To graph linear equations.

Two distinct points determine a straight line. If the graph
of an equation is a straight line, the equation is called a
linear equation.

Example

Graph the equation $y = 2x + 3$.

First, choose at least four values for x and
find the corresponding values for y. Record
each result as an ordered pair (x, y).

Next, graph the ordered pairs.

$y = 2x + 3$			
x	$2x + 3$	y	(x, y)
⁻2	2 (⁻2) + 3	⁻1	(⁻2, ⁻1)
⁻1	2 (⁻1) + 3	1	(⁻1, 1)
0	2 (0) + 3	3	(0, 3)
2	2 (2) + 3	7	(2, 7)

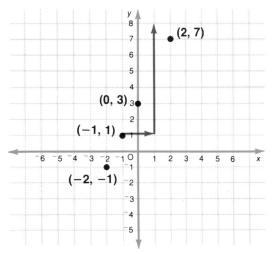

Then, draw a line through the points.
All of the ordered pairs for the points
on the line are **solutions** to the equation.
Write the equation on the graph.

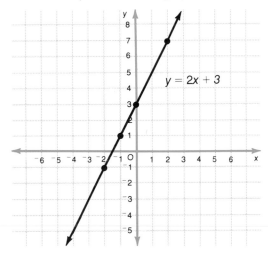

Basic: 1–29 odd; Average: 1–30; Enriched: 2–30 even

Exercises

For graph for exercises 1–2, see Teacher Guide.

**Copy and complete each chart. Then graph each equation on graph paper. Write the
equation on the graph.** Answers may vary. Typical answers are given.

1. $y = x + 4$

x	$x + 4$	y	(x, y)
⁻4	⁻4 + 4	0	(⁻4, 0)
⁻2	⁻2 + 4	2	(⁻2, 2)
0	0 + 4	4	(0, 4)
2	2 + 4	6	(2, 6)

2. $y = {}^-2x$

x	^-2x	y	(x, y)
⁻1	⁻2(⁻1)	2	(⁻1, 2)
0	⁻2(0)	0	(0, 0)
1	⁻2(1)	⁻2	(1, ⁻2)
2	⁻2(2)	⁻4	(2, ⁻4)

402 *The Coordinate Plane*

Graph each equation on graph paper. Write the equation on the graph.

3. $y = 2x$ **4.** $y = \frac{1}{2}x$ **5.** $y = x$ **6.** $y = {}^-3x$

7. $y = {}^-4x$ **8.** $y = \frac{-1}{3}x$ **9.** $y = x + 5$ **10.** $y = x - 6$

Graph each pair of equations on the same coordinate system. Tell whether the graphs intersect. Write yes or no.

11. $y = 2x + 3$ **12.** $y = \frac{2}{3}x$ **13.** $y = x - 5$

$y = 2x - 1$ **no** $y = -\frac{3}{2}x$ **yes** $y = x + 2$ **no**

14. $y = 2x + 3$ **15.** $y = {}^-x + 4$ **16.** $y = 2x$

$y = -\frac{1}{2}x + 3$ **yes** $y = {}^-x - 4$ **no** $y = {}^-3x$ **yes**

Graph each pair of equations on the same coordinate system. Then label their point of intersection with an ordered pair.

17. $y = x + 5$ **18.** $y = 3x - 1$ **19.** $y = \frac{1}{2}x + 4$

$y = {}^-x + 5$ **(0, 5)** $y = {}^-2x + 4$ **(1,2)** $y = 4x - 3$ **(2, 5)**

20. $y = 2x - 1$ **21.** $y = {}^-2x + 3$ **22.** $y = {}^-x + 2.5$

$y = {}^-3x - 1$ **(0, ⁻1)** $y = 3x - 2$ **(1, 1)** $y = x + 0.5$ **(1, 1.5)**

Graph each equation on graph paper.

23. $x + y = 2$ **24.** $y - x = 4$ **25.** $3x - y = 1$ **26.** $y = 3$

27. $x = {}^-1$ **28.** $y = 0$ **29.** $x - y = {}^-2$ **30.** $2x + 3y = 1$

This feature promotes students' mental abilities in computation and reasonableness.

Mental Math

The product of two numbers can be found mentally if the following conditions are true.

● The sum of their last digits total ten.
● Their first digits differ by one.

$$43 \times 37 = (40 + 3)(40 - 3)$$
$$= 1,600 - 9$$
$$= 1,591$$

$$71 \times 69 = (70 + 1)(70 - 1)$$
$$= 4,900 - 1$$
$$= 4,899$$

Find each product using this strategy.

1. 26×34 **2.** 89×91 **3.** 85×75 **4.** 47×53 **5.** 58×62
884 8,099 6,375 2,491 3,596

6. 94×86 **7.** 67×53 **8.** 42×58 **9.** 61×79 **10.** 35×45
8,084 3,551 2,436 4,819 1,575

PRACTICE

Estimate. Answers may vary. Typical answers are given.

1. 438
    − 287
    ___
    100

2. 49
    × 23
    ___
    1,000

3. 651
    + 273
    ___
    1,000

4. 123
    × 78
    ___
    8,000

5. $\overset{30}{17\overline{)563}}$

Add, subtract, multiply, or divide.

6. 484 + 79
   563

7. 5.68 − 2.39
   3.29

8. 34.7 × 0.35
   12.145

9. 88 ÷ 1.1
   80

10. 36 − 2.83
    33.17

Add, subtract, multiply, or divide.

11. $1\frac{3}{4} + 2\frac{1}{3}$ $4\frac{1}{12}$

12. $6\frac{7}{8} - \frac{3}{4}$ $6\frac{1}{8}$

13. $1\frac{1}{2} \times \frac{7}{9}$ $1\frac{1}{6}$

14. $28 \div 1\frac{3}{4}$ 16

15. $3\frac{3}{5} - 1\frac{7}{8}$ $1\frac{29}{40}$

16. 100 × 0.386
    38.6

17. 53.8 ÷ 1,000
    0.0538

18. 10 × 0.009
    0.09

19. 0.843 ÷ 10
    0.0843

Complete.

20. 4.3 m = ▧ cm 430

21. 428 cm = ▧ m 4.28

22. $3\frac{1}{2}$ gal = ▧ qt 14

Change each decimal to a percent. Change each percent to a decimal.

23. 16% 0.16

24. 2.4 240%

25. $7\frac{3}{4}$% 0.0775

26. 0.085 8.5%

27. 31.6% 0.316

Solve.

28. 145% of 65 94.25

29. $3\frac{1}{2}$% of 150 5.25

30. 0.5% of 82 0.41

Use the proportion $\frac{P}{B} = \frac{r}{100}$ to solve each problem.

31. 12 is what percent of 72? $16\frac{2}{3}$%

32. 24 is 75 percent of what number? 32

Find the perimeter of each figure.

33.

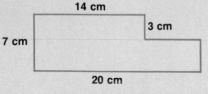

14 cm

3 cm

7 cm

20 cm

54 cm

34.

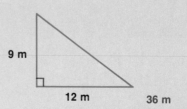

9 m

12 m

36 m

Find the area of each figure. Use 3.14 for π. Round decimal answers to the nearest tenth.

35.

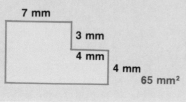

7 mm

3 mm

4 mm

4 mm

65 mm²

36.

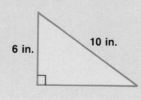

6 in.

10 in.

24 in²

37.

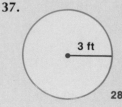

3 ft

28.26 ft²

Find the volume of each solid. Use 3.14 for π. Round each decimal answer to the nearest tenth.

38.

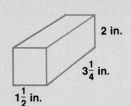

2 in.

$3\frac{1}{4}$ in.

$1\frac{1}{2}$ in. $9\frac{3}{4}$ in³

39.

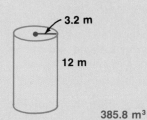

3.2 m

12 m

385.8 m³

Add, subtract, multiply, or divide.

40. ⁻3 + 8 5   **41.** ⁻6 − ⁻5 ⁻1   **42.** ⁻6 + ⁻4 ⁻10   **43.** ⁻3 × 16 ⁻48

44. ⁻5 − 8 ⁻13   **45.** 12 − ⁻3 15   **46.** ⁻5 × ⁻7 35   **47.** ⁻18 ÷ 6 ⁻3

Use the grid at the right to find the letter for each ordered pair or to find the ordered pair for each letter.

48. (3, 4) A   **49.** D (2, 0)

50. (5, 1) E   **51.** (2, 0) D

52. B (4, 3)   **53.** A (3, 4)

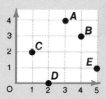

Solve each equation and check your solutions.

54. $n + 8 = 15$ **55.** $2n = 7$ **56.** $n - 3\frac{1}{2} = 5$ $n = 8\frac{1}{2}$ **57.** $\frac{n}{4} = 1.8$
  $n = 7$ $n = 3.5$ $n = 7.2$

58. $2n + 3 = 17$ **59.** $\frac{n}{3} - 4 = ⁻8$ **60.** $5n - 6 = ⁻9$ **61.** $\frac{n}{6} + 3 = 7$
  $n = 7$ $n = ⁻12$ $n = -\frac{3}{5}$ $n = 24$

Solve each inequality and check a solution. Then graph each solution set on a number line. For answers to exercises 62–69, see Teacher Guide.

62. $n - 3 < ⁻5$ **63.** $n + 6 > ⁻4$ **64.** $2n > 7.8$ **65.** $3n - 1 < ⁻3$
  $n < ⁻2$ $n > ⁻10$ $n > 3.9$ $n < -\frac{2}{3}$

66. $4n + 3 > 6$ **67.** $\frac{n}{5} - 2 < ⁻4$ **68.** $\frac{n}{4} < 9$ **69.** $\frac{n}{2} + 6 > 5$
  $n > \frac{3}{4}$ $n < ⁻10$ $n < 36$ $n > ⁻2$

Solve.

70. Gary works 15 hours a week trimming hedges. He earns $3.50 an hour. What is his weekly pay?
$52.50

71. Keiko wants to move a 34-pound lamp 9 feet, 9 inches. How much work is needed? Use the formula $W = F \times d$. $W = 331\frac{1}{2}$ **foot-pounds**

72. A circular field measures 376.8 meters in circumference. What is the length of the diameter of the field? Use the formula $C = \pi \times d$. Use 3.14 for π. $d = 120m$

73. A beginning runner buys running shoes at $45.62, socks at $3.07, and a shirt at $12.98. How much change does she get after giving the cashier four $20 bills? $18.33

18-5   Reading Graphs

Objective: To obtain information by reading a graph.

Karen Mays is developing film. She has to maintain a constant 20° Celsius temperature in the chemical solutions. Karen has only a Fahrenheit thermometer. What Fahrenheit temperature corresponds to 20° Celsius?

The linear equation $F = \frac{9}{5} C + 32$ is graphed below. The C-axis represents degrees Celsius and the F-axis represents degrees Fahrenheit. The graph can be used to estimate readings on one temperature scale when the reading on the other temperature scale is known.

Examples

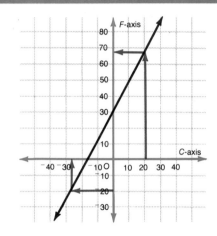

A. Estimate the Fahrenheit reading that corresponds to 20°C.

Find 20° on the C-axis. Move vertically to the diagonal line. Then move horizontally to the F-axis. The Fahrenheit reading is about 68°.

B. Estimate the Celsius reading that corresponds to ⁻20°F.

Find ⁻20° on the F-axis. Move horizontally to the diagonal line. Then move vertically to the C-axis. The Celsius reading is about ⁻29°.

The graphs of some equations are curved. Consider the graph of the equation $y = x^2 - 5$ shown in the following example.

Example

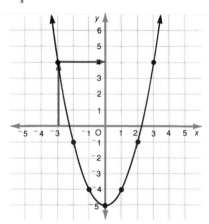

C. Find the value of y when x is ⁻3.

Find ⁻3 on the x-axis. Move vertically to the curved line. Then move horizontally to the y-axis. The value of y is 4 when x is ⁻3.

406   *The Coordinate Plane*

Exercises

For exercises 1–23, use the Celsius-Fahrenheit graph on page 406.
Estimate the Celsius reading for each Fahrenheit reading.

1. 40°F **4°C**   2. ⁻16°F **⁻27°C**   3. 4°F **⁻16°C**   4. 20°F **⁻7°C**   5. ⁻35°F **⁻37°C**

6. ⁻28°F **⁻33°C**   7. 0°F **⁻18°C**   8. 32°F **0°C**   9. 24°F **⁻4°C**   10. ⁻20°F **⁻29°C**

Estimate the Fahrenheit reading for each Celsius reading.

11. 8°C **46°F**   12. ⁻8°C **18°F**   13. ⁻32°C **⁻26°F**   14. 35°C **95°F**   15. ⁻16°C **3°F**

16. ⁻40°C **⁻40°F**   17. 0°C **32°F**   18. ⁻4°C **25°F**   19. 16°C **61°F**   20. 4°C **39°F**

Answer the following.

21. The graph crosses the C-axis at ⁻18°.
What is the value of F at ⁻18°C?
0°F

22. The graph crosses the F-axis at 32°.
What is the value of C at 32°F?
0°C

23. At what temperature are the Fahrenheit and Celsius readings the same?
⁻40°

The graph at the right shows the height of a baseball after it has been thrown into the air. The height depends on the number of seconds since the baseball was thrown.

24. How high is the baseball after 1 second? $7\frac{1}{2}$ ft

25. How high is the baseball after 4 seconds? **6 ft**

26. How high does the baseball go?
8 ft

27. How many seconds after the baseball is thrown does it reach its highest point?
2 s

28. How many seconds after the baseball is thrown does it hit the ground? **6 s**

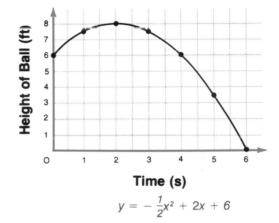

Time (s)

$$y = -\frac{1}{2}x^2 + 2x + 6$$

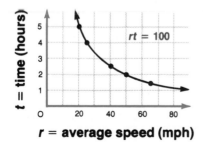

r = **average speed (mph)**

The graph at the left shows the time it takes to travel 100 miles at various speeds. The time it takes depends on the average speed.
Answers may vary. Typical answers are given.

29. How long does it take to travel 100 miles at an average speed of 55 mph? **1.8 h**

30. How long does it take to travel 100 miles at an average speed of 40 mph? $2\frac{1}{2}$h

31. What should your average speed be if you want to travel 100 miles in 2 hours? **50 mph**

32. What should your average speed be if you want to travel 100 miles in $1\frac{3}{4}$ hours? **57 mph**

33. Can you travel 100 miles in 0 hours?

How could the graph show this?
no, extend graph further to right

18-6 Using Coordinates

Objective: To identify or graph a reflection, rotation, translation, or dilation of a figure in a coordinate plane.

By moving all the points of a figure according to certain rules, new images can be formed. Some are shown below.

A figure can be **reflected,** or flipped about a line.

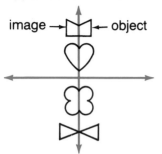

Think of an object and its image in a mirror.

A figure can be **rotated,** or turned around a point.

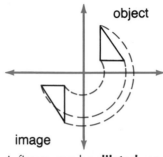

Think of an object as being on a wheel that turns.

A figure can be **translated,** or slid, in a plane.

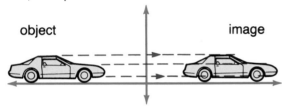

Think of an object as being pushed from one place to another.

A figure can be **dilated,** or changed in size.

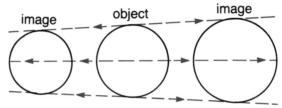

Think of a zoom lens on a camera. The image can be made larger or smaller.

Examples

A. Find a reflection of △ABC about the vertical axis.

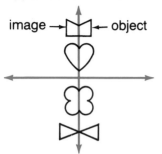

Study the triangle shown on the coordinate plane at the left.
It has vertices at points $A(1, 1)$, $B(2, 4)$, and $C(4, 1)$.

Suppose you multiply the first coordinate of each vertex by ⁻1.

$A(1, 1)$ ➡ $D(^-1, 1)$
$B(2, 4)$ ➡ $E(^-2, 4)$
$C(4, 1)$ ➡ $F(^-4, 1)$

Triangle *DEF* is a *reflection,* or flip, of △*ABC* about the vertical axis.

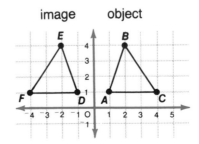

The object and its image are symmetrical with respect to the *y*-axis.
The object and its image are congruent.

408   *The Coordinate Plane*

B. Find a rotation of △ABC about the origin.

Suppose you multiply both coordinates of each vertex of △ABC by ⁻1.

A(1, 1) ⟹ G(⁻1, ⁻1)

B(2, 4) ⟹ H(⁻2, ⁻4)

C(4, 1) ⟹ I(⁻4, ⁻1)

Triangle GHI is a half-turn rotation about the origin.

The object and its image are congruent.

C. Find a translation downward of △ABC.

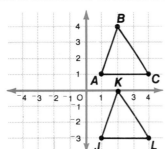

Suppose you add ⁻4 to the second coordinate of each vertex.

A(1, 1) ⟹ J(1, ⁻3)

B(2, 4) ⟹ K(2, 0)

C(4, 1) ⟹ L(4, ⁻3)

Triangle JKL is a *translation*, or slide, of △ABC down 4 units.

The object and its image are congruent.

D. Find a dilation of triangle MNP.

Suppose you multiply both coordinates of each vertex by 2.

M(2, 3) ⟹ Q(4, 6)

N(6, 1) ⟹ S(12, 2)

R(7, 3) ⟹ T(14, 6)

Triangle QST is a dilation of △MNR.

The object and its image are similar.

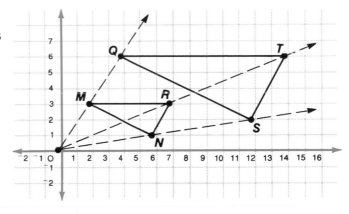

Basic: 1–12; Average: 1–14; Enriched: 1–14

Exercises

State whether each pair of figures shows a reflection, a translation, a rotation, or a dilation.

1.

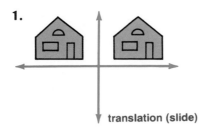

translation (slide)

2.

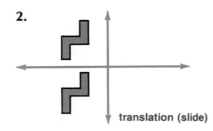

translation (slide)

3.

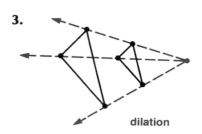

dilation

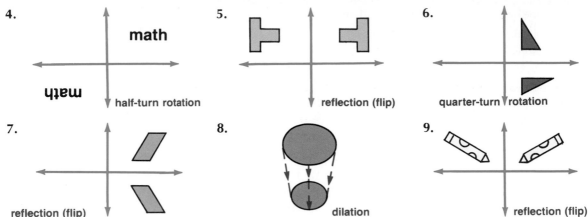

4.

math

ɥʇɐɯ

half-turn rotation

5.

reflection (flip)

6.

quarter-turn rotation

7.

reflection (flip)

8.

dilation

9.

reflection (flip)

For graphs to exercises 10–14, see Teacher Guide.

Draw coordinate axes on graph paper. Then complete the following. Label each drawing as a reflection, a translation, a rotation, or a dilation.

10. Draw a triangle that has vertices at $P(^-3, 2)$, $Q(^-1, 1)$, and $R(0, 4)$. Then add 5 to the first coordinate of each vertex. Draw the new triangle. **translation**

11. Draw a triangle that has vertices at $X(^-4, 2)$, $Y(^-3, 4)$, and $Z(^-1, 0)$. Draw the reflection of $\triangle XYZ$ about the vertical axis. Then write the coordinates of each new vertex.

12. Draw a triangle that has vertices at $A(2, 1)$, $B(1, 3)$, and $C(3, 4)$. Multiply both coordinates of each vertex by 2. Draw the new triangle. **dilation**

13. Draw a triangle that has vertices at $A(2, 1)$, $B(1, 3)$, and $C(3, 4)$. Draw the quarter-turn rotation image $\triangle DEF$ about the origin.

14. Draw a rectangle that has vertices at $K(1, 1)$, $L(4, 1)$, $M(4, 3)$, and $N(1, 3)$. Draw the 180° rotation image about the origin.

This feature presents useful ways of solving mathematical problems on a calculator.

 Calculator

Use your calculator to find $7,807 - 89$ and $196 \div 14$. As you find each answer, turn your calculator upside down and read the word formed. What kind of transformation did you use when you turned the calculator? $\frac{1}{2}$-**turn rotation**

Use a calculator to solve the following. Rotate the calculator a half-turn and read the word formed.

1. $1,547 \times 5$ **sell**

2. $81 \div 9 \times 70 + 7$ **leg**

3. $(36 - 19) \times (12 \div 4)$ **is**

4. $976 - 649 + 11$ **bee**

5. $(236 \times 14) + 269$ **else**

6. $357 \times 202 + 67 \times 78 + 5$ **shell**

7. $(2,309)^2 + 220^2 + 6^2 + 1^2 + 1^2$ **giggles**

8. $(8 \times 77)^2 + (3 \times 7)^2 + 11$ **boggle**

This feature provides general topics about the uses of a computer.

Computer

Inside a computer, only two digits are used to represent numbers. These digits are 0 and 1. These are called **binary digits** or **bits.** These two digits are used in a **base two,** or **binary,** number system.

A computer contains many tiny electronic switches. When a switch is on (current is flowing), it represents 1. When a switch is off (current is not flowing), it represents 0. Thus, a series of switches can be used to represent a number. For example, consider 5.

on
off

$(101)_{two} = (5)_{ten}$

Notice the following correspondence among binary (base two) numbers, decimal (base ten) numerals, and powers of two.

Base Two	Base Ten	Power of 2
0001	1	2^0
0010	2	2^1
0100	4	2^2
1000	8	2^3

How could you combine two of the numbers above to represent 3?

$$0001 + 0010 = 0011$$
$$1 \quad + \quad 2 \quad = \quad 3$$

What number does this represent? 0 1 1 1

$$0001 + 0010 + 0100 = 0111$$
$$1 \quad + \quad 2 \quad + \quad 4 \quad = \quad 7$$

Change each of the following to a base two numeral.

1. 5 0101　　　**2.** 9 1001　　　**3.** 11 1011　　　**4.** 12 1100　　　**5.** 15 1111

6. 6 0110　　　**7.** 14 1110　　　**8.** 10 1010　　　**9.** 13 1101　　　**10.** 7 0111

Change each of the following to a base ten numeral.

11. 10011 19　　　**12.** 10110 22　　　**13.** 10000 16　　　**14.** 10010 18　　　**15.** 11111 31

16. 10111 23　　　**17.** 11101 29　　　**18.** 10101 21　　　**19.** 100110 38　　　**20.** 100001 33

18-7 Problem Solving: Using Graphs

Objective: To solve problems using graphs.

Wade Garrett began a 700-mile
trip with 150 gallons of fuel in his
truck's fuel tanks. During the first
100 miles, the truck used 20 gallons
of fuel. During the next 150 miles,
it used 30 gallons of fuel. Was it
necessary for Wade to refuel his
truck before the end of his trip?

 Read

You need to know the amount of fuel
used in 700 miles. You know the
amount of fuel the tanks contained,
how much fuel was used in the first
100 miles, and how much fuel was used
in the next 150 miles. Assume that
the truck used fuel at the same rate
for the entire trip.

 Decide

One way to solve the problem is to
graph the given information. Then
read the graph to find the amount of
fuel used in 700 miles.

 Solve

Let the horizontal axis represent
distance in miles. Let the vertical
axis represent fuel used in gallons.
Find and graph the ordered pairs.
(100, 20), and (250, 50)
100 mi + 150 mi = 250 mi, 20 gal + 30 gal = 50 gal
Then draw the line through these points.

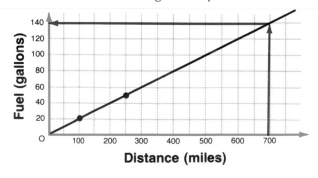

On the graph, 700 miles corresponds to 140
gallons of fuel. Wade should have had a
ten-gallon reserve at the end of the trip.

Examine You can check the solution by working backwards. Graph the ordered pairs (700, 140) and (250, 50). Draw a line through the points. The line also goes through the point (100, 20). The answer is correct.

Basic: 1–4; Average: 1–7; Enriched: 1–7

Exercises

Name two ordered pairs (x, y) that can be used to graph the information in each exercise. Do *not* solve.

1. Ryan measures the height of the steps in an office building. The third step is 1.5 feet above the floor. The fifth step is 2.5 feet above the floor. What is the height of the 17th step?
(3, 1.5), (5, 2.5)

2. Mr. Martin drives at a constant rate for 7 hours. After 1 hour he has driven 50 miles. After $2\frac{1}{2}$ hours he has driven 125 miles. How many miles does he drive in 7 hours?
(1, 50), ($2\frac{1}{2}$, 125)

Use a graph to solve each problem. Assume that the rate is constant in each problem. For answers to exercises 3–6, see Teacher Guide.

3. After driving 3 hours, Myra checks the odometer in her car. She has traveled 150 miles. After 2 more hours, Myra has traveled a total distance of 250 miles. How many more hours must Myra travel to cover a total distance of 400 miles?
3 more hours

5. Kim cuts lawns during the summer to earn extra money. After working for $1\frac{1}{2}$ hours, Kim has earned $6. After working $2\frac{1}{2}$ hours longer, Kim has earned a total of $16. How much is she paid per hour? How much will Kim earn if she works 7 hours in all? $4, $28

4. A cricket begins chirping when the temperature is about 37°F. When the temperature is 60°F, the cricket chirps about 93 times per minute. What is the approximate temperature when the cricket chirps 175 times per minute? 80°F

6. When Rosa arrived at work there were 60 completed letters on her desk. After she worked for 2 hours Rosa had a total of 220 letters completed. How many completed letters did she have after her first hour of work? How many completed letters did she have after she worked $4\frac{1}{2}$ hours?
140 letters, 420 letters

Solve. Use the graph at the right.

7. A small plane can carry 2,175 pounds of people, cargo, and fuel. The graph shows the pounds of fuel needed to fly a certain number of hours. Suppose the plane carries 495 pounds of cargo and 5 people who weigh a total of 766 pounds. About how many hours of flying time are possible? almost 5 hours

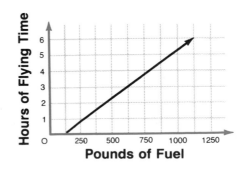

CHAPTER 18 REVIEW

Write the letter of the term that best matches each description.

1. names the location of a point on a grid e

2. horizontal distance of a point from zero k

3. vertical distance of a point from zero m

4. two perpendicular number lines in a plane that intersect at (0, 0) a

5. intersection of x-axis and y-axis f

6. an equation whose graph is a straight line d

7. mirror-image of a figure g

8. turns a figure about a point h

9. slides a figure in a plane i

10. changes the size of a figure b

a. coordinate system
b. dilation
c. graph
d. linear equation
e. ordered pair
f. origin
g. reflection
h. rotation
i. translation
j. x-axis
k. x-coordinate
l. y-axis
m. y-coordinate

Exercises

Use the grid to find the letter for each ordered pair.   Page 397

11. (0, 2) E

12. (5, 2) G

13. (2, 3) C

14. (3, 1) K

15. (6, 4) A

16. (4, 0) I

Use the grid to find the ordered pair for each letter.   Page 397

17. F (2, 6)

18. B (5, 7)

19. J (3, 5)

20. L (1, 4)

21. H (6, 6)

22. D (6, 1)

For answers to exercises 23–30, see Teacher Guide.

Draw a coordinate axis on paper. Then graph each ordered pair. Label each point with the given letter.   Page 399

23. A(5, 1)

24. B(1, $^-$5)

25. C($^-$3, 3)

26. D(0, 5)

27. E(0, 0)

28. F($^-$6, $^-$4)

29. G(2.5, $^-$2)

30. H(1$\frac{1}{2}$, 3$\frac{1}{2}$)

Copy and complete each chart for the given equation.   Pages 400–401

31. $y = x - 4$

x	x − 4	y
$^-$3	$^-$3 − 4	$^-$7
$^-$1	$^-$1 − 4	$^-$5
1	1 − 4	$^-$3
2	2 − 4	$^-$2

32. $y = 2x + 2$

x	2x + 2	y
$^-$2	2($^-$2) + 2	$^-$2
$^-$1	2($^-$1) + 2	0
0	2(0) + 2	2
1	2(1) + 2	4

33. $y = {}^-3x + 1$

x	$^-$3x + 1	y
$^-$1	$^-$3($^-$1) + 1	4
0	$^-$3(0) + 1	1
2	$^-$3(2) + 1	$^-$5
3	$^-$3(3) + 1	$^-$8

For answers to exercises 34–37, see Teacher Guide.

Graph each equation on graph paper. Write the equation on the graph. Pages 402–403

34. $y = 3x$ **35.** $y = 2x - 2$ **36.** $y = {}^-x - 4$ **37.** $x + y = 1$

For answers to exercises 38–40, see Teacher Guide.

Graph each pair of equations on the same coordinate system. Tell whether the graphs intersect. Write yes or no. Pages 402–403

38. $y = x - 4$
   $y = {}^-x + 4$ yes

39. $y = 2x - 1$
   $y = 2x + 1$ no

40. $y = x + 4$
   $y = {}^-x - 2$ yes

State whether each pair of figures shows a reflection, a translation, a rotation, or dilation. Pages 408–410

41.
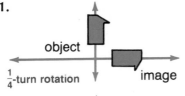
$\frac{1}{4}$-turn rotation

42.
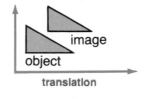
translation

43.

reflection

44.
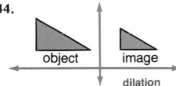
dilation

45.
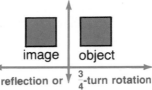
reflection or $\frac{3}{4}$-turn rotation

46.
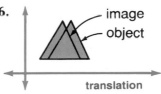
translation

Complete.

47. Three vertices of a rectangle have coordinates of (2, 1), (7, 1), and (7, 4). Graph the three given points; locate the fourth vertex; draw the rectangle. (2, 4); For answer to exercise 47, see Teacher Guide.

49. The graph at the right represents the dimensions of all rectangles with an area of 4 square meters. Use the graph to estimate the width of the rectangle if the length is 4 meters.

For answers to exercises 50–54, see Teacher Guide.

A triangle has vertices of A(2, 1), B(3, 3), and C(5, 2).

50. Draw $\triangle ABC$.   **51.** Draw a half-turn rotation of $\triangle ABC$.

52. Draw the reflection of $\triangle ABC$ about the y-axis.

53. Draw the translation of $\triangle ABC$ 3 units to the left. Then find the coordinates of each new vertex.

54. Find a dilation of $\triangle ABC$. Multiply both coordinates of each vertex by 2. Draw the new triangle.

48. Edna's age y is 26 years more than her son Carl's age x. Write an equation to show their age relationship. Find four ordered pairs to represent their ages at different times. Draw a graph. For typical answers to exercise 48, see Teacher Guide.

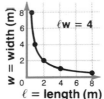

49. 1 meter. Answers may vary. Typical answer is given.

CHAPTER 18 TEST

Use the grid to find the letter for each ordered pair.

1. (2, 2) **D**   **2.** (3, 5) **E**   **3.** (1, 3) **B**

Use the grid to find the ordered pair for each letter.

4. C (5, 4)   **5.** G (5, 0)   **6.** A (6, 6)

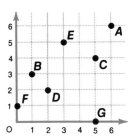

Draw coordinate axes on graph paper. Then graph each ordered pair. Label each point with the given letter. For answers to exercises 7–11, see Teacher Guide.

7. A(0, 4)   **8.** B(3, ⁻1)   **9.** C(⁻2, ⁻3)   **10.** D(1.5, 2)   **11.** E($2\frac{1}{2}$, ⁻4)

12. Copy and complete the chart at the right for the equation $y = 2x - 3$.

x	2x − 3	y
⁻2	2(⁻2) − 3	⁻7
⁻1	2(⁻1) − 3	⁻5
0	2(0) − 3	⁻3

For typical answers to exercises 13–15, see Teacher Guide.

Choose four values for x and find the corresponding values for y in each equation. Write your answers in chart form.

13. $y = 3x - 5$ **14.** $y = \frac{⁻3}{4}x + 2$ **15.** $y = 1.2x$

Graph each equation on graph paper. Write the equation on the graph. For answers to exercises 16–18, see Teacher Guide.

16. $x - y = 2$ **17.** $y = 3x - 2$ **18.** $2x + y = ⁻3$

19. Graph the equations $y = x - 2$ and $y = ⁻x + 4$ on the same coordinate system. Then describe what their relationship appears to be. For answers to exercise 19, see Teacher Guide.

State whether each pair of figures shows a reflection, a translation, a rotation, or a dilation.

20.

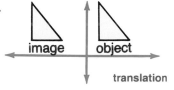

translation

21.

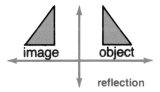

reflection

22.

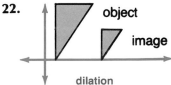

dilation

Complete. For answer to exercise 24, see Teacher Guide.

23. Mr. O'Reilly has two jobs. The first job pays $100 a week more than the second job. His total earnings are $380 per week. How much does he earn from each job? **$140, $240**

24. Draw a triangle that has vertices at A(1, 1), B(3, ⁻2), and C(4, 0). Draw the translation of △ABC upwards by 2 units. Then write the coordinates of each new vertex. **(1, 3), (3, 0), (4, 2)**

CUMULATIVE REVIEW

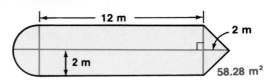

12 m
2 m
2 m
58.28 m²

1. The floor shown at the right is to be tiled. What is the area to be tiled? Pages 274–275

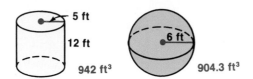

5 ft
12 ft
942 ft³

6 ft
904.3 ft³

2. Which of the two solids at the left has the greater volume? How much greater? Pages 298–299 cylinder 37.7 ft³

Name the operation that should be done first. Then solve.   Pages 322–323

3. $6 \times {}^-3 + 8$
multiply, ⁻10

4. $(17 - 3) \div 2$
subtract, 7

5. $9 \times 8 \div 4$
multiply, 18

6. $(52 + 11) \div 7$
add, 9

7. $105 \div 15 \times 6 + 2$
divide, 44

8. $(81 - 9) \div 2 \times (8 - 3)$
subtract, 180

Solve.   Pages 348–349, 367–368

9. Time and a half ($1\frac{1}{2} \times$ normal salary) is the wage paid for overtime. Joan Hudson earns $4.00 an hour. She worked 43 hours last week, 3 of which were overtime. How much did she earn last week? $178.00

10. Jorge is looking at the top of a building that is 20 feet from him. He is 6 feet tall, and the building is 48 feet tall. What is the measure of the line of sight? 46.52 ft

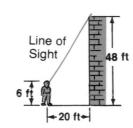

Line of Sight
48 ft
6 ft
20 ft

Express each number in scientific notation.   Pages 388–389

11. 250,000
2.5 × 10⁵

12. 890
8.9 × 10²

13. 6,090,000
6.09 × 10⁶

14. 47,300
4.73 × 10⁴

Choose four values for x and find the corresponding values for y in each equation. Write your answers in chart form.   Pages 400–401 For answers to exercises 15–17, see Teacher Guide.

15. $y = -\frac{3}{8}x + 1$

16. $y = 6x$

17. $y = \frac{1}{2}x + 2$

Use a graph to solve each problem. Assume that the rate is constant in each problem.   Pages 412–413 For graphs for exercises 18–19, see Teacher Guide.

18. Joe is climbing a mountain 10,000 ft tall. In 5 hours, he has traveled a total distance of 1,250 ft. After six more hours, he has traveled 1,500 ft more. In how many more hours will he reach the top of the mountain? 40 h

19. Mrs. Moore baked 6 cakes in 3 hours. She worked for 2 more hours, and had baked a total of 10 cakes. How many cakes had she baked after $2\frac{1}{2}$ hours? How many cakes had she baked after 6 hours? 5 cakes, 12 cakes

Basic Skills Appendix

Place Value

The chart shows the place value occupied by each digit in 2,365,789.

The 3 is in the hundred thousands place-value position.

billions	hundred millions	ten millions	millions	hundred thousands	ten thousands	thousands	hundreds	tens	ones
			2	3	6	5	7	8	9
			2	0	0	0	0	0	0
			3	0	0	0	0	0	0
				6	0	0	0	0	0
					5	0	0	0	0
						7	0	0	0
							8	0	0
								9	

Digit × Place-Value Position	▶	Number Named
3 × 100,000	▶	300,000
5 × 1,000	▶	__?__ 5,000
7 × __?__ 100	▶	__?__ 700

Name the place-value position for each of the following digits in 2,305,789.

1. the 5 1,000
2. the 8 10
3. the 2 1,000,000
4. the 7 100
5. the 3 100,000
6. the 9 1

Name the digit in each of the following place-value positions in 5,162,340.

7. millions 5
8. ten thousands 6
9. thousands 2
10. hundreds 3
11. hundred thousands 1
12. tens 4

Numbers can be interpreted in several ways. The place-value positions give other ways to name numbers.

Possible Names

Place Values ▶				
6	0	0	0	6 thousands or 60 hundreds or 600 tens or 6000 ones
	2	0	0	2 hundreds or 20 tens or 200 ones
		4	0	4 tens or 40 ones
			8	8 ones

Give the numeral for each of the following.

13. 4 thousands 4,000
14. 30 hundreds 3,000
15. 900 tens 9,000
16. 15 hundreds 1,500
17. 29 thousands 29,000
18. 75 tens 750
19. 250 tens 2,500
20. 720 hundreds 72,000
21. 20 thousands 20,000
22. 483 thousands 483,000
23. 2,456 tens 24,560
24. 5,285 hundreds 528,500

Addition

Always add in each place-value position from the least to the greatest.

First, add the *ones*.

$$
\begin{array}{r}
1 \\
297 \\
104 \\
+\ 582 \\
\hline
3
\end{array}
$$

How is the 13 recorded?

Next, add the *tens*.

$$
\begin{array}{r}
1\ 1 \\
297 \\
104 \\
+\ 582 \\
\hline
83
\end{array}
$$

How is 18 tens recorded?

Then, add the *hundreds*.

$$
\begin{array}{r}
1\ 1 \\
297 \\
104 \\
+\ 582 \\
\hline
983
\end{array}
$$

What is the sum?

Find the sum.

1. $\begin{array}{r}43\\+\ 6\\\hline 49\end{array}$	**2.** $\begin{array}{r}20\\+\ 8\\\hline 28\end{array}$	**3.** $\begin{array}{r}91\\+\ 7\\\hline 98\end{array}$	**4.** $\begin{array}{r}45\\+\ 23\\\hline 68\end{array}$	**5.** $\begin{array}{r}62\\+\ 25\\\hline 87\end{array}$
6. $\begin{array}{r}309\\+\ 40\\\hline 349\end{array}$	**7.** $\begin{array}{r}700\\+\ 37\\\hline 737\end{array}$	**8.** $\begin{array}{r}874\\+\ 23\\\hline 897\end{array}$	**9.** $\begin{array}{r}621\\+\ 138\\\hline 759\end{array}$	**10.** $\begin{array}{r}413\\+\ 453\\\hline 866\end{array}$
11. $\begin{array}{r}43\\+\ 8\\\hline 51\end{array}$	**12.** $\begin{array}{r}56\\+\ 6\\\hline 62\end{array}$	**13.** $\begin{array}{r}67\\+\ 8\\\hline 75\end{array}$	**14.** $\begin{array}{r}74\\+\ 67\\\hline 141\end{array}$	**15.** $\begin{array}{r}39\\+\ 58\\\hline 97\end{array}$
16. $\begin{array}{r}453\\+\ 87\\\hline 540\end{array}$	**17.** $\begin{array}{r}629\\+\ 95\\\hline 724\end{array}$	**18.** $\begin{array}{r}186\\+\ 85\\\hline 271\end{array}$	**19.** $\begin{array}{r}438\\+\ 292\\\hline 730\end{array}$	**20.** $\begin{array}{r}649\\+\ 393\\\hline 1{,}042\end{array}$
21. $\begin{array}{r}1{,}035\\+\ 815\\\hline 1{,}850\end{array}$	**22.** $\begin{array}{r}6{,}197\\+\ 976\\\hline 7{,}173\end{array}$	**23.** $\begin{array}{r}3{,}567\\+\ 294\\\hline 3{,}861\end{array}$	**24.** $\begin{array}{r}1{,}829\\+\ 9{,}383\\\hline 11{,}212\end{array}$	**25.** $\begin{array}{r}7{,}459\\+\ 5{,}649\\\hline 13{,}108\end{array}$
26. $\begin{array}{r}246\\4{,}075\\+\ 8{,}137\\\hline 12{,}458\end{array}$	**27.** $\begin{array}{r}12{,}647\\5{,}310\\+\ 9{,}283\\\hline 27{,}240\end{array}$	**28.** $\begin{array}{r}9{,}760\\20{,}248\\+\ 4{,}512\\\hline 34{,}520\end{array}$	**29.** $\begin{array}{r}37{,}005\\3{,}927\\+\ 17{,}481\\\hline 58{,}413\end{array}$	**30.** $\begin{array}{r}62{,}900\\40{,}283\\+\ 98{,}059\\\hline 201{,}242\end{array}$

31. 405 + 63   **468**

32. 216 + 350   **566**

33. 1,066 + 325   **1,391**

34. 205 + 4,379   **4,584**

35. 6,128 + 5,967   **12,095**

36. 3,852 + 6,979   **10,831**

37. 18 + 721 + 295   **1,034**

38. 819 + 2,073 + 7,465   **10,357**

39. 50,980 + 1,075 + 9,428   **61,483**

40. 347 + 8,706 + 71   **9,124**

41. 82 + 370 + 4,285   **4,737**

42. 367 + 9 + 78   **454**

43. 9,200 + 1,452 + 16   **10,668**

44. 95 + 2,861 + 307   **3,263**

45. 2,743 + 182 + 360   **3,285**

46. 59 + 3,842 + 175   **4,076**

47. 294 + 87 + 6,003   **6,384**

48. 609 + 8,741 + 76   **9,426**

49. 2,824 + 71 + 603   **3,498**

50. 97 + 3,701 + 659   **4,457**

51. 89 + 5,027 + 439   **5,555**

52. 1,954 + 37 + 648   **2,639**

53. 4,098 + 155 + 27   **4,280**

54. 803 + 71 + 6,428   **7,302**

55. 67 + 783 + 7,160   **8,010**

56. 704 + 35 + 9,108   **9,847**

57. 859 + 127 + 366   **1,352**

Subtraction

Subtract in each place-value position from least to greatest.

First, subtract the *ones*.

```
    785
  − 392
      3
```

Next, subtract the *tens*.

```
    6 18
    7̶85
  − 392
     93
```

Subtract the *hundreds*.

```
    6 18
    7̶85
  − 392
    393
```

You cannot subtract 9 tens from 8 tens.
So, rename the hundreds and tens.
7 hundreds is 6 hundreds and 10 tens.
Then, 10 tens + 8 tens = 18 tens.

Subtract.

1. 47 − 4 = 43	**2.** 69 − 3 = 66	**3.** 87 − 52 = 35	**4.** 46 − 31 = 15	**5.** 529 − 217 = 312
6. 6,243 − 10 = 6,233	**7.** 5,749 − 25 = 5,724	**8.** 6,862 − 730 = 6,132	**9.** 8,398 − 287 = 8,111	**10.** 9,867 − 2,026 = 7,841
11. 53 − 8 = 45	**12.** 41 − 6 = 35	**13.** 85 − 27 = 58	**14.** 94 − 46 = 48	**15.** 673 − 235 = 438
16. 826 − 686 = 140	**17.** 549 − 384 = 165	**18.** 4,925 − 751 = 4,174	**19.** 6,381 − 138 = 6,243	**20.** 7,521 − 4,003 = 3,518
21. 324 − 186 = 138	**22.** 762 − 295 = 467	**23.** 436 − 178 = 258	**24.** 853 − 677 = 176	**25.** 541 − 274 = 267
26. 1,236 − 853 = 383	**27.** 1,584 − 729 = 855	**28.** 31,453 − 9,227 = 22,226	**29.** 42,682 − 19,429 = 23,253	**30.** 73,863 − 48,295 = 25,568

31. 96 − 4 **92** **32.** 55 − 23 **32** **33.** 685 − 42 **643**

34. 72 − 5 **67** **35.** 62 − 13 **49** **36.** 382 − 66 **316**

37. 526 − 167 **359** **38.** 4,837 − 982 **3,855** **39.** 9,341 − 8,344 **997**

40. 6,475 − 2,918 **3,557** **41.** 1,625 − 907 **718** **42.** 2,754 − 1,381 **1,373**

43. 8,619 − 2,409 **6,210** **44.** 4,726 − 2,395 **2,331** **45.** 7,512 − 5,294 **2,218**

46. 1,157 − 928 **229** **47.** 5,483 − 4,721 **762** **48.** 3,256 − 2,826 **430**

Subtraction with Zeros

Sometimes you must rename in more than one place-value position in order to subtract in a particular place-value position.

First, subtract the *ones*.

```
  2 9 9 15
  3,0 0 5
 −  6 7 8
        7
```

You cannot subtract 8 from 5. So, rename 300 tens as 299 tens and 10 ones. Then, 10 ones + 5 ones = 15 ones.

How are 299 tens and 15 ones recorded?

Then subtract *tens, hundreds, and thousands.*

```
  2 9 9 15
  3,0 0 5
 −  6 7 8
  2,3 2 7
```

Subtract.

1. 403 − 36 **367**	**2.** 201 − 54 **147**	**3.** 602 − 59 **543**	**4.** 5,004 − 637 **4,367**	**5.** 7,005 − 528 **6,477**
6. 2,051 − 365 **1,686**	**7.** 4,023 − 639 **3,384**	**8.** 6,306 − 128 **6,178**	**9.** 7,250 − 3,572 **3,678**	**10.** 5,080 − 3,367 **1,713**
11. 7,004 − 359 **6,645**	**12.** 2,800 − 526 **2,274**	**13.** 6,003 − 2,497 **3,506**	**14.** 13,200 − 8,427 **4,773**	**15.** 42,005 − 5,918 **36,087**
16. 8,000 − 257 **7,743**	**17.** 4,000 − 1,928 **2,072**	**18.** 15,000 − 7,604 **7,396**	**19.** 32,000 − 10,095 **21,905**	**20.** 65,000 − 29,843 **35,157**

21. 630 − 225 **405**

22. 1,408 − 271 **1,137**

23. 5,806 − 483 **5,323**

24. 8,200 − 1,725 **6,475**

25. 6,001 − 4,095 **1,906**

26. 2,900 − 1,926 **974**

27. 14,006 − 8,259 **5,747**

28. 82,000 − 40,280 **41,720**

29. 37,000 − 28,217 **8,783**

30. 5,200 − 972 **4,228**

31. 15,008 − 9,426 **5,582**

32. 8,600 − 854 **7,746**

33. 32,500 − 30,824 **1,676**

34. 94,200 − 77,058 **17,142**

35. 45,500 − 29,721 **15,779**

36. 7,400 − 3,945 **3,455**

37. 6,800 − 897 **5,903**

38. 1,000 − 428 **572**

39. 16,000 − 9,508 **6,492**

40. 52,400 − 50,863 **1,537**

41. 9,700 − 9,284 **416**

42. 27,200 − 18,590 **8,610**

43. 4,700 − 4,058 **642**

44. 7,000 − 2,095 **4,905**

45. 8,400 − 959 **7,441**

46. 15,200 − 8,425 **6,775**

47. 19,060 − 9,150 **9,910**

48. 3,500 − 802 **2,698**

49. 22,060 − 20,158 **1,902**

50. 37,020 − 8,047 **28,973**

Estimation of Sums and Differences

On a number line, 57 is closer to
60 than to 50. Therefore, 57 rounded
to the nearest ten is 60.

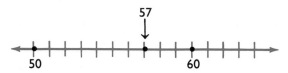

To round 2,835 to the nearest hundred, remember that 2,835 is
between 2,800 and 2,900. Then round up or down as follows.

—— Round up if the digit to the right is 5 or more.

To the nearest hundred, 2,835 is 2,800.

—— Round down if the digit to the right is less than 5.

To the nearest hundred, 2,835 is 2,800.
To the nearest thousand, 2,835 is 3,000.

Round to the underlined place-value position.

1. 35 **40**   **2.** 427 **430**   **3.** 186 **200**   **4.** 6,503 **6,500**   **5.** 3,048 **3,050**

6. 6,183 **6,000**   **7.** 9,837 **9,840**   **8.** 2,049 **2,000**   **9.** 1,842 **2,000**   **10.** 27,652 **30,000**

To estimate a sum or difference, round each number to the
same place-value position. Then, compute.

$$\begin{array}{r} 478 \\ + 321 \\ \hline \end{array} \quad\blacktriangleright\quad \begin{array}{r} 500 \\ + 300 \\ \hline 800 \end{array} \qquad\qquad \begin{array}{r} 1,826 \\ - 272 \\ \hline \end{array} \quad\blacktriangleright\quad \begin{array}{r} 1,800 \\ - 300 \\ \hline 1,500 \end{array}$$

Estimate each sum or difference.

11. $\begin{array}{r} 63 \\ + 82 \\ \hline 140 \end{array}$ **12.** $\begin{array}{r} 75 \\ + 31 \\ \hline 110 \end{array}$ **13.** $\begin{array}{r} 87 \\ + 52 \\ \hline 140 \end{array}$ **14.** $\begin{array}{r} 67 \\ - 34 \\ \hline 40 \end{array}$ **15.** $\begin{array}{r} 85 \\ - 26 \\ \hline 60 \end{array}$

16. $\begin{array}{r} 431 \\ + 25 \\ \hline 460 \end{array}$ **17.** $\begin{array}{r} 356 \\ + 41 \\ \hline 400 \end{array}$ **18.** $\begin{array}{r} 532 \\ - 56 \\ \hline 470 \end{array}$ **19.** $\begin{array}{r} 485 \\ - 31 \\ \hline 460 \end{array}$ **20.** $\begin{array}{r} 263 \\ - 59 \\ \hline 200 \end{array}$

21. $\begin{array}{r} 352 \\ + 631 \\ \hline 1,000 \end{array}$ **22.** $\begin{array}{r} 478 \\ + 304 \\ \hline 800 \end{array}$ **23.** $\begin{array}{r} 635 \\ + 283 \\ \hline 900 \end{array}$ **24.** $\begin{array}{r} 759 \\ - 261 \\ \hline 500 \end{array}$ **25.** $\begin{array}{r} 866 \\ - 528 \\ \hline 400 \end{array}$

26. $\begin{array}{r} 1,234 \\ + 405 \\ \hline 1,600 \end{array}$ **27.** $\begin{array}{r} 6,842 \\ + 340 \\ \hline 7,100 \end{array}$ **28.** $\begin{array}{r} 8,173 \\ - 338 \\ \hline 7,900 \end{array}$ **29.** $\begin{array}{r} 7,312 \\ - 673 \\ \hline 6,600 \end{array}$ **30.** $\begin{array}{r} 9,571 \\ - 862 \\ \hline 8,700 \end{array}$

31. $\begin{array}{r} 8,460 \\ + 2,952 \\ \hline 11,000 \end{array}$ **32.** $\begin{array}{r} 2,642 \\ + 8,090 \\ \hline 11,000 \end{array}$ **33.** $\begin{array}{r} 4,501 \\ + 3,862 \\ \hline 9,000 \end{array}$ **34.** $\begin{array}{r} 7,423 \\ - 3,284 \\ \hline 4,000 \end{array}$ **35.** $\begin{array}{r} 4,805 \\ - 1,783 \\ \hline 3,000 \end{array}$

Multiplication

Multiply each place-value position from least to greatest.

Multiply the *ones*.	Multiply the *tens*.	Multiply the *hundreds*.
$\overset{1}{5}43$	$\overset{2}{5}\overset{1}{4}3$	$\overset{2}{5}\overset{1}{4}3$
$\times\qquad 6$	$\times\qquad 6$	$\times\qquad 6$
$\overline{\qquad 8}$	$\overline{\quad 5\,8}$	$\overline{3,2\,5\,8}$
$6 \times 3 = 18$	6×4 tens $+ 1$ ten $= 25$ tens	6×5 hundreds $= 30$ hundreds.
How is the 18 recorded?	*Where did the 1 ten come from?*	*How is 32 hundreds obtained?*

Multiply.

1.	8 × 7 56	**2.**	9 × 6 54	**3.**	70 × 5 350	**4.**	80 × 9 720	**5.**	500 × 8 4,000
6.	23 × 3 69	**7.**	84 × 2 168	**8.**	41 × 6 246	**9.**	522 × 3 1,566	**10.**	724 × 2 1,448
11.	75 × 5 375	**12.**	63 × 7 441	**13.**	58 × 6 348	**14.**	620 × 6 3,720	**15.**	709 × 4 2,836
16.	348 × 4 1,392	**17.**	238 × 5 1,190	**18.**	917 × 9 8,253	**19.**	318 × 8 2,544	**20.**	743 × 6 4,458
21.	1,007 × 7 7,049	**22.**	8,002 × 9 72,018	**23.**	4,089 × 5 20,445	**24.**	1,890 × 7 13,230	**25.**	5,204 × 8 41,632
26.	7,284 × 3 21,852	**27.**	4,281 × 9 38,529	**28.**	2,153 × 4 8,612	**29.**	5,613 × 8 44,904	**30.**	6,381 × 6 38,286
31.	4,573 × 6 27,438	**32.**	3,365 × 5 16,825	**33.**	3,692 × 8 29,536	**34.**	9,845 × 9 88,605	**35.**	8,327 × 7 58,289
36.	10,250 × 4 41,000	**37.**	32,708 × 5 163,540	**38.**	22,006 × 8 176,048	**39.**	40,058 × 6 240,348	**40.**	51,700 × 9 465,300
41.	82,347 × 7 576,429	**42.**	15,861 × 3 47,583	**43.**	60,752 × 4 243,008	**44.**	29,954 × 8 239,632	**45.**	73,015 × 6 438,090
46.	38,270 × 9 344,430	**47.**	56,108 × 5 280,540	**48.**	44,900 × 2 89,800	**49.**	78,062 × 7 546,434	**50.**	18,456 × 8 147,648

Multiplication by Powers of 10

Multiplying by 10, 100, 1,000 or so on is easy.

8 × 10 = 8 tens or 80	37 × 10 = 37 tens or 370
8 × 100 = 8 hundreds or 800	37 × 100 = 37 hundreds or 3,700
8 × 1,000 = 8 thousands or 8,000	37 × 1,000 = 37 thousands or 37,000

What is the pattern for multiplying by 10, 100 or 1,000 or so on?
adding zeros to the non-ten number

Multiply.

1. 9 × 10 **90**
9 × 100 **900**
9 × 1,000 **9,000**

2. 7 × 10 **70**
7 × 100 **700**
7 × 1,000 **7,000**

3. 6 × 10 **60**
6 × 100 **600**
6 × 1,000 **6,000**

4. 52 × 10 **520**
52 × 100 **5,200**
52 × 1,000 **52,000**

5. 47 × 10 **470**
47 × 100 **4,700**
47 × 1,000
47,000

6. 621
× 10
6,210

7. 357
× 10
3,570

8. 841
× 100
84,100

9. 468
× 100
46,800

10. 973
× 1,000
973,000

Multiply by multiples of 10, 100 or 1,000.

6 × 30 = 6 × (3 × 10) = (6 × 3) × 10 = 18 × 10 = ___?___ **180**
9 × 400 = 9 × (4 × 100) = (9 × 4) × 100 = 36 × ___?___ = ___?___ **100; 3,600**
7 × 5,000 = 7 × (5 × 1,000) = (7 × 5) × 1,000 = ___?___ × ___?___ = ___?___
              35   **1,000**   **35,000**

Multiply.

11. 7 × 40 **280**
7 × 400 **2,800**
7 × 4,000
28,000

12. 8 × 70 **560**
8 × 700 **5,600**
8 × 7,000
56,000

13. 15 × 50 **750**
15 × 500 **7,500**
15 × 5,000
75,000

14. 74 × 30 **2,220**
74 × 300 **22,200**
74 × 3,000
222,000

15. 216 × 70 **15,120**
216 × 700 **151,200**
216 × 7,000
1,512,000

16. 435
× 20
8,700

17. 286
× 40
11,440

18. 517
× 300
155,100

19. 283
× 500
141,500

20. 4,625
× 4,000
18,500,000

21. 100
× 10
1,000

22. 1,000
× 10
10,000

23. 100
× 100
10,000

24. 1,000
× 100
100,000

25. 1,000
× 1,000
1,000,000

26. 600
× 10
6,000

27. 3,000
× 10
30,000

28. 500
× 100
50,000

29. 7,000
× 100
700,000

30. 8,000
× 1,000
8,000,000

31. 500
× 30
15,000

32. 2,000
× 50
100,000

33. 700
× 400
280,000

34. 5,000
× 700
3,500,000

35. 6,000
× 8,000
48,000,000

Multiplication by Two and Three-Digit Numbers

Multiply by the number in each place-value position as shown.

Multiply by the *ones*.

```
    3 4 7
  ×   7 6
    2 0 8 2
```

Multiply by the *tens*.

```
    3 4 7
  ×   7 6
    2 0 8 2
    2 4 2 9
```

Why must the 9 tens be placed under the 8 tens?

Now, add.

```
    3 4 7
  ×   7 6
    2 0 8 2
    2 4 2 9
    2 6,3 7 2
```

Multiply.

1. 32 × 31 **992**	**2.** 61 × 42 **2,562**	**3.** 834 × 22 **18,348**	**4.** 713 × 32 **22,816**	**5.** 624 × 21 **13,104**
6. 64 × 25 **1,600**	**7.** 59 × 36 **2,124**	**8.** 218 × 47 **10,246**	**9.** 635 × 91 **57,785**	**10.** 463 × 54 **25,002**
11. 428 × 35 **14,980**	**12.** 679 × 42 **28,518**	**13.** 508 × 63 **32,004**	**14.** 295 × 78 **23,010**	**15.** 425 × 37 **15,725**
16. 2,513 × 67 **168,371**	**17.** 4,831 × 29 **140,099**	**18.** 2,056 × 77 **158,312**	**19.** 3,009 × 85 **255,765**	**20.** 4,592 × 57 **261,744**

Be sure that partial products are placed in their place-value position.

```
    379
  × 463
    1 137      379 × 3 = 1,137
   22 74       379 × 6 tens = 2,274 tens
  151 6        379 × 4 hundreds = 1,516 hundreds
  175,477
```

```
    817
  × 407
    5 719      817 × 7 = 5,719
  326 8        817 × 4 hundreds =
  332,519      3,268 hundreds
```

Multiply.

21. 479 × 467 **223,693**	**22.** 215 × 803 **172,645**	**23.** 275 × 623 **171,325**	**24.** 807 × 382 **308,274**	**25.** 957 × 861 **823,977**
26. 5,280 × 365 **1,927,200**	**27.** 6,377 × 928 **5,917,856**	**28.** 4,982 × 756 **3,766,392**	**29.** 6,597 × 203 **1,339,191**	**30.** 8,027 × 514 **4,125,878**

Division

You multiply in each place-value position from least to greatest. Thus, you divide in each place-value position from greatest to least.

Divide the *hundreds*.

Estimate 6 hundreds ÷ 4 as 1 hundred.

$$
\begin{array}{r}
1 \\
4{\overline{)624}} \\
-\ 4 \\
\hline
2
\end{array}
$$
$4 \times 1 \text{ hundred} = 4 \text{ hundreds}$

Divide the *tens*.

Estimate 22 tens ÷ 4 as 5 tens.

$$
\begin{array}{r}
15 \\
4{\overline{)624}} \\
-\ 4\downarrow \\
\hline
22 \\
-\ 20 \\
\hline
2
\end{array}
$$
$4 \times 5 \text{ tens} = 20 \text{ tens}$

Divide the *ones*.

Estimate 24 ÷ 4 as 6.

$$
\begin{array}{r}
156 \\
4{\overline{)624}} \\
-\ 4 \\
\hline
22 \\
-\ 20\downarrow \\
\hline
24 \\
-\ 24 \\
\hline
0
\end{array}
$$
$4 \times 6 = 24$

Check: 156 × 4 = 624

Divide.

1. $4{\overline{)524}}$ = 131
2. $3{\overline{)651}}$ = 217
3. $6{\overline{)738}}$ = 123
4. $7{\overline{)952}}$ = 136
5. $5{\overline{)620}}$ = 124

6. $7{\overline{)924}}$ = 132
7. $5{\overline{)710}}$ = 142
8. $3{\overline{)984}}$ = 328
9. $6{\overline{)918}}$ = 153
10. $4{\overline{)940}}$ = 235

11. $9{\overline{)936}}$ = 104
12. $7{\overline{)868}}$ = 124
13. $5{\overline{)915}}$ = 183
14. $3{\overline{)837}}$ = 279
15. $6{\overline{)924}}$ = 154

16. $8{\overline{)952}}$ = 119
17. $6{\overline{)714}}$ = 119
18. $4{\overline{)864}}$ = 216
19. $2{\overline{)796}}$ = 398
20. $3{\overline{)762}}$ = 254

21. $6{\overline{)972}}$ = 162
22. $5{\overline{)885}}$ = 177
23. $4{\overline{)772}}$ = 193
24. $8{\overline{)896}}$ = 112
25. $9{\overline{)972}}$ = 108

26. $3{\overline{)8,559}}$ = 2,853
27. $7{\overline{)7,917}}$ = 1,131
28. $6{\overline{)6,834}}$ = 1,139
29. $4{\overline{)4,936}}$ = 1,234
30. $5{\overline{)5,885}}$ = 1,177

31. $8{\overline{)91,456}}$ = 11,432
32. $5{\overline{)68,595}}$ = 13,719
33. $7{\overline{)85,995}}$ = 12,285
34. $3{\overline{)97,011}}$ = 32,337
35. $6{\overline{)79,536}}$ = 13,256

36. $5{\overline{)32,090}}$ = 6,418
37. $4{\overline{)34,864}}$ = 8,716
38. $8{\overline{)58,520}}$ = 7,315
39. $6{\overline{)55,470}}$ = 9,245
40. $3{\overline{)47,352}}$ = 15,784

41. $9{\overline{)82,926}}$ = 9,214
42. $7{\overline{)44,247}}$ = 6,321
43. $6{\overline{)42,834}}$ = 7,139
44. $5{\overline{)38,105}}$ = 7,621
45. $8{\overline{)41,496}}$ = 5,187

46. $4{\overline{)37,096}}$ = 9,274
47. $3{\overline{)29,148}}$ = 9,716
48. $9{\overline{)77,364}}$ = 8,596
49. $7{\overline{)40,838}}$ = 5,834
50. $6{\overline{)10,470}}$ = 1,745

51. $8{\overline{)21,824}}$ = 2,728
52. $5{\overline{)22,195}}$ = 4,439
53. $7{\overline{)10,906}}$ = 1,558
54. $4{\overline{)26,668}}$ = 6,667
55. $3{\overline{)26,442}}$ = 8,814

56. $6{\overline{)14,682}}$ = 2,447
57. $9{\overline{)52,956}}$ = 5,884
58. $8{\overline{)31,952}}$ = 3,994
59. $5{\overline{)49,115}}$ = 9,823
60. $7{\overline{)59,031}}$ = 8,433

Division Using Zero

Divide in each place-value position even if the quotient there is zero.

Divide the *hundreds*.

4 hundreds ÷ 5

$$5\overline{)480}$$

Why is a zero not written in the hundreds place of the quotient?

Divide the *tens*.

Estimate 48 tens ÷ 5 as 9 tens.

$$\begin{array}{r} 9 \\ 5\overline{)480} \\ -\ 45 \\ \hline 3 \end{array}$$

How is 45 tens obtained?

Divide the *ones*.

30 ÷ 5 = 6

$$\begin{array}{r} 96 \\ 5\overline{)480} \\ -\ 45\downarrow \\ \hline 30 \\ -\ 30 \\ \hline 0 \end{array}$$

Divide.

1. $7\overline{)623}$ (89)
2. $2\overline{)156}$ (78)
3. $3\overline{)282}$ (94)
4. $4\overline{)356}$ (89)
5. $6\overline{)522}$ (87)

6. $9\overline{)738}$ (82)
7. $7\overline{)1,036}$ (148)
8. $4\overline{)2,568}$ (642)
9. $5\overline{)4,965}$ (993)
10. $8\overline{)6,736}$ (842)

Divide 2,416 by 8.

24 hundred ÷ 8 = 3

$$\begin{array}{r} 3 \\ 8\overline{)2,416} \\ -\ 24 \end{array}$$

1 ten ÷ 8 = 0

$$\begin{array}{r} 30 \\ 8\overline{)2,416} \\ -\ 24\downarrow \\ \hline 1 \\ -\ 0 \\ \hline 1 \end{array}$$

Why is the zero written in the tens place of the quotient?

16 ÷ 8 = 2

$$\begin{array}{r} 302 \\ 8\overline{)2,416} \\ -\ 24 \\ \hline 1 \\ -\ 0\downarrow \\ \hline 16 \\ -\ 16 \\ \hline 0 \end{array}$$

Divide.

11. $7\overline{)721}$ (103)
12. $6\overline{)654}$ (109)
13. $4\overline{)836}$ (209)
14. $5\overline{)950}$ (190)
15. $3\overline{)840}$ (280)

16. $4\overline{)1,628}$ (407)
17. $8\overline{)2,960}$ (370)
18. $9\overline{)4,554}$ (506)
19. $6\overline{)4,260}$ (710)
20. $7\overline{)6,335}$ (905)

21. $5\overline{)20,415}$ (4,083)
22. $3\overline{)13,521}$ (4,507)
23. $8\overline{)73,920}$ (9,240)
24. $5\overline{)35,450}$ (7,090)
25. $8\overline{)56,240}$ (7,030)

26. $6\overline{)40,020}$ (6,670)
27. $4\overline{)32,012}$ (8,003)
28. $7\overline{)28,056}$ (4,008)
29. $3\overline{)15,204}$ (5,008)
30. $9\overline{)27,036}$ (3,004)

Division with Remainders

In division, sometimes a remainder will result. A remainder can be written as a fraction in simplest form.

Divide the *hundreds*.

6 hundreds ÷ 6 = 1 hundred

$$\begin{array}{r} 1 \\ 6\overline{)652} \\ -\ 6 \end{array}$$

Divide the *tens*.

5 tens ÷ 6

$$\begin{array}{r} 10 \\ 6\overline{)652} \\ -\ 6\!\downarrow \\ \hline 5 \\ -\ 0 \\ \hline 5 \end{array}$$

Why is a zero placed in the quotient?

Divide the *ones*.

Estimate 52 ÷ 6 as 8.

$$108\tfrac{4}{6} = 108\tfrac{2}{3}$$

$$\begin{array}{r} 6\overline{)652} \\ -\ 6 \\ \hline 5 \\ -\ 0\!\downarrow \\ \hline 52 \\ -\ 48 \\ \hline 4 \end{array}$$

4 ←remainder of 4 sixths

Divide. Write each answer as a mixed numeral in simplest form.

1. $3\overline{)28}= 9\tfrac{1}{3}$
2. $4\overline{)35}= 8\tfrac{3}{4}$
3. $6\overline{)56}= 9\tfrac{1}{3}$
4. $7\overline{)48}= 6\tfrac{6}{7}$
5. $8\overline{)51}= 6\tfrac{3}{8}$

6. $4\overline{)94}= 23\tfrac{1}{2}$
7. $6\overline{)87}= 14\tfrac{1}{2}$
8. $8\overline{)98}= 12\tfrac{1}{4}$
9. $7\overline{)96}= 13\tfrac{5}{7}$
10. $5\overline{)92}= 18\tfrac{2}{5}$

11. $5\overline{)652}= 130\tfrac{2}{5}$
12. $6\overline{)785}= 130\tfrac{5}{6}$
13. $8\overline{)936}= 117$
14. $7\overline{)778}= 111\tfrac{1}{7}$
15. $4\overline{)735}= 183\tfrac{3}{4}$

16. $3\overline{)295}= 98\tfrac{1}{3}$
17. $4\overline{)359}= 89\tfrac{3}{4}$
18. $2\overline{)129}= 64\tfrac{1}{2}$
19. $8\overline{)683}= 85\tfrac{3}{8}$
20. $9\overline{)880}= 97\tfrac{7}{9}$

21. $6\overline{)3,251}= 541\tfrac{5}{6}$
22. $5\overline{)4,803}= 960\tfrac{3}{5}$
23. $7\overline{)5,271}= 753$
24. $9\overline{)6,879}= 764\tfrac{1}{3}$
25. $6\overline{)3,485}= 580\tfrac{5}{6}$

26. $8\overline{)8,016}= 1,002$
27. $3\overline{)1,210}= 403\tfrac{1}{3}$
28. $9\overline{)5,447}= 605\tfrac{2}{9}$
29. $5\overline{)1,545}= 309$
30. $7\overline{)4,956}= 708$

31. $6\overline{)1,222}= 203\tfrac{2}{3}$
32. $6\overline{)3,011}= 501\tfrac{5}{6}$
33. $8\overline{)2,456}= 307$
34. $7\overline{)2,855}= 407\tfrac{6}{7}$
35. $6\overline{)4,857}= 809\tfrac{1}{2}$

36. $3\overline{)65,852}= 21,950\tfrac{2}{3}$
37. $9\overline{)36,892}= 4,099\tfrac{1}{9}$
38. $6\overline{)48,532}= 8,088\tfrac{2}{3}$
39. $8\overline{)95,284}= 11,910\tfrac{1}{2}$
40. $7\overline{)67,893}= 9,699$

41. $5\overline{)31,123}= 6,224\tfrac{3}{5}$
42. $4\overline{)10,678}= 2,669\tfrac{1}{2}$
43. $9\overline{)24,190}= 2,687\tfrac{7}{9}$
44. $3\overline{)15,508}= 5,169\tfrac{1}{3}$
45. $8\overline{)13,395}= 1,674\tfrac{3}{8}$

46. $7\overline{)43,110}= 6,158\tfrac{4}{7}$
47. $6\overline{)45,137}= 7,522\tfrac{5}{6}$
48. $5\overline{)17,794}= 3,558\tfrac{4}{5}$
49. $8\overline{)36,413}= 4,551\tfrac{5}{8}$
50. $4\overline{)25,418}= 6,354\tfrac{1}{2}$

51. $9\overline{)22,208}= 2,467\tfrac{5}{9}$
52. $3\overline{)22,466}= 7,488\tfrac{2}{3}$
53. $7\overline{)36,531}= 5,218\tfrac{5}{7}$
54. $6\overline{)20,688}= 3,448$
55. $5\overline{)24,944}= 4,988\tfrac{4}{5}$

56. $8\overline{)44,374}= 5,546\tfrac{3}{4}$
57. $4\overline{)15,910}= 3,977\tfrac{1}{2}$
58. $9\overline{)40,273}= 4,474\tfrac{7}{9}$
59. $5\overline{)11,439}= 2,287\tfrac{4}{5}$
60. $7\overline{)16,077}= 2,296\tfrac{5}{7}$

61. $3\overline{)17,562}= 5,854$
62. $6\overline{)23,938}= 3,989\tfrac{2}{3}$
63. $8\overline{)30,189}= 3,773\tfrac{5}{8}$
64. $4\overline{)10,787}= 2,696\tfrac{3}{4}$
65. $9\overline{)50,256}= 5,584$

Division with Two and Three-Digit Divisors

Estimation can be used to determine the digits of the quotient.

$52\overline{)626}$

⬇

52 to the nearest ten is 50. Round 626 to 600. Then, mentally compute.

$$\begin{array}{r} 12 \\ 50\overline{)600} \end{array}$$

Divide the *tens.*

Estimate 62 tens ÷ 52 as 1 ten.

$$\begin{array}{r} 1 \\ 52\overline{)626} \\ -\ 52 \\ \hline 10 \end{array}$$

Divide the *ones.*

Estimate 106 ÷ 52 as 2.

$$12\tfrac{2}{52} = 12\tfrac{1}{26}$$
$$\begin{array}{r} 52\overline{)626} \\ -\ 52\downarrow \\ \hline 106 \\ -\ 104 \\ \hline 2 \end{array}$$

How can you use the estimation to see that your answer is reasonable?

Divide the *tens.*

Estimate 240 tens ÷ 26 as 8 tens.

$$\begin{array}{r} 8 \\ 26\overline{)2405} \\ -\ 208 \\ \hline 32 \end{array}$$

Note that 32 is greater than 26. So, change your estimate from 8 tens to 9 tens.

$$\begin{array}{r} 9 \\ 26\overline{)2405} \\ -\ 234 \\ \hline 6 \end{array}$$

Divide the *ones.*

Estimate 65 ÷ 26 as 2.

$$92\tfrac{13}{26} = 92\tfrac{1}{2}$$
$$\begin{array}{r} 26\overline{)2405} \\ -\ 234\downarrow \\ \hline 65 \\ -\ 52 \\ \hline 13 \end{array}$$

Divide.

1. $32\overline{)768}$ — 24
2. $41\overline{)779}$ — 19
3. $22\overline{)946}$ — 43
4. $12\overline{)888}$ — 74
5. $15\overline{)870}$ — 58

6. $47\overline{)859}$ — $18\tfrac{13}{47}$
7. $53\overline{)906}$ — $17\tfrac{5}{53}$
8. $61\overline{)775}$ — $12\tfrac{43}{61}$
9. $42\overline{)567}$ — $13\tfrac{1}{2}$
10. $73\overline{)860}$ — $11\tfrac{57}{73}$

11. $52\overline{)5,616}$ — 108
12. $65\overline{)6,760}$ — 104
13. $38\overline{)7,942}$ — 209
14. $47\overline{)9,541}$ — 203
15. $59\overline{)6,490}$ — 110

16. $72\overline{)7,739}$ — $107\tfrac{35}{72}$
17. $53\overline{)5,824}$ — $109\tfrac{47}{53}$
18. $98\overline{)9,951}$ — $101\tfrac{53}{98}$
19. $21\overline{)8,573}$ — $408\tfrac{5}{21}$
20. $68\overline{)7,050}$ — $103\tfrac{23}{34}$

21. $351\overline{)9,828}$ — 28
22. $208\overline{)7,280}$ — 35
23. $470\overline{)71,440}$ — 152
24. $258\overline{)88,752}$ — 344

25. $413\overline{)17,409}$ — $42\tfrac{9}{59}$
26. $406\overline{)20,759}$ — $51\tfrac{53}{406}$
27. $328\overline{)83,284}$ — $253\tfrac{75}{82}$
28. $591\overline{)402,942}$ — $681\tfrac{157}{197}$

29. $863\overline{)728,922}$ — $844\tfrac{550}{863}$
30. $628\overline{)295,437}$ — $470\tfrac{277}{628}$
31. $915\overline{)542,634}$ — $593\tfrac{13}{305}$
32. $748\overline{)639,827}$ — $855\tfrac{287}{748}$

Estimation of Products and Quotients

To estimate a product, round each factor to its greatest place-value position. Then, multiply.

$$\begin{array}{r} 621 \\ \times\ 37 \\ \hline \end{array} \quad \blacktriangleright \quad \begin{array}{r} 600 \\ \times\ 40 \\ \hline 24{,}000 \end{array}$$

621 to the nearest hundred is 600
37 to the nearest ten is 40
Estimate

Estimate. Answers may vary. Typical answers are given.

1. $\begin{array}{r}43 \\ \times\ 7\end{array}$ ▶ $\begin{array}{r}40 \\ \times\ 7 \\ \hline 280\end{array}$
2. $\begin{array}{r}28 \\ \times\ 34\end{array}$ ▶ $\begin{array}{r}30 \\ \times\ 30 \\ \hline 900\end{array}$
3. $\begin{array}{r}893 \\ \times\ 62\end{array}$ ▶ $\begin{array}{r}900 \\ \times\ 60 \\ \hline 54{,}000\end{array}$

4. $\begin{array}{r}64 \\ \times\ 8\end{array}$ $\begin{array}{r}60 \\ \times\ 8 \\ \hline 480\end{array}$
5. $\begin{array}{r}59 \\ \times\ 7\end{array}$ $\begin{array}{r}60 \\ \times\ 7 \\ \hline 420\end{array}$
6. $\begin{array}{r}81 \\ \times\ 3\end{array}$ $\begin{array}{r}80 \\ \times\ 3 \\ \hline 240\end{array}$
7. $\begin{array}{r}46 \\ \times\ 9\end{array}$ $\begin{array}{r}50 \\ \times\ 9 \\ \hline 450\end{array}$
8. $\begin{array}{r}46 \\ \times\ 5\end{array}$ $\begin{array}{r}50 \\ \times\ 5 \\ \hline 250\end{array}$

9. $\begin{array}{r}56 \\ \times\ 87\end{array}$ $\begin{array}{r}60 \\ \times\ 90 \\ \hline 5{,}400\end{array}$
10. $\begin{array}{r}91 \\ \times\ 15\end{array}$ $\begin{array}{r}90 \\ \times\ 20 \\ \hline 1{,}800\end{array}$
11. $\begin{array}{r}35 \\ \times\ 88\end{array}$ $\begin{array}{r}40 \\ \times\ 90 \\ \hline 3{,}600\end{array}$
12. $\begin{array}{r}71 \\ \times\ 59\end{array}$ $\begin{array}{r}70 \\ \times\ 60 \\ \hline 4{,}200\end{array}$
13. $\begin{array}{r}28 \\ \times\ 36\end{array}$ $\begin{array}{r}30 \\ \times\ 40 \\ \hline 1{,}200\end{array}$

14. $\begin{array}{r}148 \\ \times\ 52\end{array}$ $\begin{array}{r}100 \\ \times\ 50 \\ \hline 5{,}000\end{array}$
15. $\begin{array}{r}365 \\ \times\ 16\end{array}$ $\begin{array}{r}400 \\ \times\ 20 \\ \hline 8{,}000\end{array}$
16. $\begin{array}{r}821 \\ \times\ 47\end{array}$ $\begin{array}{r}800 \\ \times\ 50 \\ \hline 40{,}000\end{array}$
17. $\begin{array}{r}352 \\ \times\ 85\end{array}$ $\begin{array}{r}400 \\ \times\ 90 \\ \hline 36{,}000\end{array}$
18. $\begin{array}{r}679 \\ \times\ 38\end{array}$ $\begin{array}{r}700 \\ \times\ 40 \\ \hline 28{,}000\end{array}$

To estimate a quotient, round the divisor to its greatest place-value position. Then, round the dividend so that the quotient is easy to estimate.

$$72\overline{)348} \quad \blacktriangleright \quad \overset{5}{70\overline{)350}} \quad \text{35 tens} \div \text{7 tens} = 5$$

$$384\overline{)23{,}952} \quad \blacktriangleright \quad \overset{60}{400\overline{)24{,}000}} \quad \text{240 hundreds} \div \text{4 hundreds} = 60$$

Estimate. Answers may vary. Typical answers are given. **26.** $\overset{12{,}000}{7\overline{)90{,}000}}$ **31.** $\overset{100}{90\overline{)9{,}000}}$

19. $4\overline{)283}$ ▶ $\overset{70}{4\overline{)280}}$
20. $62\overline{)581}$ ▶ $\overset{10}{60\overline{)600}}$
21. $451\overline{)2{,}526}$ ▶ $\overset{5}{500\overline{)2{,}500}}$

22. $6\overline{)405}$ $\overset{70}{6\overline{)420}}$
23. $7\overline{)921}$ $\overset{130}{7\overline{)910}}$
24. $3\overline{)4{,}523}$ $\overset{1{,}500}{3\overline{)4{,}500}}$
25. $5\overline{)3{,}762}$ $\overset{800}{5\overline{)4{,}000}}$
26. $7\overline{)88{,}311}$

27. $59\overline{)346}$ $\overset{6}{60\overline{)360}}$
28. $72\overline{)568}$ $\overset{8}{70\overline{)560}}$
29. $34\overline{)482}$ $\overset{16}{30\overline{)480}}$
30. $75\overline{)4{,}089}$
31. $85\overline{)9{,}382}$ $\overset{50}{80\overline{)4{,}000}}$

32. $411\overline{)2{,}526}$ $\overset{6}{400\overline{)2{,}400}}$
33. $308\overline{)11{,}320}$
34. $562\overline{)47{,}770}$
35. $773\overline{)231{,}986}$

$\overset{40}{300\overline{)12{,}000}}$
$\overset{80}{600\overline{)48{,}000}}$
$\overset{300}{800\overline{)240{,}000}}$

Decimal Place Value

Decimals use powers of ten such as 10, 100, or 1000 as denominators.

$$0.5 = \frac{5}{10} \qquad \Big| \qquad 0.23 = \frac{23}{100} \qquad \Big| \qquad 0.075 = \frac{75}{1,000}$$

The chart shows the place value of each digit in 153.482.

153.482 is read 153 and 482 thousandths.
The decimal point is read as <u>and</u>.

The 8 is in the hundredths place-value position. The digit 8 and its place value name the number 0.08 or $\frac{8}{100}$.

The digit 4 and its place value name $\underline{\quad ? \quad}$. $\frac{4}{10}$
The digit 2 and its place value name $\underline{\quad ? \quad}$. $\frac{2}{1,000}$

The place values can extend in either direction.

Name the place-value position of the underlined digit.

1. 2.7<u>5</u> **hundredths**   2. 0.50<u>4</u> **thousandths** 3. 1.0<u>27</u> **hundredths** 4. 85.03<u>8</u> **thousandths**   5. 0.0<u>6</u> **hundredths**

6. 1<u>5</u>.7 **ones**   7. 4.<u>8</u>32 **tenths**   8. 2.00<u>5</u> **thousandths** 9. 0.0<u>17</u> **hundredths** 10. 35.40<u>2</u> **thousandths**

Write each of the following as a decimal.

11. $\frac{3}{10}$ **0.3**   12. $\frac{8}{10}$ **0.8**   13. $\frac{1}{10}$ **0.1**   14. $\frac{52}{100}$ **0.52**   15. $\frac{67}{100}$ **0.67**

16. $\frac{5}{100}$ **0.05**   17. $\frac{30}{100}$ **0.30**   18. $\frac{926}{1000}$ **0.926**   19. $\frac{48}{1000}$ **0.048**   20. $\frac{3}{1000}$ **0.003**

21. $7\frac{3}{10}$ **7.3**   22. $2\frac{17}{100}$ **2.17**   23. $9\frac{8}{100}$ **9.08**   24. $12\frac{375}{1000}$ **12.375**   25. $16\frac{25}{1000}$ **16.025**

26. 8 tenths **0.8**   27. 23 hundredths **0.23**   28. 74 hundredths **0.74**

29. 654 thousandths **0.654**   30. 19 thousandths **0.019**   31. 5 hundredths **0.05**

32. 5 and 2 tenths **5.2**   33. 8 and 56 hundredths **8.56**   34. 2 and 125 thousandths **2.125**

Write each of the following as a fraction or mixed numeral.

35. 0.8 $\frac{8}{10}$ 36. 0.15 $\frac{15}{100}$ 37. 0.04 $\frac{4}{100}$ 38. 0.75 $\frac{75}{100}$ 39. 0.6 $\frac{6}{10}$

40. 0.125 $\frac{125}{1,000}$ 41. 0.033 $\frac{33}{1,000}$ 42. 0.67 $\frac{67}{100}$ 43. 0.005 $\frac{5}{1,000}$ 44. 0.478 $\frac{478}{1,000}$

45. 3.6 $3\frac{6}{10}$ 46. 8.5 $8\frac{5}{10}$ 47. 2.25 $2\frac{25}{100}$ 48. 6.75 $6\frac{75}{100}$ 49. 5.07 $5\frac{7}{100}$

50. 9.375 $9\frac{375}{1,000}$ 51. 7.006 $7\frac{6}{1,000}$ 52. 4.092 $4\frac{92}{1,000}$ 53. 3.02 $3\frac{2}{100}$ 54. 2.60 $2\frac{60}{100}$

Comparing and Rounding Decimals

You can annex zeros to the right of a decimal without changing its value.

The shading in the figures below shows 0.1 and 0.10. They are the same or equivalent.

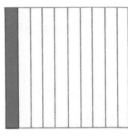

$\dfrac{1}{10}$ or **0.1**

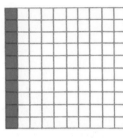

$\dfrac{10}{100}$ or **0.10**

Therefore,
0.1 = 0.10 = 0.100
2 = 2.0 = 2.00
0.04 = 0.040 = 0.0400

To compare 0.4 and 0.43, annex zeros so that 0.4 and 0.43 have the same number of decimal places.

0.4 ▦ 0.43 ▶ **0.40 ▦ 0.43** ▶ **Compare** ▶ **0.40 < 0.43**

Replace each ▦ with <, >, or =.

1. 0.2 ▦ 0.5 **<**   **2.** 0.68 ▦ 0.65 **>**   **3.** 0.03 ▦ 0.30 **<**

4. 5.4 ▦ 5.40 **=**   **5.** 0.315 ▦ 0.3 **>**   **6.** 2.05 ▦ 2.5 **<**

7. 1.010 ▦ 1.001 **>**   **8.** 1.3 ▦ 1 **>**   **9.** 0.308 ▦ 0.30 **>**

10. 0.06 ▦ 0.5 **<**   **11.** 0.08 ▦ 0.080 **=**   **12.** 4.34 ▦ 4.342 **<**

Round decimals as follows. Look at the digit to the right of the underlined digit.

Round up if the digit to the right is 5 or more.

To the nearest tenth, 24.3<u>7</u>5 is 24.4.

Round down if the digit to the right is less than 5.

Round to the underlined place-value position.

13. 2.3<u>8</u>7 **2.39**   **14.** 0.<u>4</u>17 **0.4**   **15.** 6<u>2</u>.45 **62**   **16.** 5.<u>1</u>78 **5.2**

17. 1<u>5</u>.465 **15**   **18.** 0.7<u>0</u>6 **0.71**   **19.** 7.3<u>8</u>4 **7.38**   **20.** 0.06<u>2</u>3 **0.062**

21. 0.0<u>4</u>8 **0.05**   **22.** $3.6<u>6</u>7 **$3.67**   **23.** 2<u>9</u>.75 **30**   **24.** 0.1<u>7</u>5 **0.18**

25. 7<u>2</u>.384 **72**   **26.** 0.1<u>0</u>9 **0.11**   **27.** 7.<u>6</u>58 **7.7**   **28.** $2.0<u>9</u>5 **$2.10**

Addition of Decimals

To add decimals, align the decimal points. Then add as with whole numbers.

First, add the *hundredths*.

```
      1
  4 3 . 0 7
    6 . 8 0
+   0 . 2 5
      . 2
```

How is 12 hundredths recorded?

Then, add the *tenths, ones,* and *tens.*

```
  1 1   1
  4 3 . 0 7
    6 . 8 0
+   0 . 2 5
  5 0 . 1 2
```

Add.

1. 4.8 + 3.1 **7.9**	**2.** 6.0 + 34.2 **40.2**	**3.** 15.7 + 4.6 **20.3**	**4.** 17.8 + 28.5 **46.3**	**5.** 62.8 + 129.7 **192.5**
6. 4.35 + 17.62 **21.97**	**7.** $49.04 + 17.37 **$66.41**	**8.** $68.57 + 148.04 **$216.61**	**9.** 952.35 + 68.63 **1,020.98**	**10.** 79.82 + 40.08 **119.90**
11. 4 + 3.5 **7.5**	**12.** 28.2 + 76 **104.2**	**13.** 4.82 + 6.7 **11.52**	**14.** 3.9 + 12.05 **15.95**	**15.** 65.72 + 7 **72.72**
16. 83 4.75 + 6.4 **94.15**	**17.** 15.6 8.47 + 0.5 **24.57**	**18.** 4.29 32.6 + 27 **63.89**	**19.** 0.61 7 + 15.09 **22.7**	**20.** 71.8 2.49 + 9.17 **83.46**

21. 3.5 + 7.2 + 5.6 **16.3**

22. 1.7 + 8.5 + 4.9 **15.1**

23. $35.06 + $49.17 **$84.23**

24. $12.38 + $6.27 **$18.65**

25. 16.2 + 3.17 **19.37**

26. 9.85 + 37 **46.85**

27. 6.25 + 3.7 **9.95**

28. 7.9 + 15 **22.9**

29. 3.8 + 2 + 4.67 **10.47**

30. 7.12 + 5.9 + 71 **84.02**

31. 3.04 + 6 + 5.2 **14.24**

32. 19 + 7.4 + 3 **29.4**

33. 8.275 + 3.621 **11.896**

34. 175.035 + 62.159 **237.194**

35. 13.082 + 44.71 **57.792**

36. 3.2 + 15.007 + 0.46 **18.667**

37. 50 + 2.852 + 13.6 **66.452**

38. 0.09 + 43 + 2.098 **45.188**

39. 17.3 + 843.7 + 3.92 **864.92**

40. 30.1 + 4.7 + 13.45 **48.25**

41. 1.23 + 0.451 + 5.4 **7.081**

42. 3.4 + 0.86 + 11.23 **15.49**

43. 7.9 + 0.05 + 4.632 **12.582**

44. 3.41 + 21.7 + 7.05 **32.16**

45. 6.12 + 0.06 + 2.49 **8.67**

46. 0.42 + 0.512 + 4.07 **5.002**

47. 5.78 + 1.5 + 3.753 **11.033**

48. 10 + 1.584 + 32.85 **44.434**

49. 81.7 + 27 + 6.75 **115.45**

50. $4.26 + $32.07 + $0.52 **$36.85**

51. 40.8 + 3.49 + 27 **71.29**

52. 7.38 + 12.9 + 95 **115.28**

53. 5.98 + 2.5 + 0.375 **8.855**

54. 6.81 + 9.4 + 0.54 **16.75**

55. 1.9 + 7.27 + 32 **41.17**

56. 127 + 53.6 + 8.64 **189.24**

Subtraction of Decimals

To subtract decimals, align the decimal points. Then subtract as with whole numbers.

First, subtract the *hundredths*.

$$\begin{array}{r} {}^{6\ 15} \\ 6\,3.\cancel{7}\cancel{5} \\ -\ 2\,8.6\,7 \\ \hline .\ 8 \end{array}$$

Then, subtract the *tenths, ones,* and *tens.*

$$\begin{array}{r} {}^{5\ 13}\ \ {}^{6\ 15} \\ \cancel{6}\cancel{3}.\cancel{7}\cancel{5} \\ -\ 2\,8.6\,7 \\ \hline 3\,5.0\,8 \end{array}$$

How is 75 hundredths renamed?

Subtract.

1. 62.3 − 41.2 = **21.1**	**2.** 78.9 − 43.6 = **35.3**	**3.** 94.8 − 12.5 = **82.3**	**4.** $40.86 − 21.35 = **$19.51**	**5.** $84.57 − $26.33 = **$58.24**
6. 107.95 − 64.3 = **43.65**	**7.** 64.74 − 8.91 = **55.83**	**8.** 75.35 − 9.6 = **65.75**	**9.** 45.82 − 14.06 = **31.76**	**10.** 178.53 − 69.7 = **108.83**
11. 43.81 − 27.62 = **16.19**	**12.** 485.63 − 329.47 = **156.16**	**13.** 16.1 − 8.2 = **7.9**	**14.** 27.4 − 3.6 = **23.8**	**15.** 218.3 − 55.4 = **162.9**
16. 9.41 − 3.05 = **6.36**	**17.** 68.27 − 5.9 = **62.37**	**18.** 185.84 − 66.35 = **119.49**	**19.** $47.05 − 5.98 = **$41.07**	**20.** $30.02 − 8.64 = **$21.38**
21. 13.121 − 3.47 = **9.651**	**22.** 2.956 − 0.278 = **2.678**	**23.** 52.08 − 9.81 = **42.27**	**24.** 106.31 − 18.4 = **87.91**	**25.** 91.321 − 1.873 = **89.448**

26. 59.7 − 6.8 **52.9**

27. 68.35 − 27.88 **40.47**

28. 175.04 − 62.38 **112.66**

29. 17.38 − 8.92 **8.46**

30. 49.07 − 13.8 **35.27**

31. 92.46 − 83.17 **9.29**

32. 47.1 − 7.3 **39.8**

33. 237.36 − 48.43 **188.93**

34. 67.52 − 46.8 **20.72**

35. $18.15 − $4.27 **$13.88**

36. $20.00 − $6.95 **$13.05**

37. 250.75 − 40.89 **209.86**

38. 75.248 − 10.038 **65.21**

39. 8.042 − 4.361 **3.681**

40. 10.263 − 3.294 **6.969**

41. 6.86 − 4.08 **2.78**

42. $9.48 − $3.71 **$5.77**

43. 67.34 − 4.73 **62.61**

44. $20.25 − $3.76 **$16.49**

45. 1.8 − 0.4 **1.4**

46. 32.59 − 18.7 **13.89**

47. 0.58 − 0.53 **0.05**

48. 47.5 − 8.485 **39.015**

49. $22.48 − $9 **$13.48**

50. 63.8 − 0.9 **62.9**

51. 0.65 − 0.48 **0.17**

52. 0.043 − 0.03 **0.013**

53. 86.27 − 42.9 **43.37**

54. 16.1 − 7.3 **8.8**

55. 3.22 − 1.06 **2.16**

Subtraction of Decimals with Zeros

In order to align decimal points and rename numbers, it is
helpful to annex zeros.

Subtract the *hundredths*.

$$
\begin{array}{r}
2\,0 \\
-\ 6.89 \\
\end{array}
\qquad
\begin{array}{r}
{}^{1\ 9\quad 9\ 10} \\
\cancel{2\,0.0\,0} \\
-\ \ 6.8\,9 \\
\hline
.\ 1 \\
\end{array}
\quad Note:\ 20 = 20.00
$$

Rename 200 tenths.
How is this recorded?

Subtract the *tenths, ones,* and *tens.*

$$
\begin{array}{r}
{}^{1\ 9\quad 9\ 10} \\
\cancel{2\,0.0\,0} \\
-\ \ 6.8\,9 \\
\hline
1\,3.1\,1 \\
\end{array}
$$

Subtract.

1. 8 − 2.6 **5.4**	**2.** 5 − 1.4 **3.6**	**3.** 25.2 − 8.65 **16.55**	**4.** 0.847 − 0.398 **0.449**	**5.** 0.49 − 0.214 **0.276**
6. $5.00 − 3.76 **$1.24**	**7.** 15 − 0.66 **14.34**	**8.** 0.7 − 0.28 **0.42**	**9.** $6 − 3.42 **$2.58**	**10.** 7.8 − 0.316 **7.484**
11. 0.5 − 0.284 **0.216**	**12.** 42 − 8.71 **33.29**	**13.** 1.4 − 0.675 **0.725**	**14.** 63 − 14.29 **48.71**	**15.** 0.7 − 0.403 **0.297**
16. 1 − 0.65 **0.35**	**17.** $10 − 3.67 **$6.33**	**18.** 2.6 − 0.837 **1.763**	**19.** 0.4 − 0.091 **0.309**	**20.** 8.4 − 3.518 **4.882**

21. $5 − $2.75 **$2.25**   **22.** 3 − 1.58 **1.42**   **23.** 0.9 − 0.478 **0.422**

24. 16 − 4.38 **11.62**   **25.** $10 − $8.27 **$1.73**   **26.** 54 − 27.83 **26.17**

27. 0.4 − 0.168 **0.232**   **28.** 7.5 − 0.492 **7.008**   **29.** $20 $9.67 **$10.33**

30. 3.2 − 1.054 **2.146**   **31.** 0.8 − 0.166 **0.634**   **32.** 9 − 0.875 **8.125**

33. 94 − 47.081 **46.919**   **34.** 50 − 32.795 **17.205**   **35.** 0.2 − 0.086 **0.114**

36. 0.39 − 0.246 **0.144**   **37.** 10 − 3.48 **6.52**   **38.** 1.8 − 0.416 **1.384**

39. $40 − $25.38 **$14.62**   **40.** 0.058 − 0.029 **0.029**   **41.** 64.2 − 8.98 **55.22**

42. 21.7 − 15.59 **6.11**   **43.** 36.2 − 21.73 **14.47**   **44.** $10 − $5.21 **$4.79**

45. 8.4 − 3.79 **4.61**   **46.** 28 − 9.65 **18.35**   **47.** 6.76 − 0.852 **5.908**

48. 9.48 − 7.037 **2.443**   **49.** 0.6 − 0.483 **0.117**   **50.** 0.78 − 0.754 **0.026**

51. 41.2 − 1.376 **39.824**   **52.** 1.5 − 0.415 **1.085**   **53.** 0.09 − 0.072 **0.018**

54. 0.2 − 0.098 **0.102**   **55.** $25 − $13.75 **$11.25**   **56.** 6 − 2.048 **3.952**

Multiplication of Decimals

When you multiply a whole number and a decimal, the product
has the same number of decimal places as the decimal.

Multiply as with whole numbers.

$$\begin{array}{r} \$2.47 \\ \times \quad 15 \\ \hline 12\ 35 \\ 24\ 7 \\ \hline 37\ 05 \end{array}$$

Place the decimal point.

$$\begin{array}{r} \$2.47 \quad \textit{2 decimal places} \\ \times \quad 15 \\ \hline 12\ 35 \\ 14\ 7 \\ \hline 37.05 \quad \textit{2 decimal places} \end{array}$$

Multiply.

1. $\begin{array}{r} 8.7 \\ \times\ 6 \\ \hline 52.2 \end{array}$	**2.** $\begin{array}{r} 13.9 \\ \times\ 7 \\ \hline 97.3 \end{array}$	**3.** $\begin{array}{r} 62.8 \\ \times\ 15 \\ \hline 942 \end{array}$	**4.** $\begin{array}{r} 143 \\ \times\ 6.1 \\ \hline 872.3 \end{array}$	**5.** $\begin{array}{r} 448 \\ \times\ 0.2 \\ \hline 89.6 \end{array}$
6. $\begin{array}{r} 247 \\ \times\ 4.8 \\ \hline 1,185.6 \end{array}$	**7.** $\begin{array}{r} 7.04 \\ \times\ 9 \\ \hline 63.36 \end{array}$	**8.** $\begin{array}{r} 24.46 \\ \times\ 8 \\ \hline 195.68 \end{array}$	**9.** $\begin{array}{r} \$86.15 \\ \times\ 7 \\ \hline \$603.05 \end{array}$	**10.** $\begin{array}{r} 251 \\ \times\ 7.03 \\ \hline 1,764.53 \end{array}$
11. $\begin{array}{r} 615 \\ \times\ 0.72 \\ \hline 442.8 \end{array}$	**12.** $\begin{array}{r} 587 \\ \times\ 4.92 \\ \hline 2,888.04 \end{array}$	**13.** $\begin{array}{r} \$6.85 \\ \times\ 19 \\ \hline \$130.15 \end{array}$	**14.** $\begin{array}{r} 7.04 \\ \times\ 38 \\ \hline 267.52 \end{array}$	**15.** $\begin{array}{r} 32.61 \\ \times\ 154 \\ \hline 5,021.94 \end{array}$
16. $\begin{array}{r} 415 \\ \times\ 0.031 \\ \hline 12.865 \end{array}$	**17.** $\begin{array}{r} 627 \\ \times\ 0.105 \\ \hline 65.835 \end{array}$	**18.** $\begin{array}{r} 794 \\ \times\ 0.033 \\ \hline 26.202 \end{array}$	**19.** $\begin{array}{r} 5.283 \\ \times\ 46 \\ \hline 243.018 \end{array}$	**20.** $\begin{array}{r} 0.716 \\ \times\ 208 \\ \hline 148.928 \end{array}$
21. $\begin{array}{r} 6.075 \\ \times\ 84 \\ \hline 510.3 \end{array}$	**22.** $\begin{array}{r} 198 \\ \times\ 0.076 \\ \hline 15.048 \end{array}$	**23.** $\begin{array}{r} 2.081 \\ \times\ 59 \\ \hline 122.779 \end{array}$	**24.** $\begin{array}{r} 753 \\ \times\ 0.092 \\ \hline 69.276 \end{array}$	**25.** $\begin{array}{r} 40.084 \\ \times\ 65 \\ \hline 2,605.46 \end{array}$
26. $\begin{array}{r} \$37.25 \\ \times\ 180 \\ \hline \$6,705 \end{array}$	**27.** $\begin{array}{r} 6.741 \\ \times\ 38 \\ \hline 256.158 \end{array}$	**28.** $\begin{array}{r} 925 \\ \times\ 0.643 \\ \hline 594.775 \end{array}$	**29.** $\begin{array}{r} 437 \\ \times\ 2.089 \\ \hline 912.893 \end{array}$	**30.** $\begin{array}{r} 29.005 \\ \times\ 523 \\ \hline 15,169.615 \end{array}$
31. $\begin{array}{r} 274 \\ \times\ 3.42 \\ \hline 937.08 \end{array}$	**32.** $\begin{array}{r} 18.075 \\ \times\ 28 \\ \hline 506.1 \end{array}$	**33.** $\begin{array}{r} \$62.45 \\ \times\ 92 \\ \hline \$5,745.40 \end{array}$	**34.** $\begin{array}{r} 7.073 \\ \times\ 128 \\ \hline 905.344 \end{array}$	**35.** $\begin{array}{r} 10.413 \\ \times\ 86 \\ \hline 895.518 \end{array}$
36. $\begin{array}{r} \$5.42 \\ \times\ 237 \\ \hline \$1,284.54 \end{array}$	**37.** $\begin{array}{r} 8,003 \\ \times\ 2.07 \\ \hline 16,566.21 \end{array}$	**38.** $\begin{array}{r} 392 \\ \times\ 0.045 \\ \hline 17.64 \end{array}$	**39.** $\begin{array}{r} 0.614 \\ \times\ 395 \\ \hline 242.53 \end{array}$	**40.** $\begin{array}{r} \$28.35 \\ \times\ 67 \\ \hline \$1,899.45 \end{array}$
41. $\begin{array}{r} 794 \\ \times\ 0.083 \\ \hline 65.902 \end{array}$	**42.** $\begin{array}{r} 0.057 \\ \times\ 368 \\ \hline 20.976 \end{array}$	**43.** $\begin{array}{r} 2,460 \\ \times\ 0.145 \\ \hline 356.7 \end{array}$	**44.** $\begin{array}{r} \$9.83 \\ \times\ 702 \\ \hline \$6,900.66 \end{array}$	**45.** $\begin{array}{r} 7.492 \\ \times\ 310 \\ \hline 2,322.52 \end{array}$

Multiplying Decimals by Decimals

When you multiply a decimal by a decimal, the number of decimal places in the product is the same as the sum of the number of decimal places in the factors. Multiply as with whole numbers. Then, place the decimal point.

$$
\begin{array}{r}
\textbf{2.67} \leftarrow \text{factor} \\
\times\ \ \textbf{1.3} \leftarrow \text{factor} \\
\hline
801 \\
267\ \ \\
\hline
3471
\end{array}
\qquad
\begin{array}{r}
\textbf{2.67}\quad \textit{2 decimal places} \\
\times\ \ \textbf{1.3}\quad \textit{1 decimal place} \\
\hline
801 \\
2\ 67\ \ \\
\hline
\textbf{3.471}\quad \textit{3 decimal places}
\end{array}
$$

Multiply.

1. $\begin{array}{r} 6.3 \\ \times\ 0.4 \\ \hline 2.52 \end{array}$	**2.** $\begin{array}{r} 8.5 \\ \times\ 1.3 \\ \hline 11.05 \end{array}$	**3.** $\begin{array}{r} 0.46 \\ \times\ 0.8 \\ \hline 0.368 \end{array}$	**4.** $\begin{array}{r} 7.2 \\ \times\ 0.05 \\ \hline 0.36 \end{array}$	**5.** $\begin{array}{r} 3.94 \\ \times\ 0.6 \\ \hline 2.364 \end{array}$
6. $\begin{array}{r} 17.5 \\ \times\ 1.03 \\ \hline 18.025 \end{array}$	**7.** $\begin{array}{r} \$26.85 \\ \times\ 0.3 \\ \hline \$8.055 \end{array}$	**8.** $\begin{array}{r} 64.8 \\ \times\ 2.97 \\ \hline 192.456 \end{array}$	**9.** $\begin{array}{r} 156.72 \\ \times\ 4.9 \\ \hline 767.928 \end{array}$	**10.** $\begin{array}{r} \$96.37 \\ \times\ 6.6 \\ \hline \$636.042 \end{array}$
11. $\begin{array}{r} 6.82 \\ \times\ 0.14 \\ \hline 0.9548 \end{array}$	**12.** $\begin{array}{r} 378.5 \\ \times\ 0.061 \\ \hline 23.0885 \end{array}$	**13.** $\begin{array}{r} 2.048 \\ \times\ 5.7 \\ \hline 11.6736 \end{array}$	**14.** $\begin{array}{r} \$13.78 \\ \times\ 0.15 \\ \hline \$2.0670 \end{array}$	**15.** $\begin{array}{r} 94.6 \\ \times\ 0.208 \\ \hline 19.6768 \end{array}$
16. $\begin{array}{r} 7.5 \\ \times\ 0.901 \\ \hline 6.7575 \end{array}$	**17.** $\begin{array}{r} 3.331 \\ \times\ 18.5 \\ \hline 61.6235 \end{array}$	**18.** $\begin{array}{r} 78.623 \\ \times\ 5.1 \\ \hline 400.9773 \end{array}$	**19.** $\begin{array}{r} 62.375 \\ \times\ 4.8 \\ \hline 299.4 \end{array}$	**20.** $\begin{array}{r} 37.625 \\ \times\ 15.1 \\ \hline 568.1375 \end{array}$
21. $\begin{array}{r} 8.303 \\ \times\ 62.5 \\ \hline 518.9375 \end{array}$	**22.** $\begin{array}{r} 1.83 \\ \times\ 0.105 \\ \hline 0.19215 \end{array}$	**23.** $\begin{array}{r} \$4.32 \\ \times\ 0.333 \\ \hline \$1.43856 \end{array}$	**24.** $\begin{array}{r} 16.48 \\ \times\ 2.083 \\ \hline 34.32784 \end{array}$	**25.** $\begin{array}{r} 4.048 \\ \times\ 0.75 \\ \hline 3.036 \end{array}$
26. $\begin{array}{r} 18.599 \\ \times\ 0.68 \\ \hline 12.64732 \end{array}$	**27.** $\begin{array}{r} 244.633 \\ \times\ 2.25 \\ \hline 550.42425 \end{array}$	**28.** $\begin{array}{r} \$604.52 \\ \times\ 0.075 \\ \hline \$45.339 \end{array}$	**29.** $\begin{array}{r} 80.293 \\ \times\ 1.08 \\ \hline 86.71644 \end{array}$	**30.** $\begin{array}{r} 0.728 \\ \times\ 0.49 \\ \hline 0.35672 \end{array}$
31. $\begin{array}{r} \$12.54 \\ \times\ 2.3 \\ \hline \$28.842 \end{array}$	**32.** $\begin{array}{r} 62.7 \\ \times\ 2.8 \\ \hline 175.56 \end{array}$	**33.** $\begin{array}{r} 45.6 \\ \times\ 13.2 \\ \hline 601.92 \end{array}$	**34.** $\begin{array}{r} 8.54 \\ \times\ 1.56 \\ \hline 13.3224 \end{array}$	**35.** $\begin{array}{r} \$83.46 \\ \times\ 2.6 \\ \hline \$216.996 \end{array}$
36. $\begin{array}{r} 7.08 \\ \times\ 30.5 \\ \hline 215.94 \end{array}$	**37.** $\begin{array}{r} 4.38 \\ \times\ 0.07 \\ \hline 0.3066 \end{array}$	**38.** $\begin{array}{r} 7.005 \\ \times\ 2.49 \\ \hline 17.44245 \end{array}$	**39.** $\begin{array}{r} 5.008 \\ \times\ 0.074 \\ \hline 0.370592 \end{array}$	**40.** $\begin{array}{r} 3.407 \\ \times\ 0.09 \\ \hline 0.30663 \end{array}$
41. $\begin{array}{r} 6.89 \\ \times\ 0.203 \\ \hline 1.39867 \end{array}$	**42.** $\begin{array}{r} \$37.15 \\ \times\ 0.048 \\ \hline \$1.78320 \end{array}$	**43.** $\begin{array}{r} 0.057 \\ \times\ 0.006 \\ \hline 0.000342 \end{array}$	**44.** $\begin{array}{r} 0.352 \\ \times\ 6.012 \\ \hline 2.116224 \end{array}$	**45.** $\begin{array}{r} 9.008 \\ \times\ 32.5 \\ \hline 292.76 \end{array}$

Multiplication of Decimals Using Zeros

It is often necessary to write extra zeros in order to correctly place the decimal point in the product.

1.12 2 decimal places	The factors have a total of 5 decimal places. Therefore, the product should have 5 decimal places. In order to have 5 decimal places in the product 4816, write a zero to the left of the number and place the decimal point.
× 0.043 3 decimal places	
336	
448	
4816 ▸ **0.04816** 5 decimal places	

How can you use estimation to tell that 0.04816 is the correct estimate instead of 0.48160? **1 × 0.04 = 0.04**

Copy. Then place the decimal point in the product.

1. 0.03 × 3 = 0.09	2. 0.005 × 3 = 0.015	3. 2 × 0.04 = 0.08	4. 0.012 × 6 = 0.072	5. 0.024 × 0.4 = 0.0096
6. 0.02 × 0.6 = 0.012	7. 0.068 × 0.5 = 0.0340	8. 0.16 × 0.007 = 0.00112	9. 2.07 × 0.03 = 0.0621	10. 0.212 × 0.008 = 0.001696

Multiply.

11. 0.4 × 0.2 = 0.08	12. 0.7 × 0.02 = 0.014	13. 4.6 × 0.003 = 0.0138	14. 0.03 × 0.01 = 0.0003	15. 0.04 × 2.1 = 0.084
16. 0.343 × 0.012 = 0.004116	17. 3.02 × 0.004 = 0.01208	18. 0.005 × 2.8 = 0.014	19. 0.007 × 4.15 = 0.02905	20. 0.14 × 0.22 = 0.0308
21. 0.32 × 0.007 = 0.00224	22. $0.75 × 0.002 = $0.00150	23. 0.05 × 0.12 = 0.006	24. 0.040 × 0.22 = 0.0088	25. 2.05 × 0.003 = 0.00615
26. 0.052 × 0.03 = 0.00156	27. 0.74 × 0.015 = 0.0111	28. 0.011 × 0.04 = 0.00044	29. 0.417 × 0.23 = 0.09591	30. 0.017 × 5 = 0.085
31. 0.008 × 0.14 = 0.00112	32. 2.093 × 0.026 = 0.054418	33. $12.45 × 0.008 = $0.09960	34. 0.67 × 0.045 = 0.03015	35. 0.082 × 1.09 = 0.08938
36. 0.035 × 0.76 = 0.0266	37. 5.7 × 0.019 = 0.1083	38. 0.173 × 0.028 = 0.004844	39. 0.05 × 0.073 = 0.00365	40. $0.95 × 0.067 = $0.0365

Dividing Decimals by Whole Numbers

To divide a decimal by a whole number, place the decimal
point in the quotient as shown.

$$7 \overline{)1.82} \quad \blacktriangleright \quad 7 \overline{)1{\cdot}82}$$

Then, divide as with whole numbers.

Divide the *ones*.

1 ÷ 7

$$\begin{array}{r} 0. \\ 7 \overline{)1.82} \end{array}$$

*Write a zero in the ones
place to help place
the decimal point.*

Divide the *tenths*.

Estimate 18 tenths ÷ 7 as 2

$$\begin{array}{r} 0.2 \\ 7 \overline{)1.82} \\ -14 \\ \hline 4 \end{array}$$

Divide the *hundredths*.

42 hundredths ÷ 7 = 6

$$\begin{array}{r} 0.26 \\ 7 \overline{)1.82} \\ -14 \\ \hline 42 \\ -42 \\ \hline 0 \end{array}$$

How can you use estimation to tell that 0.04816 is the
correct estimate instead of 0.48160?

Copy. Then place the decimal point in the quotient.

1. $3.2 \div 2 \overline{)6.4}$ 2. $32.1 \div 3 \overline{)96.3}$ 3. $0.02 \div 7 \overline{)0.14}$ 4. $0.003 \div 8 \overline{)0.024}$ 5. $0.07 \div 9 \overline{)0.63}$

6. $1.8 \div 34 \overline{)61.2}$ 7. $0.7 \div 25 \overline{)17.5}$ 8. $0.04 \div 54 \overline{)2.16}$ 9. $0.012 \div 86 \overline{)1.032}$ 10. $0.0036 \div 47 \overline{)0.1692}$

Divide.

11. $0.9 \div 4 \overline{)3.6}$ 12. $1.2 \div 6 \overline{)7.2}$ 13. $1.2 \div 2 \overline{)2.4}$ 14. $0.6 \div 8 \overline{)4.8}$ 15. $1.5 \div 5 \overline{)7.5}$

16. $0.09 \div 6 \overline{)0.54}$ 17. $2.19 \div 2 \overline{)4.38}$ 18. $9.03 \div 3 \overline{)27.09}$ 19. $0.61 \div 7 \overline{)4.27}$ 20. $0.09 \div 9 \overline{)0.81}$

21. $0.001 \div 9 \overline{)0.009}$ 22. $1.123 \div 5 \overline{)5.615}$ 23. $8.012 \div 4 \overline{)32.048}$ 24. $0.005 \div 3 \overline{)0.015}$ 25. $1.138 \div 8 \overline{)9.104}$

26. $2.6 \div 14 \overline{)36.4}$ 27. $0.58 \div 43 \overline{)24.94}$ 28. $0.035 \div 27 \overline{)0.945}$ 29. $2.08 \div 61 \overline{)126.88}$ 30. $0.42 \div 58 \overline{)24.36}$

31. $5.66 \div 75 \overline{)424.5}$ 32. $1.87 \div 36 \overline{)67.32}$ 33. $0.573 \div 21 \overline{)12.033}$ 34. $0.0972 \div 18 \overline{)1.7496}$ 35. $0.0925 \div 43 \overline{)3.9775}$

36. $78.4 \div 12 \overline{)940.8}$ 37. $0.543 \div 94 \overline{)51.042}$ 38. $0.0092 \div 67 \overline{)0.6164}$ 39. $0.097 \div 52 \overline{)5.044}$ 40. $0.813 \div 39 \overline{)31.707}$

41. $0.076 \div 26 \overline{)1.976}$ 42. $0.037 \div 17 \overline{)0.629}$ 43. $0.0027 \div 48 \overline{)0.1296}$ 44. $0.024 \div 83 \overline{)1.992}$ 45. $1.83 \div 76 \overline{)139.08}$

46. $0.047 \div 55 \overline{)2.585}$ 47. $0.008 \div 62 \overline{)0.496}$ 48. $1.68 \div 98 \overline{)164.64}$ 49. $0.0051 \div 23 \overline{)0.1173}$ 50. $0.039 \div 84 \overline{)3.276}$

Multiplication and Division by Powers of 10

Multiplying and dividing by powers of 10 such as 10, 100, and
1,000 is made easier by using patterns.

Multiply by powers of 10.

$0.91 \times 10 \quad = 0\,9\,1 \quad = 9.1$

$0.91 \times 100 \quad = 0\,9\,1 \quad = 91$

$0.91 \times 1,000 = 0\,9\,1\,0 = 910$

Divide by powers of 10.

$35.8 \div 10 \quad = 3\,5\,8 \quad = 3.58$

$35.8 \div 100 \quad = 3\,5\,8 \quad = 0.358$

$35.8 \div 1,000 = 0\,3\,5\,8 = 0.0358$

What is the pattern between the number of zeros and the number
of places the decimal point is moved?

Copy. Then place the decimal point in the product or quotient.

1. $5.5 \times 10 = 55.$

2. $3.8 \div 10 = .38$

3. $2.6 \times 100 = 260.$

4. $49 \div 100 = .49$

5. $24 \times 1,000 = 24{,}000.$

6. $6940 \div 1,000 = 6.94$

7. $11.4 \times 100 = 1140.$

8. $9 \div 100 = .09$

9. $0.4 \times 1,000 = 400.$

Multiply or divide. Use the patterns developed above.

10. $40 \div 10$ **4**

11. 8×10 **80**

12. $16 \div 10$ **1.6**

13. 43×10 **430**

14. $400 \div 100$ **4**

15. $80 \div 100$ **0.8**

16. 16×100 **1,600**

17. 43×100 **4,300**

18. $4,000 \div 1,000$ **4**

19. $800 \div 1,000$ **0.8**

20. $16 \times 1,000$ **16,000**

21. $43 \times 1,000$ **43,000**

22. $24.5 \div 10$ **2.45**

23. 12.8×10 **128**

24. 75.1×10 **751**

25. 8.06×10 **80.6**

26. $24.5 \div 100$ **0.245**

27. 12.8×100 **1,280**

28. 75.1×100 **7,510**

29. 8.06×100 **806**

30. $24.5 \times 1,000$ **24,500**

31. $12.8 \times 1,000$ **12,800**

32. $75.1 \times 1,000$ **75,100**

33. $8.06 \times 1,000$ **8,060**

34. 1.86×100 **186**

35. $24 \div 10$ **2.4**

36. $1.426 \times 1,000$ **1,426**

37. 5.64×100 **564**

38. $48 \div 10$ **4.8**

39. 74.4×100 **7,440**

40. $22.64 \div 1,000$
0.02264

41. $27.8 \div 10$ **2.78**

42. $400 \div 10$ **40**

43. $61 \div 1,000$ **0.061**

44. 3.1×10 **31**

45. $94 \div 1,000$ **0.094**

46. $15.9 \div 10$ **1.59**

47. 0.37×10 **3.7**

48. $37 \div 100$ **0.37**

49. 0.36×10 **3.6**

50. $3.85 \times 1,000$ **3,850**

51. $9 \div 10$ **0.9**

52. $12 \div 100$ **0.12**

53. $2.64 \times 1,000$ **2,640**

54. 94.1×100 **9,410**

55. 0.4×100 **40**

56. $0.4 \times 1,000$ **400**

57. $1.03 \div 100$ **0.0103**

Multiply or divide.

$9 \div 300 = (9 \div 3) \div 100$	$4 \times 80 = (4 \times 8) \times 10$
$= 3 \div 100$	$= 32 \times 10$
$= 0.03$	$= 320$

58. $4 \div 20$ **0.2**

59. $8 \div 40$ **0.2**

60. 9×30 **270**

61. 6×20 **120**

62. 9×40 **360**

63. $18 \div 60$ **0.3**

64. 6×800 **4,800**

65. $28 \div 700$ **0.04**

66. $81 \div 9,000$ **0.009**

67. $7 \times 8,000$ **56,000**

68. $25 \div 5,000$ **0.005**

69. $5 \times 6,000$ **30,000**

Division by Decimals (Tenths)

To divide by a decimal, multiply both the divisor and dividend by the same power of 10 so the divisor is a whole number. Then divide as with whole numbers.

$$0.7\overline{)10.01}$$

Since 0.7 has 1 decimal place, multiply 0.7 and 10.01 by 10.

$$0.7\overline{)10.0\,1}$$

$$
\begin{array}{r}
14.3 \\
0.7\overline{)10.0\,1} \\
-\,7 \\
\hline
3\,0 \\
-\,2\,8 \\
\hline
2\,1 \\
-\,2\,1 \\
\hline
0
\end{array}
$$

Divide.

1. $0.8\overline{)6.4}$ = 8.

2. $0.3\overline{)2.7}$ = 9.

3. $0.5\overline{)2.5}$ = 5.

4. $0.6\overline{)3.6}$ = 6.

5. $0.9\overline{)4.5}$ = 5.

6. $0.3\overline{)1.8}$ = 6.

7. $0.2\overline{)1.4}$ = 7.

8. $0.1\overline{)0.5}$ = 5.

9. $0.7\overline{)4.9}$ = 7.

10. $0.5\overline{)3.0}$ = 6.

11. $0.7\overline{)16.1}$ = 23.

12. $0.9\overline{)54.9}$ = 61.

13. $0.7\overline{)26.6}$ = 38.

14. $0.4\overline{)23.6}$ = 59.

15. $0.9\overline{)18.9}$ = 21.

16. $0.8\overline{)4.96}$ = 6.2

17. $0.2\overline{)1.46}$ = 7.3

18. $0.6\overline{)3.24}$ = 5.4

19. $0.5\overline{)4.45}$ = 8.9

20. $0.3\overline{)2.28}$ = 7.6

21. $0.6\overline{)0.798}$ = 1.33

22. $0.9\overline{)1.917}$ = 2.13

23. $0.3\overline{)1.893}$ = 6.31

24. $0.4\overline{)0.804}$ = 2.01

25. $0.8\overline{)2.456}$ = 3.07

26. $0.4\overline{)1.0}$ = 2.5

27. $0.8\overline{)4.0}$ = 5.

28. $0.6\overline{)1.5}$ = 2.5

29. $0.2\overline{)0.07}$ = 0.35

30. $0.8\overline{)2.24}$ = 2.8

31. $0.7\overline{)0.028}$ = 0.04

32. $0.9\overline{)0.063}$ = 0.07

33. $0.4\overline{)4.24}$ = 10.6

34. $0.5\overline{)2.045}$ = 4.09

35. $0.3\overline{)2.118}$ = 7.06

36. $0.8\overline{)0.84}$ = 1.05

37. $0.6\overline{)1.23}$ = 2.05

38. $0.7\overline{)9.52}$ = 13.6

39. $0.4\overline{)2}$ = 5.

40. $0.9\overline{)0.9027}$ = 1.003

41. $1.4\overline{)8.4}$ = 6.

42. $2.3\overline{)16.1}$ = 7.

43. $1.6\overline{)19.2}$ = 12.

44. $3.5\overline{)4.55}$ = 1.3

45. $4.8\overline{)16.32}$ = 3.4

46. $9.1\overline{)6.37}$ = 0.7

47. $5.2\overline{)4.68}$ = 0.9

48. $7.3\overline{)1.533}$ = 0.21

49. $8.7\overline{)29.58}$ = 3.4

50. $6.5\overline{)5.59}$ = 0.86

51. $2.8\overline{)1.40}$ = 0.5

52. $3.4\overline{)3.468}$ = 1.02

53. $6.1\overline{)0.427}$ = 0.07

54. $9.7\overline{)0.776}$ = 0.08

55. $2.2\overline{)14.3}$ = 6.5

56. $5.5\overline{)0.33}$ = 0.06

57. $3.8\overline{)15.39}$ = 4.05

58. $1.9\overline{)0.0152}$ = 0.008

59. $6.6\overline{)13.53}$ = 2.05

60. $4.8\overline{)456}$ = 95.

61. $12.4\overline{)37.2}$ = 3.

62. $20.1\overline{)120.6}$ = 6.

63. $26.5\overline{)18.55}$ = 0.7

64. $16.7\overline{)5.01}$ = 0.3

65. $60.3\overline{)422.1}$ = 7.

66. $81.8\overline{)130.88}$ = 1.6

67. $19.2\overline{)1.152}$ = 0.06

68. $15.8\overline{)0.79}$ = 0.05

69. $26.2\overline{)27.51}$ = 1.05

70. $31.5\overline{)95.13}$ = 3.02

Division by Decimals

Divide 19.63 by 3.02 as follows.

$$3.02 \overline{)19.63}$$ → *Since 3.02 has 2 decimal places, multiply 3.02 and 19.63 by 100.*

$$3.02 \overline{)19.63}$$ → $$\begin{array}{r} 6.5 \\ 3.02 \overline{)19.630} \\ -\ 18\ 12 \\ \hline 1\ 510 \\ -\ 1\ 510 \\ \hline 0 \end{array}$$

Name the appropriate power of 10 you would multiply by to change each divisor to a whole number.

1. 0.8 10   **2.** 1.7 10   **3.** 0.17 100   **4.** 0.017 1,000

5. 0.009 1,000   **6.** 0.04 100   **7.** 4.02 100   **8.** 0.026 1,000

Divide.

9. $0.3 \overline{)2.4}$ = 8.   **10.** $0.03 \overline{)0.24}$ = 8.   **11.** $0.003 \overline{)0.024}$ = 8.   **12.** $0.05 \overline{)0.45}$ = 9.

13. $0.9 \overline{)0.36}$ = 0.4   **14.** $0.09 \overline{)0.036}$ = 0.4   **15.** $0.009 \overline{)0.0036}$ = 0.4   **16.** $0.008 \overline{)0.056}$ = 7.

17. $0.07 \overline{)0.035}$ = 0.5   **18.** $0.06 \overline{)0.054}$ = 0.9   **19.** $0.003 \overline{)0.027}$ = 9.   **20.** $0.04 \overline{)0.28}$ = 7.

21. $0.08 \overline{)0.104}$ = 1.3   **22.** $0.9 \overline{)0.288}$ = 0.32   **23.** $0.007 \overline{)0.469}$ = 67.   **24.** $0.05 \overline{)0.195}$ = 3.9

25. $0.05 \overline{)0.40}$ = 8.   **26.** $0.006 \overline{)0.021}$ = 3.5   **27.** $0.2 \overline{)0.21}$ = 1.05   **28.** $0.08 \overline{)0.484}$ = 6.05

29. $0.14 \overline{)0.84}$ = 6.   **30.** $0.018 \overline{)0.162}$ = 9.   **31.** $3.4 \overline{)1.36}$ = 0.4   **32.** $0.56 \overline{)0.336}$ = 0.6

33. $0.029 \overline{)0.0986}$ = 3.4   **34.** $0.47 \overline{)29.61}$ = 63.   **35.** $0.61 \overline{)0.2013}$ = 0.33   **36.** $8.9 \overline{)65.86}$ = 7.4

37. $0.67 \overline{)0.0804}$ = 0.12   **38.** $0.095 \overline{)2.185}$ = 23   **39.** $0.63 \overline{)19.656}$ = 31.2   **40.** $0.044 \overline{)2.288}$ = 52.

41. $0.06 \overline{)4.2}$ = 70.   **42.** $0.073 \overline{)0.00219}$ = 0.03   **43.** $0.64 \overline{)1.6}$ = 2.5   **44.** $8.2 \overline{)0.041}$ = 0.005

45. $0.75 \overline{)6.45}$ = 8.6   **46.** $0.36 \overline{)0.0216}$ = 0.06   **47.** $0.018 \overline{)0.1089}$ = 6.05   **48.** $0.078 \overline{)0.039}$ = 0.5

49. $9.6 \overline{)289.92}$ = 30.2   **50.** $0.52 \overline{)1.066}$ = 2.05   **51.** $0.074 \overline{)0.4477}$ = 6.05   **52.** $0.46 \overline{)0.0023}$ = 0.005

53. $1.18 \overline{)0.00472}$ = 0.004   **54.** $4.07 \overline{)0.15059}$ = 0.037   **55.** $0.235 \overline{)0.00611}$ = 0.026   **56.** $0.692 \overline{)0.02076}$ = 0.03

57. $4.11 \overline{)51.786}$ = 12.6   **58.** $83.2 \overline{)124.8}$ = 1.5   **59.** $0.204 \overline{)0.04488}$ = 0.22   **60.** $0.085 \overline{)1.751}$ = 20.6

Factors

The **factors** of a number are the numbers by which it can be divided evenly. That is, the remainder is zero upon division.

$$24 \div 1 = 24 \qquad\qquad 24 \div 6 = 4$$
$$24 \div 2 = 12 \qquad\qquad 24 \div 8 = 3$$
$$24 \div 3 = 8 \qquad\qquad 24 \div 12 = 2$$
$$24 \div 4 = 6 \qquad\qquad 24 \div 24 = 1$$

factors of 24

The factors of 24 are 1, 2, 3, 4, 6, 8, 12 and 24.

State which numbers are factors of the first number.

1. 4: <u>1</u>, <u>2</u>, 3, <u>4</u>
2. 5: <u>1</u>, 2, 3, <u>5</u>
3. 9: <u>1</u>, <u>3</u>, 6, 8
4. 11: <u>1</u>, 4, 7, <u>11</u>
5. 15: <u>1</u>, <u>3</u>, <u>5</u>, <u>15</u>
6. 12: <u>1</u>, <u>4</u>, 8, <u>12</u>
7. 16: <u>2</u>, <u>4</u>, 6, <u>8</u>
8. 18: <u>1</u>, <u>2</u>, <u>3</u>, 4, 5
9. 13: <u>1</u>, 5, 8, 9, <u>13</u>
10. 20: <u>2</u>, <u>4</u>, 6, 8, <u>10</u>
11. 14: <u>1</u>, <u>2</u>, 5, <u>7</u>
12. 22: <u>1</u>, <u>11</u>, 12, <u>22</u>
13. 27: <u>1</u>, 2, <u>3</u>, <u>9</u>, 13
14. 28: <u>1</u>, <u>2</u>, <u>4</u>, <u>7</u>, <u>14</u>
15. 25: <u>5</u>, 10, 15, 20
16. 30: <u>1</u>, 4, <u>5</u>, 7, 8
17. 26: <u>1</u>, 3, 4, <u>13</u>
18. 21: <u>7</u>, 9, 11, 12
19. 35: 2, 3, <u>5</u>, <u>7</u>, 11
20. 39: <u>1</u>, <u>3</u>, 5, 7, 9
21. 40: <u>2</u>, <u>4</u>, <u>5</u>, <u>8</u>, <u>10</u>
22. 42: <u>1</u>, <u>2</u>, <u>3</u>, 5, <u>7</u>
23. 50: <u>1</u>, 3, <u>5</u>, 8, 9, <u>10</u>
24. 49: <u>1</u>, 3, 4, <u>7</u>, 10, 12
25. 60: <u>1</u>, <u>2</u>, <u>3</u>, <u>4</u>, <u>5</u>, <u>6</u>, 7
26. 45: <u>3</u>, <u>5</u>, 10, <u>15</u>
27. 72: <u>6</u>, <u>9</u>, <u>12</u>, 15, <u>18</u>
28. 36: <u>4</u>, 5, <u>6</u>, <u>9</u>, <u>12</u>, <u>18</u>
29. 64: <u>4</u>, <u>8</u>, 12, <u>16</u>, 21, <u>32</u>
30. 100: <u>5</u>, <u>10</u>, 15, <u>20</u>, <u>25</u> 30

State all the factors of each number.

31. 4 1, 2, 4
32. 5 1, 5
33. 9 1, 3, 9
34. 11 1, 11
35. 15 1, 3, 5, 15
36. 12 1, 2, 3, 4, 6, 12
37. 16 1, 2, 4, 8, 16
38. 18 1, 2, 3, 6, 9, 18
39. 13 1, 13
40. 35 1, 5, 7, 35
41. 22 1, 2, 11, 22
42. 6 1, 2, 3, 6
43. 17 1, 17
44. 26 1, 2, 13, 26
45. 28 1, 2, 4, 7, 14, 28
46. 27 1, 3, 9, 27
47. 30 1, 2, 3, 5, 6, 10, 15, 30
48. 55 1, 5, 11, 55
49. 42 1, 2, 3, 6, 7, 14, 21, 42
50. 56 1, 2, 4, 7, 8, 14, 28, 56
51. 80 1, 2, 4, 5, 8, 10, 16, 20, 40, 80
52. 72 1, 2, 3, 4, 6, 8, 9, 12, 18, 24, 36, 72
53. 38 1, 2, 19, 38
54. 32 1, 2, 4, 8, 16, 32
55. 40 1, 2, 4, 5, 8, 10, 20, 40
56. 31 1, 31
57. 48 1, 2, 3, 4, 6, 8, 12, 16, 24, 48
58. 36 1, 2, 3, 4, 6, 9, 12, 18, 36
59. 64 1, 2, 4, 8, 16, 32, 64
60. 100 1, 2, 4, 5, 10, 20, 25, 50, 100
61. What number is a factor every number? 1
62. What number is a factor of only one number? 0

Divisibility by 2, 3, 5, 9, and 10

The following rules can be used to determine whether a number is divisible by 2, 3, 5, 9, and 10. Note that if a number is divisible by a second number, the second number is a factor of the first.

2: A number is divisible by 2 if the ones digit is 0, 2, 4, 6, or 8.

5: A number is divisible by 5 if the ones digit is 0 or 5.

10: A number is divisible by 10 if the ones digit is 0.

3: A number is divisible by 3 if the sum of the digits is 3, 6, or 9.

9: A number is divisible by 9 if the sum of the digits is 9.

State whether each number is divisible by 2.

1. 12 yes	**2.** 17 no	**3.** 8 yes	**4.** 11 no	**5.** 9 no	**6.** 23 no
7. 69 no	**8.** 16 yes	**9.** 10 yes	**10.** 29 no	**11.** 37 no	**12.** 465 no
13. 157 no	**14.** 26 yes	**15.** 188 yes	**16.** 1,000 yes	**17.** 2,001 no	**18.** 2,500 yes

State whether each number is divisible by 5. Then state whether each is divisible by 10.

19. 15 yes, no	**20.** 40 yes, yes	**21.** 37 no, no	**22.** 56 no, no	**23.** 81 no, no	**24.** 18 no, no
25. 50 yes, yes	**26.** 75 yes, no	**27.** 549 no, no	**28.** 235 yes, no	**29.** 140 yes, yes	**30.** 30 yes, yes
31. 201 no, no	**32.** 60 yes, yes	**33.** 95 yes, no	**34.** 204 no, no	**35.** 185 yes, no	**36.** 380 yes, yes
37. 105 yes, no	**38.** 100 yes, yes	**39.** 2,145 yes, no	**40.** 111 no, no	**41.** 8,000 yes, yes	**42.** 7,108 no, no

State whether each number is divisible by 3. Then state whether each is divisible by 9.

Is 255 divisible by 3?	Is 3,247 divisible by 9?
2 + 5 + 5 = 12	**3 + 2 + 4 + 7 = 16**
Add again, 1 + 2 = 3.	Add again, 1 + 6 = 7.
Yes, 255 is divisible by 3.	No, 3,247 is *not* divisible by 9.

43. 27 yes, yes	**44.** 6 yes, no	**45.** 23 no, no	**46.** 17 no, no	**47.** 26 no, no	**48.** 42 yes, no
49. 9 yes, yes	**50.** 63 yes, yes	**51.** 40 no, no	**52.** 72 yes, yes	**53.** 88 no, no	**54.** 78 yes, no
55. 59 no, no	**56.** 51 yes, no	**57.** 18 yes, yes	**58.** 36 yes, yes	**59.** 99 yes, yes	**60.** 75 yes, no
61. 117 yes, yes	**62.** 139 no, no	**63.** 157 no, no	**64.** 111 yes, no	**65.** 356 no, no	**66.** 128 no, no
67. 175 no, no	**68.** 708 yes, no	**69.** 255 yes, no	**70.** 495 yes, yes	**71.** 108 yes, yes	**72.** 174 yes, no
73. 2,001 yes, no	**74.** 1,627 no, no	**75.** 3,407 no, no	**76.** 7,924 no, no	**77.** 8,838 yes, yes	**78.** 6,327 yes, yes

Primes and Composites

A **prime number** has exactly two factors, 1 and itself.

$13 = 13 \times 1$
The only factors of 13 are 13 and 1.

Therefore, 13 is a prime number.

A **composite number** has more than two factors.

$12 = 1 \times 12$
$12 = 2 \times 6$
$12 = 3 \times 4$
The factors of 12 are 1, 2, 3, 4, 6, and 12.

Therefore, 12 is a composite number.

The numbers 0 and 1 are neither prime nor composite.

State whether each number is prime or composite.

1. 16 comp.   2. 7 prime   3. 8 comp.   4. 17 prime   5. 9 comp.   6. 3 prime

7. 15 comp.   8. 10 comp.   9. 49 comp.   10. 23 prime   11. 19 prime   12. 25 comp.

13. 34 comp.   14. 2 prime   15. 41 prime   16. 30 comp.   17. 53 prime   18. 33 comp.

19. 37 prime   20. 24 comp.   21. 40 comp.   22. 91 comp.   23. 29 prime   24. 71 prime

Copy. Then complete each factor tree.

25.   26.   27. 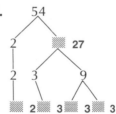   28.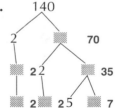

Write each composite number as a product of prime factors.
Use a factor tree to help determine the prime factors.

$27 = 3 \times 9$ $= 3 \times 3 \times 3$	$30 = 2 \times 15$ $= 2 \times 3 \times 5$	$140 = 2 \times 70$ $= 2 \times 2 \times 35$ $= 2 \times 2 \times 5 \times 7$

29. 22
2×11

30. 15
3×5

31. 25
5×5

32. 16
2×2×2×2

33. 18
2×3×3

34. 45
3×3×5

35. 24
2×2×2×3

36. 12
2×2×3

37. 8
2×2×2

38. 14
2×7

39. 48
2×2×2×2×3

40. 72
2×2×2×3×3

41. 10
2×5

42. 9
3×3

43. 42
2×3×7

44. 81
3×3×3×3

45. 96
2×2×2×2×2×3

46. 30
2×3×5

47. 36
2×2×3×3

48. 26
2×13

49. 68
2×2×17

50. 135
3×3×3×5

51. 52
2×2×13

52. 120
2×2×2×3×5

53. 32
2×2×2×2×2

54. 60
2×2×3×5

55. 90
2×3×3×5

56. 64
2×2×2×2×2×2

57. 100
2×2×5×5

58. 108
2×2×3×3×3

Greatest Common Factor (GCF)

Prime factors can be used to find the GCF of two numbers.
Find the GCF of 30 and 45.

First, find the prime factors.

Now, find the factors the numbers have in common.

$30 = 2 \times 3 \times 5$
$45 = 3 \times 3 \times 5$

The **greatest common factor (GCF)** is the product of the common factors.

$3 \times 5 = 15$

Find the GCF of each pair of numbers.

1. $2 = \underline{2}$ **2**
  $18 = \underline{2} \times 3 \times 3$

2. $12 = \underline{2 \times 2} \times 3$ **4**
  $16 = \underline{2 \times 2} \times 2 \times 2$

3. $24 = \underline{2 \times 2 \times 2} \times 3$
  $8 = \underline{2 \times 2 \times 2}$ **8**

4. $10 = 2 \times \underline{5}$ **5**
  $15 = 3 \times \underline{5}$

5. $18 = \underline{2 \times 3} \times 3$ **6**
  $30 = \underline{2 \times 3} \times 5$

6. $25 = 5 \times \underline{5}$ **5**
  $10 = 2 \times \underline{5}$

7. 9 and 12 **3**
8. 8 and 10 **2**
9. 6 and 18 **6**
10. 2 and 10 **2**

11. 5 and 25 **5**
12. 4 and 12 **4**
13. 5 and 10 **5**
14. 3 and 7 **1**

15. 12 and 3 **3**
16. 8 and 2 **2**
17. 10 and 4 **2**
18. 9 and 18 **9**

19. 3 and 11 **1**
20. 4 and 6 **2**
21. 3 and 5 **1**
22. 6 and 9 **3**

23. 2 and 4 **2**
24. 12 and 16 **4**
25. 8 and 18 **2**
26. 4 and 14 **2**

27. 15 and 6 **3**
28. 9 and 27 **9**
29. 18 and 24 **6**
30. 8 and 20 **4**

31. 14 and 16 **2**
32. 21 and 35 **7**
33. 15 and 20 **5**
34. 3 and 21 **3**

35. 18 and 12 **6**
36. 18 and 21 **3**
37. 12 and 27 **3**
38. 36 and 48 **12**

39. 5 and 45 **5**
40. 20 and 36 **4**
41. 18 and 27 **9**
42. 16 and 8 **8**

43. 36 and 45 **9**
44. 40 and 24 **8**
45. 30 and 33 **3**
46. 35 and 42 **7**

47. 24 and 56 **8**
48. 48 and 72 **24**
49. 37 and 23 **1**
50. 45 and 96 **3**

51. 54 and 36 **18**
52. 75 and 25 **25**
53. 99 and 11 **11**
54. 125 and 5 **5**

55. 42 and 56 **14**
56. 81 and 36 **9**
57. 42 and 60 **6**
58. 69 and 92 **23**

59. 39 and 54 **3**
60. 119 and 34 **17**
61. 40 and 100 **20**
62. 102 and 68 **34**

Simplifying Fractions

To change a fraction to simplest form, divide both the numerator and denominator by their GCF.

Change $\frac{21}{28}$ to simplest form.

Find the GCF of 21 and 28. $21 = 3 \times 7$
The GCF is 7. $28 = 2 \times 2 \times 7$

Divide 21 and 28 by 7. $\dfrac{21 \div 7}{28 \div 7} = \dfrac{3}{4}$

The fraction $\frac{21}{28}$ in simplest form is $\frac{3}{4}$.

Change each fraction to simplest form.

1. $\frac{2}{4}$ $\frac{1}{2}$ 2. $\frac{4}{8}$ $\frac{1}{2}$ 3. $\frac{3}{9}$ $\frac{1}{3}$ 4. $\frac{2}{8}$ $\frac{1}{4}$ 5. $\frac{3}{6}$ $\frac{1}{2}$ 6. $\frac{6}{9}$ $\frac{2}{3}$

7. $\frac{4}{10}$ $\frac{2}{5}$ 8. $\frac{4}{6}$ $\frac{2}{3}$ 9. $\frac{6}{8}$ $\frac{3}{4}$ 10. $\frac{6}{10}$ $\frac{3}{5}$ 11. $\frac{2}{12}$ $\frac{1}{6}$ 12. $\frac{2}{6}$ $\frac{1}{3}$

13. $\frac{6}{12}$ $\frac{1}{2}$ 14. $\frac{5}{15}$ $\frac{1}{3}$ 15. $\frac{4}{16}$ $\frac{1}{4}$ 16. $\frac{9}{12}$ $\frac{3}{4}$ 17. $\frac{4}{12}$ $\frac{1}{3}$ 18. $\frac{3}{12}$ $\frac{1}{4}$

19. $\frac{5}{10}$ $\frac{1}{2}$ 20. $\frac{10}{12}$ $\frac{5}{6}$ 21. $\frac{14}{18}$ $\frac{7}{9}$ 22. $\frac{10}{15}$ $\frac{2}{3}$ 23. $\frac{8}{12}$ $\frac{2}{3}$ 24. $\frac{2}{16}$ $\frac{1}{8}$

25. $\frac{12}{15}$ $\frac{4}{5}$ 26. $\frac{6}{16}$ $\frac{3}{8}$ 27. $\frac{9}{15}$ $\frac{3}{5}$ 28. $\frac{12}{14}$ $\frac{6}{7}$ 29. $\frac{9}{27}$ $\frac{1}{3}$ 30. $\frac{9}{18}$ $\frac{1}{2}$

31. $\frac{3}{15}$ $\frac{1}{5}$ 32. $\frac{10}{16}$ $\frac{5}{8}$ 33. $\frac{4}{20}$ $\frac{1}{5}$ 34. $\frac{8}{24}$ $\frac{1}{3}$ 35. $\frac{4}{18}$ $\frac{2}{9}$ 36. $\frac{7}{21}$ $\frac{1}{3}$

37. $\frac{2}{20}$ $\frac{1}{10}$ 38. $\frac{2}{18}$ $\frac{1}{9}$ 39. $\frac{14}{16}$ $\frac{7}{8}$ 40. $\frac{14}{28}$ $\frac{1}{2}$ 41. $\frac{5}{20}$ $\frac{1}{4}$ 42. $\frac{3}{24}$ $\frac{1}{8}$

43. $\frac{6}{24}$ $\frac{1}{4}$ 44. $\frac{6}{18}$ $\frac{1}{3}$ 45. $\frac{10}{20}$ $\frac{1}{2}$ 46. $\frac{6}{15}$ $\frac{2}{5}$ 47. $\frac{8}{10}$ $\frac{4}{5}$ 48. $\frac{15}{20}$ $\frac{3}{4}$

49. $\frac{25}{40}$ $\frac{5}{8}$ 50. $\frac{20}{24}$ $\frac{5}{6}$ 51. $\frac{10}{40}$ $\frac{1}{4}$ 52. $\frac{10}{25}$ $\frac{2}{5}$ 53. $\frac{20}{32}$ $\frac{5}{8}$ 54. $\frac{15}{18}$ $\frac{5}{6}$

55. $\frac{15}{100}$ $\frac{3}{20}$ 56. $\frac{28}{40}$ $\frac{7}{10}$ 57. $\frac{17}{51}$ $\frac{1}{3}$ 58. $\frac{46}{100}$ $\frac{23}{50}$ 59. $\frac{4}{44}$ $\frac{1}{11}$ 60. $\frac{13}{52}$ $\frac{1}{4}$

61. $\frac{32}{48}$ $\frac{2}{3}$ 62. $\frac{22}{55}$ $\frac{2}{5}$ 63. $\frac{24}{36}$ $\frac{2}{3}$ 64. $\frac{8}{40}$ $\frac{1}{5}$ 65. $\frac{12}{96}$ $\frac{1}{8}$ 66. $\frac{22}{48}$ $\frac{11}{24}$

67. $\frac{27}{45}$ $\frac{3}{5}$ 68. $\frac{15}{40}$ $\frac{3}{8}$ 69. $\frac{11}{55}$ $\frac{1}{5}$ 70. $\frac{28}{112}$ $\frac{1}{4}$ 71. $\frac{25}{125}$ $\frac{1}{5}$ 72. $\frac{8}{100}$ $\frac{2}{25}$

73. $\frac{50}{70}$ $\frac{5}{7}$ 74. $\frac{60}{88}$ $\frac{15}{22}$ 75. $\frac{72}{90}$ $\frac{4}{5}$ 76. $\frac{77}{110}$ $\frac{7}{10}$ 77. $\frac{35}{40}$ $\frac{7}{8}$ 78. $\frac{21}{96}$ $\frac{7}{32}$

Addition and Subtraction with Like Denominators

To add or subtract fractions with like denominators, add or subtract
the numerators. Write the sum or difference over the denominator.

Add

$$\frac{1}{8} + \frac{3}{8} = \frac{1+3}{8} = \frac{4}{8} \text{ or } \frac{1}{2}$$

$$\frac{5}{10} + \frac{5}{10} = \frac{5+5}{10} = \frac{10}{10} \text{ or } 1$$

Subtract

$$\frac{12}{20} - \frac{7}{20} = \frac{12-7}{20} = \frac{5}{20} \text{ or } \frac{1}{4}$$

$$\frac{12}{15} - \frac{9}{15} = \frac{12-9}{15} = \frac{3}{15} \text{ or } \frac{1}{5}$$

Add or subtract. Write the answer in simplest form.

1. $\frac{3}{5} + \frac{1}{5}$ **$\frac{4}{5}$**

2. $\frac{3}{7} + \frac{2}{7}$ **$\frac{5}{7}$**

3. $\frac{5}{9} + \frac{2}{9}$ **$\frac{7}{9}$**

4. $\frac{5}{11} + \frac{4}{11}$ **$\frac{9}{11}$**

5. $\frac{9}{11} - \frac{8}{11}$ **$\frac{1}{11}$**

6. $\frac{2}{3} - \frac{1}{3}$ **$\frac{1}{3}$**

7. $\frac{7}{8} - \frac{2}{8}$ **$\frac{5}{8}$**

8. $\frac{6}{7} - \frac{4}{7}$ **$\frac{2}{7}$**

9. $\frac{4}{12} + \frac{7}{12}$ **$\frac{11}{12}$**

10. $\frac{3}{10} + \frac{1}{10}$ **$\frac{2}{5}$**

11. $\frac{8}{15} + \frac{4}{15}$ **$\frac{4}{5}$**

12. $\frac{9}{20} + \frac{7}{20}$ **$\frac{4}{5}$**

13. $\frac{5}{9} - \frac{4}{9}$ **$\frac{1}{9}$**

14. $\frac{7}{8} - \frac{3}{8}$ **$\frac{1}{2}$**

15. $\frac{7}{12} - \frac{1}{12}$ **$\frac{1}{2}$**

16. $\frac{7}{10} - \frac{1}{10}$ **$\frac{3}{5}$**

17. $\frac{7}{12} + \frac{1}{12}$ **$\frac{2}{3}$**

18. $\frac{5}{18} + \frac{11}{18}$ **$\frac{8}{9}$**

19. $\frac{9}{16} + \frac{5}{16}$ **$\frac{7}{8}$**

20. $\frac{7}{24} + \frac{4}{24}$ **$\frac{11}{24}$**

21. $\frac{11}{15} - \frac{3}{15}$ **$\frac{8}{15}$**

22. $\frac{15}{16} - \frac{7}{16}$ **$\frac{1}{2}$**

23. $\frac{11}{24} - \frac{5}{24}$ **$\frac{1}{4}$**

24. $\frac{9}{10} - \frac{1}{10}$ **$\frac{4}{5}$**

25. $\frac{3}{11} + \frac{7}{11}$ **$\frac{10}{11}$**

26. $\frac{5}{24} + \frac{7}{24}$ **$\frac{1}{2}$**

27. $\frac{1}{18} + \frac{5}{18}$ **$\frac{1}{3}$**

28. $\frac{11}{20} + \frac{1}{20}$ **$\frac{3}{5}$**

29. $\frac{9}{16} - \frac{3}{16}$ **$\frac{3}{8}$**

30. $\frac{9}{10} - \frac{3}{10}$ **$\frac{3}{5}$**

31. $\frac{12}{20} - \frac{3}{20}$ **$\frac{9}{20}$**

32. $\frac{4}{9} - \frac{1}{9}$ **$\frac{1}{3}$**

33. $\frac{4}{7} + \frac{3}{7}$ **1**

34. $\frac{5}{8} + \frac{3}{8}$ **1**

35. $\frac{1}{5} + \frac{4}{5}$ **1**

36. $\frac{7}{15} + \frac{8}{15}$ **1**

37. $\frac{15}{20} - \frac{7}{20}$ **$\frac{2}{5}$**

38. $\frac{11}{14} - \frac{5}{14}$ **$\frac{3}{7}$**

39. $\frac{3}{4} - \frac{1}{4}$ **$\frac{1}{2}$**

40. $\frac{5}{6} - \frac{2}{6}$ **$\frac{1}{2}$**

41. $\frac{13}{33} + \frac{2}{33}$ **$\frac{5}{11}$**

42. $\frac{5}{18} + \frac{7}{18}$ **$\frac{2}{3}$**

43. $\frac{4}{15} + \frac{8}{15}$ **$\frac{4}{5}$**

44. $\frac{11}{24} + \frac{7}{24}$ **$\frac{3}{4}$**

45. $\frac{19}{16} - \frac{5}{16}$ **$\frac{7}{8}$**

46. $\frac{4}{3} - \frac{1}{3}$ **1**

47. $\frac{17}{12} - \frac{5}{12}$ **1**

48. $\frac{12}{9} - \frac{6}{9}$ **$\frac{2}{3}$**

49. $\frac{1}{4} + \frac{1}{4} + \frac{1}{4}$ **$\frac{3}{4}$**

50. $\frac{3}{8} + \frac{1}{8} + \frac{2}{8}$ **$\frac{3}{4}$**

51. $\frac{1}{9} + \frac{1}{9} + \frac{1}{9}$ **$\frac{1}{3}$**

52. $\frac{3}{12} + \frac{3}{12} + \frac{3}{12}$ **$\frac{3}{4}$**

53. $\frac{1}{5} + \frac{1}{5} + \frac{1}{5}$ **$\frac{3}{5}$**

54. $\frac{1}{6} + \frac{1}{6} + \frac{1}{6}$ **$\frac{1}{2}$**

55. $\frac{1}{8} + \frac{3}{8} + \frac{3}{8}$ **$\frac{7}{8}$**

56. $\frac{1}{12} + \frac{5}{12} + \frac{3}{12}$ **$\frac{3}{4}$**

450 *Basic Skills Appendix*

Improper Fractions and Mixed Numerals

The improper fraction $\frac{8}{5}$ means $8 \div 5$.

$$\frac{8}{5} \quad \blacktriangleright \quad 5\overline{)\begin{array}{l}8 \\ -5 \\ \hline 3\end{array}}^{\,1} \quad \blacktriangleright \quad 1\frac{3}{5}$$

Write the remainder, 3, as the fraction $\frac{3}{5}$. The denominator, 5, is the divisor.

Written as a mixed numeral, $\frac{8}{5}$ is $1\frac{3}{5}$.

Write each improper fraction as a mixed numeral or whole number in simplest form.

1. $\frac{9}{5}$ $1\frac{4}{5}$ 2. $\frac{8}{7}$ $1\frac{1}{7}$ 3. $\frac{10}{9}$ $1\frac{1}{9}$ 4. $\frac{5}{3}$ $1\frac{2}{3}$ 5. $\frac{7}{4}$ $1\frac{3}{4}$ 6. $\frac{24}{8}$ 3

7. $\frac{13}{7}$ $1\frac{6}{7}$ 8. $\frac{45}{5}$ 9 9. $\frac{7}{5}$ $1\frac{2}{5}$ 10. $\frac{10}{7}$ $1\frac{3}{7}$ 11. $\frac{19}{12}$ $1\frac{7}{12}$ 12. $\frac{15}{8}$ $1\frac{7}{8}$

13. $\frac{9}{2}$ $4\frac{1}{2}$ 14. $\frac{10}{4}$ $2\frac{1}{2}$ 15. $\frac{12}{9}$ $1\frac{1}{3}$ 16. $\frac{16}{4}$ 4 17. $\frac{11}{4}$ $2\frac{3}{4}$ 18. $\frac{15}{10}$ $1\frac{1}{2}$

19. $\frac{6}{4}$ $1\frac{1}{2}$ 20. $\frac{15}{6}$ $2\frac{1}{2}$ 21. $\frac{12}{10}$ $1\frac{1}{5}$ 22. $\frac{10}{6}$ $1\frac{2}{3}$ 23. $\frac{16}{12}$ $1\frac{1}{3}$ 24. $\frac{14}{10}$ $1\frac{2}{5}$

25. $\frac{72}{8}$ 9 26. $\frac{10}{8}$ $1\frac{1}{4}$ 27. $\frac{14}{4}$ $3\frac{1}{2}$ 28. $\frac{56}{7}$ 8 29. $\frac{18}{4}$ $4\frac{1}{2}$ 30. $\frac{23}{12}$ $1\frac{11}{12}$

31. $\frac{32}{6}$ $5\frac{1}{3}$ 32. $\frac{32}{12}$ $2\frac{2}{3}$ 33. $\frac{33}{9}$ $3\frac{2}{3}$ 34. $\frac{47}{6}$ $7\frac{5}{6}$ 35. $\frac{40}{16}$ $2\frac{1}{2}$ 36. $\frac{58}{8}$ $7\frac{1}{4}$

Add or subtract. Write the answer in simplest form.

$$\frac{6}{10} + \frac{5}{10} = \frac{6+5}{10} = \frac{11}{10} \text{ or } 1\frac{1}{10} \qquad \bigg| \qquad \frac{13}{4} - \frac{3}{4} = \frac{13-3}{4} = \frac{10}{4} = 2\frac{2}{4} \text{ or } 2\frac{1}{2}$$

37. $\frac{5}{9} + \frac{5}{9}$ $1\frac{1}{9}$ 38. $\frac{3}{4} + \frac{2}{4}$ $1\frac{1}{4}$ 39. $\frac{4}{5} + \frac{3}{5}$ $1\frac{2}{5}$ 40. $\frac{5}{8} + \frac{6}{8}$ $1\frac{3}{8}$

41. $\frac{6}{3} - \frac{2}{3}$ $1\frac{1}{3}$ 42. $\frac{12}{7} - \frac{6}{7}$ $\frac{6}{7}$ 43. $\frac{9}{4} - \frac{6}{4}$ $\frac{3}{4}$ 44. $\frac{7}{2} - \frac{5}{2}$ 1

45. $\frac{3}{4} + \frac{3}{4}$ $1\frac{1}{2}$ 46. $\frac{4}{9} + \frac{7}{9}$ $1\frac{2}{9}$ 47. $\frac{7}{9} + \frac{5}{9}$ $1\frac{1}{3}$ 48. $\frac{3}{12} + \frac{11}{12}$ $1\frac{1}{6}$

49. $\frac{9}{4} - \frac{1}{4}$ 2 50. $\frac{17}{16} - \frac{7}{16}$ $\frac{5}{8}$ 51. $\frac{16}{9} - \frac{4}{9}$ $1\frac{1}{3}$ 52. $\frac{31}{24} - \frac{5}{24}$ $1\frac{1}{12}$

53. $\frac{23}{32} + \frac{1}{32}$ $\frac{3}{4}$ 54. $\frac{9}{10} + \frac{9}{10}$ $1\frac{4}{5}$ 55. $\frac{7}{8} + \frac{7}{8}$ $1\frac{3}{4}$ 56. $\frac{11}{12} + \frac{5}{12}$ $1\frac{1}{3}$

57. $\frac{15}{32} + \frac{23}{32}$ $1\frac{3}{16}$ 58. $\frac{15}{24} + \frac{19}{24}$ $1\frac{5}{12}$ 59. $\frac{17}{18} + \frac{7}{18}$ $1\frac{1}{3}$ 60. $\frac{17}{27} + \frac{22}{27}$ $1\frac{4}{9}$

61. $\frac{2}{5} + \frac{4}{5} + \frac{1}{5}$ $1\frac{2}{5}$ 62. $\frac{1}{6} + \frac{5}{6} + \frac{2}{6}$ $1\frac{1}{3}$ 63. $\frac{1}{8} + \frac{5}{8} + \frac{7}{8}$ $1\frac{5}{8}$ 64. $\frac{1}{12} + \frac{10}{12} + \frac{11}{12}$ $1\frac{5}{6}$

Least Common Multiple (LCM)

You can find the LCM of two numbers by listing the multiples of each.

Multiples of 8: 8, 16, 24, 32, 40, 48, and so forth

Multiples of 12: 12, 24, 36, 48, and so forth

Some multiples, such as 24 and 48, appear on both lists.
The *least* of these, 24, is the **least common multiple**
(**LCM**) of 8 and 12.

Prime factors also can be used to find the LCM.

$$8 = 2 \times 2 \times 2$$
$$12 = \quad 2 \times 2 \times 3 \quad \cdot$$
$$2 \times 2 \times 2 \times 3 = 24$$

*Use common prime
factors only once.*

The LCM of 8 and 12 is 24.

Write the first five multiples of each number.

1. 2 2,4,6,8,10　　**2.** 5 5,10,15,20,25　　**3.** 3 3,6,9,12,15　　**4.** 6 6,12,18,24,30　　**5.** 4 4,8,12,16,20

Use the results of exercises 1–5 to find the LCM for each pair of numbers.

6. 2 and 5 10　　　　**7.** 4 and 2 4　　　　**8.** 6 and 3 6　　　　**9.** 5 and 4 20

10. 2 and 3 6　　　**11.** 6 and 2 6　　　**12.** 3 and 4 12　　　**13.** 3 and 5 15

Find the LCM of each group of numbers.

14. $6 = \quad 2 \times 3$ 12
　　$4 = 2 \times 2$

15. $15 = \quad 3 \times 5$ 60
　　$20 = 2 \times 2 \quad \times 5$

16. $21 = 3 \quad \times 7$ 105
　　$35 = \quad 5 \times 7$

17. $5 = \quad 5$ 30
　　$6 = 2 \times 3$

18. $6 = 2 \times 3$ 18
　　$9 = \quad 3 \times 3$

19. $7 = \quad 7$ 35
　　$5 = 5$

20. 15 and 3 15　　**21.** 3 and 12 12　　**22.** 2 and 8 8　　　**23.** 7 and 21 21

24. 5 and 20 20　　**25.** 4 and 9 36　　**26.** 11 and 2 22　　**27.** 5 and 10 10

28. 8 and 3 24　　　**29.** 15 and 10 30　　**30.** 16 and 8 16　　**31.** 6 and 8 24

32. 18 and 24 72　　**33.** 18 and 12 36　　**34.** 14 and 8 56　　**35.** 9 and 2 18

36. 7 and 3 21　　　**37.** 24 and 16 48　　**38.** 12 and 16 48　　**39.** 12 and 15 60

40. 10 and 12 60　　**41.** 20 and 35 140　　**42.** 15 and 18 90　　**43.** 15 and 9 45

44. 2, 3, and 6 6　　**45.** 2, 9, and 6 18　　**46.** 3, 4, and 9 36　　**47.** 4, 6, and 9 36

48. 4, 8, and 16 16　**49.** 2, 3, and 5 30　　**50.** 3, 6, and 9 18　　**51.** 4, 6, and 8 24

Equivalent Fractions and Comparing Fractions

The diagrams below show equivalent fractions. **Equivalent fractions** name the same number.

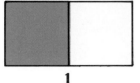
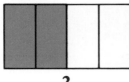
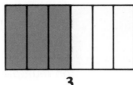
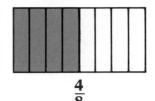

$$\frac{1}{2} \qquad \frac{2}{4} \qquad \frac{3}{6} \qquad \frac{4}{8}$$

You can multiply the numerator and denominator of a fraction by the same number (not 0) and get an equivalent fraction.

$$\frac{1 \times 2}{2 \times 2} = \frac{2}{4} \qquad \frac{1 \times 3}{2 \times 3} = \frac{3}{6} \qquad \frac{1 \times 4}{2 \times 4} = \frac{4}{8} \qquad \frac{1 \times 5}{2 \times 5} = \frac{5}{10}$$

Complete the following.

1. $\frac{3 \times 6}{4 \times 6} = \frac{\blacksquare}{24}$ **18**

2. $\frac{2 \times 4}{3 \times 4} = \frac{\blacksquare}{12}$ **8**

3. $\frac{3 \times 2}{7 \times 2} = \frac{\blacksquare}{14}$ **6**

4. $\frac{1}{3} = \frac{\blacksquare}{9}$ **3**

5. $\frac{1}{4} = \frac{\blacksquare}{8}$ **2**

6. $\frac{1}{2} = \frac{\blacksquare}{12}$ **6**

7. $\frac{1}{3} = \frac{\blacksquare}{12}$ **4**

8. $\frac{1}{4} = \frac{\blacksquare}{12}$ **3**

9. $\frac{1}{5} = \frac{\blacksquare}{15}$ **3**

10. $\frac{1}{6} = \frac{\blacksquare}{18}$ **3**

11. $\frac{1}{5} = \frac{\blacksquare}{10}$ **2**

12. $\frac{2}{5} = \frac{\blacksquare}{10}$ **4**

13. $\frac{3}{4} = \frac{\blacksquare}{12}$ **9**

14. $\frac{2}{3} = \frac{\blacksquare}{6}$ **4**

15. $\frac{4}{5} = \frac{\blacksquare}{10}$ **8**

16. $\frac{7}{10} = \frac{\blacksquare}{100}$ **70**

17. $\frac{3}{5} = \frac{\blacksquare}{20}$ **12**

18. $\frac{5}{9} = \frac{\blacksquare}{27}$ **15**

19. $\frac{3}{4} = \frac{\blacksquare}{8}$ **6**

20. $\frac{5}{6} = \frac{\blacksquare}{12}$ **10**

21. $\frac{5}{6} = \frac{\blacksquare}{24}$ **20**

22. $\frac{3}{5} = \frac{\blacksquare}{15}$ **9**

23. $\frac{7}{11} = \frac{\blacksquare}{33}$ **21**

24. $\frac{3}{4} = \frac{\blacksquare}{20}$ **15**

25. $\frac{11}{15} = \frac{\blacksquare}{60}$ **44**

26. $\frac{8}{9} = \frac{\blacksquare}{36}$ **32**

27. $\frac{5}{8} = \frac{\blacksquare}{40}$ **25**

Replace each ▦ with <, >, or =.

> Compare $\frac{2}{3}$ and $\frac{3}{4}$. The LCM of 3 and 4 is 12. Rename $\frac{2}{3}$ and $\frac{3}{4}$ so they have the same denominator. Then, compare numerators.
>
> $\frac{2 \times 4}{3 \times 4} = \frac{8}{12}$ and $\frac{3 \times 3}{4 \times 3} = \frac{9}{12}$. Since $\frac{8}{12} < \frac{9}{12}, \frac{2}{3} < \frac{3}{4}$.

28. $\frac{2}{3} \; ▦ \; \frac{3}{5}$ **>**

29. $\frac{1}{3} \; ▦ \; \frac{1}{2}$ **<**

30. $\frac{1}{6} \; ▦ \; \frac{1}{7}$ **>**

31. $\frac{3}{8} \; ▦ \; \frac{1}{3}$ **>**

32. $\frac{4}{9} \; ▦ \; \frac{8}{18}$ **=**

33. $\frac{7}{8} \; ▦ \; \frac{9}{10}$ **<**

34. $\frac{7}{8} \; ▦ \; \frac{6}{7}$ **>**

35. $\frac{5}{6} \; ▦ \; \frac{11}{12}$ **<**

36. $\frac{5}{11} \; ▦ \; \frac{7}{15}$ **<**

37. $\frac{2}{3} \; ▦ \; \frac{9}{16}$ **>**

38. $\frac{5}{9} \; ▦ \; \frac{7}{12}$ **<**

39. $\frac{12}{15} \; ▦ \; \frac{4}{5}$ **=**

Addition with Unlike Denominators

Add fractions with unlike denominators as follows. First, rename the fractions with the same denominator. Then, add.

$$\begin{array}{r}\frac{1}{15}\\[4pt]+\ \frac{5}{6}\\\hline\end{array}\qquad\blacktriangleright\qquad\begin{array}{r}\frac{2}{30}\\[4pt]+\ \frac{25}{30}\\\hline\end{array}\qquad\blacktriangleright\qquad\begin{array}{r}\frac{2}{30}\\[4pt]+\ \frac{25}{30}\\\hline\frac{27}{30}\end{array}\qquad\blacktriangleright\qquad\begin{array}{r}\frac{2}{30}\\[4pt]+\ \frac{25}{30}\\\hline\frac{27}{30}=\frac{9}{10}\end{array}$$

Add. Write the sum in simplest form.

1. $\frac{1}{12}+\frac{1}{3}$ $\frac{5}{12}$
2. $\frac{1}{4}+\frac{1}{8}$ $\frac{3}{8}$
3. $\frac{1}{2}+\frac{3}{10}$ $\frac{4}{5}$
4. $\frac{1}{4}+\frac{1}{2}$ $\frac{3}{4}$

5. $\frac{2}{3}+\frac{1}{9}$ $\frac{7}{9}$
6. $\frac{4}{5}+\frac{1}{10}$ $\frac{9}{10}$
7. $\frac{1}{6}+\frac{2}{3}$ $\frac{5}{6}$
8. $\frac{1}{2}+\frac{1}{6}$ $\frac{2}{3}$

9. $\frac{1}{2}+\frac{3}{8}$ $\frac{7}{8}$
10. $\frac{1}{6}+\frac{1}{8}$ $\frac{7}{24}$
11. $\frac{1}{7}+\frac{1}{8}$ $\frac{15}{56}$
12. $\frac{3}{7}+\frac{1}{2}$ $\frac{13}{14}$

13. $\frac{5}{8}+\frac{1}{3}$ $\frac{23}{24}$
14. $\frac{1}{4}+\frac{1}{3}$ $\frac{7}{12}$
15. $\frac{3}{5}+\frac{1}{3}$ $\frac{14}{15}$
16. $\frac{4}{5}+\frac{1}{20}$ $\frac{17}{20}$

17. $\frac{1}{6}+\frac{5}{8}$ $\frac{19}{24}$
18. $\frac{1}{4}+\frac{2}{5}$ $\frac{13}{20}$
19. $\frac{3}{5}+\frac{1}{20}$ $\frac{13}{20}$
20. $\frac{7}{10}+\frac{4}{15}$ $\frac{29}{30}$

21. $\frac{3}{8}+\frac{1}{3}$ $\frac{17}{24}$
22. $\frac{1}{3}+\frac{2}{7}$ $\frac{13}{21}$
23. $\frac{1}{4}+\frac{3}{10}$ $\frac{11}{20}$
24. $\frac{2}{5}+\frac{3}{7}$ $\frac{29}{35}$

25. $\frac{5}{8}+\frac{1}{4}$ $\frac{7}{8}$
26. $\frac{5}{6}+\frac{1}{10}$ $\frac{14}{15}$
27. $\frac{4}{15}+\frac{5}{9}$ $\frac{37}{45}$
28. $\frac{2}{9}+\frac{5}{12}$ $\frac{23}{36}$

Rename each fraction as a mixed numeral in simplest form.

29. $\frac{4}{3}$ $1\frac{1}{3}$
30. $\frac{8}{7}$ $1\frac{1}{7}$
31. $\frac{9}{6}$ $1\frac{1}{2}$
32. $\frac{25}{10}$ $2\frac{1}{2}$

Add. Write the sum in simplest form.

33. $\frac{1}{2}+\frac{7}{8}$ $1\frac{3}{8}$
34. $\frac{5}{7}+\frac{9}{14}$ $1\frac{5}{14}$
35. $\frac{2}{3}+\frac{4}{9}$ $1\frac{1}{9}$
36. $\frac{2}{3}+\frac{5}{6}$ $1\frac{1}{2}$

37. $\frac{5}{6}+\frac{1}{2}$ $1\frac{1}{3}$
38. $\frac{1}{2}+\frac{3}{4}$ $1\frac{1}{4}$
39. $\frac{5}{6}+\frac{1}{3}$ $1\frac{1}{6}$
40. $\frac{3}{4}+\frac{3}{8}$ $1\frac{1}{8}$

41. $\frac{1}{4}+\frac{5}{6}$ $1\frac{1}{12}$
42. $\frac{2}{3}+\frac{4}{5}$ $1\frac{7}{15}$
43. $\frac{2}{3}+\frac{7}{12}$ $1\frac{1}{4}$
44. $\frac{7}{12}+\frac{5}{6}$ $1\frac{5}{12}$

45. $\frac{2}{9}+\frac{5}{6}$ $1\frac{1}{18}$
46. $\frac{1}{3}+\frac{5}{7}$ $1\frac{1}{21}$
47. $\frac{3}{5}+\frac{2}{3}$ $1\frac{4}{15}$
48. $\frac{7}{16}+\frac{7}{8}$ $1\frac{5}{16}$

49. $\frac{7}{8}+\frac{4}{5}$ $1\frac{27}{40}$
50. $\frac{5}{12}+\frac{3}{5}$ $1\frac{1}{60}$
51. $\frac{7}{8}+\frac{5}{12}$ $1\frac{7}{24}$
52. $\frac{5}{8}+\frac{5}{12}$ $1\frac{1}{24}$

53. $\frac{1}{2}+\frac{1}{3}+\frac{1}{4}$ $1\frac{1}{12}$
54. $\frac{2}{5}+\frac{1}{10}+\frac{3}{5}$ $1\frac{1}{10}$
55. $\frac{2}{3}+\frac{3}{4}+\frac{1}{6}$ $1\frac{7}{12}$
56. $\frac{1}{3}+\frac{1}{4}+\frac{1}{5}$ $\frac{47}{60}$

Subtraction with Unlike Denominators

Subtract fractions with unlike denominators as follows.
First, rename the fractions with the same denominator.
Then, subtract.

$$\frac{11}{12} - \frac{2}{3}$$ $$\frac{11}{12} - \frac{8}{12}$$ $$\frac{11}{12} - \frac{8}{12} = \frac{3}{12}$$ $$\frac{11}{12} - \frac{8}{12} = \frac{3}{12} = \frac{1}{4}$$ Always simplify.

Subtract. Write the difference in simplest form.

1. $\frac{3}{4} - \frac{1}{2}$ $\frac{1}{4}$

2. $\frac{7}{9} - \frac{2}{3}$ $\frac{1}{9}$

3. $\frac{7}{8} - \frac{3}{4}$ $\frac{1}{8}$

4. $\frac{5}{6} - \frac{2}{3}$ $\frac{1}{6}$

5. $\frac{7}{10} - \frac{3}{5}$ $\frac{1}{10}$

6. $\frac{7}{12} - \frac{1}{4}$ $\frac{1}{3}$

7. $\frac{7}{15} - \frac{1}{3}$ $\frac{2}{15}$

8. $\frac{3}{4} - \frac{1}{8}$ $\frac{5}{8}$

9. $\frac{5}{6} - \frac{1}{3}$ $\frac{1}{2}$

10. $\frac{11}{12} - \frac{1}{4}$ $\frac{2}{3}$

11. $\frac{15}{16} - \frac{3}{8}$ $\frac{9}{16}$

12. $\frac{5}{6} - \frac{1}{2}$ $\frac{1}{3}$

13. $\frac{2}{3} - \frac{1}{4}$ $\frac{5}{12}$

14. $\frac{1}{4} - \frac{1}{5}$ $\frac{1}{20}$

15. $\frac{4}{5} - \frac{2}{3}$ $\frac{2}{15}$

16. $\frac{3}{5} - \frac{1}{2}$ $\frac{1}{10}$

17. $\frac{1}{2} - \frac{1}{3}$ $\frac{1}{6}$

18. $\frac{8}{9} - \frac{3}{4}$ $\frac{5}{36}$

19. $\frac{3}{4} - \frac{2}{3}$ $\frac{1}{12}$

20. $\frac{7}{9} - \frac{1}{2}$ $\frac{5}{18}$

21. $\frac{2}{3} - \frac{2}{5}$ $\frac{4}{15}$

22. $\frac{5}{6} - \frac{3}{5}$ $\frac{7}{30}$

23. $\frac{5}{7} - \frac{1}{2}$ $\frac{3}{14}$

24. $\frac{7}{10} - \frac{3}{8}$ $\frac{13}{40}$

25. $\frac{7}{12} - \frac{1}{3}$ $\frac{1}{4}$

26. $\frac{1}{6} - \frac{1}{8}$ $\frac{1}{24}$

27. $\frac{5}{8} - \frac{3}{7}$ $\frac{11}{56}$

28. $\frac{9}{10} - \frac{5}{12}$ $\frac{29}{60}$

29. $\frac{2}{7} - \frac{1}{12}$ $\frac{17}{84}$

30. $\frac{3}{10} - \frac{1}{7}$ $\frac{11}{70}$

31. $\frac{2}{9} - \frac{1}{10}$ $\frac{11}{90}$

32. $\frac{6}{7} - \frac{5}{9}$ $\frac{19}{63}$

33. $\frac{4}{7} - \frac{2}{5}$ $\frac{6}{35}$

34. $\frac{11}{12} - \frac{1}{9}$ $\frac{29}{36}$

35. $\frac{5}{8} - \frac{3}{10}$ $\frac{13}{40}$

36. $\frac{3}{4} - \frac{2}{9}$ $\frac{19}{36}$

37. $\frac{8}{9} - \frac{3}{15}$ $\frac{31}{45}$

38. $\frac{5}{6} - \frac{3}{4}$ $\frac{1}{12}$

39. $\frac{2}{3} - \frac{7}{15}$ $\frac{1}{5}$

40. $\frac{5}{18} - \frac{1}{9}$ $\frac{1}{6}$

41. $\frac{5}{6} - \frac{3}{8}$ $\frac{11}{24}$

42. $\frac{3}{4} - \frac{11}{20}$ $\frac{1}{5}$

43. $\frac{8}{9} - \frac{5}{6}$ $\frac{1}{18}$

44. $\frac{4}{5} - \frac{1}{3}$ $\frac{7}{15}$

45. $\frac{11}{15} - \frac{1}{10}$ $\frac{19}{30}$

46. $\frac{6}{7} - \frac{1}{3}$ $\frac{11}{21}$

47. $\frac{13}{18} - \frac{1}{2}$ $\frac{2}{9}$

48. $\frac{7}{9} - \frac{3}{5}$ $\frac{8}{45}$

49. $\frac{14}{15} - \frac{5}{6}$ $\frac{1}{10}$

50. $\frac{5}{8} - \frac{5}{12}$ $\frac{5}{24}$

51. $\frac{11}{18} - \frac{1}{6}$ $\frac{4}{9}$

52. $\frac{9}{10} - \frac{7}{30}$ $\frac{2}{3}$

53. $\frac{7}{16} - \frac{1}{3}$ $\frac{5}{48}$

54. $\frac{9}{20} - \frac{1}{4}$ $\frac{1}{5}$

55. $\frac{11}{12} - \frac{13}{16}$ $\frac{5}{48}$

56. $\frac{5}{9} - \frac{2}{5}$ $\frac{7}{45}$

57. $\frac{17}{18} - \frac{7}{9}$ $\frac{1}{6}$

58. $\frac{13}{16} - \frac{5}{12}$ $\frac{19}{48}$

59. $\frac{11}{18} - \frac{1}{2}$ $\frac{1}{9}$

60. $\frac{15}{18} - \frac{5}{6}$ 0

Addition with Mixed Numerals

To add with mixed numerals, follow these steps.

Add the fractions.

$$6\frac{7}{8}$$
$$+\ 1\frac{5}{8}$$
$$\overline{\frac{12}{8}}$$

Add the whole numbers.

$$6\frac{7}{8}$$
$$+\ 1\frac{5}{8}$$
$$\overline{7\frac{12}{8}}$$

Rename and simplify.

$$\frac{12}{8} = 1\frac{4}{8} = 1\frac{1}{2}$$
$$7 + 1\frac{1}{2} = 8\frac{1}{2}$$

$$6\frac{7}{8}$$
$$+\ 1\frac{5}{8}$$
$$\overline{7\frac{12}{8} = 8\frac{1}{2}}$$

Add. Write the sum in simplest form.

1. $2\frac{1}{5} + 1\frac{3}{5}$ $3\frac{4}{5}$

2. $2\frac{1}{3} + 4\frac{1}{3}$ $6\frac{2}{3}$

3. $6\frac{1}{7} + 4\frac{5}{7}$ $10\frac{6}{7}$

4. $1\frac{2}{9} + 1\frac{5}{9}$ $2\frac{7}{9}$

5. $1\frac{1}{6} + 3\frac{1}{6}$ $4\frac{1}{3}$

6. $6\frac{1}{12} + 4\frac{5}{12}$ $10\frac{1}{2}$

7. $2\frac{3}{8} + 4\frac{1}{8}$ $6\frac{1}{2}$

8. $2\frac{1}{15} + 3\frac{2}{15}$ $5\frac{1}{5}$

9. $2\frac{7}{16} + 5\frac{5}{16}$ $7\frac{3}{4}$

10. $1\frac{5}{6} + 4\frac{1}{6}$ 6

11. $2\frac{4}{5} + 3\frac{3}{5}$ $6\frac{2}{5}$

12. $7\frac{3}{7} + 9\frac{6}{7}$ $17\frac{2}{7}$

13. $1\frac{8}{9} + 3\frac{2}{9}$ $5\frac{1}{9}$

14. $2\frac{3}{8} + 1\frac{7}{8}$ $4\frac{1}{4}$

15. $9\frac{5}{6} + 1\frac{5}{6}$ $11\frac{2}{3}$

16. $5\frac{5}{8} + 4\frac{7}{8}$ $10\frac{1}{2}$

17. $4\frac{3}{4} + 4\frac{3}{4}$ $9\frac{1}{2}$

18. $8\frac{7}{8} + 1\frac{3}{8}$ $10\frac{1}{4}$

19. $2\frac{3}{4} + 4\frac{1}{4}$ 7

20. $2\frac{7}{12} + 4\frac{11}{12}$ $7\frac{1}{2}$

21. $\begin{array}{r}2\frac{8}{9}\\ +\ 1\frac{4}{9}\\ \hline 4\frac{1}{3}\end{array}$

22. $\begin{array}{r}5\frac{3}{10}\\ +\ 2\frac{4}{10}\\ \hline 7\frac{7}{10}\end{array}$

23. $\begin{array}{r}4\frac{7}{16}\\ +\ 3\frac{13}{16}\\ \hline 8\frac{1}{4}\end{array}$

24. $\begin{array}{r}3\frac{4}{15}\\ +\ 2\frac{14}{15}\\ \hline 6\frac{1}{5}\end{array}$

Add. Write the sum in simplest form.

$$16\frac{1}{2}$$
$$+\ 5\frac{5}{8}$$

The LCM of 2 and 8 is 8.

$$16\frac{1}{2} = 16\frac{4}{8}$$
$$+\ 5\frac{5}{8} = 5\frac{5}{8}$$

$$16\frac{4}{8}$$
$$+\ 5\frac{5}{8}$$
$$\overline{21\frac{9}{8} = 22\frac{1}{8}}$$

25. $2\frac{3}{8} + 4\frac{1}{4}$ $6\frac{5}{8}$

26. $6\frac{1}{2} + 3\frac{1}{4}$ $9\frac{3}{4}$

27. $3\frac{1}{3} + 4\frac{1}{15}$ $7\frac{2}{5}$

28. $2\frac{1}{3} + 3\frac{4}{9}$ $5\frac{7}{9}$

29. $2\frac{1}{10} + 3\frac{1}{2}$ $5\frac{3}{5}$

30. $7\frac{1}{6} + 5\frac{1}{3}$ $12\frac{1}{2}$

31. $2\frac{1}{5} + 3\frac{3}{10}$ $5\frac{1}{2}$

32. $2\frac{3}{8} + 4\frac{3}{4}$ $7\frac{1}{8}$

33. $4\frac{2}{5} + 3\frac{4}{15}$ $7\frac{2}{3}$

34. $8\frac{5}{6} + 3\frac{5}{12}$ $12\frac{1}{4}$

35. $7\frac{5}{18} + 1\frac{5}{9}$ $8\frac{5}{6}$

36. $6\frac{4}{5} + 3\frac{7}{20}$ $10\frac{3}{20}$

37. $5\frac{1}{2} + 3\frac{2}{7}$ $8\frac{11}{14}$

38. $6\frac{1}{2} + 3\frac{1}{3}$ $9\frac{5}{6}$

39. $7\frac{1}{5} + 11\frac{3}{4}$ $18\frac{19}{20}$

40. $9\frac{5}{8} + 8\frac{1}{6}$ $17\frac{19}{24}$

Subtraction with Mixed Numerals

When subtracting with mixed numerals, sometimes you must rename as shown below. Why must $3\frac{1}{10}$ be renamed to $2\frac{11}{10}$?

	Rename	**Subtract**
$3\frac{1}{10}$ $-1\frac{7}{10}$ $3\frac{1}{10} = 2\frac{11}{20}$	$3\frac{1}{10} = 2\frac{11}{10}$ $-1\frac{7}{10} = 1\frac{7}{10}$	$2\frac{11}{10}$ $-1\frac{7}{10}$ $\overline{}$ $1\frac{4}{10} = 1\frac{2}{5}$

Subtract. Write the difference in simplest form.

1. $4\frac{4}{5} - 2\frac{2}{5}$ $2\frac{2}{5}$
2. $4\frac{5}{6} - 3\frac{1}{6}$ $1\frac{2}{3}$
3. $2\frac{7}{10} - 1\frac{1}{10}$ $1\frac{3}{5}$
4. $8\frac{11}{12} - 3\frac{1}{12}$ $5\frac{5}{6}$

5. $3\frac{8}{9} - 2\frac{5}{9}$ $1\frac{1}{3}$
6. $13\frac{3}{4} - 10\frac{1}{4}$ $3\frac{1}{2}$
7. $12\frac{27}{32} - 5\frac{5}{32}$ $7\frac{11}{16}$
8. $5\frac{11}{18} - 3\frac{5}{18}$ $2\frac{1}{3}$

9. $7\frac{5}{12} - 3\frac{1}{12}$ $4\frac{1}{3}$
10. $3\frac{11}{16} - 2\frac{9}{16}$ $1\frac{1}{8}$
11. $17\frac{20}{21} - 6\frac{8}{21}$ $11\frac{4}{7}$
12. $9\frac{17}{24} - 5\frac{11}{24}$ $4\frac{1}{4}$

13. $8\frac{3}{4} - 2\frac{1}{2}$ $6\frac{1}{4}$
14. $7\frac{5}{6} - 5\frac{1}{3}$ $2\frac{1}{2}$
15. $12\frac{3}{4} - 11\frac{1}{8}$ $1\frac{5}{8}$
16. $8\frac{9}{10} - 8\frac{1}{5}$ $\frac{7}{10}$

17. $18\frac{3}{8} - 12\frac{1}{4}$ $6\frac{1}{8}$
18. $6\frac{9}{10} - 5$ $1\frac{9}{10}$
19. $4\frac{15}{16} - 3\frac{3}{4}$ $1\frac{3}{16}$
20. $12\frac{5}{6} - 3\frac{2}{3}$ $9\frac{1}{6}$

21. $7\frac{19}{20} - 5\frac{3}{4}$ $2\frac{1}{5}$
22. $4\frac{7}{12} - 2\frac{1}{3}$ $2\frac{1}{4}$
23. $6\frac{17}{18} - 4\frac{4}{9}$ $2\frac{1}{2}$
24. $7\frac{5}{6} - 1\frac{3}{18}$ $6\frac{2}{3}$

Rename as indicated.

25. $4\frac{1}{5} = 3\frac{\blacksquare}{5}$ 6
26. $6 = 5\frac{\blacksquare}{8}$ 8
27. $2\frac{2}{3} = 1\frac{\blacksquare}{3}$ 5
28. $5\frac{3}{8} = 4\frac{\blacksquare}{8}$ 11

29. $7 = 6\frac{\blacksquare}{9}$ 9
30. $6\frac{1}{6} = 5\frac{\blacksquare}{6}$ 7
31. $4 = 3\frac{\blacksquare}{12}$ 12
32. $2\frac{3}{4} = 1\frac{\blacksquare}{4}$ 7

Subtract. Write each difference in simplest form.

33. $3\frac{1}{5} - 2\frac{3}{5}$ $\frac{3}{5}$
34. $6\frac{2}{7} - 3\frac{3}{7}$ $2\frac{6}{7}$
35. $5\frac{1}{4} - 2\frac{3}{4}$ $2\frac{1}{2}$
36. $8\frac{3}{8} - 5\frac{7}{8}$ $2\frac{1}{2}$

37. $4 - 2\frac{5}{6}$ $1\frac{1}{6}$
38. $6 - 2\frac{1}{3}$ $3\frac{2}{3}$
39. $8 - 4\frac{3}{4}$ $3\frac{1}{4}$
40. $16 - 2\frac{2}{5}$ $13\frac{3}{5}$

41. $4\frac{5}{12} - 3\frac{11}{12}$ $\frac{1}{2}$
42. $6\frac{13}{18} - 1\frac{17}{18}$ $4\frac{7}{9}$
43. $3\frac{5}{16} - 2\frac{7}{16}$ $\frac{7}{8}$
44. $7\frac{9}{20} - 1\frac{19}{20}$ $5\frac{1}{2}$

45. $12\frac{3}{10} - 7\frac{9}{10}$ $4\frac{2}{5}$
46. $14 - 6\frac{7}{8}$ $7\frac{1}{8}$
47. $10\frac{3}{8} - 7\frac{5}{8}$ $2\frac{3}{4}$
48. $21 - 11\frac{16}{21}$ $9\frac{5}{21}$

49. $7\frac{1}{2} - 3\frac{3}{4}$ $3\frac{3}{4}$
50. $6\frac{3}{8} - 4\frac{3}{4}$ $1\frac{5}{8}$
51. $8\frac{2}{5} - 2\frac{9}{10}$ $5\frac{1}{2}$
52. $4\frac{5}{6} - 1\frac{11}{12}$ $2\frac{11}{12}$

Multiplication of Fractions

To multiply a fraction and a whole number, rename the whole number as a fraction. Multiply the numerators. Then, multiply the denominators.

$$6 \times \frac{4}{5} \quad \blacktriangleright \quad \frac{6}{1} \times \frac{4}{5} \quad \blacktriangleright \quad \frac{6}{1} \times \frac{4}{5} = \frac{6 \times 4}{1 \times 5} = \frac{24}{5} \text{ or } 4\frac{4}{5}$$

Rename 6 as $\frac{6}{1}$.

You can use the following shortcut to simplify a problem. That is, divide the factors of the numerator and denominator by their GCF.

$$\frac{3}{5} \times \frac{10}{21} = \frac{3 \times 10}{5 \times 21}$$

$$= \frac{\overset{1}{\cancel{3}} \times \overset{2}{\cancel{10}}}{\underset{1}{\cancel{5}} \times \underset{7}{\cancel{21}}} \qquad \begin{array}{l} \textit{The GCF of 3 and 21 is 3.} \\ \textit{The GCF of 10 and 5 is 5.} \end{array}$$

$$= \frac{2}{7}$$

Multiply. Write each product in simplest form.

1. $5 \times \frac{1}{7}$ $\frac{5}{7}$

2. $\frac{2}{5} \times 2$ $\frac{4}{5}$

3. $6 \times \frac{1}{9}$ $\frac{2}{3}$

4. $8 \times \frac{1}{9}$ $\frac{8}{9}$

5. $3 \times \frac{1}{9}$ $\frac{1}{3}$

6. $4 \times \frac{1}{8}$ $\frac{1}{2}$

7. $8 \times \frac{1}{2}$ 4

8. $10 \times \frac{1}{15}$ $\frac{2}{3}$

9. $6 \times \frac{3}{5}$ $3\frac{3}{5}$

10. $\frac{1}{2} \times 5$ $2\frac{1}{2}$

11. $\frac{1}{4} \times 9$ $2\frac{1}{4}$

12. $10 \times \frac{2}{3}$ $6\frac{2}{3}$

13. $\frac{5}{9} \times 18$ 10

14. $\frac{1}{6} \times 9$ $1\frac{1}{2}$

15. $\frac{2}{3} \times 6$ 4

16. $\frac{7}{8} \times 12$ $10\frac{1}{2}$

17. $\frac{5}{12} \times 18$ $7\frac{1}{2}$

18. $\frac{7}{24} \times 16$ $4\frac{2}{3}$

19. $14 \times \frac{7}{10}$ $9\frac{4}{5}$

20. $\frac{5}{18} \times 14$ $3\frac{8}{9}$

21. $\frac{1}{2} \times \frac{2}{5}$ $\frac{1}{5}$

22. $\frac{1}{8} \times \frac{3}{4}$ $\frac{3}{32}$

23. $\frac{2}{3} \times \frac{5}{9}$ $\frac{10}{27}$

24. $\frac{6}{7} \times \frac{1}{5}$ $\frac{6}{35}$

25. $\frac{3}{4} \times \frac{5}{7}$ $\frac{15}{28}$

26. $\frac{5}{6} \times \frac{7}{8}$ $\frac{35}{48}$

27. $\frac{4}{7} \times \frac{2}{3}$ $\frac{8}{21}$

28. $\frac{5}{8} \times \frac{3}{8}$ $\frac{15}{64}$

29. $\frac{2}{3} \times \frac{3}{4}$ $\frac{1}{2}$

30. $\frac{1}{8} \times \frac{4}{5}$ $\frac{1}{10}$

31. $\frac{3}{4} \times \frac{4}{9}$ $\frac{1}{3}$

32. $\frac{8}{9} \times \frac{3}{4}$ $\frac{2}{3}$

33. $\frac{4}{9} \times \frac{3}{5}$ $\frac{4}{15}$

34. $\frac{5}{8} \times \frac{4}{5}$ $\frac{1}{2}$

35. $\frac{7}{16} \times \frac{8}{9}$ $\frac{7}{18}$

36. $\frac{8}{15} \times \frac{5}{16}$ $\frac{1}{6}$

37. $\frac{3}{16} \times \frac{5}{6}$ $\frac{5}{32}$

38. $\frac{1}{6} \times \frac{24}{25}$ $\frac{4}{25}$

39. $\frac{7}{8} \times \frac{24}{49}$ $\frac{3}{7}$

40. $\frac{3}{5} \times \frac{20}{21}$ $\frac{4}{7}$

41. $\frac{5}{16} \times \frac{4}{5}$ $\frac{1}{4}$

42. $\frac{9}{16} \times \frac{5}{6}$ $\frac{15}{32}$

43. $\frac{11}{18} \times \frac{9}{20}$ $\frac{11}{40}$

44. $\frac{8}{15} \times \frac{5}{6}$ $\frac{4}{9}$

Multiplication with Mixed Numerals

To multiply with mixed numerals, first rename the mixed numerals as fractions. Then, multiply the fractions.

$$2\frac{5}{8} \times 1\frac{3}{7} = \frac{21}{8} \times \frac{10}{7} \qquad \textit{Rename the mixed numerals as fractions.}$$

$$= \frac{\overset{3}{\cancel{21}}}{\underset{4}{\cancel{8}}} \times \frac{\overset{5}{\cancel{10}}}{\underset{1}{\cancel{7}}} \qquad \textit{The GCF of 21 and 7 is 7.}$$
$$\textit{The GCF of 10 and 8 is 2.}$$

$$= \frac{15}{4} \text{ or } 3\frac{3}{4}$$

Rename each mixed numeral as a fraction.

1. $1\frac{1}{8} = \frac{(1 \times 8) + 1}{8} = \frac{\blacksquare}{8}$ **9**

2. $4\frac{2}{3} = \frac{(3 \times 4) + 2}{3} = \frac{\blacksquare}{3}$ **14**

3. $7\frac{3}{4} = \frac{(4 \times 7) + 3}{4} = \frac{\blacksquare}{4}$ **31**

4. $2\frac{5}{12} = \frac{(12 \times 2) + 5}{12} = \frac{\blacksquare}{12}$ **29**

5. $3\frac{1}{4}$ $\frac{13}{4}$

6. $3\frac{1}{3}$ $\frac{10}{3}$

7. $1\frac{7}{8}$ $\frac{15}{8}$

8. $7\frac{1}{2}$ $\frac{15}{2}$

9. $2\frac{3}{4}$ $\frac{11}{4}$

10. $1\frac{1}{5}$ $\frac{6}{5}$

11. $4\frac{1}{3}$ $\frac{13}{3}$

12. $12\frac{1}{8}$ $\frac{97}{8}$

13. $7\frac{7}{12}$ $\frac{91}{12}$

14. $6\frac{5}{16}$ $\frac{101}{16}$

Multiply. Write each product in simplest form.

15. $1\frac{2}{3} \times \frac{3}{4}$ $1\frac{1}{4}$

16. $1\frac{3}{5} \times \frac{2}{3}$ $1\frac{1}{15}$

17. $\frac{1}{4} \times 1\frac{1}{3}$ $\frac{1}{3}$

18. $6 \times 3\frac{1}{2}$ **21**

19. $\frac{2}{5} \times 1\frac{1}{4}$ $\frac{1}{2}$

20. $\frac{4}{5} \times 7\frac{1}{2}$ **6**

21. $2 \times 1\frac{5}{8}$ $3\frac{1}{4}$

22. $1\frac{5}{6} \times 9$ $16\frac{1}{2}$

23. $12 \times 2\frac{2}{3}$ **32**

24. $4\frac{3}{8} \times 2$ $8\frac{3}{4}$

25. $\frac{9}{10} \times 1\frac{1}{3}$ $1\frac{1}{5}$

26. $7 \times 3\frac{1}{2}$ $24\frac{1}{2}$

27. $1\frac{3}{8} \times 10$ $13\frac{3}{4}$

28. $4 \times 3\frac{1}{3}$ $13\frac{1}{3}$

29. $5\frac{1}{2} \times 2$ **11**

30. $7\frac{1}{4} \times 14$ $101\frac{1}{2}$

31. $1\frac{1}{2} \times 1\frac{1}{2}$ $2\frac{1}{4}$

32. $2\frac{1}{8} \times 1\frac{1}{3}$ $2\frac{5}{6}$

33. $7\frac{1}{2} \times 3\frac{1}{5}$ **24**

34. $3\frac{1}{2} \times 5\frac{1}{7}$ **18**

35. $1\frac{3}{5} \times 2\frac{1}{4}$ $3\frac{3}{5}$

36. $3\frac{1}{3} \times 2\frac{1}{4}$ $7\frac{1}{2}$

37. $8\frac{2}{7} \times 2\frac{3}{4}$ $22\frac{11}{14}$

38. $7\frac{1}{2} \times 2\frac{1}{7}$ $16\frac{1}{14}$

39. $5\frac{1}{3} \times 4\frac{1}{2}$ **24**

40. $1\frac{2}{3} \times 4\frac{3}{4}$ $7\frac{11}{12}$

41. $9\frac{1}{3} \times 4\frac{1}{2}$ **42**

42. $2\frac{7}{8} \times 1\frac{5}{6}$ $5\frac{13}{48}$

43. $2\frac{2}{3} \times 3\frac{3}{4}$ **10**

44. $1\frac{5}{9} \times 4\frac{4}{7}$ $7\frac{1}{9}$

45. $1\frac{7}{8} \times 2\frac{5}{6}$ $5\frac{5}{16}$

46. $1\frac{5}{16} \times 2\frac{4}{7}$ $3\frac{3}{8}$

47. $2\frac{1}{7} \times 1\frac{1}{6}$ $2\frac{1}{2}$

48. $1\frac{2}{3} \times 2\frac{5}{6}$ $4\frac{13}{18}$

49. $3\frac{2}{5} \times 6\frac{1}{4}$ $21\frac{1}{4}$

50. $4\frac{2}{3} \times 4\frac{2}{7}$ **20**

Division with Fractions and Mixed Numerals

Two numbers whose product is 1 are called **reciprocals**.

$$3 \times \frac{1}{3} = 1 \qquad \frac{1}{4} \times 4 = 1 \qquad \frac{5}{12} \times \frac{12}{5} = 1$$

To divide by a fraction, multiply by its reciprocal.

$$6 \div \frac{2}{3} = \frac{\cancel{6}^{3}}{1} \times \frac{3}{\cancel{2}_{1}} = 9$$

$$\frac{4}{9} \div \frac{5}{6} = \frac{4}{\cancel{9}_{3}} \times \frac{\cancel{6}^{2}}{5} = \frac{8}{15}$$

To divide with mixed numerals, rename them as fractions. Then divide.

$$5\frac{1}{2} \div 1\frac{1}{4} = \frac{11}{2} \div \frac{5}{4}$$

$$= \frac{11}{\cancel{2}_{1}} \times \frac{\cancel{4}^{2}}{5} \qquad \text{\textit{The reciprocal of} } \frac{5}{4} \text{ \textit{is} } \frac{4}{5}.$$

$$= \frac{22}{5} \text{ or } 4\frac{2}{5}$$

Name the reciprocal of each of the following.

1. $\frac{2}{5}$ $\frac{5}{2}$
2. $\frac{1}{3}$ $\frac{3}{1}$
3. $\frac{1}{8}$ $\frac{8}{1}$
4. $\frac{8}{7}$ $\frac{7}{8}$
5. $\frac{2}{9}$ $\frac{9}{2}$

6. 6 $\frac{1}{6}$
7. $\frac{4}{5}$ $\frac{5}{4}$
8. 11 $\frac{1}{11}$
9. $1\frac{2}{5}$ $\frac{5}{7}$
10. $4\frac{3}{4}$ $\frac{4}{19}$

Complete.

11. $15 \div \frac{3}{4} = \frac{15}{1} \times \frac{4}{3} = \frac{\blacksquare}{\blacksquare}$ $\frac{20}{1} = 20$

12. $\frac{4}{5} \div 8 = \frac{4}{5} \div \frac{8}{1} = \frac{4}{5} \times \frac{\blacksquare}{\blacksquare} = \frac{\blacksquare}{\blacksquare}$ $\frac{1}{8}, \frac{1}{10}$

13. $\frac{3}{4} \div 1\frac{7}{8} = \frac{3}{4} \div \frac{15}{8} = \frac{3}{4} \times \frac{\blacksquare}{\blacksquare} = \frac{\blacksquare}{\blacksquare}$ $\frac{8}{15}, \frac{2}{5}$

14. $1\frac{1}{2} \div 4\frac{1}{8} = \frac{\blacksquare}{\blacksquare} \div \frac{\blacksquare}{\blacksquare} = \frac{\blacksquare}{\blacksquare} \times \frac{\blacksquare}{\blacksquare} = \frac{\blacksquare}{\blacksquare}$ $\frac{3}{2}, \frac{33}{8}, \frac{3}{2}, \frac{8}{33}, \frac{4}{11}$

Divide. Write each quotient in simplest form.

15. $7 \div \frac{1}{3}$ 21
16. $15 \div \frac{3}{4}$ 20
17. $10 \div \frac{3}{5}$ $16\frac{2}{3}$
18. $12 \div \frac{1}{6}$ 72

19. $5 \div \frac{3}{5}$ $8\frac{1}{3}$
20. $30 \div \frac{5}{6}$ 36
21. $\frac{4}{5} \div 4$ $\frac{1}{5}$
22. $\frac{1}{2} \div 6$ $\frac{1}{12}$

23. $\frac{4}{9} \div 2$ $\frac{2}{9}$
24. $\frac{5}{7} \div 5$ $\frac{1}{7}$
25. $\frac{1}{8} \div 3$ $\frac{1}{24}$
26. $\frac{7}{12} \div 7$ $\frac{1}{12}$

27. $\frac{5}{8} \div \frac{3}{4}$ $\frac{5}{6}$
28. $\frac{3}{5} \div \frac{15}{16}$ $\frac{16}{25}$
29. $\frac{1}{6} \div \frac{3}{8}$ $\frac{4}{9}$
30. $\frac{2}{7} \div \frac{8}{9}$ $\frac{9}{28}$

31. $\frac{4}{5} \div \frac{3}{8}$ $2\frac{2}{15}$
32. $\frac{5}{7} \div \frac{15}{21}$ 1
33. $\frac{3}{4} \div \frac{6}{7}$ $\frac{7}{8}$
34. $\frac{3}{5} \div \frac{2}{5}$ $1\frac{1}{2}$

35. $\frac{2}{3} \div \frac{3}{10}$ $2\frac{2}{9}$
36. $\frac{9}{16} \div \frac{3}{5}$ $\frac{15}{16}$
37. $\frac{3}{16} \div \frac{7}{8}$ $\frac{3}{14}$
38. $\frac{8}{9} \div \frac{7}{18}$ $2\frac{2}{7}$

39. $6\frac{3}{4} \div 9$ $\frac{3}{4}$
40. $4\frac{2}{3} \div 2$ $2\frac{1}{3}$
41. $5 \div 3\frac{1}{3}$ $1\frac{1}{2}$
42. $2\frac{2}{3} \div 4$ $\frac{2}{3}$

43. $1 \div 3\frac{1}{4}$ $\frac{4}{13}$
44. $12 \div 2\frac{1}{4}$ $5\frac{1}{3}$
45. $3\frac{1}{2} \div 5\frac{1}{4}$ $\frac{2}{3}$
46. $4\frac{1}{3} \div 1\frac{5}{6}$ $2\frac{4}{11}$

Percents

Percent means per one hundred or hundredths. In the figure at the right, 40 out of 100 squares are shaded.

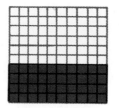

$$\frac{40}{100} = 0.40 \text{ or } 40\%$$

You can change decimals to percents and percents to decimals as follows.

To change a decimal to a percent, multiply the decimal by 100. Then, annex the percent symbol.

$$0.03 \times 100 = 0.03 = 3\%$$
$$0.625 \times 100 = 0.625 = 62.5\%$$

To change a percent to a decimal, divide the percent by 100. Omit the % symbol.

$$72\% \div 100 = 72\% = 0.72$$
$$8\% \div 100 = 08\% = 0.08$$

Name the fraction in simplest form, the decimal, and the percent for each of the following.

1.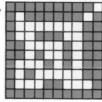

$\frac{3}{5}$; 0.6; 60%

2.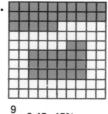

$\frac{9}{20}$; 0.45; 45%

3.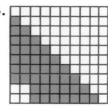

$\frac{41}{100}$; 0.41; 41%

4.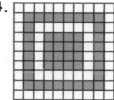

$\frac{11}{25}$; 0.44; 44%

Change each percent to a decimal.

5. 4% 0.04 **6.** 65% 0.65 **7.** 6% 0.06 **8.** 9% 0.09 **9.** 12% 0.12

10. 36% 0.36 **11.** 1% 0.01 **12.** 100% 1.0 **13.** 40% 0.40 **14.** 10% 0.10

15. 26.5% 0.265 **16.** 18.1% 0.181 **17.** 2.3% 0.023 **18.** 1.51% 0.0151 **19.** 4.3% 0.043

20. 304% 3.04 **21.** 210% 2.10 **22.** 642% 6.42 **23.** 716% 7.16 **24.** 1000% 10

25. 0.5% 0.005 **26.** 1.06% 0.0106 **27.** 0.8% 0.008 **28.** 0.017% 0.00017 **29.** 0.07% 0.0007

Change each decimal to a percent.

30. 0.06 6% **31.** 0.09 9% **32.** 0.83 83% **33.** 0.42 42% **34.** 0.17 17%

35. 0.60 60% **36.** 0.70 70% **37.** 0.1 10% **38.** 0.2 20% **39.** 0.9 90%

40. 0.125 12.5% **41.** 0.333 33.3% **42.** 0.375 37.5% **43.** 0.667 66.7% **44.** 0.177 17.7%

45. 1.00 100% **46.** 2.50 250% **47.** 3.06 306% **48.** 4.1 410% **49.** 5.8 580%

Tables

Mathematical Symbols

=	is equal to		$\sqrt{}$	nonnegative square root
>	is greater than		%	percent
<	is less than		π	pi
≈	is approximately equal to		°	degrees
⊥	is perpendicular to			

Metric System

Prefixes

thousands	hundreds	tens	ones	tenths	hundredths	thousandths
kilo-	hecto-	deka-	(no prefix)	deci-	centi-	milli-

Length
1 centimeter (cm) = 10 millimeters (mm)
1 meter (m) = 100 centimeters
1 meter = 1,000 millimeters
1 kilometer (km) = 1,000 meters

Area
1 square centimeter (cm²) = 100 square millimeters (mm²)
1 square meter (m²) = 10,000 square centimeters
1 hectare (ha) = 10,000 square meters

Volume and Capacity
1 cubic centimeter (cm³) = 1,000 cubic millimeters (mm³)
1 cubic decimeter (dm³) = 1,000 cubic centimeters
1 cubic meter (m³) = 1,000,000 cubic centimeters
1 milliliter (mL) = 1 cubic centimeter
1 liter (L) = 1,000 milliliters
1 liter = 1,000 cubic centimeters
1 liter = 1 cubic decimeter

Mass
1 gram (g) = 1,000 milligrams (mg)
1 kilogram (kg) = 1,000 grams
1 metric ton (t) = 1,000 kilograms

Time
1 minute (min) = 60 seconds (s)
1 hour (h) = 60 minutes
1 day (d) = 24 hours
1 year = 365 days

Formulas

$C = \pi \times d$	circumference of a circle
$A = l \times w$	area of a rectangle
$A = b \times h$	area of a parallelogram
$A = \frac{1}{2} \times b \times h$	area of a triangle
$A = \frac{1}{2} \times h \times (a + b)$	area of a trapezoid
$A = \pi \times r^2$	area of a circle
$V = B \times h$	volume of a prism
$V = \frac{1}{3} \times B \times h$	volume of a pyramid
$V = \pi \times r^2 \times h$	volume of a cylinder
$V = \frac{1}{3} \times \pi \times r^2 \times h$	volume of a cone
$V = \frac{4}{3} \times \pi \times r^3$	volume of a sphere
$c^2 = a^2 + b^2$	Pythagorean Theorem
$I = p \times r \times t$	interest

Squares and Approximate Square Roots

n	n^2	$\sqrt{n}$	n	n^2	$\sqrt{n}$
1	1	1.000	51	2601	7.141
2	4	1.414	52	2704	7.211
3	9	1.732	53	2809	7.280
4	16	2.000	54	2916	7.348
5	25	2.236	55	3025	7.416
6	36	2.449	56	3136	7.483
7	49	2.646	57	3249	7.550
8	64	2.828	58	3364	7.616
9	81	3.000	59	3481	7.681
10	100	3.162	60	3600	7.746
11	121	3.317	61	3721	7.810
12	144	3.464	62	3844	7.874
13	169	3.606	63	3969	7.937
14	196	3.742	64	4096	8.000
15	225	3.873	65	4225	8.062
16	256	4.000	66	4356	8.124
17	289	4.123	67	4489	8.185
18	324	4.243	68	4624	8.246
19	361	4.359	69	4761	8.307
20	400	4.472	70	4900	8.367
21	441	4.583	71	5041	8.426
22	484	4.690	72	5184	8.485
23	529	4.796	73	5329	8.544
24	576	4.899	74	5476	8.602
25	625	5.000	75	5625	8.660
26	676	5.099	76	5776	8.718
27	729	5.196	77	5929	8.775
28	784	5.292	78	6084	8.832
29	841	5.385	79	6241	8.888
30	900	5.477	80	6400	8.944
31	961	5.568	81	6561	9.000
32	1024	5.657	82	6724	9.055
33	1089	5.745	83	6889	9.110
34	1156	5.831	84	7056	9.165
35	1225	5.916	85	7225	9.220
36	1296	6.000	86	7396	9.274
37	1369	6.083	87	7569	9.327
38	1444	6.164	88	7744	9.381
39	1521	6.245	89	7921	9.434
40	1600	6.325	90	8100	9.487
41	1681	6.403	91	8281	9.539
42	1764	6.481	92	8464	9.592
43	1849	6.557	93	8649	9.644
44	1936	6.633	94	8836	9.695
45	2025	6.708	95	9025	9.747
46	2116	6.782	96	9216	9.798
47	2209	6.856	97	9409	9.849
48	2304	6.928	98	9604	9.899
49	2401	7.000	99	9801	9.950
50	2500	7.071	100	10000	10.000

Glossary

absolute value (306)   The distance a number is from zero on the number line.

accuracy (152)   The accuracy of a measurement. A measurement is only as accurate as the measuring tool.

acute angle (207)   An angle that fits inside a right angle. An acute angle measures between 0° and 90°.

acute triangle (214)   A triangle with all acute angles.

angle (205)   Two different rays that have a common endpoint.

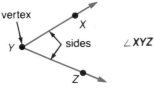

area (266)   The number of square units required to cover a surface.

arithmetic sequence (382)   A pattern of numbers in which each term is found by adding the same number to the term before it.

7, 10, 13, 16, 19, . . .

ASA rule (247)   Two triangles are congruent if two corresponding angles and the included side are congruent.

bar graph (74)   Graph that uses bars to compare data. The length of each bar represents a number.

bisect (238)   To separate into two congruent parts.

capacity (162)   The amount of liquid or gas a container can hold.

Celsius (°C) (172)   The metric unit for the measure of temperature. Water freezes at 0°C and boils at 100°C.

centimeter (m) (139)   One hundredth of a meter. Small nuts and bolts are about one centimeter long.

chance (118)   The probability of an event happening expressed as a percent. The chance of getting heads when a coin is tossed is 50%.

circle (212)   A path of all points in a plane a given distance from a fixed point (called the center) in the plane.

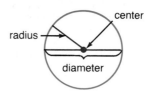

circle graph (80)   A graph that uses a circle to show parts of a whole.

circumference (262)   The distance around a circle.

complementary angles (208)   Two angles whose sum of their degree measures is 90°.

compound interest (369)   Interest computed on interest.

conclusion (224)   The part of a conditional statement that follows *then*.

condition (224)   The part of a conditional statement that follows *if*.

conditional statement (224)   A statement that can be written in *if-then* form.

cone (286)   A solid figure with a circular base and a curved surface that comes to a point.

congruent figures (233)   Figures that have the same size and shape.

construction (234)   An accurate drawing made with a compass and a straightedge.

converse (224)   A conditional statement formed by interchanging the condition and the conclusion of a given conditional statement.

coordinate plane (398)   A plane with perpendicular number lines that intersect at the zero points.

corresponding angles (244)   Angles that are in a similar position when two lines are cut by a transversal. Angles 1 and 2 are corresponding angles.

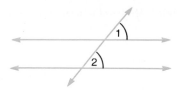

cross products (50)   In the proportion $\frac{2}{3} = \frac{10}{15}$, the cross products are 2×15 and 3×10.

cup (c) (166)   A unit of capacity in the customary system that equals 8 fluid ounces.

cylinder (284)   A solid figure with two parallel congruent circular bases.

deductive reasoning (226)   Using a rule to make a decision.

degree (°) (196)   A unit for measuring angles. It takes 360 degrees to go around a circle.

dependent events (106)   Two sets of outcomes that affect each other. Selecting a student from a classroom and then selecting another student would be dependent events.

diameter (262)   A line segment that passes through the center of a circle and has both endpoints on the circle.

dilation (409)   A change in size.

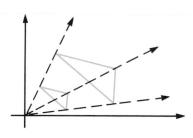

equally likely (100)   A choice or outcome made at random.

equation (331)   A mathematical sentence with an equal sign.
$$3 + 4 = 7 \qquad 3 \times a = 21$$

equilateral triangle (214)   A triangle that has all sides congruent.

expected value (122)   The number of times an event is expected to occur. The expected value for guessing 10 true and false questions correctly is 5.

expected winnings (128)   The amount that everyone who participates in a game will win.

exponent (355)   A number that tells how many times the base is used as a factor. In 10^3, the exponent is 3.
$$10^3 = 10 \times 10 \times 10$$

expression (356)   Numbers or symbols representing numbers connected by signs of operations.
$$5 \times 6 + 2 \qquad 6a - b$$

Fahrenheit (°F) (172)   The customary unit for the measure of temperature. Water freezes at 32°F and boils at 212°F.

favorable outcome (100)   The preferred outcome of an event.

fluid ounce (fl oz) (166)   A unit of capacity in the customary system.

formula (358)   A statement of a rule using letters to represent quantities and symbols of operations.
$$W = F \times d$$

frequency table (26)   A table or chart that uses tally marks to show how many times an event occurs.

function (378)   A relationship that pairs two sets so that each member of the first set corresponds to exactly one member of the second set.

gallon (gal) (166)   A unit of capacity in the customary system that equals 4 quarts.

geometric sequence (386)   A pattern of numbers in which each term is found by multiplying the same number by the term before it.
$$3, 6, 12, 24, 48, \ldots$$

graduated cylinder (188)   A cylinder used to measure the capacity of liquids.

gram (g) (161)   The basic unit of mass in the metric system. A paper clip has a mass of about 1 gram.

histogram (84)   A bar graph with no spaces between the bars.

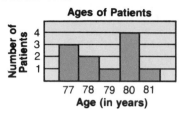

Ages of Patients

hypotenuse (218)   The longer side of a right triangle. The hypotenuse is the side opposite the right angle.

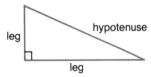

independent events (104)   Two sets of outcomes that do not affect each other. Flipping a coin and rolling a die are independent events.

inductive reasoning (226)   Making a rule after seeing several examples.

inequality (331)   A mathematical sentence that states that two quantities are *not* equal.

$$x + 4 \neq 10 \qquad 6a \geq 12$$

integers (305)   The whole numbers and their opposites.

$$\ldots, \,^-3, \,^-2, \,^-1, 0, 1, 2, 3, \ldots$$

intersecting lines (210)   Lines that meet.

inverse operations (336)   Two operations that undo each other. Addition and subtraction are inverse operations. Multiplication and division are also inverse operations.

isosceles triangle (214)   A triangle that has at least two sides congruent.

kilometer (km) (139)   One thousand meters. Five city blocks are about one kilometer long.

kilowatt hour (kWH) (192)   One kilowatt (1,000 watts) of electricity used for 1 hour.

lateral surface (284)   The surface of a solid figure excluding the bases.

leg (218)   One of the two shorter sides of a right triangle. The legs are opposite the acute angles.

line (205)   A straight path that extends indefinitely in two directions.

linear equation (402)   An equation whose graph is a straight line.

$$y = 2x + 3$$

line graph (77)   A graph that uses line segments to show change and direction of change over a period of time.

line segment (205)   The shortest path from one point to another.

liter (L) (162)   The basic unit of capacity in the metric system.

$$1 \text{ liter} = 1 \text{ cubic decimeter}$$

mean (32)   The sum of the numbers in a set of data divided by the number of addends.

$$\frac{1 + 2 + 6 + 9}{4} = 4.5$$

median (36)   The middle number of a set of data when the data is organized from least to greatest.

0.9, 1.5, 2.6, 2.9, 3.3

median

meter (m) (139)   The basic unit of length in the metric system. A car fender is about one meter high.

metric system (139)   A system of measurement using basic units and prefixes. The basic unit of length is the meter, the basic unit of mass is the gram, and the basic unit of capacity is the liter.

midpoint (238)   A point that divides a line segment into two congruent parts.

mile (mi) (144)   A unit of length in the customary system that equals 5,280 feet.

millimeter (mm) (139)   One thousandth of a meter. Wires are about one millimeter wide.

mode (30)   The number that appears most often in a set of data.

$$1, 2, ^-2, 3, 5, 5, 5, 8$$
5 is the mode

nonstandard unit (137)   Units that vary from person to person. Thumbs, spans, cubits, and paces are nonstandard units.

obtuse angle (207)   An angle that cannot fit inside a right angle. An obtuse angle measures between 90° and 180°.

obtuse triangle (214)   A triangle that has an obtuse angle.

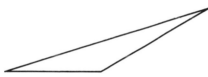

odds (117)   The ratio of the number of successes to the number of failures. The odds that a 3 shows on a die is 1 to 5.

open sentence (331)   A sentence with one or more variables.

$$3 \times a = 21 \qquad 19 - x < ^-2$$

opposites (305)   Two rational numbers whose sum is zero. 5 and $^-5$ are opposites.

ordered pair (387)   A pair of numbers where order is important.

(3, 2)

origin (398)   The point where the x-axis and y-axis intersect.

ounce (oz) (166)   A unit of weight in the customary system. A small bag of peanuts weighs about 1 ounce.

outcome (95)   A possible result of a probability experiment. One outcome of flipping a coin is tails.

parallel lines (210)   Lines in a plane that do *not* meet.

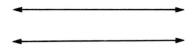

parallelogram (256)   A quadrilateral with two pairs of parallel sides.

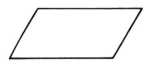

percent (56)   A ratio that compares a number to one hundred. The percent symbol is %.
53 out of 100 is 53%.

perimeter (P) (260)   The distance around a polygon.

perpendicular bisector (243)   A line that is perpendicular to a line segment and also separates the line segment into two congruent parts.

perpendicular lines (210)   Lines that intersect to form right angles.

pi (π) (262)   The ratio of the circumference of a circle to its diameter. Pi is approximately equal to 3.14 or $\frac{22}{7}$.

pictograph (73)   Graph that uses pictures to compare data.

pint (pt) (166)   A unit of capacity in the customary system that equals 2 cups.

plane (205)   The set of all points on a never-ending flat surface. The surface of a pane of glass is a model of part of a plane.

point (205)   An exact location usually represented by a dot.

polygon (255)   A closed plane figure formed by line segments called sides.

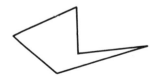

population (26)   In statistics, the entire group being studied.

pound (lb) (166)   A unit of weight in the customary system that equals 16 ounces. A hammer weighs about 1 pound.

power (355)   A number written with an exponent.
$$10^3 \qquad 8^5 \qquad 9^2$$

principal (369)   The money that earns interest.

probability (100)   The ratio of the favorable outcome to the total number of outcomes. The probability that 5 will appear on a die is $\frac{1}{6}$.

proportion (50)   Two ratios that are equivalent.
$$\frac{15}{3} = \frac{5}{1}$$

protractor (196)   An instrument used to measure angles.

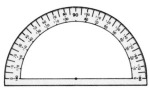

Pythagorean Theorem (218)   In a right triangle, the square of the hypotenuse is equal to the sum of the squares of the legs.

quadrant (398)   One of the four parts of a coordinate plane formed by the x- and y-axes.

quadrilateral (256)   A polygon with four sides.

quart (qt) (166)   A unit of capacity in the customary system that equals 2 pints.

radius (212)   The distance from the center of a circle to any point on the circle.

range (30)   The difference between the greatest and least numbers in a set of data.

rate (48)   A ratio of two measurements having different units.
$$\frac{483 \text{ feet}}{6 \text{ seconds}}$$

ratio (47)   A comparison of two numbers. The ratio of triangles to squares is 3 to 4 or 3:4 or $\frac{3}{4}$.

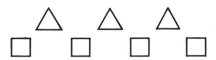

rational number (306)   Any number that can be written as the ratio of two integers.

ray (205)   A never-ending straight path in one direction.

rectangle (256)   A parallelogram with four congruent angles.

rectangular prism (281)   A prism with rectangular bases.

reflection (408)   A flip about an axis.

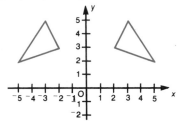

regular polygon (260)   A polygon in which all sides and all angles are congruent.

rhombus (256)   A parallelogram with four congruent sides.

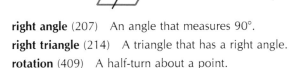

right angle (207)   An angle that measures 90°.

right triangle (214)   A triangle that has a right angle.

rotation (409)   A half-turn about a point.

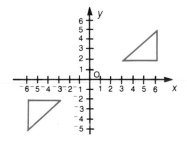

sample (26)   A representative group of a larger group called the population.

SAS rule (247)   Two triangles are congruent if two corresponding sides and the included angle are congruent.

scale drawings (52)   A geometrically similar representative of something too large or too small to be conveniently drawn actual size.

scalene triangle (214)   A triangle with *no* sides congruent.

scientific notation (388)   A way of expressing numbers as the product of a number between 1 and 10 and a power of ten.
$$3,400 = 3.4 \times 10^3$$

sequence (382)   A list of numbers following a certain pattern.

side (205)   One of the two rays that form an angle.

side (255)   A line segment that forms one side of a polygon.

significant digits (152)   The digits that indicate the results of a measurement. If a distance is measured to the nearest tenth of a meter, then 62.0 m has three significant digits.

similar figures (258)   Two figures that have the same shape but may differ in size.

simple interest (369)   Interest only on the principal and not on the accumulated interest.

solution (332)   A value for the variable that makes a mathematical sentence true.

sphere (296)   A solid figure in which all points are the same distance from the center.

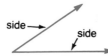

square (218)   The product of a number times itself.
$$5^2 = 5 \times 5 = 25$$

square (256)   A parallelogram with four congruent sides and four congruent angles.

square root (218)   A number whose square equals a given number. The square root of 9 is 3.

SSS rule (246)   Two triangles are congruent if the corresponding sides of the triangles are congruent.

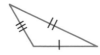

straightedge (234)   An instrument used to draw straight lines.

supplementary angles (208)   Two angles whose sum of their degree measures is 180°.

surface area (281)   The sum of the areas of the surfaces of a solid figure.

tally mark (25)   A small line used to record data.

⁗ ‖

ton (T) (166)   A unit of weight in the customary system that equals 2,000 pounds. A small car weighs about 1 ton.

translation (409)   A slide in a plane.

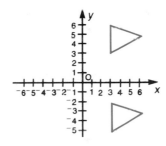

transversal (244)   A line that intersects two or more lines.

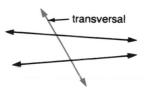

trapezoid (256)   A quadrilateral with exactly one pair of parallel sides.

tree diagram (96)   A diagram used to show possible choices or outcomes.

trend (77)   The direction of change.

triangle (212)   A polygon with three sides.

triangular number (390)   A number that can be represented by a triangle.

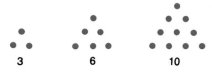

unit rate (48)   A rate with a denominator of 1.

$$\frac{55 \text{ miles}}{1 \text{ hour}}$$

variable (331)   A placeholder in a mathematical sentence.

Venn diagram (130)   A diagram using circles to illustrate data.

vertex (205)   The common endpoint of the two rays that form an angle.

vertical angles (210)   The opposite angles formed when two lines intersect. Angles 1 and 3 are vertical angles.

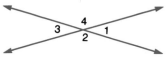

volume (288)   The number of cubic units required to fill a space.

***x*-axis** (398)   The horizontal number line in a coordinate system.

***x*-coordinate** (398)   The first number in an ordered pair.

***y*-axis** (398)   The vertical number line in a coordinate system.

***y*-coordinate** (398)   The second number in an ordered pair.

Index

A

Absolute value, 306–307, 310–311
Accuracy, 152–153
Addition
  equations involving, 334–335, 344
  estimating sums, 27, 79, 151, 198, 339
  inequalities involving, 346–348
  of decimals, 28–29
  of fractions, 108–109, 175, 349·
  of measures, 150–151, 174–175, 236–237
  of mixed numerals, 175
  of probabilities, 108–109
  of rational numbers, 310–313, 322–323, 383
  of whole numbers, 27, 209
  used in solving equations, 336–337, 345
  using calculators, 28–29
Alphanumeric data, 64
Angles, 196–197, 205–215
  acute, 207, 214
  adding measures of, 236–237
  complementary, 208–209
  congruent, 233, 236–237, 244–245, 247–249
  constructing, 236–237, 242–245, 247–249
  corresponding, 244–245, 247
  drawing, 196–197
  included, 247
  measuring, 196–197
  naming, 205–206, 210, 212
  obtuse, 207, 214
  of polygons, 221–222
  of triangles, 212–215, 221–222
  right, 207, 214, 242–243
  subtracting measures of, 236–237
  supplementary, 208–209
  vertical, 210–211
Area, 266–275
  composite, 274–275
  of circles, 272–273, 366, 371, 373
  of parallelograms, 266–268, 270, 272, 274
  of rectangles, 266–267
  of squares, 365–366, 371, 373–374, 378
  of trapezoids, 270–271
  of triangles, 268–269, 274
  surface, 281–287, 296–297
ASA rule, 247–249
Averages, 32, 38, 40

  batting, 19, 360
  means, 32–33, 36, 38–45
  medians, 36–45
  modes, 30–31, 38–45

B

Bar graphs, 74–76, 84–87, 90–92, 103
  histograms, 84–85, 91–92
  one hundred percent, 76
Bases
  in percents, 59–64
  of cylinders, 284, 292
  of exponents, 355
  of parallelograms, 266
  of prisms, 281, 288
  of pyramids, 282
  of trapezoids, 270
BASIC, 85, 249
  assignment statements, 315, 343
  GO TO statements, 225
  IF-THEN statements, 225
  LET statements, 315, 343
Binary numbers, 411
Bisectors
  of angles, 238–239
  of line segments, 238–239
  perpendicular, 243, 257
Bus schedules, 4–5
Bytes, 360
  kilo-, 360
  mega-, 360

C

Calculator mode, 249
Calculators
  and function rules, 391
  change-sign keys, 312
  command buttons, 28
  division, 235
  finding average rate, 149
  finding distances, 189
  finding percents, 81
  forming palindromes, 129
  forming words, 410
  fractions, 28, 175
  memory keys, 35
  mixed numerals, 175

  multiple-step problems, 35
  number buttons, 28
  order of operations, 323, 337
  parentheses, 337
  percent keys, 67
  pi, 263, 285
  probabilities as percents, 107
  square roots, 365
  squaring numbers, 223
  using, 28–29
Capacity, 162–168
  changing units, 164–165, 167–168, 359
  customary system, 166–168, 359
  estimating, 163, 168
  metric system, 162–165
Careers
  airline reservation agent, 61
  air traffic controllers, 398
  bank tellers, 310
  bus drivers, 4
  drafters, 234
  engineering technicians, 258
  glaziers, 196
  landscapers, 367
  licensed practical nurses, 84
  machinists, 164
  postal clerks, 382
  radio service technicians, 100
  real estate agents, 344
  sheet metal workers, 286
  stock clerks, 126
  test drivers, 30
  tool-and-die makers, 152
  tool programmers, 210
Celsius (C), 172–173, 360, 406–407
Centimeters (cm), 139–143, 154–155, 163, 359
Chances, 118–121
  and odds, 120–121
Chapter reviews, 20–21, 42–43, 68–69, 90–91, 112–113, 132–133, 156–157, 178–179, 200–201, 228–229, 250–251, 276–277, 300–301, 326–327, 350–351, 372–373, 392–393, 414–415
Chapter tests, 22, 44, 70, 92, 114, 134, 158, 180, 202, 230, 252, 278, 302, 328, 352, 374, 394, 416
Charts, see *Tables*
Circle graphs, 80–81, 91–92
Circles, 212–213
  area of, 272–273, 366, 371, 373
  center of, 212–213
  chords of, 257

K

Key skills
    addition of fractions, 108
    addition of rational numbers, 383
    changing improper fractions to
      mixed numerals, 58
    changing mixed numerals to
      improper fractions, 58
    changing percents to fractions, 118
    division of powers of ten, 142,
      165
    division of decimals, 48
    division of rational numbers, 338
    division of whole numbers, 127
    finding percents of numbers, 80
    graphing sets of numbers, 347
    multiplication by powers of ten,
      142, 165
    multiplication of decimals, 284
    multiplication of fractions, 52,
      104, 167
    multiplication of integers, 357
    multiplication of rational numbers,
      357, 387
    rounding numbers, 32
    solving proportions, 259
    subtraction of fractions, 311
    subtraction of rational numbers,
      334
    subtraction of whole numbers, 193
Kilowatt hours (kWh), 192–193
Kilowatts, 192

L

Legs, 218–220, 367
Length, 138–145, 148–158
    adding units, 150–151
    changing units, 142–143,
      148–149, 154–155
    customary system, 144–145,
      148–155, 359
    dividing units, 150–151
    estimating, 137, 140, 145
    maps, 184–185, 189
    metric system, 139–143, 152–155
    multiplying units, 150–151
    nonstandard units, 137–138
    odometers, 183
    of rectangles, 266

    precision, 152–153
    significant digits, 152–153
    subtracting units, 150–151
Light
    speed of, 361–362
    wands, 17
Linear equations, 400–403, 406
    graphing, 402–403, 406
Line graphs, 77–79, 87–92
Lines, 205–206
    constructing, 242–245
    determined by points, 402
    graphs of, 402–403, 406
    intersecting, 210–211
    naming, 205–206
    number, 305–311, 398
    of symmetry, 245
    parallel, 210–211, 244–245
    perpendicular, 210–211,
      242–243
    perpendicular bisectors, 243, 257
Line segments, 205–206
    bisecting, 238–239
    congruent, 214–215, 233–235,
      246–249
    constructing, 234–235, 246–249
    midpoints, 238
    naming, 205–206
Liters (L), 162–165, 359
    kilo-, 162–165
    milli-, 162–165, 188–189, 359
Logic
    conclusions, 224–225
    conditional statements, 224–227
    conditions, 224–225
    converses, 224–225
    deductive reasoning, 226–227
    inductive reasoning, 226–227

M

Magic squares, 199
Magnetic ink characters, 195
Maps, 184–185, 189, 204–205, 396
Mass, 161, 163–165
    changing units, 164–165, 359
    estimating, 161
Math Breaks, 5, 7, 11, 13, 15, 33,
    53, 55, 76, 83, 97, 103, 119,
    123, 141, 163, 199, 213, 215,
    245, 257, 267, 317, 319, 325,
    335, 349, 366, 387, 401

Mathematical expressions
    and tables, 377
    evaluating, 356–357
    to verbal expressions, 377
Mathematical sentences, 331
    equations, 331–339, 342–345
    inequalities, 331–333, 346–348
    open, 330–339, 342–352
    proportions, 50–53, 56–66,
      258–259
    variables, 331
Means, 32–33, 36, 38–45
Mean variations, 33
Measurement, 136–145, 148–168,
    172–189, 192–197
    adding, 174–175
    area, 266–275, 281–287,
      365–366, 371, 373–374, 378
    capacity, 162–168, 359
    changing units, 142–143,
      148–149, 154–155, 164–168,
      172–174, 176, 359–360, 378,
      406–407
    circumference, 262–263, 284,
      358–359, 362
    comparing systems, 154–155, 359
    customary system, 144–145,
      148–155, 166–168, 172–173
    density, 293
    distance, 358, 361, 372–374, 378
    estimating, 137, 140, 145, 161,
      163, 168, 173
    force, 358
    gas mileage, 359–362, 371,
      373–374
    graduated cylinders, 188–189
    length, 137–145, 148–158, 183,
      185, 359
    maps, 184–185
    mass, 161, 163–165, 359
    metric system, 139–143,
      152–155, 161–165, 172–173
    mileage charts, 3
    nonstandard units, 137–138
    odometers, 183
    of electricity, 192–193, 195
    of natural gas, 192, 194–195
    of water, 193–195
    perimeters, 260–261, 371
    precision, 152–153
    protractors, 196–197
    significant digits, 152–153
    speed of light, 361–362
    speed of sound, 362
    stopwatches, 188–189
    subtracting, 174–175
    surface area, 281–287, 296–297

for line segments, 205–206
for multiplication, 355
for operations, 29
for parallel, 244
for perpendicular, 242
for pi, 262
for rays, 205–206
for right angles, 207
for square roots, 365
UPC, 17

T

Tables, 2–27, 377–381
and expressions, 377
and functions, 378–381, 391
batting averages, 19
bus schedules, 4–5
frequency, 26–27, 73
income taxes, 14–15
making, 18–19
mileage, 3
pay schedules, 12–13
postal rates, 6–7
sales taxes, 16
square roots, 219, 365–366, 419
squares, 219, 419
tallies, 25–27
taxes, 12–16
telephone rates, 8–9
time, 4–5
withholding taxes, 12–13
Tallies, 25–27
Taxes, 12–16
income, 12–15
sales, 16, 373, 379
withholding, 12–13
W-2 forms, 14
W-4 forms, 15
Telephone rates, 8–9
Temperature, 172–173
changing units, 172–173, 360
customary system, 172–173, 360, 379, 406–407
degrees Celsius (°C), 172–173, 360, 406–407
degrees Fahrenheit (°F), 172–173, 360, 379, 406–407
estimating, 173
metric system, 172–173, 360, 406–407

Ten
powers of, 142–143, 164–165
Tests, 22, 44, 70, 92, 114, 134, 158, 180, 202, 230, 252, 278, 302, 328, 352, 374, 394, 416
Time, 174–176, 186–189, 361, 378
adding, 174–175
A.M., 186
bus schedules, 4–5
changing units, 174, 176, 378
P.M., 186
stopwatches, 188–189
subtracting, 174–175
tables, 4–5
twenty-four-hour clocks, 186–187
Tons (T), 166, 168
Transistors, 138
Translations, 408–410
Transversals, 244
Trapezoids, 256–257
area of, 270–271
bases of, 270
height of, 270
Tree diagrams, 96–98, 105
Trends, 77
Triangles, 212–215, 218–222, 255
acute, 214–215
angles of, 212–215, 221–222
area of, 268–269, 274
congruent, 233, 246–249
constructing, 246–249
corresponding angles, 247
corresponding sides, 246–247
equilateral, 214–215
hypotenuse, 218–220, 367
included angles, 247
included sides, 247
isosceles, 214–215
legs, 218–220, 367
naming, 212, 215
obtuse, 214–215
right, 214–215, 218–220, 367–368
scalene, 214–215
sides of, 212–215, 218–220, 246–249
similar, 258–259
Triangular numbers, 390–391
Twenty-four-hour clocks, 186–187

U

Units
adding, 150–151

changing, 142–143, 148–149, 154–155, 164–168, 172–174, 176, 359–360
customary, 144–145, 148–155, 166–168, 172–173, 358–359
dividing, 150–151
multiplying, 150–151
nonstandard, 137–138
of capacity, 162–168, 359
of length, 137–145, 148–158, 359
of mass, 161, 164–165, 359
of temperature, 172–173, 360, 379, 406–407
of time, 174–176
of weight, 166, 168, 359
subtracting, 150–151
Universal Product Code (UPC), 17

V

Vacuum tubes, 138
Variables, 331
in expressions, 356–357
Variations, 33
Venn diagrams, 130–131
Verbal expressions
mathematical expressions to, 377
to mathematical expressions, 377
Vertices
of angles, 205
of polygons, 255
Very large-scale integrated circuits (VLSI), 138
Volume
comparing, 298
of cones, 294–295
of cubes, 288
of cylinders, 292–293
of prisms, 288–289, 294
of pyramids, 294–295
of rectangular prisms, 288–289, 294, 298
of spheres, 296–297

W

Weight, 166, 168, 358–359
changing units, 166, 168, 359
estimating, 168

Selected Answers

Chapter 1 Charts and Tables

Page 3 Exercises

1. 1,746 mi **3.** 795 mi **5.** 996 mi **7.** 713 mi
9. 379 mi **11.** 449 mi **13.** 1,538 mi **15.** 2,114 mi

Pages 4-5 Exercises

1. Starr and Third, Maple and Lenox, Sunlawn and Miami
3. 5, Lenox **5.** Maple and Lenox, Sunlawn and Miami,
Price and Lenox, Starr and Third **7.** 11:31 A.M.
9. 2:42 P.M.

Pages 6-7 Exercises

1. 39¢ **3.** 90¢ **5.** $1.41 **7.** $1.24 **9.** $1.58
11. $3.96 **13.** $3.61 **15.** $3.18 **17.** $6.81
19. $7.66 **21.** $2.25 **23.** $1.78 **25.** $4.74
27. $1.49 **29.** Fourth-Class Parcel Post

Page 9 Exercises

1. before 8:00 A.M.; after 11:00 A.M. **3.** before 5:00
P.M.; after 11:00 P.M. **5.** all day **7.** full rate
9. 60% discount **11.** full rate **13.** 60% discount
15. direct dial night rate **17.** no **19.** Zanesville
21. 22¢

Page 11 Exercises

1. $150.50 **3.** $156.40 **5.** $147.60 **7.** $153.00
9. $140.00 **11.** $147.00 **13.** $155.80 **15.** $151.20
17. $146.20 **19.** $27 **21.** $20 **23.** $22 **25.** $18
27. $10 **29.** $3 **31.** $8 **33.** $11 **35.** $6 **37.** $25
39. $8 **41.** $25 **43.** decreases **45.** $14.00

Pages 14-15 Exercises

1. $10,762 **3.** $269.05 **5.** $1,032 **7.** make an
additional payment **9.** Ayers Trucking Company
11. 615-04-1492 **13.** $1,222 **15.** $989 **17.** $1,275
19. $883 **21.** $1,090 **23.** $1,108 **25.** $1,082
27. $876 **29.** additional payment

Page 16 Exercises

1. $0.02 **3.** 0 **5.** $0.14 **7.** $0.76 **9.** $0.89
11. $0.28 **13.** $0.45 **15.** $0.70 **17.** $0.18
19. $0.11 **21.** $5\frac{1}{2}$% **23.** $0.22 **25.** Find the amount of
tax on $16 and double it.

Page 19 Exercises

3. 18 years **5.** 1968; .237 **7.** 1956; 130 RBI's
9. 1961; 54 home runs **11.** 10 years

Pages 20-21 Chapter 1 Review

1. withholding tax **3.** sales tax **5.** tax table
7. 1,063 mi **9.** 1,748 mi **11.** 1,058 mi **13.** 12:01
P.M. **15.** 12:37 P.M. **17.** $0.39 **19.** $1.75
21. $1.41 **23.** $0.56 **25.** $2.09 **27.** $2.40
29. $4.13 **31.** $6.37 **33.** $5.43 **35.** $1.92
37. $1.89 **39.** $3.03 **41.** $1.87 **43.** full rate
45. 40% discount **47.** full rate **49.** $3.48, $0.28
51. $175.50 **53.** $161.00 **55.** $154.80 **57.** $10

59. $34 **61.** $12 **63.** $17 **65.** $1,048 **67.** $1,212
69. $1,154 **71.** $0.05 **73.** $0.06 **75.** $0.90
77. $0.45 **79.** $0.52 **81.** 1966

Page 23 Cumulative Review

1. $4.32 **3.** $3.45 **5.** $2.40 **7.** $3.61 **9.** $49
11. $31 **13.** $40 **15.** $33 **17.** $86 **19.** none
21. $0.50 **23.** $0.52 **25.** $0.04 **27.** $0.48
29. $0.06 **31.** $0.55 **33.** $0.20

Chapter 2 Everyday Statistics

Page 25 Exercises

1. 10 **3.** 11 **5.** ||||| |||| **7.** ||||| ||||| ||||| ||||| ||| **9.** ||||| ||||| ||||| ||
11. sandwich and steak **13.** high-school age

Pages 26-27 Exercises

3. other; easy listening **5.** not representative **7.** no;
people are all from same party **9.** yes; variety of people
15. 25 **17.** 11 **19.** Easier to locate and analyze.

Page 29 Exercises

1. 1,893.009 **3.** 172 **5.** 1.17 **7.** 3.52 **9.** 0.55
11. 513.2 **13.** 0.25 **15.** 0.1875 **17.** 0.1515152
19. 0.3 **21.** 0.64705882 **23.** 1.25 **25.** 20.61
kilometers **27.** $6.98

Pages 30-31 Exercises

1. 11; 5, 9 **3.** 7; 6 **5.** 0.6; 0.7, 1.0 **7.** 0.05; no mode
9. 2.6; 8.3 **11.** 7 **13.** no **15.** 9, 3 and 4 **17.** 7, 8
19. 5.7 in. **21.** 3.5 in. **23.** 7.85 in. **25.** 5.3 in.
27. 8.0 in. **29.** 4.8 in. **31.** 1.65 in. **33.** none
35. none **37.** none **39.** none **41.** 1.7 in. **43.** 5.9 in.
45. 0.05 in.

Pages 32-33 Exercises

1. 8 **3.** 5 **5.** 20 **7.** 219.2 **9.** 0.8 **11.** 3.8 or $3\frac{5}{6}$
13. 115 **15.** 37.7 yards per punt **17.** 55.1 in., 4.6 in.

Pages 36-37 Exercises

1. 16 **3.** 2.1 **5.** 83 **7.** 96.5 **9.** The same number are
greater than and less than the median. **11.** $112.50
13. median increases to 1.8 g; mean increases to 2.4 g.
15. $114.08 **17.** 16.9 mpg **19.** lowered to 13.5 mpg
21. lowered to 16.4 mpg **23.** very large or very small
values **25.** adding or dropping values that are neither very
large nor very small **27.** $8,000 **29.** $11,600

Pages 38-39 Exercises

1. mode, customers will expect to be able to afford lower
priced homes. **3.** 55 **5.** 86.5 **7.** 45 **9.** 77.5
11. Group A. Group A had both a higher mean and a
higher median because of more higher scores than group
B. **13.** 23 g **15.** 19 g **17.** 22 g **19.** $29.83, $26.50,
no mode; median **21.** $12,000, $17,909, $12,000; mean
23. 331 times at bat, 378 times at bat; 47 times at bat less

Pages 40-41 Exercises

1. mode **3.** median **5.** mode **7.** 172.4 cm; mean
9. brown; mode **11.** art; mode **13.** 154 cm
15. 154, 157.6 cm **19.** 3 passengers **21.** The best
answer for the owners is the mean, because this tells them
what the income is for the ride. **23.** $30,000 and
$100,000, $133,636.36, $100,000; median; 1 high
salary **25.** 91, 80.1, 83; median; 2 very small values

Pages 42-43 Chapter 2 Review

1. j **3.** b **5.** f **7.** e **9.** 8 **11.** 24 **13.** 卌 卌 卌 卌 卌
卌 **15.** 卌 卌 卌 卌 卌 卌 卌 卌 | **17.** no, people attend
concert because of who is performing **19.** yes, variety of
food offered **21.** 0.089 **23.** 9.75 **25.** 0.7777778
27. 5.875 **29.** 38, none **31.** no range, mode is b
33. 4.3 **35.** 162 **39.** 8 **41.** 8 **43.** 25.4 **45.** no
effect on median; mean raises to 29.2 **47.** 56.4 kg,
mean, or 57 kg, median **49.** chicken, mode **51.** Female
163 cm tall, mass of 56.4 kg, has brown hair, likes chicken
and basketball.

Page 45 Cumulative Review

1. 1:16 P.M. **3.** $1.58 **5.** $2.09 **7.** $1.24 **9.** full
rate **11.** full rate **13.** 40% discount **15.** $694
19. 68 and 75 **21.** 77 **23.** median; one very large value
affects mean **25.** mode or median; most frequent value is
also middle value

Chapter 3 Ratio, Proportion, and Percent

Page 47 Exercises

1. $\frac{4}{5}$ **3.** $\frac{4}{6}$ or $\frac{2}{3}$ **5.** $\frac{3}{10}$ **7.** $\frac{7}{4}$ **9.** $\frac{1}{5}$ **11.** $\frac{8}{9}$ **13.** $\frac{7}{20}$
15. $\frac{1}{3}$ **17.** $\frac{1}{7}$ **19.** $\frac{1}{12}$ **21.** $\frac{328}{240}$ or $\frac{41}{30}$; $\frac{240}{568}$ or $\frac{30}{71}$

Page 49 Exercises

1. $\frac{96}{4}$, $\frac{24}{1}$ **3.** $\frac{8}{2}$, $\frac{4}{1}$ **5.** $\frac{300}{6}$, $\frac{50}{1}$ **7.** $\frac{40}{4}$, $\frac{10}{1}$ **9.** $\frac{3,600}{6}$, $\frac{600}{1}$
11. $\frac{250}{2.5}$, $\frac{100}{1}$ **13.** $\frac{720}{3}$, $\frac{240}{1}$ **15.** $\frac{342}{9}$, $\frac{38}{1}$ **17.** $\frac{3.95}{5}$, $\frac{0.79}{1}$
19. $\frac{9.6}{0.4}$, $\frac{24}{1}$ **21.** $\frac{301}{3.5}$, $\frac{86}{1}$ **23.** $\frac{58,080}{11}$, $\frac{5,280}{1}$
25. 15 oz - 99¢ **27.** 49 oz - $2.57 **29.** $\frac{1}{2}$ gal - $1.32
31. $4.50 **33.** 3 hours, 20 min. **35.** 3.5 hours
37. 280 words

Pages 50-51 Exercises

1. 18 = 18 **3.** 6 = 6 **5.** 18 = 18 **7.** 24 = 24
9. 36 = 36 **11.** 30 = 30 **13.** 10 = 10 **15.** 75 = 75
17. no **19.** yes **21.** no **23.** no **25.** yes **27.** yes
29. yes **31.** no **33.** 25 **35.** 10 **37.** 2 **39.** 10
41. 5 **43.** 2 **45.** 30 **47.** 20 **49.** 7.5 **51.** 125
53. 11 **55.** 12.5 **57.** 1.68 **59.** 3 **61.** 1,395 calories
63. 3 cups **65.** 30 gallons

Pages 52-53 Exercises

1. 48 in. **3.** 192 in. **5.** 42 in. **7.** 21 in. **9.** 39 in.
11. 15 inches **13.** 6 by 9 feet **15.** 7 inches

Page 58 Exercises

1. 19% **3.** 25% **5.** 90% **7.** 225% **9.** 1,010%
11. 36% **13.** 1.5% **15.** 9.2% **17.** 60% **19.** 724%
21. 20% **23.** 1,550% **25.** 0.05% **27.** 0.12 **29.** 0.2
31. 3.04 **33.** 1.57 **35.** 0.03 **37.** 0.5 **39.** 0.005
41. $\frac{7}{10}$ **43.** $\frac{3}{100}$ **45.** $1\frac{4}{25}$ **47.** $\frac{21}{400}$ **49.** $1\frac{1}{4}$ **51.** $4\frac{1}{2}$
53. $\frac{43}{400}$ **55.** $\frac{5}{6}$ **57.** 60%

Pages 59-60 Exercises

1. 210 students **3.** 1,323 students **5.** 45 **7.** 4.59
9. 16.2 **11.** 72 **13.** 109.5 **15.** 10.1 **17.** 3.2
19. 0.74 **21.** $3.25 **23.** $126

Page 62 Exercises

1. $P = 6$, $B = 8$ **3.** $B = 40$, $r = 52\%$ **5.** $P = 18$,
$B = 24$ **7.** $P = 24$, $B = 16$ **9.** $B = 30$, $r = 116\%$
11. 50% **13.** 20% **15.** 135% **17.** 150% **19.** 50%
21. 37.5% **23.** 500% **25.** 78% **27.** 125%
29. $31\frac{1}{4}\%$ **31.** 20% **33.** 20% **35.** 50%

Pages 63-64 Exercises

1. 75 **3.** 50 **5.** $37\frac{1}{2}$ **7.** 252 **9.** $P = 6$, $r = 3\%$; 200
11. $P = 84$, $B = 300$; 28% **13.** $B = 48$, $r = 5\%$; 2.4
15. $P = 6$, $r = 12.5\%$; 48 **17.** $P = 100$, $r = 33\frac{1}{3}\%$;
300 **19.** $B = 80$, $r = 37.5\%$; 30 **21.** 140 votes
23. $30,000

Pages 65-67 Exercises

1. 210 sunfish **3.** 24 kilometers **5.** 175 pounds
7. $18.18 **9.** 5 in. by $3\frac{3}{4}$ in. **11.** A-3 students;
B-6 students; C-10 students; D-5 students; F-1 student
13. 16 oz.-$1.84 **15.** 25% **17.** $2.80 **19.** 55%
21. 825 words **23.** 1,488 miles **25.** 26 meters
27. $15,640 **29.** 136 pages

Pages 68-69 Chapter 3 Review

1. proportion **3.** ratio **5.** percent **7.** rate **9.** $\frac{3}{5}$
11. $\frac{3}{4}$ **13.** $\frac{5}{8}$ **15.** $\frac{43}{11}$ **17.** $\frac{1.20}{5}$, $\frac{0.24}{1}$ **19.** $\frac{276}{12}$, $\frac{23}{1}$
21. $\frac{2,500}{5}$, $\frac{500}{1}$ **23.** 160 = 160 **25.** 12 = 12 **27.** no
29. yes **31.** 7 **33.** 114 **35.** 7.5 **37.** 1.8 **39.** 184 cm
41. 115 cm **43.** 36% **45.** 140% **47.** 1% **49.** 85%
51. 37.5% **53.** 0.42 **55.** 0.003 **57.** 0.0125 **59.** $\frac{2}{5}$
61. $\frac{1}{200}$ **63.** 84 **65.** 17.36 **67.** $B = 8$, $r = 50\%$; 4
69. $P = 16$, $B = 50$; 32% **71.** $480

Page 71 Cumulative Review

1. 984 mi **3.** 1,760 mi **5.** 1,337 mi **7.** No, not a sample that represents all people **9.** Yes, variety of people **11.** 11,412 **13.** 371.341 **15.** 3.75 **17.** 23; 9 **19.** 18; 22 **21.** 12 **23.** 3 **25.** 45 **27.** $\frac{7}{10}$ **29.** $\frac{2}{3}$ **31.** $\frac{3}{13}$ **33.** $\frac{7}{10}$ **35.** $\frac{460}{20}, \frac{23}{1}$ **37.** $\frac{5.25}{5}, \frac{1.05}{1}$ **39.** $\frac{200}{5}, \frac{40}{1}$ **41.** 6 **43.** 20

Chapter 4 Graphs

Page 73 Exercises

1. 5 pictures **3.** 5 pictures **5.** $3\frac{1}{2}$ pictures **7.** 28 **9.** 75 **11.** 8 **13.** $3\frac{1}{2}$

Pages 74-76 Exercises

1. Average Frequency of Letters - English Language **3.** 0 and 14.0 **5.** 7.1 **7.** 13.1 **9.** 10.5 **11.** 8.2 **15.** 0 to 35,000 **17.** Asia **19.** 29,000 ft **21.** 20,000 ft **23.** 23,000 ft **25.** 20,000 ft **27.** d **29.** 9 **31.** 529 miles **33.** 2,533 cm; no **35.** 25.33 cm; yes **37.** 1 cm represents 100 mi **39.** 19 cm **43.** 23.5 cm **45.** 13.1 cm **47.** 12.7 cm **49.** 5.3 cm **51.** 25.3 cm **53.** Length of Rivers

Pages 77-78 Exercises

1. $2\frac{1}{2}$ **3.** Wednesday **5.** $295 **7.** $218 **9.** $268 **11.** from 1978 to 1980 **13.** 125 years **15.** 0-25 years **17.** about 20 years **19.** 480 ft **21.** 410 ft **23.** 440 ft **25.** 425 ft **27.** June, Aug. **29.** May, Sept. **31.** July, Aug. **33.** Apr., Sept. **35.** Feb., Mar. **37.** Mar., Apr.; May, June **39.** Mar. 10 and June 20 **43.** 40, no trend; 41, increasing; 42, increasing then decreasing

Page 80 Exercises

1. 34% **3.** 4% **5.** 4% **7.** $220 billion **9.** $67 billion **11.** social security, corporate income tax, excise tax, and other **13.** 2% **15.** 20% **17.** 28.8 billion mi^2 **19.** 51.8 billion mi^2 **21.** 92 billion mi^2

Page 85 Exercises

1. 6 age groups **3.** 57 yr, 58 yr, 60 yr, 62 yr, 63 yr, 64 yr, 65 yr, 67 yr, 68 yr, 69 yr, 71 yr, 72 yr, 73 yr, 76 yr, 83 yr, 94 yr, 95 yr, 96 yr, 98 yr, 99 yr, 100 yr **5.** 50 patients **7.** No, histograms can show only two facts. **9.** 6 families **11.** none **13.** families with children

Pages 86-87 Exercises

1. yes **3.** 5 cm^2, 1.25 cm^2 **5.** $\frac{5}{1.25}$ or 4 to 1; $\frac{5}{2.5}$ or 2 to 1 **7.** $42,000 **9.** $42,000 **11.** $40,000 **13.** D **15.** yes **17.** D **19.** 16 **21.** 2 **23.** 16

25. 12 **27.** no, only 2 more **29.** yes **31.** gives impression that more people prefer restaurant IV

Page 88 Exercises

1. 10 m longer **3.** 1980, 65 m; 1984, 67 m **5.** 1983 **7.** 23¢ **9.** over 25¢ **11.** 1968 **13.** 1978 **15.** 230 million **17.** 1990

Pages 90-91 Chapter 4 Review

1. b **3.** c **5.** a or c **7.** 43 votes **9.** 12 people **11.** 15 calls **13.** day 7 **15.** Aug. **17.** May **19.** Arctic Ocean **21.** Sept. **23.** 11 days **25.** bars will be more nearly the same length **27.** $4 per hour

Page 93 Cumulative Review

1. operator assisted person-to-person **3.** 57¢ **5.** $0.02 **7.** $0.12 **9.** $0.86 **11.** 8 **13.** 5 **15.** 2 **17.** 50% **19.** 48.6 **21.** 10 **23.** 55 **25.** 28 **27.** $6\frac{1}{2}$ **29.** 11.2 inches

Chapter 5 Probability

Page 95 Exercises

1. travel to Denver by bus; return home by bus **3.** travel to Denver by bus; return home by rail **5.** 3 outcomes **7.** 4 **9.** 2 **11.** 6 **13.** 123, 321, 312, 231, 132, 213; 6

Pages 96-97 Exercises

1. medium, regular crust, pepperoni **3.** medium, thick crust, hamburger **5.** 6 **7.** 4 **9.** 2 **11.** 8 **13.** 4 **15.** HHH, HHT, HTH, HTT, THH, THT, TTH, TTT **17.** The penny and nickel landed heads up. The dime landed tails up. **19.** 1 **21.** 3 **23.** 4 **25.** 6 outcomes **27.** 8 outcomes

Page 99 Exercises

1. 8 outfits **3.** 252 choices **5.** 24 outfits **7.** 16 outcomes **9.** 216 outcomes

Pages 100-101 Exercises

1. $\frac{1}{4}$ **3.** $\frac{1}{9}$ **5.** $\frac{1}{13}$ **7.** $\frac{1}{30}$ **9.** $\frac{10}{30}$ or $\frac{1}{3}$ **11.** $\frac{21}{30}$ or $\frac{7}{10}$ **13.** $\frac{15}{30}$ or $\frac{1}{2}$ **15.** $\frac{1}{6}$ **17.** $\frac{2}{6}$ or $\frac{1}{3}$ **19.** $\frac{4}{6}$ or $\frac{2}{3}$ **21.** $\frac{4}{6}$ or $\frac{2}{3}$ **23.** yes **25.** greatest = 12; least = 2 **27.** $\frac{2}{36}$ or $\frac{1}{18}$ **29.** $\frac{6}{36}$ or $\frac{1}{6}$ **31.** $\frac{4}{36}$ or $\frac{1}{9}$ **33.** $\frac{35}{36}$ **35.** the event will happen **37.** $\frac{11}{31}$

Pages 104-105 Exercises

1. $\frac{1}{12}$ **3.** $\frac{3}{12}$ or $\frac{1}{4}$ **5.** Sum is all possible outcomes. **7.** $\frac{1}{60}$ **9.** $\frac{1}{15}$ **11.** $\frac{1}{15}$ **13.** $\frac{1}{16}$ **15.** $\frac{3}{14}$ **17.** $\frac{81}{625}$

Pages 106-107 Exercises

1. $\frac{1}{12}$ **3.** $\frac{1}{2}$ **5.** $3 \times 2 \times 1 = 6$ **7.** $2 \times 1 \times 0 = 0$
9. $\frac{24}{504}$ or $\frac{1}{21}$ **11.** $\frac{24}{504}$ or $\frac{1}{21}$ **13.** $\frac{6}{77}$
15. 1,560,000 license plates

Page 109 Exercises

1. $\frac{7}{10} \times \frac{6}{9} = \frac{42}{90}$ or $\frac{7}{15}$ **3.** $\frac{7}{30}$ **5.** $\frac{8}{15}$ **7.** 1; Yes, since the
four possibilities account for all possible outcomes.
9. $\frac{4}{16}$ or $\frac{1}{4}$ **11.** $\frac{31}{55}$

Pages 110-111 Exercises

1. $\frac{3}{150}$ **3.** $\frac{1}{100}$ **5.** $\frac{1}{100}$ **7.** $\frac{1}{100}$ **9.** $\frac{7}{500}$ **11.** $\frac{3}{200}$
13. $\frac{1}{40}$ **15.** $\frac{1}{10}$ **17.** $\frac{3}{20}$ **19.** $\frac{1}{5}$ **21.** $\frac{1}{10}$ **23.** $\frac{3}{4}$ **25.** $\frac{1}{70}$

Pages 112-113 Chapter 5 Review

1. equally likely **3.** outcome **5.** independent
7. favorable outcome **9.** 1 **11.** 2 **13.** 3 **17.** HBT,
HBW, HFT, HFW, EBT, EBW, EFT, EFW, GBT, GBW,
GFT, GFW **19.** $\frac{1}{6}$ **21.** $\frac{3}{6}$ or $\frac{1}{2}$ **23.** $\frac{1}{18}$ **25.** $\frac{1}{36}$ **27.** $\frac{5}{6}$
29. $\frac{1}{64}$ **31.** $\frac{3}{16}$ **33.** $\frac{1}{2}$ **35.** $\frac{30}{110}$ or $\frac{3}{11}$ **37.** $\frac{3}{100}$
39. $\frac{1}{150}$ **41.** $\frac{1}{60}$ **43.** 18 outfits **45.** 6 arrangements

Page 115 Cumulative Review

1. 16% **3.** 60% **5.** $37\frac{1}{2}$% **7.** 2.15 **9.** 0.08
11. health **13.** 18% **15.** 30 min. **17.** size 7 **19.** 1
21. xyz, xzy, yxz, yzx, zxy, zyx; 6 **23.** 1 **25.** 4
27. 1,024 sets of answers

Chapter 6 Using Probability and Statistics

Page 117 Exercises

1. 7 to 5 **3.** 7 to 5 **5.** 1 to 5 **7.** 2 to 4 **9.** 3 to 3
11. 2 to 4 **13.** 1 to 5 **15.** 5 to 31 **17.** 18 to 18
19. 6 to 30 **21.** 2 to 34 **23.** 2 to 2, 3 to 1

Pages 118-119 Exercises

1. $\frac{1}{10}$ **3.** $\frac{1}{100}$ **5.** $\frac{4}{5}$ **7.** $\frac{1}{4}$ **9.** $\frac{1}{12}$ **11.** $\frac{3}{40}$ **13.** $\frac{1}{2}$
15. $\frac{3}{20}$ **17.** 50% **19.** 70% **21.** 85% **23.** 0%
25. $2\frac{1}{2}$% **27.** $16\frac{2}{3}$% **29.** 25% **31.** $33\frac{1}{3}$% **33.** 40%
35. 20% **37.** 80% **39.** 40% **41.** 50% **43.** $37\frac{1}{2}$%
45. $\frac{1}{100}$ **47.** 50% **49.** 30%

Page 121 Exercises

1. 10% **3.** 30% **5.** 50% **7.** 15% **9.** 40%
11. $66\frac{2}{3}$% **13.** $\frac{3}{5}$, 60% **15.** $\frac{1}{3}$, $33\frac{1}{3}$% **17.** 1 to 9 **19.** 3
to 7 **21.** 1 to 19 **23.** 19 to 1 **25.** 7 to 4 **27.** 2 to 1
29. 4 to 1 **31.** 5 to 1 **33.** $\frac{5}{9}$

Pages 122-123 Exercises

1. $\frac{1}{5}$ **3.** $\frac{1}{2}$ **5.** 5 **7.** 25 **9.** 9 **11.** 4 **13.** 306
15. 10 **17.** 50 **19.** 30 **21.** 3 spins

Page 127 Exercises

1. $54\frac{1}{2}$ **3.** 18 **5.** $6\frac{1}{2}$ **7.** $21\frac{1}{2}$ **9.** $\frac{64}{150}$ or $\frac{32}{75}$
11. 600,000 people **13.** $\frac{20}{125} = 16\%$; $\frac{18}{105} = 17\frac{1}{7}\%$; the
sophomore class

Pages 128-129 Exercises

1. 45¢ **3.** $\frac{6}{1,000}$ or $\frac{3}{500}$, $\frac{5}{500}$ or $\frac{1}{100}$ **5.** 10,560 prizes
7. $\frac{33}{265,625}$ **9.** 1,000 numbers **11.** 40¢ **13.** 75¢

Page 131 Exercises

1. 12,050 mi² **3.** 18,204 mi² **5.** 1,447 mi² **7.** 658
mi² **13.** 17 students **15.** 25 students **17.** $\frac{13}{30}$ **19.** $\frac{5}{30}$
or $\frac{1}{6}$ **21.** 48 people

Pages 132-133 Chapter 6 Review

1. b **3.** d **5.** c **7.** 3 to 3 **9.** $\frac{2}{5}$ **11.** $\frac{3}{8}$ **13.** $\frac{1}{8}$
15. 35% **17.** $83\frac{1}{3}$% **19.** $\frac{1}{10}$; 10% **21.** $\frac{1}{4}$; 25%
23. $\frac{1}{3}$; $33\frac{1}{3}$% **25.** 7 to 1 **27.** 7 to 13 **29.** 25 **31.** 20
33. 80 **35.** 4 **37.** 60¢ **39.** 613 **41.** 17 **43.** 22
45. 8 **47.** 5¢

Page 135 Cumulative Review

1. 82 **3.** 140 **5.** 1.35 **7.** 0.25 **11.** $24,000
13. Yes **15.** A **17.** 1959 **19.** 245 million **21.** $\frac{5}{14}$
23. $\frac{15}{56}$ **25.** $\frac{15}{28}$ **27.** 60% **29.** $37\frac{1}{2}$%

Chapter 7 Length

Pages 137-138 Exercises

1. cubit or pace **3.** thumb or span **5.** thumb **7.** pace
9. 10 paces **11.** 1 thumb **13.** 1 pace **15.** 1 cubit
17. 1 pace **19.** 48 inches **21.** 32 inches

Pages 140-141   Exercises

1. kilometer   3. meter   5. kilometer   7. centimeter
9. meter   11. mm   13. m   15. cm   17. km   19. m
21. b. 2m   23. a. 1mm   25. b. 2m   27. a. 15 cm
29. 2 cm, 20 mm   31. 6.1 cm, 61 mm   33. 8.9 cm, 89
mm   35. 11.5 cm, 115 mm   37. 8 cm, 80 mm
39. 1.5 cm, 15 mm   41. 5.6 cm, 56 mm   43. 3.9 cm,
39 mm   45. 843 kilometers

Page 143   Exercises

1. ×   3. ÷   5. ×   7. ×   9. ÷   11. ÷   13. 100
15. km   17. 1,000   19. 5,000   21. 10   23. 300
25. 8,000   27. 4   29. 1   31. 4   33. 8,000   35. 50
37. 2   39. 0.0046   41. 100,000   43. 0.00978
45. 5 cm or 0.05 m   47. 42 cm

Pages 144-145   Exercises

1. yard   3. mile   5. yard   7. inch   9. inch or foot
11. mile   13. foot   15. foot or yard   17. b. 4 ft
19. a. 10 in.   21. b. 5 ft   23. a. 7 in.   25. 1 in.
27. $2\frac{1}{8}$ in.   29. $3\frac{7}{8}$ in.   31. $4\frac{15}{16}$ in.   33. $1\frac{7}{16}$ in.
35. $1\frac{3}{4}$ in.   37. 28 yards   39. 1 yard   41. Tonia

Pages 148-149   Exercises

1. ×   3. ÷   5. ×   7. ÷   9. ft   11. 12   13. yd
15. 36   17. 120   19. 4   21. 6   23. 12   25. 180
27. 880   29. 81   31. $1\frac{1}{2}$ 33. 2, 2   35. no

Pages 150-151   Exercises

1. 13 ft 11 in.   3. 8 yd 10 in.   5. 5 ft 5 in.   7. 1 yd 2 ft
9. 8 ft 8 in.   11. 41 yd   13. 3 mi 400 yd   15. 2 yd 5 in.
17. 1 ft 6 in.   19. 2,652 feet   21. 13 feet

Page 153   Exercises

1. $3\frac{5}{16}$ in.   3. $9\frac{4}{16}$ in.   5. 56.5 km   7. 390.4 cm
9. 50.1 cm   11. 3,738.3 m   13. 2   15. 3   17. 5
19. 4   21. 4   23. 2   25. 5   27. 2   29. 2   31. 2
33. 5   35. 2   37. 2   39. 4   41. the metal ruler

Pages 154-155   Exercises

1. ≈   3. ≈   5. >   7. <   9. >   11. ≈   13. <
15. <   17. less   19. about 88 kph   21. Rocio
23. 4 inches   25. 6.16 kilometers

Pages 156-157   Chapter 7 Review

1. span   3. kilometer   5. customary   7. yard   9. pace
11. pace   13. kilometer   15. meter   17. 3.9 cm, 39 mm
19. 60 cm, 60 mm   21. ÷   23. ×   25. ÷   27. ×
29. 700   31. 0.200   33. 510   35. 1.7   37. 33
39. yard   41. mile   43. yard   45. a. 3 ft   47. b. 7 ft
49. 4   51. 31,680   53. 21,120   55. 12   57. 2   59. 6
ft 5 in.   61. 2 yd 10 in.   63. 72.34 m   65. 3   67. 2
69. 2   71. 177 cm or 1.77 m   73. more

Page 159   Cumulative Review

1. $\frac{1}{36}$ 3. $\frac{2}{36}$ or $\frac{1}{18}$ 5. $\frac{3}{36}$ or $\frac{1}{12}$ 7. $\frac{1}{16}$ 9. $\frac{9}{16}$ 11. $\frac{3}{10}$; 30
13. $\frac{1}{5}$; 20%   15. $\frac{1}{4}$; 25%   17. $\frac{1}{2}$; 50%   19. 7 to 3
21. 3 to 2   23. 25   25. thumb or span   27. cubit or
pace   29. 1 centimeter   31. 1 kilometer   33. 18 cm by
21.6 cm 35. $\frac{2}{3}$

Chapter 8   Other Common Measurements

Page 161   Exercises

1. kg   3. g   5. mg   7. g   9. kg   11. g   13. b   15. a
17. b   19. a   21. 50 mg

Pages 162-163   Exercises

1. mL   3. kL   5. mL   7. mL   9. L   11. L   13. liter
15. kiloliter   17. milliliter   19. a   21. a   23. a   25. a
27. 2,000 mL   29. 500 mL   31. 28 L

Page 165   Exercises

1. 1,000   3. divide   5. L   7. 1,000   9. 7,000
11. divide   13. 1,000   15. 4,000   17. 6,000
19. 2,800   21. 5,720   23. 7,000   25. 34,200
27. 3,000,000   29. 2,300   31. no   33. yes   35. 598 g

Page 168   Exercises

1. 32   3. 14,000   5. 1   7. 644   9. 10   11. 6,500
13. b   15. a   17. 4   19. 8   21. 1   23. 12   25. 3
27. $\frac{1}{2}$ 29. $5\frac{3}{4}$ 31. 128   33. $1\frac{1}{2}$ 35. 1   37. 14
39. c   41. a   43. 80 pints   45. 9¢   47. $1.78

Page 173   Exercises

1. 100°C, 0°C   3. 25°C   5. 30°C   7. 30°C   9. 100°C
11. 5°C   13. 80°C   15. 30°C   17. 10°C   19. 158°F
21. 104°F   23. 32°F   25. 167°F   27. 185°F
29. 95°F, too warm   31. 15°C

Pages 174-175   Exercises

1. 300   3. 2   5. 1,095   7. 2   9. 1, 30   11. 2, 12
13. 4, 2   15. 1 h 5 min   17. 110 wk
19. 7 h 25 min 28 s   21. 6 d 5 h 56 min   23. 3 wk 3 d
25. 51 min   27. 46 min   29. 1 h 20 min   31. at about
1:05 P.M.

Pages 176-177   Exercises

1. 2 quarts   3. $5\frac{1}{4}$ pounds   5. 44 minutes
7. 103,680 times   9. 12 minutes, $\frac{1}{5}$ hour   11. 1.5
kiloliters   13. 104 hours   15. 32 h

Pages 178-179   Chapter 8 Review

1. e   **3.** d   **5.** f   **7.** b   **9.** c   **11.** kg   **13.** mg   **15.** mg
17. b   **19.** L   **21.** mL   **23.** mL   **25.** b   **27.** 9,420
29. 0.001   **31.** 4.3   **33.** 1   **35.** 64   **37.** 12   **39.** 2
41. 128   **43.** 28   **45.** 131   **47.** 25   **49.** 10   **51.** 96
53. 1,095   **55.** 34   **57.** 90 min   **59.** 43 d   **61.** 30 d
63. 2 h 34 min   **65.** 40 servings   **67.** 3 qt.   **69.** 13.3
quarts **71.** 434 g   **73.** 6:05 P.M.

Page 181   Cumulative Review

1. $\frac{3}{5}$ **3.** $\frac{11}{20}$ **5.** $\frac{1}{50}$ **7.** $4\frac{1}{2}$ **9.** $\frac{131}{200}$ **11.** 150 people
13. 70,000 people   **15.** 300   **17.** 400   **19.** 6.23
21. c   **23.** 240   **25.** 30   **27.** 2   **29.** 3   **31.** 2   **33.** g
35. kg   **37.** kg   **39.** $\frac{125}{230}$ or $\frac{25}{46}$

Pages 198-199   Exercises

1. $26   **3.** $640   **5.** 32,714.4 mi   **7.** $22.91   **9.** $1,250

Pages 200-201   Chapter 9 Review

1. odometer   **3.** degree   **5.** multiply   **7.** protractor
9. 270.5 mi   **11.** 75S to 10E   **13.** 2:40 P.M.
15. 10:30 P.M.   **17.** 8:54 P.M.   **19.** 1930   **21.** 2245
23. 1 min 10.7 s   **25.** 86,201 kWh   **27.** 3,348,000 ft^3
29. 238,631 ft^3 **31.** 967,134 ft^3 **33.** 90°   **35.** 45°
43. $162.50   **45.** 226 kWh   **47.** $2.50

Page 203   Cumulative Review

1. $\frac{3}{10}$ **3.** 2   **5.** 15 ft 10 in.   **7.** 58 ft   **9.** $3\frac{3}{8}$ yd
11. 52.1 m   **13.** 3.66 cm   **15.** $\approx$ **17.** >   **19.** <
21. mL   **23.** kL   **25.** L or kL   **27.** 3,000   **29.** 3,500
31. 0.51   **33.** 64   **35.** 40   **37.** 9,000   **39.** 35°C
41. 48°C   **43.** 45°C   **45.** 50°C   **47.** 2 to 2; 3 to 1

Chapter 9   Reading Measures

Page 183   Exercises

1. 55,624.8   **3.** 31,396.2   **5.** 2,178 4 mi   **7.** 238.1 mi
9. 14,155.9 miles

Pages 184-185   Exercises

1. 80E   **3.** 66W to 81S to 40W to 30W   **5.** 3 ways
7. 250 mi, 4:45   **9.** 588 mi, 14:00   **11.** 1,180 mi,
23:45   **13.** Columbus and New York City, Denver and
Kansas City, St. Louis and Columbus   **15.** 1,957 miles
17. 43.8 mph or 44 mph   **19.** 44.8 mph or 45 mph

Pages 186-187   Exercises

1. 1:52 A.M.   **3.** 11:46 A.M.   **5.** 9:50 P.M.   **7.** 12:30 A.M.
9. 6:05 P.M.   **11.** 6:50 A.M.   **13.** 1500   **15.** 0530
17. 1930   **19.** 2330   **21.** 0416   **23.** 2047   **25.** 1752
27. 2127   **29.** 2030   **31.** 2200   **33.** 1030, 2230
35. 0912, 2112   **37.** 0015, 1215   **39.** 2:00 P.M.
41. 7:15 A.M.

Pages 188-189   Exercises

1. 5.8 s   **3.** 10.7 s   **5.** 7.6 s   **7.** 22.6 s   **9.** 24.7 s
11. 20 s   **13.** 2.5 mL   **15.** 8.7 mL   **17.** 7.4 mL
19. 100 cylinders   **21.** 3.8 mL   **23.** 45 s

Pages 193-195   Exercises

1. 15,825 kWh   **3.** 38,568 kWh   **5.** 5,762 kWh
7. 238,700 ft^3 **9.** 620,100 ft^3 **11.** 129,800 ft^3
13. 12,400 ft^3 **15.** 238,631 ft^3 **17.** 9,613 ft^3
19. 834 ft^3 **21.** 3,162 ft^3 **23.** 349 ft^3 **25.** 1,524 ft^3
27. a. 28,300 ft^3, b. 18,000 ft^3, c. 7,800 ft^3, d. 2,200 ft^3,
e. 2,400 ft^3

Page 197   Exercises

1. 35°   **3.** 10°   **5.** 90°   **7.** 180°   **9.** 40°   **11.** 20°
13. 135°   **15.** 10°   **17.** 160°   **19.** 32°   **21.** 115°
23. 70°   **25.** 80°   **39.** 360°

Chapter 10   Geometry

Page 206   Exercises

1. $\overline{AP}$ or $\overline{PA}$ **3.** $\overline{BD}$ or $\overline{DB}$ **11.** XY begins at X and
extends beyond Y; YX begins at Y and extends beyond X.
13. Z   **15.** $\overrightarrow{PU}$ or $\overrightarrow{UP}$ **17.** $\angle CAT$ or $\angle TAC$ **19.** $\angle YAM$
or $\angle MAY$ **21.** $\overline{AC}$, $\overline{AR}$, $\overline{AT}$, $\overline{RC}$ or $\overline{CR}$ **23.** $\overline{AC}$, $\overline{AT}$
25. an unlimited number   **27.** an unlimited number
29. an unlimited number

Page 207   Exercises

1. acute   **3.** acute   **5.** right   **7.** right   **9.** acute
11. acute   **13.** obtuse   **15.** acute   **17.** acute
19. obtuse angle

Pages 208-209   Exercises

1. 90   **3.** complementary (C)   **5.** supplementary (S)
7. S   **9.** N   **11.** N   **13.** S   **15.** C   **17.** 39°, 129°
19. 25°, 115°   **21.** 3°, 93°   **23.** 16°, 106°   **25.** 44°, 134°
27. $\angle AOB$ or $\angle DOB$ **29.** $\angle AOB$ and $\angle DOB$, $\angle AOC$
and $\angle DOC$ **31.** right angle

Pages 210-211   Exercises

1. 70°   **3.** $\angle 1$ and $\angle 3$, $\angle 2$ and $\angle 4$ **5.** c   **7.** a   **9.** d
11. no   **13.** 63°   **15.** 27°   **17.** 27°   **19.** 153°
21. 160°   **23.** 70°   **25.** 90°   **27.** Yes, the sum of their
measures is 180°.   **29.** 75° and 105°, supplementary
31. parallel lines   **33.** parallel lines

Page 213   Exercises

1. P   **3.** A, B, C, D, E   **5.** $\overline{PB}$, $\overline{PC}$, $\overline{PD}$, $\overline{PE}$, or $\overline{PA}$
7. $\overline{DC}$, $\overline{DB}$, $\overline{BC}$ (or $\overline{CD}$, $\overline{BD}$, $\overline{CB}$)   **9.** 3 planes   **11.** a
point   **13.** a sphere, a circle is limited to a plane

1. scalene 3. isosceles 5. right 7. obtuse 9. $\overline{BC}$ and $\overline{CA}$ 11. isosceles; $\overline{AC}$ and $\overline{AB}$ are congruent. Yes, $\angle B$ and $\angle C$. 13. $\triangle ABC$, $\triangle ADE$ 15. $\triangle BDF$, $\triangle CEG$ 17. none 25. not possible

1. 4 3. 49 5. 196 7. 144 9. 625 11. 2,116 13. 5,929 15. 7,056 17. 1,764 19. 6,561 21. 2 23. 6 25. 8 27. 12 29. 7 31. 20 33. 16 35. 14 37. 42 39. 82 41. legs: 90 in., 120 in.; hypotenuse: 150 in. 43. legs: 1.5 m, 2 m; hypotenuse: 2.5 m 45. legs: 13 cm, 84 cm; hypotenuse: 85 cm 47. legs: 36 ft, 77 ft; hypotenuse: 85 ft 49. 20 Km 51. 15 in. 53. 34 yd 55. 65 m 57. 50 mi 59. 25 ft 61. 100 yd 63. 50 cm 65. 68 mi 67. yes 69. no 71. yes 73. no 75. 13 feet 77. 5 inches

1. 10 triangles 3. 1,080° 5. 138° 7. 13 sides 9. 70 sit-ups 11. $148 13. 7,776 recipes 15. 11 boys

1. a number is even, it is divisible by two. 3. the degree measure of an angle is 120°, it is an obtuse angle. 5. the sum of the degree measures of two angles is 180°, they are supplementary angles. 7. we cook pizza, the smoke alarm goes off. 9. If an animal is a mammal, then it is a bear. original-true, converse-false 11. If a triangle is equilateral, then it has three congruent sides. original-true, converse-true 13. If the sum of the degree measures of two angles is 90°, then the angles are complementary. original-true, converse-true 15. If a month has 31 days, then it is named May. original-true, converse-false 17. Yes. It cannot snow without clouds.

1. 30, 35 3. 16, 25 5. 1,000; 10,000 7. no decision 9. no decision 11. deductive 13. inductive 15. deductive 17. You have an excellent voice.

1. k 3. c 5. g 7. h 9. i 11. $\overleftrightarrow{FX}$ (or $\overleftrightarrow{XE}$, $\overleftrightarrow{FE}$, $\overleftrightarrow{XF}$, $\overleftrightarrow{EX}$, $\overleftrightarrow{EF}$); $\overleftrightarrow{NX}$ (or $\overleftrightarrow{NI}$, $\overleftrightarrow{XI}$, $\overleftrightarrow{XN}$, $\overleftrightarrow{IN}$, $\overleftrightarrow{IX}$) 13. $\angle FXN$, $\angle FXI$, $\angle IXE$, $\angle EXN$ (or $\angle NXF$, $\angle IXF$, $\angle EXI$, $\angle NXE$) 15. $\overrightarrow{XF}$, $\overrightarrow{XN}$ 17. obtuse 19. right 21. 9°, 99° 23. 47°, 137° 25. $\overleftrightarrow{AC}$ (or $\overleftrightarrow{AD}$, $\overleftrightarrow{CD}$, $\overleftrightarrow{CA}$, $\overleftrightarrow{DA}$, $\overleftrightarrow{DC}$) is parallel to $\overleftrightarrow{EF}$ (or $\overleftrightarrow{FE}$) 27. $\angle BCA$ (or $\angle ACB$) and $\angle DCF$ (or $\angle FCD$); $\angle BCD$ (or $\angle DCB$) and $\angle ACF$ (or $\angle FCA$) 29. $\overline{CM}$ or $\overline{MT}$ ($\overline{MC}$ or $\overline{TM}$) 31. $\angle CMT$ (or $\angle TMC$), $\angle MTC$ (or $\angle CTM$), $\angle TCM$ (or $\angle MCT$) 33. scalene 35. yes 37. yes 39. 13 ft 41. true; true 43. inductive 45. 10 cm

1. 16 oz - 89¢ 3. 8 oz - $1.25 5. 3 7. 50 9. 180 11. 3 13. 4 15. 300 17. 140 19. 1 min 40 s 21. 2:43 A.M. 23. 10:50 A.M. 25. 12:20 A.M.

27. 5:15 P.M. 29. 12:00 midnight 31. 16.3 s 33. 22.6 s 35. 20.8 s 37. $\overrightarrow{AB}$ 39. $\overleftrightarrow{HI}$ or $\overleftrightarrow{IH}$ 41. $\overrightarrow{NM}$ 43. 38 kilometers 45. 20 inches 47. 384.4 miles

Chapter 11   Constructions

1. not congruent 3. not congruent 5. congruent 7. 27, 3

13. yes

13. yes 15. no

13. It forms two right angles and separates the line into two congruent parts.

1. 2 3. 7 5. 48° 7. 48° 9. 132° 11. 132° 13. $\angle 3$, $\angle 5$, $\angle 7$

1. $\overline{MN}$ 3. $\overline{NQ}$ 5. ASA 7. SSS 27. No triangle is possible

1. congruent 3. perpendicular 5. transversal 7. congruent 9. congruent 27. 55° 29. 55° 31. 55° 33. 125° 37. $\overline{ED}$ 39. $\angle EDG$

1. 22.5 years 3. 5-10 years 5. 73 feet 7. $55.00 9. $55.00 11. 42°, 132° 13. 58°, 148° 15. 73°, 163° 17. 66°, 156° 19. 15°, 105° 21. $\overleftrightarrow{EA}$, $\overleftrightarrow{BI}$; $\overleftrightarrow{JH}$, $\overleftrightarrow{BI}$ 23. Yes. Both lines are perpendicular to the same line. Therefore they are perpendicular.

Chapter 12   Polygons and Circles

1. yes 3. yes 5. yes 7. no 9. no

1. E 3. A, B, C 5. B 7. false 9. true 11. true 13. true 15. rhombus 17. parallelogram 19. rectangle 21. square 23. trapezoid 25. trapezoid 27. no 29. no 31. yes 33. no 35. no 37. yes

Page 259   Exercises

1. 16 mm   **3.** 20 km   **5.** 30 m   **7.** 18 ft

Pages 260-261   Exercises

1. 16 m   **3.** 15 in.   **5.** 36 cm   **7.** 36 cm   **9.** 28 m
11. 24.8 cm   **13.** 9 cm   **15.** 9.5 cm   **17.** 9.75 cm

Page 263   Exercises

1. 15.7 in.   **3.** 31.4 cm   **5.** 18.84 cm   **7.** 1,507.2 m
9. 37.68 m   **11.** 62.8 ft   **13.** 157 yd   **15.** 31.4 ft
17. 75.36 mm   **19.** 40.82 m   **21.** about 220 inches

Page 267   Exercises

1. 72 m²   **3.** 54 yd²   **5.** 42 cm²   **7.** 120 yd²
9. 168 m²   **11.** 115 km²   **13.** 195 cm²   **15.** 52.5 ft²
17. 81 yd²   **19.** 370 ft²

Page 269   Exercises

1. 7.5 ft²   **3.** 297 cm²   **5.** 24 m²   **7.** 54 cm²   **9.** 24 yd²
11. 143 in.²

Page 271   Exercises

1. 81 m²   **3.** 50 m²   **5.** 45.57 m²   **7.** 13.5 m²
9. 18 cm²   **11.** 800 ft²

Page 273   Exercises

1. 28.26 cm²   **3.** 616 km²   **5.** 78.5 in.²   **7.** $38\frac{1}{2}$ ft²
9. 113.04 km²   **11.** 3,850 cm²   **13.** The radius is
one-half of the diameter.   **15.** 28.26 m²   **17.** 616 cm²
19. ≈ 452.16 ft²   **21.** ≈ 127.17 m²   **23.** ≈ 27,475 ft²

Page 275   Exercises

1. 432 cm²   **3.** 46.28 m²   **5.** 140 m²   **7.** 260.48 ft²

Pages 276-277   Chapter 12 Review

1. a   **3.** j   **5.** q   **7.** k   **9.** h   **11.** c   **13.** no   **15.** yes
17. no   **19.** trapezoid   **21.** rectangle   **23.** parallelogram
25. $2\frac{2}{5}$ m   **27.** 20 in.   **29.** 15 m   **31.** 25.12 yd
33. 31.4 cm   **35.** 180 m²   **37.** 46.2 cm²   **39.** 20 m²
41. 45 mm²   **43.** $19\frac{1}{2}$ ft²   **45.** 36 ft²   **47.** 264 in.²
49. 3,850 cm²   **51.** 24.64 in.²   **53.** I can

Page 279   Cumulative Review

1. 2.1 in., no mode   **3.** 30 days   **11.** no   **13.** no
15. no   **17.** 55.2 cm   **19.** 56.25 yd   **21.** 68 m
23. 83.75 yd   **25.** 31.6 m

Chapter 13   Surface Area and Volume

Page 281   Exercises

1. 190 cm²   **3.** 192 cm²   **5.** 249 yd²

Pages 282-283   Exercises

1. 16 m²   **3.** 22.4 m²   **5.** 144 cm²   **7.** 105.6 cm²
9. 100 in²   **11.** 210 in²   **13.** 10 m²   **15.** 108.7 m²
17. 546 cm²   **19.** 260 ft²   **21.** 324 ft²

Page 285   Exercises

1. 628 cm²   **3.** 879.2 cm²   **5.** 62.8 in.²   **7.** 100.5 m²
9. 276.3 m²   **11.** 314 mm²   **13.** 37.7 m²
15. 345.4 cm²

Page 287   Exercises

1. 44.0 cm²   **3.** 12.6 ft²   **5.** 125.6 yd²   **7.** 427.0 cm²
9. 501.6 cm²   **11.** 84.8 cm²   **13.** 157 m²
15. 175.8 mm²   **17.** 354.1 in.²   **19.** 254.3 cm²
21. 1,099 m²   **23.** 125.6 m²   **25.** 373.7 cm²

Page 289   Exercises   1. 120 cm³   **3.** 108 in.²   **5.** 576
in.³   **7.** 8 ft³   **9.** 27 in³   **11.** 1,246.3 cm³   **13.** 341 in³
15. 124.2 cm³   **17.** 280 ft³   **19.** 1,940 cm³   **21.** 681.6
cm³   **23.** 128 ft³   **25.** 512 ft³   **27.** 10 gal

Pages 292-293   Exercises

1. 502.4 cm³   **3.** 25.12 cm³   **5.** 6,154.4 cm³
7. 840 cm³   **9.** 208 in.³   **11.** 212.5 ft³   **13.** 930 in.³
15. 115.2 m³   **17.** 317.2 m³   **19.** 331.7 m³   **21.** 166.5
ft³   **23.** 131.88 m³   **25.** 904.32 cm³

Pages 294-295   Exercises

1. 192 cm³   **3.** 600 cm³   **5.** 560 cm³   **7.** 520 cm³
9. 272 cm³   **11.** 10,048 cm³   **13.** 1,356.5 cm³
15. 452.2 in³   **17.** 317.9 ft³   **19.** 6,330.2 mm³
21. 1,884 ft³   **23.** 512.9 in³

Pages 296-297   Exercises

1. 1,256 in², 4,186.7 in³   **3.** 201.0 ft², 267.9 ft³
5. 5,024 in², 33,493.3 in²   **7.** 744.7 m², 1,911.4 m³
9. 72.3 in², 57.9 in³   **11.** 764.2 ft², 1,986.8 ft³
13. 651.1 m²   **15.** 904.3 ft³   **17.** 201,000,000 mi²
19. 18 gal

Page 299   Exercises

1. B   **3.** 297 cm³   **5.** C   **7.** 401.9 cm³   **9.** 392.5 cm³
11. neither, volumes are the same   **13.** 2 times as much

15. $\frac{1}{8}$

Pages 300-301   Chapter 13 Review

1. cylinder or rectangular prism   **3.** face   **5.** $\pi r (r + s)$
7. Bh **9.** radius   **11.** $4\pi r^2$ **13.** 216 in²   **15.** 552 cm²
17. 100.6 ft²   **19.** 177.4 cm²   **21.** 1,018.9 in²
23. 7,850 in²   **25.** 115 in³   **27.** 135 in³   **29.** 18.3 ft³
31. 20.9 in³   **33.** 551.9 in.³   **35.** 65,416.7 in.³
37. 528 ft³

Page 303   Cumulative Review

1. m   **3.** 1,000   **5.** 0.6   **7.** multiply   **9.** 1,000
11. 1 h 57 min 57 s   **13.** 2 wk 5 d   **15.** 172,600 ft³
17. 27°   **19.** 80°   **21.** 45°   **23.** 40°   **25.** 247 cm²
27. 94 yd³   **29.** 216 ft³

Chapter 14   Rational Numbers

Page 305   Exercises

1. $^-9$ **3.** $^-10$ **5.** $^-1$ **7.** $12°$ **9.** 400 **11.** $^-7$
13. $^-8$ **15.** $^-42$ **17.** $^-36$ **19.** $^-32$

Pages 306-307   Exercises

1. $-2\frac{1}{3}$ **3.** $\frac{4}{5}$ **5.** $^-5$ **7.** F   **9.** C   **11.** E   **13.** $>$
15. $>$ **17.** $>$ **19.** $=$ **21.** $^-2, 0, 4, 5, 7$ **23.** $^-15, ^-8,$
$3, 6, 7$ **25.** $^-3.5, ^-3, 0, 3, 3.5$ **27.** $^-0.75$ **29.** $^-25$
31. 9 **33.** 12 **35.** 4 **37.** 1.5 **39.** $\frac{2}{3}$ **41.** 3
43. gain of 4 yards   **45.** $^-3\frac{1}{8}$ **47.** $^-282$ **49.** $^-1,290$ ft

Pages 308-309   Exercises

1. pattern continues indefinitely   **3.** circle at 4·   **5.** a dot
on the line at 5   **7.** greater than or equal to   **9.** F
11. G   **27.** $\{^-1, 2, 3\}$ **29.** $\{4, 5, 6, ...\}$ **31.** {all
numbers > 0}   **33.** {all numbers ≥ 4}   **35.** {all numbers
between $^-2$ and 2}

Pages 311-312   Exercises

1. $2 + 6 = 8$ **3.** $7 + ^-8 = ^-1$ **9.** 33 **11.** 5 **13.** $^-18$
15. $^-24$ **17.** $^-31$ **19.** $\frac{1}{24}$ **21.** $\frac{41}{50}$ **23.** $\frac{5}{7}$ **25.** $\frac{5}{6}$
27. $^-7\frac{3}{4}$ **29.** $^-8\frac{11}{24}$ **31.** $\frac{^-3}{5}$ **33.** $2\frac{3}{10}$ **35.** $^-\frac{1}{8}$ **37.** $\frac{1}{6}$
39. $^-1\frac{5}{12}$ **41.** $\$59$ **43.** 18th floor   **45.** 29 yard line

Pages 314-315   Exercises

1. $^-1, ^-2, ^-1, ^-2$ **3.** 1 **5.** $^-7$ **7.** $^-7$ **9.** $5 + ^-2$
11. $^-16 + ^-16$ **13.** $5 + 4$ **15.** $0.7 + ^-0.5$
17. $-\frac{7}{10} + (-\frac{3}{10})$ **19.** $^-3 + 46$ **21.** 0 **23.** $^-37$
25. 16 **27.** $^-8$ **29.** $^-26$ **31.** 1 **33.** $^-5$ **35.** $^-72$
37. $^-21$ **39.** $^-75$ **41.** 1.8 **43.** 11 **45.** $^-1.8$
47. 2.7 **49.** 2.6 **51.** $^-8.8$ **53.** $\frac{1}{5}$ **55.** $\frac{4}{5}$ **57.** $6\frac{1}{2}$
59. $^-18\frac{1}{4}$ **61.** $25,380$ ft   **63.** $2.8°F$ **65.** $49°F$
67. about $41.5°F$ **69.** about $2,227$ years old

Pages 318-319   Exercises

1. $8, 4, 0, ^-4, ^-8$ **3.** $18, 9, 0, ^-9, ^-18$ **5.** negative
7. negative   **9.** positive   **11.** positive   **13.** $^-18$ **15.** 5
17. 0 **19.** $^-45$ **21.** 96 **23.** 147 **25.** $^-1,296$
27. $2,324$ **29.** $^-192$ **31.** $^-112$ **33.** 32 **35.** 144
37. 0.03 **39.** 6.24 **41.** $-\frac{3}{32}$ **43.** $\frac{^-1}{4}$ **45.** 13 **47.** $\frac{35}{72}$
49. $1,760$ gallons   **51.** $^-45$ yards

Pages 320-321   Exercises

1. positive   **3.** negative   **5.** positive   **7.** negative
9. negative   **11.** positive   **13.** $^-9$ **15.** 1 **17.** 0
19. $^-6$ **21.** $^-42$ **23.** 0 **25.** $^-0.7$ **27.** $^-70$ **29.** 7
31. $^-0.8$ **33.** 3 **35.** $^-3$ **37.** $1\frac{3}{4}$ **39.** $^-5\frac{1}{4}$ **41.** $^-1\frac{1}{3}$

43. $5\frac{1}{5}$ **45.** $^-3$ **47.** 15 **49.** 0 **51.** $^-17$ **53.** 16
55. 7 **57.** $1,156$ people per year

Page 323   Exercises

1. add   **3.** subtract   **5.** multiply   **7.** multiply 3×2
9. $^-32$ **11.** 14 **13.** $^-22$ **15.** 15 **17.** $^-8$ **19.** 2
21. 81 **23.** 3 **25.** 98 **27.** 83 **29.** $^-88$
31. $85\frac{1}{2}$ or 85.5 **33.** 12 **35.** 20 **37.** 9 **39.** $\$12.08$

Pages 324-325   Exercises

1. 950 feet   **3.** 137 points   **5.** $\$10.08$ **7.** $^-44$ **9.** No
11. 50 ft^2

Pages 326-327   Chapter 14 Review

1. h   **3.** e   **5.** b   **7.** f   **9.** 37 **11.** $\$75$ **13.** $>$
15. $>$ **17.** $<$ **19.** $<$ **21.** 11 **23.** $3\frac{2}{3}$ **27.** 9
29. $^-71$ **31.** $^-2.6$ **33.** 9.23 **35.** $\frac{1}{8}$ **37.** $4\frac{3}{4}$
39. $9 + ^-10$ **41.** $6.36 + ^-4.37$ **43.** $^-9$ **45.** $^-17$
47. $^-0.5$ **49.** $^-10.2$ **51.** $\frac{1}{4}$ **53.** $1\frac{4}{15}$ **55.** negative
57. negative   **59.** $^-96$ **61.** 182 **63.** 0 **65.** $^-20.8$
67. $\frac{1}{4}$ **69.** $8\frac{1}{8}$ **71.** positive   **73.** negative   **75.** $^-12$
77. $^-14$ **79.** $^-3$ **81.** 3 **83.** $\frac{^-9}{14}$ **85.** $\frac{1}{2}$ **87.** 65
89. 72 **91.** 13 units   **93.** a depth of 43 meters
95. $^-1,233$ persons   **97.** $^-\$20$

Page 329   Cumulative Review

1. $\$8,050$ **3.** 12; $\overline{AB}, \overline{AC}, \overline{BD}, \overline{CD}, \overline{EF}, \overline{EC}, \overline{EG}, \overline{AG}, \overline{DF},$
$\overline{FH}, \overline{BH}, \overline{HG}$ **5.** 5 planes   **7.** 96 m^2 **9.** 433.3 in.^{2}
11. 75.4 cm^2 **13.** $>$ **15.** $<$ **17.** $<$ **19.** $=$ **21.** $=$
23. $<$

Chapter 15   Solving Open Sentences

Page 331   Exercises

1. true   **3.** open   **5.** open   **7.** false   **9.** open   **11.** true
13. true   **15.** true   **17.** open   **19.** $35 + t = 53$

Page 333   Exercises

1. 4 **3.** 5 **5.** $^-5$ **7.** $3, 4, 5, ...$ **9.** $11, 12, 13, ...$
11. 2 **13.** 4 **15.** 0 **17.** 7 **19.** 13 **21.** $^-1$ **23.** 3
25. 8 **27.** 4 **29.** 6 **31.** $^-7$ **33.** $t + 6 = 22$; 16
35. $n \times 11 = 99$; 9 **37.** $n - 6 = 13$; 19 years old

Page 335   Exercises

1. $n + 2 = 6$; remove 2 from each side; $n = 4$
3. $t + 4 = 5$; remove 4 from each side; $t = 1$ **5.** $2, 6$
7. $6, 7$ **9.** $7, 6$ **11.** $12, 13$ **13.** 11 **15.** 11 **17.** $^-53$
19. $^-446$ **21.** 1.0 **23.** $^-2\frac{5}{6}$ **25.** 0.51 **27.** 2.03
29. 55 **31.** 115.2 **33.** $x + 37.5 = 52$; 14.5 miles

494   *Selected Answers*

Pages 336-337 Exercises

1. subtraction **3.** addition **5.** Undo the indicated operation. **7.** 6, 17 **9.** $1\frac{1}{2}$, 5 **11.** 9, 32 **13.** 12, 24 **15.** 0.08, 1.88 **17.** 18, 42 **19.** 6, 27 **21.** 1, 2, 3 **23.** 22 **25.** 30 **27.** 55 **29.** 3 **31.** 17 **33.** 1 **35.** 55 **37.** 7 **39.** $^-$4 **41.** 5.9 **43.** $^-$13 **45.** $^-$33 **47.** $^-$29 **49.** $^-$7.2 **51.** $\frac{7}{8}$ **53.** $1\frac{1}{15}$ **55.** $\frac{^-3}{4}$ **57.** $3\frac{9}{10}$ **59.** $t + 12 = 40$; 28°F **61.** $38 + n = 62$; 24 grams

Page 339 Exercises

1. $2t = 6$; Remove 1 beaker and 3 weights; $t = 3$ **3.** $3n = 9$; Remove 2 beakers and 6 weights; $n = 3$ **5.** 4, 5 **7.** 7, 3 **9.** 2, $^-$7 **11.** $^-$6, 8 **13.** 19 **15.** $^-$18 **17.** 7 **19.** $^-6\frac{2}{5}$ **21.** $^-$0.27 **23.** 0.6 **25.** $\frac{1}{10}$ **27.** $-\frac{2}{3}$

Page 343 Exercises

1. multiplication **3.** division **5.** Undo the indicated operation. **7.** 7; 84 **9.** 8; 88 **11.** 12; 132 **13.** 6; 48 **15.** 117 **17.** 42 **19.** 1,020 **21.** 705 **23.** 30 **25.** $^-$78 **27.** 60 **29.** 3.42

Page 345 Exercises

1. $-, \div$; 6 **3.** $-, \div$; 10 **5.** $-, \times$; 16 **7.** $-, \div$; 2 **9.** $-, \times$; $^-$10 **11.** 8 **13.** 1 **15.** $^-$3 **17.** 8 **19.** 12 **21.** $^-$50 **23.** 10 **25.** 8 **27.** 5 **29.** 2 **31.** $^-$3.5 **33.** $\frac{1}{6}$ **35.** $\frac{11}{36}$ **37.** $2\frac{1}{2}$ **39.** $^-9\frac{1}{3}$ **41.** $5t + 11 = 56$; 9 **43.** $10 + 6r = {}^-14$; $^-$4 **45.** $\frac{t}{2} + 8 = 11$; 6 **47.** $20 + \frac{y}{3} = 25$; 15 **49.** $2n + 6 = 22$; 8 **51.** $3d - 4 = 38$; 14 years old

Page 347 Exercises

1. $x + 2 > 5$ **3.** $t + 4 < 7$ **5.** $\times 8$; $t < 72$ **7.** $^-4$; $5 > a$ or $a < 5$ **9.** $\times 8$; $56 > c$ or $c < 56$ **11.** $+ 6$; $y < 30$ **13.** $x > 23$ **15.** $w < 15$ **17.** $r < 8$ **19.** $t < 432$ **21.** $m < 18$ **23.** $m < 93$ **25.** $f < {}^-10$ **27.** $z > {}^-2$ **29.** $n > 6.6$ **31.** $t > 4.8$ **33.** $m > {}^-2.1$ **35.** $p > \frac{3}{4}$ **37.** $120 + f > 270$

Page 349 Exercises

1. $22.50 or more **3.** 156 seconds **5.** $1.70 or less **7.** 12 **9.** 5 or more **11.** 275 meters **13.** 7°F **15.** $860 **17.** $304

Pages 350-351 Chapter 15 Review

1. solving **3.** inequality **5.** open sentence **7.** true **9.** false **11.** false **13.** $8 + m = 40$; 32 **15.** $^-3h = 21$; $^-$7 **17.** 3 **19.** 19 **21.** 1.2 **23.** $\frac{3}{4}$ **25.** 12 **27.** 30 **29.** $1\frac{5}{8}$ **31.** 0.7 **33.** 3 **35.** $^-$19

37. $^-4\frac{1}{2}$ **39.** $\frac{5}{8}$ **41.** 28 **43.** $^-$63 **45.** $^-$30 **47.** 0.84 **49.** 7 **51.** $^-$8 **53.** 12 **55.** 1.6 **57.** 10 **59.** $3z + 5 = 35$; 10 **61.** $\frac{x}{5} + 2 = 6$; 20 **63.** $\frac{k}{2} - 6 = 1$; 14 **65.** $2n - 10 = 28$; 19 **67.** $y > 11$ **69.** $j < 24$ **71.** $^-6 < z$ or $z > {}^-6$ **73.** $t < {}^-0.5$ **75.** $b < 59$ **77.** $^-24 < m$ or $m > {}^-24$ **79.** $4x = 348$; 87 coins **81.** $x - 20 = 52$; 72 mL **83.** 16 years old **85.** $x + 3.75 \leq 30$; $26.25 or less

Page 353 Cumulative Review

1. $\angle PNM$ and $\angle MPN$ **3.** right **11.** trapezoid **13.** rectangle **15.** trapezoid **17.** $^-4 + ({}^-2) = {}^-6$ **19.** true **21.** open **23.** $3y = 27$; $y = 9$ **25.** $\frac{30}{x} = 5$; $x = 6$ **27.** $x + 21 \geq 30$; $x = 9$

Chapter 16 Using Formulas

Page 355 Exercises

1. 3^2 **3.** p^3 **5.** m^3 **7.** $2^2 w^2$ **9.** 16 **11.** 8 **13.** 1 **15.** 2^6

Page 357 Exercises

1. 10 **3.** 4 **5.** 45 **7.** 4 **9.** 40 **11.** $^-$20 **13.** 6.4 **15.** 3 **17.** $^-$12 **19.** 42 **21.** 4 **23.** $^-$36 **25.** 47 **27.** 6 **29.** 8 **31.** $^-$8 **33.** 36 **35.** 125 **37.** $^-$35 **39.** 81 **41.** 16 yd^2

Pages 359-360 Exercises

1. 45 ft-lb **3.** 729 ft-lb **5.** 3,038 ft-lb **7.** 66 ft **9.** 176 km **11.** 31.4 yd **13.** 20.41 ft **15.** 119 **17.** 139 **19.** 122 **21.** 141 **23.** 116.5 **25.** 10.34 **27.** 10.16 **29.** 4.8 **31.** 120 **33.** 19 **35.** 2.16 **37.** $\frac{1}{2}$ **39.** $9\frac{1}{2}$ **41.** 1 **43.** 4 **45.** $B = \frac{h}{a}$ **47.** $F = \frac{9}{5} C + 32$

Pages 361-362 Exercises

1. $d = 60$ mi **3.** $r = 40.3$ mph **5.** $t = 8$ hours **7.** $d = 3$ mi **9.** $r = 170$ mph **11.** $t = 1.25$ hours **13.** $s = 25$ **15.** $s = 32.4$ **17.** $m = 323$ **19.** $g = 11$ **21.** $g = 9.2$ **23.** $s = 44$ **25.** 12.56 **27.** 20.41 **29.** 53.38 **31.** 10 **33.** 7 **35.** 6 **37.** 2.5 **39.** 47.1 **41.** ≈ 55 meters **43.** 93.5 km/h **45.** $\approx 6,782.4$ miles

Page 366 Exercises

1. 4 **3.** 100 **5.** 400 **7.** 2,500 **9.** 121 **11.** 2 **13.** 6 **15.** 30 **17.** $^-$9 **19.** $^-$1 **21.** 13 **23.** $^-$17 **25.** 21 **27.** 87 **29.** $^-$26 **31.** 361 **33.** 841 **35.** 3,481 **37.** 6,889 **39.** 1,764 **41.** 2, 3 **43.** 6, 7 **45.** 8, 9 **47.** 10, 11 **49.** 8, 9 **51.** 3.162 **53.** $^-$4.899 **55.** 6.481 **57.** $^-$8.246 **59.** $^-$6.782 **61.** $^-$4.583 **63.** 5.477 **65.** 9.220 **67.** 5 yd

Page 368 Exercises

1. $c = 5$ **3.** $a = 10$ **5.** $a = 16$ **7.** $a = 20$ **9.** $a = 11$
11. $c \approx 7.810$ **13.** $c \approx 9.220$ **15.** $b \approx 8.660$ **17.** 12
in. **19.** 13 ft **21.** 11 ft **23.** ≈ 1.732 m

Pages 370-371 Exercises

1. $106.09 **3.** $266.52 **5.** $525.48 **7.** $10.60
9. 6% **11.** $35.70 **13.** 45% **15.** 8.464 cm²
17. ≈ 47.1 cm **19.** 121 **21.** 48 mph **23.** ≈ 47.434 ft

Pages 372-373 Chapter 16 Review

1. h **3.** b **5.** d **7.** g **9.** 27 **11.** 49 **13.** 1 **15.** 64
17. 100,000 **19.** 9 **21.** 26 **23.** 120 **25.** 7 **27.** 24
29. 6 **31.** 4 **33.** $^-4$ **35.** 4 **37.** $^-8$ **39.** 40 **41.** 60
43. 0.5 **45.** $r = 32$ mph **47.** $t = 3$ hours **49.** $g = 8$
51. $m = 192$ **53.** $g = 9$ **55.** 62.8 **57.** 15 **59.** 7.5
61. 81 **63.** 225 **65.** 1 **67.** $^-7$ **69.** 4 **71.** 12
73. $^-14$ **75.** 441 **77.** 1,296 **79.** 6,561 **81.** 676
83. 5,476 **85.** $c = 13$ **87.** $b = 20$ **89.** $c \approx 8.062$
91. $a \approx 9.165$ **93.** $157.59 **95.** $1,273.63
97. ≈ 6.481 m **99.** 4 ft **101.** 15%

Page 375 Cumulative Review

1. 20 in. **3.** 40 ft **5.** 89 mm **7.** 52.6 ft **9.** 69.08 mm
11. 82.87 in. **13.** 508.68 yd **15.** 47.63 cm
17. 1060.8 cm² **19.** 53.6 ft² **21.** 287.5 yd² **23.** 5.6
25. $^-20$ **27.** 6 **29.** $^-100$ **31.** $^-4.7$ **33.** $-9\frac{32}{3}$
35. $196 **37.** 9.42 in³

Chapter 17 Patterns and Functions

Page 377 Exercises

1. 90% **3.** 40% **5.** $87\frac{1}{2}$% **7.** $x - 3$ **9.** $6x + 2$
11. 16, 27 **13.** $\frac{3}{4}, \frac{1}{5}, \frac{4}{7}$ **15.** $\frac{1}{2}, \frac{3}{4}, \frac{4}{5}, 1\frac{1}{4}, 3\frac{5}{8}$

Pages 378-379 Exercises

1. 1; $1\frac{1}{2}$; 4; $\frac{300}{60}$, 5 **3.** 205; $220 - 24$, 196; $220 - 39$,
181; $220 - 42$, 178; $220 - 56$, 164; $220 - 65$, 155
5. $4(42 - 40)$, 8; $4(54 - 40)$, 56 **7.** 8, 7, 13

Pages 380-381 Exercises

1. $x + 5$ **3.** $5x$ **5.** $t = s - 2$ **7.** The sum of the
measures of the angles of a quadrilateral is 360°. **9.** $s =$
$(w - 1) + 50$

Page 383 Exercises

1. 0.1 **3.** $^-3$ **5.** 26, 32, 38 **7.** 69, 83, 97 **9.** $^-265$,
$^-285$, $^-305$ **11.** $\frac{1}{4}, \frac{1}{2}, \frac{3}{4}$ **13.** $\frac{1}{2}$, 1, $1\frac{1}{2}$ **15.** $^-2$, $^-10$,
$^-18$ **17.** $^-0.7$, $^-0.4$, $^-0.1$ **19.** 1, 3, 5, 7, ...
21. $435

Page 387 Exercises

1. 2 **3.** $^-4$ **5.** 64, 128, 256 **7.** 625; 3,125; 15,625
9. 14, 7, $3\frac{1}{2}$ **11.** 486; $^-1,458$; 4,374 **13.** $^-2,592$;
15,552; $^-93,312$ **15.** $1\frac{9}{16}, \frac{25}{64}, \frac{25}{256}$ **17.** 12, 15, 19
19. 19, 18, 20 **21.** $2\frac{1}{2}, 2\frac{3}{4}$, 3 **23.** 72, 29, 92
25. 24,300 bacteria

Page 389 Exercises

1. 1 **3.** 3 **5.** 5 **7.** 2 **9.** 2 **11.** 1 **13.** 5.3×10^2
15. 6.42×10^2 **17.** 9.27×10^2 **19.** 1.2×10^3
21. 3.65×10^4 **23.** 9.25×10^8 **25.** 4×10^7
27. 1,300 **29.** 16,600 **31.** 3,710 **33.** 8,930
35. 142,000,000 **37.** 3.2×10^5; 320,000
39. 5×10^{11} cans; 500,000,000,000 cans

Page 391 Exercises

1. 21 **3.** twentieth (210) **5.** $1 + 3 + 5 + 7 + 9 = 25$
7. eleventh (121) **9.** $3 \times 3 = 9$; $10 \times 10 = 100$

Pages 392-393 Chapter 17 Review

1. square numbers **3.** function **5.** scientific notation
7. 70% **9.** 80% **11.** 12.5% **13.** $x - 10$ **15.** $5\frac{x}{5}$
17. 9 less than a number **19.** Divide a number by 3.
Then subtract 2. **21.** $\frac{30}{10}$, 3; $\frac{60}{10}$, 6; $\frac{75}{10}$, $7\frac{1}{2}$; $\frac{110}{10}$, 11
23. $(4)^2 + 1$, 17; $(10)^2 + 1$, 101; $(12)^2 + 1$, 145; $(\frac{1}{2})^2 + 1$,
$1\frac{1}{4}$ **25.** $x - 2$ **27.** 19, 22, 25 **29.** $6\frac{1}{2}, 5\frac{1}{2}, 4\frac{1}{2}$
31. 512; 2,048; 8,192 **33.** $^-48$, $^-96$, $^-192$ **35.** 8, 5, 9
37. 5, $^-1$, $^-8$ **39.** 2.6×10^2 **41.** 7.56×10^5 **43.** $6 \times$
10^3 **45.** 4.6×10^4 **47.** 2,600 **49.** 8,200,000
51. 89,400,000 **53.** 130,000 **57.** $p = 18 + s$
59. 3×10^{10}

Page 395 Cumulative Review

1. If the sum of the measures of two angles is 180°, then
they are supplementary. original - true, converse - true
3. If two lines in a plane are parallel, then they are
perpendicular to the same line. original - true, converse -
false **5.** We will go to the park. **7.** It is not Sunday.
9. 9, 36 **11.** 1, 6 **13.** 0.02, 1.84 **15.** $1\frac{1}{2}$, 4 **17.** $\frac{1}{2}$
19. $1\frac{2}{3}$ **21.** 37 **23.** $66.7 \frac{cm}{s}$ **25.** 58; 42; 39; $90 - 11$,
79; $90 - 9$, 81; $90 - 3$, 87 **27.** 0.2 **29.** $^-0.1$

Chapter 18 The Coordinate Plane

Page 397 Exercises

1. Z **3.** N **5.** J **7.** I **9.** D **11.** A **13.** (4, 5)
15. (7,2) **17.** (10,10) **19.** (5.7, 0)

Page 399   Exercises

1. $x = 1$, $y = 1$ **3.** $x = {}^-8$, $y = 0$ **5.** $x = {}^-3$, $y = {}^-6$
7. II   **9.** I   **11.** none   **13.** IV   **15.** IV   **17.** (6, 2)
19. $({}^-5, 4)$ **21.** (2, 10)   **23.** (0, 5)   **25.** $({}^-9, 11)$
27. location of streets

Pages 400-401   Exercises

1. 1, 3, 6   **3.** $^-10$, $^-2$; $^-4$, 0; 2, 2; 5, 3   **5.** $^-2({}^-3)$, 6;
$^-2({}^-1)$, 2; $^-2(0)$, 0; $^-2(2)$, $^-4$ **7.** (x, y), $({}^-1, {}^-2)$, $(0,0)$,
$(1, 2)$, $(2, 4)$ **9.** (x, y), $({}^-1, {}^-5)$, $(0, 0)$, $(1, 5)$, $(2, 10)$
11. (x, y), $({}^-1, 6)$, $(0, 0)$, $(1, {}^-6)$, $(2, {}^-12)$ **13.** (x, y),
$({}^-1, {}^-2)$, $(0, 1)$, $(1, 4)$, $(2, 7)$ **15.** (x, y), $({}^-1, 0)$, $(0, 5)$,
$(1, 10)$, $(2, 15)$ **17.** (x, y), $({}^-1, 7)$, $(0, 3)$, $(1, {}^-1)$, $(2, {}^-5)$
19. (x, y), $({}^-1, -\frac{1}{2})$, $(0, 0)$, $(1, \frac{1}{2})$, $(2, 1)$ **21.** (x, y),
$({}^-1, -\frac{3}{4})$, $(0, 0)$, $(1, \frac{3}{4})$, $(2, 1\frac{1}{2})$ **23.** (x, y), $({}^-1, {}^-2\frac{1}{3})$,
$(0, {}^-2)$, $(1, {}^-1\frac{2}{3})$, $(2, {}^-1\frac{1}{3})$ **25.** (x, y), $({}^-1, 5)$, $(0, 3)$, $(1, 1)$,
$(2, {}^-1)$ **27.** (x, y), $({}^-1, 8)$, $(0, 7)$, $(1, 6)$, $(2, 5)$ **29.** (x, y),
$({}^-1, 11)$, $(0, 6)$, $(1, 1)$, $(2, {}^-4)$ **31.** $y = x - 3$; (x, y),
$(40, 37)$, $(30, 27)$, $(20, 17)$, $(4, 1)$ **33.** $y = 0.1x + 100$;
(x, y), $(10, 101)$, $(100, 110)$, $(200, 120)$, $(500, 150)$

Pages 402-403   Exercises

1. $^-4 + 4$, 0, $({}^-4, 0)$; $^-2 + 4$, 2, $({}^-2, 2)$; $0 + 4$, 4, $(0, 4)$;
$2 + 4$, 6, $(2, 6)$ **11.** no   **13.** no   **15.** no   **17.** (0, 5)
19. (2, 5)   **21.** (1, 1)

Page 407   Exercises

1. 4°C   **3.** $^-16$°C   **5.** $^-37$°C   **7.** $^-18$°C   **9.** $^-4$°C
11. 46°F   **13.** $^-26$°F   **15.** 3°F   **17.** 32°F   **19.** 61°F
21. 0°F   **23.** $^-40$°   **25.** 6 ft   **27.** 2 s   **29.** 1.8 h
31. 50 mph   **33.** no, extend graph further to right

Pages 409-410   Exercises

1. translation (slide)   **3.** dilation   **5.** reflection (flip)
7. reflection (flip)   **9.** reflection (flip)

Page 413   Exercises

1. (3, 1.5), (5, 2.5)   **3.** 3 more hours   **5.** $4, $28
7. almost 5 hours

Pages 414-415   Chapter 18 Review

1. e   **3.** m   **5.** f   **7.** g   **9.** i   **11.** E   **13.** C   **15.** A
17. (2, 6)   **19.** (3, 5)   **21.** (6, 6)   **31.** $^-1 - 4$, $^-5$; $1 - 4$,
$^-3$; $2 - 4$, $^-2$ **33.** $^-3({}^-1) + 1$, 4; $^-3(0) + 1$, 1; $^-3(2) +$
1, $^-5$; $^-3(3) + 1$, $^-8$ **39.** no   **41.** $\frac{1}{4}$-turn rotation
43. reflection   **45.** reflection or $\frac{3}{4}$-turn rotation
49. 1 meter

Page 417   Cumulative Review

1. 58.28 m²   **3.** multiply, $^-10$ **5.** multiply, 18
7. divide, 44   **9.** $178.00   **11.** 2.5×10^5 **13.** $6.09 \times$
10^6 **15.** (x, y), $({}^-1, 1\frac{3}{8})$, $(0, 1)$, $(1, \frac{5}{8})$, $(2, \frac{1}{4})$ **17.** (x, y),
$({}^-2, 1)$, $({}^-1, 1\frac{1}{2})$, $(0, 2)$, $(2, 3)$ **19.** 5 cakes, 12 cakes

Photo Credits

Cover: Aaron Haupt

2, *Commercial Image;* **4, 5,** *Pamela J. Willits;* **7,** *Commercial Image;* **9,** *Edna Douthat;* **13,** *Gerard Photography;* **15, 18, 24, 27,** *Commercial Image;* **33,** *Brian Parker/Tom Stack & Associates;* **36,** *Hickson-Bender Photography;* **39, 41,** *Commercial Image;* **46,** *Larry Hamill;* **48, 50, 56,** *Commercial Image;* **60,** *Cobalt Productions;* **61,** *David R. Frazier;* **62,** *file photo;* **63,** *Cobalt Productions;* **65,** *Brian Heston;* **67,** *file photo;* **72,** *Cobalt Productions;* **79,** *Steve Lissau;* **80,** *Commercial Image;* **84,** *Cobalt Productions;* **86,** *Commercial Image;* **88,** *LPI/MY/FPG;* **89,** *file photo;* **94,** *Pictures Unlimited;* **96,** *Doug Martin;* **100, 105,** *Cobalt Productions;* **106, 107,** *Larry Hamill;* **108,** *Barry L. Runk from Grant Heilman;* **110,** *Commercial Image;* **111,** *Bob McKeever/Tom Stack & Associates;* **114,** *Bogart Photography;* **116,** *NASA;* **118,** *Zimmerman/FPG;* **120,** *David R. Frazier Photolibrary;* **122,** *Cobalt Productions;* **126,** *Commercial Image;* **128,** *Cobalt Productions;* **136,** *courtesy of Ford Motor Company;* **138**(t) *First Image,* (tc, bc) *file photos,* (b) *courtesy of Intel Corporation;* **140,** *Ted Rice;* **143,** *Pictures Unlimited;* **145,** *courtesy of TRW, Inc.;* **148, 150, 153,** *Doug Martin;* **155,** *Kevin Syms/Frazier Photolibrary;* **160,** *NASA;* **162,** *Paul Brown;* **169,** *Cul-*

ver Pictures; **174,** *Commercial Image;* **177,** *Rick Kocks;* **182,** *Latent Image;* **186, 192, 196,** *Cobalt Productions;* **198,** *Gerard Photography;* **204,** © *Copyright by Rand McNally & Company, R.L. 87-S-52;* **208,** *Steve Lissau;* **210,** *Tom Carroll/FPG;* **212,** *James A. Surgar/Black Star;* **218,** *Allen Zak;* **222, 224, 227,** *Doug Martin;* **232,** *file photo;* **234, 236,** *Doug Martin;* **244,** *Larry Hamill;* **246,** *Allen Zak;* **254,** *Grant Heilman Photography;* **258,** *Doug Martin;* **280,** *Larry Hamill;* **283,** *M. Timothy O'Keefe/Tom Stack & Associates;* **286,** *Allen Zak;* **296,** *courtesy of American Iron & Steel Institute;* **304,** *Steve Ogden/Tom Stack & Associates;* **306,** *Doug Martin;* **310,** *Allen Zak;* **313,** *H.M. DeCruyenaere;* **314,** *National Park Service;* **318,** *David R. Frazier;* **320,** *James N. Westwater;* **322,** *Doug Martin;* **330,** *Tom Tracy/After Image;* **333,** *Roger K. Burnard;* **335, 338,** *Cobalt Productions;* **342,** *Shay Photography;* **344,** *Allen Zak;* **348,** *Commercial Image;* **354,** *courtesy of National Earthquake Information Service;* **356,** *Cobalt Productions;* **358,** *Orville Andrews;* **360,** *Joseph Nettis/Photo Researchers, Inc.;* **360,** *Doug Martin;* **361,** *NASA;* **367, 369,** *Doug Martin;* **376,** *Chuck Armstrong/Aperture;* **379,** *Allen Zak;* **380, 382,** *Doug Martin;* **386,** *First Image;* **396,** *Orville Andrews;* **400,** *Doug Martin;* **412,** *Milt & Joan Mann.*

1 2 3 4 5 6 7 8 9 10 11 12 13 14 15 — 97 96 95 94 93 92 91 90 89 88 87